WITHDRA

Praise for *The Color of Words*

"From *Abie* to *Zulu*, with slurs of nearly every U.S. ethnic group, ethnic euphemisms, and key terms in multicultural debates, *The Color of Words* provides the wherewithal to understand the politics of language and the language of racial politics." –Amazon.com

"This book promises to become a classic in the field of multicultural literature."
–Paul Pedersen, Professor, Department of Human Studies, The University of Alabama at Birmingham

"A writer and editor trained as an anthropologist, Herbst has created a balanced, scholarly treatment of intercultural communication. This work will help define the language of cultural relations."
–*Library Journal*

"An essential reference book and a readable short history of ethnic slurs." –*American Studies International*

"Thank you, Philip H. Herbst, for bravely becoming the lexicographer of U.S. ethnic bias in your new book, *The Color of Words*. You add both light and depth to our understanding of the power and perils of language." –George Simons/George Simons International

"As politicians and scholars consider regulating hate speech and individuals express concern about using appropriate and respectful terms in their everyday speech, this book will serve as an essential guide to the language of our multicultural society."
–Anti-Defemation League/*Multicultural Review*

"This unique reference book will be helpful for anyone living or working in a multicultural setting and interesting to anyone who is curious about the language." –*The Evanston Review*

"Highly recommended." –*MultiCultural Review*

"Thorough and enlightening. An essential purchase for every reference collection." –*American Reference Books Annual*

"Ask anyone who has ever tried to engage in a conversation about race—it is much easier said than done. *The Color of Words* can support this dialogue by guiding students in understanding ethnic labels and racist language. This well-researched reference tool avoids a 'politically correct' tone." —*Teaching Tolerance*

"This dictionary is more than about the color of words. It is also about the power of words. For individuals who take trips across ethnic and racial boundaries, this book is equivalent to a well-drawn map or correctly calibrated compass." —George Henderson/Dean/ College of Liberal Studies/The University of Oklahoma

"An interesting and informative resource which may be read cover-to-cover or used as a reference source. Helpful in all academic and public libraries to sensitize people to the problems that their words may cause. It will also be a valuable addition to a traditional dictionary reference collection as it adds breadth to the coverage." —*Booklist*

"*The Color of Words* fills a need by bringing together definitions, etymologies, and commentary on the language of ethnic relationships in the United States. This book will be of interest not only to libraries, but to anyone interested in American society and the American language." —Jean Alexander/Reference Librarian/ Northwestern University Library

"Author Philip Herbst has produced a unique and thought-provoking work that will have readers pondering over the power of language and how, throughout history, it has expressed anger, bias and hatred toward 'others.'" —James W. Stockard/Professor/ School of Education, Auburn University at Montgomery

Wimmin, Wimps & Wallflowers

Wimmin, Wimps & Wallflowers

An Encyclopædic
   Dictionary of Gender and
   Sexual Orientation Bias
   in the United States

Philip H. Herbst

INTERCULTURAL PRESS INC.

First published by Intercultural Press. For information contact:

Intercultural Press, Inc.
PO Box 700
Yarmouth, Maine 04096 USA
001-207-846-5168
Fax: 001-207-846-5181
www.interculturalpress.com

Nicholas Brealey Publishing
36 John Street
London, WC1N 2AT, UK
44-207-430-0224
44-207-404-8311
www.nbrealey-books.com

© 2001 by Philip H. Herbst

Book design and production: Patty J. Topel
Dust jacket design and production: Patty J. Topel

Printed in the United States of America

05   04   03   02   01   1   2   3   4   5

Library of Congress Cataloging-in-Publication Data

Herbst, Philip H.
    Wimmin, wimps & wallflowers: an encyclopædic dictionary of gender and sexual orientation bias in the United States/ Philip H. Herbst.
        p.   cm.
    Includes bibliographical references
    ISBN 1-877864-80-3
        1. Heterosexism—United States—Dictionaries.   2. Sexism—United States—Dictionaries.   I. Title: Wimmin, wimps, and wallflowers.   II. Title

HQ76.45.U5 H47   2000
306.74'6'097303—dc21   00-059729

Table of Contents

Foreword ix

Acknowledgments xi

About This Dictionary and Its Entries xiii

How to Use This Dictionary xxiii

Dictionary Entries 1

Core Works Consulted 311

Foreword

Phil Herbst's first book, *The Color of Words,* takes on terms and expressions that malign ethnic groups or create controversy and confusion where such groups are concerned. In *Wimmin, Wimps & Wallflowers* he addresses two additional categories where language bias is often found: gender and sexual orientation.

It is at times a disconcerting book to read, so infested is our language with words that are spoken or written to hurt others. Open the book to any page and the words fly out at you: *loose woman, limp-wrist, pervert, Tinker Bell, trash, trollop.*

Many of the words and expressions in this painstakingly researched dictionary are recognizable at once for their bias; others are words we often use without realizing their underlying meaning or without knowing how their meanings have been twisted to suit the purposes of those who demean others who are different from themselves and therefore are objects of fear and scorn. Take, for example, the word *honey,* an everyday term of affection among both men and women or among parents to their children. Besides sometimes being a patronizing word, connotations of sexuality that are rude and demeaning have crept in, befouling the term's common meaning.

Writing a book that includes seventy-three cross-references for the term *lesbian,* alone, cannot be an easy task for anyone. Author Phil Herbst found the project, at times, daunting and discouraging. Discovering the degree to which women have been linguistically victimized and abused by men and often by other women and to which gays have been verbally attacked by homophobes was disheartening, to say the least. However, the research does not lie, and Herbst consulted all aspects of the media—popular magazines, journals, newspapers, scholarly books, movies, television, and the Internet—as well as talking with informants from many different walks of life. I commend him for a next-to-impossible job well done.

To claim that Herbst is totally unbiased in the construction of his definitions would be a bit of an exaggeration. As he explains to the reader in his introduction, "My biases will be evident." Among these are his efforts to expose the myth conveyed by language that certain ways of being feminine and masculine are natural, rooted in biology, or part of God's plan, while other ways and gender identities are deviant, sick, or sinful. The insistence that the standard, whether it be the male or the heterosexual, is the natural, best, or only way serves to prop up the privileges of some while promoting intolerance toward others.

I share Herbst's hope that this dictionary will help bring to light the inequalities and misunderstandings between groups and to open lines of communication. For whatever biases it might harbor, the dictionary overall is a balanced, descriptive effort that forces us to confront our gender and sexual orientation prejudices and challenges us to be aware of alternatives that are less discriminatory and more enriching for everyone.

—Morris Dees
Southern Poverty Law Center
2001

Acknowledgments

I owe a debt to many who helped in the making of this book. Numerous experts were consulted, some of the most important of whom are acknowledged under "Sources and Methods" in "About This Dictionary and Its Entries" or listed in "Core Works Consulted." Equally valuable were the colleagues or assistants who met with me and answered my questions or who sent their thoughts, advice, or research to me. Among these contributors were Jacquelin Pegg, Sukie de la Croix, Amy Partridge, Carrie Porter, and Angela Rickwalt. Not the least in the cast of professionals were Dr. Susan Stryker and Dr. Heather McClure.

I also want to gratefully acknowledge Morris Dees, founder and executive committee chair of the Southern Poverty Law Center, who provided the funding for hiring assistants, and Jim Carnes, director of the Center's Teaching Tolerance project. Thanks also goes to the Gender Studies Department at Northwestern University for its grant of a visiting scholarship for researching the project.

I am particularly grateful to Toby Frank, president, and David S. Hoopes, formerly editor-in-chief, of Intercultural Press for their insights and ongoing support of my writing and for publishing this volume in sequence with *The Color of Words: An Encyclopaedic Dictionary of Ethnic Bias in the United States*. Special thanks go out to managing editor Judy Carl-Hendrick, who provided both essential editorial expertise and (yes, Judy) a sustaining sense of humor.

For any errors in either fact or judgment that remain in what was a daunting project, I take full responsibility.

About This Dictionary and Its Entries

Exploring the histories and uses of words of gender and sexual orientation, including the many omitted from standard dictionaries, can be a linguistic adventure. But it can also be an unsettling experience, threatening to turn our conventional notions about gender, gender privilege, and sexual identity into questions. The entries in *Wimmin, Wimps & Wallflowers* take the reader on just such a journey. These terms and expressions shed light on how our lives are shaped by learned ideas of gender and sexual orientation; in particular, how words are used to put some groups down and privilege others.

Most of the terms included here are current or at least still-recognized U.S. language usages. Many reflect and embody gender standards and relations and are used to control departures from them; many are derogatory, devaluing those who fail to meet the standards. However, a number of the entries—such as *wimmin* and *herstory*—are words that, despite (or because of) the controversy surrounding them, have provoked a questioning of our gender standards and relations. Some terms (e.g., *queer)* that have been used to hurt people have been reclaimed by the targeted group, while other entries, such as *looksism,* *homophobia,* and *sex object,* are meant to throw light on other entries in the dictionary.

Gender and sexual orientation are treated together because they are inseparable in our culture. It is impossible, for instance, to discuss words that censure gay men (e.g., *fairy, pansy)* without understanding our society's expectations of what it means to be male. Similarly, words disparaging lesbians (e.g., *bull, marimacho)* point to expectations of femininity.

In general, the words in this dictionary are ones that have carved a deep place in our culture and define us as a people.

Patterns of Language Bias

Virtually all of us are targeted for linguistic disparagement or control for one reason or another: race, ethnicity, age, social class, appearance and mannerisms, physical or mental disability, faith, occupations and interests, the region we reside in, or how we cast our vote, as well as gender and sexual orientation. The breadth of epithets in our society is a reminder of the increasing diversity of our nation, our fragmentation, our many competing worldviews, the pervasive inequalities among groups, and the ways dominant groups have found to mask, ignore, or justify these inequalities.

But while everyone may experience biased language, there are certain distinguishing patterns and principles behind its use. This is true of gender-related language. I want to make only three general points in this regard. The first is that the brunt of our language bias with regard to gender and sexual orientation falls on marginalized groups, specifically, heterosexual women and lesbian, gay, bisexual, and transgendered (LGBT) people. By sheer count of words in this dictionary, not to mention the vulgarity and scornfulness of many (e.g., *skank, faggot, pervert),* it is clear that women and LGBT groups meet with more bias and intolerance than do heterosexual males. The second point is that to insult a man, especially a heterosexual man, is not the same as insulting a woman. Many men are in a stronger position than women and better equipped to deal with verbal attacks.

Finally, individuals are targeted not just for their gender or sexual orientation, but also for how these identities interlock with, for example, those of race, class, age, or disability. Typically, the more marginal a person's intersecting identities, the more stigma that person may be subject to. For example, black women have to deal with racially rooted bias as well as that of gender, biases fused in such epithets as *Jezebel* and *Sapphire.* Poor men of color feel the barbs of both racist and classist slurs. On the other hand, although educated, affluent black people often experience the same racism as the poorer members of their racial group, they stand on firmer footing because of their social class; and if heterosexual, they will generally be favored over lesbian or gay African Americans of the same social background.

In other instances, uneducated, rural, or small-town white men suffer a variety of "redneck" slurs, and old men sometimes get tagged with ageist epithets such as *old coot, buzzard,* and *geezer.* However, these words are seldom as demeaning as slurs directed at old women, such as *hag, witch,* or *battle-ax.*

Creating "Women's Place"

Those who control language have in their possession the means to acquire and exercise power (Lakoff 2000). Such individuals or groups are able to use words to construct meaning in ways that serve them. In addition, those who have power are largely spared having to deal with negative labels themselves or are granted a certain immunity from them. Keeping in mind the differences, say, of race or class discussed before, this freedom and power are much more characteristics of men than of women.

Men are indeed victimized by the influence of language but usually with different intent than that associated with the stereotyping and devaluation of women. For example, men may be harmed psychologically and socially by such cultural imperatives as being "macho" or acting like a "real man," and men, regardless of sexual orientation, who cannot or choose not to meet these cultural standards are shamed with loaded words such as *candy-ass* and *sissy*. Yet men enjoy certain linguistic privileges and protections.

To begin, by virtue of gender alone, many men are better equipped than women to deal with linguistic attacks. For example, a man can proudly label himself a sexist when he and his male friends and mainstream society at large have already dismissed feminism as bra-burning silliness and political correctness as the beat of the liberal elite. Also, in many circumstances, a man who calls himself a sexist draws attention only to himself as an individual. This obscures the existence of sexism as part of a larger political and cultural structure, thus guarding male privilege. Women, too, have been able to reclaim words used against them, but they do so on less privileged grounds and with different aims and consequences than do men.

Men are protected in other ways, too. For example, men may be disparaged with the same insulting words used against women, but the words may have very different implications. For example, although men may be labeled "pigs," the charge against them more often suggests sloppy habits than obesity (though men have also been called "pigs" for racist behavior). However, neatness is not implied as an essential or expected attribute of men as a group, while women—whose essential worth is often assessed in our culture in terms of youthfulness and lean figures—are more likely than men to be called a pig for appearing fat and unattractive.

That men are not vulnerable like women, and also enjoy control over them, is consistent with the fact that despite a number of changes in our society in recent decades, men and the male experience—particularly the middle-class, white, heterosexual experience—still come off as the norm. In other words, men define women as "other" and use language to put women "in their place." Women have been conventionally defined, among other ways, as subordinate (see, e.g., *wife)*, weak and emotional (e.g., *weaker vessel, hysteria)*, and even aberrant and unclean (e.g., *female problems, curse)*.

Although the predominant public discourse in the United States today increasingly avoids overtly prejudicial usage against women (e.g., words such as *spinster* are on the way out, and *coozie* would raise eyebrows in the widening political correctness circles), the culture continues to send sexist messages through language. These culturally pervasive messages objectify, silence, belittle, or debase women and even sometimes dismiss their existence. Far more often than men, women are reduced to sex objects, such as *just another pretty*

face, sex goddess, or, more vulgarly, a *punchboard*. They are viciously objectified through such words as *piece of meat* or *cunt*. Women are also depicted in
terms of animals more commonly than men are—especially animals that are
ugly, domesticated, eaten, and ridden. Women are called scrumptious metaphorical "dishes" and "tasty morsels" and are depicted as passive and stupid.
Even if such slights and debasements are increasingly disavowed, speakers
may use their disavowel only to hide more subtle forms of sexism.

A number of entries in the dictionary—see, for example, discussions under *rape* or *temptress*—also indicate how men, by using sexist language, can
make themselves out to be the victims of women's behavior, thus deflecting
guilt from themselves to women. "Jailbait" gets blamed for Casanova's promiscuity.

In conclusion, many men, including some gay men, are in a different position linguistically from many women. In particular, men can and do benefit
from linguistic sexism—in the home, workplace, or courtroom, although it
may not be directly perpetrated by them. Even everyday innocuous terms such
as *mother* and transcendental expressions such as *Eternal Feminine* give an
advantage, usually unacknowledged, to men. The deeply rooted assumption
that such characteristics as nurturance or passive sexuality are "natural," fixed,
and innate in the female personality allows men to deny or justify gender inequality and to avoid the argument that they are being self-serving by sub-
scribing to these conventional notions of "womanhood."

"Faggots" at the Stake

The labeling of women that helps define them as a category finds its counterpart in the homophobic images of gay men and lesbians and the prejudices
against the transgendered communicated in our culture. The loaded and often
mean (especially when used by heterosexuals) epithet *faggot* sums up much of
the antigay prejudice. This slang term has been traced to the Old French word
fagot, meaning a bundle of sticks of the kind said to have once been used in
burning homosexuals at the stake as heretics. The etymology is dubious, but
the heat of oppression is nevertheless still real for persons in LGBT groups.

The language of homophobia and transphobia is rooted in our dominant
social discourse and is much more abundant and contemptuous than are expressions of hostility toward mainstream heterosexuals (for examples of the
latter, see *breeder* or *heterosexual [het])*. This biased language follows in lock-
step with, and in support of, the conventional dual-sex (or "opposite sex")
concept—men and women as fixed categories—embedded in our gender ideology. The heterosexist lexicon is full of stereotypes and dismissals of those
who cross these gender boundaries. Lesbians, for example, are typically represented as "mannish" and gay men as "effeminate" or "limp-wristed."

The social climate in recent decades has become, in some ways, more open to lesbians, gay men, and bisexuals and perhaps to a small degree even to the transgendered. Yet while they may be "out and about" in society more than ever before, and without all the rabid "man-hating"/"pervert" rhetoric once heaped on them (though sometimes more *because* they have come out), these communities remain targets of both verbal and physical assaults. Political and verbal attacks on LGBT individuals and communities have been readily justified on unyielding religious, moral, and sometimes also medical grounds.

Gay men today are accused unfairly of being "AIDs carriers," and gay men and lesbians are labeled "biological errors" and "sick" or "sinful" and are warned against "flaunting" their homosexuality. Meanwhile, the transgendered, a concept and a community fundamentally incompatible with mainstream society's construction of a dual-sex paradigm, remain probably the most misunderstood group in society.

In addition, in the "culture wars" over the rights of gay and transgendered people, antigay activists use language to define gays as socially dangerous, thereby solidifying the heterosexual political advantage. For example, such activists have tainted the gay struggle to obtain the same rights enjoyed by straight people by referring to "the gay agenda." On the surface a deceptively neutral term, this usage suggests that while straights are entitled to their rights, gays have an agenda. The implication is that gays and lesbians are in search of "special" rights and more entitlements than those enjoyed by the more "deserving" heterosexual population, who are not likely to acknowledge that they in fact are the privileged ones.

Exposing Prejudice

It hurts to face our prejudices. We shy away because acknowledging them exposes special or unfair privileges we may enjoy, makes us think about the consequences of these privileges, and may even bring into question our very way of life. Language helps us to express while at the same time disguise our prejudices (even transmuting them into moral righteousness), but it can also be used to reveal and control them. A main aim of this book is to make more visible some of the attitudes and inequities in our relationships that are so easily distorted, ignored, denied, or dismissed as relics of some unprogressive past.

Biased Word Use among Women and LGBT Groups

Oppressed groups' perceptions of threat to their community and identity are also reflected linguistically. The dangers they find, however, are not just the ridicule and stereotyping that come from dominant groups.

Intragroup name-calling may occur to scold group members for deviating from some group standard or for giving in to the other side (e.g., *Uncle Mom*).

Usage can simply reflect arguments over what constitutes danger to the community. Thus, some lesbians challenge the inclusion of bisexual women into the lesbian community because these lesbians perceive the threat of betrayal in a woman who sleeps with men as well as women. This perception is both influenced by and in turn contributes to the negative value they give to the word *bisexual*. Similarly, those lesbians designated as "crunchies" differ in lifestyle from or disagree philosophically with the so-called "lipsticks," while some gay men refuse to acknowledge politically conservative gay men as *gay*, an honorable term for the gay activist, limiting the conservative's identity to *homosexual*. The latter connotes only sexual orientation and may imply that conservative gay men are willing to be labeled by a term considered by many gay men to be heterosexist.

Naming Oppression and Self-Definition

If language provides a channel for bias, political attacks, and self-serving definitions of others, it also offers its comebacks and ways of speaking up. These, too, are described in this dictionary.

By naming their problems and oppressions, heterosexual women and LGBT communities have been able to better understand these problems, break through some of the silence, and encourage more accurate and fair representation in the media. Words such as *sexist, herstory, homophobia, patriarchy, sexual harassment*, and *transgender*, for example—though most of these have been rendered controversial in a backlash against efforts to procure full rights for gays and lesbians and other women—have served these ends.

Self-definition follows closely from naming oppression. For example, today an adult woman who calls herself "girl" may see herself not as childlike and dependent, but as partaking in "girl power," while gay men and lesbians have, as I mentioned earlier, reclaimed *queer* as a term of protest and dissent. Even *bitch* has been used self-descriptively among women to convey their solidarity. These negotiations of the meanings of words that dominant groups impose on others remind us that people can sometimes resist dominant definitions, with their attached stigma and stereotyping, and devise ways to help defend and negotiate their identities.

Audience and Clarification of Purpose

Wimmin, Wimps & Wallfowers is designed for a wide audience: educators, writers and editors, speakers and other media professionals, foreigners and nonnative speakers of English, students of language and society, and, of course, anyone involved or interested in issues of gender and sexual orientation.

The dictionary is meant only as a guide to our understanding of gender language usage. The terms are not meant as descriptions of people, nor are words that may be offensive to certain groups or classes of people being promoted. To the contrary, the aim is to emphasize that words are merely labels for the classifications that people make in society and that these classifications are often made for reasons of manipulation, mischief, and the degradation of others. In writing the word definitions I have tried to emphasize the words, meanings, and perceptions, and not to confuse them with people themselves.

Readers are also reminded, however, that even words that carry a heavy load of bias are used in historical contexts (in print today often with quotation marks), in fiction, or when quoting a speaker. They are also used in private, when the user and the person addressed are on familiar terms, or in related forms of social interaction without the degrading connotations they take on in other circumstances. When spoken, their meanings are colored by tone of voice and other paralinguistic factors. The situation and the intentions of the speaker are always at work, shaping the use and meaning of these words.

What's Covered and How

The almost 1,100 entries in *Wimmin, Wimps & Wallfowers* make for a book that is unusually comprehensive, although we omitted a number of terms and expressions that we deemed dated, socially insignificant, or obscure. Some readers may notice the omission of a word or some meanings or aspects of a word that they regard as important. I welcome your suggestions for a second edition.

Most of the basic components of lexicography are here: spellings, definitions, usage notes, etymologies, and cross-references that direct the reader to related entries of interest. (Some lists of *see also* references are gold mines of information about gender bias in themselves.) Readers interested in knowing about the social context of usage and the stereotyping or linguistic control of groups because of gender or sexual orientation will also find ample information. References, many of them scholarly and current, should aid readers who want to learn more about specific gender or word topics.

Virtually all gender and sexual orientation group bias is covered. In fact, during the extensive examination of our culture required to write this book, I made an active effort to locate words applied to and against heterosexuals, especially heterosexual men and white men. Wherever possible, views have been balanced—it is important for more liberal groups, for example, to know and understand how conservative Christians feel and think about homosexuality and to pry open the tightly closed door to communication.

Still, my biases will be evident. Certain commentary will strike some readers as more political and moral than exacting and scientific. For this I offer no apology. Those dictionary makers who mask the political agenda of dominant groups behind pretensions of "lexicography" do us no favor. I expect that the majority of readers who approach this subject matter will value pluralism and respect the integrity of all individuals, regardless of gender or sexual orientation and identity. Perhaps others can learn to do so, too, from this book.

Sources and Methods

The references listed in "Core Works Consulted" at the end of the dictionary represent a body of nonfiction texts that call for special acknowledgment. Many were consulted to cull words, their spellings, and definitions. Discrepancies between sources were often resolved by resorting to the more recent or scholarly works or, sometimes, by drawing from primary sources or conferring with individuals whose experience or identity gave them special access to uses and meanings of words and expressions.

Among the core reference books that I found especially valuable in this research are the following, listed alphabetically by author or editor:

Chapman, Robert L. *American Slang*

Flexner, Stuart Berg, and Anne H. Soukhanov. *Speaking Freely: A Guided Tour of American English*

Lighter, J. E. *Historical Dictionary of American Slang,* vols. 1 and 2

Maggio, Rosalie. *Talking about People*

Spears, Richard A. *Slang and Euphemism*

Two other very useful sources were Hugh Rawson's *Wicked Words: A Treasury of Curses, Insults, Put-Downs, and Other Formerly Unprintable Terms* and Clarence Major's *Juba to Jive: A Dictionary of African-American Slang,* consulted for words in black English.

Wherever possible, for spellings of entry words and related lexicographic information, I have tried to follow standard dictionaries used in publishing, particularly *Merriam-Webster's Collegiate Dictionary.* Also frequently consulted was *The Oxford English Dictionary.* Other dictionaries used are listed under "Core Works Consulted." Many of the words here are not found in these dictionaries, however. In such cases I relied on specialized dictionaries and my own citation data from a wide variety of sources.

Journals, especially *American Speech,* provided useful information, and recent issues of editorial newsletters, such as *Copy Editor,* helped to keep me current on issues of spelling and acceptance of words by U.S. presses. Some of the listed classic works in feminism and gender studies were essential, and their ideas are incorporated throughout the book.

Yet these various documented sources, however central to the research, represent only a part of the total effort. Current newspapers, magazines, and other periodicals were searched, sometimes through the use of Lexis-Nexis, available to me at the Northwestern University Library. Other media also played a role: movies (a favored source), radio and television, novels and short stories, song lyrics, and the Internet. In many phases of the research, personal assistants, listed in the Acknowledgments and hired under the generous auspices of the Southern Poverty Law Center, made valuable contributions.

How to Use This Dictionary

The entries in this dictionary explain words and expressions used in the United States today that carry gender or sexual orientation bias or are commonly regarded as controversial or confusing. Many of the entries present social and historical background to the terms and their biases as well as basic lexicographic information. More on what constitutes the entries can be found in "About This Dictionary and Its Entries."

The dictionary has been designed for readability and flexibility. There are no recondite abbreviations or special symbols that require the reader to flip forward or backward in the book to some key to understand. Nor is there a rigid formatting imposed on entries. Entries do follow a general plan, however. A boldface entry word (or words) is always found at the beginning of the entry; a general definition immediately follows the entry word in most instances; and cross-references, if any, are placed at the end. Following are a few notes about the components, formatting, and mechanics of entries.

Boldface Entry Words

Entry words, in boldface type, are alphabetized letter-by-letter, without regard to spaces or punctuation. Articles (*a, an, the*) that in conversation or print would appear before the entry word do not appear with the entry word or, if they do, are shifted to the end of the boldface entry (following a comma) and not taken into account in alphabetization.

The first entry word is sometimes followed by another boldface word, a different form of the first word with a related meaning. In such instances, the two terms are separated by a semicolon (e.g., **AIDS**; **AIDS victim**).

The entry word usually presents the standard spelling and is sometimes followed by boldface variant or nonstandard spellings. Variants are listed roughly according to use or familiarity today. The reader should be aware, however, that many slang words are not standardized in spelling; "variant" slang spellings offered may be more or less equal variants and are not exhaustive.

Definitions, Usage Notes, and Social Commentary

The boldface entry word is followed directly by an explanation of its meaning. The focus is on meanings relating to gender or sexual orientation, though some of the words clearly may have other meanings as well. As with variant spellings, the inclusion of other senses is not necessarily exhaustive.

Other basic information about the word may include its stylistic status (e.g., slang, offensive, vulgar), comments or cautions about usage, and any current body of opinion about the word, often from published scholarly sources, including social and political commentary. I have diligently tried to document usage authorities unless their views were a matter of common knowledge and not special to any one authority. In addition the use of a word elsewhere in the English-speaking world may be noted, as may U.S. regional usage.

Illustrative Examples

Many entries contain at least one example, often included with or following the explanation, showing the use of the entry word in a typical or, sometimes, variant sense. Occasionally the example is of a different but related form of the entry word. Examples illustrate usage or help to expand or clarify the definition or attest to a new or variant meaning. Examples are drawn from a wide array of sources, cited parenthetically after the quotation (see "References" below).

References

There are two types of reference citation: one for illustrative examples and one for documenting statements from authorities and other sources. Within entries, full publication data are not given for sources of illustrative examples. They are attributed by author (except often when a news story or letter to the editor is cited), work, year (and day and month in the case of periodicals), and—unless there have been many editions of a book—page number and are enclosed in parentheses (e.g., Lev Raphael, *The Edith Wharton Murders,* 1997, 13). Sources for other statements or authorities are cited by the author-date system: the author's name and year of publication, followed by a page number where appropriate, also enclosed in parentheses (e.g., Feinberg 1998). Complete information for these latter references is grouped alphabetically by author under "Core Works Consulted" at the end of the dictionary.

Etymologies, Histories, and Dates

Within the entry body, etymologies, tracing the use of the word back in English and from one language to another, commonly appear, especially where there is some etymological controversy that may be of interest to the reader. Etymologies are kept as simple as possible, though comments about the status of etymologies are included in a few instances.

Time of origin or common use is frequently designated by a decade, a larger part of the century, or a historical period. Dates of earliest use are typically dates of earliest known printed or written use. Not all entries have such dates, indicating either that they did not turn up in the course of research or, if they did, that they could not easily be confirmed. The absence of a date may also mean that the usage is fairly recent. There may be further historical notes about people, the social milieu in which they became the targets of bias, and the origins of stereotypes defining them.

Cross-References

Following an entry word without an explanation, *see* is used to refer the reader to the main entry where the term is discussed (e.g., **chickie**. See CHICKEN). At the end of an entry, *see also* references steer the reader to other entries in the dictionary that may also be of interest. *See also* references point to words with similar meanings, to other words used for the same group, sometimes to words that contrast in meaning, or to other related subject matter.

A

abbess. See -ESS.

aberration. See PERVERT.

abnormal. See NORMAL, PERVERT.

abomination. See PERVERT.

AC-DC. See BISEXUAL.

acey-deucey. See BISEXUAL.

actress; **AMW**. Actress, once a euphemism meaning a prostitute or promiscuous woman. This use was an expression of moral disapproval of women's involvement on the stage, which was regarded as an unrespectable place for women, who were believed to be ordained for the home. Formerly, men had played women's roles in the theater. When women did appear on the English stage, a practice allowed by proclamation of Charles II in the seventeenth century, they were called "actors" along with men. *Actress* for a woman stage performer came into use in the early eighteenth century, but the masculine *actor* remained the generic term.

Although the long-standing puritanical attitude toward actresses began to ease up near the end of the nineteenth century, it carried over for much of the twentieth. "The actress and the singer were considered nothing much more than prostitutes with a sideline" (Stephen Longstreet, writing of New Orleans before 1917, in Holder 1996). Many people still link the acting profession with morally "loose" women, owing in part to the notion that actresses sleep around with male producers—who do not sacrifice their own reputations for doing so—in order to make it on the stage or in Hollywood. The male actor, however, is not necessarily exempt from being stereotyped; some heterosexual men cast him as effeminate.

Actress also occurs in gay communities in reference to gay men.

AMW stands for *actress-model-what-ever*, meaning a female prostitute. Some prostitutes, however, seeking a higher professional level, do identify with those roles, and both *actress* and *model* may be used by those involved in these professions without implying sexual activity.

See also –ESS, LADY (lady of the stage), PROMISCUOUS, PROSTITUTE, SCARLET WOMAN.

admitted/avowed/declared homosexual. See HOMOSEXUAL.

adulteress. See LOVER.

African goddess. See GODDESS.

agfay. See FAG.

aggressive. See GENDER-SPECIFIC ADJECTIVES.

A.H. See ASS (asshole).

AIDS; **AIDS victim**; **innocent victims of AIDS**; **AIDS carrier**. AIDS, an acronym for acquired immunodeficiency syndrome, an infectious, transmittable disease involving damage to the body's immune system in varying, often progressive degrees. Throughout the world, AIDS has taken on a highly politicized meaning, tending to attract attention as a feature of groups that are already stigmatized. In the United States homophobic people perpetuate the myth that homosexual persons are capable of transmitting their "lifestyle" to innocent children. Homosexual males have been feared and despised even more for transmitting the human immunodeficiency virus (HIV) through having gay sex—for which they are supposedly being punished by contracting the AIDS disease! In fact, however, about 70 percent of persons with AIDS are heterosexual, and about 90 percent of reported cases occur in the developing world.

Senator Jesse Helms once asserted that AIDS is a disease transmitted by people who deliberately engage in "unnatural acts." In response, Mrs. Jeanne White-Ginder, whose young son Ryan died of AIDS after acquiring the disease from a blood transfusion, asked whether Senator Helms felt the same about Americans dying of cancer because they smoke.

Like the disease, the language of AIDS has been surrounded by controversy and is often loaded with bias. The main entry terms, especially *AIDS victim*, carry connotations to which persons with AIDS or their families and friends may object. Although people in the gay community say that *AIDS patient* and *AIDS sufferer* have found a level of acceptance, all of these terms suggest weakness, passivity, and dependence, which is not the way many people with AIDS face the disease. Death is often implied as well.

Pressure groups in the 1980s, when the language of AIDS was becoming emotionally charged, tried to replace such terms with the abbreviation *PWA* for a "person (or people) with AIDS." *PWA* arose as an outcome of the second AIDS forum in Denver, Colorado, December 1983, becoming current by the early 1990s (*Oxford Dictionary of New Words* 1991). Variants on *PWA* are *PLWA* and *PLA*, which stand for the very politically correct "person living with AIDS." These variants stress "living with" rather than "dying from" AIDS. Still, some object to dismissing the idea of victimization. This "uniquely brutal disease" is a victimizing experience, argues Shilts (1987), and the euphemisms can misrepresent the realities of the disease. Gay historian Sukie de la Croix (personal communication, 2 October 1998) acknowledges regretfully that "the disease has become so devastating in gay communities that the terms used are not the main issue anymore."

Innocent victims is sometimes used for persons who contract AIDS through blood transfusions or for children who have AIDS. "This term contains the implication that others with the disease are somehow guilty of something" (*GLAAD*

Media Guide n.d., 36).

Persons who have been infected with HIV (believed to cause AIDS) and who are HIV-antibody-positive, may be dehumanized by being called *AIDS carriers*. This term "can easily be misinterpreted as implying that AIDS, like typhoid, is casually transmitted by 'carriers'" (*GLAAD Media Guide* n.d., 33). "Words like 'faggots' and '... AIDS carriers' were used by officers the night they brutally searched the house [where private gay parties were held] and the thirty men inside" (*Leatherfolk,* 1991, xii). *AIDS incubator* is a synonym for *AIDS carrier*, suggesting someone who does not deserve compassion—or life.

See also GAY PLAGUE, VICTIM.

airedale. See DOG.

airhead. See DITZ, SPACE GIRL.

alley cat. A person considered disreputable, often a woman, who hangs out in city streets or in back alleys like a tomcat—which is a male cat (in other words, behavior regarded as inappropriate for a woman); especially, a woman considered sexually promiscuous or a female prostitute who carouses at night, like a stray cat. This is early- to mid-twentieth century slang.

In the traditional Southern lexicon, *alley cat,* meaning an illegitimate child, suggests the disreputable behavior of the mother (see also BASTARD).

See also BAT (alley bat), CAT, PROMISCUOUS, PROSTITUTE, TOM.

all man. See MAN.

all woman. See WOMAN.

alternative lifestyle; gay lifestyle; lifestyle choice. *Alternative lifestyle,* a way of life outside mainstream or conventional society, especially that of lesbians and gay men, bisexual individuals, and the transgendered. The term has been in general currency but has been especially prevalent in the mainstream press to hint at sexual orientation other than heterosexuality. "People who lead an alternative lifestyle say they feel particularly vulnerable to harassment and violence at school" (Matthew Cardinale, Fort Lauderdale *Sun-Sentinel,* 3 June 1998, 14). Although the phrase is commonly perceived as favorable or expressing tolerance, even sometimes as implicitly critical of the heterosexual orientation, *alternative* (or *alternate*) usually implies that heterosexual behavior is, or should be, the norm, and that individuals who identify themselves as homosexual are therefore deviant, peculiarly "other."

In addition, the diversity in gay communities is lost with this usage. Gay or lesbian people do not live according to some single lifestyle, as stereotypes dictate. Gay business executives, gay photographers, and gay bag boys in supermarkets, to name just a few examples, are likely to live very different lifestyles. The journalistic word *lifestyle* may also imply a casual way of life that one is capable of changing, not a significant aspect of gay identity.

Also commonly heard is *gay lifestyle,* which is usually accepted as a neutral term in the straight community but frowned upon in the gay. When spoken by the religious right (whose members made the expression popular), in particular, the term takes on subtly negative but often deeply offensive connotations. "A local minister...was an extremist given to frequent denunciations of the 'gay lifestyle'" (Lev Raphael, *The Edith Wharton Murders,* 1997, 13).

Lifestyle choice has many of the problems of the term *alternative lifestyle* plus those of *choice*: most gay men and lesbians do not consider their sexual orientation something they have simply chosen. Less often heard—in the United States, anyway—are *alternative sexuality* (homosexuality) and *alternative proclivity* (ascribed to a gay). Such expressions carry much the same biased implications as does *alternative lifestyle,* though the emphasis is on the psychological or sexual orientation rather than on the lifestyle.

See also DEVIANT, SEXUAL PREFERENCE.

amateur. Term meaning a young woman who is not a "professional," that is, who does not take money for sex but who is said to practice promiscuous sex. "Then he realized suddenly that Ramona had made herself into a sort of sexual professional (or priestess). He was used to dealing with vile amateurs lately" (Saul Bellow, *Herzog,* 1992, 17). If a woman does start to take money for her sexual services, she is said to have "lost her amateur standing." The word comes from the mid-nineteenth century, when it had a somewhat different meaning: a prostitute who also held down a respectable job.

See also PROFESSIONAL, PROMISCUOUS, PROSTITUTE.

Amazon. In its capitalized form, a member of a warlike group of women of Asia Minor known in Greek mythology. The word comes from the Greek *Amazōn,* often labeled as of obscure origin in dictionaries, although *The American Heritage Dictionary* (1992) notes a probable Indo-European, specifically Iranian, origin. Kramarae and Treichler (1992), however, argue for a non-Indo-European origin. Drawing on the work of Carol F. Justus, they note that the non-Indo-European root word *mag-* gave us the Gothic *magan* (to have power), to which *Amazon* is sometimes linked. This constitutes, they claim, a linguistic trace of a "prepatriarchal social organization" (however much this claim may be disputed, to some feminists it constitutes an affirmation of their foremothers' identity).

Originally (and still) applied to the women of classical Greek fame, *Amazon* came to mean any female warrior, then a tall or masculine woman, one who did not conform to the "feminine" ideal.

Often today it means a sexually attractive young woman (e.g., 1980s black singer and actress Grace Jones was often described as an amazon, though African American feminists have resented representations of amazons as black, especially when they are seen as animals [hooks 1981]). The sexual sense, appearing in lowercase form, has been U.S. slang since at least the mid-twentieth century. *Amazon* may also mean a sexually aggressive lesbian (lesbians are often stereotyped by heterosexuals as "masculine" in looks and sexual motivation or performance) and "a virago" (since the mid-eighteenth century). Any woman regarded as strong, tough, and domineering may be labeled, often pejoratively, an amazon. Sometimes, on the surface anyway, praise is intended, as for women considered able to endure in the face of suffering. Yet hooks (1981) calls this into question in relation to black women: "Much of what has been perceived by whites as an Amazonic trait in black women has been merely stoical acceptance of situations we have been powerless to change" (83). (See BLONDE [dumb blonde, quotation].) In some cases *amazon* refers to a tall person, regardless of sex. See BERDACHE for the use of *amazon* in certain cultures in the sense of a cross-dresser.

It is not known for certain whether there is any historical basis for the mythological Amazons of Asia Minor. Some feminists have argued that male scholars tend to dismiss Amazons as mythical. In any case, the idea of these women did capture the imagination of writers, who have depicted them as ruling independently of men and threatening male dominance. To maintain their numbers, the Amazons had intercourse with male outsiders, but male children were sent away or mutilated or even exterminated. Any male members of the group were held in servile positions.

Amazons secured their independence, integrity, and self-containment by taking on the traditional male roles, including that of warrior and ever-vigilant protector. Female children were said to have had the right breast (sometimes also the left) burned off to make it easier to use the bow and lance in the pursuit of enemies or game. Thus, some language students believe the Amazons derive their name from the Greek term meaning those who have no breasts, which *The Oxford English Dictionary* (1989) calls "popular etymology of an unknown word." Others warn that men have played up the idea of the breast mutilation to argue that the enjoyment of power robs women of femininity. Still others suggest that the breast was not removed, explaining the appearance of a single breast showing through the tunic as a product only of the artist's conventional rendering of Amazons.

Late-twentieth-century feminists turned to the ancient myth of matriarchal Amazons in search of social and political ideals and even appropriated certain symbols (e.g., the moon sickle) to represent feminist power and identity. Di Leonardo (1991, 3) notes that this quest for signs of an early form of female power paralleled an aim of the French Revolution, whose adherents found their models of political virtue in the ancient Athenian republic.

See also LESBIAN, MATRIARCHY, SHE-MALE, VIRAGO.

AMW. See ACTRESS.

Amy. See MISS ANNE.

androgyny; androgyne. From the Latin *androgynus*, meaning hermaphrodite, from the Greek roots meaning male and female. The Greeks sometimes applied the word *androgynos*, meaning man-woman, in scorn for what they viewed as a PASSIVE partner in a same-sex encounter. *Androgyny* has commonly, especially in the past, been used derogatorily to suggest hermaphroditism, effeminacy, and sexual ambivalence, all of which have often had negative images in Western culture. Androgynous Romantic-era images of slim, foppish young men and boyish, sexless women suggested "sexual pathology, the macabre, and the diabolical" (Singer 1976, 32). Yet *androgyny* has also acquired the positive sense of wholeness or completeness. In some cultures androgyny, the joining of the features of both sexes, has even been regarded as an ideal state.

An androgyne, or androgynous person, is one who has the characteristics conventionally associated with both male and female, such as being both nurturing and aggressive. The androgyne is also sometimes defined as having features that cannot easily be gender-typed, that are neither distinctively feminine nor clearly masculine. *Androgyne* has been used since the sixteenth century for a hermaphrodite, a eunuch, or an effeminate man. The last two senses, however, are now obsolete, and *androgyne* is now often distinguished from *hermaphrodite* by emphasizing, instead of biology, the possession of the moral and psychological characteristics associated with both masculinity and femininity.

Androgyne has come into currency to describe lesbians or gay men who display both masculine and feminine traits and therefore are difficult to categorize by gender. For example, androgynous lesbians would be those with a physical appearance that is not specifically male or female, or a woman with some masculine body traits who attempts to balance this image by dressing or behaving in a conventionally feminine way. A female bodybuilder, with lean, hard muscle mass, may also be regarded as androgynous, while male performers such as Michael Jackson, who blends masculine and feminine physical characteristics and adornment, cut across culturally defined gender boundaries. The concept of androgyny has in-

trigued feminists for its power to challenge the conventional sexual duality of masculinity/femininity and the notions that this duality is natural and unchangeable. However, the paradox, says Mary Anne Warren (in Kramarae and Treichler 1985), is that "it is itself formulated in terms of the discredited concepts of masculinity and femininity which it ultimately rejects." Others add that it is hard to be good at playing both gender roles because, for example, some of them are contradictory (e.g., being competitive and being affiliative). The idea of "gender role transcendence" attempts to get around such problems by allowing individuals to develop their own personalities without regard to biological sex or cultural pressures (Ashcraft 1998, 121).

See also EFFEMINATE, EUNUCH, GENDER AND SEX, GENDER BENDER, HE-SHE, HERMAPHRODITE, HIM-HER, OPPOSITE SEX (third sex), SHE-HE, SHE-MALE, TRANSGENDERIST.

angel. Most commonly used in the domain of the spiritual and virtuous: a spiritual being possessing greater power than humans, a celestial attendant or messenger of god, a guardian spirit, or someone with the beauty or purity associated with angels. The word comes ultimately from the Greek *angelos* (messenger).

This word, however, is also applied to humans, especially women and sometimes homosexuals, often in biased ways. Western society has traditionally entertained a dual notion of women: a woman's body is dangerous, threatening, and impure, both physically and morally corrupting to men. At the same time, woman is seen as mother-Madonna—pure, beneficent, and emotionally as well as physically nourishing. The polarization is between good and evil, fertile and barren, pure and contaminating. The angel, although often a masculine figure in Judeo-Christian thought, or even of indeterminate sexuality, has come to represent the good and pure in woman.

Contemporary culture has borrowed heavily from these stereotypes: some women are angels, others morally sullied. (Mae West, as she made clear in her 1933 movie, *I'm No Angel,* refused to be put on a pedestal, where men could control her.) Sometimes, however, the term *angel* carries the meanings of its polar opposite, expressing the dominant idea of being sexually available. Angels are often represented as having wings, suggesting flying, which may connote sexuality (as in Erica Jong's *Fear of Flying,* 1973). A woman described as "heavenly" or "divine" is probably not a spiritual person but a sex object. *Charlie's Angels,* for example, titular heroes of the 1970s TV crime show, were criticized for sexualizing women, showing them using sexuality only to get their way, even on the job (Douglas 1994, 212). Some men have played with the term ironically, as in the expression for a lustful woman: *an angel looking for Peter,* where *Peter* makes a double entendre.

When the wings are thought of as gossamer and frail, then delicacy—another feminine attribute in traditional views—is evoked. "In the Victorian era, the ideology of separateness was expressed in the cult of the wife as 'the angel of the house,' who was imagined to be too delicate to face the rigors of the outside world" (Sally Helgesen, *Everyday Revolutionaries,* 1998, 72).

Angel is also slang for a gay man, connoting the stereotypical femininity of male homosexuals or the view of some heterosexuals that gay men are somehow of indeterminate sex. *Angel food* has been gay slang for an Air Force serviceman (see also DISH). However, *fallen angel,* as applied to a gay man, suggests moral disapproval. In the mid-twentieth century, after the production of the 1938 movie *Angels with Dirty Faces* (about two boyhood buddies who grow

up on opposite sides of the law), a man who was timid about expressing his homosexual inclinations was known as an "angel with a dirty face."

Among its other senses, the term *angel* is also used for beloved children of either sex; for a partner in love, reflecting on his or her innocence or charm; or by a father for his (often spoiled) daughter (a boy will resist being called by this feminine name). Once referring to a woman who was angelic by temperament but not necessarily in appearance, *angel* came to be a playful tag referring to a woman's attractive face, as in *angel face* or *angel puss. Angel* is also often racialized, a representation of white womanhood. Contrast with JEZEBEL; see also SNOW WHITE.

In the U.S. women's suffrage movement, the angel, with the theme of enlightenment, served to represent women's role as culture-bearer and preserver (Kramarae and Treichler 1992).

See also GODDESS (sex goddess), MADONNA, MAIDEN, VIRGIN.

angry white male. Expression meaning a white man, usually politically conservative, who sees himself as the victim of programs for minorities and women believed to be taking away his job opportunities.

> The political phenomenon of the "angry white male," and the growing divergence in political views held by men and women, has been fueled by the widespread perception among certain men that women's growing presence in the work world has deprived them of the secure and well-paying jobs to which they, as men, are somehow entitled. (Sally Helgesen, *Everyday Revolutionaries,* 1998, 66)

The expression is not likely to be self-descriptive; instead, it is usually a dismissal by liberals of those with antifeminist or anti-affirmative-action viewpoints. Liberals accuse these men of using their anger in ways that enable them to ignore or counter the argument that they benefit from sexism and racism. See also VICTIM.

animal. An allusion to passion in women, commonly stereotyped in Western culture as being more instinct-driven than men, less governed by reason. For a man, it may refer to uncouthness, brutality, rowdiness, athleticism, or sexual virility. The male reference probably came before the female, by the early twentieth century in popular U.S. usage, but it is not always as disparaging as the female reference may be in some contexts. Especially when used by men for other men, it may be a sign of respect for their prowess or excesses, which are still tolerated forms of male behavior in our culture. Rotundo (1993, 229) notes that in the late nineteenth century, beliefs about manhood evolved in the direction of putting a positive value on male passion, making virtues of aggression and competitiveness. In his 1903 novel, *The Call of the Wild,* Jack London earned fame for his depiction of the wild animal lurking behind the civilized veneer of men.

Animal has also been applied contemptuously to someone whose sexual orientation or related lifestyle is regarded as deviant. When used for gay people, it can suggest sodomy with an animal. "[The police] called us animals. We were the lowest scum of the Earth at that time" (drag queen who had been at the 1969 Stonewall riot in Greenwich Village, in Witt, Thomas, and Marcus 1995, 215). *Animal* may also see contemptuous use for poor people or people of color whose behavior does not conform to middle-class standards of conduct. However, the term may also be used as a covert word of affection between love partners in reference to their sexual performance.

Animal house, originally a 1950s campus term, usually refers to a college fraternity house noted for its uncleanness and rowdiness.

See also BEAST, BEAVER, BIRD, BULL, BUNNY, BUTTERFLY, CAT, COW, DOG, FILLY, FISH, FOX, GORILLA, HORSE, HUNTER, KITTEN, LAMB, LIZARD, MEAT, MINK, PET, PIG, PUSS, SHREW, SQUIRREL, STALLION, STUD, TIGER, TOM, VIXEN, WOLF, WOMEN AS ANIMALS, WORM, ZOO.

antimale. A term used especially by men or antifeminists who object to feminist thought or view profemale (or any egalitarian) attitudes as being antithetical to men's (they might say society's) interests. The user may wish to imply that disagreement with men and their control of society's institutions are somehow aberrant. A synonym is *man-hating,* the use of which can distract from the fact that hatred of women has so often been entwined with the attitudes associated with male dominance.

See also MAN-HATER.

antisexist. See FEMINIST.

anus queen. See PASSIVE.

ape. See GORILLA.

apple pie. See MOTHER.

apron; **apron strings**. *Apron,* a reference to a woman, from the name of the garment that stereotypically links women with kitchen chores. The term was used in the slang sense mostly early in the twentieth century, but the reference is still heard. A young man "tied to his mother's apron strings" is said to be dominated by her, or to be a sissy. Similarly, a man may be tied to his wife's apron strings and thus be regarded as servile to her, a culturally unacceptable role for a man.

See also CANDY-ASS, EFFEMINATE, FLOWER, MAMA'S BOY, MILKSOP, MILQUETOAST, NAMBY-PAMBY, PANSY, PUSSY-WHIPPED, SISSY, SKIRT, WIMP, WUSS.

armpiece. A slang reference to a woman who, especially because of her good looks, is asked to attend social functions as a man's escort. The allusion is thus to being on a man's arm (i.e., at his side, subordinate), and *piece* may suggest the woman as a sex object. Lighter (1994) notes that this term, dated to about the early 1980s, usually appears in journalistic contexts.

See also MISTRESS, PIECE.

arrow. See STRAIGHT.

ass. A reference, usually regarded as a vulgar, to a man's or woman's posterior or anus (from Middle English *ars*). It is also used for a person (often a woman but also a gay man) regarded as a sexual partner or prey (a woman reduced to genitals; a gay man, to the act of anal intercourse). It may also mean sexual activity or gratification. The ass, compared with the penis, connotes passivity, and thus fits the cultural stereotype of women and gay men. In male conversation it has commonly been used to suggest a man's dominance over either other men or women. During the presidential campaign of 1984, for example, vice presidential candidate George Bush got into hot water for referring to a debate with Geraldine Ferraro by saying, "We tried to kick a little ass last night." By this, he later explained, he meant "doing well" (beating his opponent) as opposed to referring literally to Ms. Ferraro or her posterior. *Ass* in the sense of a person or sexual activity has been in use since the nineteenth century.

Tail and *piece of ass* are synonyms for *ass* in the anatomic and sexual senses. Today, the meaning usually implies a woman as a sex object, although *tail* was originally a reference to a man's parts: *penis* is the Latin word for tail. Given this linguistic connection, Panati (1998, 349) goes so far as to say, "The word is, in a way, a curious male projection of his desire for a woman onto that woman herself." In the 1970s Continental Airlines, alluding to its attractive female airline attendants, came up with the sexist ad, "We really move our tail for you!" (see HUNK [of tail]).

Ass finds a place in a number of word combinations usually considered vulgar and often derisive as well, those included here being only a sample. *Ass bandit* (from mid-twentieth century) is a reference to a person who seduces young women. *Ass bandit* also means a "homosexual anal sodomist," specifically, the one who takes the active role. (see also SODOMY). Related words are *ass-king* and *ass-burglar*. Aman (1987, 17) gives the usage *baked ass,* applied in the Ozarks for a woman believed to be "stingy with her charms." *Ass peddler* means a female or male prostitute (although it apparently sees little use in gay communities, especially compared with HUSTLER; see also CRACK [crack salesman], PROSTITUTE). *Charity ass* refers to a prostitute who gives out a sexual favor (or to the act of intercourse with her) for no charge. A CANDY-ASS is a male seen as weak or cowardly (see also SISSY), or sometimes a female, though in the latter case, it may mean a sexy young girl. *Fat-ass* is a word for a heavy person or a reference to anyone you don't like.

Asshole (abbreviated to *a-hole* and *A.H.*) and *shit-ass* objectify a person regarded as obnoxious, mean, or worthless. They commonly apply to men, as does *bad-ass*. *Asswipe,* reported by Risch (1987) as being used by young college women for men, has similar meanings but can also suggest fawning behavior (see also LOUSE).

See also ASS MAN, BOX, CUNT, GASH, GINCH, HOLE, PASSIVE, PIECE, TWAT.

ass man. A reference to a man (usually by another man) believed to frequently indulge in sexual activity with women (see also LECHER) or a man who is sexually aroused by a woman's posterior. The expression is not usually insulting to the male referred to and may even be flattering to the man proud of his particular fetish. It does, however, definitely degrade the woman whose rear he admires. Both senses are from at least the mid-twentieth century.

See also ASS, LEG (leg man), MEAT (breast man), TIT MAN.

aunt; auntie; aunteater. Literally, a kinship term meaning the sister of one's mother or father. *Aunt* has, however, also a number of biased meanings. They cluster around kinds of women, including lesbians, and—reflecting a heterosexual view of homosexual men as feminized—gay men.

Aunt may be used endearingly for any woman who acts like a concerned relation. *Auntie* or *aunt* has also served as a term of address in the South, first by white people and then also by black, for an old black woman, especially a nursemaid. This usage is now usually regarded as offensive. To a slave master, an "auntie" was a black female slave no longer able to breed. *Aunt* has also meant any old woman or female gossip; though dated in this sense, *aunt* may still carry the mildly disparaging connotation of a somewhat conservative or staid older woman (see also GOSSIP). In addition, it has found euphemistic employment for the madam of a brothel or for a female prostitute, often an older one (see also PROSTITUTE). In *The Winter's Tale* Shakespeare wrote,

Summer songs for me and my aunts
While we lie tumbling in the hay.

In British and U.S. slang, *aunt* has been used to mean menstruation, as in such expressions as "My aunt is paying me a visit" or "Aunt Flo's in town" (see CURSE).

In gay communities, *aunt* or, more often, *auntie* (or *aunty*) refers to older gay men, especially fastidious, effeminate ones (from the early twentieth century). At one time, it had mildly disparaging ageist connotations, taken from the stereotype of an aunt as a useless old woman who gossips over tea. Rodgers (1972) lists it as denoting any homosexual persons over age thirty who seem, to very young gay men, to have nothing to show for their age. However, around the turn of the twentieth century, *auntie* communicated respect for a senior gay man but also often for the fact that he was not viewed as a sexual partner (*mother* was used in a similar, even more respectful way). Currently, especially among middle-aged or older gay men, the word may identify a dear or old, nonsexual friend. Gay men often lose their families when they "come out," and they replace them with close friends, using family terms. The idea is that "family" are those with whom you have significant, nonsexual relationships, not simply those people with whom you have only blood ties.

Rodgers notes related words, all also once carrying ageist connotations as used in gay communities. Thus, for example, an *auntie queen* is a young gay man who seeks an older man as a partner. Note the variable use of such terms—some may occur in affectionate contexts. Their description here is not meant to stereotype gay communities as having ageist tendencies.

Aunteater is part animal metaphor and part a play on *aunt;* it refers to a gay male. It is usually regarded as vulgar or derogatory.

See also HEN (old hen), SISTER.

Aunt Tom; Aunt Thomasina. From the mid-1900s, *Aunt Tom* has been a disparaging reference to a woman who does not support the goals of feminism and is thus regarded by those who do as docile in respect to men. The term comes by way of analogy from *Uncle Tom,* the African American ingroup slur for a subservient black man, from the 1852 novel *Uncle Tom's Cabin* by Harriet Beecher Stowe. The related *Aunt Thomasina* has been in use for a black woman who is servile to white people or accommodat-

ing to white society.
See also UNCLE MOM, UNCLE TOM.

avowed/admitted/declared homosexual.
See HOMOSEXUAL.

B

babe; **baby**. *Babe*—probably of imitative origin (from the infantile sound *baba*)—first used in the late fourteenth century to mean an infant. *Fowler's* (1996) regards it as mostly an affectionate or old-fashioned variant of *baby*, meaning a young child.

From the late nineteenth century, the Americanism *babe* has traditionally been a term of endearment and form of address for a woman, especially a pretty one, suggesting cuddliness and cuteness. It may still be considered complimentary by some women but is patronizing and offensive to many others. Babies are known for infantile behavior, dependence, whining, and underdeveloped intelligence (see also BIMBO), a feminine stereotype that contributes to the connotations of this usage as applied to women. *Babe,* however, occurs in black English as a friendly term of address for a spouse or lover or more generally for any man or woman (often man to woman and even man to man). Recently, female students have applied it in the sense of a handsome young man, and among young people generally, it signals a "hot" guy. *Babe* was also used generally to mean a sweetheart, regardless of sex, and as a term of address for a man, especially one outstanding in some way (mid-nineteenth century). Babe (George Herman) Ruth, born in Maryland, illustrates the use of the term as a pet name for a boy or man in the South. A "babe in the woods" is an innocent or inexperienced person, male or female. A "righteous babe" is a woman that feminists might see as a model.

Baby has had similar meanings (though not the student sense above). As a term for a sweetheart, especially a woman, it may be heard with sexual connotations: for example, "My Baby Gives It Away" was the title of a song sung by Pete Townshend and Ronnie Lane. With a female market in mind, Virginia Slims cigarettes devised a motto they believed would convey the idea of women's growing independence: "You've come a long way, baby." Ironically, the condescending use of *baby* was a cause of some feminist grief. *Baby* also occurs in slang usage for anything that may be the object of a man's pride or affection, that is, a car or fishing rod as well as a woman.

When referring to a man who is not behaving according to society's expectations of a man, *baby* suggests a SISSY or WUSS. "Blubberin' like a baby!... A big guy like you" (John Steinbeck, *Of Mice and Men,* 1937). It can serve to censure a boy or man for being weak, dependent, soft, complaining, or overly emotional—that is, too much like a baby or, more pertinent here, like the stereotypical woman. Similarly, *crybaby*, a common jeer among children, is a label most boys fear, and one that may restrain them from seeking aid or comfort when they need it. *Crybaby* is also applied to girls. A "babyface" is a man who is too pretty, youthful, or soft to be mean. In wrestling lingo, he is the good guy.

Associated with immaturity, *baby* is also applied as a negative sanction by adults or other children to control a child's behavior. Although the parent does not take the word as a slur, *baby* is a despised identity for most children, regardless of sex (Cahill 1986, 301–02). Being called a baby undermines a child's assertion of competence and independence. As the identifying labels "boy" and "girl" become increasingly important to children, they learn to appropriate gender identity as a way of avoiding being identified as a baby.

Baby also has been applied to gay men, probably suggesting an unmanly softness, though apart from private endearments, it is not used this way in gay communities. However, *babycakes,* popularized by Armisted Maupin's gay soap opera, *Tales of the City,* which began as a fictional series in the *San Francisco Chronicle* in 1976, is used as an endearment in gay communities. It is also used to mean "sweetheart" among straight people (see also CUPCAKE).

Baby also occurs in a number of slang word combinations. *Baby-doll,* for instance, refers to a pretty young woman, especially one seen as having guileless charm (see also DOLL), perhaps intended as a compliment but often regarded today as sexist, connoting a plaything or helpless child. "Did I hurt my little baby's arm?... Where I hurt little baby's arm?... My sweet baby doll" (Archie to his twenty-year-old wife in Tennessee Williams' *Baby-Doll: The Script for the Film,* 1956, 367). *Baby pro* (sometimes abbreviated *BP*) refers to an underage prostitute (see also LOLITA) or to child prostitution.

See also JAZZ (jazz baby), TOOTSIE.

bachelor. In its common sense, an unmarried man. It has, though, had other meanings related to young men, such as, historically, a novice knight. Generally a positive word, *bachelor* must be understood in the context of men's versus women's domains. Women have traditionally been defined within the world of marriage and family, so to fall outside that domain was likely to incur reproach rather than favor. Unlike men, at least until recently, women have not been able to enjoy the freedom to have "bachelor's parties" or "bachelor's pads" or been bestowed with such laurels as "most eligible bachelor" (said to be a "good catch"). Yet, while *bachelor* is generally positive, *confirmed bachelor* may suggest euphemistically that a man is gay; in gay communities, it may imply a closet homosexual.

See also BRIDE, DIVORCÉE (divorcé), OLD MAID (bachelorette), PLAYBOY, SINGLE, SPINSTER.

bad-ass. See ASS.

badger. Used since the early nineteenth century for an old man. It is often disparaging, unless applied to a native of Wisconsin, the Badger State.

See also BUZZARD, COOT, CUSS, DUFFER, FART, FOGY, GEEZER, GOAT, OLD FART.

bag; baggage. *Bag,* a pouch or pack, from Middle English *bagge.* By the late nineteenth century, *bag* came to be used to ridicule a middle-aged or old woman, especially one seen as slatternly, or to reproach a prostitute or sexually promiscuous woman, often an old one or one who appears aged or dumpy. The sexual sense of *bag* gains reinforcement from *bagnio* (from Italian *bagno,* bath), meaning a brothel, as well as from its onetime use in the sense of the womb or female genitals. Today it usually means simply any woman who does not meet male standards of attractiveness or submissive temperament. "After he stopped thinking of her as 'an old bag,'...he started thinking of Cora as a lush" (Tennessee Williams, "Two on a Party," in *Hard Candy,* 1954). Mills (1989) notes that this is one of a few words (see also DISH, WEAKER VESSEL) suggesting women as containers—empty until filled up by a man. The idea of what goes into a bag—often garbage—no doubt adds to the scurrilousness of the word. There seems to be a long-standing connection between *bag* and the idea of a woman. We see this in a quotation from the querulous Saint Odon of Cluny (879–943): "But if we refuse to touch dung or a tumor with the tip of the finger, how can we desire to kiss a woman, a bag of dung?" (Arango 1989, 23).

Bag is also used for any person regarded as low or despicable; Spears (1991) notes this slang usage as a truncation of DOUCHEBAG. *Scumbag,* on the other hand, has a tradition of application to men, though not exclusively. In April of 1998 Dan Burton, Republican representative from Indiana, slandered President Clinton, then under investigation for allegedly having had an affair with a White House intern and covering it up, as a "scumbag." The term derives from *scum,* meaning semen in slang usage, and *bag,* or condom.

An unrelated expression is *bag lady,* meaning a homeless woman, often elderly, who totes her few worldly possessions around in shopping bags. This word, from the 1970s, suggests destitution. As such, LADY is euphemistic, glossing over the social problem. Another problem is that *bag lady* is not parallel with *bag man,* who, far from being destitute, collects money for mobsters. (*Bagman* has had derogatory male use in the sense of a commercial traveler.) Although *bag lady* does not necessarily carry derogatory connotations, it has come to be used to mean any scruffy woman.

Funbag is a dismissive term for a female prostitute in police jargon. A "haybag" is a female prostitute or vagrant who may also be considered fat and lacking in moral restraint. *One-bagger* means an ugly person, especially a woman; the idea is that her facial ugliness can be hidden by placing a single bag over her head. Even worse is the "two-bagger." A "bag of bones" (also "skin and bones") is a person regarded as emaciated or just too thin to meet the cultural standards of physical beauty.

Baggage comes from the French *bague,* meaning a bundle. In addition to its common meaning of luggage, it has also been associated with refuse and things that get in the way. At one time, part of the "baggage trains" of European armies were the so-called camp followers, women who accompanied the soldiers from military camp to military camp, valued for giving—or selling—their sexual services to them. Indeed, *baggage* has referred to women since at least the sixteenth century (and denot-

ing a corpulent or burdensome woman since the early twentieth century).

See also BAT (old bat), FAG BAG, GEEZER (geez bag), HOSE (hose bag), HAG, HO (hobag), PROSTITUTE, SLATTERN.

bait. Since the mid-twentieth century, slang meaning a sexually attractive young woman not yet of legal age (age of consent). Figuratively, *bait* is allurement or temptation, dangerous to the predator (the male is held blameless for the "seduction"). A "squid bait" is a young woman viewed as seductive by sailors (see also FISH).

See also JAILBAIT, LOLITA, QUAIL (San Quentin quail), SEDUCTRESS, SIREN, TEMPTRESS.

baked ass. See ASS.

ball and chain. Twentieth-century slang meaning a man's wife or girlfriend (especially one insisting on getting him to the altar), regarded as restraining or domineering. "I ain't tied down…I'll be there, if I can get rid of the ball and chain" (Joel McCrea referring to getting away from his new wife [Ginger Rogers] in the 1940 movie *The Primrose Path*). While often meant to be whimsical, the expression reflects a cultural emphasis on the so-called right of men, chafing at female-imposed restrictions, to exercise their freedoms. Note from the illustrative quotation that the man is taking action on a woman regarded as an inanimate object. There is no comparable expression that women can use to suggest being weighed down by men. *Ball and chain* can also be used by men in reference to marriage.

There seem to be some cross-cultural equivalents. In Spanish, for example, *esposa* means wife, while *esposas* means handcuffs.

See also APRON, IRON MAIDEN, OLD LADY, PUSSY-WHIPPED, SQUAW, WARDEN, WIFE.

ballbreaker; **ballbuster**; **ballcutter**. Slang words for a tough boss, relentless taskmaster, or any vexatious person, but often a vulgar male reference to a woman seen as demanding, bossy, or nagging, that is, who attacks a man's masculinity (figuratively, his testicles; thus, she castrates him). The first two boldface forms are from the mid-twentieth century; the third came a little later. "There must be more ballcutters among those *grande dames* who never held a job in their lives...than among women who supervise shipbuilders' unions and direct troops" (quoted in Gittelson 1972, 354).

See also AMAZON, BARRACUDA, BITCH, CASTRATING, MANEATER, MOM (momism), NAG, VIRAGO.

BAM, Bam. Acronym for a "broad (or big)-assed marine," an offensive reference used in the military, especially by men, for a female marine.

See also BROAD.

bambi. See FAWN.

bandit. See ASS (ass bandit).

bar girl. See GIRL.

Barbie doll; Barbie. *Barbie doll*, an attractive woman regarded as empty-headed or bland and conformist in appearance. Only sometimes does it refer to a man, but the connotations are the same. The epithet comes from the trade name (Mattell Corporation) for a blue-eyed, blonde, teenage doll designed in 1959 for children and known for its depiction of glamour and conventional femininity (since the 1980s, she has had some racially diverse company in the market, but all are equally glamorous in style). Recently, she has taken on digital form in Mattel's Barbie Interactive line. Interestingly, the doll, named after designer Ruth Handler's daughter, was modeled on a German sex doll, Lilli, though the manufacturer does not draw attention to this shady origin.

Critics view the doll as contributing to a distorted perception of femininity, one, for instance, that readers of *Play-*

boy might appreciate. They also point, for example, to the extremely thin waist associated with starvation diets, bulimia and anorexia, and surgery. But others argue that having dated Ken (her male partner, also conventional) but never marrying him, and always paying her own way, Barbie conveys an image of independence. She has also been defended as opening a broad range of fantasies for girls, including entering such unconventional female careers as astronaut (Martin 1998) and as serving to model assertive behavior.

Barbie, meaning a girl or young woman who behaves superficially, appears to be used primarily among Euroamerican high school and college girls (Sutton 1995, 293). *Barbie doll* is probably also largely, but not entirely, limited to these school groups.

In 1992 Carolyn Levy taught a course on community-based theater script development. Some of the dialogue that emerged dealt with our society's biased sex roles as reflected in an imaginary companionship between the feminine Barbie and the masculine GI Joe dolls:

> Barbie: (Giggles.) Hi.
> GI Joe: Well, hello.
> Barbie: Where are you going?
> GI Joe: On a dangerous secret mission to slay my evil enemies. And you?
> Barbie: Malibu.
> GI Joe: Perhaps we should go together.
> Barbie: (Giggles.) You'll have to put my shoes on first.
> GI Joe: No! I'll carry you! (Slings her over his shoulder.)
> Barbie: Ooo! You're much more interesting than Ken!
> (in Buchwald, Fletcher, and Roth 1993, 232–33)

See also BLONDE (dumb blonde), DOLL, LOOKSISM.

barefoot and pregnant (keep them). A cliché that has come to be used by feminists as a shorthand way of expressing what they see as men's traditional desire to keep women dependent and tied down—to the home and the domestic role. Boles and Hoeveler (1996) note that local chapters of the National Organization for Women (NOW) once offered "Barefoot and Pregnant Awards" to men in mockery of acts of egregious sexism. The German equivalent is *Kinder-Küche-Kirche,* meaning children, kitchen, church.

See also FRAU, HOMEMAKER, MOTHER, WIFE, WOMAN'S PLACE IS IN THE HOME.

barker. See DOG.

barney. A man seen as socially inept, homely, or plainly dressed; a nerd. In the 1960s TV comedy sitcom *The Andy Griffith Show,* Don Knotts was aptly named Barney Fife, an inept if zealous deputy sheriff often described as one of the "naïve but noble rubes" who made that show and others with a similar rural orientation popular. The word is closer to "cute" than to "contemptuous." Compare it with more demeaning words for homely or backward women, such as BIFFER, DOG, or DOUCHEBAG (the emphasis in the attacks on women is more on appearance than on competence).

barracuda. Fish metaphor meaning a woman who is more aggressive or assertive than her society approves of. "The lady's a killer. She's a barracuda" (psychologist, played by Bob Newhart, speaking of a tough female TV interviewer, *Newhart,* 1998 rerun). The epithet comes from the name of a warmwater fish that has a large mouth with many sharp teeth. Large barracudas have been known to attack human swimmers.

See also BALLBREAKER, BITCH, CASTRATING, FISH, SHREW, VIRAGO, WOMEN AS ANIMALS.

barren. See GENDER-SPECIFIC ADJECTIVES.

baseborn child. See BASTARD.

bastard. Deriving from Old French *bastart,* a usually abusive word for an "illegitimate" child, a person born of unmarried parents, or any person considered despicable, cruel, or selfish; typically restricted to males. *Bastard* was not a term of disapproval at the onset—"There was a mysterious glamour of having an unknown father who might be a hero. But the Anglo-Saxons eventually reasoned, probably to bar a son of an unknown father from legal inheritance, that the state of bastardhood was a dishonor" (Una Stannard, in Kramarae and Treichler 1992). In the sixteenth century, Shakespeare used the word in the sense of a contemptible person, and by the eighteenth century the word had begun to replace the now archaic *whoreson,* meaning, literally, the son of a whore, with all that word's derisiveness (see also WHORE). It has been a popular aspersion in the twentieth century: "Americans were…weak, smelly, self-pitying—a pack of sniveling, dirty, thieving bastards" (Kurt Vonnegut, *Slaughterhouse Five,* 1966). *Bastard* may also be used affectionately, although the man's mother is somehow always morally in question.

There are other terms used for persons of unmarried parents, most of them negative; for example, *baseborn child,* a traditional Southern term, the first syllable of which carries a highly disparaging tone.

See also ALLEY CAT, BUZZARD, COCK, FUCKER, JERK, PRICK, SCHMUCK, SON OF A BITCH.

bat. A reference to a female prostitute who prowls the streets at night for customers (most bat species forage at night) or to any woman of ill repute (see also CHICKEN, OWL, QUAIL), first appearing in the seventeenth century. By the twentieth century, *bat* came to mean a woman considered difficult or quarrelsome, usually middle-aged or older (often as *old bat;* see also BAG), or an ugly woman or man. A mother-in-law, as an example of someone supposedly difficult to get along with, may be the prototypical "bat." Partridge (1984) says the more recent meaning may have derived from the association of bats with witches. *Bat* may also suggest the nocturnal VAMP, since vampires were thought to sometimes assume the form of bats. Unlike the prettier or domesticated birds, which also serve as metaphors for women, the nocturnal, rodent-faced bat—an anomaly in the animal world as a flying mammal and worse yet, one that sleeps upside down (symbolic of being an enemy to the "natural" order)—has traditionally been the subject of stories about ghouls. It suggests an ugly underworld remote from the orbit of human domestication (as some women may be thought of who escape male control). In Europe bats were once imagined to take form as demons that cohabited at night with women.

A variant term, *alley bat,* meaning a promiscuous or slovenly woman, emphasizes the connection with nocturnal disreputability (see also ALLEY CAT).

See also BATTLE-AX, BIMBO (bimbat), CRONE, HAG, HARRIDAN, HARPY, MOTHER-IN-LAW, SCOLD, SHREW, WITCH.

bathing beauty. See BEAUTY.

battle-ax. A woman regarded as having characteristics displeasing to men: she is often old, unattractive (a deformed face was once said to be "battle-axed"), sharp-tongued, and difficult to manage. She may be a domineering woman, such as the stereotypical mother-in-law (often the husband's) or a spouse like the bossy wife of Mr. Peterson (John Fiedler), the meek character who was a psychology patient in the 1970s TV sitcom *The Bob Newhart Show*. Like the synonyms *battering ram* and *battlewagon,* more rarely used, and *warhorse* (see HORSE), this expression also suggests belligerence. It comes from the late nineteenth

century but probably not, as stories have it, from the decoration used by the Battle-Ax Cut Plug chewing tobacco company in Lexington, Kentucky. Supposedly, because of the little red axes adorning tin tags attached to the plugs, the women workers at the plant, already enjoying reputations as a formidable lot, came to be known locally as battle-axes (Rawson 1989). Daly and Caputi (1987) give the meaning a feminist twist, defining the word as an "unconquerable crone," offering Carry Nation, the temperance leader, as an inspiring example.

See also BAT, BOMBSHELL (quotation), CRONE, CROW, HAG, HARPY, HARRIDAN, HATCHET, MOTHER-IN-LAW, SCOLD, SHREW, VIRAGO, WITCH.

battle of the sexes. A slogan and war metaphor applied to gender, referring to conflict and discord between men and women. Although popularly accepted as eternal, perhaps as a way of justifying or tolerating such behavior, strife between men and women is not universal or built-in but is the result of local social and political conditions that act on gender relations. "The battle of the sexes is not immediately implied in the anatomy of man and woman" (de Beauvoir [1952] 1974, 797). Maggio (1997) notes that the expression implies more equality in the struggle than, in fact, exists.

In the mid-twentieth century, there were rumblings about a crisis in American masculinity reflecting a battle between men and women in which women, many male experts mourned, were winning. "The 'Battle of the Sexes' is a reality, and one of its results has been rather extensive psychological castration of the male" (Ferdinand Lundberg and Marynia Farnham, in Ehrenreich and English 1978, 241). In a highly publicized tennis match in 1973, tennis champion and feminist Billie Jean King beat former champion Bobby Riggs, a self-described male chauvinist, in a contest billed as the "Battle of the Sexes." CBS followed up on the widely watched King-Riggs match by airing *The Challenge of the Sexes* and *Celebrity Challenge of the Sexes*, shows that also pitted women against men. The labeling of such competitions led many to infer that *battle of the sexes* was coined to describe the feminist urge to get revenge on men or to indicate men's backlash.

bawd. From Middle English *bawde* and Old French *baude*, a prostitute or madam, the woman who runs a house of prostitution. Originally applied mostly to men, in the sense of a lecher or pander, since 1700 the term has come to be restricted to women (the procuress). Deriving from *bawd* are *bawdry*, meaning suggestive or obscene language, and *bawdy*, lewd or boisterously indecent. In reference to the lecherous, Shakespeare wrote that "the bawdy hand of the dial is now upon the prick of noon" (*Romeo and Juliet*). A bawdy house is a bordello.

See also BROAD, MADAM, PROSTITUTE.

B.D. woman. See BULLDYKE.

beach bunny. See BUNNY.

beagle. See DOG.

beard. A usually vulgar word referring to female pubic hair or external genitals since at least the eighteenth century. In gay communities, it refers to a woman who dates a gay man to "front" him, that is, to make him look heterosexual in heterosexual society (Rodgers 1972). In this sense, it alludes to the beard as a masculine symbol and disguise (putting a masculine "face" on the gay man). She may also be said to be his "drag," that is, his disguise, making him out to be a heterosexual (see DRAG). Lesbians may also use the term for a male date, usually for a function where a male spouse is expected.

See also BEAVER, BUSH, HAIR, HAT, PUSSY, WHISKER, WOOL.

beast. Making its way into English from the Old French *beste,* a word meaning animal. Although it was first used to include humans, later it acquired the sense of a "lower" animal. As a gender-related epithet, it has different meanings, referring to both women and men.

Applied to women, it may allude to their supposed base animal sexuality or their stereotypically wild, threatening aspect as experienced by some men. When Western culture was still under the sway of Aristotelian thought, the womb was often depicted as a raging "beast," which helped to explain the alleged excessive lust of women and their assumed lack of rational control. Women (to men) are different, and *beast* serves to convey their "otherness." According to George Sanders, playing a banker-turned-artist in the 1942 movie *The Moon and Sixpence,* "Women are strange little beasts." In slang the word can mean a sexually attractive woman or one deemed ugly, unpopular, and distasteful but also sexually promiscuous (see also BIFFER). Both senses are from about the mid-twentieth century, typically associated with student use. In the sense of a cheap female prostitute, *beast* was in use somewhat earlier. Also in use is *beastie*, especially for a woman regarded as ugly. In the phrase *beast of burden,* often associated with women, the connotations are of property and subservience.

In the classic folk story "Beauty and the Beast," popularized in the eighteenth century by Madame Leprince de Beaumount, the woman is the BEAUTY, and the man, a beast, though he was in fact a handsome prince who had been bewitched. We may still refer to a beautiful woman and a homely or crude man together as "beauty and the beast." Men are often considered beasts for their size and aggressiveness, attributes associated with masculinity, and also because of their sexuality, which—in Victorian times at least—was regarded as a feature especially of the male. When applied to men, the sense of savagery or animality may not necessarily be insulting and in fact may be complimentary (male cruelty has been celebrated). Yet in British slang, *beast* is used for a sex offender, usually male, and men viewed as mean or despicable are often disparaged as brutes or beasts. Brigitte Bardot once took them to task: "Men are beasts and even beasts don't behave as they do" (in Fikes 1992).

In racist white supremacist thinking, black males are contemptuously called "beasts," since they are misperceived as closer to the bestial than are other categories of people (see BUNNY (jungle bunny).

See also ANIMAL, BIRD, CAT, COW, DOG, FOX, GORILLA, HORSE, LOOKSISM, PIG, TIGER, WOLF, WOMEN AS ANIMALS.

beauty; **bathing beauty**. *Beauty*, in its standard meaning, loveliness or prettiness, appearing in the early nineteenth century as a tag for an attractive woman. There were many kinds of "beauties," often by region of the country: Southern beauties, New England beauties, and New Orleans beauties, among others, all representing women as mere decoration. The tag *beauty* is still nearly ubiquitous in reports of women, even when physical appearance is irrelevant to what they do; and the expression is often accompanied by adjectives that focus on particular physical features, such as hair color. "The raven-haired beauty co-starred in a number of movies including *Nighthawks* with Sylvester Stallone" (Diedre Johnson, *Star,* 8 September 1998, 44). Women are also said to be "lovelies," a close synonym.

To succeed, it helps to be beautiful, especially if you're a woman, to whom the word *beauty* is closely and unfairly linked in our culture. French writer Ernest Renan summed up the expectation: "It is the duty of a woman to be beautiful."

> I have to pretend to be eaten up by my dresses, my jewels, my vanities. I make myself beautiful, often with an aching heart. (Margaret Scott, as the character Roxana in the 1936 British film *Things to Come*)

According to Naomi Wolf (1991), belief in the importance of outward beauty weighs heavily on many women. Women are encouraged by society to starve themselves and to submit to plastic surgery in order to conform to contemporary arbitrary standards (largely white male) of beauty. Beauty is like a "third shift" for women. Wolf argues that just as newly working women had to work a "second shift," taking care of house and children, now women are pressured into performing a "third shift": makeup, hair, diet, and exercise. The hidden agenda behind the beauty myth, says Wolf, is to take over where the myths about motherhood, domesticity, chastity, and passivity are no longer sufficiently coercive in a patriarchal society.

Some critics have attacked the emphasis on female beauty as a form of objectification that is pornographic (Griffin 1981) and an entirely passive accomplishment for women (Lakoff and Scherr 1984). Clearly, beauty is a form of power for those women considered beautiful, given their allure and their greater ability (compared with other women) to impress others, manipulate men or women, and evoke envy and admiration. Beauty has even been represented as dangerous to men, an aspect reflected in our use of SIREN or VAMP. Lakoff and Scherr's argument, however, is that "the power of beauty is the power of the weak" (26), meaning that women squander much of their human potential when they compete in the beauty game. A beautiful woman might manipulate men, but it is usually men who have the real power to make things happen for the woman doing the manipulating (see also GOLD DIGGER). Beauty, though not something we want to dispense with in our lives, may for a woman be more like a meal ticket than a source of real power.

Bathing beauty, used for a woman who appears in a beauty contest in a bathing suit, dates to the second decade of the twentieth century. At the time, Mack Sennett, a showman who was having problems getting press, discovered the value of displaying young women who were dressed only in bathing suits during a comic's performance. The Mack Sennett Bathing Beauties, as they were called, hired solely for their figures without regard to their acting abilities, made quite a hit. According to Flexner and Soukhanov (1997, 372), this was the first word for a woman that acknowledged that female prettiness was a matter of having a good figure as well as a pretty face. *Beauty contest* dates to the 1890s, while *bathing beauty contest* was widespread in the 1920s.

See also BEAST, BELLE, FACE THAT LAUNCHED A THOUSAND SHIPS, JUST ANOTHER PRETTY FACE, MISS AMERICA, PACKAGE, QUEEN (beauty queen), SEX OBJECT.

beaver. A twentieth-century slang term, often considered vulgar, meaning female pubic hair or external genital organs. In a more recent (since the 1960s) sense, it refers to a woman reduced to that part of her anatomy. It is often said to be a play on the expression *flat tail*, which is a nickname for a beaver, and *tail*, suggesting a woman's posterior or genitalia. A later, related use of *beaver* is any form of pornography featuring female nudity: a "beaver shot" (a "beaver shooter" is a man who seeks such a view) or "beaver" (girlie) flick. Though normally pejorative in reference to a woman, the term has been self-descriptive among women CBers, as suggested, for example, by "This is Little Beaver from Tallahasee" (Rawson 1989).

In addition there are the related *beaver patrol*, slang for girl-watching or young men (i.e., "beaver chasers") out seeking women; *beaver hunt*, a search for women, especially while driving; and *beaver-retriever*, a lecher. These three terms, while not generally offensive to the man whose activities are so labeled, are considered vulgar by most people and regarded as demeaning by many women and men today.

See also BEARD, BUNNY, BUSH, CAT, CUNT, HAIR, HAT, MINK, PUSSY, SQUIRREL, WOMEN AS ANIMALS, WOOL.

bed-bunny. See BUNNY.

beddy. A pretty young woman regarded (usually by men) as sexually promiscuous. This largely 1980–1990s California usage is based on *bed*, which the man supposedly—or wishfully—finds it easy to get her into, but *beddy* also sounds like the female given name Betty. "Some beddy, huh?" (one teen boy to another, eyeing a poster of a sexy woman, 1992 movie *Encino Man*).

See also BETTY, PROMISCUOUS.

bedworthy. See FUCKER (fuckable).

beef; beefcake. *Beef,* a vulgar reference to the genitalia, either female (usage beginning in the eighteenth century) or male (since the nineteenth century). *Beef* also refers to an attractive woman (since the mid-twentieth century) or any woman seen as a source of sexual gratification, including a prostitute. *Beef* has also been a name in male Jamaican use for a black woman. In gay slang it refers to masculine men.

Beefcake (from mid-twentieth century, patterned after the feminine CHEESECAKE) can refer to displays or pictures of muscular men in partial undress or (since the 1970s) to any muscular, sexually appealing man (see also HUNK). The word was originally U.S. slang, sometimes labeled in the dictionary as humorous. "As for the beefcake, 'What comes through is how narcissistic he is'" (reference to the late John F. Kennedy Jr., who posed as the biblical Adam in his magazine, *George* [quoted in *People,* 25 August 1997, 106]). In gay slang *beefcake* designates male pinups, who, before Stonewall, were portrayed only in "muscle mags" that masqueraded as health magazines (see *Beefcake: The Muscle Magazines of America 1950–1970,* by F. Valentine Hooven III, 1995). Unlike *cheesecake, beefcake* connotes a food that is more substantial than the feminine "cheese."

Partridge (1984) notes that the now obsolete phrase "to be in a man's beef" meant to wound him with a sword, whereas "to be in a woman's beef" meant to have sexual intercourse with her. Both usages reflect the judgment of the male speaker, indicating a striking difference in attitude toward women compared with that toward men.

Both *beef* and *beefcake* reflect one-sided views of masculinity, especially in relation to the body, suggesting how the structure of patriarchy, so often accused of distorting women's relations to their bodies, has done the same to men.

See also MEAT, MUTTON.

beef trust. People considered grossly fat, often women, such as the fat women performing in carnival sideshows (Lighter 1994). This is twentieth-century objectifying slang derived, according to Chapman (1987), from the muckraker term for those in control of the meat business.

See also BIG BERTHA, BOB, BRICK SHITHOUSE, HOGGER, LOOKSISM, PIG, SOW, YETI.

belle. Stressing female beauty, from the French word *belle* (beautiful). "The belle of the ball," sometimes still in use for the woman in the room on whom all men's eyes fix, may also be used today ironically for a woman who assumes the airs of such an idealized woman. But it is still often meant to be flattering, since gender standards encourage women to cultivate an attractive appearance (often above other qualities). "Melanie Griffith is the belle of the ball in a full-skirted satin gown" (*Star,* 13 October 1998, 32).

Used for a gay male, especially a young one who acts in feminine ways (it derives from the word as used for a woman, but is also related to the gay-disparaging term TINKER BELL), *belle* has had currency in gay communities since the early to mid-twentieth century, sometimes synonymous with QUEEN. As a dated term, however, when used today it may also date the speaker, highlighting his age. Rodgers (1972) says it has also had some pejorative use to mean loss of sexual attractiveness, getting old, fading in one's beauty.

See also BEAUTY, COQUETTE, EFFEMINATE, GAY, LOOKSISM, MARY, TACO (taco belle).

belle mère. See MOTHER-IN-LAW.

berdache. A Native American biological male who adopts the dress and ways of a woman. Native American women, too, have had a similar institution and might also be called berdaches, though AMAZON has had some use in referring to the female counterpart of the generally male concept of berdache. Certain non-Native American cultures also have this kind of institution, but while the term *berdache* might be applied to them, the common practice is to use culturally specific identity labels, such as *mahu*, meaning of either sex in the Hawaiian language.

The origins of the term are uncertain, but it appears to be derived from the Arabic *bardaj* (slave), from the Persian *bardag*. It was probably imported into English from Spanish *bardajo* or *bardaja* (kept boy); the Italian variant, *bardaccia,* CATAMITE or male prostitute; and the French *bardache*. Williams (1986, 9) writes that the 1680 edition of *Dictionnaire française* defined the word as "a young man who is shamefully abused (Caesar was the *bardache* of Nicomedes)."

Because of these etymological associations and because of the term's pejorative use by European colonizers, who reduced the role to one of sexual servicing of members of the same sex, it is now regarded as objectionable by many Native Americans and is often discredited by anthropologists as ethnocentric. In many American Indian communities, *two spirit* (sometimes capitalized and hyphenated), referring generally to Native Americans who are gay, transgendered, or lesbian, is replacing *berdache*. Still, there is a considerable history of use without overt or intended bias, and some Native Americans may even regard *two spirit* as problematic. Gary Bowen, a transgendered Native American cited in Feinberg (1998), explained that he doesn't use the term *two spirit* to describe himself. Where he grew up it was a pejorative term for a person of mixed blood. Further, there is no consensus as to just who is referred to by the term *two spirit*, and if translated into Native tongues, it acquires unfortunate meanings.

> Among my people it means "ghost-haunted"—a powerful concept and important in many Native spiritual systems, but having nothing to do with gender or orientation. (75)

Two-spirit individuals, or berdaches, have lived openly in their androgynous roles and traditionally took accepted, sometimes prestigious roles in Indian societies. Some two spirits served as shamans. Sexual contact with such a person endowed with the ability to communicate with the supernatural was considered to confer magical benefits (Churchill 1967, 81). Two spirits might exercise their capacity for biological reproduction, or become a spouse to another member of their culture. Because of their twin perspectives—male and female—they have

been viewed as being able to mediate between women and men.

The cultural role is viewed as demonstrating that sexual orientation is not simply a matter of two "opposite" sexes, man and woman, defined anatomically. *Male* and *masculine* are not at one pole and *female* and *feminine* at the other. Terry Tafoya has described his sense of gender as a Native American as being more appropriately represented as a circle, with individuals being located at many different points on the circle (Susan Stryker, January 1999; personal communication, citing from the video *Two Spirit People*). Will Roscoe has described Native American gender identities as matters primarily of spirituality: persons follow the unique gender paths of their particular spiritualities. Given these points of view, gender becomes a personal, idiosyncratic practice, more aptly seen as myriads of possible combinations of individualized choices (Susan Stryker).

See also ANDROGYNY, CROSS-DRESSER, DRAG (drag queen), TRANSGENDERIST, TRANSVESTITE.

Betty; Bettyfuss. *Betty*, the diminutive form of Bet, an abbreviation of Elizabet, or Elizabeth. A female pet name, once fashionable, as *The Oxford English Dictionary* (1989) claims, *Betty* is now often rustic. However, in recent U.S. slang, the word has been used for a young woman regarded as attractive or sexy, especially among young men or male students viewing the woman as a sex object. A "Betty Coed" is an average female student or member of a college sorority (see also COED). *Betty* or *Bettyfuss* usually refers contemptuously to a man who gives himself over to the kinds of household chores commonly viewed as "women's work" (see also HOMEMAKER [househusband], MARY [Mary Ann]). A "Bettyfuss" may also be thought of as a fussbudget.

See also BEDDY.

bi; bicycle. See BISEXUAL.

biddy. As the diminutive or affectionate form of the female name Bridget, "a woman." Among the Celtic Irish, Brigit, meaning exalted, was a pagan goddess of fertility and healing who was later Christianized and known as St. Brigit. In the eighteenth century the name, slipping from these spiritual heights, became a popular Christian name and then, in the nineteenth century, a generic for an Irish maid. It came to be used in this latter sense especially in the United States (the male equivalent was Mike, an Irish laborer). Perhaps this working-class context reinforced the idea of a biddy as a SLATTERN or PROSTITUTE, a sense it had also acquired in the eighteenth century. In the mid-twentieth century the word was heard among black speakers for an attractive little girl or small old woman (see Major 1994, who spells it *biddie*).

The common meaning of the word in the United States is an elderly woman, especially one regarded as fussy or mean or as a gossipy busybody (often as "old biddy"). *Biddy* also takes its connotations from the word's use for a chicken or hen. "The English hens had a contented cluck as if they never got nervous like Yankee biddies" (Louisa May Alcott, *Little Wives,* 1868).

See also BIRD, GOSSIP, HEN.

biffer; biff. Twentieth-century slang, largely in black English, for a woman viewed as ugly or distasteful, especially one who compensates for her homeliness by being promiscuous (Chapman 1998). (See also BEAST.) The more recent *biff* is college slang for a stupid young woman.

big bad wolf. See WOLF.

Big Bertha. Primarily a military expression for a piece of heavy artillery (a Big Bertha was a German gun used to shell Paris during World War II). By extension, in U.S. slang, the term has also been applied derogatorily to a very large or obese woman. In gay male communities, it has seen camp use for big, usually "overweight" men who are also often seen as effeminate.

See also BEEF TRUST, BOB, BRICK SHITHOUSE, HOGGER, PIG, SOW, YETI.

billy goat. From the nineteenth century, a man considered lecherous. Also a cantankerous man, often as "old billy goat," synonymous with "old coot." Both senses are somewhat dated now.

See also BADGER, BUZZARD, COOT, CUSS, DUFFER, GEEZER, GOAT, LECHER, OLD FART.

bimbo. A disrespectful slang word for any young woman, especially one thought to be empty-headed, frivolous, or, sometimes, hard-bitten; also used in the sense of a young, promiscuous woman or "tramp." The more recent sense of the term is that of a dumb but sexy woman. *Bimbo* may come from the Italian *bimbo,* meaning baby (perhaps by way of the Sicilian Mafia in U.S. society during the 1920s) and then following the English word BABY in eventually acquiring the meaning of "woman." Like a baby, a woman is stereotypically believed to have little developed intelligence. Chapman (1987), however, suggests that in the sense of a prostitute, *bimbo* may be related to *Bimbo,* the name of a monkey or monkey doll, which in turn is related to the monkey seen with street organ-grinders, usually Italian.

Bimbo, in the sense of a woman of loose morals, caught on during the Roaring Twenties and in the 1930s detective novel. The detective story helped popularize the notion of a beautiful but dumb blonde woman taken out for a night on the town in exchange for sexual favors (*Webster's Word Histories* 1989). *Bimbo* became a vogue term in the 1980s. Governor Bill Clinton, when deciding whether to run for president in 1988, supposedly had his gubernatorial chief of staff draw up a list of women with whom he had allegedly had affairs to determine who might talk to the press. This chief of staff described herself as a guardian against "bimbo eruptions" (*Newsweek,* 9 June 1997, 34). *Bimbo factor* appeared in the early 1990s in reference to how philandering affects a male politician's campaigning.

Bim, for a woman, comes to us from the early twentieth century and most likely derives from *bimbo.* While *bimbo* has had use throughout much of the twentieth century, *bimbette* (the jocular, diminutive form, even more connotative of a woman as a plaything) is relatively new, from the second half of the century. *Bimbat,* a blending of *bimbo* and *bat,* suggests an old, empty-headed woman or an old woman of ill repute. A "dimbo" (*dim* suggesting *dim-witted* or *dumbo*) is a "dumb bimbo"—with some redundancy in meaning—but may be used for either sex.

Bimbo may also be used derisively to describe men, usually in the sense of a mean and aggressive man or an undistinguished, unimportant man, particularly a bozo, but since the 1980s it has had lighter overtones (see also TOYBOY). A derived term for a man is *himbo*; he is supposed to be very good-looking but doesn't have much in the way of a mind. White women in particular have also been reported to use *mimbo* in much the same sense.

See also BLONDE (dumb blonde), BOW-HEAD, BUNNY (dumb bunny), DITZ, DUMB DORA, FEMINISM (bimbo feminism), SPACE GIRL, TWINK (twinkie).

biphobia. See HOMOPHOBIA.

bird. Animal metaphor meaning a woman, more common in British usage (where *burd* once meant a lady). *Bird* has been used in this sense in English since the fourteenth century, often disparagingly but also with easy familiarity. *Bird* is an animal metaphor suggesting domestication and pets, youth and prettiness (an aged bird becomes an "old crow"), or

game to be hunted (see also HUNTER). Birds, supposedly like women, are also not known conventionally for their intelligence, as the expression *birdbrain,* meaning dumb, suggests. A pet bird may also be a caged animal, "locked up" in the home as housewives are sometimes thought to be and, in fact, traditionally, in some important ways, have been.

Birds that are symbols of intelligence, power, or nobility, such as the cock, hawk, eagle, and falcon, are not typically used to represent women. They are masculine symbols, although not the only birds that have been used to represent masculinity. The gander (the adult male goose), for example, gave its name in the nineteenth century to a man who lived away from home (*gander* can mean to wander); in mid-twentieth-century gay slang, *gander* was used to designate a gay man who took the "active" role. (For other bird metaphors applied to men, see BUZZARD, PEACOCK.) In the past, however, birds were often positive feminine symbols. For example, the stork—once a symbol of spring or rebirth, now a bird of folklore believed to deliver babies—was believed to be a female deity in some prehistoric cultures.

Bird has also been used for female prostitutes and for lesbians. Also, both *bird* and *bird's nest* may mean the female genitals (compare with the masculine COCK). *Birdie* saw some student use around the middle of the twentieth century for an effeminate man, suggesting SISSY, as well as for a lesbian.

Bird has also served as an epithet for men in such terms as *jailbirds,* "prisoners," suggesting a cage; and specifically for gay men, (mis)represented in feminine terms. In twentieth-century usage, the word usually suggested an eccentric type of man, as in *odd bird* or *queer bird* (before the gay connotations of *queer* arose; however, *queer bird* has also had derogatory heterosexual use for a lesbian), or an older man (*old bird*). *Duck* is used similarly to *bird* in these general senses (*queer duck* or *old duck*). *Bird-watcher* is slang for a man who keeps his eyes on young women—a "girl" watcher.

See also BAT, CANARY, CHICK, CHICKEN, CROW, GROUSE, HEN, OWL, PATO, PET, PIGEON, QUAIL, WOMEN AS ANIMALS.

biscuit; biscuit bitch; biscuit eater. *Biscuit,* from the nineteenth century, an Americanism meaning a young woman seen as a sex object.

Biscuit bitch refers to a female volunteer in the American Red Cross. It is a military usage patterned after *Donut Dolly,* the official U.S. Red Cross moniker, but usually considered vulgar. Lighter (1994) associates *biscuit bitch* largely with use by U.S. soldiers during the Vietnam War. *Biscuit eater,* besides referring to a dog, serves as a euphemism for *bitch* in such phrases as *son of a biscuit eater* (especially in the South). Thus, *biscuit,* too, is sometimes used in the sense of *bitch.*

See also BITCH, CUPCAKE, DISH.

biscuit getter. See BREADWINNER.

bisexual. Standard English generally used today for a person who is sexually interested in both men and women and capable of consummating sexual activity with either. The term *bisexual* came originally from botany, meaning a plant with the functioning sex organs of both sexes (known also as a hermaphrodite, which is not usually used in this sense today).

A diversity of types of behavior is covered by the term in its current sense. These include serial experiences with members of the same and other sex. Some individuals who have had such experiences, however, may not identify themselves as bisexual but rather as heterosexual or homosexual, or they may prefer not to label themselves at all. In fact, among the questions raised about bisexuality is whether children who ex-

periment with same-sex partners before developing a heterosexual orientation may be considered bisexual; or married people who leave their other-sex spouses for someone of the same sex; or prisoners who have same-sex experiences but only in the limited context of prison. Such different sets of experiences— along with underlying questions of identity and intention as well as questions about the role of biology, learning, and circumstances in shaping desire and gender—point to the complexity of what so many call bisexuality.

The term *bisexual* rose to prominence as an adjective in the sexology studies of the nineteenth century. At the time that such sexologists as Richard von Krafft-Ebing spoke of "psychosexual hermaphroditism" (see also HERMAPHRODITE), *heterosexual* was actually the word applied to people with a bisexual inclination. Until the 1920s *bisexual* was applied to persons who displayed both "feminine" and "masculine" emotional and physical characteristics and was not yet used to describe sexual choice (Chauncey 1994, 49). In the mid-twentieth century, *bisexual* gained general currency in its modern sense by way of medical usage. It still carries a clinical tone.

The range of misleading connotations of *bisexual* includes promiscuity (someone willing to try "it" with anyone), infidelity, confusion about who one is, and experimentation. The last was fashionable in some quarters at one time but quickly faded with the advent of the AIDS crisis, since the heterosexual majority felt especially threatened by intimate contact with bisexuals. A popular stereotyping joke goes, "I'm trisexual— I'll try anything." Woody Allen's version is "I'm a practicing heterosexual...but bisexuality immediately doubles your chances for a date on Saturday night" (in Richter 1993). The term *bisexual* may also suggest just another kind of QUEER, expressing a common prejudice against bisexual people among heterosexuals. In the 1960s and 1970s many bisexual individuals began to see themselves as another victimized minority. However, some gay men, in self-reports of sexual orientation, have indicated that they are bisexual, a supposedly less stigmatizing term than *homosexual*. *Bisexual* may also be applied to lesbians or gay men by heterosexuals, who often ignore the distinctions in sexual-orientation diversity.

Among gays or lesbians, the word may connote a betrayal of one's homosexual identity (the bisexual person, unlike the gay person, is afforded the freedom to play straight) or simply a reluctance to commit oneself in sexual orientation. Where bisexuality is not accepted as a coherent, unique sexual orientation, bisexual people are often pressured by homosexuals and heterosexuals alike to choose one or the other identity. Many bisexuals argue that this kind of thinking offers an impoverished view of the range of possible sexual desire and orientation. Some have even found in bisexuality the utopian sexual rule of the future, replacing the narrow, limiting forms of exclusive heterosexuality and homosexuality.

Slang epithets applied to bisexual persons are not necessarily derogatory. However, heterosexual speakers or those of other sexual orientations, clinging to a notion of their orientation being the only acceptable or most respectable one, may load considerable bias into them. Jacqueline Susann illustrates this in *Valley of the Dolls* (1966) with a disparaging use of *double-gaited*: "And now Ted was taking it out on her. Where in hell was he? Probably cruising, the double-gaited sonofabitch" (256). Gay men and lesbians may also turn to such words to express linguistic bias against bisexual persons. Although within the gay and bisexual community, *bisexual* and even *bi* (an abbreviation for *bisexual*) are usu-

ally acceptable, other, mostly slang terms (e.g., *bicycle, AC-DC*) are sometimes used to suggest a cop-out (the individual may be regarded as ashamed of his or her homosexuality). Some expressions, such as *two-way baby,* are biased because they contain a word commonly taken as biased, in this case, *baby*. A common theme among the slang words for a bisexual is two-sidedness or changeability.

AC-DC (AC/DC, a.c.-d.c.), from the abbreviation for alternating current/direct current, has had jocular and euphemistic use since the mid-twentieth century.

Electrical current suggests sexual desire. The term may imply someone who can alternate his or her object of sexual desire; or *alternate* may mean different sex and *direct*, same sex. The idea of alternating may also suggest homosexuality, that is, the alternative to the cultural norm of heterosexuality (see ALTERNATIVE LIFESTYLE). Among gay people, *AC-DC* may be applied to those in the closet who pretend in public to be straight, or to heterosexuals who think about experimenting with homosexuality. The expression can also refer to a gay man who varies between taking a "female" and a "male" sexual role.

A synonym is *acey-deucey*, which also suggests *ace*, a British slang word for female genitals, and *juicy*, which sometimes means lusty (Richter 1993).

AM-FM comes from the abbreviation for amplitude modulation/frequency modulation, the two types of broadcasting systems (i.e., contrasting options).

See also HALF-AND-HALF, HETEROSEXUAL, HOMOPHOBIA (biphobia), HOMOSEXUAL, JASPER, LESBIGAY, SEXUAL PREFERENCE.

bit; bitty. See PIECE.

bitch. Generally an abusive word for a woman regarded as malicious, domineering, blunt, brassy, or spiteful; or for any highly disagreeable woman or thing. A common implication is that the woman does not know how to hold her tongue (she talks in ways that do not conform to men's ideas of femininity; see also NAG, SEEN BUT NOT HEARD). But the word implies more than this, defining—and degrading—women in terms of an animal metaphor, a female dog.

Bitch derives from the Old English *bicce,* and its original sense, still common, means a female of the dog species or other carnivorous mammals (e.g., wolves and wild dogs)—that is, a member of the sex capable of reproduction—to which the human female came to be compared in terms of receptivity and temperament. While a dog in heat need not be an object of contempt—Barbara Walker says that *bitch* was a sacred title of the ancient goddess Artemis-Diana, who led the hunting dogs (Kramarae and Treichler 1992)—we know the female dog protecting her litter as one that may bite the hand that feeds it. Dunayer (1995, 14) points out that dog breeders have traditionally treated the female dog (euphemistically called *lady dog* or *she dog*) with scorn, a serviceable animal whose only purpose is to create a profitable litter. Meaning may vary with the speaker or the intent of the speaker, but *bitch* is often contemptuous when used by males whose tendency, like that of dog breeders, is to see women's bodies as exploitable. For much of the nineteenth century, because of the sexual potency of *bitch* in the ears of Victorians, the word nearly fell out of use among the delicate American public. Henry Miller (*Sexus,* 1965), seldom delicate in his wording, suggests which of the sexes he regards as steely strong and which writhes in passion, evoking the lewdness sometimes connoted by *bitch*: "She was just like a bitch in heat, biting me all over, panting, gasping, wriggling like a worm on the hook" (180). We still have expressions such as *hotter than a*

bitch-wolf to describe women viewed as lustful and willing to engage in sex.

Bitch has often been used in the sense of a lewd or lascivious woman or, in early use, a prostitute (*bitchery* was once used for prostitution).

> I wish I were a fascinating bitch:
> I'd never be poor—I'd always be rich.
> I'd live in a house with a little red light.
> I'd sleep all day and work all night.
> —Traditional college sorority song in Goldman 1981, 57

Some men may claim to use *bitch* affectionately for a woman (though the contexts for that use would be very limited), while Sutton (1995) reports that some California female undergraduates do use it *among themselves* as a term of affection. Among women, says Sutton, it is a signal of solidarity. In addition it may be used by some women self-descriptively as an acronym of independence—that is, *B*eing *I*n *T*otal *C*ontrol of *H*erself.

Bitch even appears to be increasingly used by young women for a man. In the 1996 film *Girls Town,* a teenage girl calls a rough, obnoxious man a "bitch." But as applied to a man, the word has often lacked the opprobrium associated with use for women and may be regarded as whimsical (*The Oxford English Dictionary* 1989). It may even suggest something extraordinary about a person, usually a man, as in "He's a bitch on the horn."

Bitch also commonly means a complainer, and the verb *bitch* (to gripe) is stereotypically associated with menstruation (the verb *bitch* also means to womanize). *Bitch box* is slang for a public address system loudspeaker viewed as brassy and nagging (see also NAG). *Bitch kitty* is a name used in the sense of a highly unpleasant or heartless woman, and *megabitch* (also *turbobitch*) is slung at a woman considered especially treacherous. The mixed metaphor *cocky bitch* alludes to a self-confidence that often still seems culturally out of place for a woman (a self-confident male is known by the more positive *cocksure*). When applied to a woman, *bitchy* means sexually provocative as well as rude and complaining (effeminate men may also be accused of bitchiness). When a woman is wealthy—more wealthy than a woman should be by most standards—she may be censured as a "rich bitch" (also the name of a song performed by D.O.A.).

When used by black people, *bitch* suggests an ill-tempered or malicious female, or it may be used for any woman (and sometimes even a black man). "When I off a nigger bitch, I close my eyes and concentrate real hard, and pretty soon I get to believing that I'm riding one of them bucking blondes" (character in Eldridge Cleaver's *Soul on Ice,* 1968, 161). However, African Americans have been known to adopt white slurs but give them a different or inverted meaning: "That woman is a bitch" or "She a tough bitch" may, among black males, be intended as complimentary (Dillard 1976, 121), used in such senses as strong or self-possessed. In any case, the black usage does not carry the sense of personal malice heard in the more common usage; Thorne (1990) calls the black overtones more proprietorial or condescending. How it is taken, however, is another matter. In the 1990s concern was expressed among black people that the use of *bitch* in rap music was degrading to African American women and to women in general. "So what about the bitch who got shot…?" (NWA, "Straight Outta Compton," in Stanley 1992, 244).

The Bitch Manifesto was a feminist paper written by Jo Freeman (Joreen), founder of Chicago Women's Liberation Union, and first published in 1969 (Roszak and Roszak 1969, 275–84). It claimed to speak for women who were marginal in society because they had rejected the feminine stereotype. The Manifesto described bitches as "independent cusses" who seek their identity "strictly through themselves and what they do." "If something gets in their way, well, that's why they become Bitches" (276). The author attempted to reclaim the word with the slogan "Bitch is beautiful," patterned after the 1960s civil rights slogan "Black is beautiful," and called for an organization of strong women to work toward women's liberation.

In other senses, in gay communities, *bitch* suggests a gay man who plays the PASSIVE role in sex or an ill-tempered, resentful, or haughty homosexual man. But there are variations: *beach bitch*, for example, means a gay man who cruises beaches to make sexual contacts. *Bull bitch* applies to a woman with "masculine" characteristics (see also BULLDYKE). In still other contexts, a *gangsta bitch* means a young woman who is a member of or hangs around a street gang. William James' *bitch goddess success*, the worship of which he claimed gave Americans a bad case of moral flabbiness, refers to one's career or standard of living as a negative force—like a woman threatening to bring bad luck or ruin.

In addressing the issue of whether the slur *bitch* is actionable, courts have generally concluded that it is not. In May 1998 Supreme Court judge Herman Cahn of Manhattan ruled that Gay Culverhouse, a Manhattan businesswoman who was called a "rich bitch" by the president of the Cooke Center, was not justified in claiming the slur to be defamatory. The term was too "imprecise," said the judge (*Copy Editor,* June–July 1998, 2).

See also BALLBREAKER, BARRACUDA, BLUFF, BOB, BULL (bull bitch), CASTRATING, COCK (cock bite), CWA, DOG, FOUR-LETTER MAN (five-letter woman), GAB, HAG,

HARPY, HARRIDAN, HEN (henpecked), NAG, SCOLD, SHE-DEVIL, SHREW, SON OF A BITCH, STEPMOTHER, TERMAGANT, VIRAGO, WICKED WITCH OF THE WEST, WITCH, WOMEN AS ANIMALS. For the male equivalent, see BASTARD.

black pearl. See PEARL.

black rose. See ROSE.

black widow. See WIDOW.

blonde; dumb blonde; blondie. *Blonde,* a woman with blonde hair (coming in many shades, e.g., strawberry or platinum, from nature or the drugstore) and, often, light complexion and blue or gray eyes; from the Middle French *blond*, masculine; *blonde*, feminine. The gender distinction in spelling is sometimes still observed, though the nonbiased preference is to use *blonde* as an adjective for both a man's and a woman's hair color.

In the case of the noun, gender bias enters in when an obviously feminine part of the woman, the hair, is allowed to represent the whole woman. This is not so for the man, of whom we may say "He's blonde" but not so often "He is a blonde." Blonde is a color of symbolic appeal and legend in Western culture. "Gentlemen always seem to prefer blondes" are the often-quoted words of Anita Loos, from her best-selling novel *Gentlemen Prefer Blondes* (1925), in which she satirized the flappers and gold diggers of the Jazz Age. Mystery story writer Raymond Chandler gave us the unforgettable line, "It was a blonde. A blonde to make a bishop kick a hole in a stained-glass window" (reference to a photograph in *Farewell My Lovely,* 1940). Chandler's is a comment on men's experienced loss of control in the face of female sexuality (see also BOMBSHELL).

Dumb blonde refers to a white, blonde-haired woman viewed as empty-headed. She need not be young or attractive but if so, she is even more likely to be viewed as light in the head, as singer Dolly Parton once bemoaned the stereotype (*Ms.,* June 1979). Among other stereotypical characteristics of the much maligned dumb blonde are a squeaky voice, large breasts (often as *buxom blonde*), and a lack of "class." She's only good for partying ("Blondes have more fun"). In *Soul on Ice* (1968) Eldridge Cleaver contrasted the blonde stereotype with that of the black woman and laid the blame in both cases on the white man. "The myth of the strong black woman is the other side of the coin of the myth of the beautiful dumb blonde. The white man turned the white woman into a weak-minded, weak-bodied, delicate freak, a sex pot, and placed her on a pedestal; he turned the black woman into a strong, self-reliant Amazon and deposited her in his kitchen" (162).

There is a series of "dumb blonde" jokes that both put down blonde women and make fun of women's stereotypical "stupidity." They may go like this one:

> Do you know how to get a blonde's eyes to light up?
> Shine a flashlight in her ear.
> —Elizabeth Powell, in
> Buchwald, Fletcher, and Roth
> 1993, 112

Blondie is an epithet used largely by black men for white women, although black women may use it also. It reduces a woman to hair color, specifically the lighter hair of many white women. *Golden girl* conveys an image of a successful or popular young woman—virtually always white.

See also BARBIE, BOMBSHELL (blonde bombshell), BUNNY (dumb bunny), DUMB DORA, FAIR SEX.

blowser. A slang term used over the past three centuries or so to mean variously a coarse or slatternly woman, a female prostitute, or any woman regarded as offensive. *Blowze* appeared in English in the sixteenth century, meaning a wench, and *blowzy* entered the language about a century later in the sense of having a red, bloated face or slatternly appearance. *Blowzy* was sometimes also applied to men.

See also PROSTITUTE, SLATTERN.

Bluebeard. A lascivious man (*blue* has long had associations with sexuality), mostly in British slang. Also, based on the stories of seventeenth-century author Charles Perrault, *Bluebeard* denotes a merciless man who marries, then kills his wives: a literal lady-killer.

The true-life Bluebeard was a boy molester who raped and killed as many as a hundred peasant boys in his Brittany castle (Brownmiller 1975, 323). The story that was passed down, however, was that of a rake who killed his wives rather than a murderous molester of boys. It has often been discussed as a story that satirizes notorious historical wife killers such as Henry VIII. But even if the modified story was used as satire, this probably wouldn't account for why the story was changed. As Brownmiller suggests,

> It is almost as if the *truth* of Bluebeard's atrocities was too frightening to men to survive in the popular imagination—but turned about so that Bluebeard's victims were acceptably female, the horror was sufficiently diminished (not, of course, to women). (323–24)

The name *Bluebeard* lends itself to sensational journalistic writing, but its fairy-tale-like quality does not reflect the ugliness of a tyrannical husband, let alone one who murders his wives—or young boys.

See also LADY-KILLER.

blueberry pie. See PIE.

bluestocking. A woman considered to have, in the eyes of ridiculers, pretentious literary or intellectual interests and therefore is supposedly "unfeminine." In the

mid-eighteenth century, this word was used for women and men who attended literary discussion groups in the salon of Elizabeth Montagu in London. It is said to derive specifically from an allusion to Mr. Benjamin Stillingfleet, a noted botanist and poet and a member of the clique. Mr. Stillingfleet was too poor to wear formal black silk stockings but was assured that the everyday blue stockings would do. The group members came to be called the "Blue Stocking Society."

Within a few decades, in both the United States and England, the term came to be used to belittle any woman with literary, intellectual, and, sometimes also, feminist interests. The ability to think, after all, was attributed only to men. In the 1850s, for example, when fiction written by women was at a high tide, author Nathaniel Hawthorne, in a letter to his publisher, condemned the "mob of scribbling women" known as "bluestockings" who were producing some of the literary work of the day (in Fred Pattee, *The Feminine Fifties,* 1940, 110). Mothers in the nineteenth century who feared that their daughters might become overly learned, and thus scare off suitors, discouraged their daughters from being bluestockings.

Bluestocking is still heard, perhaps seldom with any of the original scoffing connotations, but Mills (1989) reports an example of use from the 1980s indicating that the word implies that learning can still make a woman less attractive to many men. *Bluestocking* also acquired the meaning of a flirt, a young woman who displayed her learning as a way of attracting a man. The term has also seen some biased application to lesbians and gay men.

bluff. Mid-twentieth-century slur on a lesbian, possibly a blend of the words BITCH and FLUFF.

See also LESBIAN.

bob. Stands for "big ol' bitch," that is, an extremely obese woman.

See also BITCH, HOGGER, LOOKSISM, PIG.

bog queen. See QUEEN.

bombshell. A term meaning a stunningly sexy woman or a woman of explosive energy, especially common in the 1930s to 1950s, when such Hollywood superstars as Jean Harlow (who gave us one of her best performances in the 1933 movie *Bombshell*) and Marilyn Monroe were known as "blonde bombshells." The term often occurs in tabloids alliteratively, such as "bleached bombshell," "busty bombshell," and "bombshell bimbo" as well as "blonde bombshell" or as "airhead bombshell." While a bombshell is merely the casing of a bomb, it suggests the devastation contained inside. It is similar in a sense to *firecracker,* which suggests the explosiveness of passion, and synonymous with *sex bomb.* All these terms are military metaphors implying that among men, female sexuality is experienced as a kind of dangerously explosive weapon: it has the power to "blow" men away. In *Proving Manhood,* Timothy Beneke (1997) discusses female sexuality as a "powerful physical force" that distracts, overpowers, angers, tests, and even devastates men.

In a *Life* magazine article on sexist language in 1970, Ann Bayer wrote of a fictionalized woman concerned with "rampant sexism" in our society. Hyperia, as she was called, complained of how close men's insulting language was to their compliments: "If you're not a *bombshell,* what are you? A *battle-ax"* (Nilsen et al. 1977, 2).

See also BLONDE, FEMME FATALE, GENDER-SPECIFIC ADJECTIVES (ravishing), HAMMER, HOT, KNOCKOUT, LOOKSISM, SEXPOT, WOMEN AS STORMS.

boom-boom girl. A term since the mid-twentieth century for an East Asian female prostitute, especially a Vietnamese woman sought by soldiers during the Vietnam War. "At dusk, the boom-boom girls arrived. From the bunker roof, I'd spot a cloud of dust in the distance, and ten minutes later, they'd roar up on their Hondas, seated behind their pimps" (*The River,* Paul Clayton, 1996, www.vietvet.org/river.htm). *Boom boom* is pidgin for "sexual activity."

See also EXOTIC, PROSTITUTE.

boondagger. See BULLDAGGER.

boss, the. See WIFE.

boss lady. See LADY.

bossy. See COW.

bovine. See COW.

bowhead. Derogatory slang since the 1980s for a female college student or sorority "girl" who customarily wears bows in her hair and is known as shallow or dumb.

See also BIMBO.

bowser. See DOG.

box; Pandora's box. *Box,* a slang term since the sixteenth century for the female genitals, suggested by the idea of a box as a container (in gay parlance, *box* sometimes means male genitals). *Box* later came to mean a woman reduced to that part of the female anatomy. There are variations, too, such as *poxbox,* which uses rhyming syllables to refer to a woman believed to carry syphilis (or any woman viewed as promiscuous). Usage in all these senses is primarily male.

Richter (1993) suggests a relationship between *box* in the sense of female genitals and death, since *box* is also used to mean a coffin. He notes that orgasm is a "little death" of sorts. *In the box,* said of men, stands for sexual intercourse but also connotes death.

Female sexuality, particularly as represented by this part of the anatomy, has long been viewed among men in Western societies as a threat to men. In one version of the ancient Greek myth of Pandora, this First Woman, who was endowed by the gods with both sensuous appeal and a dangerous curiosity and deceitfulness, is sent to Epimetheus as a gift from Zeus. Epimetheus, however, fails to heed the warning of his brother, Prometheus, who was skeptical of gifts from Olympian gods. Zeus in fact sends Pandora as a form of recompense for the fire Prometheus stole from heaven for the benefit of mortals. Once with Epimetheus, Pandora, out of curiosity, opens a vase, or jar, in her possession that she was expressly forbidden to open, thereby letting loose on the world all manner of pain and evil. Centuries later, the scholar Erasmus mistranslated Hesiod, the Greek storyteller, rendering "vase" as "box," thus giving us today's standard expression *Pandora's box*. It has since come to mean any source of troubles. As Hays (1964, 86) has suggested, Pandora's box can be viewed as a symbol of the womb, also of the vulva, long depicted in myth and belief to be a source of evil magic to men.

In the 1928 German silent movie *Pandora's Box*, Louise Brooks tempted men into moral destruction.

See also ASS, BEAUTY, CUNT, FEMME FATALE, GASH, GINCH, SEDUCTRESS, SHE-DEVIL, SIREN, TEMPTRESS, VAMP, VIXEN, WITCH. Compare with FALLEN WOMAN.

boy. From the thirteenth-century Middle English term *boi*, possibly from the Old French *embuié* (servant) a term commonly used to mean a male child. *Boy* has a variety of other uses, however, some of them biased.

When used for a man, *boy* may be a way of evoking immaturity, frivolous or prankish behavior, dependence, or other preadolescent conditions or qualities. In this example—"Just three days after sentencing in DUI, rap bad boy [Bobby Brown] romped with disco blonde" (*Globe*, 17 February 1998, 4)—*boy* suggests a man who is a troublemaker because he has never grown up. Or, in the words attributed to pianist Liberace, "The difference between men and boys is the price of their toys." *Boy* also suggests innocence, as when politicians, seeking support for a war, speak of getting behind "our boys" going overseas to fight, appropriating their youthfulness for political ends. Male solidarity, too, may be evoked—"He's one of the boys"—as is, sometimes, exculpation, as in the expression "Boys will be boys."

> Sexual harassment in schools is dismissed as normal and unavoidable "boys will be boys" behavior; but by being targeted, girls are being intimidated and caused to feel like members of an inferior class. (Sadker and Sadker 1994, 13)

When intimacy is an issue, *boy* is often suffused with homosexual eroticism (e.g., *lavender boy* [see LAVENDER]). Connotations of subservience, immaturity (the gay man as a child), and effeminacy may come into play. *Pretty boy* (we typically apply *pretty* to women) and especially *Percy boy* also suggest an effeminate or gay man, while *boy toy* applies to a man or woman as a sexual plaything (see also DOLL). Women have nonsexual girlfriends; when a man has a boyfriend, however, he is probably a sexual friend.

Boy is also commonly applied to males as a way of suggesting the inferiority of their race, ethnicity, or occupational status. *Boy* has a long history in English meaning someone of low or menial status, such as a "houseboy" or a "ship's boy," who occupies the lowest station among mariners.

Similarly, *boy* has been applied to any male who works as a porter, a courtesy helper in a grocery store, or an elevator operator, suggesting low status. Also, in biased ethnic discourse, *city boy* is a code word for, and subtle slur on, a Jew, based on the traditional association of Jews with cities, especially New York. The overt slur would be *Jewboy. Gayboy* has long been a slur on gay men (see also GAY).

Boy was used by white colonists in North America for males who were indentured servants, Indians, or black slaves and was later restricted to mean black male slaves of almost any age, with emasculating connotations. It was heard commonly in the South, especially when the black man's first name was not known, since white Southerners did not traditionally use titles of respect for black people.

White people still sometimes use this pejorative today for black males, though less so because of greater social disapproval of the term as an overt slur. Of Frederic Morrow, the first black assistant to a president of the United States (Eisenhower), David Halberstam wrote, "When he attended social events as a member of the White House staff, people occasionally gave him their coats, saying 'Boy, take care of this'" (interview in *Booklist*, 15 September 1993, 105). Black people have returned the insult with such black English slang forms as *grayboy* and *whiteboy*.

On the other hand, an expression such as *fair-haired boy* (or *blue-eyed* or *white-haired boy*), where the person named is a white man or boy, refers to someone who is favored in some way, given special attention, or destined to become a leader of his group. *Good ol' boys,* meaning a group or organization of men that display male solidarity, may be used pejoratively by black people, women, or Northerners. *Boys' club* is used sardonically by women.

Boy is also frequently heard in gay communities. The term *boystown* refers to any location where gay men gather, deriving from the 1938 cult film *Boys Town,* which dealt with male juvenile delinquents (Thorne 1990). In Chicago, for example, a six-block area on the north side of the city is popularly known—and among gay men, with pride—as "Boys Town," because of the number of gay men living there and the gay-owned businesses that cater to them.

Commonly topping the popular music charts today are such "boy groups" as Backstreet Boys and Boyzone.

See also BULLY (bully-boy), CALL BOY, CATAMITE, CHERRY (cherry boy), CHICK (boychick), CHICKEN, CHORUS BOY, GAL (gal-boy), GAZOONEY, GENDER AND SEX, GIRL, GOOD OL' BOY, GUNSEL, HOMOSEXUAL, LEATHER (leather boy), LOVER (loverboy), MAMA'S BOY, MAN FRIDAY, NANCY (Nancy boy), OLD BOY, TOMBOY, TOYBOY.

BP. See BABE (baby pro).

bra burner. Derogatory reference to a feminist regarded as militant or strident; a stereotype of the women's movement and both an invention of and common code label in the media. Since its appearance, it has been used for feminist-bashing.

Bra burner arose from an incident at the Miss America pageant in Atlantic City in 1968. Women protesting the image of women as sex objects tossed such typically feminine items as spike-heeled shoes, false eyelashes, undergarments (including padded bras), and traditional women's magazines into a "freedom trashcan" on the Boardwalk. Never mind that the items were never actually burned, as those who participated insist. The press, generally sympathetic with the pageant, and alluding to the draft-card-burning incidents of the antiwar movement of the 1960s, reported burning, and the label (if not the bras) caught fire. We hear it still today as a reference to women with a feminist take on politics, inequality, or sex. "Women are judged by their jugs.... The question for a woman is how to deal with this, and that's where I part ways with the bra-burners" (Jan Breslauer, *Playboy*, July 1997, 66).

It may be that the fashion among some young women of the day to go without bras reinforced the label, though the practice was much more than just a fashion to many in the women's movement.

See also FEMINAZI, FEMINISM, FEMINIST, LIBBER, WOMEN'S LIBERATION.

bra-buster. A woman whose breasts are so big they more than fill a bra. This men's talk is usually considered coarse and is reductive of women.

See also COW (milker), GIRLS, HOOTERS GIRLS, MEAT (breast man), TIT MAN.

breadwinner. The wage earner in a patriarchal nuclear family. The woman has been expected to be the HOMEMAKER and the man, the breadwinner. Given this gendered division of labor—which most sociologists refuse to consider as biologically determined (and as today's common two-career family should testify)—it is assumed that the breadwinner is to be strong and protective, the homemaker, submissive and nurturing. Many people—women as well as men—regard the male breadwinner as a source of well-being for the whole family. Some even insist on the role as a burden on men, a benefit for women. Referring to the conflict he experienced over the rise of the women's movement, playwright August Strindberg wrote,

> Man's prospects of winning the battle [against women's independence] are very dubious, considering his inborn respect for woman—to say nothing of the privileges he bestows on her by being the breadwinner and giving her the leisure time to prepare her battle plans. (from *A Madman's Defense*, in Roszak and Roszak 1969, 13)

But those of Strindberg's political persuasion have been said, in fact, to be limiting a woman's choices.

Breadwinner—or *provider*, as Maggio (1997) recommends—can today be applied to women as well as to men. However, in some groups or social classes, the homemaker-woman may be financially dependent on a man and feel

the need of his protection. A woman may also lack control over certain kinds of resources, such as pocket money (the woman has "housekeeping money") or a car in a single-car family, since she is not the breadwinner. Families where women are the breadwinners, departing from the male breadwinner norm, may be regarded disparagingly as deviant.

A man who is inadequate as a breadwinner, whatever the reasons, may be slandered by any of the following terms, among others: *bum, deadbeat, dead-beat dad, good-for-nothing, loser*. Although some of these terms may also be used for females (*loser* is probably gaining ground here as women increasingly enter the competitive public sphere), they seem to be coded primarily for males. On the other hand, the more productive a man is as a breadwinner, whatever his personal faults as a husband or father, the more society tends to glorify his virtues.

Biscuit getter has served as a joking reference to a man who puts the food on the table for his family.

See also BUM, DEADBEAT, GENDER-SPECIFIC ADJECTIVES (aggressive), GOLDBRICK.

breast man. See MEAT, TIT MAN.

breeder. Someone who breeds, that is, who has sex with the intent of having children. The term, from the sixteenth century, has been applied as recently as the 1980s by homosexuals to a heterosexual person or straight couple, that is, people who are usually interested in procreation—especially when they are enthusiastic about childbearing. The implication is that reproduction is not everything, that gay men and lesbians also have a contribution to make to society. The usage has also been picked up by some confirmed single heterosexuals.

Originally associated with Chicago lesbians (Kramarae and Treichler 1992), *breeder* is usually derogatory slang. It was apparently also used earlier in the twentieth century by progressive-thinking women who did not accept the role of mothering over that of developing a career.

In another sense, it has referred to a woman who is used for her reproductive functions to carry and bear a child for someone else, usually couples who cannot for one reason or another have children. Raymond (1993, xxii) describes the "breeder" as a woman who is "procured" by surrogate contract ("reproductive purchase order") in a system of breeding that is called "surrogacy" in the United States but more bluntly "baby farming" in the third world (see also MOTHER [surrogate mother]).

In the antebellum South, a breeder was either a man or a woman kept for purposes of reproducing field hands; *breeding woman* was similarly used by slaveowners but apparently without an equivalent term for men. Slaveowners took an interest in reproducing their slave "property," especially when injury, mistreatment, and malnutrition resulted in low birth rates. Sometimes enslaved women resisted being treated as breeders, for example, through natural forms of contraception (breast-feeding). Other language associated with female slaves was *childbearing woman, too old to breed,* and *not a breeding woman.*

Among white supremacist groups today, echoing Nazi notions, women may take pride in being "breeders" for the white race, and white women are especially valued for their ability to reproduce that race in face of the perceived challenge of supposedly fertile women of color.

See also HETEROSEXUAL.

brick shithouse. An expression, usually considered vulgar, meaning a big, solidly built woman, especially one large across the beam. She may also be said to be "built like a brick shithouse." The same expression applied to a man may be somewhat more respectful, implying strength and statuesque qualities. From the mid-twentieth century.

See also BEEF TRUST, BIG BERTHA, BOB.

bride. To many, a lovely word, and in nearly everyone's lexicon, an acceptable one. One of the rare words in English once used for men as well as for women in the fifteenth and sixteenth centuries (the sixteenth-century *brydegrome* was simply a young man who was a bride), it never picked up derogatory or sexual meanings as it became specific to women (Mills 1989), as so many other words for women have. Yet it does reflect, or conceal, bias.

In the context of marriage and weddings, which carry a feminine emphasis in U.S. culture, here is an exception to the general principle that the masculine form of a related pair of words is stronger than the feminine. There are a number of ways this asymmetry can be illustrated. For example, a number of terms are formed with *bride* or *bridal,* including *blushing bride, bridal gown, bride-price, bridesmaid, bridal shower* (compare with *bachelor party*), *bridal attendant,* and *bridal wreath.* On the other hand, the only compound found in the dictionary made with *groom* that is not labeled "rare" is *groomsman,* usually the best man. We talk about a "bride and groom," while in many other constructions—for example, "men and women," "host and hostess"—it is the masculine word that goes first. Nilsen (1998, 401) views such facts as these as linguistic evidence that weddings have more significance to women than to men.

Mail-order bride is worrisome, as it reflects treatment of women as objects of trade.

See also MRS., WIFE.

broad. A derogatory slang term for a woman. Originally she was thought of as a sexually promiscuous woman,

woman of low morals, mistress, or prostitute. Soon, however, *broad* became a term for any woman, though especially a young one. Its use is largely male, coarse, and impolite, often even contemptuous. Probably to avoid offending an increasingly politically correct public of the 1960s, the U.S. Olympic Committee changed the name of the track-and-field event once called the "broad jump" to "long jump." Some women, however, might use *broad* jocularly or self-descriptively (e.g., Bette Midler in her 1980 book, *A View from a Broad*). Since the 1980s the word has taken on the additional meanings of a gay male who takes the PASSIVE role (this is restricted largely to prison slang) and a big, outspoken or authoritative woman.

Attempts have been made to derive the term from words related to anatomy, such as *broad-ass* or *broad in the beam* (originally a phrase describing a ship with a wide base). These terms suggest not only the buttocks but also an objectifying image of a promiscuous woman in a position putting that part of her body to use. The nearly sound-alike BAWD, a "prostitute" or "madam," could also have been an influence, as could other, now obsolete senses of *broad*, such as being coarse and loud or sexually loose.

B and B is military slang for "booze (or beer) and broads," probably a take-off on *rest and recreation* (R and R). *Outlaw broad* means a female prostitute who works the streets independently, that is, without a pimp (at least around the mid-twentieth century). *Silk broad* is a black male term for a white woman, while a lesbian may be disparaged as a "double-barreled broad." A variant form of *broad* is *broadie*.

See also DICK (dicky broad).

broiler. See CHICKEN.

broken-wrist. See LIMP-WRIST.

bronco. See HORSE.

brother. See SISTER.

brownie hound. See FUDGEPACKER.

bruiser. Slang since the eighteenth century for a large, husky man, especially one considered pugnacious; a hired thug, or a prizefighter, often in the expression "the big bruiser." It is frequently used to label men considered crude and lower-class and may be taken as offensive, though it may also be affectionate.

See also BULLY, CAVEMAN, CRIMINALS, GORILLA, LUG.

brute. See BEAST.

Bubba; Bubbette. *Bubba*, a man's nickname, probably from a child's pronunciation of *brother*. *Bubba* has been in use among African Americans as a form of address for a male sibling and is still heard as a nickname among black people and, nonpejoratively, among pro football players. The word is also associated with a white Southern man, also known as a "good ol' boy" (see BOY). Outside the South, however, the image is negative—an unsophisticated, boorish white man: "Look at the southern characters on television in the 1960s: the Beverly Hillbillies, Gomer Pyle, the Real McCoys... morons one and all...many of them sporting such yokel names as Bubba, Slick Mavis, or Billie Joe Bob" (*Jane & Michael Stern's Encyclopedia of Pop Culture,* 1992, 415).

Bubba has been in use in the formation of a number of terms, especially since the 1992 presidential campaign, when then Arkansas governor Bill Clinton was a candidate (*American Speech,* Spring 1993, 100-02). For example, *Bubba and the brother* refers to a political coalition between white Southerners and black people.

A less frequently heard female version, *Bubbette*, means a white Southern female of the same ilk as a Bubba, although the *-ette* ending suggests that when men talk politics, they still view women as little versions of men (see

-ETTE). A "Faux Bubba" is a man who might appear to be a member of the social class to which the Bubba belongs but in fact attended an Ivy League school or made a lot of money.

> The national media may call Bill Clinton and Al Gore the Bubba ticket, but...Bubbas don't go to Harvard and Yale.... No, Clinton and Gore are Faux Bubbas—Fake Good Ol' Boys, Counterfeit Crackers, Weekend Billybobs. (29 September 1992 *Louisville Courier-Journal*, quoted in *American Speech*, Summer 1993, 184)

bubblehead. See SPACE GIRL.

bud. See FLOWER.

buffalo; **buffarilla**. *Buffalo,* a pejorative term sometimes used for a big woman seen as homely (a variant, *water buffalo,* may also connote aggressiveness or dominance). *Buffalo* may also be used disparagingly for a black man, or sometimes any man. From *buffalo* plus *gorilla* comes *buffarilla,* used since the mid-twentieth century for a young woman considered fat or ugly.

See also HOGGER, LOOKSISM, PIG, YETI.

bufu. A blend of *butt* and *fuck. Bufu* is usually considered a vulgar, derogatory reference to a gay man thought of as a pederast. Also anyone considered loathsome.

See also ASS (ass bandit), BUGGER, BUNNY (chocolate bunny), FUDGEPACKER, HERSHEY BAR, SODOMY.

bugfucker. An insulting reference to a man with a very small penis, or, more generally, any man considered worthless or contemptible. Accusing a man of having a small penis is a powerful way of diminishing his entire stature as a man. A synonym is *needle-dick* (see also DICK). In the 1987 movie *Outrageous Fortune,* Bette Midler says, "You've heard of needle-dick? The big bugfucker?" She is referring to a man (a corpse, actually) with a small penis. To counter the belief that

the corpse was her boyfriend, she is supplying evidence that her boyfriend must still be alive—he was well endowed.

See also PRICK.

bugger. A term of varied uses, including a term of abuse for a man or a disagreeable person of either sex, or simply a word for any fellow or chap. However, the common meaning of the term, as it has been used since the sixteenth century (and now altered in American usage; see below), is a sodomite. Near the end of the seventeenth century, *buggery* began to replace *sodomy* in the colonial statutes prohibiting such sexual activity. A sodomite may be someone who engages in noncoital sex—usually anal or oral—with a person of the other sex, but most commonly (and dictionaries often lump these together), it is a person who copulates with someone of the same sex (again, usually by anal or oral means) or with an animal (see also SODOMY).

Since at least the eighteenth century, *bugger* has also come to mean a rascal, bastard, or worthless person, especially a man. Today *bugger* might be used in the sense of any man or child, though sometimes specifically for a despicable person, again often a man (see also BASTARD, BUFU).

Bugger derives from the Medieval Latin *Bulgarus* (Bulgarian), from the onetime association of Bulgaria with the Bogomils (Lovers of God). The Bogomils were members of a medieval heretical religious sect who believed that a true Christian abstained from marriage, regarded the body as the work of Satan, and felt that the perpetuation of the human species was a mistake. They were thought to practice sodomy, since that form of sexuality could not be as evil as the procreative variety. Religious heretics, especially when a religious majority seeks to stamp out their beliefs, have often been unfairly suspected of "unnatural" sexual acts. In the historical sense of a heretic, *Bugger* is capitalized.

The word may be seen as deriving much of its expressive force from the taboo placed on this form of sexual activity. What's more, it draws from the masculine images of violence and conquest implicit in the idea of anal sex. Not only can submission be forced on a woman through sodomy performed on her, but—and perhaps even more important in the male worldview—it can be on a man. Arango (1989, 66) points out that common expressions of triumph in male conversation, such as "I want to have his ass," reflect metaphorically on men's wish for domination over other men. *Sodomy,* as Arango discusses it, is a form of emasculation by which a man is made a woman.

In noting its slang usage in England, White (1994) writes that

> in Bloomsbury *bugger* was the preferred term, presumably because it was salty and vulgar enough to send those rarefied souls into convulsions of laughter. One pictures Virginia Woolf discussing "buggery" with Lytton Strachey; how they must have relished the word's public school, criminal and eighteenth-century connotations. (72)

The only "decent use," as *The Oxford English Dictionary* (1989) puts it, has been as a legal term (e.g., in England, *buggery* was used in official military court-martial documents).

The use of *bugger* in the sense of a sodomite is still known in the United States but not commonly. It has also come into a new life, heard in such nonsexual expressions as "He's a cute little bugger."

bull. A word ranging in meaning from a virile, sexually active male to an aggressive gay man to an aggressive lesbian (as in *bull bitch*, BULLDAGGER, BULLDYKE). The common denominator is the connotation of aggressive masculinity (a bull is the adult uncastrated ox or the male

of other large, powerful animals). Each sense (but not the terms in parentheses above) comes from about the mid-twentieth century. America's prudery about the animal word *bull*, which connotes sexual potency, resulted in a prohibition on its use for much of the nineteenth century and even the early twentieth, resulting in what Mencken (1962, 113) called "a number of grotesque euphemisms," including *gentleman cow, top cow, cow critter, the gentleman,* and *the master.* The raw masculinity of the term notwithstanding, the bull as a symbol of the power of nature was originally, in some ancient cultures, associated with goddess worship; it was later appropriated by patriarchal religion and, in Christian iconography, became identified in terms of Satan (Eisler 1988, 22). *Bullheaded,* meaning stupidly stubborn, and often used for a man, corresponds to *stupid cow*, applied to a woman, though the latter is more disparaging.

See also BUTCH, COW, HORSE, STUD.

bull bitch. See BULL.

bulldagger. A "masculine" (butch) lesbian or one who takes an aggressive role in sexual activity. *Bulldagger* is often considered largely a black or Southern usage. A type of "new woman" in the early twentieth century, who chose to be independent, unmarried, and linked with other women in strong supportive networks, was the "mannish lesbian" in Lucille Bogan's "B.D. [bulldagger] Woman's Blues." "I'm glad I had a chance to be a bull-dagger before it became fashionable to be a lesbian" (Duberman 1997, 267). This usually stigmatized lesbian is said to have been vital in creating working-class lesbian communities in various ethnic groups in the United States (Mankiller et al. 1998). Her more feminine admirers of the time, incidentally, were not regarded as lesbians.

Bulldagger is almost always derogatory when used by heterosexuals. However, Grahn (1990) views the term as one of empowerment, since it suggests a castrating woman, "something Lesbians are often accused of being merely by our existence" (140). The word suggests the swordlike implement said to have been used by priestesses in sacrificing bulls in religious ceremonies. Used among lesbians self-descriptively today, *bulldagger* implies strength and willingness to fight to defend one's way of life and community.

Boondagger is a variant, also usually disparaging but less often used.

See also BULL, BULLDYKE, DYKE, HE-SHE, LESBIAN, MANNISH, MARIMACHO, SHE-MALE.

bulldyke. Among heterosexuals, usually a very provocative slang word meaning a "masculine" (butch) lesbian, sometimes any lesbian, or any woman regarded as "mannish." *Bull* adds further connotations of masculinity and toughness to *dyke*. The pejorativeness of *bulldyke* stems from use by men or by heterosexual people in general (often by but not limited to working-class background) with stereotypical notions of womanhood. Even in the lesbian community, there is some aversion to the term, of which Grahn (1990) says, "Only truly, obstinately honest and tough dikes use the word *bulldike* about themselves" (135). The term first appeared in writing in the early 1920s, when it was a part of black American slang. *Bull-dyker* and *bulldyking woman* were also used among blacks, the latter being shortened to *B.D. woman*.

The Oxford English Dictionary (1989) says the origin of the term is unknown. However, romantic speculation links the term to the name of the Celtic warrior-queen Boadicea, who organized an insurrection against the colonizing Romans. Relating the word to the office of the ancient bull-slayer priestess, Grahn (139) suggests that Boadicea—

whose name she claims was actually Boudica, pronounced "Boo-uh-*dike-ay*"—may have performed the ritual killing of the bull, which was viewed as a god. Given the vengeful policies of the Romans against Boadicea and her people, continues Grahn, no doubt her name was driven underground as a taboo, tainted word few people would have wanted to mention. Grahn's perspective is usually regarded as historically and philologically untenable ("impossible," according to Dynes 1990). Yet it has been important for presenting a myth that suggests and glorifies women's former power and explains their oppression.

Some speculation links the term to the Germanic *tyke* (bitch, in the sense of a female dog), thus suggesting the meaning "a bitch that behaves like a bull," that is, one that is masculine (Dynes).

See also BULL, BULLDAGGER, DYKE, HE-SHE, LESBIAN, MANNISH, MARIMACHO, SHE-MALE.

bully. A man given to blustering and browbeating, especially one seen as cruel to those weaker than he. But while smacking of masculine connotations, the word is also sometimes directed at women. *Bully* probably comes from the Middle Dutch *boel,* meaning a lover of either sex. In its earliest use in English, in the sixteenth century, it meant a sweetheart, a woman as well as a man. After entering English, it soon began to make a shift in use toward men, taking on different meanings: a fine young fellow, a fop, an impostor, a pimp, and, coming closer to the modern sense, a swindler or hoodlum. At least some words for men—like so many for women (see, e.g., HARLOT, QUEEN)—it appears, have also suffered a slide in meaning. The word is still also applied to a pimp (perhaps suggesting the earlier "lover," though now in criminal form) or a thug. Outside of the original meaning, the themes throughout the history of the word focus on male dress or appearance, deception, criminality, and cruel or brutish behavior. *Bully-boy*, sometimes used for a hired ruffian, suggests the immaturity of the bully (see also BOY).

See also BRUISER, CRIMINALS, GORILLA.

bum. A term meaning a despicable person, freeloader, idler, drifter, derelict, loser, or any incompetent or irresponsible person. From the early to mid-1800s, when large numbers of German immigrants arrived in the United States, *bum* may have been formed (as a back-formation) from *bummer*, from German *Bummler*, (idler, loafer, or tramp).

Typically applied to men, as are such related terms as *vagabond, parasite,* and *sponger,* it refers to those who do not meet society's expectations for males regarding work, self-reliance, and responsibility, especially being the BREAD-WINNER of the family. It comes down harder on men than does the similar *bag lady* on women (see BAG [bag lady]). In *To Renew America* (1995, 78), conservative Speaker of the House Newt Gingrich—though himself accused of failing to provide adequate child support for his two teenage children—referred to "deadbeat" fathers as bums. In his story "God's Wrath," Bernard Malamud suggested a similar meaning: "Helen's husband, a drinker, a bum, supported her badly…" (*The Stories of Bernard Malamud,* 1983, 258).

A one-time president of what was known as the Hobo College in Chicago in the early twentieth century developed a classification of homeless men in which he included the "bum" in the sense of a derelict: "A hobo," he noted, "is a migratory worker. A tramp is a migratory non-worker. A bum is a stationary non-worker" (quoted in Nels Anderson, *The Hobo,* 1923, 87).

The disparaging sense of idleness also comes through in expressions such

as *ski bum, beach bum,* and *tennis bum.* But they are often used self-descriptively. Speaking of "shifting," the linguistic process by which words change into new meanings or forms, Plotnik (1996) noted that, "Now a bum (noun) with a bum (adjective) leg can bum (verb) a ride to Arizona and bum-trip (adverb-like) on peyote" (137). Employing *bum* in a positive way, fans of the former Brooklyn Dodgers referred to themselves with affection as "dem bums," while Chicago Cubs fans today proudly call themselves "bleacher bums."

See also DEADBEAT, GOLDBRICK, TRAMP.

bunny. Slang, meaning a young, attractive woman. This is largely a patronizing and often offensive male usage connoting stereotypical young, cute, and cuddly femininity (see also PET). The term has been used for any young woman since the seventeenth century. In the twentieth century the most famous "bunny" was Hugh Hefner's Playboy variety, beautiful young women once employed in the Playboy clubs to serve, ostensibly, in such roles as waitperson, while displaying their physical attributes (see also PLAYMATE).

An animal metaphor, *bunny* is also sexualized through its connection with *bun* in the sense of female genitals/posterior (see also HOT DOG [bun]; *bunny* has also had gay use for a male hustler, probably suggesting anal intercourse; see also ASS). As the diminutive of *bun,* meaning tail, *bunny* suggests an animal with a little tail. Along with rabbit ears, the Playboy Bunny once sported a fluffy "tail" as part of her costume, and *cottontail* is a synonym for *bunny* in this feminine sense. *Bunny* may also be related to the notion of the rabbit as an animal with a proclivity for mating (hence the expression "fuck like a wild bunny"), but it seems to relate more to the idea of rabbits as domesticated or as small game hunted for sport (Kramarae and Treichler 1992).

In another sense that adds to its connotations, the term *bunny* also reflects on the stereotypical role of the woman as soft, tender, helpless, and weak. In Beatrix Potter's stories the male rabbits (Peter and Benjamin) were out and about, but the females—Flopsy, Mopsy, and Cottontail—stayed at home like good bunnies. If she's a "dumb bunny," a woman's intelligence is also in question. "'Lucy, what does a [car] jack look like?' 'Oh, Ethel, you're such a dumb bunny'" (1998 rerun of TV sitcom *I Love Lucy*).

Of the other types of "bunnies," the following commonly scamper through our sexist language: A "beach bunny" is a bikini-clad young woman who hangs around the surfing crowd at the beach but does not surf or swim herself. The expression connotes a man's idea of femininity that is sexy, cute, and cuddly, with no better ambition than frolicking in the sun with the guys. "Ski bunnies" and "snow bunnies" simply frolic in a different climate, while "show bunnies" are young women, especially performers asked to show off their physical assets. When those assets are considered especially provocative, a woman may be called *sex bunny*. And when men perceive them as invitations to go to bed, they demean the woman with the vulgar expression *fuck bunny*. The origin of most of these expressions is the 1960s, although as indicated above, the term *bunny* for a sexy young woman is much older.

Cuddle-bunny saw mid-twentieth-century use for a young woman considered affectionate and sexy, while a "bed-bunny" is a young woman thought of (often wishfully) as making herself sexually available to men. The allusion in *chocolate bunny*, applied to any black person, is to skin color, but used for a woman or gay male, it can also be to the more "feminine" qualities of sweetness and softness (or in the case of a gay male, to the color brown, associated with anal intercourse; see also FUDGEPACKER, HERSHEY BAR). It may be jocular or affectionate only within the community; used by a white person or heterosexual male, it would probably be taken as offensive. *Jungle bunny*, contemptuous when applied to an African American or members of other ethnic groups, alludes to "racial" primitiveness; applied to black men, it is also emasculating (see BEAST).

See also BEAVER, FAWN, KITTEN, PUSSY, SQUIRREL, WOMEN AS ANIMALS.

bush. Usually considered a vulgar reference to the pubic hair, the female pudenda, or, by extension, to a woman as a sex object. The anatomic sense derives from the seventeenth century, the slang meaning "woman" from the mid-twentieth century.

See also BEARD, BEAVER, CAT, HAIR, HAT, HIDE, PUSSY, WHISKER, WOOL.

business girl. Twentieth-century euphemistic reference, and often self-descriptive, for a prostitute. *Business* can allude to either a woman or sexual intercourse and prostitution.

See also GIRL, PROSTITUTE.

butch. A nickname and U.S. slang for a young boy, especially a tough young man (as in "Butch" Cassidy, the American outlaw), first appearing in the late nineteenth century (perhaps deriving from *butcher*). As an adjective for either sex, connoting strength, toughness, and assertiveness, it may express mild ridicule, but it can also be intended jocularly, often affectionately.

Applied to women, *butch* has been used disapprovingly among nonlesbians who tend to view any woman seen as having a hard, "mannish" look, short-cropped hair, and domineering traits as "butch" regardless of that person's own identity.

Among gay men, where it probably sees less use, the term denotes a type of look that represents a reaction against the effeminate stereotype of gay men—an obvious display of masculinity, such as that associated with the Marlboro man (a positive association; see also MACHO). In homosexual communities, gay as well as lesbian, *butch* constitutes a common chosen identity, though it has been challenged, especially among some lesbian feminists in the 1970s and 1980s, who view it as a patriarchal way of relating to other lesbians.

By the 1940s *butch* was in use for a style of short haircut worn first by men and then adopted by some lesbians, especially in urban working-class culture. But *butch,* in the sense of a type of lesbian identity, was in use from the 1930s. The identity itself, and its pairing with that of the FEMME, probably reached its principal importance in the lesbian community, both black and white, between at least the 1940s and the early 1960s. The sexual identity of the butch is usually seen in contrasting or complementary relation with that of the femme. For example, Steven Capsuto (Witt, Thomas, and Marcus 1995, 107) describes the characters Oscar and Felix, in the TV sitcom *The Odd Couple,* as "butch/femme roommates," even though they did not play explicitly homosexual roles (in fact, the series had both men dating women). The butch, however, is more visible in society than the femme; since the butch lesbian may have to fight to protect her way of life, the term may connote the tough warrior.

In butch-femme relations in the lesbian community (once known in that community as Butch and Marge), a language of sexual and emotional bonding has evolved. In a successful relationship each woman nurtures the other's sexual-emotional identity. Dynes (1990), however, notes that the femmes, contrary to stereotypes, may be strong, aggressive

women, and the butch role is not comparable to masculinity. In addition, these roles and terms vary with social class, "race," and region (in the black New York lesbian community, e.g., according to Dynes, BULLDAGGER and STUD were more common than *butch*). The butch-femme style is only one among a diverse array of relational styles in the lesbian community, but it was the first publicly visible one among lesbians in this country.

Bigendered or transgendered lesbians—individuals with biologically female bodies who identify as masculine and may be attracted to other women—may call themselves *stone butch*, though without negative connotations (see also CHICK [boychick], DYKE [mandyke], TRANSGENDERIST). *Stone* may mean "very" in slang, but it also implies "untouchable" in a sexual sense—not wanting to be touched during sexual relations. Also heard self-descriptively in lesbian communities is *soft butch,* meaning a woman who looks and acts "feminine" but may have some butch mannerisms or traits, such as being athletic or tomboyish, without self-identifying as a butch. A "baby butch" is a young lesbian with a masculine appearance or air.

See also BULL, DYKE, HEN (crested hen), LESBIAN, MANNISH, SHE-HE, TOMBOY.

buttercup. Flower allusion to a young man, boy, or gay male seen by straight men as soft and effeminate. "Can you believe this buttercup?" (teenage bully to his submissive half-brother, in the 1991 made-for-TV movie drama *My Son Johnny*). The term was common in the early twentieth century but is still in use today to disparage men seen as not living up to the culture's traditional standards of masculinity.

See also DAFFODIL, DAISY, EFFEMINATE, FLOWER, GLADIOLA, LILY, PANSY.

butterfly. An insect metaphor used sometimes for an effeminate or gay man, one stereotyped as frail, pretty, or flighty. The Gay Liberation Front attempted a short-lived reclamation of the image in the 1970s, perhaps to represent the colorful magnificence of the butterfly (or man) emerging from a cocoon after so much time in the dark, but also probably as an extension of the idea of the elusive and free "fairy." A woman may be disparaged as a butterfly if she is considered flighty or as someone who rushes indiscriminately from man to man. Lennert and Willson designate it as a "symbol of the clitoris" (Kramarae and Treichler 1992).

Even when women are tough and aggressive, they may be reminded of their "place." England's former prime minister Margaret Thatcher, sometimes known as the Iron Lady, was also dubbed the Iron Butterfly.

See also EFFEMINATE, FAIRY, FLAPPER, FLIT, MARIPOSA.

buzzard. A person seen as contemptible, one who, like the scavenger bird, feeds off the weakened state of others; especially a despicable old man (as in *old buzzard*). Although used in the sense of a foolish or unlikable person since the seventeenth century, the term is restricted largely to the sense of an old man today. In the nineteenth century it was particularly associated with the Old West. As a nickname for an inhabitant of Georgia (supposedly from nineteenth-century legal protection of the bird), *buzzard* is accepted as jocular. Also of Southern origin is *old salty buzzard*, meaning a testy old man. *Buzzard* was also heard in hobo slang early in the twentieth century for homeless men who lived in transient groups in sites such as near railroad crossings or on the outskirts of cities, where they subsisted on the leavings of others' meals.

See also BADGER, BASTARD, BIRD, COOT, CUSS, FOGY, FUTZ, GEEZER, JACKAL, OLD FART.

C

cad. See HEEL, LOTHARIO, ROMEO.

cake. Connoting a sweet food and often associated with black usage since about the 1930s, a young, sexually attractive woman, one also considered "foxy"; also the female genitals, breasts, or buttocks. In another sense, common earlier in the twentieth century, the term means a ladies' man.

See also CAKE-EATER, CHEESECAKE, COOKIE, CREAMPUFF, CUPCAKE, DISH, HONEY, JELLY ROLL, MUFFIN, PIE, SWEET, TART.

cake-eater; cookie-pusher. *Cake-eater,* in heterosexual talk, a man viewed as a sissy; in particular, a young man whose clothes or attendance at such events as fussy tea parties may stigmatize him as wealthy and effeminate. The term has been in use since the early 1900s but not in gay communities. A synonym is *cookie-pusher* (sometimes also *cookie-cutter*), almost always a man who engages in "effeminate" or "sycophantic" activities. The cookie-pusher may simply like unmanly events or seek the company of those among whom he can promote himself. The term is used derogatorily in political talk for a government official, especially one in the State Department, thought of as focusing too much on protocol and social life. *Cookie-pusher* may also be used for a waitress.

See also CAKE, DISH, EFFEMINATE, SISSY.

calendar girl. See GIRL.

call boy; call girl. References to a male and female prostitute, specifically those who make appointments for "dates" when clients call them on the telephone (necessary especially where streetwalking is outlawed), usually through individual referrals. These prostitutes attend to their clients either at their own place of residence (where they are "called on") or at their clients'. *Call girl* (also sometimes *C-girl*) is always used with a sexual meaning, which is characteristic of many words for women and thereby distinguishes them from their male counterparts. *Call boy* (spelled as one word), on the other hand, can also mean a bellhop or page.

There are some other differences between *call boy* and *call girl*. *Call girl* came first, originating as slang in the early twentieth century, and has worked itself into standard English. *Call boy,* a colloquial back-formation from *call girl,* appeared in about the middle of the century in reference to male prostitutes but is rarely heard. Furthermore, *call girl* can sometimes extend to female prostitutes who work out of brothels, whereas *call boy* is restricted to a male prostitute who relies on the telephone.

Popular media representations of call girls would often have us believe that they are all high-class, professional sex workers, either independent or operating under a classy white madam. In fact, many of them ply their trade in cheap hotels and rely on an organization for recruiting clients. Of course, there are also call girls who cater to the rich: "With most uptown call girls, the choice is not between starvation and life, but…between $10,000 and $50,000" (prostitute taped by Kate Millett, in *Woman in Sexist Society,* ed. by Vivian Gornick and Barbara K. Moran, 1971, 100).

> "You can't let Latka marry a hooker."
> "She's not a hooker…she's a call girl."
> —TV sitcom *Taxi,* 1998 rerun

See also BOY, GIRL, HUSTLER, PROSTITUTE.

camp. From London theatrical slang (but existing before that) and associated with gay parlance, a word with various related meanings associated with a type of wit, especially one relying on innuendo, intonation, or affectation. Men once played women's parts in the theater, giving us images of men with humorously exaggerated feminine characteristics or mannerisms called *camp.*

Although not exclusive to gay communities, the term is widespread in that arena, describing a gay man who exaggerates effeminate homosexual behavior, such as a strong lisp or a mincing gait. Another meaning is the flamboyant behavior or speech exhibited by a gay man. *Camp* may also refer to a place where homosexual males gather (e.g., a camp bar). The notion of *camp* still has resonance in gay communities, where its theatricality is seen as challenging and mocking conventional notions of gender.

The term is apparently not related to *camp* in the sense of a place of temporary dwelling; its origins are obscure. Chapman (1998) relates *to camp it up,* meaning to act in a humorously affected or exaggerated way, to the French verb *se camper* (put oneself in a bold, provocative posture). Whatever its origins, *camp* is linked with the arts. Suárez (1996) says that an early form of "camp sensibility" was performed by the surrealists with their "dandy-like appreciation of…excess, artifice, and flamboyance" (44).

Drag, grounded as it is in theatricality, may be considered a form of camp but only if it is clearly an artifice. Some heterosexual people may negatively stereotype gay men as flamboyant, but the term *camp* does not usually carry any derision. Among many gay men, camp behavior may be thought of as promoting the subversion of those identities based on the heterosexual male model (see Tyler 1991 for a discussion of flamboyance in drag roles).

Camp may also be used for a brothel. See also DRAG, EFFEMINATE, FLAMER, GAY, MINCE.

canary. A demeaning bird metaphor for a girl or woman—canaries are generally regarded as pretty, frail, and domesticated. In the 1934 romantic comedy movie *It Happened One Night,* Roscoe Karns delivered a line expressing another take on the bird comparison: "Women should be kept illiterate and clean, like canaries." In the slang of the music industry, *canary* refers to a female vocalist. Lighter (1994) points to a related resemblance in his citation from a nineteenth-century source that describes a canary as a woman who carries the tools of a burglar and watches outside (perhaps to alert her fellow thieves to an approaching party by "singing"). Both senses, a woman and a vocalist, are from the mid- to late-nineteenth century. The term was also once used in the sense of a whore or mistress.

See also BIRD, CHICK, CHICKEN, PIGEON, WOMEN AS ANIMALS.

candy-ass, candyass; **candy kid**. *Candy-ass,* from the mid-twentieth century, usually a vulgar term meaning a coward or unmanly man. As an adjective (often with the *-ed* suffix), *candy-ass* describes a person considered timid, weak, or sissified, usually a man (synonymous with *wimpy*). From earlier in the century comes *candy kid,* referring to a sweet boy (see SWEET) or man, often implying a pretty boy, a sissy, or a mama's boy. Both expressions tend to reinforce the social expectation that men are to be brave, tough, and independent.

Candy-assed can also describe a diminutive woman, especially one narrow across the beam. *Candy* can also indicate sexual gratification and may be used to objectify women.

See also APRON (apron strings), CAKE-EATER, CHICKEN (coward), EFFEMINATE, FLOWER, GIRL, LIMP-WRIST, LITTLE LORD FAUNTLEROY, LOLLIPOP, MAMA'S BOY, MILKSOP, MILQUETOAST, PANSY, SISSY, TINKER BELL, WIMP, WUSS.

canned fruit. See FRUIT.

career girl. See GIRL.

Casanova, casanova. A name referring to a ladies' man, seducer of women, especially one who is unscrupulous. "A regular Casanova" is a man with a reputation for amorous undertakings—a man sometimes said to "love them and leave them."

The name is taken from that of Giovanni Giacomo Casanova, whose byname was Jean-Jacques, Chevalier de Seingalt. Born in 1725 in Venice, Italy, Casanova was a writer, friar, soldier, spy, and diplomat, but he is known today mainly as an Italian adventurer whose *Memoirs*—a record of the amours and rogueries of his dissolute life—made his name synonymous with *debaucher* (later in his life, he was treated with mercury for having contracted gonorrhea and syphilis).

Flem (1997) derives this libertine's devotion to women from a childhood of illness and the hurt supposedly caused by his beautiful mother, who withheld her affection. The term may be employed by men and women alike for men who "play the field," with some admiration or envy, or with a jocular or ironic note, as in the following quote. "If Bob Neal is a 'real ladies man,' then Don Knotts is Casanova" (Judith Exner, *My Story,* 1977, 112).

It is characteristic of words used for men with active libidos that they carry little, reluctant, or no opprobrium. They may even be romanticized. Carpineto (1989) writes,

> Today's "womanizers," were yesterday's "roués," "gallants," "ladies men," "Don Juans," and "Casanovas." With the old labels these men could be perceived as romantic figures, as men who were helpless to prevent the adoration that they received from women and the secret envy that they inspired in less-appealing men. (11)

Even the very slangy synonym *sack artist,* meaning a womanizer, carries the positive *artist.*

A number of words exist for women who demonstrate this kind of behavior toward men, but most are negative—they are seducers, bewitchers, or whores rather than lovers—and such women are called by names like *vamp, hussy,* or *slut.*

See also DON JUAN, LADIES' MAN, LOTHARIO, LOVE MACHINE, LOVER, PLAYBOY, ROMEO, ROUÉ, SCUTZ, WOMANIZER.

case. See CLOSET (closet case).

castrating. An adjective meaning being deprived of the testes, thus, figuratively, rendering a man impotent. Although it may also be used about women (*Merriam-Webster's Collegiate Dictionary*, 10 ed., says *castrating* can mean depriving of the ovaries), the term is most frequently used by men for women. It alludes to them as domineering and making men appear or feel victimized or demasculinized. When a man's male traits are removed, he is believed to be degraded; when stolen by a woman, anything can happen.

In the 1950s it became fashionable to make fun of confused and cowed husbands, like the cartoon character Dagwood, and to speak of such men as the outcomes of castrating women. But the evil attributed to men can also be blamed on such women. In his novel *The Diary of a Rapist* (1966), for example, Evan Connell, telling the story of a diffident, middle-class clerk who was a psychopathic rapist, gives him a nagging, bitchy, "castrating" wife.

Yet the fear of castration can also be a real psychological burden placed on men. As Goldberg (1976, 23) has argued, such concepts as "castration anxiety," "fear of failure," and "impotence" may have the effect of pushing men into greater self-consciousness, guilt, and distrust of their own sexual reponses.

See also BALLBREAKER, EUNUCH, GENDER-SPECIFIC ADJECTIVES (aggressive),

HARPY, HARRIDAN, HEN (henpecked), IM-
POTENT, MANEATER, MOM (momism),
SCOLD, SHE-DEVIL, SHREW, VIRAGO, WITCH.

cat. Originally a contemptuous term for either sex but later came to refer to a
woman considered "loose" or sexually
promiscuous. Until the end of the nineteenth century, *cat* was used especially
for a prostitute, dating back to at least
the sixteenth century. *Cathouse,* from the
early 1900s, is still used in the United
States for a brothel (*cat wagon* in the Old
West). A "painted cat" (or "painted
lady") was a prostitute marked for her
profession by heavy makeup. In keeping with the common sexual overtones
of the word, *cat* may also refer to the
female genitals in what is often considered vulgar usage; a cat's fur may call
to mind a woman's pubic hair. The
French *chat* can mean female genitals
as well as cat (see also PUSSY).

Cat is also applied to a woman regarded as spiteful, backbiting, and malicious, especially one who belittles
other women (see CATTY, from which *cat*
in this sense may derive rather than the
other way around [Thorne 1990]). *Cat
fight* refers to the mutual belittling between two women, viewed as having
their "claws" out. This term, for example, was sometimes used for incidents
between ice skaters Nancy Kerrigan and
Tonya Harding, archrivals, when they
appeared in public together.

Although in some cultures cats have
been honored as a sacred animal, and in
ours they are frequently loved as household pets, there have also been connotations of evil and power in the word, as
in the association of black cats with
witches. Philosopher Friedrich
Nietzsche, though an admirer of some
women, described woman's "nature" as
"the genuine, cunning suppleness of a
beast of prey, the tiger's claw under the
glove" (in Roszak and Roszak 1969, 9).
More recently, in the 1992 movie

Batman Returns, Catwoman (Michelle
Pfeiffer) played a nemesis of the Caped
Crusader, meeting a grisly fate as her
punishment for terrorizing men. A synonym linking women with evil is *hellcat.*

Applied to men, however, *cat* (from
the slang verb *tomcat,* sometimes still
used for male activity) takes on different, sometimes even positive connotations. As a verb, *cat* refers to a man pursuing amatory relations with women
(something heterosexual men are by
convention proud of doing); said of either sex, it means to be sexually unfaithful (as in to *cat around*).

In black parlance *cat* has been used
to refer to a man or boy who is a flashy
dresser or "dude" (the female version in
this context is a "chick") or, in the jazz
community, to a male musician or fan
of jazz. It may also be used among "hip"
white people for a man with progressive
tastes in music or dress. In some contexts, it means simply any fellow. In
hobo usage, a cat was a hobo or migrant
worker, aptly applied since the cat was
classically a symbol of freedom. In the
early-twentieth-century *gaycat,* hobo
slang for a gay male youth, *cat* may be
related to the animal metaphor or derive
from CATAMITE.

See also ALLEY CAT, ANIMAL, BEARD,
BEAST, BEAVER, BISEXUAL (gray cat), BUSH,
HAIR, PUSSY, TIGER, TOM, WHISKER, WOMEN
AS ANIMALS, WOOL.

catamite. A term for a boy "kept" for homosexual purposes or one considered to
be the PASSIVE sexual partner, from the
Latin *catamitus*, referring to the
cupbearer to the god Jupiter.

Catamite is actually the Latin version
of the Greek *Ganymede*, a term for a gay
boy restricted in use largely to literary
circles. In Greek mythology, Ganymede
was a beautiful Phrygian boy who, while
playing a flute and tending his father's
sheep, was abducted by Zeus and carried up to Olympus to serve as cupbearer
to the gods.

Although *catamite* is from the sixteenth century, it did not become a standard term for a homosexual until the nineteenth century. The word is regarded as dated and is not likely to be heard in gay communities; however, it still appears in dictionaries and other reference sources to describe a gay youth. The *-ite* ending is often considered to carry a derogatory tone.

See also BOY, GAZOONEY, GUNSEL, PUNK.

cattle. See COW.

catty. Like a cat; in particular, slyly malicious or spiteful. *Catty* is frequently restricted to descriptions of women (and probably also to use by female speakers), especially women viewed as gossips (see also GOSSIP). Female author Kitty Kelley, known and sometimes maligned for her biographical books on such personalities as Frank Sinatra, Nancy Reagan, and Britain's royal family, was nicknamed "Catty Kitty" by the press. In some ways *catty* is the opposite of *kittenish*, the latter connoting youthful charm (see also KITTEN).

Some schoolteachers have been reported to use sexist language such as *catty* to control female students who get out of hand. Katherine Clarricoates noted that some adjectives used for female students are the usually derogatory *bitchy, giggly,* and *silly* as well as *catty.* Those applied to boys, on the other hand, imply more masculine, often positive qualities: *aggressive, assertive,* and *adventurous* (in Abbott and Wallace 1997, 101).

See also CAT, GENDER-SPECIFIC ADJECTIVES.

caveman. A handsome, virile man or a man considered boorish or crude, often depicted as hairy and rugged in physique. In the cartoon style of a Neanderthal, the legendary shuffling caveman drags women around by their hair. *Caveman* is often ironically applied to men, who may take it as either jocular or insult-

ing. The sexist assumption is that women love his rough, domineering style. John Corbin's novel *The Cave Man* (1907) is said to be the source of the expression in this sense; in the sense of a prehistoric cave dweller, it dates to 1865.

The caveman image not only insults both the men to whom it is applied and the women thought to adore them, but it also disparages the prehistoric people believed to have dwelled in caves. The Stone Age Neanderthal people, only some of whom actually lived in caves (in the Dordogne area of France, limestone cliffs provided shelter during the Ice Age), have been transformed into a very similar trivializing cartoon, and the word *Neanderthal* is also often used for a boorish or crude man.

> Some people use the word *Neanderthal* to describe dim-witted, ugly people who are like apes, an insult aimed at [prehistoric people] they consider stupid.... But there is every reason to believe that they were expert hunters and beings capable of considerable intellectual reasoning. (Brian M. Fagan, *People of the Earth,* 1998, 97)

The rugged popular cartoon depiction of Stone Age cavemen even seems to have once been echoed in the now-challenged anthropological view of the rugged "Man the Hunter," a perspective that made cooperative male hunting the chief force behind human evolution and ignored women's substantial contribution to their foraging economies.

In prizefighting, *caveman* means a fighter with a strong punch.

See also BRUISER, GORILLA, HE-MAN, HUNTER, MACHO, MAN, TARZAN.

cedarchest sissy. See CLOSET (closet case).

centerfold. A picture of a nude or seminude person (usually a woman) on the foldout that constitutes the center spread of a magazine, an Americanism from the early 1950s. Also, any sexually attractive person regarded as a subject of a centerfold (hence, a sex object). Although men may be centerfolds (actor Burt Reynolds opened the way with his seminude centerfold appearance in *Cosmopolitan* magazine in 1972; smiling, he covered his genitals with one hand, spoofing skin magazine images), this term is still coded for women.

See also CHEESECAKE, GIRL (cover girl).

chain gang. See DAISY CHAIN.

charity ass. See ASS.

charity cunt/girl/worker. See CUNT.

chaser. See SKIRT (skirt-chaser).

chaste. See GENDER-SPECIFIC ADJECTIVES, VIRGIN.

chatter; chatterbox. See GOSSIP.

chauvinist pig. See MALE CHAUVINIST PIG.

cheap. See GENDER-SPECIFIC ADJECTIVES.

cheesecake. Photographs of clothed or, especially, scantily clothed women shown in sexy poses featuring their breasts, hips, or legs; a good-looking young woman or group of such women. Chapman (1998) derives the term with some uncertainty from the appreciative remarks of one or another early-twentieth-century photographer who took pictures of women at the New York City ocean-liner docks to feature their legs, pronouncing the pictures "better than *cheesecake.*" In a complementary explanation, Mills (1989) suggests tracing the word to the practice of New York restaurants displaying large cheesecakes in their windows, just as large publicity photos outside theaters exhibited the charms of their actresses or chorus girls.

Whatever the precise origin, the word is akin to *cheesy*, meaning cheap, and is associated with *cheese* (from the photographer's inducement to smile), used in the sense of an attractive young woman. It is also clear that a "piece of cheesecake" is something sweet and delectable, to be "consumed" by a man.

Cheesecake is less commonly used for photographs of handsome young men (see BEEFCAKE). The difference between the sexualized *cheesecake* and the more affectionate *cupcake* is illustrated in the joking line, "Hey, guys, that's no cheesecake. That's my cupcake" (young man protesting a sexual comment about his girlfriend, TV sitcom *Newhart,* 1998 rerun).

See also CAKE, CAKE-EATER, CENTERFOLD, COOKIE, CREAMPUFF, CUPCAKE, DISH, JELLY ROLL, LOOKSISM, MUFFIN, PIE, SWEETIE, TART.

cheesehole. See HOLE.

Cherchez la femme! See FEMME.

cherry. Slang reference, often considered in bad taste, used for the hymen (small pinkish fold of tissue that partly closes the vaginal orifice) or, often snubbingly of either sex, virginity or a sexually uninitiated person. In these senses, it has been common throughout the twentieth century, though references to *cherry* in the sense of a virgin or the hymen are no doubt much older. The related French *chérie* means "beloved," explaining why *cherry* has also long been in use as a term of endearment, usually for a woman (it may also be a first name of a female). Variations, such as *cherry pie* (dated), allude to sweetness (see also PIE, SWEET); *cherry pie* also once referred to the crotch of a virgin and to anything "available" or "easy" to come by. Another association is between the cherry (the fruit), with its dark red color, and the blood of a woman who has had sexual intercourse for the first time.

Cherry orchard (from the name of the play by Anton Chekhov) refers to any place where young women live or gather. Suggesting a sexual pun (but also taken from the cherished trees of Japanese gardens), the epithet *cherry blossom* is used for a Japanese woman, or East Asian women in general, reflecting a stereotype of Asian women as deferential and servile to men, sexually or otherwise (see also EXOTIC). Also in biased ethnic discourse, *chocolate-covered cherry* refers to a black woman. *Cherry picker* refers to a man said to prefer sexual relations with young girls (i.e., virgins) or with gay male youths. *To lose one's cherry* means having sexual intercourse for the first time; *to cop a cherry* means to deflower a virgin. A male virgin may be called a "cherry boy," and male recruits in the army have been referred to contemptuously as "cherries" ("real men" are not virgins). *Cherry,* by extension from the virginal sense, may also describe any novice.

See also DISH, FRUIT, PEACH, VIRGIN.

chick. Originally an endearment used for any child. As early as the fourteenth century, *chick* was applied to a girl or young woman. In the early twentieth century, it was applied more disparagingly in the sense of a prostitute, then quickly acquired connotations of a liberated woman (perhaps prostitutes were thought of as free of attachments). Today *chick* may refer to a woman viewed as sexy, cuddly, and cute, superficial characteristics that may be valued by men.

The word is often associated with the 1930s entertainment scene, the 1950s beat generation (e.g., *hip chick*), and the 1960s counterculture, when it meant not just a young woman but one who was progressive in her views of sex. It has long been a part of street talk: "Oh, look at all those muscles. Bet the chicks like all those muscles" (1979 film *The Warriors*). It hangs on in the vernacular in such expressions as "chick with attitude" (CWA), which may refer to a woman with a temperament not considered pleasant by men or, from a woman's point of view, something more assertive and positive: "Grrrls just wanna have fun: From Spice pop to comic-strips to CD games glam girls—the chicks with attitude are taking over" (Jan Howells,

4 February 1997, *The Daily Telegraph,* lexis-nexis.com/univers).

Variant forms include *chickie* (usually a prostitute), *chickabiddy, slick chick, chickadee* ("My little chickadee" is what W. C. Fields called Mae West, hardly a woman of that bird's size or temperament, in the 1940 film by that name), and *chicklet.* The variant *chiclet,* restricted mostly to young girls, is suggested by *Chiclet,* trade name of a brand of chewing gum. *Home chick,* a woman from one's neighborhood, is a term for a young African American or Hispanic woman who is a member of a street gang (also known as *homegirl*). As an adjective, *chick* is heard in the sense of "applying to or interesting only to women," for example, "a chick magazine." *Chick* may also apply to a male prostitute whose clients are men. Bigendered lesbians—individuals with biologically female bodies who identify as masculine and may be attracted to other women—may call themselves *boychicks*, without negative connotations (see also BUTCH).

See also BIRD, CANARY, CHICKEN, DOVE, GIRL, PIGEON, WOMEN AS ANIMALS.

chicken. A bird metaphor with a number of different meanings, many of which suggest youth, girlishness, lower status, and vulnerability. Applied to a woman, it connotes domestication, weakness, or something of little value.

Since the fifteenth century, *chicken,* though referring to an adult bird, has meant any child or young person, often, especially since the nineteenth century, a young woman (once used in direct address with *my,* in the sense of "dear"). From at least the seventeenth century, it has referred to a person considered weak, cowardly, inexperienced, or foolish.

In eighteenth- and nineteenth-century use it also meant a prostitute, but since the mid-nineteenth century it has been used as a name for either a prostitute or any woman, especially a young, attractive one, viewed as a sex object. "The Oriental girls wore tight dresses over their skinny bodies, along with high heels and makeup, looking like classy *gai* ('chickens,' or whores)" (Normal Wong, "Disneyland," *Boys Like Us,* 1996, 254). Sometimes it occurs also as the demeaning *chicken meat* or, in black English, *chicken dinner* (see also MEAT). *Chicken* may also mean the act of intercourse with a woman, while *chicken ranch* refers to a rural brothel. Here *chicken* may refer to the female prostitutes who work there—"cooped up"— or to the chickens, as one story goes, exchanged by farmers for the prostitutes' services (Thorne 1990).

Chicken has also been used affectionately as a man's personal nickname for his wife or girlfriend. In the 1949 film *My Friend Irma,* for example, Irma's boyfriend called her by the pet name "Chicken." *Chicken inspector* (jocular) refers to a man who devotes himself to watching and pursuing women. "No spring chicken" is an uncomplimentary idiom referring to a woman viewed as past her prime. She may also be seen as trying to act younger than she is. *Spring chicken* was once a nickname for a prostitute but may also connote naivete as well as youth. *Chicken legs* may refer to a woman with skinny legs. See also BAT, BIDDY, BIRD, CHICK, OWL, PIGEON, QUAIL, WOMEN AS ANIMALS.

In the sense of a coward, an easily frightened person, or a SISSY, words like *chicken* and *coward,* still largely reserved for boys and men, are applied where expectations of manliness are held. Goldberg (1976) speaks of the "hero-image bind" in which a man is likely to engage in behavior that is self-injurious if he accepts challenges to his masculinity, and to face the accusations of other men if he doesn't, "particularly peers who will label him 'coward,' 'chicken-shit,' 'sissy'…[words] that will have a devastating impact on his self-image" (889). *Chicken* was heard as a children's taunt in the United States by the early 1950s. *Chicken-shit* (see quotation above) is a synonym, and *chicken-livered* (also *lily-livered*) is the adjectival equivalent. See also CANDY-ASS, WIMP.

In the nineteenth century, in the Navy, *chicken* was a term used for a ship's boy and may still be used for a young recruit. In particular, it has had currency among sailors and soldiers for the younger partner in a boy-man (or boy-older boy) relationship in which homosexuality is at least implied. It may still be used for an adolescent boy or young man (also called *chickie,* usually pretty and blonde) in prison and gay male parlance. In the lingo of street prostitution, a chicken is a boy prostitute. See also BOY.

Chickenhawk (or *hawk;* also *chicken queen*) refers to a gay man who is attracted to young adult male sexual partners. As predatory as the image of a hawk may seem, the word itself is not now usually used with those connotations in gay communities, nor with the implication that the younger gay man, implied as a victim, is incapable of making sexual decisions. He is a consenting partner. What it may suggest, however, is an older man who "swoops" down on younger ones in the bars. It may be self-descriptive: "[Architect Philip] Johnson described himself and [gay industrialist] George Gallowhur as 'chickenhawks'— gentlemen who preferred the company of younger men" (Kaiser 1997, 11). In the 1980s Liberace's lover, Scott Thurston, made news by referring to the pianist as a "chickenhawk" (see also QUAIL, TROLL, VAMP [vampire]). In addition, *chickenhawk* may refer to a male heterosexual who preys (here the predatory image is appropriate) on adolescent girls. See also PEDERAST.

Chicken porn movies show men sexually abusing children. The free market system also offers chicken porn magazines as forms of entertainment for men.

"To run around like a chicken with its head cut off" means to act crazy, or brainless.

chickenhawk; **chicken queen**. See CHICKEN.

chickie. See CHICKEN.

China doll. A Chinese or any East Asian woman viewed as being deferential and existing to serve men. Also, any woman regarded as feminine, small, or delicate. "My friend Tina's was a fascinating house to visit because of her mother, Florida—a small, blonde china doll with a brain like a steel trap" (Marie Stokes Jemison, in Alexander 1984, 46).

See also CHERRY (cherry blossom), EXOTIC, PEARL (pearl of the Orient).

chippy, **chippie**. Suggestive of youth, inexperience, and vulnerability, especially that of a woman. The meanings of *chippy*, primarily from the mid-nineteenth to early-twentieth century, include a young person or novice and a loose or sexually promiscuous young woman, often a poor woman or a prostitute. "That's where we were Wednesday night—out with a couple of chippies we picked up on Lake Shore Drive" (1959 film *Compulsion*). Henry Seidel Canby, writing of the 1890s, reduced the "chippy" to a woman's male-exploited physical charms:

> Her pretty face, her shapely limbs, were all there was to a "chippy"—companionship, friendliness never entered to complicate a simple and exciting relationship. (quoted in Rotundo 1993, 125)

Chippy-chaser refers to a male philanderer (see also SKIRT [skirt-chaser]); *chippy joint* (or *chippy house*), to a brothel. *To chip* or *to chippy* (sometimes with *around*) means for a man to be promiscuous or adulterous. In black English, *chippy* may mean any young woman or girl, or a young woman who is a sometime or amateurish user of strong drugs, not yet addicted (this latter sense is also in general slang use). Gamblers may use *chippy* in the sense of a sucker.

There have been different attempts to find the hazy origin of *chippy*. One explanation relates it to the practice of paying women who worked in Western brothels in chips, which they could then cash in; another traces it to the French word *chipie*, meaning a mean woman. Still another theory derives the word from the sound *cheap*—supposedly made by streetwalkers to get the attention of men (*cheap*, in the sense of "sleazy," might also have a role in reinforcing the sense of a promiscuous woman or prostitute). A bird metaphor may also come into play—the chipping sparrow (see BIRD).

See also DIRTY GERTIE, EASY LAY, HARLOT, LOOSE, PROMISCUOUS, PROSTITUTE.

chitchat. See GOSSIP.

chocolate. See BUNNY (chocolate bunny), CHERRY (chocolate-covered cherry), HERSHEY BAR (hot chocolate).

chorus boy; **choirboy**. *Chorus boy,* a male singer or dancer in a chorus, from the 1940s; also, *chorus boy* can connote a young man viewed as sissified. *Choirboy* refers to a rookie in the police force; also any innocent, naive, or righteous young man or a man who feigns innocence. Both terms may carry derisive overtones.

See also BOY, EUNUCH, SISSY.

chunk of meat. See MEAT.

cissy. See SISSY.

closet; **closet queen**; **closet case**; **closet queer**. References to a person who is unwilling to be open about her or his homosexuality. The closet metaphor suggests that dark place at the margin of society where one's same-sex impulses are hidden from all but oneself—or at most, a very close circle of friends or family—to convey the impression of being heterosexual.

The term *closet* implies a scandalous personal secret, or skeleton, in the family closet. In the case of a gay person, it refers more precisely to *being* the skeleton in the family's closet. (Grahn 1990, 23)

Grahn says that before gay civil rights were recognized, the word *closet* in this sense was itself once guarded as something of a secret, not spoken of in the presence of heterosexuals. However, Chauncey (1994, 67) claims that although *closet* is a central metaphor in retrospective thinking about gay men before the 1960s, the term does not appear in any of the records or literature of gay men or lesbians before that time, cautioning us against using it uncritically and ahistorically to refer to pre-1960s gay society. Gay men before Stonewall tended instead, Chauncey argues, to speak of their negotiation with the often hostile straight world as "living a double life" in which they often passed as straight (even married). They saw themselves as "wearing a mask" that was taken off to participate in the "gay world"—a more expansive idea of the space in which they were able to express themselves.

Closet queen is a name for a gay man who keeps his homosexuality a secret. (His orientation may also be considered LATENT, or unconscious.) He may be thought of as a shy person who does not get out often to make friends, especially among homosexuals, or the term may be a way gay men scold a man whose only way of being heterosexual is to impersonate the role. *Closet queen* emerged from the underground language of gays in the early 1970s, when an increasing number of gay men were "coming out of the closet" to publicly acknowledge their homosexuality.

Coming out has not always carried the current connotations of exiting "from a hiding place." As Chauncey (7) notes, the expression derives from the language of women's culture, referring to the formal introduction of a debutante to her peers' society. Thus, while gay men since the 1960s have come out *of* the closet, freeing themselves of isolation, gay men of the early twentieth century experienced a "coming out" that initiated them *into* gay society, by way of the drag ball. (Note also that *coming out of the closet* implies a voluntary action; *being outed* refers to being forced out by others.)

Closet case and *closet queer* (or *queen*) may refer to either gay men or lesbians. These terms may be pejorative in gay communities because of feelings there that the closeted individual is "selling out" to the heterosexual majority (see also UNCLE TOM). *Case* suggests someone in need of help, and when used by heterosexual persons, *queen* and *queer* usually carry offensive overtones. Rodgers (1972) lists a number of related words once in use in at least some regions of the country, all suggesting that a gay man or, when applicable, a lesbian, has hidden, squelched, or in some way limited his or her feelings and identity. Among these are *canned* (or *crushed*) *fruit* (see also FRUIT), *cedarchest sissy* (see also SISSY), *pink tea* (a person who assumes a gay identity only after hours), *undercover fag* (or *man/punk/sissy*), and *closet dyke* (lesbian who is not candid).

See also LILY, QUEEN, QUEER.

coarse piece. See PIECE.

cock; cocksucker. *Cock,* a rooster metaphor with strong overtones of virility, reserved mostly for men (see CHICKEN for the very different female version). The name for an adult male chicken, *cock* was created through onomatopoeia, echoing the "cock-a-doodle-doo" made by a rooster. When applied to male genitalia (since the seventeenth century, it has meant the penis), it is suggested by the image of the erect comb of the rooster. The sexual meaning is also sometimes said to derive from the spout or watercock sense of the term. Although the word has been considered vulgar since the early nineteenth century, from the fifteenth through the eighteenth century it was standard English. Men once thought of themselves as "proud cocks."

In the sixteenth century, it meant the supreme leader or boss of a group. By the seventeenth century, it also was used for a man who fought with pluck. A "cock-of-the walk" is a strutting, bossy man or bully. In Chaucer's day, it has been suggested, this expression referred to a man who patrolled the streets of a town at night, awakening slumberers at daybreak. But it is also related to the fact that barnyard fowls are fed on a "walk," where cocks may fight one another. A man who "cries cock" claims victory, while one who "rules the roost" is in charge—that is, of the "hens." *Cock* has also been used for a spirited, hearty, or jolly man (often as *old cock,* since the seventeenth century) or simply any buddy. When applied negatively to a person, reducing a man to the implied part of the anatomy, *cock* (also *prize cock*) came to be synonymous with BAS-TARD in the sense of a despicable man. It has been used this way since at least the mid-twentieth century (see PRICK). The masculinity of the term is affirmed in other expressions: we say (often of a man, but also women) that he is cock-sure (very confident; contrast with *cocky bitch*) or cocky (bold, conceited) (see also HOT DOG).

Cock may also mean the act of intercourse with a woman (or with a man), a vulgar usage since the nineteenth or early twentieth century that reduces intimacy to anatomy (see also PUSS). It may also refer to the female genitals (mostly Southern use) or, derived from this sense, to a woman as a sex object. *Cockbite* is synonymous with BITCH in the sense of a woman regarded as castrating (it may also refer to oral sex). *Cockhound* (see also DOG) has been heard predominantly in the South and

the West since about the 1940s and means a lecher; *cocksman* refers to an ardent womanizer (see also STUD). Though often considered vulgar, these two latter terms may be used self-de-scriptively, even in pride. *Rooster* carries similar meanings.

Cocksucker combines the obscenity of *cock* with the often disturbing sensuality of the word *suck.* Usually applied contemptuously, it means a person of either sex, but often a man (for a woman, it probably still usually refers to a fellatrix, but it is now seeing some use for any woman considered contemptible). Since the early twentieth century, *cocksucker* has been an epithet for either a straight or a gay male, synonymous with SON OF A BITCH. The negativity of the epithet stems from what is regarded by heterosexuals as the despised homoerotic activity (see also FLUTE). "I hate that little prissy cocksucker" (man-to-man talk in the 1997 film *In the Company of Men*). Since a man might conceivably be cursed as a "tit-sucker" but is not, the expressive power of the term apparently comes from what is regarded among heterosexuals as taboo behavior for men. It is most frequently used by men to abuse other men. "If it wasn't for the spooks couldn't a damn one of you white cock suckers *ever* get laid" (James Baldwin, *Another Country,* 1962). It may also be said of a rascal or scamp, in a jocular vein, or of a sycophant. *Cockteaser* (or *cocktease* or *C.T.*) refers usually to a flirtatious woman but also to a gay man, especially one who lures a man into sexual behavior but denies him intercourse (also *prickteaser* or *dickteaser*). It may carry a hint of cunning.

See also BIRD, BULL, KING (king of the jungle), PEACOCK, STAG, STALLION, STUD, WOLF.

codger. Since the eighteenth century, an often elderly fellow considered somewhat eccentric, as in the phrase "old codger" (sometimes women are spoken of in these terms, too). *Codger* is now standard English. It may be used self-descriptively or affectionately, but it can also be mildly pejorative and be taken with offense. Besides connoting oddness, and sometimes unpleasantness, it may also suggest sexlessness; sometimes it connotes meanness or miserliness. Still, it usually does not carry the negative connotations that such words as *hen, hag,* or *crone* do, all applied to women. *Codger* appears to be a variant of *cadger* (an itinerant salesman or hawker).

See also BUZZARD, COOT, CUSS, DUFFER, FOGY, GAFFER, GEEZER, OLD FART.

coed. A shortening of *coeducational student,* a reference to a student in an institution that enrolls both sexes. It is nearly always, however, applied to females, often to those stereotyped as cute and preppy. Speaking of entering college in the 1960s, Sadker and Sadker (1994) remarked on an official college women's rule book in which "Female students were 'coeds'; male students were 'gentlemen'" (177). Although used since the 1890s, this locution began to slowly fall out of use as coeducational institutions became more common and when feminists objected to the word because of some pejorative overtones and the absence of a counterpart word for males. In September 1962, in *Esquire* magazine, then-burgeoning feminist Gloria Steinem published "The Moral Disarmament of Betty Coed" in which she argued that female college students were beginning to thumb their noses at the double standard and reject those social dictates that made them feel compelled to choose between a career and marriage.

Coed still enjoys currency as an adjective ("a coed school") and may be used without bias if applied to both women and men. However, in the context of sex advertising—it is often placed in alliterative word pairs, such as *kinky coed*—it is frequently used as though female sexual availability were coded into it.

See also BETTY (Betty Coed).

cold fish. See FRIGID.

colt. See HORSE.

coming out; coming out of the closet. See CLOSET.

commodity. See SEX OBJECT.

coo, cou; cooch. The female genitals or women regarded as sex objects. *Cooch* can also refer to a hootchy-kootchy dance, an erotic, suggestive dance usually performed by women for men.

From the first sense above comes the gay use of *cooch* to mean any woman or an effeminate man (see EFFEMINATE).

See also BOX, COOZIE, CRACK, CUNT, GASH, GINCH, NOOKY, PUSS.

cookie. An epithet often used for people, from a Dutch term meaning "little cake." In the sense of a young, good-looking person of the other sex, it usually applies to a woman (since the early twentieth century), alluding to sweetness or a "good enough to eat" quality. It also applies to a woman regarded as promiscuous. In the lesbian community, and suggesting traditional femininity, it may refer to the lesbian partner thought to take the "passive" role. When describing a man, *cookie* is often constructed with *tough* (a *tough cookie*) or *shrewd,* but *tough cookie* is also frequently applied to women who are assertive or liberated.

> Not too long ago, we were called dolls, tomatoes, chicks, babes and broads. We've graduated to being called tough cookies, foxes, bitches and witches. (Barbra Streisand [1992], in *The American Women's Almanac* [1997], ed. Louise Bernikow)

In her 1998 novel, *Gingersnaps,* Delorys Welch-Tyson calls her African

American female characters after the titular cookie because they are "spicy, and hard, brown and bold—women who refuse to let their cookies crumble when faced with a challenge." In black English, *cookie* or *cookies* can mean the female genitals.

See also CAKE, CAKE-EATER, CHEESE-CAKE, CREAMPUFF, CUPCAKE, DISH, JELLY ROLL, MUFFIN, PIE, SWEET, TART.

cookie-pusher. See CAKE-EATER.

cooler. Slang word for a woman who, because she is regarded as homely, cools a man's ardor. In use since the late eighteenth century.

See also COYOTE, DOG, GANGSTER GIRL, HOGGER, LOBO, LOOKSISM, PIG, SCUD, SKAG, YETI.

coot. Since the eighteenth century, someone regarded as harmless or simple, usually an unpleasant, foolish, old, or senile man. It is often heard as *old coot*. "Shut up and stop complainin', ya half dead ol' coot" (young man to old one, in 1995 made-for-TV movie *It Came from Outer Space II*).

The coot, an aquatic bird characterized by a shrill cry and zany antics, also gives us an alliterative descriptive for insanity, *crazy as a coot*. *Mad coot* dates to at least the sixteenth century. One species of the coot bird has a wide white plate on the front of its head, giving us yet another sometimes offensive expression, *bald as a coot*.

See also BUZZARD, CODGER, CUSS, DUFFER, FOGY, GEEZER, GOAT, OLD FART.

coozie, coozey. Since the mid-twentieth century, a vulgar and objectifying slang term used mostly by men for women. *Coozie* is synonymous with *cunt*, in the sense either of the female genitals or of a despicable or sexually promiscuous woman, or any woman viewed as a sex object. It may also mean copulation with a woman. *Coozie* found its way into the language early in the twentieth century. Its origin is unclear. *Coozey* has also been used to

designate someone regarded as a sexual "pervert," for example, a gay male youth having a sexual relationship with an older male (Spears [1991] calls this U.S. underworld slang of the mid-1900s). *Cooze* has also been used for a lesbian.

See also BOX, COO, CRACK, CUNT, FLOOZY, GASH, GINCH, HOOZIE, NOOKY, PROMISCUOUS, PUSS.

coquette. A woman seen as flirtatious or a woman who tries to gain the attention of men through sexual teasing or by making insincerely amorous overtures. *Coquette* is the feminine form of *coquet* (flirtatious man), diminutive of the French *coq,* meaning cock, first appearing in English around the early seventeenth century and referring then to both sexes. In early use, however, as Mills (1989) points out, "male coquets were gallant; female ones...were wanton, immodest or prettily pert." The word also acquired connotations of cunning and deceptiveness, traits morally frowned upon, especially in a woman. In their coverage of the 1996 Summer Olympics in Atlanta, some commentators referred to a female gold medalist as a "calculating coquette."

See also BELLE, HOYDEN, HUSSY, TEASE, VAMP.

corker. See KNOCKOUT.

corral. Livestock metaphor meaning a group of prostitutes working usually for a pimp, sometimes for a madam. Heard mostly in the U.S. underworld (twentieth century), this term suggests the enclosure used to pen horses, cattle, or other animals. The implication is that the women are domesticated and controlled, lacking in freedom and useful only for serving the needs of those who pay for their services.

See also HORSE, PROSTITUTE, WOMEN AS ANIMALS.

corset crowd. A disparaging reference to women, alluding to the nineteenth-century woman, believed to be useless in the worldly affairs of men. Such women—more precisely, "ladies"—were said to spend much of their time in such nonproductive activities as gossiping. The expression has also seen some use in the twentieth century.

A corset is a tight-fitting undergarment worn to shape the waistline, hips, and breasts. According to early-twentieth-century sociologist Thorstein Veblen (1953), enforced useless activity was precisely the purpose of the garment.

> The corset is, in economic theory, substantially a mutilation, undergone for the purpose of lowering the subject's vitality and rendering her permanently and obviously unfit for work. (121)

Veblen argued that the corset enhanced the prestige especially of the husband of the wearer, since he was advertising his ability to afford such leisure.

See also GOSSIP, HEN, LADY.

cottontail. See BUNNY.

cover girl. See GIRL.

covey. See QUAIL.

cow. Once a metaphor for any timid person and later one of many farm and animal metaphors for a woman, especially one considered coarse or a prostitute. The earliest date attesting to this latter use of *cow* is 1696, according to *The Oxford English Dictionary* (1989). The cow has long been a feminine symbol because of its life-giving milk, associated with the plentifulness of the maternal earth. The demeaning basis of comparison with human females, however, appears to be based on several other, or related, attributes of the bovine.

A cow, the mature female of cattle and other large animals, is a domesticated animal that is usually fat or dumpy-looking. It is a dull, low-status animal, passive and docile and easily "husbanded" when fed—as a woman

supposedly should be, according to some traditional sexist thinking. The cow also possesses large mammary glands (hence *cow* or *milker* for a large-breasted woman, *dairies* for her breasts). Dunayer (1995) says that our perception of the cow's passiveness comes from her stall confinement, which makes it impossible for her to nurture a calf, "so that milking becomes something done *to* her rather than *by* her" (13).

A number of expressions link the human female with cows. Both *bovine* and *bossy* (a popular nickname for cows, but here also a double entendre) have been applied to women. A woman may be looked over like a "prize cow," or she may be easily "cowed" by a man, although that term can also apply to men. The expression "Why buy a cow when milk is so cheap?" means "Why take a wife when it is so easy to find a sexually available woman?"

An obese woman may be disparaged as a "cow" or an "udder." HEIFER, meaning a young cow, is also used for women, often for plump ones, while *livestock* has found some use in referring to women as sex objects. *Cow pilot* is airline talk that insults a female flight attendant. Although "fresh cow" can be said of a man, that is, to just be showing the symptoms of gonorrhea, it's a good guess that the reference to *cow* here is at least reinforced by the idea of a promiscuous woman or prostitute having given the disease to him. Finally, the old expression "called to straw" refers to a woman going into labor, alluding to a cow giving birth.

Rodgers (1972) claims that *cow* has also found use in gay communities for a heavy or clumsy gay man.

See also COWBOY, HOGGER, HORSE, PIG, SOW, WOMEN AS ANIMALS.

coward. See CHICKEN.

cowboy; **drugstore cowboy**; **cowgirl**. *Cowboy*, originally used in England to mean simply a boy or man who looks after cows. When *cowboy* entered American English, however, it took on new meanings. The first was a Revolutionary War designation for pro-British colonists who harassed the rural areas of Westchester County, New York. These raiders were said to hide in the bushes with guns and cowbells that they tinkled to deceive patriots hunting for cows (Barnhart and Metcalf 1997).

Cowboy later took on the more characteristic American sense of a mounted cattle-ranch hand and rodeo performer. The legend of the Western cowboy as we know it today developed after the Civil War, particularly in the 1870s and 1880s, when a rough breed of horsemen, working for low wages and in the most challenging circumstances, roped and branded cattle and drove them from Texas to the Colorado and Kansas railroads.

No doubt arising from legend, the sense of *cowboy* since at least the 1930s is that of a rash, risk-taking, or unscrupulous man. In more specific senses it may refer to a man who drives a car or pilots a plane recklessly, an impulsive criminal or gunman, or an undisciplined politician. It may also connote a man who is rough, swaggering, or rowdy— like the cowboy hero of lore, an all-around macho man. During his presidency, Ronald Reagan was sometimes called a cowboy, an allusion to what some considered his tendency to act before thinking but also to his strong stance on the military.

For many *cowboy* conjures up images of a patriarchal society: guns, violence, and the domination of women. A cartoon of President Reagan as a cowboy with a big hat and gun read, "A gun in every holster; a pregnant woman in every home. Make America a man again" (Andrea Dworkin, in Buchwald, Fletcher, and Roth 1993, 17) (see also HE-MAN, MACHO).

Major (1994) notes a use in black

English (Watts and South-Central L.A.) meaning a "badass nigger." Major also claims that in colonial America, while African slaves who tended cows in the South were known as cowboys, which was emasculating because of both syllables, white men were always called cattlemen (see also BOY, COW). In general usage, however, the *cow* in *cowboy* carries none of the demeaning connotations seen with *cow* when applied to women. And the earlier cow*boys* were usually just that—boys or very young men.

Cowboy, since about the mid-twentieth century, has also been employed for a male prostitute or gay man, connoting one with masculine characteristics. Also, there is the "midnight cowboy" (used in the name of the 1969 movie in which Jon Voigt goes to New York to become a male prostitute).

Drugstore cowboy is used for a young man who hangs around drugstore soda fountains, lunchrooms, or similar places to meet women and show off. He may also be a man who affects the look and manners of a real cowboy but may be regarded as a phony; or simply, any callow man. The term also suggests an effeminate man, that is, one who is not the "real thing." Mencken (1962, 333) says that comic-strip creator Thomas A. (Tad) Dorgan is attributed with introducing the term.

Cowgirl may evoke some MANNISH (if not immature) qualities but does not carry the masculine connotations of wild west action and adventure that those bred on Western stories and movies have come to associate with *cowboy*. Originally, *cowgirl* referred only to female performers in wild west shows or competitors in rodeos. Unlike hired male hands on ranches who call themselves cowboys, few women in such positions ever call themselves cowgirls. However, for as long as there have been cattle and horses in North America, women—Native American, Latina, African American, or European American—have worked with them (Mankiller et al. 1998).

coy. See GENDER-SPECIFIC ADJECTIVES.

coyote. A usually demeaning term for women regarded either as very homely (see also COOLER, DOG, GANGSTER GIRL, HOGGER, LOBO, SCUD, SKAG, YETI) or as flirtatious and sexually aggressive (see also VIXEN). In obsolete British usage, *coyote* meant the female genitals. The name is also used in the West for any contemptible person, for a smuggler of undocumented workers into the United States, or for a Native American or person of mixed Native American descent.
See also JACKAL, WOLF.

crack; crack salesman. *Crack,* since the sixteenth century, an epithet for the female genitals. Once used also for a female prostitute, in early-twentieth-century U.S. slang, *crack* came to stand for any woman regarded as a sex object. *Crack salesman* has been used either for a PIMP—more disparagingly of the female prostitute than of the pimp—or for a gay male prostitute (the association here is probably with the crack in the buttocks; see also ASS [ass peddler]).
See also COO, COOZIE, CUNT, GASH, GINCH, HUSTLER, NOOKY, PROSTITUTE, PUSS.

cracked pitcher/piece. See DAMAGED GOODS.

creampuff, cream puff. Twentieth-century slang for someone viewed as weak or soft (like a pastry). The term is often applied to a man in the same demeaning vein as SISSY (see also CAKE-EATER, EFFEMINATE, WIMP, WUSS). Like so many words that censure a man for effeminacy, a creampuff may also be a woman.
See also CAKE, CHEESECAKE, COOKIE, CUPCAKE, DISH, HONEY, JELLY ROLL, MUFFIN, PIE, SWEET, TART.

crested hen. see HEN.

crime against nature. Euphemistic expression for sodomy, or any nonorthogenital sex, originating in the nineteenth century. The idea is that sodomy violates the "natural" order of things human—it is believed by the speaker to be deviant, perverted, and unnatural. This tendency to euphemize what society views as an unutterable idea such as sodomy is also reflected in such references as "the Cities of the Plain" (rather than "Sodom and Gomorrah"). The Latin *crimen innominatum* (the crime [or offense] that is not to be named), has also been applied euphemistically to sodomy; a synonym is "the love that dare not speak its name." Also reflecting evasiveness are such expressions as "Is he one of them?" or "Is he that way?"
See also DEVIANT, NORMAL, PERVERT, SODOMY.

criminals. Term applied to people convicted of a crime, most commonly implying men. Throughout much of the nineteenth century, and much of the twentieth, because of men's far greater participation, visibility, and opportunities in public life, women were not known to commit crimes in the same numbers as men, except for prostitutes. Popular notions of women did not even recognize them as having roles in crime, except perhaps under a man's coercion or direction. Even when a wife and husband were accused of a crime, it was the husband who was taken as the initiator and performer; the woman was viewed as merely his passive partner. Women, it was thought, lacked the aggressiveness, intelligence, and creativity to be criminals (see also WEAKER VESSEL). Even today, in the face of increasing crime by women, the prevailing view is one of female innocence. Women's crimes are seen as largely involuntary, a result of provocation or of defense against male aggression (Pearson 1997).
Our language is rich in words that

suggest a link between crime and males. Thus, such terms as *burglar, crook, gangster* (note that a "gangster girl" is not a gangster but an unattractive woman), *hood(lum), mug* (any lout as well as a hoodlum), *mugger, killer, mobster, outlaw, pickpocket, racketeer, stalker, swindler, terrorist, con artist* (or *con man*), and *thief* usually suggest a male perpetrator. *Hooligan*, for a juvenile delinquent, also usually implies a male. Murder is supposedly a male activity. Even though women commit violent crimes, men are also virtually always believed to be the serial killers, rippers, stranglers, hit men (the female hired killer may be called by the non-parallel term *hit lady*), and slashers.

White-collar criminals evokes men in dark, pin-striped suits. An unknown "suspect" in a crime is often assumed to be a man. In many cases, especially street hustlers, pimps, and deadbeats, the language suggests stereotypical images of African American men; Latino men or poor men, especially young ones, are also more likely to be criminalized than are other categories of men.

In 1976 James Ney published a paper in *Etc.: A Review of General Semantics* (Nilsen et al. 1977) in which he presented his research using free association and semantic differentials with university students. His student subjects showed a clear tendency to mark such words as *killer, murderer, robber*, and *attacker* as masculine. Also illustrating a bias against males, Ney pointed to the absence in English of a pejorative word describing women in terms such as *rapist*. Ney concludes that in English, if

> speakers want to call a man something bad, there seems to be a large vocabulary available to them, but if they want to use a term which is good to describe a male, there is a small vocabulary available. The reverse is true for women. (312)

There is, in fact, a large vocabulary

of negative and disparaging words describing women, and many such words labeling men are simply not as bad as those applied to women. Yet in the realm of crime, or wherever men, especially those who are poor or of color, are believed to hurt people or possess the power to impinge on others' lives detrimentally, there is some linguistic bias against men.

As Pearson (1997, 153) has pointed out, when women do commit violent crimes and brutal murders, they are more likely than men to receive nicknames that make light of their deeds (and, consequently, of their victims). Nicknames such as "Arsenic and Old Lace Killer," "Giggling Grandma," and "Old Shoe Box Annie" inappropriately insert comedy into descriptions of killers.

The view of criminals as men is part of a long Western tradition of embodying certain strengths in masculine terms. Along with what we sense to be evil in the criminal is energy and dynamism. We see the same masculine energy in male roles such as those of HUNTER and HERO. Philosopher Friedrich Nietzsche saw this when he wrote of his great *Übermensch*, or overman (sometimes superman) as deriving from the character of the criminal, and the creative male energy of the criminal as being suppressed by a society of tame, mediocre, "feminine" ideals.

See also BRUISER, BULLY, BUM, GORILLA, MOLL, RAPE, ROUÉ.

crone. A woman considered ugly, withered, and old, sometimes, alliteratively, a "cackling crone," since the fourteenth century. *Crone* comes from Old North French *carogne* (carrion, cantankerous woman), in turn possibly from Vulgar Latin. It has been used synonymously with WITCH or HAG. "At least you're pretty. You should see some of the crones who come through here" (obnoxious boss to his employee [Jane Fonda] on her first day at work, 1980 movie *9 to 5*).

The term has been given a positive turn by many spiritual women and feminists today. Mary Daly and Jane Caputi (1987), who refuse to let meanings stand where they are, trace the word to the Greek *chronios* (long-lasting). Thus, they link it with the idea of survival— "of the perpetual witchcraze of patriarchy" and of the "early stages of the Otherworld Journey," an inner voyage in which a woman discovers the depths of her strength, courage, and wisdom. Daly thus defines a crone as the "Great Hag of History," or "long-lasting one," and gives as examples Harriet Tubman, the abolitionist born a slave who struggled to free slaves, and Ding Ling, a Chinese feminist activist who survived numerous political purges (114).

See also BAG, BAT, BATTLE-AX, CROW.

cross-dresser, **X-dresser**. A person who dresses like someone of the other gender. *Cross-dresser* is traced to Magnus Hirschfeld, who, in 1910, coined the Latinate German neologism *Transvestiten,* which was translated into English by Edward Carpenter in 1911. The term is used by those who engage in cross-dressing behavior and participate in the transgender subculture (see TRANSGENDERIST). It has been pointed out, however, that the idea of "crossing" unfortunately strengthens the conventional, rigid notion that there are only two sexes and two genders. *Cross-dresser* is also misused or misunderstood by those who are not familiar with transgender behavior or who are biased against it. The term is often thrown about haphazardly to embrace all sorts of people.

Cross-dresser is most accurately applied only to individuals who consider themselves to be members of one sex or gender but who wear the clothing they know to belong conventionally to what they consider the other sex or gender.

Commonly, in North American usage, it is a self-applied identity label for males with social and legal identities as men but who dress as women on certain occasions; who are usually sexually oriented toward women; and who do not usually consider themselves to be gay men or drag queens.

The rubric appears never to be used for self-identification by people, including transgendered people, who have been socialized into gay/lesbian/bisexual/queer subcultures (Susan Styker, personal communication, January 1999). Those who do self-apply the term generally see it as more neutral than TRANSVESTITE, which is often regarded as a pathologizing term. *Cross-dresser* is sometimes misapplied to transsexuals, individuals who feel they properly belong to a sex other than the one to which they were assigned at birth (see TRANSSEXUAL). For example, male-to-female transsexuals who wear skirts would not be cross-dressing, just dressing. Dressing validates and acknowledges their self-perceived gender identity.

Male cross-dressers are common in many cultures, including ours, where they tend to be more visible and less tolerated than female cross-dressers. However, there is a long history of women dressing as men to claim opportunities, jobs, or liberties available only to men. For example, an estimated four hundred women cross-dressed to serve as soldiers in the Civil War.

There is no way of simply categorizing cross-dressing, which is a complex, varied, and widespread phenomenon. The spectrum of cross-dressing behavior ranges from dressing in only a single item of clothing of the opposite gender to a total burlesque of that gender, from brief tampering with gender identity or comic impersonation to an earnest, lifelong effort to live as someone of the other gender.

Ritual cross-dressing has occurred in

many cultures for religious ceremonies, and cross-dressing takes place in heterosexual celebrations, as when football players impersonate cheerleaders at high school pep rallies or men in military barracks perform skits or dances dressed in women's clothes. It also has a role in political lampoon. Cross-dressing can be understood in terms of the public and private dimensions. The performance of a man said to be "in drag," which is a public act, differs considerably from more private behaviors, such as married men wearing panties and bras to enhance sexual arousal.

Medicine and psychiatry have reduced cross-dressing to a pathological deviation from social norms. From this milieu of biased medical thinking comes a host of clinical, confusing, and sometimes objectionable labels, which, because they are too numerous or obsolete, will not be listed here.

In most cultures dressing symbolizes gender differences. In our culture it helps to mark the distinction of "masculine" and "feminine," and crossing from one domain to the other violates socially accepted boundaries. However, though often an expression of gender identity, cross-dressing does not necessarily represent a sexual matter. For much of history, in fact, it was not seen in sexual terms. Not until the nineteenth century did cross-dressing enter the medical consideration of sex. It was also at this relatively recent time that it came to be regarded as a "mental illness." Other cultures have viewed cross-dressing simply as variant human behavior and have even assigned special significance to it. For example, Nanda (1990) describes the class of people in India known as *hijras,* with the distinct status of "not man/not woman," as members of traditional social organizations—part cult, part caste, and worshipers of the goddess Bahuchara Mata.

By connoting gender violation

through what is misperceived as duplicity and falseness, *cross-dresser* may have its pejorative uses. For example, in his speech at the Republican National Convention in 1992, former presidential candidate Pat Buchanan tried to disparage the Democrats as "cross-dressers." His intent was to draw on the designation as a way of linking the Democratic Party with such supposedly undesirable elements as feminists, lesbians, and gays. But what he was doing was directly disparaging the transgendered by using a transgender term he believed to refer to a morally inferior status.

In recent years, *X-dresser*, meaning "cross-dresser," has gained in currency. It is common, for example, in personal ads in publications, used as a space-saving device, an informal abbreviation, or simply a way of being "cute." It appears to have no other particular significance. Also employed are *CD* or *XD,* meaning cross-dress, and *CDer* or *XDer,* meaning cross-dresser. These are usually merely abbreviations, but they could also serve as codes among those who seek discretion or who speak only to those "in the know."

See also BERDACHE, DRAG, GENDER BENDER, HE-SHE, HIM-HER, KNOBBER, LEATHER, OPPOSITE SEX, SHE-MALE.

crow. A woman seen as unattractive or unpleasant, especially an old one. It is commonly found in the form "old crow" and has been used since the mid-nineteenth century. No doubt carrying over some of its feminine connotations, the epithet is also sometimes meant for a difficult or old man. The crow is a plain, unpopular bird with a call that can be abrasive and a reputation in American folklore for being associated with death and witchcraft.

Feminists and lesbians, however, have reclaimed the term, giving it the sense of a sage woman elder.

The same word, much in the sense of *bird,* has been used throughout the twentieth century for any young woman.

See also BAG, BAT, BATTLE-AX, BIRD, CRONE.

crunchie. A term for a type of lesbian. *Crunchies*, as opposed to *lipsticks*, are distinguished by a less fashionable lifestyle, a more aggressive manner, or utopian ideas. According to Thorne (1990), both were originally different groups at Yale University in the 1980s. The appellation may be used with mild derision among those lesbians who oppose the viewpoints of those so labeled. But it is also used in fun, connoting a sturdy, wholesome type of woman. It calls up the idea of granola and such related things as vegetarianism, environmentalism, and earth-mother types of religion.

See also LESBIAN, LIPSTICK LESBIAN.

crushed fruit. See CLOSET (closet case).

crybaby. See BABY.

cry rape. See RAPE.

cuckold. The husband of an unfaithful wife. The word comes from the Middle English *cokewold* (the spelling used by Chaucer), in turn from French words referring to the cuckoo bird. Samuel Johnson claimed that husbands were once warned of the approach of an adulterer by the call of "cuckoo" (*Brewer's Dictionary* 1970). The allusion is to the parasitism of some female Old World cuckoos: they lay their eggs in other birds' nests, where they are then tended by the resident nesters (the cuckolded male thus finds himself looking after another male's brood). Cuckoos are also known for changing mates often. Because of this behavior, the bird has been associated figuratively with unfaithfulness.

"Call your husband a cuckold in jest, and he'll never suspect you" (H. G. Bohn, in James 1984, 2). Since there is no comparable term for a woman who has been betrayed, the use of *cuckold*

leads men to believe that they are susceptible to victimization by women and gives tacit support to a double standard, allowing men greater freedom in being unfaithful. As a verb, *cuckold* means to make a cuckold of a man.

cuddle-bunny. See BUNNY.

cunt. A slang term for a woman's external genital organs, from Middle English *cunte* (hollow space), and related to Middle Low German *kunte* (female pudenda), and Latin *cunnus* (vulva). This has been its primary sense since the thirteenth century. Often considered extremely vulgar, it is burdened with more taboo than are words referring to men's body parts (compare the more innocuous *dick* or even *prick*). This word has for some time been largely unprintable and unspeakable in polite or mixed company. In the 1995 movie *Boys on the Side,* Whoopi Goldberg's worldly character successfully encourages a rather "goody-goody" young woman to say the dreaded word instead of her childhood euphemism *hoo-hoo.*

The unregenerate quality of *cunt* derives from its particularly strong obscenity. This in turn comes from its ability to expose to public view a sexual side of women (represented by an anatomical organ) that is normally supposed to be kept private and which may be a turn-on (see Arango [1989] on the power of taboo). The deep ambivalence and disgust—Greer (1970) spoke of "cunt-hatred"—some men feel about female genitals add to the sense of taboo (the usage reflects a deep-seated loathing of female sexuality). The term also has a phonetic force and masculine assertiveness that can be compared with those of the obscenity FUCK. Because of taboos on use of the word, it may politely be known as the "c-word" (or, in Pig Latin form, *unt-cay,* a slight disguise).

The word has also been used in English for coitus with a woman; for a woman regarded as a sex object, especially a woman believed to be sexually available for men; or generically for any woman. *Cunt* has also been used since the early twentieth century for a woman regarded as despicable or degraded (see also BITCH). Although it may be used as an abusive term for any person, the perspective is almost always that of a man. "You can forgive a young cunt anything" (Henry Miller, *Tropic of Cancer,* 1961, 114). We rarely hear a woman calling another woman a "cunt." Strainchamps (1971) tells us that male philologists have traditionally regarded this term one of the most "sexually energizing" words in English, "an opinion that surely disregards women's sexual response, if any, to these words" (354). If a woman is just a "cunt," she is indistinguishable sexually from other women and can thus be brought down with a slur if she dares to challenge men's status. Thus, in a variation on an old degrading "joke": "Know what they call a woman with a Ph.D. (or seat in Congress or position on the board of directors)? A cunt." When the word is qualified—such as *black cunt,* meaning an African American woman—the qualifier (race, in this instance) may compound the slur.

Cunt has also been used since the mid-nineteenth century in the sense of a low, despicable man, and in the Navy, derogatorily for a yeoman. In the gay male community, it may mean a despised gay man, while *boy-cunt* is a gay man said to take the feminine "passive" role. Applied to men, gay or straight, the term serves to linguistically emasculate (he is said to be like a woman).

Among other, related, and usually vulgar slang expressions are the following. *Charity cunt* (or *charity girl/worker*) means a sexually promiscuous woman or a prostitute who gives out sexual favors for no charge. *Cuntish* is used to describe things that are WOMANISH. *Cunthead* means an idiot or BASTARD, that

is, a despicable person, while a lecherous man may be called a "cunt-hound" (or said to be "cunt-struck"). *Cunt-lapper* refers either to a despicable person or to a lesbian, and *cuntface* connotes an ugly person (*cuntface* may also mean a despicable person). *Cunt-teaser* is a label given to someone who arouses a woman sexually but denies her intercourse or is unable to perform because of impotence (this is usually a heterosexual male but may also be a lesbian; see also TEASE).

Like other locutions of gender, *cunt* reflects on the relative social standing of men and women. As said earlier, while the male counterpart *prick* may also be used abusively, it does not convey the obscenity of *cunt*; and *balls* (testicles) may actually carry positive connotations—a sign of courage and other male virtues, except perhaps when applied to women. Note, for example, the sex-biased expression for strength, *testicular fortitude.*

Some feminists have been inspired to reclaim the insult *cunt.* It is, after all, related to *cunning,* with its positive connotations of power, craftiness, and insight. It is also capable of being construed positively as a potent part of the female anatomy, and we hear it in such positive turns of phrase as *cunt art* (meant to celebrate female imagery created by woman artists) and *cunt history* (a lesbian reference to the lesbian past), while lesbians sometimes refer to their lovers as "cunts."

[Inga] Muscio's cultural analysis [*Cunt: A Declaration of Independence,* 1998]…is a long-overdue call to reclaim "cunt," the word; cunt, the body part; and cunt, the attitude—via a social and political philosophy of cuntlove. (Lisa Miya-Jervis, *Bitch,* Wint-O-Green, 1998, 53)

For the present, however, most women would not likely want themselves reduced to an anatomical part, however upgraded the term may be.

See also ASS, BOX, COO, COOZIE, CRACK, GASH, GINCH, HAIR, HIDE, HOT (hot pants), HOT DOG (hot dog bun), NOOKY, POONTANG, PUSS.

cupcake. A person regarded as eccentric; a gay or effeminate man (one considered soft and unmanly; or (used patronizingly) a sweet, good-looking young woman. "Hey, guys, that's no cheesecake, that's my cupcake" (TV sitcom *Newhart*, 1998 rerun). *Cupcakes* has been used for the buttocks, especially those shaped like the pastry. A close synonym, especially in the sense of an attractive woman, is MUFFIN.

See also BABY (babycakes), CAKE, CAKE-EATER, CHEESECAKE, COOKIE, CREAMPUFF, DISH, EFFEMINATE, HONEY, JELLY ROLL, PIE, SWEET, TART.

cur. A mongrel or worthless dog, also used for a person considered mean, cowardly, or surly, usually a man. George Washington is said to have called Philip Freneau, the poet of the American Revolution, "that barking cur." The word is probably as close as male-specific slurs come to the usually female-specific *bitch*, though that term is more common as invective and in related uses.

See also ANIMAL, DOG.

curmudgeon. In the earliest, sixteenth-century sense of the term, a miser (Charles Dickens' Scrooge was a prime example of a curmudgeon). It later came to refer to a mean person and then a testy, blunt man, but not one all that bad. Ciardi (1980) claims the shift to a man who is gruff but basically decent probably came with Franklin Delano Roosevelt's Secretary of the Interior Harold L. Ickes, who pronounced himself "an old curmudgeon." The word is almost always used for men and implies age. Although ill-tempered, the curmudgeon is not vicious, as a HARRIDAN, who is always a woman, is thought to be.

See also BUZZARD, CODGER, CUSS, FOGY, GEEZER, OLD FART.

curse, the; the curse of Eve. Slang references to the menses, or menstrual period, since the nineteenth century. *Curse* may have influenced or been influenced by the word *course(s)*, also meaning menstruation. The anxiety and ambivalence that surround this natural biological process in our society are reflected in taboos on speaking about it except in such euphemisms as "little friend" or "the curse of Eve": "The most damning euphemism attached to menstruation reflects the belief that the monthly flow of blood is the curse God laid upon woman for her sin in Eden" (Weideger 1975, 90).

Fear and ambivalence toward menstrual blood occur across cultures. Patterns of avoidance (taboo), purification, or punishment of menstruating women are common, though there is great variability in practices and meanings. Examples of controls are the avoidance of menstruating women among traditional Inuit men for fear that the blood causes bad luck in hunting; women's seclusion in "menstrual huts" in many cultures to protect the community from female "pollution"; and the threat of death among some Native Americans for women who did not alert the community of their period.

The long-standing superstition among Americans about the unluckiness of walking under ladders has been attributed to an old fear of passing under bridges or clotheslines when menstruating women were around, lest any contaminating blood fall on their heads (Delaney, Lupton, and Toth 1988, 9). Feminist Gloria Steinem (in Nelson 1997, 127) wonders whether male menstruation wouldn't have resulted in a glorification of the menses.

Many explanations have focused on menstruation taboos as male-imposed constraints on women. For example, Jungian theorist M. Esther Harding (1976) argues that men create scapegoats of women for the evil that men fear in themselves. Also writing from a psychological perspective, Weideger (110–13) adopts Gregory Zilboorg's theory regarding the mythical act of primal rape and the consequential devaluation of women. Man, the scenario goes, envying and fearing woman, sexually assaulted her and then subjugated her. Viewing women's bodies as unclean was a way men had of reinforcing their power. The economic consequences were that men came to treat women as property. Women's economic dependence on men as well as anxiety over rape then led women to accept men's claim of the corruption of the female body.

Contemporary anthropology provides alternative views of attitudes toward menstruation. Taboos are not necessarily indicative of female oppression. In some cultures, women might actually use the taboos as a way of exercising power to their own ends rather than just reacting to the imposition of men's power (see, e.g., Delaney, Lupton, and Toth) on women's use of the local menstruation taboo in a Portuguese village).

Menstrual taboos are also not necessarily about gender ideology. Susan Rasmussen's research on the Kel Ewey Tuareg of Niger shows that taboos serve to highlight not gender divisions but such social principles as class distinctions between elites and peasants (*Dictionary of Anthropology* 1997, 320). What's more, some societies attribute positive powers to menstrual blood. The menstrual state may in some ancient societies have been regarded as sacred and life-giving. In Taiwan, according to Charlotte Furth and Shu-yueh Ch'en (*Dictionary of Anthropology,* 320), while men tend to denigrate women's periods, some women view them as a source of

good health. In still other societies, women may regard menstrual segregation from their community as a break from the usual work routine, a time to socialize with other women, and even a source of spiritual strength.

The practice of some women in industrialized societies of devising their own rites to celebrate the menstrual cycle may help women to ultimately reclaim the "curse" as a form of empowerment.

Brumberg (1997) notes how social and medical changes in the late nineteenth century led to some devaluation of the "curse" expression, replacing it with clinical language: "The new hygiene provided middle-class mothers with a safe script for their private conversations with their daughters. Instead of talking about the 'curse of Eve'…they focused on the logistics of 'sanitary protection'" (40).

The multifarious other expressions, slang terms, and euphemisms for this biological process include *Aunt Flo, become a Lady, domestic affliction, falling off the roof, female disorder, full moon, grandma* or *the granny, mother nature, the thing, woman's home companion,* and *Zelda.*

See also AUNT, DOG (dog days), FEMALE PROBLEMS, FLOWER (flowers), MENOPAUSE, SICK.

cuss. An alteration of *curse*, used since the eighteenth century for a man (also sometimes an animal), often in the phrase *old cuss* or *strange old cuss*. It is also heard in the sense of an odd or perverse creature.

See also BADGER, BUZZARD, COOT, CURMUDGEON, DUFFER, FOGY, GEEZER, GOAT, OLD FART.

cutie; **cutie-pie**. See GENDER-SPECIFIC ADJECTIVES (cute), PIE.

CWA. A "Chick with Attitude." *Attitude* here suggests pugnacity, something not conventionally associated with or acceptable in women. The expression often carries positive connotations, especially among women. "Grrrls just wanna have fun: From Spice pop to comic-strips to CD games glam girls—the chicks with attitude are taking over" (Jan Howells, 4 February 1997, *The Daily Telegraph,* lexis-nexis.com/univers).

See also CHICK, GIRL.

D

daddy; sugar daddy. *Daddy,* a dated slang name used as a familiar address for an older man. It has also been used among African Americans to designate one's paternal father or any old black man (see also AUNT), while *big daddy* signifies a man with power or influence in the black or Southern community, as was the cotton planter nicknamed "Big Daddy" in Tennessee Williams' 1955 play, *Cat on a Hot Tin Roof.* Sometimes, by extension, *daddy* occurs as a reference to any man in a dominant position in society.

> The passing of Mrs. Goodwife from the American scene marks the passing of man as master and husband as hero. Almost everywhere, Big Daddy is dead. (Gittelson 1972, 9)

It is also used to name the best or largest example of something ("It was the daddy of all volcanoes") or to indicate the most respected man in a field ("Hitchcock was the daddy of movie directors").

Since at least the beginning of the twentieth century, *daddy* has also meant a woman's male lover, especially one who supports his girlfriend, often an older male lover, or a husband or pimp. The usage conveys a patronizing attitude toward the woman. "All you 'chickens' take notice—a loving 'daddy' is in town" (Jack Hanley, *Let's Make Mary,* 1937, 36). There have been other, related uses, too, including (often in prison talk) the partner who takes the dominant or "active" role in a homosexual relationship. Speaking of a county jail for women, Elaine Brown wrote,

> The daddy tank was solitary confinement, so called because it was reputedly run by tough lesbian guards who were like men, "daddys." They would have their way with a violator if she ever wanted to see the light of day. (*A Taste of Power,* 1992, 173)

A long form, *sugar daddy* (from the early twentieth century), is, in the heterosexual world, a man (usually an older one) who keeps a young mistress or supports a sweetheart, especially one interested largely in his money, the "sweet" things in life he can provide her (see also GOLD DIGGER). A gay man may also play a sugar daddy role to a "kept boy," consistent with heterosexual use (see CHICKEN [chickenhawk] for a stereotype of older men in gay relationships). There are no truly parallel words for women. Maggio (1997) suggests *meal ticket* as an inclusive alternative.

Disneyland daddy or *zoo daddy* are terms of disapproval for men who are separated or divorced and visit their children rarely, usually to take them on an outing to entertain them. See also DEADBEAT (deadbeat dad), FREAK (freak daddy).

daddy's girl. See GIRL.

daffodil. A flower metaphor used by straight people for an effeminate young man, sometimes implying a gay man. It is likely to give offense. "Where I come from, the only thing we pick by hand is little yellow daffodils" (American soldier to a Canadian soldier, supposedly "hand-picked" for an assignment, 1968 movie *The Devil's Brigade*). The term is not used in gay communities.

See also BUTTERCUP, DAISY, EFFEMINATE, FLOWER, GLADIOLA, LILY, PANSY, VIOLET.

daisy; daisy chain. *Daisy,* a person or thing that is a prime, remarkable, or admirable example of something (This tool is a real daisy). Given the female connotations of this flower metaphor, there may be a touch of irony when used in this sense (compare with DADDY). It can also mean a good-looking young woman (dated in this sense, though it may still be heard as a woman's given name). Since the early to mid-twentieth century, in usually derogatory "straight" usage that draws on the feminine connotations, it can refer to a gay man, any effeminate man (see also BUTTERCUP, DAFFODIL, FLOWER, GLADIOLA, LILY, PANSY, VIOLET), or a "feminine" lesbian.

Daisy chain refers to a line or circle of homosexuals (the term may have originated among gay men) or heterosexuals, each taking an "active" and "passive" role to someone else in simultaneous sexual intercourse. "You have to do more than take a little gas, or slash the wrists. Pot? Zero! Daisy chains? Nothing! Debauchery? A museum word" (Saul Bellow, in *The Oxford Dictionary of Modern Slang*, 1992). When homosexuals are involved in tight-knit groups, implying SODOMY, the association may be referred to derisively as a daisy chain. However, since AIDS, this sexual activity has largely disappeared, associated today in gay communities with the 1970s.

damaged goods. Sexist expression meaning a woman, viewed as property, who has lost her virginity (had sexual intercourse) or been raped and thus has supposedly lost her value to men. This term has been used throughout the twentieth century, occasionally for men, too. Also, *cracked pitcher* or *cracked piece* often suggest promiscuity. *Undamaged goods* refers to a female virgin.

See also VIRGIN.

dame. A slang term for a woman, usually disrespectful today. The word comes originally from the Latin *domina*, meaning mistress of the house and the feminine form of *dominus* (master). In earliest use, *dame* was used in reference to a woman of high social standing.

While titles of honor for men, such as *baronet*, tend to retain their honor, many of those for women have been tainted over the years. As early as the seventeenth century, *dame* began to denote a woman of lower standing or an older housewife. This leveling was especially true in the United States, where there was no system of aristocratic titles, compared with England, where *dame* still means the wife of a baronet—or, as a female appointee to the first or second class of the Order of the British Empire, a woman of high standing in her own right. The American version eventually came to connote much the same meaning as do BROAD and DOLL.

Although a bit dated in the slang lexicon, known mostly through movies and books, *dame* is often associated with the "lower" class, street, and criminal environments of earlier decades. *Dame* belittles women, describing them as either sexy or sexually available, as in the lyrics to the song "There Is Nothing Like a Dame" (Oscar Hammerstein II, musical *South Pacific*). It also marks the speaker for social class: "Do you know what he [hard-boiled police detective] calls women?...'Dames!'" (*Laura*, 1944 film).

It is also found in the expressions *dizzy dame* (see DITZ) and *Dame Fortune*. The proverbial term *wisecracking dame* means a woman considered smart, cynical—and often bitchy.

Dame may also be used affectionately among women without derogatory connotations.

See also DAMSEL, DUCHESS, GOVERNESS, MISTRESS, PRINCESS, QUEEN (woman).

damsel. Dated term meaning a young woman or maiden. The word derives from the Old French *dameisele* (the feminine form of *damoisel,* a squire) from the Vulgar Latin *domnicella,* the diminutive of *domina* (lady). In spite of this noble beginning, however, by the fifteenth century the word had acquired other meanings: a maid-in-waiting, attendant, or country girl. Especially in such expressions as *damsel in distress* (now regarded as quaint but sometimes heard ironically), *damsel* suggests a helpless woman dependent on men.

See also DAME, LADY, MADAM.

dark meat. See MEAT.

date. See JOHN.

date rape. See RAPE.

deadbeat; deadbeat dad. *Deadbeat,* an Americanism from the nineteenth century, used in the sense of a worthless man or bum. Usually reserved for men, it connotes the unwillingness to do the things men are expected to do: be a provider, be productive, and pay one's bills. *Deadbeat dad* refers to a noncustodial father who refuses or does not make a good-faith effort to pay child support. In unfair use, however, it labels a father who cannot make his payments or stereotypes all noncustodial fathers; it is applied disproportionately to poor men.

See also BREADWINNER, BUM, DADDY (zoo daddy), GOLDBRICK.

dead meat. See MEAT.

dear. In use since the thirteenth century, a term of affection for a loved one, a sweetheart, or any endearing or likable person. In certain contexts of familiarity, the usage may be appropriate for either a man or a woman. But in many contexts it applies mostly to a woman and is often patronizing. It can express affection, condescension, or even anger (though meant to soften it).

Alette Olin Hill (1986, 86) reported being in a restaurant where the waitress addressed her husband as "sir" but called her "dear." Attempting to explain this, she notes that Wolfson and Manes (in *Women and Language in Literature and Society,* 1980) found that two of the dominant modes of addressing women (*dear* and *ma'am*) may occur in the same kind of situation. In other words, either *dear,* a term of endearment, or the more formal *ma'am,* or both, may be used by a person for a woman in essentially the same setting or circumstances. However, *dear* (and related forms, such as *hon*) may strike the listener as insincere or phony or represent a form of ingratia-

tion. A woman's subordination to a man is evoked as the heart of the matter. The waitress who addressed her as "dear" while the husband was "sir" was being superficially friendly, while condescending to her as a woman. Such a usage may also serve to raise the speaker's self-esteem.

See also HONEY, SUGAR, SWEET.

declared/avowed/admitted homosexual. See HOMOSEXUAL.

defloration. See VIRGIN.

degenerate. See DEVIANT, HETEROSEXUAL, HOMOSEXUAL, PERVERT.

depraved. See PERVERT.

deviant. Label for a person whose behavior or attitudes depart in some way from the dominant accepted standards of a society and who is likely to be stigmatized, censured, and penalized for it. *Deviant,* when applied to people in this way, is often a convenient term for those who take their biases for granted and presume to know what is normal and abnormal, what is good and bad. Those who make such judgments seldom ask how the standards came about in the first place, what makes some people seem to resist or violate them while others manage to conform, and what it means to be stigmatized for transgressions or to feel good to be on the side of "normality." What they do experience is the need to categorize the deviant and control what may be viewed as his or her threatening "degeneracy." Homosexuality is an example:

> Science discovered homosexuality in the middle of the nineteenth century.... Practitioners of forensic medicine...were searching for physical differences that would allow scientists to identify deviants, making the job of the policeman much easier. (Higgins 1993, 117)

Regarding others as deviant—for instance, a gay man who resists heterosexual relations or a single mother who refuses to rely on a man to help raise her children—usually leads to their devaluation or stigmatization and often exclusion. Labeling others as "pathological" distances the "normal," virtuous us from a "sick" other. More specifically, the term can contribute to the criminalization of the poor, discrimination against gays and lesbians, and coercive attempts to ensure the sexual acquiescence of women to men. But determining just who is deviant is a tricky matter. The type of person or characteristic so labeled depends on the social perspective and circumstances of the labeler. For example, "terrorists" become "freedom fighters" to those who share their cause. Attempting to grapple with the difficulties of understanding deviance, social scientists see it not as a type of person or personality trait but rather as characteristics of a society, such as the organization of the family, social control, or differences in wealth and power among classes of people. In some instances people may embrace a deviant identity as a way of resisting domination. Lesbian theorists, for example, have tried to replace *deviant* with *counterculture*.

Sexual orientations that are labeled deviant are associated with numerous negative character traits in order to delineate and naturalize the "deviance." Daniel Mangin (in Witt, Thomas, and Marcus 1995, 76), for example, notes that in the movies gay men have often been stereotypically portrayed as mentally disturbed individuals or failures: child molesters, neurotics, promiscuous predators, psychopaths, sissies, and sad young men. Meanwhile, lesbians have been misrepresented as deceitful, jealous, "just waiting for the right man," predatory, sexually immature, and hard-edged. Yet some gay and lesbian activists have used the deviant label self-descriptively, even applying "Sexual deviant—OK!" to T-shirts.

How useful is deviance analysis? According to Stewart (1995), "The group of sexual deviants picked out by deviance analysis is so diverse that such analysis seems about as useful as analysis of society by brand of toothpaste."

A *deviate* is someone regarded by straight people as sexually perverse or a sodomite. This has been a euphemism since the nineteenth century, in use largely among heterosexuals.

See also ALTERNATIVE LIFESTYLE, DIRTY OLD MAN, EXHIBITIONIST, HOMOSEXUALITY AS DISEASE, LEFT-HANDED, NORMAL, PEEPING TOM, PERVERT, SICK, TWISTED, TWINK.

devil. See GOD, SHE-DEVIL.

dick. A term for penis since the late eighteenth century, in what is usually considered vulgar language linked with British military use.

In noun form, *dick* can mean, among other things, a man, especially one considered odd or foolish; also a police officer or a detective, usually as *private dick* (a female police officer may be disparaged as a "Dickless Tracy," a pun on *dick* [penis] and the Chester Gould comic-strip detective).

As a word for a man (since the sixteenth century), it comes from *Richard*, of which *Dick* is the pet form. Chapman (1998) suggests derivation from the practice of using affectionate names for the genitals or from the earlier British word *derrick* (penis). In a popular explanation of *derrick*, Panati (1998) recounts how spectators of executions in seventeenth-century London watched eagerly for the erect penis that spontaneously resulted when a man was asphyxiated by hanging. Since one especially ruthless executioner in London at that time was named Derrick, his name (eventually abbreviated to *Dick*) was given to that anatomical phenomenon. In addition, *dick* can mean sexual intercourse with a man (here the anatomical part represents the whole sex act) or a despicable man, as in the derogatory sense of the rhyming word *prick*.

In verb form *dick* has various meanings, including botching or screwing up, cheating or deceiving, and having sexual intercourse with a woman. These senses all share an aggressive meaning. Chapman notes the possibility of the survival from Middle English *dighten,* to have sex with. A sentence such as "He dight her" would be pronounced as "He dicked her."

The insulting *limp-dick,* which Major (1994) says is of black origin though its use is more widespread, means a man considered weak, ineffectual, or impotent (see also LIMP-WRIST). *Dickbreath* is mid- to late-twentieth-century slang for a man considered despicable—a "cocksucker"—often with that term's implications of homosexuality, and *dickhead* means a stupid man. *Dickweed* and *dickwad* also convey contempt for a man, usually for his stupidity. (It is possible to hear some of these terms applied to women, too, whatever the masculine connotations of *dick.*) For fellators and gay men there are also the disparaging *dicksucker* and *dick(ey)-licker* as well as *deadeye dick* (*deadeye* referring to the anus). *Dick peddler* refers to a male prostitute, and *dicky broad* has use among lesbians for a lesbian viewed as aggressive or having a long clitoris. *Dickhound* is black slang for a sexually promiscuous woman, or SLUT. For an explanation of *dickteaser,* see COCK (cockteaser).

However strong the contempt may be in these usages, they do not carry the taboo or compare in virulence to CUNT, applied to a woman.

See also BUGFUCKER (needle-dick), DIESEL (cock-diesel), JACK, PRICK, SCHMUCK, TEASE (dicktease).

diesel; diesel dyke. A lesbian viewed as tough or aggressive or having other "masculine" traits. The stereotype is the lesbian who cuts her hair short, dresses in leather, and wears the heavy working shoes called Doc Martens. She is also known as a "truck driver."

Diesel, from the surname of the man who invented this type of engine, is the mechanical equivalent of the animal BULL, as in BULLDYKE; in either case, the associations are "butch." In use since the mid-twentieth century, *diesel dyke* was apparently a variation of *bulldyke* invented in the gay underground. Whereas *diesel* in this lesbian context tends to be offensive, especially when not used by lesbians, in the word combination *cock-diesel,* said of a muscular or well-built man, it may be flattering.

See also BUTCH, DYKE, LESBIAN.

dike. See DYKE.

dimbo. See BIMBO.

dinge; dinge queen. *Dinge,* a vulgar and usually contemptuous term for a black person deriving from *dingy* (dark, discolored), used since the mid-twentieth century for a black gay man.

In gay communities *dinge queen* refers to a white gay man who prefers black men sexually. It has also seen some use for a black man. Although no rudeness was intended (for the most part) when the term was current, as political correctness took hold in the 1980s, expressions such as *dinge queen,* the synonym *midnight queen, snow queen* (a black gay who seeks fair-skinned males), and *rice queen* (a white man who dates Asian men) came to be widely frowned upon as racist in gay communities.

Although *Merriam-Webster's Collegiate Dictionary* (1997) says the origins of *dingy* are unknown, other sources suggest a relationship to *dung* (Rawson 1989).

See also QUEEN.

dinner. See DISH.

dinner hound. See DOG (hound), GOLD DIGGER.

Dirty Gertie. A rhyming nickname for a woman viewed as sexually assertive or promiscuous, used mostly during the first half of the twentieth century. It was an easy way to dismiss a woman for not conforming to the standards of her gender by being forward.

See also DIRTYLEG, LOOSE, MUDKICKER, PROMISCUOUS.

dirtyleg; hard leg. *Dirtyleg,* a female prostitute or, more consistent with the degrading tone of this word, a slut. *Hard leg* refers to a woman viewed as ugly or debased, often a prostitute who has been on the streets for a long time. *Leg* here is probably a reference to female anatomy, though it might also allude to streetwalking. Major (1994) says that *hardleg* may also be used in black slang for any man.

See also DIRTY GERTIE, FLOOZY, LEG, MUDKICKER, PROSTITUTE, SLUT.

dirty old man. A lecher, especially an older one; from the early twentieth century. This hackneyed expression, referring to a middle-aged or old man whose seemingly excessive interest in young women, sex, or pornography appears DEVIANT, is usually regarded as sexist and ageist, although there are sometimes ironically Victorian, even affectionate, tones to the phrase. A common stereotype is that of a middle-aged or elderly man dressed in a raincoat. The abbreviated form *D.O.M.* is also in use.

Speaking of the hazards of the male experience, Goldberg (1976, 35) writes that whether an older man who pursues a young woman is considered a "dirty old man" or "hip and interesting" often boils down to his wealth and position. Strainchamps (1971) wrote that "The Mrs. Robinsons are given points for initiating inexperienced males, while the Humbert Humberts [see LOLITA] are ostracized as dirty old men" (360).

Since the mid-twentieth century, the expression has also been used in gay communities for a homosexual man who is considerably older than his male partner. In this context, the usage typically carries no derogatory connotations; though it may be mocking and ageist, it may also be affectionate. A gay modification of the expression would be *dirty old queen*, a gay man who is much older than his partner. This usage, too, would be largely affectionate (see also QUEEN).

See also EXHIBITIONIST, LECHER, PEEPING TOM, PERVERT.

dish. Probably since at least the seventeenth century, but still common at the beginning of the twenty-first, an objectifying reference to a very pretty young woman, or sometimes also to a man (as food). As Nilsen (1998) has pointed out, food, when used as a metaphor for women, is something passive, "just sitting there waiting to be eaten" (404). *Dish* can also be used to allude to a woman as a container (suggested by the female genitals). Combining the idea of *dish* as a suggestion of sexuality with that of something sweet and delectable, Norman Mailer wrote of Marilyn Monroe that "sex with her would be like eating ice cream" (*Marilyn: A Biography,* 1987, in Smith 1989, 98). We often hear of a woman being described as "good enough to eat," a "feast for the eyes," or perhaps a "tasty morsel," something that makes a man's mouth water. Such expressions may also apply to men, though men are less likely than women to be thought of as culinary delicacies. Gay men, however, have their own food references to other gay men (see ANGEL [angel food]).

A similar metaphor for a woman is *dinner,* which is mostly black usage.

See also BEEF, CAKE, CHEESECAKE, COOKIE, CREAMPUFF, CUPCAKE, DONUT HOLE, EATING PUSSY, FLAVOR, FRUIT (fruit plate), HONEY, JELLY ROLL, LOLLIPOP, LOOKSISM, MEAT, MUFFIN, PEACH, PIE, POTATO, SEX OBJECT, SPICE, SWEET, SWEET MEAT, TABLE GRADE, TAMALE, TART, TOMATO, TREAT, WOMEN AS ANIMALS, WOMEN AS STORMS.

displaced homemaker. See HOMEMAKER.

ditz; ditzy. *Ditz,* a person viewed as flighty or frivolous, an airhead; a mid- to late-twentieth-century usage. "She [actress Lisa Kudrow] has to prove she can be something besides the ditz that everyone likes" (*People,* 5 October 1998, 77). As a noun and in adjective form (*ditzy* or *ditsy*), this term is often said of a woman, for example, *ditzy blonde* (also sometimes styled *dizzy blonde*), which is like *bubblehead*. "A lot of my female students complained about a science teacher who persisted in referring to them as 'dizzy' or 'ditzy' or 'airhead'" (Sadker and Sadker 1994, 95). Chapman (1987) suggests that *ditzy* is a blend of *dizzy* and *dotty*. Men have been nicknamed "Dizzy" without insult; witness jazz trumpeter and composer Dizzy Gillespie (John Birks Gillespie) or baseball's Dizzy Dean (Jay Hanna Dean).

See also BLONDE (dumb blonde), BUNNY (dumb bunny), DAME (dizzy dame), DUMB DORA, GENDER-SPECIFIC ADJECTIVES (scatterbrained), SPACE GIRL, TWINK (twinkie).

divorcée. A woman who was formerly married (from French, feminine of *divorcé,* from Middle French *divorse*). Not only does *divorcée* sometimes carry negative connotations (and the final feminine-marking -*e* seems prissy by today's linguistic standards) but also the male equivalent, *divorcé,* is not used as often. Men who have been divorced are more likely to be called simply "divorced," "unmarried," or a "bachelor."

A large part of the biased overtones of this term derives from the way our culture has questioned women who are without a man. At one time, divorced women were treated with disdain, stigmatized as undesirable and immoral. The *Washington Post* banned the term from its newspaper in 1970. It sees less use today than formerly.

See also OLD MAID, SPINSTER.

dog. A term with numerous meanings, complex and sometimes contradictory, referring to and often disparaging both men and women. From Old English *docga,* from at least the eleventh century, the common use of *dog* is for the domesticated canine that guards our house and plays with our children. Until the late nineteenth century, *dog* referred to the male of the species; *bitch,* to the female (this is still the case among breeders).

A common symbol of fidelity and protection, the dog has also represented depravity and baseness. Since the fourteenth century, for example, *dog* meant a despicable man, a scoundrel, or an untrustworthy person. This sense survives in such expressions as *dirty dog, lazy dog,* and *surly dog,* while ageist connotations are found in *old dog* ("You can't teach an old dog new tricks"). In twentieth-century black English, probably patterned after the original sense of a scoundrel, *dog* became a slur on a white man, and it has also been in use to refer to a brutal policeman.

> After we [Black Panthers] were arrested...we were all put into the Drunk Tank, a large room with nothing in it but us. No bed, no blankets, nothing. This kind of treatment you expect from a racist dog. (Warren Tucker, in Mario Van Peebles, Ula Y. Taylor, and J. Tarika Lewis, *Panther,* 1995, 36)

Dog may also mean a LECHER (mid-twentieth century). But along with these slurs directed largely at men, the word *dog* has also been wielded against women, though more often focusing on their physical appearance and sometimes also temperament. Since the early twentieth century, *dog* has often been a man's slur on a woman regarded as very unattractive or uncouth, that is, one compared in looks or behavior to a canine. "Why do you call her [a college girl] Lassie?... Are you calling her a dog?" (male student, 1981 movie *Porky's*).

A woman in this sense might be thought of as someone treated abusively, that is, "treated like a dog." To justify such treatment of women, "men must view them as a separate species, like pigs or dogs or cows...and dominating a lowly dog or cow can hardly be very satisfying" (French 1992, 181). As the male abuser experiences doubt about the significance of controlling the woman he has designated as lowly, he relies all the more on abusiveness. Dunayer's (1995, 12) explanation of the use of the label for women starts with the speciesist outlook on dogs as nonhumans with a bad image. Calling a woman a dog causes her to share in that negativity, and implies that she—unlike men, who are seldom referred to as dogs for reasons of physical appearance—has a special obligation to look good.

The breeds and varieties of "human dogs" are numerous. *Airedale, beagle,* and *bowser* have all been used for a woman regarded as unattractive. A woman who suffers the barking sounds made by men knows that they are alluding to her "doglike" qualities, though she may also see the sounds as reflections on the animal-like crudeness of the men making them. Dog sounds are also suggested in the student epithet *barker,* referring to a woman who vocalizes during sex (Sutton 1995).

The slang expression *dog days* has had some use as a metaphor for the menstrual period, when a woman is accused of being "bitchy." *Dog's mother* (or *mamma*) refers to a woman as a "bitch," as does *dogess,* and singer David Bowie's "diamond dog" is a woman also known as a "rich bitch." *Dogface* and *dog meat* apply to any person considered ugly, while *kennel club* means any place where a male goes to find a date many men would regard as unattractive. *Mutt* is used to mean a homely woman, but originally represented a sheep, not a dog. *Hound,* meaning a hunting dog, has a male cast:

cunt-hound (see CUNT) and *glory hound* (a man who seeks personal glory).

In the jazz world *dog* means something more like fox, a sexy woman. It can also mean simply a man (fellow). In black communities in particular, *dog,* in addition to its use in tagging brutal white men, has been used at different times for a woman regarded as a whore, an untrustworthy man, or among women, an offensive or abusive man. *Doggish* describes a sexually irresponsible man (Major 1994).

Other expressions, such as *a dog's life* (either a miserable one or, ironically, a comfortable one); *sick as a dog* (very sick); *going to the dogs* (ruin); and *mad dog,* meaning a crazy person or evil man, suggest our ambivalence toward dogs and our lack of linguistic loyalty to them.

See also ANIMAL, BEAST, BITCH, COOLER, COW, COYOTE, CUR, FOX, GANGSTER GIRL, GAY (gay dog), HOGGER, LOBO, LOOKSISM, MINK, MINX, PET, PIG, SCUD, SKAG, WOLF, WOMEN AS ANIMALS, YETI.

doll. Term, often viewed as patronizing or offensive, used to describe a woman. Originally a nickname for *Dorothy,* later acquiring the sense of a mistress (Shakespeare used it this way in *Henry IV*), *doll* has taken on a number of meanings. Since at least the late eighteenth century, it has meant a pretty girl or woman, especially one who is looked upon as an empty-headed decoration (she needn't know how to talk or do anything); also any woman who is stylish, lively, or piquant; or a young woman with a babyish face. Because the word also applied to a child's toy (first recorded in this sense in the early eighteenth century), the implication is that men view women, especially young and attractive ones, as playthings.

Dolly, once used to mean harlot, refers generally to a pretty young woman, as does *living doll,* though this term can carry the broader meaning of any very special or competent woman.

A living doll, everywhere you look.
It can sew, it can cook,
It can talk, talk, talk....
My boy, it's your last resort.
Will you marry it, marry it, marry
it.

—Sylvia Plath, *The Applicant,*
1966 (in Rogers 1994)

Dolly mop means a street prostitute or sexually promiscuous young woman. *To be all dolled up* indicates that a woman (though it is sometimes used for men, too) is dressed up in her best.

The conventional middle-class image of a doll is a pretty, blonde, blue-eyed woman or girl. A doll may also weep or pout on command. Drawing from this image is the epithet *Barbie doll,* from the trade name for a blue-eyed, blonde, teenaged doll designed in 1959 for young children and known for its depiction of glamour and conventional femininity (since the 1980s, she has had some racially diverse company in the market, but her friends of color are also glamorous and feminine).

Also applied to women is the trademark name "Kewpie" doll, describing a short plump woman who may or may not, like the toy doll by that name, have a topknot of hair, or, more often, a girl or woman overly made-up and almost too cute. (The spelling *cupie,* sometimes capitalized, showed up in a Web search a few hundred times more often than *Kewpie.*) *Paper doll,* used for a doll made of paper or cardboard, can also indicate a woman; she is only two-dimensional and quite frail.

Doll also came to take on the sense of a good-looking man, though usually less belittling in this context. It can suggest an effeminate or gay man, especially one regarded as a "queen." Also carrying feminine connotations, it has been in use in homosexual communities for a youth having a sexual relationship with a man or for a PASSIVE lesbian. In gay male communities, it may simply mean

any very attractive man, sometimes implying youthfulness, or an attractive, pleasant, or popular person of either sex.

To cut out (paper) dolls means to be insane.

See also BABE, BARBIE, DONUT HOLE (DONUT DOLLY), MOLL, PET, PLAYMATE.

D.O.M. See DIRTY OLD MAN.

domestic affliction. See CURSE.

domestic arts. See HOMEMAKER.

dominatrix. See GOVERNESS.

Don Juan. A philanderer, a man seen as always on the make. The name comes from the legend of a man who was the son of a leading family in Seville, Spain, in the fourteenth century.

The name Don Juan became a synonym for a rake and libertine. In Mozart's opera *Don Giovanni,* a musical version of the story, the Don's valet says that his master had 700 mistresses in Italy, 800 in Germany, and over 1,000 in Spain. Byron's Don Juan was also a Spanish aristocrat, though of a restless, romantic temperament, more an adventurer than a roué. But his travels offered him many amatory episodes, including being sold into slavery to the sultana of Constantinople, whom he angers by making love to one of the young women in the sultan's harem.

A man might not mind being called a Don Juan; the name carries none of the stigma borne by terms for women with strong romantic or sexual inclinations. However, because it is a Spanish name, it may contribute to stereotyping a Hispanic or Latino man as a "lady-killer."

See also CASANOVA, LADIES' MAN, LOVE MACHINE, LOVER, LOTHARIO, PLAYBOY, ROMEO, ROUÉ, SCUTZ, WOMANIZER.

donut hole. Recent Army slang for a woman volunteering with the American Red Cross, usually considered a vulgar phrase. According to Lighter (1994), the term is suggested by *Donut Dolly,* the official name for American Red Cross female volunteers, while *donut* suggests being edible and *hole* alludes both to the vagina and to emptiness (being without a man).

See also DISH, DOLL (dolly), HOLE.

douchebag. Since the 1940s, a term of contempt, however supposedly humorous, for a woman viewed as loathsome and homely, sometimes an old woman. "That douche bag has slept with nearly every woman on the 'yard'" (tongue-lashing given to a female prisoner, Bentley and Corbett 1992, 59). The physical object called a douche bag is a device for flushing out the vagina. A man regarded as despicable may also be called a douchebag, in which case this female-related slur is even more scornful. A person who has "a face like a douchebag" is considered very ugly indeed. Rhyming slang: *toe-rag*.

See also BAG, DOG, HOSE (hosebag).

drag; **drag queen**. *Drag,* cross-dressing, or wearing the clothes typical of the other gender, especially for theatrical effect. *Drag,* however, can be used to mean any dress that is regarded as appropriate for a particular role or activity, thus, a temp-agency worker could be said to go to work in "office drag." From at least the 1920s, the term itself has seldom been intended as disparaging (compare with its offspring, *drag queen*), but mainstream society's current images of people in drag, depending on the context, may carry a significant load of anything from humor to scorn.

Starting in the mid-nineteenth century *drag* was used for female clothing (specifically, a petticoat) worn by a male actor on stage in a female role. It was said to drag across the floor when he walked. The term was also applied to women's attire worn by transvestites (including female impersonators—or impressionists, as they may prefer to be known—in a drag show).

More generally, it is apparel of the other sex. Used for a woman (sometimes as *man drag* or *male drag), drag* implies BUTCH. Since the late 1800s *drag* has also meant a party (drag party or drag ball) for gay people or transvestites, where the dress of the other sex is worn. A related sense is a bar where transvestites gather. In addition to these senses, in homosexual slang *drag* may refer to a young woman escorted to a dance or party or to a boy's girlfriend (see BEARD).

Whatever its recent meanings, however, the common lexicographic explanations of the term do not acknowledge what Grahn (1990, 95–96), known for alternative explanations of gay-related terms, says is its more venerable, spiritual history. Grahn describes medieval practices in which being "in drag" referred to cross-dressing that took place during the Fool's King New Year's procession, when cross-dressing men, playing the person of the female god or queen mother, or cross-dressing women, taking the part either of the male god or the god-king Puck, were pulled through the village in carts. These people were also said to be "in a cart" (*drag*, according to Eric Partridge, cited in Grahn, [95], was once slang for "cart" or "coach").

Others who have explored the origins of the word speculate that it has an even more ancient meaning. Romans castrated a man by "dragging" his testicles out. The eunuch that resulted from the cruel operation sometimes dressed in women's clothes.

Under the rubric of *drag queen* are subsumed a wide range of transgender identities and practices. Some drag queens are gay men, some are transsexual women, and some are professional entertainers. The complexity of the concept is reflected in the attempt at definition offered by members of the Gay and Lesbian Historical Society of Northern California, who say that queens are

MTF [male to female] transgendered individuals who tend to live socially as women some or all of the time, who might or might not pass as nontransgendered women, who tend to be sexually involved with men, and who might or might not engage in hormonal or surgical body alteration to help sustain their gender presentation. The category "queen" overlaps and intersects with populations of gay men, MTF transsexuals, and nontranssexual women in a complex manner that reveals the boundaries between those three groups to be somewhat more porous than one might naively assume them to be. (1998, 351)

Probably most commonly, both in the heterosexual and in the homosexual communities, the term *drag queen* refers to a gay man who dresses in flamboyant, exaggerated women's attire for the purpose of performance art—a drag show. Sometimes synonymous with *female impersonator*, the term can be used offensively, though it is often self-descriptive. The drag queen's performance can be anything from an on-stage show to a group of friends "dragging up" and going on a bar crawl, making a mini-traveling show, or to any gay or straight man's adoption of feminine behavior and clothes, especially when flamboyant, for the sake of performance.

Although the expression *drag queen* is as recent as the 1930s, modern drag queens are merely continuing an age-old theatrical tradition. Men dressing up as women on the stage dates back before Shakespeare (the DYKE, too, can trace her history to stage productions). In the seventeenth and eighteenth centuries, aristocrats in Europe sometimes dressed in the clothing of the other sex. This practice made its way to other classes of people through theatrical productions involving female and male impersonators. Alternatively, the aristocrats in certain countries may have been aping the original drag queens in their society, the peasants reveling during Mardi Gras.

Some people consider the drag queen to be mocking or burlesquing women, but this is not necessarily true. Although sometimes taken as conveying an ambivalence toward women, expressing both envy and hostility, the drag queen could also be regarded as subverting gender identity:

> She [the drag queen] has made gender identity more than frighteningly easy to lose, she has questioned its reality at a time when it has attained the status of a moral absolute and a social imperative. (White 1994, 74)

Drag king, recent slang for a female transvestite, is modeled on *drag queen.*

See also ANDROGYNY, BERDACHE, CAMP, CROSS-DRESSER, GENDER BENDER, HUSTLER (drag prostitute), OPPOSITE SEX (third sex), QUEEN, TRANSGENDERIST, TRANSVESTITE.

drama queen. See QUEEN.

dressing. See CROSS-DRESSER.

drugstore cowboy. See COWBOY.

dryballs; dry-nuts. Both somewhat dated slang expressions, alluding to a condition of the testicles and referring to an impotent man, that is, one unable to have or sustain an erection. Often regarded as vulgar, and likely to be taken as offensive for the idea of emasculation, these expressions were most widespread during the mid-twentieth century.
  ‣ See also IMPOTENT.

dry goods. Women regarded as sexual objects. This is one of several terms (see also SKIRT) drawing on the idea of clothes or household stuff as a way of objectifying women. Twentieth-century slang.

duchess; duke. Since the fourteenth century, *duchess* has been the title of a wife of a duke or a woman who holds the rank of duke herself. While still a high noble title, *duchess* has strayed (i.e., from the "straight" point of view) in meaning in the direction of drag queens, especially, in gay communities, those regarded as "piss-elegant." *Dutchess* served as a form of address for a woman or girl in black slang early in the century.

As a gender identity found in gay communities, *dutchess,* in the sense of a PASSIVE gay man, was common in earlier decades. Writing of the construction of gay personas among "fairies" in turn-of-the-century New York, Chauncey (1994) quotes the Mazet Committee's investigation of Paresis Hall, on the Bowery: "These men…act effeminately; most of them are painted and powdered; they are called Princess this and Lady So and So and the Duchess of Marlboro" (33).

See also -ESS, GOVERNESS, MISTRESS, PRINCESS, QUEEN (woman).

duffer. Someone viewed as worthless or objectionable, usually a man; an oaf; often a foolish old man (frequently as *old duffer*), a GEEZER. Originally (mid-nineteenth century), *duffer* was a British term for a worthless thing. Although the term may be applied with at least mild contempt, it often carries affectionate tones ("He's a nice old duffer"), as though an old, sexless man is somehow innocuous.

In black usage, *duffers* designates young women who provide oral sex in exchange for cocaine (Major 1994).

See also BADGER, BUZZARD, CODGER, COOT, FART (old fart), FOGY, GOAT, JASPER.

duke. Since the twelfth century, duke has been a title for a male ruler of a continental European duchy or a nobleman of the highest hereditary rank. Unlike DUCHESS, *duke* more closely retains its original aristocratic meanings, although it has acquired additional masculine, if not entirely noble, meanings. It has been used for a headman or boss or a tough or combative man. Lighter (1994) notes these as primarily prison usage. Usually as a plural, it can mean a fist or fisticuffs (as in "put up your dukes," a stereotypical image of the pugnacious male). It is also found as a personal name

given to males. American moviemaking recognizes only one "Duke," Western star John Wayne.

See also KING, PRINCE.

dumb blonde. See BLONDE.

dumb bunny. See BUNNY.

dumb Dora; dumb Isaac. *Dumb Dora,* a woman seen as stupid or empty-headed; a slang expression since at least the 1920s, from the personal name for a woman. *Dumb Isaac* means a stupid man, but this term sees little if any use today.

See also BLONDE (dumb blonde), BUNNY (dumb bunny), DAME (dizzy dame), DITZ, GENDER-SPECIFIC ADJECTIVES (scatterbrained), SPACE GIRL, TWINK (twinkie).

dutchess. See DUCHESS.

Dutch girl. Euphemism for a lesbian, based on the association of The Netherlands with "dikes."

See also DYKE, LESBIAN.

dyke, dike. Originally, any lesbian; today, in particular, a lesbian who takes an aggressive role and adopts "masculine" behavior (the stereotypical "swaggering, cigarette-puffing lesbian" [Rodgers 1972]; see also MANNISH). *Dyke* has been in use since at least the 1930s (original use was in the heterosexual community). The term is usually a strong put-down when coming from nonlesbians, but since the 1970s it has often been used among lesbians as a blunt, political, and conscious self-designation. Reflecting this redefinition, for example, is DAM, "Dyke Action Machine," a New York-based lesbian propaganda group, and the 1970s' lesbian periodical titled *Dyke*.

There are distinctive kinds of women labeled *dyke* within the lesbian community. Besides the so-called "mannish" BULLDYKE, there are a number of others; for example, *leather dyke* (see LEATHER), *root dyke* (one whose dress reflects ethnic "roots"), *lipstick dyke* (see LIPSTICK LESBIAN), and *granola dyke*. Bigendered lesbians—individuals with biologically female bodies who identify as masculine and may be attracted to other women—may call themselves *mandykes*, without negative connotations (see also BUTCH).

Among heterosexuals, *dyke* may be applied to any lesbian, the generalization all the more a term of contempt. In fact, some men find the "dyke" label convenient for putting down women who are seen as unattractive, who do not act "feminine," or who show no interest in them. "No Means Dyke," a sign appearing in a men's dorm window in Canada, 1989, demonstrates a kind of self-serving distortion by male culture of "no means no," and the graffiti "Kill a Dyke, Rape a Feminist" (*Ms.,* January/February 1992, 6) shows how the lesbian and feminist are linked in the mind of the misogynist. Only within the lesbian community is the term applied with impunity.

Although dictionaries often label the origin "unknown" or "obscure," some suggest a relationship to *morpha[o]dyke*, a dialectal pronunciation of *hermaphrodite*. Chapman (1998) also calls attention to the similarity to *dick* (penis, a symbol of masculinity) and to an 1896 source that lists *dyke* as meaning vulva. Rawson (1989), though largely dismissive, and Flexner and Soukhanov (1997) suggest a connection with *dike,* meaning to overdress or wear fancy clothes. Furthermore, *dike* also once referred to male clothing, so that when applied to women, it connoted having an appearance that nonlesbians would link with "masculinity." Richter (1993) adds yet another possibility: the obsolete British use of the term for female genitals, in turn from a standard meaning of *dyke*, a ditch.

In a highly speculative argument, Grahn (1990, 46–48) sees *dyke* as being of the spirit, linking it with the name of Dike, a goddess of ancient Greece. Dike was a storm goddess who made war against those who departed from the old female-oriented traditions. Granddaughter of Gaia, her name denoted "the way," meaning specifically the path between one world and another, and her role was to preserve a natural balance of forces.

Dyke has also been used as a verb, meaning to behave like a lesbian is believed to act (hence, *de-dyke*, among lesbians, means to act as one's parents or straight friends think one should act). The usually disparaging *dykey* (or *dikey*) means having lesbian characteristics, especially aggressiveness. *Van dyke* refers to a lesbian with a hint (or more) of a moustache on her upper lip or hair on her chin. Rodgers (1972) also notes 1970s San Francisco use for a lesbian truck driver (see also BULL, BULLDYKE).

See also CLOSET (closet dyke), DRAG, DUTCH GIRL, HE-SHE, LESBIAN, MARIMACHO, MOLL (molly dyke), TOMBOY.

E

easy lay; **easy make**. Twentieth-century slang expressions for a woman who supposedly can be easily persuaded to have sex, as on the first date. These terms may also be used for men, also sometimes (mainly mid-twentieth century) known as "pullovers" (the earlier, comparable word for a woman is *pushover*). *Woman of easy virtue* is a dated euphemism for a woman viewed as sexually free or a whore. The vulgar *walk-up fuck,* suggesting how easy a man believes it is to have sex with a woman, is still in use.

Easy lay also, as an ironic term in dark humor, refers to a drug, also known as a "date-rape" drug, used by men who wish to incapacitate women—who unwittingly take the drug—in order to rape them. The drug is ostensibly manufactured and sold as a sleeping pill or a preanesthethic.

See also CHIPPY, COOZIE, DIRTY GERTIE, EASY RIDER, GOOD LAY, HARLOT, HAT, HIDE, HOOZIE, HUMP, JOB, LOOSE, MATTRESSBACK, MINK, MINX, NYMPH, PROMISCUOUS, PROSTITUTE, PUNCHBOARD, SKEEZER, SLATTERN, SLUT, STRUMPET, TART, TRAMP, TROLLOP, TUNA, WENCH, WHORE.

easy rider. Black slang meaning an irresponsible man who lives off women, especially prostitutes (thus a PIMP), or by gambling. While suggesting a man looking for a "free ride" or an "easy mark," *easy rider,* as spoken by men, may also be dismissive of the young woman involved for being regarded as sexually promiscuous—someone who is easily persuaded to have sex.

See also EASY LAY, GOLD DIGGER, LOOSE, MACK, PIMP.

eating pussy; **eatin' stuff**. Allusions to women as food, metaphorically, a passive substance to be consumed. The reference to "pussy" also reduces the woman to a sexual part of the anatomy. *Stuff* was once used to denote something either worthless or indecent and lustful (today we speak of "hot stuff"; see HOT). See also DISH, MEAT, PUSS.

effeminate. From Latin *ex-* plus *femina*, meaning "woman," a description of a man in terms of what are viewed as "inappropriate" (for a man) feminine characteristics—overly delicate, soft, weak, or wimpy. The word is not usually applied to women. Although regarded as a euphemism, *effeminate* draws disparagement from society's stance that feminine characteristics are inferior, and lacking those characteristics is in a man's best interest. "Any qualities in a man that a woman finds useful, she calls *masculine;* all others, of no use to her or to anyone else for that matter, she chooses to call *effeminate"* (Esther Vilar, quoted in *On the Contrary,* ed. Martha Rainbolt and Janet Fleetwood, 1984, 6). More positively, it could suggest a man who is gentle and docile, which is how the word was used in the sixteenth century without diminishing a man's character.

Effeminacy has been central in marking men as not "real" men. Until the middle of the twentieth century, it was even more significant than homosexual behavior per se in identifying men as "queer" (Chauncey 1994). Men were once labeled "queer" only because of their manifestation of womanly behavior or playing of "female" roles. In Chauncey's words,

> The abnormality (or "queerness") of the "fairy"…was defined as much by his "womanlike" character or "effeminacy" as his solicitation of male sexual partners; the "man" who responded to his solicitations—no matter how often—was not considered abnormal, a "homosexual," so long as he abided by masculine gender conventions. (13)

Effie, from *effeminate,* insults a man in abbreviated form.

See also BIRD (birdie), BOY, BUTTERCUP, CAKE-EATER, CANDY-ASS, COO (cooch),

DAFFODIL, DAISY, EUNUCH, FAIRY, FEMME, FLAMER, FLOWER, GAL, GIRL, GLADIOLA, GUSSIE, LA-DI-DA, LESS-THAN-NOTHING, LILY, LIMP-WRIST, LISPER, LITTLE LORD FAUNTLEROY, MAMA'S BOY, MARIPOSA, MARY, MILKSOP, MILQUETOAST, MINCE, MOL-LYCODDLE, NAMBY-PAMBY, NANCE, NELLY, PANSY, PUSS, PUSSY-WHIPPED, SEYMOUR, SHE-HE, SHE-MALE, SISSY, SKIPPY, SKIRT, SQUAW, SWEET MEAT, SWISH, TINKER BELL, TUTTI-FRUTTI, TWIT, VIOLET, WIMP, WOMANISH, WUSS.

enchilada. See TAMALE.

English disease. See HOMOSEXUALITY AS DIS-EASE.

escort. See PROSTITUTE.

-ess. A suffix that entered Middle English from the Old French *-esse,* used in forming nouns meaning female persons and female animals. Linguists refer to this ending as a way of semantically and formally "marking" a term. The unmarked *lion*, for example, may indicate a male in some contexts, but can also be used for either a male or a female. Said to be "neutral," *lion* is actually the base word from which the word for the female of the species—*lioness*—is formed by the addition of the *-ess* suffix. The marked term differs from the unmarked one by being restricted in use to females or, as *mayoress* (mostly in British usage) sometimes does, to wives. It may seem to be a kind of decoration added to the "real" word, which, feminists have complained, is the more powerful word, the *-ess* ending carrying low-status, disparaging, or even humorous connotations. *Fowler's* (1996) notes that *The Oxford English Dictionary* lists more than one hundred words with the *-ess* ending denoting female persons or animals. Although some of them have survived longer than others, some have not lasted at all, and others, such as *farmeress* and *preacheress*, have not gone beyond being jocular or fanciful. In 1838 author James Fenimore Cooper tried out

Americaness in "Home as Found," but it did not catch on (Mencken 1962, 591). Terms such as *doctress, lecturess,* and *conductress* enjoyed favor for the most part only among some women's rights advocates in the United States in the nineteenth century, possibly as ways of calling attention to the expanding roles of women outside the private domain (Flexner and Soukhanov 1997). Such words as *countess, duchess* (here the *-ess* ending means wife of), and *empress* (as titles of nobility), *goddess* (in goddess religions and feminist spirituality), and *priestess* (in historical contexts or feminist literature) have survived in our language. Also, *abbess,* meaning a woman in charge of a convent of nuns, a position of high respect, is a title no one has challenged.

Other terms that have survived, however, are now often regarded as quaint if not unnecessary (e.g., *paintress*) and even sometimes offensive (e.g., *Jewess, Negress*). But offensiveness does not necessarily result in a dwindling of the lexicon of *-ess* words. It is renewed with slang words—for example, *veepess, muggess*—perhaps, as Chapman (1998) suggests, *because* the standard use is now so often taken as offensive.

In recent decades *waitress* has shown some signs of being replaced by *server, waitperson,* or *waiter;* the last is now often regarded as appropriate for both sexes. (In the military, *orderly* is used to expunge the feminine connotations of waiting on someone.) *Waitron* (the *-on* is said to have been modeled on the suffix in *automaton,* suggesting the robotic-like work of waiting on tables, but more likely comes from *neutron* [neuter]), appearing around the early 1980s, has lost ground altogether. *Waitstaff* is a collective common-gender form. Other occupational terms are also giving way, for example, *airline stewardess* or *hostess* to *flight attendant. Authoress,* which *Fowler's* (1996) tells us was never prominent in the sense of a female author, has lost further ground as *author* comes increasingly into use for both sexes, except when sex may be significant to point out. Similarly, many speakers feel increasingly comfortable with *actor* used for women as well as for men.

See also ACTRESS, DUCHESS, -ETTE, GODDESS, GOVERNESS, MATRON (patroness), MISTRESS, PRINCESS.

Eternal Feminine. See FEMININE.

-ette. From the Old French *-ete,* a suffix that entered English to create diminutive feminine nouns to match the masculine *-et.* An early example is *cigarette* (1835), "a small cigar"; a later one, *kitchenette* (1903), "a small kitchen." In some cases, smallness is not an intended meaning, however, as in *launderette.* In other cases, however, *-ette* indicates not smallness but insignificance or falseness, as in *leatherette.*

In the twentieth century, the ending came to imply femininity. This apparently fit with the schemes of "smallness," in a figurative as well as literal sense. *Suffragette* (from 1906; see SUFFRAGIST) was adopted by female advocates, especially British, of women's suffrage; later came such terms as *drum majorette* (1938) and team names like Rockettes and Trojanettes. More recently, as *Fowler's* (1996) notes, some sexist male writers began peppering the language with pejoratives such as *bimbette, editorette,* and *snoopette.* Although seldom lasting, these usages have contributed to a pattern of bias. Although the historically significant *suffragette* is embedded in English, words such as *usherette, bachelorette,* and *farmerette* are now usually regarded as biased and, by some, offensive, the implication being that women are cute little versions of men.

See also -ESS.

eunuch; **capon**. *Eunuch,* a castrated man; originally from the Greek *eunouchos,* meaning to have charge of the bed, in use in English since the fifteenth century. In ancient China and the Middle East, eunuchs served as guards and servants in harems and as chamberlains in palaces. Because they had been castrated, often voluntarily, they were regarded as suitable for taking charge of the wives or concubines of a ruler.

Kathryn M. Ringrose (in Herdt 1994) says that in late antiquity and Byzantine society, *eunuch* suggested someone who had chosen to withdraw from the world and refused to procreate; eunuchs in these periods were employed to regulate access to the emperor, to carry messages between persons constrained from meeting directly, and to care for the dead—all intermediary functions. Political eunuchs, serving as advisers and officials, were also employed in different areas of the world, and rapists and men conquered in war have in some cultures been humiliated or punished through emasculation. Boys were once made eunuchs in Italy to prepare them to be adult soprano singers, a practice brought to an end by Pope Leo XIII in 1878, while the Romans offered "toy boys" to wealthy women for sexual pleasure (the women did not have to be concerned about becoming pregnant), and eunuch teachers in ancient Greece were believed to be safe to teach children.

Also known as eunuchs were Christian men who castrated themselves as a way of showing their devotion to God, and the category of people, neither men nor women, of India known as *hijras* (see CROSS-DRESSER). Other men have been called eunuchs because their testes never developed, and Ernest Hemingway's character Jake Barnes of *The Sun Also Rises,* who suffered genital injuries in war, might also be called a eunuch.

Because a castrated male by definition does not have testes (sometimes the penis either), the term *eunuch* has been employed as a put-down for a man regarded as weak or weak-willed, incomplete, lacking in virility, or, in slang, lacking "balls." When a man's masculine traits are removed, he is thought to be degraded. There is no equivalent term for women.

Capon, meaning, literally, a castrated cock, applied in the sixteenth and seventeenth centuries in the sense of a eunuch, has come to mean a gay male (i.e., a man whose sexual life does not result in procreation) or an effeminate man. *Capon* is a euphemism in use among heterosexuals. Major (1994) describes it as a pejorative African American usage of the 1930s and 1940s (see also CAS-TRATING).

Synonyms are *androgyne, bob tail, castrato, gelding, rascaglion, spado, third sex.*

See also CHOIRBOY, EFFEMINATE, FRIGID, OPPOSITE SEX (third sex).

Eve. See FALLEN WOMAN.

exhibitionist. A person whose actions involve exposure of the private parts of the body in a lewd manner in public. In legal discourse an exhibitionist is a male. *Black's Law Dictionary* (Black 1990) cites the Model Penal Code, paragraph 213.5, on indecent exposure:

> A person commits a misdemeanor if, for the purpose of arousing or gratifying sexual desire of himself or of any person other than his spouse, he exposes his genitals under circumstances in which he knows his conduct is likely to cause affront or alarm.

The acts of such a person, whom we usually regard as a sexual DEVIANT, reflect an underlying cultural assumption that the male sexual drive is more powerful and vital than that of the female, thus requiring more regulation. As Strainchamps (1971, 360) points out, a man who watches a woman undress in front of a window can be arrested as a voyeur or Peeping Tom. The same man undressing in front of a window and seen by a woman can be arrested for indecent exposure.

Sometimes women, especially prostitutes or strippers, are disparaged by being called "exhibitionists," but that usage does not correspond to the legal definition quoted above. The female exhibitionist is likely to be disparaged not because of her own "inappropriate" arousal but because she is believed to cause that of the man. However, women who work in industries that require exposing their bodies for men's pleasure are not commonly known as exhibitionists, though many, usually disparaging slang terms may apply. The term *flasher,* for someone who suddenly exposes the genitals in public, is almost always used for a man, even though female prostitutes and striptease dancers may "flash."

See also DIRTY OLD MAN, PEEPING TOM.

exotic. Description of black, Asian, third world, and other "racialized" people, often women, in the eyes of white Western people. This categorization stems from an ethnocentric attitude that attributes qualities of foreignness, strangeness, and exoticness to women of other ethnicities. Black and Asian women or women of mixed racial heritage have been depicted in literature, advertising, and the media as seductive and mystifying. These women are known variously as "Shebas," "Miss Saigons," "queens of the jungle" (see also QUEEN), and by many other names. Western male travelers to Asia may even purchase packaged holidays on the basis of the promise of the exotic sexuality available, and U.S. men have sought wives by mail from, for example, the Philippines, often hoping not only for the exotic femininity of the Asian woman but her stereotypical obedience and submissiveness as well. This notion of female sexuality is created out of racist as well as sexist assumptions.

Sharp (1993) describes "exotic erotic" as

> some folks' fantasy psychosis which sees all Black women as simultaneously strange, fascinating, primal and childlike, uninhibited, earthy, sensuous and highly sexed. (39)

See also BOOM-BOOM GIRL, CHERRY (cherry blossom), GODDESS (African goddess), HOOCHIE, LBFM, MAMA (mama-san), PEARL (pearl of the Orient).

F

face that launched a thousand ships, the.
An allusion to the ancient Trojan of
Greek legend, Helen of Troy, immortal-
ized for female beauty and representative of it. Though wedded to Menelaus,
king of Sparta, Helen eloped with Paris,
son of the king of Troy, bringing about
the launching of the Greek fleet that
sailed for Troy to avenge Menelaus, the
subject of Homer's *Iliad*. The phrase itself derives from Marlowe's play, *Dr.
Faustus* (1588). Marlowe's apostrophe
to Helen became well known:

> Was this the face that launched a
> thousand ships
> And burnt the topless towers of
> Ilium?
> Sweet Helen, make me immortal
> with a kiss;
> Her lips suck forth my soul, see
> where it flies!

The stereotypical seductive powers
of beautiful women (see also SEDUC-
TRESS) are naturalized in such expressions. The modern version of the cliché,
however, has taken an ironic turn to the
negative—female ugliness: "He's very
handsome but have you seen his wife?
Talk about the face that launched a thousand ships!" (Kirkpatrick 1996).

Similarly expressive of the limited,
stereotyping definitions of women is the
cliché, "Her face is her fortune."

See also BEAUTY, BELLE, FEMININE
(Eternal Feminine), JUST ANOTHER PRETTY
FACE, LOOKSISM, QUEEN, SEX OBJECT, TEMPT-
RESS.

fag bag. A term for a woman who is married to a gay man. Used largely in the
gay male community since the mid-
twentieth century, this word tends to
deride the woman.

See also BAG, FAGGOT, FAG HAG, FISH
(fishwife).

faggot; fag; feigele. *Faggot,* a degrading
epithet for a gay man and occasionally

today for a lesbian woman. It has been
common in U.S. slang since the early
twentieth century, first seen in print in
Portland, Oregon, in 1914.

Faggot is typically a highly disparaging epithet in use by homophobic
people (often men) who hate and bru-
talize gay men. Expressions such as
"Kill the faggot" and "We're going to
teach this faggot a lesson" are commonly
used prior to and during vicious assaults
on gay individuals. For example, some
high school boys who kicked, punched,
and threw a gay man off a bridge to his
death in 1984 left behind a spray-painted
message on the bridge, "Faggots Jump
Here."

> Straight cats invent faggots so they
> can sleep with them
> without becoming faggots them-
> selves.
> —James Baldwin (in Katz
> 1995, 103)

Yet the slur may be used even by those
more moderate in their attitudes, commonly applied with equal contempt to a
heterosexual male seen as effeminate,
one who looks like the stereotypical homosexual male, or any man deemed
weak or cowardly. For example, *faggot*
is one of the drill sergeant's favorite
terms of abuse to suggest to his male
recruits that they lack manhood: they are
"faggots" until they become soldiers. For
the most part, only gay or lesbian people
may use the term among themselves
without the implications of hatred.

The origin of *faggot* in the sense of a
homosexual is very unclear, surrounded
by myth and an abundance of speculation. In the popular imagination it has
been linked with *fagot,* from Old French,
meaning a bundle of sticks or kindling.
"The very word *faggot* means a bundle
of sticks that were burned in the fire.
When homosexuals were burned at the
stake as heretics, they were called 'faggots'" (Farrell 1993, 211). Although
many lexicographers find this derivation

untenable, if not historically impossible, there seems to be a need in gay communities to find the source of the word, the more rooted in the past the better.

Besides disparaging gay men, *faggot,* since the mid-twentieth century, has also been in use pejoratively for a lesbian, especially one thought of as "butch," or for a woman considered ugly. The derogatory application to women is actually much older than that for men, dating to before the seventeenth century. Indeed, as a slur, *faggot* has been used in English since the sixteenth century (and up to the early twentieth) for women and children. It has meant a bad-tempered, shrewish, or dissipated, slatternly woman—one no better than a "fagot" in the sense of sticks—and has been directed at children in reproof of undesirable behavior. Although some dictionaries (e.g., Thorne 1990) claim a weak connection, the sense of a gay man most likely derives from this slur on women and children, since gay men are often ridiculed for supposedly effeminate and immature behavior.

Faggotry is usually pejorative for homosexuality or the gay world. Adjective forms describing homosexuals or effeminate men or their behavior are *faggoty, faggy,* and *fagola* (the last word may also be a noun). *Bed faggot* refers to a bed companion, either female or male, or a prostitute.

From the early twentieth century, *fag,* short for *faggot,* has also been applied, sometimes even more scornfully than *faggot,* to a gay or effeminate man (also known as *fag-bait*) or sometimes to a pimp, known for showy dress, like that of a woman. In 1998 one of the signs carried by antigay protesters at the funeral of a gay man murdered in Wyoming by two homophobic men read, "No Fags in Heaven." *Fag* in this sense has been linked with *fag* meaning cigarette, the tie-in supposedly being that at one time, "real" men smoked cigars because cigarettes were believed to be effemi-

nate. It is also interesting to speculate whether the meaning of the earlier verb form *fagge* (to droop), may not have carried over to resonate with the idea of limpness sometimes stereotypically associated with gay men. Chauncey (1994) says that in the 1930s *fag* was in widespread use but mostly by heterosexuals. Gay men, though black gay men more than white ones, preferred *faggot.*

Fag once meant a servant, including a boy retained as a menial. Some of these boys, as in the English public schools, were used for sexual purposes by older boys. This, too, however, is usually regarded as an unlikely explanation of the origin of the gay meaning, since the homosexual sense of the word appeared in the United States before it was known in England.

Fag is also used by students and teenagers for any disliked person or someone viewed as offensive. That person may also be slurred as a "three-letter man," after the three letters in the word (see also FOUR-LETTER MAN). Young children, even without understanding the meaning of sexual orientation, may use *fag* to insult boys (even sometimes girls) with the implication of being a "sissy" (Thorne 1993, 116–17).

As a verb, *fag* means to act as a gay person does or to make someone resemble a gay person, as by subjecting the person to homosexual sex. A magazine featuring male nudity may be called a "fag mag"; use is within gay communities. *Fag factory* (or *-joint*) refers to a place where gay men gather.

Feigele (faygeleh), meaning little bird, from a Yiddish word, *faygl,* has been used as an epithet for a gay person. A bird usually evokes feminine characteristics, but also has wings—like a fairy. It is most likely influenced by *fag* but without that term's negative connotations.

Alternate spellings of *faggot* include *fagot* and *faggit.*

See also CLOSET (undercover fag), FAG BAG, FAG HAG, FAIRY, HOMOSEXUAL.

fag hag. A term usually for a heterosexual woman, though she might be lesbian or bisexual, who prefers the company of gay men. To the woman so named, gay men may be sexually nonthreatening and can more easily be taken into one's confidence. The back-cover copy to Robert Rodi's *Fag Hag* (1992) describes the heterosexual "fag hags" as "women who love men who love men" (in the novel, the man she loves "sees her more as sidekick than siren").

This Americanism dates to the 1920s, when, in spite of the use of the disparaging *hag* (probably chosen largely because it rhymes with *fag*), it may have carried some positive associations, since the straight woman companion became a part of gay lore and probably helped the community to bridge with straight society.

When straight women (and the heterosexual world in general) became even more aware of the existence of gay men in the 1960s, the term became more widely known but acquired some derogatory connotations as the gay liberation movement rendered homosexual men less dependent on the fag-hag role.

Although it is often still self-descriptive, the term's pejorative use occurs both among heterosexuals (especially straight men who may resent or distrust the association of heterosexual women with gays) and in the gay male community, where there has also been some misogyny. "Most gigolos were homosexuals…and the matrons who mothered them were often privately referred to, even by their subsidized suitors, as 'fag hags'" (Talese 1980, 530). A synonym is *fag* (or *faggot's*) *moll* (see also MOLL); also once, *queen bee* (see also QUEEN).

Before this gay sense, around the mid-twentieth century, *fag hag* was used by young people for a woman who smoked, since during World War I *fag*

came to mean a cigarette.

See also FAG BAG, FAGGOT, FISH (fishwife), FRUIT (fruit fly), HAG.

fair-haired boy. See BOY.

fair sex. Hackneyed, dated, and patronizing term that characterizes women as gentle and soft, at least as seen from the traditional gender perspective of men. Casanova wrote, "I felt myself born for the fair sex" (*Memoirs*, in Corey 1997, 59). *Fair sex* may also allude to skin color and related white-male racist standards of beauty.

We hear most about *fair sex* from the nineteenth-century. Philosopher Arthur Schopenhauer, in his "Essay on Women," manifests considerable distaste for the female body: "It is only the man whose intellect is clouded by his sexual impulses that could give the name of *the fair sex* to that undersized, narrow-shouldered, broad-hipped and short-legged race" (in Hays 1964, 210). Ambrose Bierce seemed to be denying the attributive and more when he defined a female as "One of the opposing, or unfair, sex" (in Rudolf Flesch, *The Book of Unusual Quotations,* 1957).

See also FEMALE, FRAIL, GENDER AND SEX, WEAKER VESSEL, WOMAN, WOMEN AND CHILDREN FIRST.

fairy. A term with two different meanings since the nineteenth century, both reflecting on femininity and tending to degrade it. It was once used for women, but its common slang use today, probably American in origin, is (especially among heterosexuals) to disparage a gay man. "Work your ass off so some of those goddam fairies can sit around and act like women" (Norman Mailer, *The Naked and the Dead,* 1948). This slur, however, may be slung at homosexual people in general, and a lesbian is also sometimes called a "fairy lady." The *Dictionary of American Regional English* (1991) notes that although the use of *fairy* is widespread in the United

States, it is chiefly encountered in the North and northern midland.

The usage has now been adopted by gay communities, where it may be heard in a friendly and even advocative manner. Its use is encouraged as part of the Radical Fairy movement, a group started in the late 1970s by gay activist Harry Hay as a protest against the mainstreaming of gay communities.

> Our all-volunteer magazine (with our loud covers of gay fairies, s/m dykes, queer ministers and transgendered lesbians) is having a direct impact on the problem of invisibility with thousands of mental health practitioners and family members. (Laura Markowitz, *In the Family,* October 1998, 2)

Originally from the Latin *Fata,* goddess of fate, *fairy* came into English in the fourteenth century with the meaning in folklore of a small mythical being, female or male, usually having magical powers. Evans (1977), who has explored European symbols relating to fairies as they bear on the contemporary gay community, found a common denominator in the supposed matriarchal traditions of the ancient Celts, traditions long forced underground. In a similar (some would say misleading) attempt to find egalitarian and spiritual roots for gay people, Grahn (1990, 76–82), drawing from the work of anthropologist Margaret A. Murray, speculates on the existence of a real group of small-statured people indigenous to the British Isles and elsewhere in Europe before the arrival of the Celts.

By the mid-nineteenth century, perhaps from the sense of diminutive people and magic, the term acquired the sense of a girl or woman, sometimes but not necessarily young and pretty (British slang had it as an ugly or debauched woman). Carrying the feminine connotations over, and possibly also as a result of earlier hobo talk in the United States, it came to be applied to a gay or effeminate man (also sometimes, as *fairy-lover,* for a lesbian). Rawson (1989) claims that the first apparent mention of the word in the gay sense occurred in an article in the January 1896 issue of the *American Journal of Psychology.* Called "Sex and Art," the article described a supposedly secret organization of New York gay men called "The Fairies," who were said to gather to pursue such feminine avocations as knitting and crocheting. Writing of gay culture in the early twentieth century, Chauncey (1994) says,

> As the dominant pejorative category in opposition to which male sexual "normality" was defined, the fairy influenced the culture and self-understanding of all sexually active men. (47)

(See Chauncey for a discussion of the fairy as a gendered persona and the largely working-class background of "fairies.")

Among the related terms that may still be heard, though they would sound dated to many and are not necessarily still common usages in gay communities, are the following: *fairy godmother* (the homosexual tutor or initiator of a homosexual relationship); *hair fairy* (an effeminate gay man who gives special attention to his "coiffure"); *screaming fairy,* a gay male who acts in a blatantly "homosexual" way; and *twinkle-toes,* a related derogatory term, restricted in use largely to straight speakers, meaning an effeminate gay man (see also TWINK).

Especially in straight society, *fairy* is a very derogatory word. In the 1950s during the infamous Army-McCarthy hearings, which addressed the issue of homosexuality as a "security threat," Senator Joseph McCarthy charged that one of the Army's bases harbored homosexual soldiers he believed to be communist government infiltrators. Asked where he had gotten his facts, McCarthy said from "a little pixie." An Army lawyer then quipped that "a pixie is a close relative of a fairy" (Steven Capsuto, in Witt and Marcus 1995, 108).

See also BUTTERFLY, EFFEMINATE, FAGGOT (feigele), FEY, FLIT, HOMOSEXUAL, MARIPOSA, MINCE QUEEN.

fallen angel. See ANGEL.

fallen woman; **Eve**. *Fallen woman*, a euphemism meaning a morally degraded woman.

> Girls in this way, fall every day,
> And have been falling for ages;
> Who is to blame? you know his name,
> It's the boss that pays starvation wages.
> —Joe Hill, "The White Slave,"
> *Little Red Songbook,* 1913

The woman designated is believed to have "fallen from grace," usually because she has lost her chastity, is promiscuous, or works as a prostitute. *Fallen* in this sense has largely dropped out of use, having acquired a somewhat antiquated ring, since the issue of chastity is not as central to women's lives as it was in the Victorian culture of the nineteenth century. Then, the fallen woman was pictured as a woeful woman clutching an infant as her shamed father throws her out into a blizzard. Regarding the moral code of the 1830s and 1840s, one historian wrote,

> Of the attitude of the respectable women towards their fallen sisters little is to be said—they were not supposed to know of their existence, and many, miraculously, did not…heroine and hero [of contemporary literature] were spotless. (Carl Russell Fish, *The Rise of the Common Man,* 1929, 155)

Even though the term sounds dated, the depiction of women as "fallen" survives. *Fallen* is often heard today in an ironic sense in references to current negative depictions of women:

> One has only to look at American television twenty-four hours a day for an entire week to learn the way in which black women are perceived in American society—the predominant image is that of the "fallen" woman, the whore, the slut, the prostitute. (hooks 1981, 52)

The biblical story of Adam and Eve may be regarded as the Judeo-Christian account of the original "fallen woman." While the account in Genesis has woman and man created in God's image, thus promoting the idea that all people are sacred in God's eyes and deserving of respect, the myth of Adam and Eve has often been interpreted as dividing men and women into two very unequal categories. As Kate Millett (1970) put it, the story represents "the most crucial argument of the patriarchal tradition in the West" (52).

In earlier mythology, the mother goddess, of whom Eve is a kind of deposed representative, was, like Yahweh, a creative force (see also GODDESS). Reflecting this is Eve's Hebrew name, *Havvah*, she who gives life (but also close in form to Semitic words meaning snake, which may imply wisdom and immortality as well as destruction). In the biblical myth of the Fall, however, Eve—now human, deposed from the station of goddess to that of woman—is assigned the responsibility for human sin and suffering. According to the Yahwist's tenth-century B.C. narrative (Gen. 2:4b–3:24), Yahweh formed "man" (Adam, from an ancient Hebrew name interpreted as meaning humankind, suggesting androgyny [Miller and Swift 1991, 18]) from earth's dust, breathing life into his nostrils. Later, Yahweh fashioned Eve from Adam's rib to relieve him of loneliness. The original couple then lived together in the Garden of Eden in primeval innocence. Although the two were not yet conscious of "knowledge" (read "sexuality"), Eve, intellectually awakening, was tempted by the serpent into eating the forbidden fruit of the tree of knowledge of good and evil. Adam, seduced by Eve, then followed her in tasting the forbidden fruit.

The account of God's swift justice for this disobedience provides both an explanation for and a justification of traditional male-dominated relations. The punishment for man is a cursed ground, which makes man's life as a laborer difficult; hence, the expression "the curse of Adam," meaning having to work for a living. The punishment for woman is pain in childbirth (see also CURSE) and a destiny of being ruled by men.

Eve may refer euphemistically to a woman regarded sexually. *Piece of Eve's flesh* is a slang expression for a woman as a sex object (see also MEAT, PIECE) and can also mean copulation (Spears 1991). *Eve's customhouse* was used mostly in the eighteenth century for the vagina. The phrase *daughter of Eve* refers to a woman, but also suggests feminine curiosity and, like the term *Eve* itself, sinfulness (compare *daughters of Eve* with the spiritual *sons of God*). Referring to the menses is *the curse of Eve,* which carries a heavy freight of notions of pollution (see also CURSE). *Rib* (or *Adam's rib*) has been used for women or wives, suggesting their dependence on men.

See also BOX (Pandora's box), PROSTITUTE, SCARLET WOMAN, SEDUCTRESS, SIREN, TEMPTRESS.

fall guy. See GUY.

fancy pants; **fancy Dan**. References to a man who overdresses or shows off—a dandy. *Fancy pants,* which uses an item of clothing to represent the man (see also PANTS, SKIRT), in particular, suggests effeteness or fastidiousness. Used since at least the mid-twentieth century, *fancy pants* has been popular, especially as a taunt among children. *Fancy Dan* can mean a ladies' man, but it is also heard in sports for an athlete (usually a man) who has some clever moves but can't produce results. A fancy Dan is often a boxer who is skilled but lacks punch.

fart. See OLD FART.

fast woman; fast life. *Fast woman,* "a prostitute," in use since the nineteenth century. *Fast* in this sense, used since the eighteenth century, refers to wantonness. A man may have a fast car, but unless he is a sprinter, he is seldom called "fast" himself. *Fast life* refers to prostitution, usually female.

See also PROSTITUTE.

father. See MOTHER.

fattism. See LOOKSISM.

fawn. A girl or young woman considered pretty but helpless and submissive, that is, cute and cuddly, like the young of a deer. Sutton (1995, 288) reports that her data from California undergraduate students indicate *fawn* is used almost exclusively by men. Sutton (291–92) also reports the use of *bambi* and *thumper* among female students for a woman considered promiscuous.

See also BUNNY, KITTEN, PET, WOMEN AS ANIMALS.

feast for the eyes. See DISH.

feigele. See FAGGOT.

female. A girl or woman; ultimately from Latin *femella,* diminutive of *femina* (woman). The Middle French *femelle* was taken up by Middle English in the fourteenth century. However, in order to agree with its opposite, *male,* though unrelated etymologically, the term quickly became *female.* In other words, *female* does not derive from *male* (which comes from the Latin *masculous*), as some feminist semanticists once claimed in their argument that *female* should be banned from the language.

In earlier centuries since entering English, *female* came to be used to mean things weak or inferior. Also, during the nineteenth century, some controversy mounted over the suitability of the term because of its association with female biological function and animals. According to Strainchamps (1971, 351–52), the late nineteenth-century edition of *The Oxford English Dictionary* noted the noun *female* as a term of opprobrium. The culture wars of the mid-nineteenth century involved a feminist campaign against the word *female,* which, some women protested, was ambiguous and disparaging. It was more commonly used than *male* and just as likely, it was argued, to mean mares or she-asses as women. Women's rights advocate Sarah Josepha Hale wrote editorials in the magazine *Godey's Lady's Book,* substituting *male* for *man* to poke fun at her critics. She once reported an arrest that had been made of certain "males who had robbed the mails" (Pattee 1940, 104).

By the beginning of the twentieth century, the word had been withdrawn from print and "polite conversation" and was largely replaced by LADY (which in turn suffered vulgarization). Even Matthew Vassar eventually mandated that the word *Female* be chiseled from the stone of the front building of Vassar Female College, as it was once called, leaving a curious blank space.

Of course, the word *male* is also applied to animals as well as humans, yet this stronger masculine word has been spared the charge of being impolite or vulgar. In her acclaimed 1952 book, *The Second Sex,* philosopher Simone de Beauvoir, speaking of defining *woman* in biological terms, noted that "In the mouth of a man the epithet *female* has the sound of an insult, yet he is not ashamed of his animal nature; on the contrary, he is proud if someone says of him, "He is a male!'" (1974, 3).

In the twentieth century, the term became especially applicable when females of different ages are referred to, or on official forms. It has also been used to denote women as a biological cat-

egory, that is, those of the species who are typically capable of bearing offspring and whose cell nuclei contain two X chromosomes. This biological sense is distinguished from the emphasis on femaleness as a social construction (see GENDER AND SEX) and from the popular (and most feminists would say sexist) use of *feminine* to refer to the qualities conventionally construed as essential or "natural" to women, such as softness, beauty, and nurturance. In other contexts, however, *female* gave way to *woman.* Around the 1980s some feminists advocated the term *fe-person* as a way of eliminating what they regarded as the sexist affix *male*; this locution has not caught on.

Most women today, unless they regard femaleness as inherently inferior, do not find anything derogatory in the word *female.*

Female-oriented and *female-identified* are sometimes heterosexual references to lesbians, seemingly avoidances of the blunter term *lesbian* (see also WOMAN [woman-identified-women]).

See also FEMME, MALE, WOMAN.

female impersonator. See DRAG.

female problems. A euphemism (along with *female complaints, female disorders,* and *female troubles*) used to describe certain conditions and maladies, mental or physical, identified with women and even construed as a part of "womanhood." In particular, these are symptoms, ailments, or disturbances associated with female reproductive or sexual functions (though some, such as "hot flashes," are not recognized in other cultures). Common examples of physical conditions are menstrual cramps, the menses, and genito-urinary problems such as yeast infections and urinary tract infections. Also included in this catch-all expression are such maladies as ovarian cysts, excessive menstrual bleeding or hemorrhage, and other medical maladies that most men (and some women) prefer not to name directly. The *Dictionary of American Regional English* (1991) dates earliest use from the 1930s, but such expressions no doubt precede that date by at least a few decades.

Traditionally—and still today—the life course of women has been seen as problematic, a result of cultural notions of women being both different from and, in significant ways, inferior to men. Because Western women's roles have been primarily those of mother and homemaker, their bodies—especially their reproductive functions—rather than their minds have been of great concern to society. Women have commonly been stereotyped as "victims" of female biological processes and "pathologies," these problems being used as justifications for attempts at male control of the female.

This conception of female biology in turn comes to be used as an explanation for certain mental states or difficulties associated with women. For example, the premenstrual syndrome (PMS) has been linked by some studies (critiqued by many as flawed) to violent behavior, eating problems, psychological distress, suicide, and accidents. PMS has also been used both as a legal defense for violent female behavior and as a justification to exclude women from positions of power.

Medical intervention for "female problems," which some feminists see as the use of male scientific knowledge to control natural female biological processes, may involve hysterectomies (now much less common) or hormone replacement therapy (supposedly a help for osteoporosis, but also for retraining female receptivity to penetrative sexual intercourse).

The idea that hormonal treatment can cure many of the problems from which women suffer—"female problems"—has resulted in the no-

tion that control can be exercised from menstruation to menopause. (Abbott and Wallace 1997, 128–29)

Some feminists also reject the view that menopause and its related symptoms require vigorous drug and other treatment. Others have revealed inconsistencies and inappropriateness in the medical response to women's symptoms, from denial that symptoms exist to excessive treatment with drugs.

See also CURSE, DOG (dog days), HYSTERIA, MENOPAUSE, NERVOUS DISORDER.

feminazi, femiNazi. A pejorative blend of *feminist* and *nazi*, stigmatizing almost any feminist or liberal female activist. "[Radio talk show personality] Rush Limbaugh thinks it is cute to refer to people with whose views he disagrees as 'feminazis'" (Anthony Lewis, in Goshgarian 1998, 207). Limbaugh has also been fond of the disparaging *feminutsy*. These slurs, thought to be jocular by some people, are not likely to be used outside politically far right discourse and have been on the wane even there.

See also FEMINIST, LIBBER.

feminine; Eternal Feminine. *Feminine*, a term used to assign a grammatical gender to nouns and related words, also referring to a particular society's definition of femaleness. When first entering English in the fourteenth century, *feminine* designated biological differences in animals and people.

We do not use the term symmetrically with MASCULINE, even though it may appear to be used in that manner. In many ways, our definitions of the feminine often suffer in comparison with the masculine. In U.S. society, although ideas of femininity vary, it may still, as in earlier centuries, evoke stereotypical images of weakness and frilliness, passivity, womanly wiles (see WILES, FEMININE), and dubious "female logic." The qualifier *feminine* in *feminine logic* implies that logic is natural to men; feminine logic is something other than logic, or the absence of it. Graham (1975, 61) notes that we tend to label what we consider the exception to the rule, as with woman doctor or male nurse. Use in these ways, and to praise women for fulfilling their ascribed traditional roles, reinforces a gender system in which women are viewed as different from (inferior) and subordinate to men. Many today would argue that to be truly "feminine," just as to be truly "masculine," is not to be a whole person.

Eternal Feminine is an expression that objectifies women, emphasizing physical youth and beauty, passiveness, and other stereotypical features. It is womanhood idealized and essentialized, capable of launching a thousand ships and selling even more cars and colognes. It is often said to have arisen from the so-called ancient Great Mother myths, mixing feelings of respect for womanly strength with fear of those powers believed to come from a mysterious realm outside of men's knowledge. Germaine Greer (1970) wrote of the Eternal Feminine as

> the Sexual Object sought by all men, and by all women. She is of neither sex, for she has herself no sex at all. Her value is solely attested by the demand she excites in others. All she must contribute is her existence. (50)

See also BEAUTY, FACE THAT LAUNCHED A THOUSAND SHIPS, FEMALE, FEMME, GENDER AND SEX, LOOKSISM, SEX OBJECT, WOMAN.

feminism. From the French *feminisme,* an English derivative referring to a belief in the full equality of men and women, first used in the late nineteenth century by French women's rights advocates. In the United States, the term first appeared in print in a book review published in *The Athenaeum* in 1895. However, the word was used only occasionally for a few years, finally gaining currency in the early twentieth century among women's rights advocates who sought more for women than just winning the franchise.

There has always been confusion about what feminism is and attempts to attack it as a kind of aberration of femaleness. The Christian Right, for example, has depicted it as a form of "moral perversion." As with FEMINIST, considerable bias has been attached to the word, making it virtually a term of reproach among many men and antifeminists. Among the attempts to degrade feminism, the word *strident* is often applied to it, whatever its tone, as though women are supposed to hold their tongues—keep their opinions to themselves and not speak out—according to the male ideal of femininity (e.g., see BITCH, NAG).

The opprobrium heaped on the word has caused some to speak softly or ironically of the "F-word." At the same time, Russ (1998) has noted an increased (and she believes ominous) depoliticization of the term. This she relates to attempts to construe it more broadly so that it now often means anything related sympathetically to women that does not ignite the subject and draw opposition. Also increasingly vague, Russ says, is *women's movement,* which may now "include… everything from learning to read the tarot to discussing summer vacations" (2).

Dictionary definitions seldom do justice to *feminism,* but we can say generally that it has taken on at least two broad, related senses. The first is a perspective on social, economic, and political inequality between the sexes. The other is an organized movement, also known as the feminist or women's liberation movement, concerned with furthering the rights and interests of women and giving them equal status with men, if not a world better than that in which there is mere social equality.

Although some historians prefer to

see feminist thought and activity as a single movement occurring since the nineteenth century, feminism has had its swings. In North America, the nineteenth-century phase of the women's movement is known as the "first wave"; it emphasized women's suffrage, a movement beginning in 1848 and culminating in 1920 in the passage of the Nineteenth Amendment to the United States Constitution, which gave women the right to vote in national elections.

The "second wave" gained momentum in the late 1960s. It dealt with broad public issues of discrimination and sexuality, encouraged activism in such areas as abortion rights and violence against women, and promoted "consciousness-raising" groups under the slogan "The personal is the political." The vaguer term *third wave* has been in popular circulation only since about 1995. It was used in the title of the feminist anthology *The Third Wave: Feminist Perspectives on Racism,* published in the mid-1980s, and began to be used in 1992 following the Clarence Thomas-Anita Hill hearings and the trial of William Kennedy Smith, found not guilty in a case of rape. At that time young feminist activists organized a political network called "The Third Wave."

Third wave is often characterized by the activities of young feminists who look back at the women's movement as a "piece of history" and who attempt to navigate feminism's contradictions—historical, cultural, and psychological (Orr 1997, 12). In particular, it involves renewed attempts to include women of color and poor women in feminist activism and is an attack on those feminist views that proposed political and sexual separatism for women.

As a perspective and a movement, feminism is a heterogeneous set of concepts, proposals, practices, and calls for action. Although feminists agree that women are subordinated to men and that

a goal of the movement is to seek ways to liberate women, they disagree on many things, including what the discrete goals of feminism should be, how to explain the causes or agents of oppression, and how to proceed to free women.

Even notions of equality and notions of the basis of the rights of women vary among feminists contesting its meaning. Some see women as being just like men and thus entitled to the same rights; others prefer to make distinctions, arguing that women should have the right to represent themselves.

> When students reject the label "feminist,"…it is because they don't really know what the term means and haven't yet had help in figuring it out. They don't realize yet that it comprises contradictory voices. (Aaron Rosenfeld, *Chronicle of Higher Education,* 12 September 1997, B3)

Liberal, or *mainstream feminism,* seeks to expose the immediate forms of discrimination against women and to promote legislative, workplace, and other reforms designed to eliminate discrimination and promote equality of opportunity. Beyond this venue, there is also *Marxist feminism,* which finds the source of women's problems in the traditional exclusion of women from the workforce and holds that women need to liberate themselves from the ruling forces of capitalism.

Also attempting to get at the root causes of female oppression is *radical feminism,* which views patriarchal domination as culturally pervasive, universal, and destructive of women's "true nature." Radical feminism proposes the elimination of society's artificial assumptions about differences between the sexes in order to achieve equality. *Dual-system feminism* combines Marxist and radical feminism. *Cultural feminism* asserts the superiority of women over men, celebrates female differences, advocates a feminist counterculture that it sees as capable of bettering society, and often encourages the separation of women and men. Emphasizing a women-first approach, *lesbian feminism* merges radical feminism and women's separatism, though separatism is less an issue today than it was in the 1970s.

Postmodern feminism, which opposes the idea that there is a female or male "nature" and examines divisions between men and women in terms of historically and culturally specific knowledge, is another important form of feminism. *Black feminism* argues that sex and race create a situation for black women different from that for white women. Adding to the list are such varieties as *American Indian, Arab American, Asian American, Chicana, Latina, Puerto Rican,* and *Jewish feminism* as well as *international feminism* and *ecofeminism*.

Still other ways of designating the varieties of feminism, and sometimes suggesting their alleged flaws, include the adjectives *academic* (intellectualized, and often criticized as being remote from women's lives); *amoral* (e.g., the French theory); and *moralistic* (e.g., the academic feminism of Catharine MacKinnon). *Career feminism* was used by Myra Marx Ferree and Beth B. Hess in *Controversy and Coalition: The New Feminist Movement* (1985). It emphasizes women's right to pursue individual goals and occupational freedom and to create women's networks. As Tuttle (1986) notes, it is the kind of feminism accepted by those who partially disavow feminism. *Bimbo feminism* refers derisively to the advocacy of education, careers, *and* attractiveness to men (see also BIMBO).

This is not an inclusive list of feminist thought and labels, and the definitions oversimplify the issues involved, for example, different understandings of the relevance of culture, race, class, and sexuality. Nor does this list mean to convey the impression of unity of thought under each rubric. Each type of feminism may have different advocates holding different points of view.

See also SEXIST, WOMEN'S LIBERATION.

feminist. A person who subscribes to beliefs that advocate the social, political, and economic equality of women with men. The feminist also typically supports activities organized to secure the interests and rights of women, seen as being in a subordinate position to men, and, more generally, to achieve a better world for all. But the definitions vary, and different feminists disagree, for example, over just what *equality* means and how it can be achieved. The American use of *feminist* stems from French usage in the 1890s, but the adjective form preceded the noun form, which did not appear until the early twentieth century.

> I myself have never been able to find out precisely what feminism is: I only know that people call me a feminist whenever I express sentiments that differentiate me from a doormat.
>
> —Rebecca West, 1913, in Faludi 1991, xxiii

The term is a loaded one: who defines it (and how) will influence how the speaker sees the person labeled, just as one's worldview will shape the definition of the term. It carries strong negative connotations for many moderate to conservative people who feel that it suggests an antifamily attitude, especially a rejection of the value of bearing and raising children. Although caricatures have lessened in recent years, feminists are still often stereotyped as losers: unattractive women who are humorless, dogmatic, man-hating (see MAN-HATER), and unwilling to respect the roles of mother and housewife. Feminist ideas are often disparaged as "extremist"; they have been stereotyped as lesbian, drawing

upon negative associations with homosexuality, and in some circles the term
may still evoke the sensationalist "hairy-
legs" caricature. Even by many liberal,
educated people, feminists have been
branded as a peculiar breed of women,
off doing things that range from trivial
to subversive (or both at the same time).
But the contradictions in stereotyping go
unnoticed because the stereotypes and
distancing serve the important function
of confirming the general notion of
"real" women: those who are submissive, pleasingly heterosexual, and apolitical.

In mainstream society, especially in
the media, the term has come to gener-
ate enough heat that it may, sometimes
ironically and mockingly, be called the
"F-word." Advocates of feminism will
say it's not a four-letter word. Others
have their ways of evading its implications. Some women may proclaim, "I'm
not a feminist, *but....*" What follows is
their advocacy of equal pay for equal
work, enjoyment of the same educational and professional opportunities as
men, abolishment of sexual harassment
on the job, and other feminist issues. The
user of this near motto is only disavow-
ing the term, not the philosophical position.

Russ (1998) has noted an increasingly depoliticized use of the term, so
that more women today than in earlier
decades are willing to label themselves
as feminists, even when their understanding of the issues of women's liberation do not correspond to those of the
women who were involved in 1970s activism. Russ associates this with, among
other things, the (she believes ominous)
abandonment of confrontation, so that

> the air no longer rings with horrid
> tales of ball-breaking dykes, man-
> hating neurotics, vicious and para-
> sitic wives, and the rest of the tiny
> train of male-imagined phantoms. (3)

Among those who are serious about

one or another variety of feminist views,
there has been a kind of tug-of-war over
ownership of the term *feminist.* Who are
the "true" feminists?

> When anti-porn feminists say,
> "Susie Bright isn't really a femi-
> nist," or when pro-porn feminists
> say, "Andrea Dworkin isn't really a
> feminist," part of what they're ar-
> guing about is what they consider
> to be dangerous to women (objecti-
> fication and violence against
> women vs. repressive censorship).
> (Greta Christina, in Queen and
> Schimel 1997, 34)

However, some feminists are increasingly becoming aware that many views,
however inadequate by themselves, contain partial truths and contribute to an
overall understanding of gender roles
and relations in society. At the same
time, some theorists have dropped the
term *feminism* altogether because they
believe it amounts only to one more
-ism.

Domestic feminist has been applied
to women, especially in the nineteenth
century, who sought to educate women
and enhance their legal status not for the
sake of their liberation but to make them
better wives and mothers. The term is
regarded today as a misnomer.

Men who regard themselves as antisexist may prefer to be called profeminist rather than feminist, although the
latter is sometimes used for men (86
percent of the usage panel of *The American Heritage Dictionary* [1992] apply
feminist to a person of either sex). *Men
against sexism, effeminists,* and *profeminist man* as well as the adjective *antisexist* have sometimes been preferred by
men in the men's liberation movement
(beginning in the late 1960s) who declared their loyalties to the women's liberation and gay liberation movements.
To these individuals *men's liberation*
was objectionable because it appeared
to imply an opposition to women's lib-

eration. *Male feminist* is an oxymoron to some feminists.

See also BRA BURNER, FEMINAZI, FEMINISM, LIBBER, SISTER.

fem lib. See LIBBER.

femme; *Cherchez la femme! Femme,* a word based on the English FEMININE or FEMALE but made to look like the French word for woman. It may be used for a girl or woman. In this sense, it has been in widespread use since at least the late nineteenth century. Not necessarily derogatory, it nevertheless suggests, at least, some variant of woman construed as the "second sex." To conservatives, however, it may imply simply more traditional femininity.

Carrying the idea of female, *femme* is also applied to an effeminate gay man or a lesbian believed to adopt the "passive" role, which in fact is a misnomer and does not define femininity as many women see it. In the lesbian community, the term that was sometimes used was *Marge* (see also BUTCH, FISH, MOM) or, since the 1930s, also *femmie* or *femmy.* FLUFF has been used with similar connotations. Among lesbians, the meanings of *femme* constitute a chosen identity but not one that corresponds in any simple way to the heterosexual wife role.

Among heterosexuals, *femme* as applied to any woman may carry some derogatory or trivializing connotations. For example, *femme D.,* a play on *M.D.,* is a jocular and dismissive way of referring to a female physician.

Cherchez la femme! is a French expression, often used in English, meaning "Seek the woman!" It was first used in the form *cherchons la femme* (Let's find the woman), by French writer Alexandre Dumas *père* in *Les Mohicans de Paris* (1864). The expression is associated with a style of mystery writing where the trouble or conflict that sparks the plot is believed to start with—who else?—a woman, and to find the woman

is to find the key to the mystery. "Erotic rivalry between men can only have a single origin. *Cherchez la femme!*" (Arango 1989, 75).

See also FEMME FATALE.

femme fatale. A beautiful temptress or seductress; an image of a woman both desired and despised or feared by men, whom they cannot handle and who is thus fatal to them. The expression comes from the French *femme fatale* (fatal woman), and the stereotype was found throughout the twentieth century. "He saw me the first time in my old slacks and my sloppy old jersey, and then I rolled into the restaurant, nothing less than a *femme fatale,* and he didn't know how to have me, he couldn't say a word all evening" (Doris Lessing, *The Golden Notebook,* 1981, 9). The image remains common in popular fiction such as John Bradley's *My Juliet* (2000), featuring a sultry New Orleans "seductress" up to no good to get her family manse.

See also BOMBSHELL, KNOCKOUT, SEDUCTRESS, SIREN (ravishing), TEMPTRESS, VAMP, WILES (FEMININE). For a term for men, see LADY-KILLER.

fe-person. See FEMALE.

fetish. See TRANSVESTITE.

fetishist. See CROSS-DRESSER.

fey. A twentieth-century usage for a gay man or, especially in Britain, used as an adjective similar to *gay.* In standard English, it has been used to mean whimsical or strange, disordered or excited in state of mind, or having a supernatural or fairylike quality (see also FAIRY). The word as applied to sexual orientation is typically descriptive, with no disparagement involved: "The more fey an act, the more media play it got, affecting everyone from hard rock acts like Blue Öyster Cult to R&B groups like Labelle" (Jim Farber, *The Advocate,* 10 November 1998, 76).

See also GAY.

filet. In the late-twentieth-century slang sense, usually very offensive, a sexually attractive young woman regarded as a "piece of meat." In standard English, a fillet, from the Middle French *filet*, diminutive of *fil* (thread), means a ribbon or narrow strip of material, including a slice of boneless meat or fish. In the same semantic field, *prime cut* is a vulgar slang word meaning vagina (see also MEAT). The word may also be construed as a variation of *filly*, an animal metaphor for a girl or young woman.

See also FILLY, MEAT, PIECE, WOMEN AS ANIMALS.

filly. Any girl or young woman, often one considered attractive or wanton (from the French *fille*, "girl," but also, in the familiar, "whore"). *Filly* for a woman has been in use since the seventeenth century, becoming at one point a euphemism for a lewd woman. During the 1930s the term was especially popular in the sense of a frisky young woman, and Spears (1991) labeled the usage "U.S. stereotypical Western jargon." Because another sense of the word is a young female horse, or young mare—a domesticated animal that a man "rides" for his pleasure or use—the likeness is considered offensive by many women, though it is positive compared with the intentionally insulting *old nag*. "'The blonde filly?' 'She's not a filly. Her name's Lady Arlington'" (1939 film *Man About Town*, starring Jack Benny). Compare the connotations with that of the masculine STALLION.

See also FILET, HEIFER, KITTEN, MEAT, WOMEN AS ANIMALS.

finger artist. Usually (especially among heterosexuals) a derogatory term for a lesbian, reducing her to a form of sexual technique.

See also LESBIAN.

firecracker. See BOMBSHELL.

first lady. See LADY.

first skirt. See SKIRT.

fish. Among its many meanings, paralleling the development of other food and animal metaphors, a term for a woman, used since the seventeenth century; also, in the nineteenth century, for the vagina (today, sometimes, the penis); and for copulation with a woman. Its related slang meanings include a female prostitute, a female heterosexual or any woman (usually used disparagingly in gay male communities), and a lesbian who acts or looks feminine (among lesbians) (see FEMME).

The association of *fish* with women is reinforced by the sense of searching for or catching something (to "hook") but also by the idea of a "dish" to be eaten (flesh), food for sale in the (meat) "market," or something that smells (odor is suggested by the genital sense of the word) (see SKANK). Also reinforcing the usage is the notion that women who are not sexually willing are "cold," as in a "cold fish" (a term also applicable to very emotionless men). In some cultures, the fish, like women, has been regarded as both holy (see VIRGIN) and threatening.

At one time, also, *mermaid* was a reference to a female prostitute. Although connected with the idea of fish, this usage may also be a product of the sexual fantasizing of sailors at sea for long periods of time. Major (1994) gives *fresh water trout* as a dated expression for pretty young women. Among gay men *fishwife* means a woman who is married to or the consort of a gay man (an earlier sense of *fishwife* was a scolding, ill-tempered woman; see also FAG BAG). *Seafood* is used by gay men for handsome sailors but also by heterosexual men for a woman considered edible. Chapman (1987) notes the pun on *c food*— "cuntfood." *Fishy,* in the sense of something odd or irregular, may refer to a gay man (see also QUEER [queer fish]).

See also BAIT (squid bait), BARRACUDA, DISH, MEAT.

five-letter woman. See FOUR-LETTER MAN.

flamer; **flaming**. *Flamer,* a word for a gay man of conspicuous or flamboyant effeminacy. From roughly the mid-twentieth century, the word may not be considered an overt slur by either straight people or gay men, yet it may be taken offensively, especially when used by straight speakers. The adjective *flaming,* referring to the conspicuousness of a man's effeminacy, often precedes such derogatory words as *fag, faggot, queen, queer,* or *asshole.* "What a fancy restaurant. Everything came out flaming, including the bus boy" (Rhoda, on the TV sitcom *Mary Tyler Moore,* 1997 rerun). Within gay communities, however, *flaming queen* is not a slur. It may be considered slightly "bitchy," but more often it is affectionate and is in fairly widespread use. Today the behavior often described as flamboyant may be said to promote the subversion of those identities based on the heterosexual male model (see also CAMP).

Writing of early-twentieth-century urban gay culture, Chauncey (1994) says,

> The fact that many ["homosexual"] men referred to "flaming faggots" or "swishes" as "obvious types" or "extreme homosexuals" suggests the extent to which they saw themselves as part of a continuum linking them to the public stereotype [of gay men]. (104)

See also EFFEMINATE, FAGGOT, MINCE, QUEEN, SWISH.

flamboyant. See CAMP, FLAMER.

flapper; **flap**. *Flapper,* a term especially prominent in the years 1910 to 1930 for a young woman known for her worldliness and freedom from conventional female dress, conduct, and sexual codes, characteristics that made her a very controversial figure to say the least. Nilsen et al. (1977, 28) also suggests that the term indicates frivolity or unimportance,

much like SOCIAL BUTTERFLY. A BIRD image is evoked as well: an unfledged, flighty bird "flapping" its wings, suggesting the popular dance of the 1920s called the Charleston.

Breaking away from many of the inhibited manners and gender ideals of the older generation, the flapper of the 1920s was known to party without a chaperon, smoke cigarettes in public, and dance to jazz with her skirt raised above her knees. Attested to by H. L. Mencken (1962), the term was popularized by writers Harry Leon Wilson (see MRS. [Missus] for a quotation) and F. Scott Fitzgerald, and the lifestyle was discussed with moral concern in the magazines of the day.

> This was the generation whose girls dramatized themselves as flappers, the generation that corrupted its elders and eventually overreached itself less through lack of morals than through lack of taste. (F. Scott Fitzgerald, *The Crack-Up,* [1931] 1945, 15)

However much the stereotypical flapper frustrated society with her alleged licentiousness, heralding a sort of "new woman" (largely middle-class European American), she did not ally herself with the feminist movement of the time. She welcomed freedom of a sort, focusing on her right to control her body; but she did not support the feminist goals of equality with men in social, political, and economic life.

Since the seventeenth century, and through the mid-twentieth century, *flap* (also later a short form of *flapper*) was used for a supposedly flirtatious, disreputable, or loose woman, or one who could not be taken seriously (it finds its equivalent in a contemporary British term *flap,* denoting an unsteady young woman). *Flap* also had some currency in American slang from the 1880s for a young girl and in the late nineteenth century in Britain for an adolescent female prostitute. In this nineteenth-century use, sexual precociousness with lack of physical maturity was often highlighted and not lost in the way the word was used by the next generation.

flasher. See EXHIBITIONIST.

flatbacker. See PROSTITUTE.

flat-cock. See BEAVER.

flaunt (one's homosexuality). To engage in certain conduct, such as kissing or holding hands, which heterosexual people can do in public without notice but which often elicits strong disapproval if gay people are seen doing it. Women may flaunt, or display ostentatiously, their curves, appearing disreputable in the process, and men may flaunt their muscular development, seeming egotistical, but we usually only speak of gays and lesbians as "flaunting their sexuality." Although they are no more likely to be parading or displaying that behavior than heterosexual people are (in some public places, they are less likely), the fact that society takes the normative heterosexual behavior for granted, while the gay behavior is regarded as DEVIANT, makes some people—usually heterosexuals—accuse gays of "flaunting" their homosexuality. Gay privacy, says the *GLAAD Media Guide,* is defined differently from that of heterosexual people.

flavor. Black slang meaning a pretty young woman, since the 1960s. The allusion is to taste.

See also DISH.

flibbertigibbet. From a Middle English word, *flepergebet,* a silly, flighty, frivolous person; a scatterbrain, especially one who can't stop talking—often a woman. The idea is that women are closely associated with mindless chatter. Even when used for a man, the term brings to bear its derisive feminine connotations. When American writer Henry David Thoreau carelessly started a for-

est fire near his native Concord in the 1840s, he said that some of the owners of the burned tract of land bore their losses "like men," while others continued to shout insults at him, acting like "flibberty-gibbets" (*Concord's Happy Rebel,* Hildegarde Hawthorne, 1940, 85).

See also GOSSIP.

flit; frit. Heterosexual epithets meaning a gay or effeminate man. The former comes from the 1930s, the latter is as recent as the 1960s. *Flit* is suggestive of a "fairy," especially a winged one, or one that "flits about," relating also to the feminine sense of BIRD. "He assured me that he had a luscious ass.... Flits have always been attracted to me" (Mary McCarthy, *The Group,* 1963). *Flitty* disparages a homosexual or someone or something effeminate. *Frit* may come from blending *flit* with *fruit,* a common slur on a homosexual.

See also BUTTERFLY, FAIRY, FRUIT.

floozy, floozie, floosie; flooze. From about the turn of the twentieth century through at least the middle of that century, an Americanism meaning an attractive but usually flashy and uncultivated young woman. She is likely to be thought of as flirtatious, promiscuous, or predatory (living off the generosity of a "sugar daddy") and sometimes slovenly as well. For most of the twentieth century the term has been used synonymously with *tramp* or *prostitute.* "Frank's [Gifford] floozy stole my hubby, too" (Larry Haley, *National Enquirer,* 19 August 1997, 29). *Flat floozy* is a name for a prostitute who works out of a room or a flat (the idea of being flat on one's back to work probably reinforces the meaning).

The origin of the term is obscure. Related terms, however, are the now archaic *flossy* (a young woman, prostitute, or, as an adjective, showy or shiny), from which *floozy* may derive, and the dialectal *floosy,* meaning "soft" and "fluffy" (see also FLUFF). It is also said to have been influenced by the South African *vlossi,* the name of a plane that transported women, and even the female personal name, Flora, "flower."

Also rendered *floogie, faloosie, flugie.*

Floosie is a usually derogatory slang reference to a gay man.

See also COOZIE, HOOZIE, LOOSE, PROMISCUOUS, PROSTITUTE, SLATTERN, TRAMP.

flower. A metaphor applied to women and gay men. There are numerous cultural and linguistic connections between flowers and traditional notions of femininity. Flowers, suggesting pretty, soft, and decorative things, are often associated with women, especially young ones, who, to men, as de Beauvoir ([1952] 1974) once wrote, "must incarnate the marvelous flowering of life" (177). *Flower* may also be used in the sense of the vulva or hymen (regarding "defloration," see VIRGIN), while *flowers* refers to the menses (see also CURSE), and *passion flower* is a woman considered sexually passionate. In the 1946 movie *Duel in the Sun,* Jennifer Jones played a seductive, tortured, mixed-race (part Indian) woman said to be a "wildflower." *Bud* is a dated term once used to refer to a virgin—a "flower" not yet in bloom.

Among the more common flower terms applied to people are *pansy* and *rose.* Consistent with the femininity of the term, *pansy* can represent a gay man, especially an effeminate one—straight men take themselves to be stronger, more rugged than a flower. This gay usage has been in the language since the early twentieth century. Sometimes it may apply insultingly to any effeminate male (who may also be known by the synonym *lily*). Chauncey (1994, 15) says that in the 1920s and 1930s, gay men were labeled so commonly after the names of flowers that they also became known simply as "horticultural lads."

Given our gender stereotypes, it is not surprising to see *rose,* as an object of beauty, a flower valued for its shape, scent, and extraordinary colors (and handled cautiously for its prickly stems), applied to women. *Rose* is found either as a given name or in other references, such as *black rose,* occurring in literary descriptions of beautiful black women. As a color, *rose* is close to pink, an association that strengthens the female connotations.

In a discussion of words that label women as things, Alleen Pace Nilsen et al. (1977, 323) notes the practice of naming girls after flowers, such as Rose, Lily, or Daisy. She asks us to compare these names with boys' names such as *Martin,* "warlike"; *Ernest,* "resolute fighter"; *Nicholas,* "victory"; *Val,* "strong" or "valiant"; and *Leo,* "lion" (33).

See also BUTTERCUP, DAFFODIL, DAISY, EFFEMINATE, GLADIOLA, LILY, PANSY, PEARL, SEX OBJECT, VIOLET, WALLFLOWER.

fluff, a bit of/a piece of. A stereotype of a young woman or young women in general; also the vagina (Major [1994] gives the latter as a black usage); in addition, a lesbian seen as feminine and PASSIVE—femme, the opposite of butch (see also LESBIAN)—or an effeminate gay man. The first sense entered the language about the beginning of the twentieth century; the homosexual usage came about midcentury.

Fluff alludes to a downy surface, as on a fabric, suggesting something soft, light, airy, something that gives (in), hence lacking in substance, inconsequential—traditional stereotypes of women. The connotations are also of something belonging to the house, as a woman has traditionally been pegged. Since the late nineteenth century, the term has also been used to refer to female pubic hair.

"If a woman learns and uses women's language, she is necessarily considered less than a real, full person—she's a bit of fluff" (Lakoff 1975, 61).

See also BLUFF, FEMME, FLOOZY (floosy), FRAIL, SKIRT, WEAKER VESSEL.

flute. A term for a gay man; perhaps from *flute* as a metaphor for the erect penis, or the idea of "playing the skin flute" (see also COCK [cocksucker]), or a mispronunciation of the usually disparaging term FRUIT, in the sense of a homosexual. *Flute* is usually considered inappropriate language, but while it may be only mildly disparaging, it reduces a man to a part of his anatomy. The term is restricted largely to straight use, when used at all.

See also HOMOSEXUAL.

fly; **fly-girl**. Somewhat dated terms for a woman deemed of questionable character, one seen as wanton or loose. *Fly* comes from the late nineteenth century. While a *flyboy* (in addition to its sense of aviator) is a clever or sophisticated man, a *fly-girl* is a pretty or sexy woman or one of easy morals, a prostitute. *Fly-girl* is also applied to female airline flight attendants.

See also EASY LAY, FRUIT (fruit fly), GIRL, LOOSE, PROSTITUTE.

fogy, **fogey**. A term for a dull, conservative, or eccentric person, frequently constructed with *old*. Even a young person with old ideas may be regarded as an "old fogy." "My sons' prominent use of the phrase 'the old man' connotes to me that they color me in the graying shades of old fogyism" (Will Manley, *Booklist*, July 1998, 1834). The term may apply to a woman but is far more commonly used for a man. *Fogy* is said to be of Scottish origin, though its beginnings are unclear, but it is known to date from the eighteenth century. *Old fogy* once had related meanings in the military, referring to an old or disabled soldier (*fogy* may still connote someone who is decrepit). A nearly synonymous expression, also frequently but not exclusively applied to men, is *old stick-in-the-mud.*

See also BADGER, CODGER, COOT, CUSS, DUFFER, FRUMP, FUDDY-DUDDY, GEEZER, GOAT, OLD FART.

fooper. According to Spears (1991), a name for a gay man, possibly from the usually derogatory British *poof*, "a gay or effeminate man." In use since the mid-twentieth century.

See also EFFEMINATE, HOMOSEXUAL.

forbidden fruit. An allusion to the tree of knowledge, the fruit of which God forbade Adam and Eve to eat in the biblical story in Genesis. The allusion is to a young woman, specifically a virgin. In use throughout the twentieth century, the word's meaning is similar to that of JAIL-BAIT.

See also FRUIT, TEMPTRESS, VIRGIN.

forty-four. See WHORE.

four-letter man; **five-letter woman**. *Four-letter man,* a man who is said to be stupid, boring, or detestable; a euphemistic characterization of someone who can be summed up in words of four letters, such as *dumb,* but also *shit* or HOMO. In use since the 1920s, it was originally a reference to a male student who had earned four varsity letters (a letterman). Based on this idea, but mostly a British usage of the early twentieth century, is *five-letter woman,* that is, a "bitch."

See also FAGGOT (three-letter man).

fox; **foxy**. *Fox,* as an animal metaphor, a person regarded as crafty ("sly like a fox") or, very frequently, a sexy or pert young woman (she may be clever as well). As applied to a woman, *fox* was probably originally a black usage from the 1940s, possibly from the black jazz scene: "the spendidly ambiguous expression *fox,* which emanates from the Chicago ghetto" (Greer 1970, 262). The term was popularized in the 1960s by boxer Cassius Clay, later known as Muhammad Ali, soon coming to mean an attractive person of either sex or (in prison) a PASSIVE partner in a lesbian relationship. Probably, however, the animal metaphor as applied to women is an old one.

Fox, referring to a woman, implies something to chase, make sport of, take aim at, or perhaps "fire a shot at" (in the sense of ejaculation) (see also HUNTER). When a man is described as a fox, the term alludes to such things as slyness or the "beast" in him. For either men or women, the word may refer to sleek good looks. *Fox* derives from the Old High German *fuhs* (fox)—the modern German being *Fuchs* (close in sound to *fucks*)—and perhaps the Sanskrit *puccha*, meaning tail. In medieval art the fox was, among other things, a symbol of lust.

Whereas the domesticated dog gives us a derogatory term for men and women, the wild fox suggests something wild, cunning, attractive, independent, elusive, and predatory—an ambivalent creature, much more exciting than the domesticated dog. The fox is known for carrying off farmers' livestock—that is, what are usually men's resources. Yet, however strong or positive the image may be, its meanings in reference to women derive largely from the judgment of the male name-caller. The wearing of fox furs by women and the association of the female genitals with "fur" (in particular, the bushy tail of the fox) may reinforce the female sense of the term.

Foxy generally applies to women, meaning stylish, sexy, and inclined to lovemaking (mid-nineteenth century); often as *foxy lady,* which can also mean a sexually attractive man in the gay community. *Foxy* is also used among women to refer to a good-looking young man. In black English, it means stylish, showy, fine, or, as said of women, sexy; and *stone fox* means an unquestionably beautiful woman, perhaps cold or untouchable as well.

See also ANIMAL, BEAST, CAT, DOG, FOX, VIXEN, WOLF, WOMEN AS ANIMALS.

frail; **frill**. *Frail,* a stereotypical attribute of women that denotes weakness and carries feminine connotations. At one time *frail* suggested the kind of moral fragility believed to be natural to women, that supposedly made a woman susceptible to evil influences, such as devilry and sexual promiscuity. The nineteenth-century euphemism *frail sisters* was used for prostitutes. By the end of the nineteenth century, *frail* came to signify not just a prostitute but any woman, carrying the more general idea of the "weaker sex." Thorne (1990) places it in the Raymond Chandler era of crime fiction, claiming it was condescending but not intended to be offensive. It has also occurred in prison talk for a "passive" woman in a lesbian relationship (Lighter 1994).

Frill, a mildly demeaning term for a girl or woman, may be related to the idea of females as decorative or frivolous, but it is also said to be related to *frail* (see e.g., Thorne).

See also FAIR SEX, GENDER-SPECIFIC ADJECTIVES, WEAKER VESSEL.

frame. A woman regarded as attractive or sexy (it rhymes with DAME). *Frame* here alludes to the figure, or physique, used since the early twentieth century, but somewhat dated now. *Frame* is also applied to a male heterosexual who attracts gay men.

See also LOOKSISM.

Frau; **Hausfrau**. *Frau,* a German word meaning woman or wife and occurring as a title equivalent to *Mrs. Frau* is sometimes also used in English [it is capitalized, following the German practice of capitalizing all nouns] with similar meanings but often with a hint of contempt for women. Similarly, the German word *Hausfrau* (housewife), entered English with demeaning overtones. It suggests an unattractive woman with few interests outside of cleaning, cooking, and ironing.

See also BAREFOOT AND PREGNANT (KEEP THEM), HOMEMAKER, MRS., WIFE.

freak. Since the early twentieth century, a term that has been used for a homosexual person or man (sometimes woman) whose sexual practices or androgynous looks are regarded as very unconventional, unacceptable, or deviant. "Is [transsexual] Christine Jorgensen a man or a woman?" "She isn't anything.... She's a freak" (quoted in Feinberg 1996, 7). The term may suggest "freak of nature" (see NORMAL). Lighter (1994) places the term in prison and prostitution slang and claims it is also applied to a prostitute's customer.

Since the middle of the twentieth century, *freak* has also been applied to a young woman considered sexy, often connoting a nymphomaniac in black (also Latino, especially male) usage. Sutton (1995, 293) reports a variety of West Coast senses of *freak:* a promiscuous or slutty girl, a beautiful girl (also *watch queen*), or a cute girl or even boy. *Peek freak* refers to a gay voyeur (see also PEEPING TOM). *Freakish* can describe sexual deviance, homosexuality, or nymphomania. *Freak daddy* is a name for a sexually attractive man, and *freak mommy,* a sexually attractive woman. During the 1960s long-haired, pot-smoking, counterculture "freaks" took some pleasure in reclaiming the term as applied to them in the sense of weird people—like members of a freak show.

See also DEVIANT, FUCKER (fuck freak), NYMPH (nymphomaniac), PERVERT.

free woman. See LIBERATED WOMAN.

fresh cow. See COW.

fresh meat. See MEAT.

fresh water trout. See FISH.

friend of Dorothy's. GAY; an expression deriving from the character played by Judy Garland in the 1939 film classic, *The Wizard of Oz,* in which one of her friends was the sissified, cowardly lion. Garland, because of both her singing and her tragic life, has been popular among gay men, for whom Garland herself was known to have had an affinity. The Stonewall riot in New York City took place on the night of her funeral.

As a code word, the expression once found use among gay men in referring obliquely to their sexual orientation, thus helping them to render themselves visible to one another and invisible to a hostile straight world (a gay man could introduce himself to a man he thought was gay by asking, "Excuse me, are you a friend of Dorothy's?"). This method of introduction perhaps found its greatest popularity in San Francisco and England.

frigid. Lacking in ardor, having an aversion to sexual intercourse, or being nonorgasmic. This term goes back to the seventeenth century, when it was applied to men as well as women. *The Oxford English Dictionary* (1989) quotes from Jonathan Swift's eighteenth-century *Beasts' Confession:* "He was not much inclin'd To fondness for the female kind.... Not from his frigid constitution." The word, however, became specific to women by the twentieth century. The "condition" is often blamed on the woman, the implication being that she is emotionally cold or is perhaps a PRUDE or even a lesbian or "masculine" woman. In any case, she is unavailable, which is often the reason the user of this disparaging term applies it.

At the same time women, blamed for their own lack of ardor, may also be blamed for men's *impotence.* However, as Spender (1980, 177) has pointed out, because a woman's frigidity could be regarded as a form of reluctance—to respond to *his* sexuality rather than to use her own—it takes on the appearance of a form of power against men ("passive resistance or unavailability"). Men's impotence, on the other hand, is more a form of physical handicap, not a matter of choice (see IMPOTENT).

A woman may also be put down in such related slang expressions as *frosty* and *sitting on a frozen custard* or be dismissed as a "wet smack" (*smack* may allude either to sex or to a cold slap) or an "ice cube with a hole in it" (alluding to the absence of the woman's body—the woman herself—except for the vagina). A sexually or emotionally unresponsive woman may also be called a "cold fish" (see FISH). If she is really unresponsive, she may be labeled *glacial*. Men are rarely described as frigid today; they are "hyposexed" or labeled as a EUNUCH.

See also GENDER-SPECIFIC ADJECTIVES (barren), ICEBOX.

frit. See FLIT.

frosty. See FRIGID.

fruit; **fruitcake**. *Fruit,* a usually hurtful putdown for a gay or effeminate man, heard since the early part of the twentieth century. Fruit, the food of a plant, is soft, sweet, and is "eaten"—all stereotypical female attributes that can be used to call into question a man's masculinity (see PASSIVE). It may also be thought of as EXOTIC or ripe, also usually female categories (young female virgins were once known as "unripe fruit"). In addition *fruit* is associated with color, as are gay men, often stereotyped as fashion designers and decorators; and with scent, the use of which has been another stereotypical characteristic of gay men. The term found earlier use in the sense of a promiscuous woman. Fruit is also symbolically linked with feminine attributes in the biblical story of Adam and Eve, in which the fruit was a forbidden food that Eve picked off the tree (see also FORBIDDEN FRUIT). Representing temptation to sin, "fruit" as applied to a homosexual person might suggest that heterosexuals are fighting a homoerotic attraction (tasting it may mean one's "fall" into homosexuality).

There have been some attempts to reclaim the word in the second half of the twentieth century. Early gay programs on the radio, beginning in the 1960s, included KPFA's *Fruitpunch*, also once broadcast under the name *Gay Talk*. Former Fruitpuncher Philip Maldari recalls that the original members were recruited en masse one night at a gay coffeehouse in downtown Oakland (Witt, Thomas, and Marcus 1995, 125).

Synonyms, also still mostly pejorative, especially when spoken by heterosexuals, are *fruitbar, fruit basket, fruit plate* (see also DISH), *fruitcake, fruiter, fruit-loop,* and *fruit punch.* A "fruit hustler" is a straight expression for either a man who robs gay men or a male prostitute. *Fruit fly* is a name for a woman who is attracted to gay men (see also FAG HAG, FLY). *Fruit picker* refers to a heterosexual man who from time to time looks for a homosexual partner. *Canned fruit* has been used for a gay man who conceals or denies his homosexuality. Early in the twentieth century, *fruit for the monkeys* referred, often contemptuously, to extreme moral looseness.

Fruit, fruit-loop, and *fruitcake* can also mean a crazy or eccentric individual, that is, a "nutty" person.

See also DISH, EFFEMINATE, HOMOSEXUAL, POTATO, TOMATO, VEGETABLE.

frump. A term for a person seen as drab, staid, or dowdy, especially an unattractive, old-fashioned woman; also, ugliness itself. Probably from the early nineteenth century, from *frumple*, to wrinkle, referring here to facial wrinkles. *Frumpy* is the adjective form.

See also FOGY, FUDDY-DUDDY, GENDER-SPECIFIC ADJECTIVES (dowdy), LOOKSISM, SPINSTER.

fuckboy. See SCREWBOY.

fuck bunny. See BUNNY.

fucker; **fuck**. *Fucker,* a man considered promiscuous or one regarded as offensive, mean, base, or formidable. The term may be used in the sense of a buddy or affectionately for any nice man ("He's a pleasant old fucker") as well as derisively, but it is almost always seen as vulgar. It is one of the most forceful, sexually charged words in the English language, usually taboo in polite social conversation. Among men, it may also refer to a woman considered promiscuous, but not necessarily mean or base. In the sense of a man who copulates, it derives from the sixteenth century; in the sense of a despicable man, or BASTARD, it has had use at least throughout the twentieth century and into the twenty-first. Nineteenth-century usage included a male lover, and the term may still be applied to the penis.

In many contexts the idea of aggression (*fuck* can mean to deceive, injure, or destroy; *fuck over*, to cheat or beat up) and that of sexuality (the verb *fuck* means to copulate) are virtually fused. Like other words for copulation (e.g., *penetration, poke, screw*), it suggests something that men *do to* women. The related Middle Dutch word *fokken* and German *ficken* also both mean to strike as well as to copulate with.

Fuck, meaning a partner in sex (sex object, as in "an easy fuck") or a despicable person, can be used for either sex, increasingly in recent decades by women for men. But like its synonym (in the first sense of a sex object), *screw*, it is most closely associated with male use for a woman (or for the "passive" partner, whatever the sex). It carries definite masculine connotations; the word can also refer to sexual vigor in men. "To get fucked" is an expression that mixes meanings of sexuality with conquest and debasement. In our culture, the female (or "passive" gay male) is viewed as the recipient of the action (the conquered); the male is expected to be the active doer (the conqueror). *Fuckable* usually describes a woman—one seen as sexually attractive and approachable (synonyms include *punchable* and *bedworthy*); *fuck freak* refers to a woman disparaged as a

nymphomaniac. Further, the fact that the same term can be applied to either a despicable person or a sex partner, and to both conquest and debasement, reflects on our—many would say *men's*—ambivalence toward sex and probably also our fear of it.

It is also known, among many other disguises, as the "F-word."

See also COCK, GENDER BENDER (gender fucker), GROUPIE (celebrity fucker), MOTHERFUCKER, PRICK, PROMISCUOUS, SCREWBOY, SON OF A BITCH.

fuddy-duddy; **fud**. *Fuddy-duddy*, a person, often a man, viewed as prissy, stodgy, or a foolish old person or one who is old-fashioned; often constructed as *old fuddy-duddy*. It was in use throughout the twentieth century, though its origins are unknown. *Fud*, having the same meaning, is probably a shortening of *fuddy-duddy*, but likely influenced by the character in Bugs Bunny cartoons named Elmer Fudd. It may also designate an EFFEMINATE man, especially one who is meticulous or conservative. Also *fug, fuddy-dud, fuddie-duddie*.

See also FOGY, FRUMP, OLD FART.

fudgepacker. Alluding to the color of excrement, a vulgar and derisive slang term, spoken largely by heterosexuals, meaning a gay man, especially an anal sodomist; of fairly recent coinage (1980s). Related slang terms are *Mr. Brown, brownie hound*, and *turd burglar.*

See also ASS (ass bandit), BUFU, BUGGER, BUNNY (chocolate bunny), HERSHEY BAR, SODOMY.

full moon. See CURSE.

funbag. See BAG.

funny. In the sense of peculiar, odd, or suspiciously different, a usage from the mid-twentieth century describing an effeminate or gay man. It is a kind of "polite" version of the derisive *queer*, but it sees less use today than in previous decades.

See also ODD, QUEER.

furburger. See MEAT.

futz. A slang word for a man viewed as repulsive, often an old one. From the early
twentieth century. It may be constructed
as "old futz."

See also BUZZARD, JACKAL.

F-word. See FEMINISM, FEMINIST, FUCKER.

G

gab; gabby. *Gab,* a verb meaning to talk fast and without thought to what one is saying, often considered something that women do; *gabby,* an adjective meaning talkative, also often stereotypical of women. A "gabfest," a gathering where there is a lot of conversation, is something that many are likely to believe that women indulge in. Talkativeness—"the gift for gab"—is a stereotypical attribute of women but one that Spender (1980, 106–37) claims is demonstrably not characteristic of women. It is men, she insists, who talk more, and male dominance is threatened when women are given free voice. Spender argues that men exercise intimidation to ensure that women's talk does not undermine male primacy, and when that fails, attempt to discredit what women have to say. *Gab* is only one of the dismissive terms that men can use to discount women's talk; others include *babble, bitch, cackle, chatter,* NAG, *natter, prattle,* and *whine* (note that a few of these words are also applied to children, whose "nature" women are sometimes assumed to share). For another perspective on how women use language, see Deborah Tannen's *You Just Don't Understand: Women and Men in Conversation* (1990).

Both *gab* and *gabby* are occasionally applied to old men, who are sometimes lumped with women, and both words tend to trivialize. George "Gabby" Hayes, the 1940s Western movies character actor, could jaw with the best of them. The actor Walter Brennan also often played gabby old men.

See also BIDDY, FLIBBERTIGIBBET, GOSSIP, SEEN BUT NOT HEARD, YENTA.

gaffer. One's father (a British contraction of *godfather* or *grandfather*) or simply an old man. Whatever its original intention of conveying respect, perhaps when society valued older people, the epithet has now taken a slide into moderate disparagement of an aged man. Also used to mean a boss.

See also BADGER, BUZZARD, CODGER, COOT, CUSS, DUFFER, FOGY, FUDDY-DUDDY, GEEZER, OLD FART.

gal. An informal usage for a girl or woman. *Gal* first appeared in the mid- to late-eighteenth century and became current slang in the twentieth. *The Oxford English Dictionary* (1989) describes it as a "vulgar or dialectal pronunciation of *girl.*" This colloquialism is sometimes also described as "lighthearted," although it was used euphemistically for a prostitute in the nineteenth century. "What a gal" may still be heard among older people for a woman regarded as someone special, both beautiful and intelligent.

Somewhat dated since the late 1960s, the word has become objectionable to many women. It is considered the female equivalent of *guy,* but as an informal variation of *girl,* which indicates youth and immaturity, it lacks the more positive connotations of *guy. Gal* was also once used as a verb to mean to look for a woman (go courting).

Gal Friday (or *girl Friday*) refers to a woman who serves as an assistant or helper, usually in an office. The expression comes from *Robinson Crusoe,* Daniel Defoe's 1719 novel in which the faithful servant to Defoe on his desert island is named Friday. The male counterpart, *man Friday,* employs the more dignified *man* rather than *boy.*

Gal-boy (sometimes *girl-boy*) is slang for a woman regarded as masculine or for a gay male youth having a sexual relationship with an older man (see also HE-SHE). Major (1994) gives *gal officer* as a black Harlem pejorative meaning HARPY or LESBIAN (see also SERGEANT). *Gayl,* from a blend of *gay* and *gal* (and sounding like *Gail*), is a positive slang coinage heard probably only among lesbians.

See also GIRL, GUY, LADY.

Gal is also used among men in the disparaging sense of a "sissy" or "faggot": "We got us two gals on our patrol" (reference to two soldiers who resisted their sergeant's command to rape a Vietnamese woman, in Brian De Palma's 1989 film, *Casualties of War*).

See also EFFEMINATE, FAGGOT, SISSY.

game. See HUNTER, QUAIL (game hen).

gander. See BIRD.

gangbang. See RAPE.

gangster girl. A woman regarded as unattractive. This meaning is very different from *gangster,* which is usually linked with men and refers to a member of a criminal gang or a mobster (see also CRIMINALS).

See also COOLER, COYOTE, DOG, HOGGER, LOBO, LOOKSISM, PIG, SCUD, SKAG, YETI.

gash. A term first appearing in the eighteenth century to mean vulva and used throughout most of the twentieth century by men for a woman (or women collectively) as a sex partner (object) or prostitute and for a man's enjoyment of the sex act with a woman. Usually considered vulgar, if not violent, it is highly depersonalizing of women, reducing them to genital tissue. It is consistent with Freud's idea of women's genitals as a "wound." Freud wrote, for example, of a young boy being frightened at his first knowledge of the vagina and regarding any traces of blood that he might find on his mother's bed as a sign that his father has injured her (Freud 1966, 317–19). Today, *gash* is found in rap lyrics meaning girlfriend, though many listeners will still hear the blatant sexual connotations.

Gash may also be applied to a male homosexual youth, especially one said to take the "passive" role. *Gash-hound*

is applied to a man who seeks out women for sex, that is, a lecher. *Slit* may be synonymous with *gash.*

See also ASS, BOX, COO, COOZIE, CRACK, CUNT, GINCH, NOOKY, PUSS.

gay. A term used for and by someone who self-identifies as a homosexual, especially a male. It has known a long history of semantic change and having more than one meaning at a time.

Gay, meaning merry or lively in mood, is clearly adopted from the Old French *gai,* high-spirited, mirthful. It does not derive from the Old High German *gahi* (impetuous), as is sometimes claimed. Uses for women were among the earliest. Up until the early twentieth century, *gay girl* or simply *gay* (originally applied to any young female and later a self-referential term for a lesbian) had been in use for a female prostitute or a woman conventionally regarded as morally degraded. *Gay ladies* and *gay bit* were also nineteenth-century slang usages meaning a female prostitute.

Gay dogs and *gay Lotharios* were terms applied to men considered dissipated. These senses may have arisen from the close interaction—or lumping together in the imagination—of gay men and female prostitutes in the nineteenth century, both groups being marginalized people who shared a common slang. The early-twentieth-century underworld expression *gaycat* (a tenderfoot, boy tramp, or errand boy for a gang of criminals) suggested homosexuality, since *gaycat* referred to a young man who bonded with an older, more experienced hobo or vagrant in a relationship that might sometimes have involved sexual activity.

Gay, with homosexual connotations, was entered in *Underworld and Prison Slang* in 1935, the first dictionary that treated it. However, *gaycat* (homosexual boy) had appeared two years earlier in Noel Ersine's *Dictionary of Underworld*

Slang. At least a decade before that, *gay boy* had appeared in slang use, first in Australia, for a male homosexual (see also BOY).

The gay and lesbian community adopted *gay* as a code word, using it among and for themselves with an apparent sense of irony and self-satirization, given the word's dubious slang background. As code, it thus became a linguistic stratagem for keeping "the gay world hidden from the straight while rendering it visible to the gay" (Chauncey 1994, 24). Chauncey notes, however, that originally *gay* did not mean simply homosexual, referring to a sexual object choice. Rather, it referred to gendered behavior associated with gay life, especially flamboyance in dress and speech (17). An early public reference to the word in this behavioral sense occurred in the 1938 screwball comedy *Bringing Up Baby*, in which Cary Grant, playing a forgetful zoologist who finds himself donning a negligee, exclaims that he's "gone gay."

The decades of the 1930s and 1940s saw the term gaining popularity in homosexual communities, especially among a younger generation of men who increasingly regarded *queer* as disparaging. Chauncey claims *gay* was a hip term among New Yorkers a full decade before gay liberation brought it to the general public (20). Recording linguistic change in these decades, novelist Gore Vidal observed that "The words 'fairy' and 'pansy' were considered to be in bad taste. They preferred to say that a man was 'gay,' while someone quite effeminate was a 'queen'" (*The City and the Pillar*, [1948] 1965, 156). *Gay* was current in the theatrical world in the 1960s, by which time it had acquired the status of a euphemism.

Less formal than *homosexual,* lacking that word's medical and psychological tones, and one of the few words in the lexicon of male homosexuality that did not link gay identity explicitly with sexual activity (as opposed to affectional and cultural preference), *gay* caught on around the 1970s. Many men (and women, too) adopted the term as one that helped them to declare their self-respect and to "come out." By the 1980s it had become widespread in both the gay and straight communities, used broadly to refer to all men engaged in some form of homosexual activity, although the media continued to ban the use of the word, except in names of organizations or in quotations, until well into the 1980s. Some gay men, too, especially activists, resisted applying the term to a conservative or apolitical homosexual, while others continued for some time to complain that its use as a noun (*gay* was introduced into the gay community as an adjective) implied that sexual identity is fixed and the totality of what a person is. This latter objection no longer seems to be much of an issue.

As the term gained currency in the 1970s, heterosexuals and some gay men complained. Heterosexuals thought it implied that heterosexuals were dreary, but more commonly they complained that it preempted the more common, festive sense of *gay*, "having high spirits." Thus, it seemed impossible to say "I'm having a gay old time" any longer without suggesting that the speaker was gay, or to live on a street called "gay" without some embarrassment on the part of the straight residents. Fowler (1996) quotes Paul Johnson to illustrate some of the heterosexual opposition (note the "we-they" attitude): "There is no historical case for homosexual ownership of 'gay.' So can we have our word back please?" Similarly, historian-speechwriter Arthur Schlesinger Jr. once complained, " 'Gay' used to be one of the most agreeable words in the language. Its appropriation by a notably morose group is an act of piracy" (*Unnatural Quotations,* Leigh Rutledge, 1988). Schlesinger's assumption is that the dominant group "possesses" words, which can be pirated by "unsavory" groups.

Unfortunately, not homosexuals but heterosexuals—specifically, homophobes—have been the ones to pack the term with bias. By using it to call men's masculinity and morality into question, they have made the term seem inappropriate for other uses. They have even rendered it troublesome for themselves, as suggested by the use in some contexts of the evasive "g word." But language is flexible, words susceptible to many colorings, and no one "owns" them. As Dynes (1990) points out, many words in English have more than one distinct meaning, and that generally gives us no trouble.

Some dissatisfaction has also been expressed with the term because it may still suggest lightheartedness, as when it is spelled like the French word *gai* (merry, jolly) or heard in the black English expression *gaycat* (to have a good time). To some gay men, especially in the 1970s, these were inappropriate meanings to attach to a serious political movement. But most opposition to the word within gay communities arose from an older generation of men who had been taught not to rock the boat with cries of "gay power" or "gay rights."

The use of *gay* has also reflected some division between gay men and lesbians. In the early 1970s, with the rise of the gay liberation (or gay lib) movement, those lesbians who identified with gay activism tended to call themselves gay women; those who aligned with the women's movement preferred to see themselves as lesbian women. This distinction, however, did not last, as lesbians began to set their own agendas and develop their own identities separate from gay liberation. Today, while *gay* often refers to female as well as male homosexuals, there are many references to gay and lesbian or lesbian and gay;

lesbians (who may prefer *lesbian* to *gay*) may give their allegiance to both terms.

Gayola is often a disparaging epithet for a homosexual, but it may also refer to bribery, extortion, and blackmail paid by gay men or businesses to police in order to protect themselves and their investments. *Gay-bashing* means the harassment of gays and lesbians because of their sexual orientation.

See also ALTERNATIVE LIFESTYLE, BOY (gayboy), FEY, FRIEND OF DOROTHY'S, GAY AGENDA, GAY PLAGUE, GAY POWER, HOMOSEXUAL, LESBIAN, LESBIGAY, LOTHARIO, QUEER.

gay agenda; special rights. *Gay agenda,* a loaded term implying a definite, political program on the part of gay people. In a community as diverse as that of the combined lesbian and gay population, there is no single political agenda, nor is there a movement toward having any kind of "special" rights or control over heterosexuals.

Gay and lesbian activists and advocates seek an end to homophobia, discrimination, and hostility against all people on the basis of sexual orientation. They promote the inclusion of sexual orientation provisions in all those laws that now bar discrimination on grounds of race, creed, gender, national origin, and disability in private employment, public accommodation, housing, and access to credit and insurance. But to call these efforts at claiming equal rights or basic civil rights with all other citizens of the United States "special" rights or a "gay agenda" is to slant the argument against the gay population. "[Police officer] Gallardo called the one-hour [homophobia] class 'worthless,' an attack on Christians, and a push to influence police with 'the homosexual agenda'" (P. J. Engelbrecht, *Outlines,* 23 December 1998). Such opinions make gay and lesbian people sound as though they want special privileges or more entitlements than the rest of society. *GLAAD Media Guide* (n.d.) says,

> In spite of the right-wing attacks launched against the gay and lesbian movement, accusing us of seeking "special rights" or having a specific "gay agenda," the movement simply seeks the removal of all forms of public and private discrimination that currently exist against us. (25)

What is "special" about any gay issue is that it so often seems problematic to heterosexuals, who may turn it into an attack against gay people. When homophobic people make any gay issue an emotionally charged and politically controversial matter with heightened media coverage, gay and lesbian people are exposed to higher risk of being harassed and physically attacked.

The use of the word *gay* in such terms as *gay agenda* and *gay lifestyle* in antigay arguments may constitute a kind of sly attack on gay people. Because homosexual people self-identify as gay and often prefer the term, the use of *gay* may sound sympathetic and respectful while delivering an underlying message of the alleged unsavoriness of the gay community.

See also GAY, GAY PLAGUE.

gayl. See GAL.

gay lifestyle. See ALTERNATIVE LIFESTYLE.

gay plague; **gay disease**. Fingerpointing and inaccurate terms given to AIDS (acquired immunodeficiency syndrome) since the 1980s as a result of its original and stereotypical association in the United States with gay men. However, as the *GLAAD Media Guide* (n.d.) points out, "AIDS is not a 'gay disease.' It does not discriminate on the basis of age, race, gender, economic status, or sexual orientation. AIDS is a threat to everyone" (29). The expression sometimes also occurs as *gay cancer.*

Throughout the world AIDS has often taken on a highly politicized and discriminatory connotation, tending to attract attention as a feature of groups that are already stigmatized.

See also AIDS, GAY.

gay power. A motto of the 1970s, patterned after *black power,* the motto of the 1960s movement among militant African Americans. Those who made gay power their motto sought freedom from discrimination based on their sexual orientation and demanded the same rights that other U.S. citizens enjoy. In June 1969 the New York City police raided a gay bar, the Stonewall in Greenwich Village, and met resistance from a group of gay men and lesbians. One of the resisters in the crowd outside the bar shouted "Gay Power"; thus began the gay movement. It took a while, however, for the concept of gays as either militant or a legitimate minority to catch on in gay communities.

Also used as a slogan was "Gay is good."

See also GAY, GAY AGENDA.

gazooney. A boy seen as green or inexperienced. Among hobos or in prison, the word has been used in the sense of a young gay male. It may also mean a man believed to be ignorant, odd, or loutish. All senses are from the early twentieth century.

See also BOY, CATAMITE, GUNSEL, PUNK.

geezer. Slang meaning a man considered odd, eccentric, or offensive; a "duffer" or a dull-witted old man. Although originally used mostly for women, *geezer* came to be an epithet aimed at men. It may be an alteration of the Scottish *guiser* (one who wears a disguise, thus a quaint figure) from the late nineteenth century. It is sometimes used among older men for each other but is often considered derogatory and ageist when applied by a stranger or a younger person. At other times it is used affectionately or regarded as colorful. Also spelled *geeser. Geez,* for short.

Geez bag, nearly synonymous with *old fart,* is heard primarily among teenagers. Also heard is the slang expression *old gee,* "fellow." Here, though possibly influenced by *geezer,* the term may be an imitation of the French given name, *Guy,* for a man (Lighter 1994).

See also BADGER, BUZZARD, CODGER, COOT, CUSS, DUFFER, FOGY, GAFFER, GOAT, OLD FART.

gender and sex. Coming ultimately from the Latin *genus* (birth, race, kind), *gender* has long been used to mean a person's sex and was reserved largely for the grammatical categories known as masculine, feminine, and neuter.

Some conservative language users have preferred to restrict it to that latter sense. However, by the 1970s, it was commonly identified with the social division between men and women. As such, it has provided a context for understanding the lives of historical women and men, explaining differences in power relations between them and the legitimization of those relations.

In addition, the concept enables us to question the gender paradigm that marginalizes individuals, such as homosexuals and transsexuals, who cross gender lines.

Although gender is sometimes still used in the sense of the biological category of sex, many social scientists would prefer to make a distinction between sex and gender. In the social sciences, for example, gender denotes not only individual identity and personality but also the cultural symbols and stereotypes of masculinity and femininity and society's sexual division of labor (*The Concise Oxford Dictionary of Sociology* 1994). Gender in this sense is not a given at birth: "One is not born...a woman" (Simone de Beauvoir [1952] 1974, 301). Rather, it varies with time and group, and, as gender theorists such as Martine Rothblatt (1995) contend, there may be as many genders as there are individual human beings.

Although some cultural determinists have even been skeptical of the concept of sex as purely biological, realizing that it, too, is imbued with social meaning, other social scientists refuse to dismiss biology as merely another aspect of social discourse.

The exact meaning of the term and its implications in the social sciences and feminist thought are also surrounded by some disagreement and confusion (Gefou-Madianou and Iossifides 1996). Among the different approaches to gender, the "essentialist" stance, rejected today by many feminists, holds that there is a "woman's nature." This nature is believed to be determined by certain biological constants across cultures. It is presocial, underlies culturally diverse behavior, and is reflected in various social concepts of women and men.

The "constructionist" viewpoint, on the other hand, sees gender differences arising through social interaction and a society's ways of giving meaning to the world. In the United States, to illustrate the now-popular constructionist viewpoint, gender roles manifest themselves as ways of acting, talking, dressing, and communicating identity as well as a form of social control urging individuals to conform to the system of dual gender (men are supposed to do one thing; women another) characteristic of U.S. society. Far from being "natural," such behavioral attributes as female nurturance and male aggression are created out of social pressures and learning and are internalized in a process called "gendering" (Oakley 1972). They are not universals. In *Sex and Temperament* ([1935] 1963), anthropologist Margaret Mead noted that children in our society are pressed into gender conformity by invoking gender as the reason a child should prefer pants to skirts or dolls to baseball bats—"Girls don't do that," or "Don't you want to grow up to be a real man like Daddy?"—and in the process often inducing fears in children that they may not belong to their assigned gender at all. In other societies that Mead studied, however, without a rigid gender dichotomy, adults invoke considerations of behavior as socially defined—"Don't behave like that; people don't do that"—rather than gender-determined conduct.

Many theorists have challenged the assumption that biology shapes gender, a view that tends to imply that women are born with attributes that incline them to subordination, while men tend to be dominant. At the same time, constructionism, which promises to free women and men from the constraints placed on them by gender systems if social institutions can be changed, has had to tackle the problem of the apparent existence of women's subordination to men across many cultures. Such a cultural constant would not be expected in the absence of biological constants.

Numerous ideas other than biology have been proposed to explain female subordination. Briefly, they include male control of language (Spender 1980), technology, and worldviews; economic relations, including the sexual division of labor; the role of biological reproduction and mothering in women's lives and the social assignment of women to the domestic sphere; and the association of women with matters carrying less prestige than men's affairs.

In spite of this long-standing concern with gender inequality, more recent work has debunked the notion of the universality of such inequality. Women, even in the same society, have many different experiences of sexism and oppression. Both male and female gender roles must be understood in terms of different races, classes, ethnicities, ages, nationalities, physical abilities, and other specific contexts, not to mention individual differences. In dealing with the ideas of equality and subordination, we are also cautioned by anthropologists that these Euro-American constructs can bias our depictions of the position of women and the relation between the sexes in other cultures.

As mentioned, also challenged has been the popular stance that so-called sexual categories—male and female—are biological. Foucault's work (1978) describes sex as a historically Western category, and Laqueur (1990) has shown how the Euro-American model of two sexes is a fairly recent invention. Women were thought to be inverted men in a one-sex model that was part of Western culture for centuries. In so-called poststructuralist perspectives, sex, rather than describing biological differences, is a social idea exploited to justify women's subordination. Still, while we may be able to speak of what sex is only in any particular society, sex and gender remain central analytical categories in many social and psychological studies.

Neuter gender, or just *neuter,* was a heterosexual colloquialism referring to a gay man, implying that he had no gender.

See also ANDROGYNY (gender role transcendence), BERDACHE (circle of gender), FEMININE, GENDER BENDER, GENDER-SPECIFIC ADJECTIVES, HETEROSEXISM, HOMOPHOBIA, MASCULINE, OPPOSITE SEX, OPPRESSION, SEXIST, SEXUAL PREFERENCE, TRANSGENDERIST.

gender bender; **gender blender**; **gender fuck**. *Gender bender,* in technical language, a piece of equipment for changing electrical plugs to the opposite (electrical) gender (also, *gender changer*). Informally, and from the early 1980s, it is a rhyming, somewhat emotive though usually nonpejorative word for a person who dares to cross the gender boundary, thus "bending" the rules of how males or females are to act, look, and dress. "You can only be considered gender-bent in a society that is gender-rigid" (Feinberg 1996, 97).

Gender bender has appeared in journalistic writing in reference to androgynous rock performers such as David Bowie, Boy George, Michael Jackson, and Madonna, but also, for example, to Milton Berle and Flip Wilson, who built their comedy careers in part by appearing in drag on stage, and to transgendered or even gay people in general. The term is also used to describe any situation in which what is normally expected of one sex has been changed or reversed. For instance, in 1997, when the National Basketball Association hired two female referees, the alteration in the all-male status quo in basketball refereeing was referred to in the news as "gender-bending."

Gender blender, first used in the 1980s, is similar in meaning to *gender bender* but implies a less forceful playing with the rules, as by mixing the elements of gender: a woman wearing a tie, a rock performer adopting a cross-gender name, or women's lingerie modeled after men's underwear.

The deliberately more vulgar and hostile but also playful *gender fuck* denotes the act of mixing male and female attire, usually for the purpose of creating a sense of discord and absurdity. The person who does it is called a *gender fucker.* In San Francisco the term appeared around 1969, used primarily in reference to people who were politically militant sexual liberationists and to people who did street theater. By 1970 the first explicit gender-fuck group, the Cockettes, arose from the Haight-Ashbury neighborhood. After the fashion of "gender fucking," a man may perform on stage wearing combat boots and a miniskirt or a tutu and a motorcycle jacket. The term is still in use today.

See also ANDROGYNY, CROSS-DRESSER, DRAG, GENDER AND SEX, HE-SHE, HIM-HER, OPPOSITE SEX, SHE-HE, TRANSGENDERIST, TRANSSEXUAL.

gender dysphoria. See TRANSSEXUAL.

gender-specific adjectives. Modifiers in English that are sometimes totally or at least partially gender-linked. Such usages perpetuate gender stereotypes, working to naturalize "masculine" and "feminine" traits as biologically based and determined. However commonly used and seemingly innocuous some appear to be, they set up a framework of thinking that fosters the disparagement and exclusion of one gender or the other. Most of the following examples (hardly exhaustive of these adjectives) are biased against women, but there is bias here against men as well.

Aggressive. Because men have traditionally been held to such expectations (and burdens) as breadwinning, competing in sports, and soldiering, we have come to associate the male and the male role with aggressiveness. There is a large body of lore and pseudoscientific literature explaining and rationalizing aggression in males. The male has also been ascribed the social and economic independence and leverage to earn the descriptor *aggressive,* usually without its being a put-down. In fact, it may be considered a compliment: "real men" stand up for themselves, fight when deemed necessary, and learn to "make moves" on women. Such behavior may be so expected that it is not even commented on, whereas an aggressive woman is suspect in more than one way. A woman called aggressive is still believed by many to have an unfeminine taint and may be disparaged as pushy or uppity (see also *pushy* and *uppity,* below). *Aggressive* may also be a code word among men for a lesbian or a feminist, suggesting an unacceptable nonconformity to the conventional rules of being feminine. A man is disparaged only if he lacks aggressiveness, in which case he may be called a "milksop," "milquetoast," "pansy," or "wimp." Despite our culture's notions of who has the right to behave aggressively, anthropology has indicated that whether it is men or women depends on the culture (Mead [1949] 1975). See also PASSIVE.

Barren. A woman unable to become pregnant has traditionally been stigmatized as "barren," as though only she and never the husband is responsible for the infertility. As the source of reproduction in any society, women are enjoined to be fertile: "Be fruitful and multiply," in the words of God in Genesis. Barrenness is often regarded as a curse; in some cultures a woman is believed to be punished with barrenness for her sins. Compare with FRIGID.

Blowsy. The English dialectal word *blowse* meant a wench, and this term, describing slovenly or frowsy appearance, is more often applied to a woman than to a man. See also *dowdy,* below; SLATTERN.

Calculating female. This stereotype is used against women to mean tricky or conniving, as a GOLD DIGGER, for example, is believed to be. See COQUETTE for a quotation.

Chaste. This adjective, meaning pure in one's thoughts and desires and innocent of sexual relations, may be used of men but often still conjures an image of female virgins and innocent maidens. Chastity appears to have long been considered a female virtue and a condition forced on women; it was women, not men, who wore the chastity belt. See also STRAIGHT.

Cheap. Applied to a woman, *cheap* describes her supposed sexual promiscuity. Applied to a man, it indicates an unwillingness to provide for or escort a woman without concern for financial cost. See also CHIPPY.

Coy. Women who are described as coy are viewed as cute and coquettish, especially those who affect modesty or shyness in order to gain attention.

Cute. A woman considered attractive, especially in a dainty or pretty way, is often referred to as "cute." Typically a woman's word, this adjective is used for other women, for some men, or for small, cuddly creatures (see also LITTLE WOMAN). "A cute number," usually reserved for a young woman, connotes a sexually attractive woman, especially in an impersonal or casual relationship (she may be someone a man ogles before picking up). When it means impertinent or smart-alecky, it may be applied to either sex. The noun *cutie,* for a charmingly attractive person, is more often used for women than for men. "[Anna] Kournikova, who is well on her way to becoming the most marketable female athlete in history, is different from all the other cuties" (*Details,* July 1998, 138).

As Beneke (1997) points out, men, more often than women, may refer sarcastically to other men's actions as "cute." Here it is applied in the sense of "clever, but incompetent," a way of denigrating other men (42).

Dowdy. A dowdy woman is one who is not tidy or tasteful in her dress or who gives the appearance of being old-fashioned. The word reflects the emphasis the culture places on women's looks. See also *blowsy,* above.

Frail. See FRAIL.

Giddy. Meaning frivolous, impulsive, or flighty, this adjective has been in common use for women, but it has also, in gay communities, taken on the meaning of "gay."

Hot. See HOT.

Impulsive. A man may be called *impulsive,* though this word is somewhat more likely to be reserved for a woman; rather than referred to as impulsive, the man is more likely to "think on his feet."

Little. See LITTLE LADY, LITTLE SHIT, LITTLE WOMAN, MAMA (little mama).

Mannish. See MANNISH.

Perky. A woman who typically exudes self-confidence and has a briskly cheerful air about her is sometimes called "perky." We also hear it used to describe a woman's body parts—"perky breasts."

Pretty. See BOY (pretty boy), MAMA (pretty mama).

Profligate. Usually applied to men, *profligate* labels those seen as licentious and self-indulgent.

Pushy. This unflattering term may still be used more for women than for men. See also *aggressive,* above.

Randy. This adjective does not derive from the man's given name but from the obsolete *rand* (to rant), and it means lecherous or lustful, an adjective commonly reserved for men.

Ravishing. Virtually never used for a man, this adjective means strikingly attractive. "Ravishing in red, [Princess] Diana wowed the crowd" (*National Enquirer,* 8 September 1998, 24). The verb *ravish* implies a forceful action of seizure. See also BOMBSHELL.

Saucy. Meaning impudent or forward, *saucy* is largely restricted to young women.

Scatterbrained. This label, meaning flighty, thoughtless, and incapable of focusing, usually describes women. Such actresses as Judy Holliday often played "scatterbrained" women with good hearts. See also DITZ, DUMB DORA, SPACE GIRL.

Shapely. This adjective, meaning having a pleasing body shape, is almost always said of women. There are many other body-oriented adjectives that are also female-linked, such as *voluptuous* and *curvy* or *curvaceous.*

Straitlaced. See PRUDE.

Strident. See FEMINISM.

Sweet. See MAMA (sweet mama), SWEET, SWEET MEAT.

Uppity. *Uppity* usually refers to a black person, often a man, who appears self-important or puts on airs, but it can also be applied to other marginalized groups, including women. "[First Lady] Hillary Clinton's experience graphically demonstrates the risks facing 'uppity women' who become associated with feminism" (in Rhode 1997, 89).

Vivacious. A vivacious woman is one who is considered lively or spirited. Being an animated speaker or an outgoing hostess has traditionally been a valued characteristic of women in our society. Referring to a man as a vivacious man may sound incongruous to some speakers, although there is no reason that it should.

See also GENDER AND SEX.

gentler sex. See WEAKER VESSEL.

gigolo. A term for a man kept by a woman, usually in exchange for his personal and sexual attentions; a paid male escort; or a pimp. The word derives from the French *gigolette,* meaning a female prostitute or dance-hall girl. Since its appearance in 1922, it has carried disparaging connotations from association with a role conventionally regarded as a female one. In the 1980 movie *American Gigolo,* Richard Gere gave his version of a male prostitute. See FAG HAG for an illustrative quotation.

See also GOLD DIGGER, HUSTLER, LOUNGE LIZARD, MACK, MISTRESS, PIMP, PROSTITUTE, TOYBOY.

ginch. Since the 1930s a derogatory word for a woman, especially one sought by men solely for sexual gratification; also refers to copulation with a woman or to the female pudenda. The origin of the term is not known, but it appears to be heard largely among motorcyclists. It has also been used for an effeminate gay man.

See also ASS, BOX, COO, COOZIE, CRANK, CUNT, GASH, NOOKY, PUSS.

girl; girlie. *Girl,* from Middle English *gurle,* a term used throughout the thirteenth century and up until about the fifteenth century for a young person of either sex. Boys were a kind of girl; more specifically, they were *knaves* or *knave girls,* while young females were known as *gay girls.* In the fifteenth century, *girl* came to mean a female young person, especially a young unmarried woman. This was the beginning of the term's use in its many new, often off-color senses. During the seventeenth and eighteenth centuries, it was also used to designate a serving girl (i.e., low class but unmarried and thus supposedly virginal, as *girl* implies). Later still, it came to mean a prostitute—commonly known now as a working girl, *call girl*, or MISTRESS— among other senses, usually suggesting someone who services a man (all connotations of virginity are lost in this use).

In the informal sense of any woman, regardless of age, *girl* takes on its more current overtones. When writer Dorothy Parker coined the couplet, "Men seldom make passes/at girls who wear glasses" or when F. Scott Fitzgerald wrote to his daughter, "A great social success is a pretty girl who plays her cards as carefully as if she were plain," they were not talking about preteen female children. Recent opposition to the term in this sense focuses on the term's undesirable connotations of childlikeness, dependence, and inferiority. Whereas *girl* has commonly denoted a female of almost any age, *boy*, with some exceptions (see BOY), is more clearly restricted to young males. Feminist protest of the usage mounted in the 1970s, with female office workers, in particular, objecting to being called "girl" by their male bosses, who were often younger than they were. In the following decades, the use of *girl* for an adult female declined.

In some contexts, the use of *girl* removes the sexual connotations of *woman*. It stresses youth, which may seem flattering, but it also evokes frivolity and immaturity. A girl is not to be entrusted with important decisions; a girl is not to be taken seriously. Men competing with women for jobs have been able to subtly diminish them by tagging them as "girls."

The asymmetries of the language abound when we look at words formed with *girl*. *G-girl*, for example, was used in the 1930s for a woman employed by the federal government, while a male employee, specifically of the Federal Bureau of Investigation, was called a *G-man*. *Bar girl* (also *b-girl*) often referred to a prostitute, while *bar boy* has the very different meaning of a man who tends bar. *Schoolgirl*, stereotyped, for example, as frivolous and a crybaby, is not symmetrical with *schoolboy*, which may connote immaturity or prankishness but is also used for a young man whose education may be taken more seriously than his sister's. A "career girl" (largely ceded today to *career woman*) and a "career man" are both seen as professionals, but the language tells us who is believed to be more important (*career man* is not in common use, being restricted largely to government service). *Les girls*—there appears to be no male equivalent—ironically combines the English *girls* with the French plural article, suggesting either women as sex objects or women seeking male attention. Although men can do quite well without it, women still seem to need a euphemism for a lavatory, such as "little girls' room" or "rest room." There is probably no popular expression as diminishing to men as "diamonds are a girl's best friend" is to women (the phrase comes from the song popularized by such diverse performers as Carol Channing, Marilyn Monroe, and Pearl Bailey).

Girl Friday (see also GAL) is a name for a woman who serves as an assistant or helper, usually in an office. The expression comes from *Robinson Crusoe*, Daniel Defoe's 1719 novel in which the faithful servant to Defoe on his desert island is named Friday. The male counterpart is *man Friday,* using the more dignified *man* rather than *boy* (see also MAN FRIDAY).

Fowler (1996) argues that still remaining largely unchallenged are such usages as *girlfriend* used by a woman for an intimate female friend (though men seldom call their male buddies "boyfriends") and *single girl.* Also still common, says Fowler, is *glamour girl* (such as a beautiful female model or movie star) and *cover girl* (a model, specifically a woman featured on the cover of a magazine).

Nevertheless, these words may be questionable, at least in certain contexts. For example, *girlfriend* is sometimes used by men to deride a man seen as effeminate. *Single girl* has no *single boy* counterpart (we say *single man* or *guy*); and *glamour* (or *glamor*) and *cover girl* indicate women considered desirable to look at, that is, sex objects (see also LOOKSISM, SEX OBJECT). In addition, besides its sense of a woman featured on a magazine cover, *cover girl* can refer to an attractive young woman sitting in the front seat of a car; truck drivers use the term to notify other drivers by radio that they are nearing the woman (Spears 1991). Finally, the male counterpart to *glamour girl*—*glamour boy*—suggests vanity and shallowness, taking on its derision through association with so-called womanly attributes. There are no real male equivalents for *showgirl*, *go-go girl*, *calendar girl,* and *working girl.*

Pinup girl became popular during World War II. U.S. soldiers, sailors, marines, and pilots hung up photographs of their favorite actresses—especially popular were Dorothy Lamour, Betty Grable, and Rita Hayworth—in their barracks and lockers and in bars around the world. A photo of Rita Hayworth was said to have been taped to the atomic bomb dropped on Hiroshima in 1945. *Sweater girl*, originally used in the 1940s by Hollywood press agents for a young woman whose upper-body shapeliness was enhanced by a sweater (Lana Turner was dubbed the "Sweater Girl"), was revived in the 1990s among teenagers (see also SKIRT).

Girl is also used for a boy or man to censure what may be regarded as inappropriately feminine or soft behavior. "Army drill sergeants in the early '90s still humiliated lagging male recruits by calling them 'girls'" (Linda Bird Francke, "In the Company of Wolves," *Time*, 2 June 1997, 38). "You throw [or run] like a girl" is a young boy's taunt hurled at boys (or girls) who manifest what men often stereotype as a lack of athleticism associated with a girl. Like *girlfriend, girl-boy,* and *gal-boy* are derogatory references to a feminine boy or young gay man (see also EFFEMINATE, HE-SHE). *Girl* has also been used in the drug subculture for cocaine, perhaps because it is believed to "serve" the user or, more likely, because it supplies a sexual charge upon use.

A "daddy's girl" is a nice girl (sometimes, a grown woman) who is accommodating to her father, who pleases him as he does her, and who may even be said (at least in some psychological quarters) to have a "romantic" attachment to her father. *Daddy's girl* carries positive connotations compared with *mama's boy*, probably because a girl is expected to learn how to be attractive to a man (starting with her father), while the boy is taught to scorn things feminine.

All these negative and biased uses notwithstanding, *girl,* especially when used by women for other women, may carry no derogatory meaning outside the context of childhood. It has commonly been used among women to signal camaraderie and strength. Beginning in the 1990s, it was popular, especially among younger women, viewed as a "word-with-attitude," as in such expressions as "You go, girl," and "Hey, girlfriend." The Spice Girls ("girl-power" singing group), Tank Girl (a comic-book heroine who refuses to accept conventional femininity and stands up to male opponents), quake girls (female computer gamers who compete aggressively in male action games), and Riot Grrrls (who embrace female empowerment though participating in such traditionally male activities as motorcycle racing) have all given the word "attitude plus." The *grrrl* in *Riot Grrrl*, whose coining is often attributed to punk band singer Kathleen Hannah, "is meant to subvert the image of girlhood innocence and evoke an angry grrrowl" (*Periodical Abstracts,* 1997, 7).

Much of this positive use of *girl* has been influenced by black English. Among African American women, regardless of age, *girl* has been used reciprocally and affectionately since the 1930s for another woman. It may be used by black men, too, but not necessarily with the same affection. Used for a black woman by someone other than a black person, however, the term might still be taken as racist, since it was used for African American women, especially those under forty years of age, as part of the code of race relations in the Old South (see also AUNT, BOY).

Girlie, a nineteenth-century affectionate designation for very young girls, has been applied since the 1920s to magazines, movies, and other related entertainment featuring young women in the nude or partial dress.

> Many customers became aware of the full variety of the merchandise,...eventually getting to know the counter clerks well enough to gain flipping privileges with the girlie magazines without having to buy one. (Talese 1980, 69)

Girlish, meaning being like a girl, says very little that is positive about whoever is referred to. It may mean many different things, though it is largely associated with immaturity. *Girl kisser* is directed at lesbians (see also LADY LOVER).

See also BUSINESS GIRL, CALL BOY (call girl), CHICK, CUNT (charity girl), FLY (flygirl), GOOD OL' BOY (good old girl), GOS-SIP (girl talk), HAREM (harem girl), LADY, OLD BOY (old girl), PARTY GIRL, PLAYBOY (playgirl), PRISSY (girly-girl), SPACE GIRL, SPICE, TOMBOY, WENCH, WOMAN.

girl talk. See GOSSIP.

glacial. See FRIGID.

gladiola. A flower metaphor that may be considered disparaging, suggesting weakness and effeminacy when directed at a man.

See also BUTTERCUP, DAFFODIL, DAISY, EFFEMINATE, FLOWER, LILY, PANSY, VIOLET.

goat. A usually degrading, though sometimes semiaffectionate, animal metaphor for a man counted as lewd or lecherous or as an unpleasant old man. The latter sense is a twentieth-century usage; the former sense is much older, dating from the sixteenth century. In either case the word is now often used with *old,* usually suggesting unlikability or a mild character flaw or sometimes a fool. "We all love Hugh Hefner, that old geriatric goat, rutting his way through the nightclubs at an age when he should be showing his grandkids how to make paper hats" (Neil Steinberg, *Chicago Sun-Times,* 13 September 1998, 18A). Only sometimes is a woman a goat. In the nineteenth century, however, *goatmilker* was used for a prostitute.

The goat as a symbol of lust and lechery and as an element of devil lore is ancient. According to English and Scots folklore, a goat couldn't be seen at a certain time of the day because it was visiting the devil to have its beard combed. The devil has also been portrayed as a goat or with the cloven feet of a goat. "To separate the sheep from the goats" derives from the Bible, Matthew 25: 32–33, in which the good (sheep) are parted from the evil (goats).

Goat is also slang for body odor. *Goatish* means sexually aroused.

See also BADGER, BILLY GOAT, BUZZARD, COOT, CUSS, DUFFER, FOGY, GAFFER, GEEZER, LECHER, OLD FART, RAKE.

God. The supreme or transcendent being and ultimate reality. The word derives from Old English and is akin to Old High German *Gott*, "God."

It is no surprise, given the cultural emphasis on masculine principles throughout much of Hebrew and Western history, that the Judeo-Christian God is depicted in terms of male symbols and metaphors, with Sunday-school pictures of God as king sitting on His throne in heaven. This conceptualization of "God-He" overrides theologians' claims that God is androgynous and spiritual (John 4:24: "God is spirit"), the fact that Spirit is female in Hebrew, and the use of some feminine metaphors in the Bible to depict God (e.g., God as a nursing mother or a mother bear). Whereas mystical traditions have found God to be indescribable, a God who was completely transcendent would have no relation to people, and we could have no name or image for such a God. So we talk about God through analogies derived from human experience—in the case of Western societies, largely *patriarchal* experience.

Although God may be viewed as having "feminine" attributes, such as compassion and mercy, the male image is strong in the term *God,* as it is also in *Father, Lord,* and *King,* also applied to the deity. For that matter, we see maleness in such biblical metaphors as shepherd, judge, and warrior. Consistent with this is the idea of the "God of the patriarchs," namely, Abraham, Isaac, and Jacob (the Hebrew prophets were men).

A theme running throughout Western religious thought is that men are somehow closer to God than are women, and drawing upon masculine metaphors to depict God lends credence to that notion. In the Genesis story of the Fall, Eve, deposed from her position in earlier mythology as a unified creative force who gave life but also brought death, has been split in function. In the Judeo-Christian account of the origin of humanity (read "man"), God became the creator (the progenitor, or father), and Eve, descended from a goddess, was assigned the role of destroyer of life.

An Inclusive Language Lectionary, a product of the National Council of Churches begun in 1980, uses language that is inclusive of males and females. God is thus referred to as "Sovereign One" instead of "Lord," and "Son of God" is replaced by "Child of God." R. Reuther (in Ashcraft 1998, 295) prefers "Redeemer," "Source of Being," and "Liberator." Many feminists and others view revision as essential to avoid the male-dominated language of the Bible that they see as adding to and perpetuating gender inequality. Feminist theology views sexism as a fundamental manifestation of human sinfulness (Gentz 1986). But others see the revision as an unnecessary and irreverent tampering with the Holy Scripture. Furthermore, as some male-perspective proponents have argued, few object to the depiction of Satan as "Father of Lies" as equally sexist (August 1998, 432). However, Satan, as God's chief enemy and possessor of power over the world and death, is not an image of weakness as are many depictions of women in sexist discourse.

Outside of feminism, certain individuals and religious groups have recognized the feminine side of the Christian God. Thus, for example, the medieval English Christian mystic Julian of Norwich, a woman, spoke of God as Mother. In the eighteenth century, the Shaker Mother Ann Lee (regarded by Shakers as the female incarnation of Christ) and the Shaker people, who established communities in the United States based on the idea of gender equality, referred to God as Mother. In the nineteenth century, Mary Baker Eddy, founder of the church called Christian Science, spoke of the Father-Mother God.

Miller and Swift (1991) write hopefully of a time when women, freeing themselves to reflect on their own experiences and longings, will be able to create "new images and symbols. These will bring into being not a 'feminine' or even a feminist theology, but new, more inclusive ways of describing the indescribable" that will benefit all believers (89).

See also GODDESS, OLD LADY (old man).

goddess. A female deity. The term *goddess* has had different meanings. A goddess may be viewed as a female divinity embodying great powers or as a symbol of the natural order, including life, fertility, birth or creation, death, communitarianism, and wholeness. She may also represent the power and potential of women themselves; worship of the goddess by women today serves to give a dimension to their lives that is simultaneously cosmic and earth-centered.

In certain religions, such as Hinduism and many African religions, she is a focus of worship, while in Western culture she offers a balance to the Judeo-Christian monotheistic emphasis on God. Robert Graves' *The White Goddess* (1948)—about the early European deity who governed birth, love, and death and was the muse of poetry—became a chief source of feminists' quest in the 1970s for some ancient matriarchy. In *The First Sex* Elizabeth Gould Davis (1971) constructed images of goddesses serving in the spiritual life of humans in ancient civilizations. Also, in *The Paradise Papers* (1976) and *Ancient Mirrors of Womanhood* (1979), Merlin Stone looked further into goddess worship and its history, including views of its suppression with the rise of patriarchal religion.

A common belief running throughout much of the work on goddesses is that goddess worship was debased at some point and placed under the shadow of patriarchal sky gods and warring societies, though never completely lost. Not everyone accepts this belief in a primordial Ur-goddess and her following, however. In his critical evaluation of neopagan feminist spirituality, Philip Davis (1998) places the roots of what he calls the Goddess Movement in nineteenth-century radical romanticism.

"The first god was a goddess," wrote E. B. Renaud in 1929, speaking of the Venus of Willendorf, a Paleolithic female figurine. Such female figures have been found throughout the world and from different times; they are used as evidence of the extensiveness of goddess worship before the rise of patriarchy and monotheism. They have often been understood as goddesses, especially mother goddesses, even though they may be depicted realistically and some may have no special female characteristics except for breasts. But such figurines are difficult to interpret, and according to modern archaeologists may not, in at least some instances, represent goddesses at all.

Similarly, visions of past matriarchal societies that ruled in better, more peaceful ways than did men are not archaeologically sound, though they may have served certain feminist agendas. Nelson (1997) notes about the Virgin Mary, "Her statues are ubiquitous where women have little power" (153).

Ancient goddesses are nevertheless still believed to have governed the principles of both life and death, to have enjoyed large powers, and to have controlled their own sexuality. If the goddess was a model for mortal women, then she communicated the need to enjoy rather than constrain and debase a woman's sexuality, since she never played the role of wife but often had many lovers.

As a positive vision of women, however, these images of the ancient goddess have been largely lost in Western views that devalue women's powers and sexuality. For example, Aphrodite, the Greek goddess of love, beauty, and fertility, and the Roman goddess, Venus, have given their names to our language in ways that link women with sexuality. Thus, from *Aphrodite* is derived *aphrodisiac,* arousing sexual desire; and from *Venus* comes *venereal,* referring to infections transmitted through sexual intercourse, and *Venus's curse,* meaning a venereal disease. We have come to adore such female figures not for their strength, courage, or industry, for which we revere the gods, but because of their beauty and charm. The devaluation of *goddess* is seen in such expressions as *sex goddess, love goddess,* and *Hollywood goddess*—all objects that many men accept as untouchable. *African goddess* is a name used by lesbians for an attractive, dark-skinned black woman, connoting eroticism (as does *black goddess*). *Goddess* may also suggest something that is sought and worshiped, such as wealth or fame, the very antithesis of the spiritual values of deity.

See also ANGEL, -ESS, FALLEN WOMAN (Eve), GOD.

God's gift to women. See LADIES' MAN.

goldbrick. From the early twentieth century, a person—usually a man—believed to shirk his work; an idler, loafer, or malingerer, as originally used in the Army. The epithet was also once used in the naval academy for an unattractive or unpleasant young woman (Lighter 1994).

See also BUM, DEADBEAT, TRAMP.

gold digger. A woman who acts as consort to a man in order to marry into his wealth. The term comes originally (1830) from the sense of a person who digs for gold. Figuratively, the gold digger is working a rich vein and staking a claim. "I am not going to leave my fortune to some gold-digging scum who is no better than a whore" (father to his son, in 1999 TV movie *Murder in a Small Town*).

The word carries demeaning connotations, since it stresses a side of a

woman not usually acceptable in our culture: she is utilitarian and realistic, asking not what she can do for her boyfriend or family but "What's in it for me?" Love takes a backseat to money and comfort for this "schemer," as she is known, this emotionless "calculator" who strategizes on how to please a man in order to advance her own purposes. The first issue of *Playboy* carried a lead article called "Miss Gold-Digger of 1953." It sympathized with divorced men forced to pay high alimony. In this sense the term has been in use throughout most of the twentieth century. See also BEAUTY, DOG (dinner hound), GENDER-SPECIFIC ADJECTIVES (calculating).

The term is sometimes also used for a man who wheedles money or other material gain out of a woman. When used for a man, the term suggests something very similar to a gigolo, a role considered inappropriate for a man, traditionally positively stereotyped as the BREADWINNER (see also EASY RIDER, GIGOLO). But men may be more likely to be called fortune hunters, a tag more easily worn than gold diggers.

Also acknowledging mercenary motives, but stressing moral degradation, is *gold digger* in the sense of a prostitute, a somewhat dated usage (see PROSTITUTE).

golden girl. See BLONDE.

good enough to eat. See DISH.

good lay. Typically and originally, a woman regarded as sexually pleasing, that is, a sex object, but also used for a man. Also, any loose woman. This is twentieth-century U.S. slang.

See also EASY LAY, LOOSE, PROMISCUOUS.

good ol' boy; **good old girl**. *Good ol' boy,* a loyal Southern man, often one considered a redneck, or a man in a network that supplies support to the other men in the network. *Good old girl* refers to a Southern woman, often viewed as crude in manner or from the working class, or a woman in a network that supplies support to the other women in the group. Although it sounds parallel, it is more of a parody of *good ol' boy.* "The group [Digital Dames, a support network of female executives] was started a year ago by Christine Comaford, CEO of PlanetU, who deliberately set out to start an old girls network" (Elizabeth Weise, *Chicago Sun-Times,* 28 August 1997, 34).

See also BOY, GIRL, OLD BOY.

goody two-shoes. A young person seen as very virtuous, used for men as well as women but for a long time carrying feminine connotations. The term is usually applied mockingly or in contempt, implying prissiness and often hypocrisy. "Although they talk about being 'nice' girls, they are far from goody two-shoes" (Thorne 1993, 95).

The expression comes from an eighteenth-century nursery story believed to be by Oliver Goldsmith, in which a poor girl expresses her unbounded joy to everyone she meets after acquiring a second shoe, pointing out her "Two shoes!"—hence taking the name of Goody Two-shoes. Through diligence, she learns how to read, becomes a schoolmistress, and marries a wealthy man.

See also PRUDE.

gooey. See HONEY.

gorilla. From the nineteenth century and applied throughout the twentieth, an epithet for a man viewed as brawny, crude, dumb, ugly, or brutal or as a thug (as a ruffian, also spelled *gorill*). During the Civil War it meant *guerrilla* (a fighter engaged in irregular warfare), which seems to have influenced the usage (Lighter 1994). Also during the Civil War, Southerners referred to President Abraham Lincoln disparagingly as the "Gorilla" (his own secretary of war referred to him as the "Original Gorilla").

The expression clearly stems from the large anthropoid ape by that name, which in fact, although strong, is generally a more gentle creature than humans and can be quite intelligent. Later in the twentieth century *gorilla* developed the sense of a large or overweight and unattractive woman. Major (1994) lists *gorilla pimp* as black usage for any crude or tactless hustler or pimp with more brawn than brains.

Also emphasizing size, strength, and apishness is *King Kong,* an epithet for a man derived from the 1933 movie by that name about a big gorilla that climbs the Empire State Building.

See also BRUISER, BULLY, CAVEMAN, CRIMINALS, LUG.

gossip. Originally, a sponsor in baptism. Old English *godsibb* meant a kinsman or kinswoman in the Lord. By the mid-sixteenth century, *gossip* began to take on derogatory meanings related to women, especially those regarded as engaging in idle chatter. A gossip, or person who passes on rumors or personal and sensational reports about others, can be either a man or a woman, but in our culture, we still associate gossiping with women.

Gossip is a trivializing term, often a male rendering of what women supposedly do among themselves, that is, talk without having much of importance to say. The gossip is judged as having a problem, or perhaps as simply doing what comes "naturally" for women, but the name-caller may pay little attention to the conditions surrounding the "gossip's" life, with whom (or what) she is being compared when she is said to be gossipy, or the social functions of gossip. "The gossip suffers from 'perversity of the tongue as an expression of the perversity of her mind'" (Tenenbaum 1936, 330). Blondie and Tootsie, two female characters from the comic strip *Blondie*, created by Chic Young, are depicted as inveterate gossips.

In some circumstances gossiping may be a form of capitulation to a life hemmed in by restrictions, including the inability to get out of the house or neighborhood; or it may simply be the same thing men do when they are at their jobs or "out with the boys" (where they "shoot the bull"). Spender (1980) argues that the idea of women as the talkative sex involves measuring them against some yardstick: "The talkativeness of women has been gauged in comparison not with men but with *silence*" (42).

One of the disadvantages of gossip, according to Sheila Rowbotham (in Mills 1989), is that it can hold women down by directing itself against any kinds of signs of liberation on a woman's part. But Rowbotham acknowledges that gossip can also be subversive of patriarchy. Erica Jong quipped about men's response: "Men have always detested women's gossip because they suspect the truth: their measurements are being taken and compared" (*Fear of Flying*, 1973).

Deborah Tannen says that gossip plays a role in establishing intimacy, enhances one's status through learning the secrets of high-status people (and being able to prove that you know them), and exercises social control. She notes also that men have less use for gossip than women do because of men's lower affiliation need and also because men do not gain status so much through whom they are close to as through their achievements. Men may also be more averse than women to the risks of showing weakness through sharing secrets and passing on information that could be used against them (1990, 96–122).

Related terms that trivialize women's language and social life are *chatter* and *chatterbox, chitchat, girl talk,* and *mother's meeting.*

See also BIDDY, FLIBBERTIGIBBET, GAB, HEN (hen party), NAG, SEEN BUT NOT HEARD, YENTA.

governess. Originally, a powerful goddess or a woman who governed; by the eighteenth century, a woman entrusted with the education and care of a child, a kind of glorified baby-sitter. "In her successful bid for the Connecticut governorship, the late Ella Grasso had to contend with the opposition's slogan 'Connecticut Doesn't Need a Governess'" (Lederer 1991, 56).

It is noteworthy that although *governor* (ruler), as well as other such titles for men in positions of authority, has retained its honorableness, *governess* obviously has not. How did this decline come about? As men exercised control over the emerging European state, women increasingly lost any hold over positions of governance they once had. The domestication of women meant that teaching, especially in private homes, offered one of the few outlets for women to be employed in a middle-class position. Although at one time often a woman of relatively high social standing, the governess entered employment closer in rank to a servant and has even been depicted as poor. The semantic shift toward the domestic and powerless opened the term to weakened connotations.

Male teachers in private employment eventually even abandoned the relatively strong title *governor* (which finds its only real pejoration in Cockney speech) in favor of *tutor*. Many now prefer to use *governor* for the person in authority, regardless of sex. For the person who teaches, titles such as *tutor* or *private teacher* are acceptable (*child mentor,* used in the 1976 Department of Labor's *Dictionary of Occupational Titles*, never seemed to find ground).

Governess was also once used euphemistically in the sense of a female bawd. It has also had use as a synonym for *dominatrix*.

See also DUCHESS, -ESS, GODDESS, MISTRESS, PRINCESS, QUEEN (woman).

Government Inspected Meat. See MEAT.

grandma. See CURSE.

grand old man. See MAN.

granola dyke. See DYKE, LIPSTICK LESBIAN.

grass skirt. See SKIRT.

grass widow, widower. See WIDOW.

grayboy. See BOY.

Griselda, patient Griselda. In fading use, a wife who acts patient and humble in the face of trials laid on her by her husband. There is no equivalent in English for a husband who submits himself in all humility to the tests presented to him by his wife, probably because such submission is traditionally not expected of a man. We have only such terms as *henpecked* (see HEN) *pussy-whipped,* and *ball and chain*, which tend to demean the wife even more than the husband and do not reflect on his virtues.

The name is based on medieval legend. Among the different versions of the story of Griselda is that told by Chaucer in *The Canterbury Tales*. In the "Clerk's Tale" a marquis marries a beautiful and virtuous but lowborn woman, Griselda. To prove his wife's steadfastness—specifically, her willingness to please him—the marquis orders two of her children to be taken from her, telling her they are to be slain, and then sends her from his house, commanding her before she goes to prepare it for the new bride he says he is about to take. Griselda is remarkably submissive through all this. Finally, satisfied that he has a most constant wife, the marquis stops testing her tolerance of abuse and tells her that the woman coming to the house is not a new bride but his daughter.

Also spelled *Grisilda, Patient Grisel,* or *Grizel*.

See also WIFE.

groom. See BRIDE, HORSE.

groupie. Since the mid-1960s, a fan or devotee, usually of a rock musician or a pop group (the musical groupie preceded the other varieties) or athletes, who worshipfully follows the group or team on tour. Although the term may be applied to an ardent male fan, to a gay man, or to other kinds of enthusiasts, it is most frequently associated with young women, often teenage girls, especially those seen as willing to offer sexual favors to their idol. It was Frank Zappa, in *Rolling Stone* (15 February 1969) who launched the mythology of the "groupie." The word soon became derogatory. It may be offensive to those who consider themselves merely fans, not "groupies."

> In some respects she [Desiree Washington] should have known that when you go to the room of an athlete [i.e., boxer Mike Tyson] at three o'clock in the morning, who is used to groupies, you better make it *very, very* clear that you are not a groupie. (Alan Dershowitz, quoted in Jeff Benedict, *Public Heroes, Private Felons,* 1997, 41)

Because of the sexualization of the term, it may be used as an apologetic for rape.

Synonyms considered vulgar are *celebrity fucker* and *star fucker,* which can be used to dismiss any woman who wants to be close to a celebrity or gain attention or success through the relationship (see also FUCKER).

grouse. A word for a young woman; also, sexual intercourse with her. In the animal kingdom, a grouse is a bird of the pheasant family that men hunt (see also QUAIL). The word has been in use since the nineteenth century.

See also BIRD, HUNTER.

gumdrops. See SUGAR (quotation).

gun moll. See MOLL.

gunsel. A callow or inexperienced boy, a CATAMITE, or a young gay male—often someone viewed as loathsome. From the Yiddish *gendzl* or *gantzel* (gosling, or young goose) and probably also English *gun*, this Americanism is derisive and associated largely with dated hobo and prison slang from the early twentieth century. Humphrey Bogart, playing Sam Spade in the 1941 movie version of *The Maltese Falcon*, makes little of the Joel Cairo character by calling him a gunsel. It may also be used to suggest a stupid or despicable man, and it has come by way of misreading to mean a gunman. Also seen as *gonsil, gonsel,* or *gonzel.*

See also BOY, FEIGELE, GAZOONEY, PUNK.

gussie. A man regarded as effeminate, gay, affected, or foolish, from the personal name "Gussie," and used mostly in the first half of the twentieth century.

See also EFFEMINATE.

guy. A man or a fellow, an informal usage since the mid- to late-nineteenth century. Damon Runyon paired it with *dolls* in his stories and in his play *Guys and Dolls* (the stronger, male *guys* always appears before *dolls*). Since the 1940s, in the plural and often following *you*, the term has also served as a reference to people in general or a group of women, and *guy* is becoming a common-gender term, though some still resist this trend.

In largely British usage (often capitalized), *guy* has denoted an effigy of Guy Fawkes, who masterminded a plot to blow up the houses of Parliament; the effigy is paraded through English towns and burned on Guy Fawkes Day. The grotesque effigy resulted in using *guy* for a man, often an old one, of odd or ridiculous appearance. This sense was heard largely from the 1820s through the early twentieth century. *Guy* was also used in the mid-nineteenth to early twentieth century for a man regarded as a comical character or smart aleck.

Fall guy, meaning someone who is easily duped or is a scapegoat, is rare among masculine terms for its suggestion of victimhood. *Tough guy, wise guy,* and *smart guy* may carry some negative connotations, or suggestions of low status, but they primarily suggest the aggressive roles of males.

See also MAN.

H

hag. Originally, since the fourteenth century, an old woman deemed ugly and sometimes vicious; since the sixteenth century, a witch. The Old English *haegtesse*, appearing in Anglo-Saxon writing, referred to a spirit who seized her victims, usually men, from whatever safety they enjoyed (see also HARPY and HOOKER for words applied to women said to have similar intent). A "hag-ridden" man was one who was tormented in his sleep by satanical beings. In Western art and iconography, evil and death have been personified as a horrible, white-haired old hag, who may fly on bat wings and cut down the living with an axe.

Hag later shifted in meaning to something less diabolical, usually any unattractive woman regarded by men as either sexually worthless or bad-tempered. "I don't care how old she is, so long as she's not a hag" (Henry Miller, *Tropic of Cancer*, 1961, 115). It has also been used for women in general or for the stereotypical ugly, domineering mother-in-law. In student use it may suggest a homely young woman believed to make herself sexually available (in this sense, the word is ironically sexualized). A "hag and stag party" is one for both women and men (see also STAG for differences in connotation between it and the more derogatory *hag*).

In some feminist interpretations, the hag is a female archetype, creative in nature, wise and knowing, and helpful to those who have lost their way.

See also BAG, BAT, FAG, HARRIDAN, LOOKSISM, MOTHER-IN-LAW, SCOLD, SHREW, TERMAGANT, VIRAGO, WIFE, WITCH.

hair. Female pubic hair; probably since the sixteenth century. This use of *hair* gives us the sense of a woman regarded as a sex object. In the form *hairburger*, it means either the vagina or a woman considered sexually (see also MEAT). *Hair* may also refer to a gay male hairdresser.

See also ASS, BEARD, BEAVER, BOX, BUSH, CAT, CUNT, GASH, GINCH, HAT, HIDE, PUSS, SQUIRREL, WHISKER, WOOL.

hair fairy. See FAIRY.

hairy-legs. See FEMINIST.

half a man. A demeaning slang, usually prison epithet, for a PASSIVE gay man. This term also alludes to the devastation to a man's ego when he is disabled. "If the public ever perceived the extent of his [Franklin Delano Roosevelt] disability, he would have been seen as only 'half a man' and would never have been electable" (Will Manley, *Booklist*, August 1997, 1852).

See also HOMOSEXUAL, MAN.

half-and-half. Slang since about the 1930s for a hermaphroditic or bisexual person. It is not necessarily intended as derogatory but may give offense. This term is not likely to be used in gay or transgendered communities.

See also BISEXUAL, HERMAPHRODITE.

hammer. Slang, primarily black, used for a girl or woman viewed as sexually attractive (sometimes now also for a man), dating to the mid-twentieth century. Although it is usually intended to convey admiration, the term is likely to be taken offensively. The hard tool metaphor suggests two possibilities: the more likely is an image of an act of male aggression on the supposedly passive female (*pound* and *nail* both mean to copulate with a woman); thus, a woman is someone who is said to be "hammered." The second is a weapon wielded by the woman rather than the man, placing this epithet in the category of female sexuality as potentially harmful (see also BOMBSHELL).

Note that the male *hammer man*, also in black English, is not characterized by his sexuality, but by the authority he wields over others.

See also KNOCKOUT, STUD (stud hammer).

happy homemaker. See HOMEMAKER.

happy hooker. See HOOKER.

harassment. See SEXUAL HARASSMENT.

harem. From Arabic *harīm*, meaning something forbidden; the part of a Muslim household or palace reserved for the women in the household, including the female relations of the male head of the family and his wives, concubines, entertainers, and servants. Although the harem was a part of pre-Islamic civilizations, the practice of having a harem is still commonly associated with Muslim countries. Some interpretations of the Koran support the seclusion and veiling of women, though there are Muslims who disagree with these interpretations. The elaborate harem of the imperial Turkish sultan was known as a *seraglio* (from Italian *serraglio* or enclosure), the administration of which was overseen by the sultan's mother. Sometimes the women in the harem and their sons were influential and, especially in pre-Islamic courts, had important political functions.

In American usage the term carries bias against women, viewed as sex objects—"harem girls"—owned and lorded over by men (see also GIRL).

harlot. Usually a harsh word meaning a female prostitute or whore or a woman viewed as such. In the early thirteenth century, when the word was first recorded, it referred to a man of no fixed occupation, a beggar, or a vagabond, from the Old French *herlot*. In Chaucer's day the term took on a meaning similar to that of rogue, rascal, or lecher, still masculine in sense. It was also used for male clowns, jugglers, itinerants, and servants.

In the fourteenth century, *harlot* began its shift toward women, being used for actresses, dancers, and unchaste women. By the seventeenth century, when *varlet* had come to be used for a rogue, the largely feminized word *harlot* acquired the primary sense of a female prostitute, though it never became as sharp as *whore*. Mills (1989) notes that while we seldom use *harlot* today except to capture its archaic flavor, when it is used, it may still carry some of the connotations of *rascal*, making it less offensive than either *whore* or *prostitute*. Thus, *harlot* is more likely to be heard in a jocular vein: "'They say she sleeps around.' 'The harlot!'" (joke line on TV sitcom comedy *Newhart*.) There is no comparable male term.

See also CHIPPY, COOZIE, DIRTY GERTIE, EASY LAY, GOOD LAY, LESBIAN (lesbia), LOOSE, MATTRESSBACK, MINK, MINX, NYMPH, PROMISCUOUS, PROSTITUTE, PUNCHBOARD, SADIE THOMPSON, SKEEZER, SLAG, SLATTERN, SLUT, TART, TRAMP, TROLLOP, TUNA, WENCH, WHORE.

harpy. A person seen as rapacious or predatory, but more commonly, a woman considered shrewish. Although the word, when still used, may be applied to men—for example, "He is a regular harpy" usually signifies a man who takes from others whatever he wants—it is most often reserved for women. It typically connotes women as being difficult (women are traditionally expected to be pleasant and submissive). There is no male term that carries comparable connotations of scolding and ill-temper, characteristics stereotypically ascribed to women. The word has also been used in the sense of a female prostitute, and it has acquired the meanings among gay men of an aging or difficult drag queen, especially one who applies makeup in such a way as to create a repulsive image; or a lesbian, often stereotyped as mannish and domineering.

Harpy comes from the Greek *hárpuiai*, "snatchers" (see also HAG and HOOKER for similar meanings). In Greco-Roman mythology, the Harpies (capitalized in the classical context) were birdwomen. The earlier versions were not the loathsome creatures they later became; they were possibly ghosts (they appear in tomb friezes) or, as in Homer's *Odyssey*, winds that carried people away. In later representations, however, Harpies became monstrous, with the wings of a bird and the face and breasts of a woman. Bearing a starved-like look and living in filth and stench, they polluted everything they came near.

See also BITCH, CURSE, CASTRATING, GAL (gal officer), HARRIDAN, HEN (quotation), NAG, SCOLD, SHE-DEVIL, SHREW, TERMAGANT, VIRAGO, WITCH.

harridan. A woman viewed as old and scolding, a shrew; from at least the early eighteenth century and believed to be from the French *haridelle*, old horse or nag. Over the century, the meaning migrated from a woman viewed as a bawd or old strumpet to one who was vicious, nagging, and generally disagreeable. No longer a haggard prostitute, she became an ill-tempered woman, someone like the stereotypical mother-in-law. There is no real equivalent term for a man.

See also BITCH, CASTRATING, HAG, HARPY, HORSE, MOTHER-IN-LAW, NAG, SCOLD, SHE-DEVIL, SHREW, TERMAGANT, VIRAGO, WITCH.

hat. In the eighteenth and nineteenth centuries, a slang term for the female genitals; also used by the British for a prostitute, especially an old one. In the United States, mostly in underworld slang, it has meant sexual satisfaction from a man's point of view, a so-called loose woman, or a woman generally, including a girlfriend or wife. The term may have originated with the felt once used for hats, suggesting a woman's vulva and pubic hair, or with the idea that a woman, like a hat, is to be "felt." *Hat* is also used for a homosexual, either in the female sexual sense or from the expression "wearing a different hat," suggesting that one is different (Richter 1993). *Old hat,* which we now think of as meaning "old news," was also once an expression for a woman's genitals or

sexual intercourse (from a man's point of view).

See also BEAVER, BUSH, HAIR, LOOSE, PROMISCUOUS, SQUIRREL, WHISKER, WOOL.

hatchet. A woman seen as sexually unappealing, debauched; since the nineteenth century. The reference may be to *hatchet-faced* (ugly) or to something hard or difficult to handle.

See also BATTLE-AX, LOOKSISM.

Hausfrau. See FRAU.

hawk. See CHICKEN (chickenhawk), DOVE.

haybag. See BAG.

head; **headhunter**. *Head*, a term used, among other ways, to mean sexual gratification. At one time the term was just a shortened version of *maidenhead* (hymen). *Head* has also been applied to objectify a girl or woman, especially one seen as having sex appeal or making herself sexually available. A headhunter is a lecher—a man out looking for "heads."

See also LECHER.

heffa. See HEIFER.

heel. See LOUSE.

he-haw. A seldom-used heterosexual aspersion on gay men from the mid-twentieth century, based on the sound-alike expressions *he-whore* (see also WHORE) and *hee-haw* (allusion to the donkey, known for having large genitals). The term is offensive for its reduction to sexual activity and private parts.

See also HE-WHORE, HOMOSEXUAL.

heifer. Literally, a young cow or female calf but also applied to young women, especially ones viewed as attractive. Along with youth, it may suggest virginity (a heifer is usually a cow that has not yet had a calf). The rest rooms in many restaurants with western themes are labeled "heifers" and "bulls." The differences in connotations allude to popular stereotypes of the sexes.

Being plump or chatty are yet other

qualities that may be suggested by the word. Also as *heffa*.

Even when in jocular use, this word may be taken as offensive. For the full meanings of the cow metaphor and how it demeans women, see COW.

hellcat. From at least the seventeenth century, a woman regarded as high-spirited, ill-tempered, or dangerous; also a witch or practitioner of sorcery. Women who are stronger or more aggressive than cultural standards allow or who don't conform to similar expectations of femininity have traditionally been viewed as wicked. Note that *hell-raiser*—for someone known for causing disturbances, and more commonly associated with males—alludes to a defiant spirit, thus often having more positive connotations than *hellcat*.

See also KITTEN (hellkitten), SHE-DEVIL, WITCH.

hellpig. Late-twentieth-century student usage for a girl or woman considered hellish, especially one regarded as fat and ugly (Spears 1991).

See also HOGGER, KITTEN (hellkitten), LOOKSISM, PIG, SOW.

he-man. An Americanism from the early nineteenth century referring to a man seen as tough, strong, and virile. "NOW has dedicated itself to caricaturing the group as a modern-day Women Hater's Club, its he-man members bent on padlocking women to the stove" (Laura Ingraham, "Men Who Can Do Nothing Right," the *New York Times,* 10 July 1997, A21).

Since the 1960s, especially with the rise of the feminist movement, this term has come to be almost stigmatizing, as if too much masculinity may be deviant.

See also CAVEMAN, IRONBALLS, MACHO, TARZAN.

hen; **henpecked**. *Hen,* an adult female chicken; as a metaphor, a disparaging word for a woman since at least the sev-

enteenth century. The word applied to women has at one time or another been used jocularly, has denoted a mistress, or has meant an officious woman. Dunayer (1995, 12–13) says that comparing women to hens communicates contempt, since hens are valued only for their flesh and for their ability to lay eggs. What's more, hens "cluck," as women are sometimes said to do in disparaging male talk.

Today *hen* is likely to be reserved for a middle-aged or an older woman, especially one seen as fussy, or a housewife. An "old hen" has lost any attractive features that the young "chick" may have enjoyed and may even sprout the flapping, scolding wings of a HARPY: "The hen-harpy is but the Cinderella chick come home to roost" (Philip Wylie, *Generation of Vipers,* 1955, 197).

Mother hen suggests a MOTHER who controls and hovers over her "brood." *Old hen* may also still occur in some quarters of gay male communities as a slur on an aging gay male (see also AUNT). *Hen hussy* was used early in the twentieth century for a man with womanlike qualities. A derisive slur on a lesbian is the male-female animal metaphor *crested hen*, meaning butch. *Hen party* connotes a clique of ladies clucking away about the trivialities of their lives. See also STAG (stag party). Also compare *hen party* with the more favorable men's *bull session.*

To *henpeck* (from at least the seventeenth century) means to nag and dominate one's husband. James Thurber depicted his character Walter Mitty as a weak-spirited, daydreaming, henpecked hero in the short story, "The Secret Life of Walter Mitty" (1942).

Because of the male bias..., not only do women who exercise power receive no reward for it in the form of prestige or deference, but they are actually punished. They are "henpecking" their husbands. They are "castrating bitches." (Jessie Bernard, in McPhee and FitzGerald 1979, 45–46)

See also BIRD, BITCH, CHICKEN, CORSET CROWD, NAG, OLD BOY (old hen), PUSSY-WHIPPED, QUAIL (game hen), WOMEN AS ANIMALS.

her majesty. See WIFE.

hermaphrodite. A term in use in English since the fourteenth century and originating from mythology, with a number of related meanings having to do with something that combines diverse elements, especially an animal or a person with both male and female reproductive organs. Anatomical human hermaphroditism, now often known as intersexuality, involves a number of different types of intersex conditions, including, for example, those that are chromosomal, those that are hormonal, some that result in ambiguous genitalia, and some that involve atypical development of secondary sex characteristics. Probably the most common assumption is that intersexuality involves ambiguous genitalia, in which case it is usually a matter of some sexual characteristic falling outside what is deemed the "normal" range, for example, an elongated clitoris or a double scrotum, each containing one testicle.

In classical mythology, Hermaphroditos was a son of the goddess Aphrodite and the god Hermes. As an adolescent, he bathed in a fountain where a fountain nymph, Salmacis, fell in love with him and pleaded with the gods to make them both one. Her wish granted, the two were united into one body without losing either sex (although the double-sexed creature retained the male name Hermaphroditos, Salmacis being subsumed under the male identity). In practice, as opposed to mythology, the ancient Greeks and Romans, as their societies became increasingly sex-segregated, were not so tolerant of intersexu-

ality. They regularly killed—sometimes burned to death—hermaphrodites at birth.

Different cultures have had different views of intersexuals and different mythological representations of hermaphroditism. Hermaphroditic or androgynous figures have been both appealing as images of balance or unity and rejected for violating the supposedly "normal" boundaries between the sexes. Westerners have usually dealt poorly with anatomical indeterminacy or contradiction, and since the middle of the twentieth century, anyway, surgeons and hormonal specialists have been brought in to eliminate ambiguity upon the birth of a child with intersexual characteristics. Mythological and fictional hermaphrodites in Western tradition are often depicted as monstrous anomalies, and they are still generally thought of in these terms. However, in Hebrew tradition, Adam, the first man in the book of Genesis, was androgynous, bearing both the male and the female (Eve) principle. Having been made in the image of his Creator, or Yahweh, Adam is said to reflect the androgyny of Yahweh.

At various times, the word *hermaphrodite* has been used for effeminate men or masculine women, for cross-dressers, euphemistically for gay men, and for anyone with androgynous characteristics. "The glam revolution…took [David] Bowie as its hermaphroditic patron saint" (Jim Farber, *The Advocate*, 10 November 1998, 76).

The term has sometimes been applied as just another way of stereotyping gay men as "womanish." However, a male having "feminine" characteristics of behavior or personality or a female having "masculine" characteristics is not the same as intersexuality, or physical hermaphroditism. Adding to the confusion, psychologists early in the twentieth century began using the term *psychosexual hermaphrodites*. By this they meant a number of different things, including bisexuals, but perhaps the term came closer in meaning to invert, referring to a kind of INVERSION that is manifested mentally, not physiologically.

Although *hermaphrodite,* often derogatory in its uses, is being replaced by *intersexual,* considered a neutral medical term, there has been considerable reclamation and use of the term *hermaphrodite* within the political intersex movement. Having fallen out of favor in the medical establishment, *hermaphrodite* may be used among intersexuals in the same way that the word *queer* has its contemporary, nonpejorative uses.

Intersexual people, or hermaphrodites, also affectionately known within the transgender communities as "herms," have a strong activist group named Hermaphrodites With Attitude.

> A dozen members of Hermaphrodites With Attitude and Transsexual Menace picketed outside the George Washington University Hospital, protesting GWU's cutting of intersexed infants' genitals. Hermactivists call this medical intervention intersex genital mutilation (IGM). (*Transgender Tapestry,* Fall 1998, 10)

A useful source of information on the hermaphrodite movement is the Intersex Society of North America.

See also ANDROGYNY, BERDACHE, CROSS-DRESSER, EFFEMINATE, HALF-AND-HALF, MORPHADITE, OPPOSITE SEX, TRANSGENDERIST, TRANSSEXUAL, TRANSVESTITE.

hero; heroine. Two terms, both from the Greek *hērōs,* of which the feminine form is *hērōinē,* with only somewhat similar denotations and very different connotations. The first definition for a hero in *Merriam-Webster's Collegiate Dictionary* (1997) is "a mythological or legendary figure often of divine descent endowed with great strength or ability." The heroine—though said, like the hero, to be admired for achievements and qualities—is defined as "having the qualities of a hero." She seems, then, to be almost a derivative of the hero. The hero, according to the same dictionary, can also be an illustrious warrior, one that shows great courage, or an idol. None of these attributes is mentioned for the heroine.

Although either a hero or a heroine may be a principal character in a dramatic or literary work, the term *heroine* has been used more exclusively in this sense throughout the centuries than has *hero.* The term *hero* is richer in connotative power. Traditionally, we have tended to think of the hero as the one whose occupation is the masculine affairs of danger and war. He is a "man of action" (see MAN), an adventurer who courts death, and he often surrounds himself with other men to whom he proves his loyalty. Moreover, whether a selfless and magnanimous defender of the social order or the brave but antisocial rebel that Paul Zweig (1974) calls an "adventurer," much of what he is and does can be defined against the woman and her expectations of him. From Achilles to Natty Bumpo to James Bond and Chuck Norris, the hero or adventurer is not often likely to hook up with women, at least, not permanently. "The adventurer is in flight from women," writes Zweig, since he does not do well at coping with what he sees as their erotic and social hegemony (61).

Robin Morgan (1989), drawing from Joseph Campbell's work on world mythology, places the hero—by which she means the man with a calling to, for example, save his family or avenge his people—in a darker perspective of patriarchal values. The hero's destiny, as he knows, leads him to descend into death, but his very power depends on that fatedness. When woman appears as someone other than merely a source of aid to him, she changes shape from the

Medea rescuing Jason from her vengeful father, or from the supportive Virgin Mary, to the temptress. Once a boon, she is now a danger from whom he takes flight or whom he must conquer. "Because she represents life, she is the ultimate destroyer of what he values most—death" (70).

Unlike the hero, continues Morgan, and his quest, which draw from men's experiences, the token heroine does not suffice to represent women and their experience. "She is no more a true representative of most women than the airbrushed *Playboy* centerfold is a true representative of most women's bodies" (59–60).

Of course, there are authentic heroines in the world: women such as Harriet Tubman, the abolitionist born a slave who struggled to free slaves, and Ding Ling, a Chinese activist who survived numerous political purges. But when heroism in fiction involves acts of aggression, as Pearson (1997) points out, social roles may constrain women to turn the aggression against themselves. Thus, "The outlaw heroines Thelma and Louise in Hollywood's 1991 film hurled themselves into a canyon. Self-destructive heroines are far more memorable within our culture than female warriors" (21–22).

In recent decades the number of women authors has increased dramatically; not surprisingly, child, teen, and adult heroines have kept pace. It is no longer so difficult for girls or women to find heroines with whom to identify.

Shero(e) is an alteration of *hero*. This word is a feminist coinage (first used by Maya Angelou in a speech) designed to create a word that identifies women as heroes, avoiding the assumption that a hero is always a man and the exclusion of women leaders from history books. So far it has had little use outside certain feminist writers, but there it has taken hold. "As sheroes, all women can

fully embrace and embody their fiery fempower and celebrate the unique potency of our gender tribe" (Varla Ventura, *Sheroes,* 1998, xv).

See also GOD, HUNTER, MEAT (hero sandwich).

Hershey bar. A usually vulgar epithet for a gay man. The allusion is not to eating chocolate, but to its color, which is similar to that of feces, suggesting anal intercourse.

See also ASS (ass bandit), BUFU, BUGGER, BUNNY (chocolate bunny), FUDGEPACKER, SODOMY.

herstory. Women's history, heritage, knowledge, and contribution to society; also the ways in which women's position and ideas have been devalued in Western history and in other cultures. The term was coined by Robin Morgan, former editor of *Ms.* magazine, in the early 1970s and entered journalistic writing in the 1980s.

> Radical feminists have also been concerned to uncover her-story, to recover for women their history and their cultural heritage and to reveal the ways in which women's knowledge has been devalued both historically and in other societies. (Abbott and Wallace 1997, 34)

The word has been a thorn in the side of language purists, who make an etymological point. *Herstory* is not simply a female equivalent of *history*. *History,* meaning the record of past events, derives from the Latin *historia,* which has no relation to the English words *his* and *story*. The male equivalent of *herstory* would be *his-story*. In any case, the point of this punning coinage is not simply to flout etymology. The idea is that until recently, history has been *his* story, told mostly by men and telling very little about women's roles in history.

Editor Varda One referred to *herstory* and *manglish,* her name for the English language, as words that act as "reality-violators and consciousness-raisers" (in Miller and Swift 1991, 146). They help to point out the taken-for-granted privileges of men and to suggest the ways women and their lives have been ignored or underrated in standard history texts. Whatever one may think of *herstory* or the political views behind it, that it is in use cannot be denied.

With recent changes in men's roles and challenged notions of what men should be, the history of men, like that of women, has been taking off as an independent study.

See also HERO (shero), MALESTREAM, WIMMIN.

he-she. A term for a lesbian, "passive" gay or effeminate male, transsexual person, cross-dresser, or androgynous person, especially a young woman who dresses or acts like a boy. Such indiscriminate use is a result of a general lack of understanding of gender behavior that does not fit the rigid dual-gender system of mainstream America. The hyphen joining the two pronouns is a sign of what is often believed to be a contradiction, "since sex and gender expression are 'supposed' to match" (Feinberg 1996, 97). The term has been in use among heterosexual speakers since at least the mid-twentieth century and is still current.

However, the word also has uses as a self-identifying label, referring to a masculine-appearing female-bodied person. In Leslie Feinberg's novel *Stone Butch Blues,* the narrator Jess speaks of working with he-shes on the shop floor of factories in Rochester, New York, by which she means females who pass as men to hold certain jobs and to survive in public life generally.

See also ANDROGYNY, BULLDAGGER, CROSS-DRESSER, DYKE, EFFEMINATE, GAL (gal-boy), GENDER AND SEX, GENDER BENDER, GIRL, HIM-HER, HOMOSEXUAL, LESBIAN, SHE-HE, SHE-MALE, TRANSSEXUAL.

het. See HETEROSEXUAL, STRAIGHT.

heterosexism; heterocentrism. *Heterosexism,* an "ism" arising in the late 1970s, referring to biased views that favor heterosexual people and their sexual orientation and encourage prejudice against homosexual, bisexual, and transgendered people. Although *heterosexism* is not always defined the same as *homophobia,* which is often regarded as a psychological condition, there is considerable overlap in meaning, heterosexism also involving an aversion to and discrimination against homosexual people and others whose sexual orientation is not heterosexual. Among some lesbians and gay men, *heterosexism* is comparable to and preferred over *homophobia.*

Heterosexism takes form in a number of assumptions that indicate that the "straight" orientation is considered normal and is institutionalized in the traditional family and the larger patriarchal society. For example, it is often assumed that *couple* means only a man and a woman, that everyone is straight unless they indicate otherwise, and that there is something inappropriate about same-sex partners celebrating an anniversary of their relationship (commitment, the norms tell us, occurs only within heterosexual marriage).

Also coming out of the 1970s, *heterocentrism,* which is at the core of heterosexism, designates heterosexuality as the measure by which all other sexual orientations are judged. It is at the *center,* all other orientations being considered marginal and deviant. In the heterocentrist view, the heterosexual orientation is normal and, indeed, superior, and the other orientations are judged by that standard. This outlook assumes that everyone is heterosexual unless they state otherwise. Thus, a historical figure whose behavior might lead some to suspect homosexuality is asserted to be straight from the heterocentrist point of view, usually out of some felt need to keep the person's name from being sullied.

Labeling someone a "heterosexist" may not have the force of "sexist" or the charge of "racist," but it can still be used against people to dismiss their views. When used too indiscriminately or smugly by gays or lesbians against heterosexuals, it may turn away their sympathies for homosexual rights.

See also HOMOPHOBIA, OPPRESSION, SEXIST.

heterosexual; heterosexuality. *Heterosexual,* a person whose main emotional or romantic and sexual attraction is to people of the other sex. Though a standard, accepted English term (from the Greek *heteros,* other, different), the term has had some biased uses, and the historically specific concept it represents is in dispute. "I think rigid heterosexuality is a perversion of nature" (Margaret Mead, in Higgins 1993, xi).

Jonathan Ned Katz (1995) has argued that the heterosexual categorization is a historically specific, modern phenomenon—"a weird concept of recent origin but terrible consequences" (Gore Vidal, in Katz, vii). The origin of the concept, as Katz (whose views inform much of this entry) sees it, lies in the last four decades of the nineteenth century in Western Europe and the United States, when "the experience of a proper, middle-class, different-sex lust began to be publicly named and documented" (51).

Both *heterosexual* and *homosexual* were coined by the mid-nineteenth century Austro-Hungarian sex reformer Karl Maria Kertbeny, who defined heterosexuality as a form of sexual gratification of the majority of people. By emphasizing "numbers as the foundation of the normal," Kertbeny marked "a historic break with the old qualitative, procreative standard" (Katz, 523). However, Kertbeny's heterosexual was perfectly capable of sexual "degeneracy" and "license," indulging in both "natural" (procreative) and "unnatural" (nonprocreative) sexual activity.

In the United States the term *heterosexual* first appeared in a medical journal article by Dr. James Kiernan, who defined heterosexuality as an abnormality characterized by the expression of a sexual interest in both sexes (*hetero* here meant interest in two different sexes rather than in the "opposite" sex). Kiernan's heterosexual was "deviant" also in taking an interest in nonprocreative sexual activity. The German neurologist Richard von Krafft-Ebing helped to spread the use of the term in the United States in the 1893 U.S. publication of his treatise *Psychopathia Sexualis,* where the term referred to interest in one different sex and implied procreative desire. But Krafft-Ebing's interpretation of *heterosexual* was also linked with "perversion." In fact, for some time, *heterosexual* in the medical and psychiatric literature signified sexual perversion.

In 1915 in *Sexual Inversion,* sexologist Havelock Ellis deleted the term from the list of sexual deviations. By the 1930s, owing to the social changes of the Roaring Twenties, including removing the stigma from nonprocreative sex, *heterosexuality* had "come out," acknowledged and sanctified as the dominant, normative type of sex—sex between a man and a woman.

In our society, heterosexuality is considered the rule, the preferred form of sex, while other orientations are commonly regarded as deviant. Boys at a fairly early age learn to see heterosexuality as basic to masculinity—it is associated with being "a real man"—while girls similarly learn to see heterosexuality as central to femininity. But it is not usually an identity in the way or degree to which homosexuality may be. Heterosexuality is not marked as is homosexuality, and most people we would call heterosexual give little thought to themselves in this role, and make little use of the term, unless they are confronted with homosexuals. The privileged status of heterosexuals frees them from having to deal with labeling, which is part of the privilege.

Compulsory heterosexuality (sometimes also *obligatory heterosexuality*) is a term used especially by some feminists to suggest society's systematic and coercive production of a different-sex eros (Rich 1980). The expression implies that women are deprived of the right to choose their sexual orientation pleasures; for that, they are dependent on men. Rich cites the former use of the death penalty for lesbian sexual activity and severe punishments for women's adultery as examples of the denial of choice (183). Women's sexuality is viewed as established by men and prescribed in their interest; abuse, such as the verbal attacks described in this dictionary, is only one way that society has of restricting options to heterosexuality. Implicit in institutions such as marriage and family, compulsive heterosexuality becomes a means of structuring gender relations and keeping women dependent sexually, emotionally, socially, and economically. Its enforcement also serves to exclude homosexuality as an acceptable choice.

Het is an abbreviated adjectival slang form also used as a noun, derisively by nonheterosexual people or simply as an informal reference. "So what's your trip? Trying to turn the heathens into hets?" (Carol Queen, *The Leather Daddy,* 1998). The dismissive *hettie* may also be heard, as are the colloquial *hetero* and *heter*.

See also BISEXUAL, BREEDER, FRAME, HOMOSEXUAL, OPPOSITE SEX, SEXUAL PREFERENCE, STRAIGHT, TWINK.

he-whore. From the mid-twentieth century, an epithet for a gay man or gay male prostitute. The degradation in the term comes from both the *whore* element (see WHORE) and the resemblance in sound to *hee-haw* (the donkey alluded to is known

for having large genitals). The term thus reduces the man to sexual activity and to his private parts.

See also HE-HAW, HOMOSEXUAL, HUSTLER.

hide. A term once in use for the vulva or vagina (see also CUNT, TWAT). *Hide* has since come to mean young woman or women viewed as sex objects. In the early twentieth century in particular, *hide* was a word for a prostitute. *Hide* or *piece of hide* refers to sexual intercourse with a woman from a man's point of view. The chief reference is to skin (thus, the term reduces a woman to a part of her anatomy; see also HAIR). However, allowing for puns, there are suggestions of going into hiding, as a prostitute might on the streets. But if a woman is promiscuous, she may also be regarded as having nothing private enough to want to hide.

Hide has also been applied to a young gay male (see also HOMOSEXUAL).

See also LOOSE, PROMISCUOUS, PROSTITUTE.

himbo. See BIMBO.

him-her. A term for a gay man or androgynous person since the mid-twentieth century. Also heard as *himmer*. Both may be very disrespectful.

See also ANDROGYNY, GENDER BENDER, HE-SHE, SHE-HE, SHE-MALE.

his-story. See HERSTORY.

ho, hoe, 'ho. Twentieth-century variant pronunciation and respelling of *whore*, "prostitute." This usually demeaning epithet is based on black English pronunciation but is used also by white people. *Ho* may also refer to any woman regarded as sexually promiscuous—sometimes any woman: "You don't have to *be* one to be called one" (Sharp 1993, 39). In any case, *ho* is likely to be taken offensively. "In my brief lifetime we have gone from a people who would greet each other as brother and sister to folks who salute one another as 'gangsta' and 'ho'" (W. J. Musa Moore-Foster, in Buchwald, Fletcher, and Roth 1993, 424). However, Sutton (1995), reports that some California undergraduates claim *ho* is used between women as a term of affection (a signal of solidarity), and others indicate that it may even be neutral (288).

"Bros before hos" is an expression of male solidarity: a man's male friends come before women. *Weekend ho* refers to a part-time prostitute; *hoe layer,* to a man who spends a lot of time having sex with women. Among other variants for women regarded as sexually promiscuous is *skank ho* (see also SKANK); and for women considered ugly, *hobag* (see also BAG).

See also PROMISCUOUS, PROSTITUTE, WHORE.

hog. See PIG.

hogger. A young woman seen as homely and obese. The term, from about the mid-twentieth century, is suggested by the usually contemptuous use of *hog* meaning a fat, ugly person. The usage is recorded mostly as student language. The use of *hog* for a locomotive, another metaphor for a big person, reinforces the sense.

See also BEEF TRUST, BIG BERTHA, BOB, BUFFALO, COOLER, COYOTE, DOG, GANGSTER GIRL, HELLPIG, LOBO, LOOKSISM, PIG, SCUD, SKAG, SOW, YETI.

hole. The anus since the fourteenth century, and the vagina since the sixteenth. This slang usage, usually considered vulgar, has been applied in the twentieth century to sexual intercourse with a woman and to women as sex objects. As an epithet for a woman, *hole* reduces her to an anatomical part (the difference between the anus and the vagina seemingly irrelevant) and suggests hollowness. Mills (1989) has discussed men's views of women as sexual receptacles or containers.

In slang use the term is also used for the mouth (see also GOSSIP, NAG). As a term of negativity, it is not surprising to find *hole* used in other negative expressions, such as *hole in one's head* (lacking good judgment) and *hole in the wall* (a tacky or disreputable room or place).

Hole is also one of many slang slurs, largely in prison use and usually considered vulgar, for a PASSIVE gay man (see also HOMOSEXUAL). In gay male communities *manhole* has also had some use for a gay male said to take the passive role. Although it is not necessarily meant to be disparaging as used among gay men, it is reductive.

Variant expressions are *cheesehole* and *stimey hole*.

See also ASS (asshole), CRACK, CUNT, DONUT HOLE, FRIGID (ice cube with a hole in it), NOOKY.

home chick. See CHICK.

homemaker; housewife. *Homemaker,* from the late nineteenth century, a person who manages a household, usually as a principal (but nonwage labor) occupation. Such a person may be a man, but traditionally and usually still—despite many social changes that emphasize such roles as day-care workers and au pairs—the word applies to a woman, specifically the wife and mother. American society has assigned great social significance to the role, though at the same time bringing some devaluation through the backdoor.

> Wanted—More Mothers: We are short on homes; *real* homes. We are short on mothers; *real* mothers.... God designed woman as the *homemaker*.... (from an advertisement in a Christian fundamentalist journal, 1921, in French 1992, 55)

The word *home* derives from Old English *hām* (village). By the fourteenth century, it came to mean one's birthplace; in the sixteenth, one's own place or country. The word did not come to carry the meaning of a sentimentalized family life, the small circle where women were thought to belong, until at least the eighteenth century. This new sense coincided with the emergence of a virtual social cult around the home. With this evolution *home* took on connotations lacking in *house*. The former is a symbol that has the full sanction of American society: a warm hearth and security. The latter is merely the physical place we inhabit. *Happy homemaker,* which now may be used ironically, conveys the idealized traditional values surrounding women as the primary managers of the family home.

Housewife, from the thirteenth century, is nearly synonymous with *homemaker* but, of course, stresses the idea of a married woman and lacks some of the positive connotations provided by *home*. In the thirteenth century, *housewife* was used for a woman who not only occupied herself with menial household chores but exercised palpable power in managing the household as well.

In subsequent centuries, however, the term came to be associated with low status and even sex. The German *Huswif,* for instance, once denoted a woman seen as girlish or worthless, and a nineteenth-century slang meaning of *housewife* was vagina. While today housewifery is a way many women have of identifying themselves, for others it may connote the dull, drudgelike work of a married woman and can be taken as offensive for defining women's tasks in relation to a man. Maggio (1997) points out that the respectable word *work* is often reserved for what men do; domestic work is too tedious to warrant a dignified name. Some sociologists have argued that it is not the women's movement that has denigrated the housewife role but the male-dominated culture that has created certain conditions (i.e., not making homemaking a legal occupation but a low-status position) or allowed them to exist. The term *househusband* is almost considered jocular (see also BETTY).

The stereotype of the traditional homemaking role as oppressive has, however (according to some feminists as well as antifeminists, though their reasons differ), been exaggerated and is even potentially harmful. To many Asian or black women, for example, the adoption of Western middle-class or white feminist values is not necessarily a happy retreat from the alleged oppressiveness of the familial role. In fact, some black women defend the family as their primary institutional shoulder to lean on, a way of rebuffing racism (Brah 1986). For women of many different ethnic or class backgrounds, the family is regarded as providing a means of subsistence and a supportive network of kinspeople.

See also BAREFOOT AND PREGNANT (KEEP THEM), FRAU, HUSSY, LADY (of the house), MOTHER, MRS., WIFE.

homewrecker. A term for someone who does something to ruin a family's life, such as sleep with a married man; virtually always used for a woman, serving to protect the male adulterer from blame.

See also TEMPTRESS.

homo. Short for *homosexual*, often referring to a gay male. Usually offensive and intended by heterosexuals as disparaging, *homo* dates to the 1920s as street slang, about fifty years after the coining of *homosexual*. In the nineteenth century, however, it had served as psychiatric jargon referring to male sexual "perversion."

Words that have been abbreviated, such as *homo* or *JAP*, often take on special derogatory force. In the movie *The Distinguished Gentleman* (1992), Eddy Murphy goes for a laugh at the expense of gay men in a scene in which he thinks that a U.S. senator may be "going homo." "Cause if you are," Murphy exclaims, "I'm gonna whup you." *Homo* lost ground once *gay* became popular in the 1960s, but it lives on as a slur against gay men. In 1998 Representative Dick Armey of Texas called Representative Barney Frank of Massachusetts a "homo." *Homo-cide* is what some police may use to dismiss the murder of a homosexual, and the single syllable *mo* may be heard among students as a derisive way of referring to a gay or effeminate male.

Yet beyond all the conventional nastiness, the word may take on a certain panache when used by those within homosexual communities or those who are supportive of them:

> As the homo population becomes larger and more demanding, policies promoting everything from harassment-free high schools to queer partnership are very slowly coming to pass. (Danya Ruttenberg, *Bitch,* 1998, 45)

See also FAGGOT, FOUR-LETTER MAN, HOMOSEXUAL.

homophile. See HOMOSEXUAL.

homophobia. A reference to a conscious or unconscious aversion to and fear of homosexual—also bisexual or transgendered—people, homosexuality, and homosexual communities and culture. Often today it is discussed as the fear of *being* homosexual. The term is said to have been coined as early as the 1950s and occurred as *homoerotophobia* in a 1967 study of attitudes toward homosexual people by Wainwright Churchill.

The concept was developed and the term popularized by heterosexual psychotherapist George Weinberg in his 1972 work, *Society and the Healthy Homosexual* (Weinberg claimed the word was a condensation of *homosexualphobia*). A person with this particular type of antipathy is called a "homophobe," also sometimes a "gay-basher," though a person may be homophobic without necessarily attacking homosexual people, especially not physically. Yet homophobia often goes much further than

just fear or antipathy; it is an attitude that readily leads to discriminatory acts and violent abuse, including murder.

Unlike *heterosexism*, a word that generally encompasses matters of social discrimination and politics as well as belief that heterosexuality is the only "normal" sexual orientation, *homophobia* often signifies a psychological condition. However, more than just a xenophobic reaction to people seen as different or fear of their sexuality, homophobia represents hostility toward the perceived violation of cultural sex-role stereotypes. This hostility is reflected in many of the slurs in this dictionary that disparage men for being effeminate or women for appearing mannish. Homophobia also assumes institutional form, reflected, for example, in antigay laws or policies and society's general refusal to provide gay people with legal protection against discrimination.

Among those who have debated the merits of the term *homophobia* are some who argue that homophobia is generated and directed in an institutional setting. Yet the term tends to locate the hatred instead in individual pathology. Pellegrini (1992), also regrets that the term *homophobia*, meaning literally fear of the same, displaces the burden of responsibility onto its targets. "An analysis of homophobia may all to [sic] easily become an investigation into what it is about gay men and lesbians that 'makes' heterosexuals hate us so" (44).

In part the homophobic attitude may be reflected in distorted and simplistic views of gay or lesbian people that take the place of facts and resist change in the face of contrary evidence. For example, all lesbians are portrayed as "butch" or "losers," all gay men as "sissies," "queens," or "child molesters." However, the exact nature of the stereotyping slur doesn't matter as much as the charge that someone is a homosexual: "The category itself—and whatever it means to the individual using it—is the main accusation: 'Faggot!' 'Dyke!'" (Young-Bruehl 1996, 143). Also often said to be characteristic of homophobia are conflict over sexual guilt and a preoccupation with homosexuality as a sin, sickness, perversion, and menace.

Homophobia is commonly seen as a way for people, men especially, to distance themselves from their own homoerotic desires and convince others that they are heterosexual. Studies focusing on heterosexual male prejudice against gay men reveal homophobia as a form of SEXISM: an expression of male hatred of femininity, including the femininity they sense in themselves. But homophobic persons cannot be thought of only in terms of self-hatred. For example, heterosexual men who are homophobic are more afraid of homosexuality as a threat to male dominance and heterosexuality than they are of any unconscious homosexual desire on their part.

> Visible gay men are the objects of extreme hatred and fear by heterosexual men because their breaking ranks with male heterosexual solidarity is seen as a damaging rent in the very fabric of sexism. (Pharr 1988, 18)

There are, of course, other points of view about antigay attitudes. Some claim such views are not irrational or pathological, as the term *phobia* implies, but expressions of religious or cultural rules. Some fear that *homophobia* only points an accusatory finger, going on the offensive against those whose views gay people are said to dismiss. But proponents of antigay attitudes, however rationalized, usually fail to acknowledge the damage done to gay and lesbian people, their communities and relations with their communities, not to mention their health and physical safety. Such attitudes are thus not only destructive to a large group of people but dehumanizing for everyone involved.

Biphobia has been used to refer specifically to fear of bisexual people, *transphobia* to fear of the transgendered, and *lesbophobia* for aversion to lesbians.

See also HETEROSEXISM, OPPRESSION.

homosexual; homosexuality; homophile. *Homosexual*, a person who is emotionally or romantically and sexually attracted to people of the same sex. Some would add that the term applies only when the sexual desires are directed entirely or primarily toward those of the same sex and when practice coincides with inclination, although one need not have any homosexual experience to identify as such.

In fact, a definition of the term does not come easy. Homosexuality expresses itself in very different ways: mere homoerotic fantasies, having a single homosexual experience or two in one's lifetime, having a period of homosexual experimentation or practice (institutionally prescribed for youth in some cultures at certain stages of life), or exclusive selection of same-sex partners. Moreover, whatever others may call one's behavior, that person may deny that it is homosexuality on the grounds that the situation does not fulfill certain criteria he or she thinks define homosexuality.

For many gays and lesbians today, the use of *homosexual,* originally restricted largely to the medical world, is unacceptable as a clinically objectifying usage. It is also somewhat cumbersome. In addition, unlike *gay,* it does not usually signal self-identification as a homosexual person, although *homosexual identity* has been a favored term since the 1980s.

What is most objectionable to many is the use of the word in such biased journalistic contexts as "homosexual murderer" (homosexuals tend to be more the victims than the instigators of murder); "homosexual rape" (why don't we also distinguish "heterosexual rape"?); "The police arrested prostitutes, drug addicts, and homosexuals" (lumping diverse categories together as deviant groups); or such slanderous, stereotypical expressions as "promiscuous homosexuals." For others, however, *homosexual* is generally acceptable as one of the most neutral terms available for discussing people of same-sex orientation.

Homosexual is a relatively new term. Jonathan Ned Katz has argued that the homosexual-heterosexual categorization is a historically specific, modern phenomenon. Both terms, he says, were coined by a nineteenth-century Austro-Hungarian writer and journalist, Karl Maria Kertbeny (1995; 1997b, 177–80).

First used in a letter written by Kertbeny to a colleague, Karl Heinrich Ulrichs, *homosexual* made its initial public appearance in 1869 in a petition against a German law that criminalized "unnatural fornication." Although competing with other linguistic offerings of the day, such as Ulrichs' *Urnings* (after the Greek *Urania*), it was *homosexual* that quickly achieved international currency. The notion of a same-sex orientation as a fixed, inherent aspect of personality was just emerging at this time.

About two decades later, the German neurologist Richard von Krafft-Ebing distinguished between *homosexual* and *heterosexual* in his treatise *Psychopathia Sexualis,* which drew on "degeneracy" theory, once a very popular explanation of everything from mental retardation to urban crime (see also DEVIANT). Mondimore (1996) states that it was due largely to Krafft-Ebing's book "that the scientific consideration of homosexuality remained inextricably intertwined with the study of mental illness for the next eight years" (35). Perhaps the first written use of the word in the United States was in an 1892 article by Dr. James Kiernan in the *Chicago Medical Recorder*. In the article Kiernan, defining what we would call today a trans-

sexual, defined the homosexual as a person who felt like someone of the other sex: a homosexual man wanted to be a woman, argued Kiernan, and a lesbian wanted to be a man. In little more than a couple of decades, the term *homosexual* had been appropriated by medicine.

Before the 1890s *sissy* had been used to talk about effeminate men, who had become an acceptable topic of conversation around the 1870s and 1880s. A variety of other terms had been in use, including *love* (as in *Greek love), friendship, boy/man, chicken, sodomite, bugger* (the latter two words were and are typically highly negative), and *pederasty* (a positive term in the ancient Greek context, where the activity was considered healthy for a young man, but today often connoting a pedophile [who is more likely to be a heterosexual than a homosexual male] or child molester).

Such language conveyed different types of same-sex eroticism. But there are many differences between these terms and *homosexual;* for one example, the former were probably restricted exclusively to men. Similarly, the earlier terms denoted only sexual acts that, theoretically anyway, could have been those of anyone—there was at that time no concept of homosexuality or of a type of person with such a "nature" or condition. By the turn of the twentieth century, however, these older terms were "subordinated under one single, powerful, unifying medical sign: 'homosexuality'" (Katz 1997a, 231).

In 1892 a medical journal defined both *homosexuality* and *heterosexuality* (which had not yet taken on its current meaning) as sexual perversions. By about the 1920s, however, heterosexuality had begun to be construed as the sexual standard; those practicing it were labeled the "normals," while those deviating from it, the "perverts," were perceived as inferior to heterosexuals in their brand of eroticism. Gradually these dual categories became commonplace but still did not enjoy widespread currency until the 1970s. Meanwhile, however, the word *homosexual* itself was not seen in print in family newspapers or heard on radio or in the movies until the 1940s. Not only was the idea of this kind of orientation bothersome to the majority of Americans, but also the word's emphasis on *sexual* was disturbing to many.

Between the end of the nineteenth century and the 1960s, the new terms *heterosexual* and *homosexual* had edged their way together into popular American culture. The images accompanying them were those of

> a sexual solid citizen and a perverted unstable alien, a sensual insider and a lascivious outlaw, a hetero center and a homo margin, a hetero majority and a homo minority. (Katz 1995, 112)

In 1987 the *New York Times*, thanks to the influence of GLAAD (the Gay and Lesbian Alliance Against Defamation), began to replace the term *homosexual* with the term *gay* for males. *Gay* is now preferred by many in gay communities.

Homosexual has had varied uses depending on the speaker or context. Traditionally, society has not looked upon female homosexuality as so serious an "affliction" as male homosexuality. Perhaps one outcome of this less scornful attitude toward female homosexuality is that the term *homosexual* came to refer largely to the male category. Thus, we have seen expressions such as "homosexuals *and* lesbians." Today, *homosexual*, rather than *gay*, remains a common usage in newspaper articles, law courts, and other contexts. Gays and lesbians, however, often apply it with some derision to those who remain in the closet.

The term *homophile* ("same" plus "love") is an adjective meaning homosexual, though it extends to nonsexual, affectional as well as sexual relations

between members of the same sex. The term, which had a place in the Dutch homosexual rights movement following World War II, was adopted in the 1950s among U.S. homosexual activists for reasons of political expediency and came into currency in the 1960s. It does not see much use today, being regarded in gay communities as a euphemism (it was replaced by *gay* with the rise of the gay liberation movement), though it may be used to describe organizations campaigning for gay rights.

An even broader term in reference to same-sex relations is *homosocial*, which refers to general bonding between men or between women. However, *homosocial* has also had the more specific meaning of male social bonding that reinforces male dominance.

Avowed, admitted, and *declared homosexual* are biased terms. When we admit or avow something, it is like making a confession. A crime, sin, or weakness is suggested. *GLAAD Media Guide* (n.d., 14) says that all three of these terms "imply something unsavory." *Openly lesbian* or *openly gay* are preferred in designating those who self-identify as gay or lesbian in their public or professional lives.

Since language has become a battlefield where traditional or religious views and progressive ideas confront each other, it is worth mentioning that the term *homosexual* is not found in the Bible. "No extant text or manuscript, Hebrew, Greek, Syrian or Aramaic, contains such a word" (John Boswell, in Gomes 1996, 148). Gomes adds that the subject is not brought up either in the Ten Commandments or in the Summary of the Law.

> Jesus himself makes no mention of it, and homosexuality does not appear to be of much concern to those early churches with which Saint Paul and his successors were involved. One has to look rather

hard…to find any mention of homosexuality at all. (147)

See also ANGEL, BITCH, BOY, BUGGER, BUFU, FAGGOT, FAG HAG, FAIRY, FLAMER, FOUR-LETTER MAN, FUNNY, GAL (gal-boy), GAY, HAT, HE-SHE, HE-WHORE, HIM-HER, HOMO, HOMOPHOBIA, INVERSION, LA-DI-DA, LATENT, LAVENDER, LEATHER, LEFT-HANDED, LESBIAN, LESBO, MOLLY, MINCE, NELLY, ODD, OLD BOY (old girl), ONE OF THOSE, OPPO-SITE SEX, OTHER WAY, PANSY, PERVERT, PUNK, PUSS, QUEEN, QUEER, SEXUAL PREFERENCE, SEYMOUR, SHE-HE, SHE-MALE, SICK, SISSY, SISTER (sis), SHIT, SODOMY, SQUAW, SWISH, TART, TRADE, TRASH, TWINK, UNCLE TOM, UNNATURAL, VEGETABLE, VIOLET, WOLF, WOMAN.

homosexuality as disease. One way U.S. culture categorizes homosexuality. The notion of homosexuality as a disease emerged near the end of the nineteenth century in the United States, where medical doctors drew upon the "deviance" model of such German sexologists as Richard Krafft-Ebing.

The idea, which probably gained acceptance in part to reinforce then-challenged traditional views of sexuality, soon spawned a spate of medical and psychiatric theories. These included physical defects, hormonal imbalance, masochism, and other pathologies, none of which was ever shown to have any validity—but all of which have been stigmatizing.

After World War II, psychiatrists in the United States regarded homosexuality as a form of mental illness, and it was entered as such in *The Diagnostic and Statistical Manual of Psychiatric Disorders* until 1973. At that time the American Psychiatric Association—as a result of a postal vote—dropped homosexuality from its list of disorders. The Immigration and Naturalization Service, however, continued to regard homosexuality as a mental illness until 1990, using that classification as a basis for ex-

cluding immigrants and visitors, and the World Health Organization continued the classification throughout the twentieth century.

Antigay or homophobic people persist in pathologizing homosexuality, including evoking the myth of contagion, that is, that one person can "catch" homosexuality from another, like tuberculosis. It has also been seen as just another kind of addiction. In 1998 U.S. Senate Majority leader Trent Lott, scaling the moral high ground during that year of sexual scandal in Washington, D.C., compared homosexuality to certain unrelated behavior disorders: "You should try to show them a way to deal with [homosexuality] just like alcohol…or sex addiction…or kleptomaniacs" (*Time,* 26 October 1998, 34). Among some people of color, homosexuality may be looked upon as a white people's disease. When antigay people of color see it in their own community, it appears to them to be a form of genocide.

If behavior is constructed as a disease, it is also likely to have its "cures." In the case of homosexuality, these have ranged from giving homosexuals the opportunity for sexual experience with the other sex (sexologists employed prostitutes for this purpose) to surgical removal of the testes or ovaries to X-ray treatment and even lobotomy (see Don Romesburg in Witt, Thomas, and Marcus 1995, 225–27). Other cures put forward have included diet, electroconvulsive therapy, the power of prayer, and treatment with LSD. Commenting on what he thought was the power of LSD to cure homosexuality, 1960s drug guru Timothy Leary gave an account of a young woman who visited his training center in Mexico.

> She was a lesbian and she was very attractive sexually, but all of her energy was devoted to making it with girls. She was at an LSD session at one of our cottages and went

down to the beach and saw this young man in a bathing suit and—flash!... Her subsequent sexual choices were almost exclusively members of the opposite sex.

—Leigh Rutledge, *Unnatural Quotations*, 1988

Today we are more likely to hear about "reorientation therapy," psychiatric treatment usually regarded as unethical and scientifically unsubstantiated, and religious "conversion therapy" as ways of "curing" gay people of their homosexuality.

Seeing homosexuality as a disease category "scientizes" it. On the one hand, this may seem to save gay people from the charge of engaging in sin or morally degenerate practices, thus making them more the objects of compassion than of harsh judgment. This patronizing attitude has also been said to have played a role in the removal of some oppressive antihomosexual laws. On the other hand, having one's inclinations compared with diseases such as TB or leprosy cannot be expected to win favor in gay communities.

For one thing, the disease argument probably makes it easier to challenge and even prohibit homosexuality than does the moral argument, since the so-called rationality of science is more acceptable to much of the public than are moral or religious taboos alone. The implication—that homosexuality, if a disease, requires a cure—also allows those who are antigay to disavow any homophobia ("We hate the disease, not the person"). No one wants to be accused of homophobia, which is becoming increasingly unacceptable to many in heterosexual society. Furthermore, when the "cure"—such as surgery or electroconvulsive therapy—is painful, expensive, demeaning, or even just inconvenient, it is hard to distinguish cure from punishment. The latter makes for a harder sell in a liberal society, even if it is "for their own good."

There are also political implications to the disease concept. Sullivan (1995) writes that a liberal society cannot

engage someone who simply asserts that another citizen is diseased and that society has an obligation to impose a cure. In the case of homosexuality, where the overwhelming majority of homosexuals reject the notion that they are sick at all, such politics would require an essential cessation of civil relations. It would have to treat some citizens as subcitizens, adults as children, fellows as patients. (23)

The prevalent view of homosexuality as a disease and an aberration has been challenged and to some extent countered by contrary evidence and opposing positions. Studies as early as the 1940s and 1950s drew into question the idea of homosexuality as mental illness. Alfred Kinsey's 1948 study—*Sexual Behavior in the Human Male*—revealed that more than one-third of the male population surveyed admitted to some form or degree of homosexual activity. Clellan Ford and Frank Beach's 1951 report, *Patterns of Sexual Behavior*, showed that forty-nine out of seventy-seven cultures the researchers studied regarded male homosexual activity of one sort or another to be normal or acceptable.

Quickly following these studies, Evelyn Hooker's psychological research reported that the homosexuals studied indicated no such thing as a "homosexual personality" and no more signs of mental pathology than heterosexuals, although some homosexuals did suffer victim status (reported in the *Journal of Projective Techniques*, 1957, 59).

Today, many regard homosexuality as healthy or neutral, "an alternative sexual orientation...and that falling under or choosing this alternative has all the moral and health implications of being a woman rather than being a man or of being black rather than being white, namely nil" (Ruse 1988, 203).

The national slur *English disease* refers to male homosexuality.

See also DEVIANT, HOMOSEXUAL, INVERSION, NORMAL, PERVERT, SICK, SINFUL, TWISTED.

honest woman. An expression used for a woman who is "properly" married before having sexual relations with a man and before getting pregnant. "Make an honest woman of her" means to get married. This cliché, dating to the nineteenth century, suggests the immorality of a woman having a sexual relationship outside of marriage. Reflecting a double standard, there is no equivalent traditional expression for a man, although Kirkpatrick (1996) says that today's emphasis on sexual equality has given rise to the inverse phrase "make an honest man of."

honey. A food metaphor alluding to sweetness, softness, and passiveness. As a term of endearment, *honey* has been used in English since the fourteenth century. It is generally accepted and appropriate in contexts of intimacy between men and women (its use for men by women is relatively recent) and is heard between members of the same sex. It is often applied paternalistically as well as endearingly to females, such as one's "sweetheart" or any attractive girl or woman, a use common in the United States since at least the mid-nineteenth century.

Outside a familiar relationship, however, the usage may be offensive. In this context, it is usually applied to someone regarded in one way or another—because of age, gender, or job position—by the speaker as an inferior or subordinate. Although regarded as sexist by some women, however, *honey* has never suffered the demotion of meaning to "prostitute," as have such words as *tart*.

In the eighteenth century *honey-pot* was used to denote the vagina, and then it came to refer to the woman herself. Since *pot* suggests woman as a container, *honey* thus acquired the connotations of semen (see also SEXPOT). But the more obvious connotations heard in *honey* are those of softness, also carried by similar metaphors, especially *gooey*, an adolescent usage meaning girlfriend, mostly of the late 1980s and early 1990s.

Hon is a shortening. *Honeybun,* which plays on the word *bun* in either its food sense or that of the buttocks, is synonymous with *honey*, and like *honey,* it may be a term of endearment. "Honeybun" was also the name of a 1940 Richard Rodgers and Oscar Hammerstein song: in the film version of *South Pacific,* the role of Honey-Bun was played by a man in grass-skirt drag, at whom a sailor lobs a dart that strikes the man's rear end, i.e., "buns."

Honey-bunch is another synonym. *Honey-baby* enjoys some use, too (see also BABY). *Honeyfuck,* meaning a woman considered sexually attractive, reduces her to the act of sexual intercourse.

See also CAKE, CHEESECAKE, CHERRY, COOKIE, CREAMPUFF, CUPCAKE, DEAR, DISH, JELLY ROLL, MUFFIN, PIE, SUGAR, SWEET, SWEET MEAT, TART.

hoochie, hootchie. In black English, especially known in rap music, a woman considered sexually available; also occurs as *hoochie mama. Hoochie* appears to be related to *hootchie-kootchie,* denoting a suggestive dance performed by a woman—the term first appeared in the 1880s to denote a type of belly dance—and has also had the meaning of "fooling around" sexually. The first "hootchie-kootchie girl," as she came to be known, was Fahreda Mahzar, an Egyptian dancer who performed at the World's Columbian Exposition in Chicago in 1893, where she created a sensation—and legend—that did not fade in men's imaginations for some years. The dated *hoochie-coochie man* referred to a man who pursued women (see also LADIES' MAN). *Hoochie* may also be applied in the sense of the pudenda; thus, when used for women, it is a reductive, or synecdochic, term. The origin of *hoochie* is obscure.

See also EXOTIC, PROMISCUOUS.

hooker. Colloquialism for a female prostitute, in use since the mid-nineteenth century. Lighter (1997) cites an 1859 source that derives the term from "Corlear's Hook," a red-light district in New York City that sailors once frequented. Thorne (1990) mentions the popular version of the term's origin as the encouragement the Civil War commander General Hooker supposedly gave to his men to visit brothels.

Whatever the exact origin, the term suggests the stereotypical idea of a woman putting her "hooks" into a man to use him as she pleases (see also HAG and HARPY for other words applied to women with the sense of seizing men). Singer Frank Sinatra apparently had this sense in mind when he berated the news reporters who harassed him: "It's the scandal men that bug you and drive you crazy, and the hookers—the broads of the press are the hookers" (in Fikes 1992).

A woman is also said "to have her hooks" in a man when she has managed to manipulate him into proposing marriage to her. Mills (1989) suggests that the reasoning behind viewing prostitutes as having hooks is to absolve men of "their guilt for seeking to satisfy their desire for illicit sex: a hook, like a talon or a magical charm, is difficult to escape from." It is reminiscent of "the childhood cry, 'But (s)he made me do it.'"

The word is much less offensive than *whore*. Yet those prostitutes who make their appointments with men by the telephone and wish to avoid the coarse connotations of *hooker* may prefer to be identified as "call girls." *Hooker* may sometimes also be used for a male prostitute, but *hustler* (used also for a woman) has more commonly been applied to male prostitutes who serve gay men.

Happy hooker suggests a prostitute as a person who has fun in an immoral sort of way. The image evoked is of a woman lounging around her madame's high-rise apartment or hanging out in the bars of high-class hotels—fun, but not real work.

See also CALL BOY, HUSTLER, PROSTITUTE, TROLLOP.

hooligan. See CRIMINALS.

Hooters Girls. Name used by Hooters of America, Inc., for its female servers (the company does not hire male servers). *Hooters* is a slang term (typically in male use, often considered vulgar and obnoxious), for a woman's breasts. It is sometimes applied also to a big-breasted woman. The scantily dressed servers known by this company name wear a midriff-bared T-shirt that bears an owl logo whose eyes look like a woman's breasts and nipples on the front, while the slogan "More than a mouthful" appears on the back.

Hooters suggests something to "hoot" about. It may also play on the British word for a car horn—squeezed with the hand. It dates to about the mid-twentieth century, after World War II and the popularity of the female pinup.

See also BRA-BUSTER, BREAST MAN, COW (milker), GIRL, TIT MAN.

hoozie. Slang word for a woman reputed to make herself sexually available; a prostitute. This term appears to be related to *floozie,* while the initial letter is probably suggested by that of *hussy.*

See also COOZIE, FLOOZY, HUSSY, LOOSE, PROMISCUOUS, PROSTITUTE.

horse. A metaphor that has been applied to both men and women. Men have been called a horse for being big, strong, wild, or formidable (in many cultures the horse has symbolized strength, youth, and masculine sexuality) but sometimes unattractive or stupid as well. A man may also be impugned as a "horse's ass." Sometimes *Horse* or *Hoss* (Norwegian for good luck) is simply a nickname or a term of address for a male (Hoss was one of Ben Cartwright's sons on the TV western *Bonanza*). *Horse* has also been used in police talk for a male officer who is honest and hardworking (Chapman 1998), and *workhorse,* meaning a hardworking person, is also usually reserved for a man.

Colt, meaning a male horse that is young or sexually immature, is also applied to a young man new to a position. *Stallion* and *stud* connote male sexuality or virility; both are often used positively, even self-descriptively. *Bronco* is a term for a young, inexperienced gay man considered "rough, and at times intractable to the advances of the homosexual; from the cowboy term for an unbroken, half-wild horse" (*The Guild Dictionary of Homosexual Terms* 1965).

When horse metaphors are used for women, they take on different, often more demeaning connotations. Women's sexuality is conveyed in *filly* and *nelly* (both connoting youth and smallness), *jade* (a "loose" or disreputable woman), the degrading *horseflesh* (see MEAT), *mare,* and *pony* (a chorus or burlesque dancer). *Harridan* is derived from a French word meaning old horse, the same meaning carried by *nag. Hot to trot* (which can also be used for a man) does not convey sexual vigor when applied to women but, rather, passion and availability (but it most likely derives from the sense of "eager to dance").

Horse has also implied a prostitute who works in a pimp's "stable" (a bunch of them is a "string of ponies"). In addition, *hobbyhorse,* the word for a toy horse that can be ridden, was a British colloquialism meaning a prostitute or loose woman. In both senses the person is viewed as little more than a body that will give someone, usually a man, pleasure or profit. For similar reasons, *mount*

has seen some slang use meaning a promiscuous woman or, at one time, a wife.

Women may also be disparaged as big and ugly with either the noun or an adjective form (*horse* or *horsie*): "I saw her picture...big horsie-looking bitch" (man-to-man talk in 1997 film *In the Company of Men*). *Horsewoman,* also used for a woman regarded as unattractive, is a heterosexual disparagement of the so-called masculinity of some lesbians, including what is seen as their "horsey" masculine clothing and "gait" (*Guild Dictionary*).

Horses and ponies are also subordinate to the people riding them. An old Chinese proverb says that "a wife married is like a pony bought; ride her and whip her as you like" (in Fikes 1992).

A woman may be regarded as formidable and determined with the expression *warhorse,* but her aggression is not as acceptable as that of a man referred to as a horse. Rather than being admired for her strength, she is more likely to be chided (see BATTLE-AX).

See also ANIMAL, BEAST, BISEXUAL (double-gaited), CORRAL, FILLY, HARRIDAN, HOT TO TROT, JADE, MAIDEN, MARE, NELLY, OLD GIRL, STALLION, STUD, WOMEN AS ANIMALS.

hose. A vulgar slang word for the penis since the nineteenth century; also found in the sense of a young woman's boyfriend (the relation in meaning is not coincidental). The epithet is reductive, probably often derisive, but not necessarily always intended as derogatory. *Hoseman* is used for a man regarded as sexually promiscuous (carrying similar connotations to those of STUD). Among the female usages, *hose, hosebag,* or *hosie,* usually regarded as offensive, may refer to a woman seen as homely, loathsome, or sexually promiscuous (compare with DOUCHEBAG). *Hose monster* refers to a person, usually a woman, who is believed to be very sexually active. *Monster* suggests something capable of devouring a "hose," or penis (see also NYMPH [nymphomaniac]). *Hoser* and *hose queen* (see also QUEEN) also mean a sexually active woman (*hoser* is also used for a promiscuous man or a con man). Except for *hose* in the sense of the penis and *hoseman*, which is in the general slang lexicon, these are largely high school and college usages of relatively recent currency.

hot. In the sense of sexy or lustful, a term originally used for women. In current usage *hot* is popular slang for someone who is considered sexy, exciting, or good-looking. *Hot* may also be heard in the gay male community in reference to men. It is said to have been in use in the lustful sense since Chaucer's time. A woman (and sometimes also a man), as said also of other mammals, is sometimes described as "in heat," that is, ready for sex.

In addition to the sense of strong physical desire, *heat* can connote something too dangerous to touch, such as a bomb or a firecracker or the stereotypically "fiery spitfire," also used as a metaphor for women (see BOMBSHELL, SPITFIRE). It also suggests the color red, associated with passion and blood.

There have also been a number of terms formed with *hot* that emphasize female lust or passion (though the male is not necessarily excluded in all instances). A "hot number," for example, where *number* suggests an attractive or sexually available person of the (often) other sex, frequently implies a woman (it may also refer to her telephone number). *Hot chocolate* means a sexy, young black woman. "Seal [male musician] squeeze Tyra Banks [supermodel] redefines hot chocolate" (*Maxim,* January/February 1998, 19) (see also BUNNY [chocolate bunny]). *Hottie* gives diminutive form to a woman considered sexy, while *hot* can also mean angry, applied to both sexes.

Hot pants is a slang reference to a woman seen as lustful and willing to have sex (it sometimes also refers to a sexually eager man). The phrase is often contructed as "to have hot pants (for someone)" (similar to "to have the hots for"), which may be used today by and for both sexes. Hot pants, a style of women's tight-fitting shorts designed to show off the legs and accentuate the curves in the buttocks, took their name, as bestowed by *Women's Wear Daily* in 1971, from the slang word. The idea is that the skimpy shorts represent both female sexuality and the woman herself (see also PANTS, SKIRT).

Hot mama alludes to a woman regarded as lustful and accessible for sex with a man. When she's so hot she turns color, she's a "red-hot mamma" ("I'm the Last of the Red Hot Mamas" was a hit song of 1929; see also MAMA). *Hot stuff* (see also EATING PUSSY) often means a woman considered highly sexed or sensuous (applied to a male, it may mean one who thinks he is "hot shit"). Playing on the spiciness of Mexican food, *hot tamale* refers to a Mexican woman—or any woman—regarded as very sexy, while a passionate woman may be known as a "hot tomato" (see also TOMATO).

See also BITCH (hotter than a bitch wolf), GENDER-SPECIFIC ADJECTIVES, HOT DOG, HOT TO TROT, MEAT (hot piece of dark meat), SPICE, TAMALE.

hot dog; hot shit; hotshot. *Hot dog*, someone taken as a show-off, especially a cocky athlete to exhibit his flashy skills. Typically used for men, but possibly applying to women also, *hot dog* was used throughout the twentieth century in this sense and also for the penis; thus, a "hot dog bun" is a woman.

Hot shit refers to a boy or man said to think a lot of himself—a very egotistical person (sometimes a woman, too). *Hotshot*, a brash person, is often a cocky young man (this expression would seem to be a euphemism for *hot shit*). *Hot nuts* is one patently sexual term applied to men: it means one who is quite lustful (see also LECHER, ZIPPER). Whatever the formation with *hot,* when it is used for women, it commonly implies sexuality; for men, though having some sexual connotations, it refers more often to accomplishment or attitude toward oneself.

See also HOT, HOT TO TROT.

hot to trot. An expression, meaning sexually aroused, often used for a woman, and considered rude or offensive. *Trot* is used for purposes of rhyme, but it may also suggest a FILLY, used for a young woman who is mounted like a horse for sexual purposes. Spears (1990), however, says *hot to trot* derives from the more general expression which means "eager to dance." When applied to a man, *hot to trot* is more likely to mean simply eager or ready to act.

A similar, somewhat dated expression is *hotter than a little red wagon* (*wagon* meaning a woman).

See also HOT, HOT DOG.

hound. See DOG.

househusband. See HOMEMAKER.

housewife. See HOMEMAKER.

hoyden. A girl or woman depicted as saucy, bold, and carefree. "She took pleasure in the various guises she could use: for instance, being a hoyden in lean trousers and sweaters, and then a siren...wearing a dress which made the most of her full breasts" (Doris Lessing, *The Golden Notebook,* 1981, 9).

Hoyden probably comes from an obsolete Dutch word, *heiden* (country lout), in turn from a Dutch word meaning heathen. In the earliest examples in writing in English, it meant an ignorant fellow or bumpkin, that is, a man. By the nineteenth century, the term came to be restricted to women, suggesting disapproval of their supposedly rude appearance or low-class behavior. The word reminds us that women, according to traditional expectations, are not supposed to appear loud, ill-bred, or tomboyish.

See also COQUETTE, HUSSY, TOMBOY.

hubby. See HUSBAND, HUSSY.

humanity; humankind. See MANKIND.

hump. A slang word referring to sexual intercourse (especially from a man's point of view), usually considered vulgar today. The term can also refer to a person—especially a woman, including a female prostitute—regarded as sexually available; for example, "That woman is a good hump." Applied to a man, it carries the sense of someone who is mean or loathsome, though it may also suggest a gay man who takes the PASSIVE role. In the sense of a sexual partner, the usage has been in U.S. slang since at least the 1920s. *To hump,* meaning to have sexual intercourse, has been in English from the eighteenth century.

See also LAY.

hunk. A large-built, "beefy" man, often one regarded as slow-witted (since the nineteenth century). Terms such as *hunk, hunky,* and *bohunk* were late-nineteenth- and early-twentieth-century epithets that disparaged unskilled immigrant workers from central or eastern Europe, who were regarded as men with the muscles—not brains—requisite for manual labor. *Hunk* was also used, mostly in the South, for a country man and for a white person. From a woman's point of view, a hunk is a sexually attractive man, such as a well-built athlete (mostly since the 1970s). Variations are *superhunk* and *megahunk,* for those men who exceed the standards of "hunkiness." *Hunk of tail* (or SKIRT, among many other possibilities) has also been used to designate a woman as a sex object.

In most senses of the term a purely physical attribute—a person as brawn or flesh—is suggested. Applied to men, the word suggests how patriarchy, so often blamed for distorting women's relations to their bodies, has done the same to men. In the case of men, however objectified they may be by the word, it may contain some sense of usefulness: they may be workers or athletes. The woman's only usefulness is as a sex object.

See also ASS (tail), BEEF (beefcake), MEAT.

hunter. A word for a person who pursues and kills game, often connoting masculinity and power. Virtually all depictions of real (vs. mythical) hunters in Western culture, regardless of the historical period, are of men. In Western civilization the "huntress" usually had a smaller role in this activity, if any, outside of classical mythology (e.g., Artemis, or Diana, presided over the hunt). Not that women haven't hunted: in the history of the United States, Rebecca Bryan Boone is known to have kept meat on her family's table when her husband Daniel was ill, and Stange (1997), writes that about one in ten American hunters is now female. Nonetheless, they are overshadowed by "man the hunter" (1).

Hunting implies virility, adventure, the hero quest, and the chase. The hunt as a rite of passage has played a role in the acquisition of a male identity among many men. Perhaps this is why Robert Bly (1990), a leader of the men's movement, advocates bolstering traditional masculinity with such metaphors as that of the hunt. Although Stange has discussed as stereotypes the contention that men are necessarily the predators, women and animals always the prey, the male objectification and control of animals cannot easily be separated from the objectification and control of women (Kheel 1995). Women are commonly pursued in the male metaphorical hunt and are even viewed as "meat"—sexual conquest. Such words as *target, quiver* (the case that holds the hunter's arrows), and *bullseye* have sometimes denoted women, more exactly, the vagina. In

British usage *game* refers to women as sex objects that men pursue. "Man is the hunter; woman is his game" (Alfred, Lord Tennyson, *The Princess*, 1947, part v). When women pursue men—or set their "traps"—they take on the image of a predator rather than a sportsman, their "prey" being "helpless" male victims (see also SEDUCTRESS, SHE-DEVIL, VAMP). Although hunting can also signify survival—providing necessary food for the domestic group—and can offer a connection with nature for men and women alike, it is also often closely tied with aggressively mastering one's environment in order to exalt in that mastery—in one sense, lording it over animals, and sometimes, women.

The aggressiveness implied in the male hunter role also comes through in related words in our language. Thus, according to Random House *Webster's College Dictionary* (1991), *venery* has had two meanings: the practice of hunting (dated to the thirteenth century) and the gratification of sexual desire (from the fifteenth century). If hunting involves killing and eating an animal, then the second sense of *venery* implies rape (Adams 1995, 74). In some ways, the carnivorous animals themselves have served as a paradigm for male behavior.

In some traditional hunting cultures, where the hunter was necessary for survival, the myth of the mother GODDESS complemented and balanced that of the hunter. The goddess symbolized fertility and the wholeness of life, while the hunter took life in order to preserve those of his kind or band. However, during the Western Bronze Age, according to Baring and Cashford (1991), the myth of the hunter evolved into that of the masculine warrior-hero, and the link with the myth of the goddess was severed.

So important has the concept of "man the hunter" been that most anthropologists, at least until recent decades, accepted the notion that men as hunters were responsible for the rise of human intelligence and culture. Women, on the other hand, seemingly tied to gathering plants, cooking, and breast-feeding, were portrayed as dependent, passive, and static in their cultural role.

More recent research on women, however, indicates that women as gatherers of food and as child tenders also contributed to the evolution of human capabilities. Women have made substantial contributions to the food supply—up to 90 percent of the diet—in both foraging and agricultural societies, women hunt in many societies, and they are not necessarily devalued, even when men are primarily the hunters. Addressing the work of Lyn Wadley, Nelson (1997) notes her use of the term *meat provider* rather than *hunter* as a way of shedding "all the baggage of implied masculinity and the implications of the hero's quest" (98).

See also CAVEMAN, FOX, GROUSE, HERO, MACHO, MEAT, PIGEON, QUAIL, TARZAN, WOLF.

hurricane. See WOMEN AS STORMS.

husband. Deriving from Old English *hūs* (house) and Old Norse *bōndi* (a freeholder or yeoman, from *bua*, to dwell), originally meaning a houseowner, a man at the head of the household, thus coming to mean a married man. *Husbandry*, though later restricted to farm management, referred to what the husband did as the head of the household. *Husband* came to carry connotations stronger than those of *wife*. "'To husband' draws dignity, whereas 'to wife' is hardly a verb but when said brings to mind her sexual duty" (Gouëffic 1996, 71). Ephesians 5:22–24 tells us that "The husband is the head of the wife, even as Christ is head of the church." The Christian Right has taken its cues in its antifeminist agenda from Ephesians and buttressed itself ideologically in favor of the husband.

Both wives and husbands are often said to "cheat" on their spouses, but unlike wives, husbands, traditionally believed to be more naturally restless, have also been said only to "stray." Language becomes a subtle linguistic justification of male unfaithfulness. Our common ordering of spouses—*husband and wife*—also suggests the term's strength.

Husband is not without its weakness, however. The male spouse has come to suffer a few stereotypes, and in a context like *househusband,* the image of *husband* is not strong enough to counteract the humor sometimes suggested.

Husband also occurs in prison slang for a dominant partner in a homosexual relation, especially one who is bisexual or has sex with men only because women are not available. Early in the twentieth century in gay communities, the term referred to men who conformed to masculine standards but engaged in sexual activity with other men at least some of the time. (See AUNT for a discussion of kinship terms in gay culture.)

See also MASTER, MOTHER (father), WIFE.

hussy. A term meaning a saucy, mischievous young woman or a brazen or lewd woman. Formerly this term meant the female head of a household, or housewife (sixteenth-century Middle English *huswife*). Starting in the seventeenth century, as men participated increasingly in the public sphere, enhancing their power there, and as household work came to be thought of as "women's work" or peasant labor, the term acquired the pejorative meanings of a rustic, rude, or bossy woman. Later it was sexualized, first taking on the meaning of a pert young woman, then denoting a lewd woman or prostitute. It is often preceded by such clearly negative modifiers as *bold* (supposedly too aggressive for a woman), *shameless*, or *brazen* (all of which only give emphasis to what the word already connotes). Also seen as *huzzy*.

See also COQUETTE, HEN (hen hussy),
HOYDEN, JADE, JEZEBEL, PROSTITUTE, SADIE
THOMPSON, TRAMP.

hustler. An energetic, go-getter type of a
person or a swindler, commonly applied
to a man. A woman called a hustler is
usually a prostitute. A male prostitute,
or any man regarded as working "fast"
with women, has, since the early twentieth century, also been called a hustler,
a use perhaps even more common than
the female sense. When applied to males
today in the sexual sense, especially in
gay communities, the term indicates a
male prostitute with homosexual male
clients. The male hustler, however, is not
necessarily gay (or may deny that he is);
he may be straight or bisexual, though
sexual orientation may not be stabilized
among adolescent male prostitutes.

P. Maloney gives us the names of
several different types of male hustlers
with male clients. These are the *punk*
(offered protection in exchange for
sexual services, especially in prison), the
"drag prostitute" (a transvestite or
presurgery male-to-female transsexual),
"brothel prostitutes" (working in a house
of prostitution), the *kept boy* (who benefits materially from having a long-lasting relationship with a sugar daddy), the
relatively high-status *call boy*, "bar hustler," and the low-status "street hustler"
(in Herdt 1989, 133).

See also CRACK (crack salesman),
HOOKER, JAG, KNOBBER, PROSTITUTE.

hysteria. Ultimately from Greek *hysterikos*,
from *hystera* (womb) plus *–ikos*, originally describing a condition of women
believed to suffer from disturbances of
the womb. Hysteria, the disorder that
psychiatrists now call conversion reaction, or more generally, psychoneurosis,
was said to be characteristic of women.

Supposedly prone to loss of emotional restraint and related disturbances
in the body, women were commonly
believed to be afflicted with hysteria
because of the malfunctioning of the
uterus, though the medieval church took
a religious stance and deemed the condition a result of bewitchment (see also
WITCH). In the eighteenth and nineteenth
centuries, medical doctors viewed the
uterus as floating, thus explaining
women's so-called emotional outbursts.
Men, so *they* said, were emotionally
stable, not given to losing control as
women were believed to do, but then,
men lacked uteruses. Although some
nineteenth-century physicians began to
suspect that women manifesting such
symptoms as fainting and fits were only
malingering, evading their duties at
home and with their husbands, the condition continued to be regarded as medical.

The comparable medical condition
that men commonly suffered when hysteria was epidemic among nineteenth-
century women was called neurasthenia.
But rather than being attributed to some
innate biological weakness, neurasthenia was said to be the result of the hard
work and mental labor characteristic of
the middle-class professional man. Not
typically denigrated for his condition as
women were sometimes condemned for
hysteria, the neurasthenic could excuse
himself as being a victim of his own success (Rotundo [1993] contrasts the two
conditions in his chapter on work and
identity among men).

Sigmund Freud viewed such "hysterical" symptoms in women as para-
lyzed limbs, blindness, vaginal spasms,
and fainting spells not as indications of
bewitchment or malingering but as
symptoms of a real illness. Claiming that
hysteria was passive, and assuming a
natural disposition to passive sexuality
on the part of women—an assumption
reinforced by the Victorian climate—
Freud tried to explain why this "illness"
seemed more specific to women. But
what Freud and psychiatry in general
have tagged clinically as "hysteria" in

many ways corresponds to the behavior or attributes traditionally *expected* of women: the body alienated as object, emotionalism, unanalytic thinking, and dependence on others for an identity and sense of security. This behavior, in fact a product of a marginalized social status, was, by use of the medical model, *reduced* to a "disease"—a physical manifestation or personal problem.

Women's "problems" have often been described in terms of "disease" (see FEMALE PROBLEMS) and women themselves as "patients" (Ehrenreich and English 1978). Some historians, however, have also tried to explain the "female disorder," tremors, or fits that have been labeled hysteria as an acceptable outlet for rebelliousness, rage, or despair for the overly domesticated woman, especially of the repressive Victorian era in which women were not allowed to express independence or dissatisfaction with their lives (Smith-Rosenberg 1972).

Since the nineteenth century, feminism has also often been dismissed as the product of women's alleged "hysterical" tendencies. Feminists generally view the stereotype of hysterical women as a means by which men deny privilege and opportunity to women; for example, women cannot be presidents, we are still sometimes told, because they are prone to illogic and emotional volatility, thus allowing men to protect their positions of authority as a male domain.

Robert Jean Campbell's *Psychiatric Dictionary* (1989) notes five ways the term *hysteria* may be used, including the "hysterical personality," but it concludes with the following use: "loosely, as a term of opprobrium." *Hysterical* is what men (and some women, too) still call women who express anger or other signs of what men deem as irrational, especially when it is not becoming to the traditional subordinate role of women. To many men the behavior is just another trial laid before them by women. "Hysteria is a natural phenomenon, the common denominator of the female nature. It's the big female weapon, and the test of a man is his ability to cope with it" (Tennessee Williams, *The Night of the Iguana*, 1961, in Stibbs 1992).

See also CURSE, FEMALE PROBLEMS, GENDER-SPECIFIC ADJECTIVES (impulsive), MOTHER (the mother), NERVOUS DISORDER, QUEEN (drama queen).

I

icebox; ice queen; ice princess. *Icebox*, any person believed to lack emotional warmth but applied to women in particular, especially in male use. *Icebox* was in use at least throughout the twentieth century. Similarly, *ice queen* or *ice princess* (see also PRINCESS, QUEEN) means a woman lacking in emotion (late twentieth century). "Powerful women often attract some unflattering names: 'troublemaker,' 'difficult,' or even 'ice queen'" (Arlene Weinbraub, *Working Mother,* June 1998, 13). *Ice queen,* however, has also been adopted as a persona name by female computer gamers participating in aggressive fighting games in competition with men.

Men, of course, are often viewed as lacking in emotional expression compared with women, yet they are less likely than women to be tagged pejoratively for it.

See also FRIGID.

ice cube with a hole in it. See FRIGID.

impotent. Said of a man who lacks physical vigor, especially one who is unable to perform sexual intercourse, from the Latin *impotentia* (lack of power). The implication is that a man's strength stems from his ability to perform sexually, an extremely limiting criterion for masculinity. More broadly, an impotent male is one viewed as inadequate or lacking in effectiveness in other areas where men are expected to excel. As a medical term referring to the inability to attain or sustain a penile erection as a part of the male sexual function, the inability to ejaculate, and even sterility, *impotence* carries a heavy load of meaning liable to diminish a man's ego. In the spring of 1998 the American Medical Association's manual of style for medical writers abandoned *impotence* for the supposedly more descriptive and precise *erectile dysfunction*. Although the latter may be dis-missed as jargon and euphemism by many, it is beginning to establish itself in technical contexts (*Copy Editor,* June-July, 1998, 6).

Unlike *frigid,* which is viewed today as a sexist usage describing a woman, *impotent,* while often a put-down, still carries less political weight. Women may even be blamed for a man's impotence, thus making the impotent male seem like a victim of the woman and often her stereotypical dominance or overbearing manner (see also BITCH). What's more, as Spender (1980, 177) has pointed out, because a woman's frigidity can be regarded as a form of reluctance—to respond to *his* sexuality rather than to use her own—it takes on the appearance of a form of power against men (passive resistance or unavailability); men's impotence, on the other hand, is viewed more as a form of physical handicap, not a matter of choice.

See also CASTRATING, DRYBALLS, FRIGID.

impressionist; impersonator. See DRAG.

impulsive. See GENDER-SPECIFIC ADJECTIVES.

Indian princess. See PRINCESS.

intersexual. See HERMAPHRODITE.

inversion; sexual invert. *Inversion,* a term used euphemistically for homosexuality, from the Latin *vertere* (to turn). Once understood as a turning in toward one's own sex rather than outward to the other sex, *inversion* also came to mean the adoption of the behavior, manners, or sentiments of the other sex—a reversal from the "normal" pattern.

The concept was first developed by the German psychiatrist Karl Friedrich Otto Westphal and translated into English as "inverted sexual proclivity" in 1869 in a paper of his reviewed in a British journal (in Haeberle and Gindorf 1998, 123). The idea of inversion, which Freud helped to introduce into our discourse, suggests what Foucault (1978) called the "disease of effeminacy" in men; hence, its unfortunate clinical connotations. The term is still heard in behavioral science contexts, where it is meant to be descriptive. "Once popular images of the 'Drag Show' and 'transvestite queen'...seem a mixture of stereotypic inversion and camp protest against stigma" (Herdt 1989, 8). Yet lesbians and gay men have been skeptical of terms, however seemingly descriptive, used in academic discourse that make them "objects" of study.

Invert, first recorded in 1838, indicates a gay man, especially an effeminate one; a lesbian; or a transvestite. In each case, it commonly connotes a sexual misfit. Somewhat like *pervert*—which, however, implies misdirection of sexuality rather than reversal—*sexual invert* was once regarded as a technical term and enjoyed currency among medical doctors, police, and the socially conscious. "He has frequented gay bars, attended 'drags,' and invaded so-called 'circles' where inverts gather" (Robert Lindner, *Must You Conform?* 1956, 49). However, whatever neutral use *invert* may have once had, now it often carries negative connotations.

With heterosexuality established as normative in society, the concept of homosexuality implies a standing of things on their head, a change in the normal order of things, a reversal in gender behavior or desires, a subversion of heterosexual people, or just being mixed up.

See also DEVIANT, HOMOSEXUAL, HOMO-SEXUALITY AS DISEASE, OPPOSITE SEX (third sex), PERVERT, SICK, TRANSGENDERIST, TRANSVESTITE, TWISTED.

ironballs. A man, often an army officer, regarded as overly tough or harsh. The allusion is to having hard testicles, which represent a social norm of masculinity.
See also CAVEMAN, HE-MAN, MACHO.

iron lady. See LADY (iron lady).

iron maiden. Originally, a term applied to a torture device, supposedly medieval, formed of a hollow iron statue or coffinlike frame shaped like a woman and often painted with a woman's smiling face. This hollow structure enclosed a victim who was either starved to death or impaled on spikes lining the inside. The inquisition-like menace and the severity of the cruel machine have been transferred to a woman viewed as an inanimate object having some of the same harsh and unyielding characteristics. Ironically, a maiden was soft and virginal, but many words for women are ambivalent, even to the extreme. Today, many rock enthusiasts probably know the term as the name of an English rock combo that plays uncompromisingly heavy metal, named after the instrument of torture.
See also BALL AND CHAIN, LADY (iron lady), MAIDEN.

iron man. See LADY (iron lady).

J

jack. A name and also an epithet derived from the Middle English Jacke, a nickname for Johan (John) and long used as a familiar term of address for a man regarded as low-bred or socially inferior. *Jack* has acquired a plethora of uses, many quite innocuous, including as a term of address for a man whose name is not known and as an intensifier in such phrases as *every man jack* (every individual man). It is also a historical epithet (often capitalized) for sailors and has been applied to servants (the playing card jack is a figure of a servant or soldier) and other workingmen as well as serving as a shortened form of *lumberjack*.

A "jack-of-all-trades" might be a woman (more appropriately, a "jill-of-all trades"), but the term's masculine cast is suggested, for example, by the sometimes added "*master* of none." *Jack* has also denoted various kinds of mechanical devices and animals: the jack hare is a male animal, as is the jackass, which also gives us a name for a stupid person or fool. Perhaps related to *jackass* is *jack* used as a derogatory reference to a black man (Spears 1990). *Jack* can also be used in the sense of a "blockhead" or "jerk."

Jack sometimes carries sexual meanings and sometimes a vulgar tone. For example, although a jack-in-the-box is a toy figure, such as a clown's head that springs up when the lid of the box is raised, formerly, primarily in British slang, the word referred to the penis inside the vagina (see also BOX) and also to syphilis; and *jack's house* (or *place)* is a dated term for a privy. The earlier sexual senses of *jack*—the penis (usually as *John Thomas*) and to have sexual intercourse (from a male point of view)—are preserved in *jack-off,* used contemptuously for a male masturbator or a doltish man. The vulgar *jack-shit*

means a worthless or stupid man. Thorne (1990) notes also that Jack, as a racier form of John, has often carried overtones of raffishness. Prostitutes may refer to their customers as "Jacks."

See also DICK, JACKAL, JOCK, JOHN, PRICK, SCHMUCK.

jackal. An animal metaphor meaning a lackey who helps someone commit base or disreputable acts—and, by extension, any loathsome person—probably most often applied to men. *Jackal* comes from the idea of jackals preceding lions to flush out their prey. It probably picks up some of the connotations of the male word *jack.*

See also BUZZARD, FUTZ.

jackass. See JACK.

jack-off. See JACK.

jack-shit. See JACK.

jade. From the Middle English *iade*, a fourteenth-century term originally applied contemptuously to a horse (and may still be used for a broken-down, useless, or vicious horse). By the sixteenth century, and through at least the nineteenth, it also designated a woman regarded as worthless, shrewish, or disreputable. *Jade* may also be used for a flirtatious girl, similar in meaning to *hussy,* and it is applied disparagingly to an old woman. This association between a horse and a woman is not coincidental; *horse* has long been a degrading metaphor for women.

See also HORSE, HUSSY, NAG, SHREW, WOMEN AS ANIMALS.

jag; jagoff. *Jag,* a reference to a gay male prostitute, from the mid-twentieth century. Spears (1991) describes it as a verb meaning "to be a male prostitute to other males." Although he identifies it with homosexual use, the term appears, according to informants, to have little currency, if any today, in gay communities (see also HUSTLER). *Jag* can also mean a drinking spree (or a drunk man) or a sensational experience, from which the drinking sense probably derives; or an odd or incompetent man—a "jerk." In verb form, it means to have sexual intercourse with a woman.

Jagoff, typically considered vulgar, is a man who masturbates regularly or, based on that sense, a worthless man. Like *jag,* it is usually found in male talk. See also JACK (jack-off).

jailbait. Since the early twentieth century, a girl who men are uncomfortably aware is not yet of legal age (age of consent) to engage in sexual intercourse. She is regarded as so dangerous that just flirting with her is believed to cause a man to end up in jail for statutory rape. " 'Who's that?' [man pointing to beautiful young woman] 'That's jailbait… Good for ten to fifteen years, with little chance for parole'" (made-for-TV movie *Netherworld,* 1992).

The word is also used for any woman whose sexual provocativeness is believed to be powerful enough to make a man do something that would lead to his arrest. Sometimes considered a linguistic deflection of guilt, the temptress-jailbait is deemed at fault for whatever sexual assault or other criminal behavior a man may inflict on her. *Jailbait* may also be used in gay communities for a male under the legal age of consent.

See also BAIT, FORBIDDEN FRUIT, LOLITA, QUAIL (San Quentin quail), TEMPTRESS.

Jane. A woman's given name that has taken on a number of meanings in colloquial or slang talk, including any woman or girl, a man's sweetheart, a woman that a man might pick up in the streets (including a prostitute), and a woman's lavatory. In England King Edward IV's sexual mistress, Jane Shore, a name that rhymes with *whore,* gave us *Jane* in the sense of a prostitute. Holder (1996), however, notes that Americans may prefer to find the derivation in the Hungar-

ian word *jany,* meaning a girl. A "plain Jane" is known for her drab appearance, a "Jane Doe" is any anonymous woman, and a "Calamity Jane" is a woman who is prone to disaster or is viewed as deficient in optimism.

In the 1960s feminists used *Jane Crow* (patterned on *Jim Crow*) to describe the way the system worked against women. Whereas *John Q. Public,* the "man on the street," is commonly heard in the sense of an average person, establishing the male citizen as the standard, *Jane Q. Public* is modeled on the male expression and is usually restricted in sense to the female public. *Jane* was also the name that Edgar Rice Burroughs gave to Tarzan's sweetheart, aka Jane Porter. Her relationship with the wild man who was lord of the jungle may be summed up in the apocryphal line, "Me Tarzan, you Jane (see also TARZAN).

See also JOE, JOHN.

Jane Q. Public. See JOHN (John Q. Public).

JAP. See PRINCESS (Jewish American Princess).

jasper. From the given name for a male, and believed to represent a common name for a country man, a term in use since the late nineteenth century in the sense of *yokel* or *hick*—derisive terms usually intended for men, as though only men, perhaps because of enjoying greater public prominence than women and representing the norm, can be rubes. Sometimes *jasper* is also used in the sense of any fellow man, an odd fellow, or one who does not seem to amount to much.

See also BARNEY, DUFFER, GEEZER.

In black English, largely during the mid-twentieth century, *jasper* sometimes meant a lesbian or bisexual woman. This usually derogatory use probably draws from the masculine sense of the term, reinforcing a stereotype of lesbians as women who have stepped outside the gender role assigned to women. Rodgers (1972) locates this usage in New York City.

See also LESBIAN.

jazz; jazz baby; jazzbo. *Jazz,* a term used in several senses in addition to the standard one, a form of music evolved in the United States and associated with African Americans. Slang meanings include the usually vulgar one of copulation, generally seen from a man's point of view, and women regarded by men as sex objects.

Jazz baby may be used for a young woman who takes an interest in jazz music or a woman reputed to be sexually promiscuous (see also BABY). *Jazzbo* is an expression for a man who plays or listens to jazz music or who wears stylish clothes. Its alternative, derived senses are a black man (only sometimes derogatory) and a fool.

All of these uses probably date to the late nineteenth or very early twentieth century.

jelly roll. A twentieth-century black English expression, from the name of a small cake rolled up with jelly, meaning the genitals of a man or a woman, sexual intercourse, or one's lover. As a woman's male lover, however, it may have less use. Thorne (1990) notes that the metaphor works better for a woman, deriving from the "rolling motion, the supposed resemblance of the cake to the vulva, and the notion of 'sweet reward.'" The sense of a male lover Thorne traces to the idea of a "*sweet*heart."

See also CAKE, CHEESECAKE, COOKIE, CREAMPUFF, CUPCAKE, DISH, PIE, SWEETIE, TART.

Jewboy. See BOY.

Jewess. See -ESS.

Jewish mother. See MOTHER.

Jezebel. Phoenician princess and queen of Israel, wife of Ahab, known in the Old Testament (1 Kings) as an idolator. In common use since the sixteenth century, *Jezebel* has served to describe an alluring woman said to be scheming, shameless (often a prostitute), or evil and betraying. A "painted Jezebel" was an expression applied to a woman reputed to be of "easy virtue." Although the epithet may be used for a woman of any race, when applied to an attractive black woman, it is a derogatory reference to her alluring ways regarded as tempting white men.

Collins (1991), sees the image of the Jezebel arising as a result of the need among white men during slavery to justify their frequent sexual assaults on black slave women (77).

> In these streets out there, any little white boy from Long Island or Westchester sees me and leans out of his car and yells…Say there, Jezebel!… Bet you know where there's a good time tonight. (Lorraine Hansberry, *To Be Young, Gifted, and Black,* 1969, 98)

The term may also serve to censure a black woman regarded as selling out her people in order, for example, to support a feminist cause.

See also QUEEN (woman), TEMPTRESS.

joanie. An adjective used to describe something or someone out of date, from the speaker's point of view, or old-fashioned. Thorne (1990) places *joanie* in the Valley Girl lexicon of the 1970s. He also notes that although its origins are obscure, it could reflect an antipathy to what is regarded here as an older-generation name or to such previous-generation performers as Joan Crawford or Joni Mitchell in particular. The usage suggests a cultural tendency to select a feminine word connected with age to connote something taken to be worthless.

See also OLD LADY.

job. A person deemed to be attractive, sexually available, or tough. Slang dictionaries typically note that *job* can describe either a man or a woman but tends to be directed mostly to women. In use for much of the twentieth century.

See also LOOSE, PROMISCUOUS.

jock; jockstrap. *Jock*, probably from the common Scottish form of the name Jack, used as slang for the penis beginning at least as early as the eighteenth century. As a verb, from a male point of view, it meant to copulate (both uses now obsolete).

The word has changed in meaning since the nineteenth century (at that time it also denoted female genitals), but it continues to carry masculine overtones. In the late nineteenth and early twentieth century, *Jock* or *jocker* was used in underworld slang for a pederast, in particular, a tramp who sought a younger boy companion for a sexual partner or to beg for him (the youth, or "prushun," was believed to be a virtual slave to his elder protector). In prison slang, *jock* was used for a gay male who takes the "active" role (see also PASSIVE, PEDERAST, WOLF).

As a shortened form of *jockstrap,* meaning athletic supporter (the meaning of which derives from the slang sense of *penis)* since the mid-twentieth century, *jock* has also carried the meaning of someone—usually still a man but increasingly also a woman—who participates in athletics, sometimes thought of disparagingly as large and dim-witted.

Lighter (1997) reports pejorative student use for a white, conservative, middle-class male athlete usually thought of as convivial but not very perceptive. Educational researcher Penelope Eckert (1989), who studied teenage subcultures in high schools in the Detroit metropolitan area, found that the generally endorsed "jock" identity embraced respectable middle-class values, such as living a "clean lifestyle," accepting the authority of the school officials, and participating in such activities as student government as well as (but not necessarily) athletics. The opposing identity in these

schools was that of the working-class "burnout," associated with alienation from school and contempt for the "jocks." The school massacre that occurred in 1999 in Littleton, Colorado, brought the animosity between such identity groups to light.

Jockstrap is also applied to a supposedly dumb or obnoxious male, especially among young men.

Jocko, applied to an athlete, has also found use to name a boy or man considered dumb. *To be on someone's jock,* late-twentieth-century slang, is said of a female who is pursuing a man for sexual or romantic purposes.

Reflecting positive use for women, the magazine *Girljock,* started in the 1990s by editor Roxxie, is for women who participate in sports.

See also TOMBOY.

jocker. See JOCK.

Joe. A name suggesting a man who represents the average American, an ordinary, white working- or middle-class guy— the "typical" one pollsters interview to ascertain what people in general are thinking. The use of *Joe* for an ordinary fellow dates to the early twentieth century. A likable woman may also be a "Joe," or "good Joe."

Joe (sometimes lowercase) was used during World War II for any American, especially one in the military. *Joe Blow*, meaning any man, is a 1920s-derived usage from black musicians (perhaps from the idea of blowing a horn). *Joe Sixpack* (Mr. Average) may be as recent as the 1970s (the allusion here is to the six-pack of beer always at his side). The implications of these terms, for which there are no exact female equivalents (compare with JANE), is that men represent the norm—"the people"—and women are not worth consulting for their points of view. *Joey,* heard around the middle of the twentieth century among blacks for a white man, also suggests someone in the mainstream. Such usages as *Joe* and its variants may sometimes be derisive but not typically insulting like the related expressions *Joe Schmo* and *Joe Zilch,* both meaning a man who is nondescript and not much of anything—a real nobody.

See also JOHN.

John. From the given name for a man, an average man or any man, especially one whose name is not known; a group of people collectively; or a prostitute's male client. Applied as a euphemism for the penis (often as *John Thomas* or *johnny),* the term carries a heavy masculine tone (see also JACK).

John has been used since the eighteenth century as a name for a man who represents or personifies some group, such as John Bull personifies Englishmen, the British collectively, or Great Britain. *John Q. Public* is commonly heard in the sense of an average person, the "man on the street," establishing the male citizen as the standard (unless used in parallel with *Jane Q. Public*).

John Chinaman was once used as a personification of all Chinese, reflecting white people's view of a homogenized mass of people. Popular when Chinese immigrants to the United States were primarily laborers (and still mostly male), the usage revealed a patronizing attitude toward the Chinese as drudges. Applied to a Native American, the word is also disparaging and patronizing. To call an Indian man *Johnny Navajo* is to obscure his individuality.

In theater talk since the early twentieth century, *John* has referred to a man who tries to establish intimacy with the actresses, chorus "girls," or strippers. In related usage, *John* (sometimes lowercase) has signified a rich, gullible man who keeps a showgirl or prostitute and, commonly since at least the mid-twentieth century, any man who patronizes a prostitute.

Major (1994) says that in the black

community, a "John" in this sense is usually used to mean a white man. Just as female prostitutes are usually targeted for legal action more often than their male patrons are, prostitutes have been given much more linguistic attention. The names for the customers number only a few—*John,* TRICK, *date*, or TRADE—while well more than a hundred terms, many of them scornful, have been slung at prostitutes. *John* may be used by a male prostitute as well as by a female (see also SCORE).

Related meanings of *John,* usually mildly disparaging, include a man who has been victimized by a swindler (a "sucker") or one who fraternizes with lesbians (use is restricted mostly to lesbian communities). A more common use has been as a colloquialism for a toilet.

Johnny has also served a number of uses but most commonly means any man, a young man in particular, or one who is shallow and devoid of substance.

See also JANE, JOE.

Johnny. See JOHN.

joyboy; joy girl. *Joyboy,* a man who always clowns around, to the point of appearing obnoxious or, ironically, a glum, serious man. *Joy boy* (two words) has been used for a gay male or any male viewed as sexually active. *Joy girl* derives from the French *fille de joie,* meaning a prostitute (*joy sister* was an early-twentieth-century variant). The joy in *joy girl* is meant for men. Both these terms appeared around the second decade of the twentieth century.

See also PROSTITUTE.

Juliet. See ROMEO.

just another pretty face. A young woman, whatever her talents and intellect, who is dismissed as just another sex object. This expression has come to be applied to men as well as women, commonly implying that he or she is ordinary.

See also BEAUTY, FACE THAT LAUNCHED A THOUSAND SHIPS, LOOKSISM, SEX OBJECT.

K

Ken. From the name for the male counterpart of the Barbie doll and referring to a man viewed as blandly handsome and conformist in appearance.

See also BARBIE DOLL.

kept boy. See HUSTLER, KEPT WOMAN.

kept woman. A woman whose services are said to be maintained at the disposal of (usually) a man. The term implies female passivity: she is the one kept, while the man does the keeping. It is not a term that most women, even those who are financially supported, would likely apply to themselves, though a woman might use it for another woman. The man supporting the woman is not called a "keeper"; he might, though, be called by the patronizing DADDY or, if he is expected to buy expensive gifts for her, *sugar daddy*. The closest male equivalent in the heterosexual world would be *toyboy,* but gay men might also have a "kept boy" (see also HUSTLER).

Keptie is a derived slang word meaning a mistress.

See also EASY LAY, LOOSE, MISTRESS, PROMISCUOUS, PROSTITUTE.

Kewpie doll. See DOLL.

killer. See LADY-KILLER.

king. From Old English *cynn* (kin), a male sovereign or monarch. There is ample linguistic evidence that the king tends to "bump" the queen as a paradigm of rule or preeminence.

King, like the equally masculine *lord,* is also used as a reference to God and Christ (along with the *kingdom of God*) and to any person or thing outstanding in its class ("king of the mountain"). The king is also the chief piece of each color in chess, a piece in checkers that has been crowned, and a playing card bearing the picture of a king—and which "takes" a queen. "King-sized" is bigger than "queen-sized." We may still hear

"Every man is a king in his own castle," although the term is probably carrying increasing irony among men.

The King's English refers to the standard English spoken in England and traditionally respected. In England during the reign of a woman, it is normally changed to *the Queen's English.* However, in the United States, in reference to English, *King's* is usually retained even during a woman's reign in England, and *kingdom* rather than *queendom* is always employed during a woman's reign.

From political talk comes *kingfish,* meaning a powerful organizer (like Huey P. Long, governor of Louisiana, known by the nickname of "the kingfish"). *King Shit,* usually considered vulgar—and which may have sarcastic or ironic overtones—is a man regarded as a big leader. A woman considered a leader of her community may be called a king only when she is a lesbian, suggesting the stereotype of masculinity.

See also DRAG (drag king), DUKE, PRINCE.

King Kong. See GORILLA.

kink; **kinky**. See PERVERT.

kitten. A small, cute, cuddly baby cat and also a nickname given to girls or young women seen as having those same qualities. For example, the youngest daughter (played by Lauren Chapin) in the 1950s TV sitcom *Father Knows Best,* known as Kathy to everyone else, was "Kitten" to her father.

In some contexts, however—especially as *sex kitten* (dating to 1940), popularized by gossip columnists in Hollywood—it connotes a woman, specifically, a young woman, as a sex object. *Kitty* was originally a pet name for a woman, but at one time it also acquired the meaning of a loose woman or prostitute. It is also used for the vagina, as illustrated in the double-punned saw: "A thrifty tom-cat puts something in the kitty every day" (Holder 1996).

Also, at least throughout the mid-twentieth century, *kitty* has been used in black slang, with feminine connotations, for a Cadillac: it purrs, it can be ridden, and a man gets inside it. Inside every kitten, a man might say, lurks a cat. Of Daniela Bianchi, who played Tatiana Romanova, James Bond's "girlfriend" in *From Russia with Love* (1963), *Maxim* magazine wrote "The Soviet sex kitten who's instructed to find Bond and do *whatever* he wants—thereby unwittingly sabotaging her own country" (January/February 1998, 57). At the same time, *hellkitten* has been used as a persona name by female computer gamers who participate in aggressive fighting games; the hellkitten does not purr or let men have their way with her (see also HELLCAT).

See also BEAST, BITCH (bitch kitty), BUNNY, CAT, FAWN, PET, PLAYMATE, WOMEN AS ANIMALS.

knave. See SLATTERN.

knobber. A term for a male transvestite or female "impersonator," often one who is a prostitute, used especially among police. Chapman (1998) notes it may come from their wearing of false nipples or breasts, also known as "knobs," or from giving "knob jobs," that is, fellatio.

See also CROSS-DRESSER, HUSTLER, PROSTITUTE, TRANSVESTITE.

knockout. Anything considered thrilling for some reason or a person of some overwhelming quality, but often a very good-looking or sexy person; in use since at least the nineteenth century. Although the term may apply to either sex, it is probably more often meant for a very beautiful woman, who might also be known by the synonym *stunner*. The idea of the knockout is that she is seen as capable of disabling (or flooring) a man, as by a punch. Another synonym is *corker,* which also means a hard blow. The references to aggression reflect on the male experience of women's sexuality as a kind of weapon.

See also BOMBSHELL, FEMME FATALE, GENDER-SPECIFIC ADJECTIVES (ravishing), WOMEN AS STORMS.

L

la-di-da, **la-de-dah**. A slang expression used since the mid-nineteenth century to describe behavior that is considered affected, pretentious, or precious in manner. It is applied to someone considered a fop or any effeminate young man. Usually with negative connotations, the expression may stereotype a gay male as flamboyant or feminine in behavior.

See also EFFEMINATE, PRISSY.

ladies' man, **lady's man**. A term for a man who prefers to spend his time with women, who is attentive to them, and is likely to think that they like him. "He is a ladies' man, and that's why I'm attracted to him" (young woman on TV talk show *Jenny Jones,* 10 March 1998). This term dates to the early nineteenth century.

Most men called by this name would not likely find it objectionable (a contemptuous synonym is *lady-monger*). It is flattering to most men to think that they are suave and able to please women. At worst, the word may suggest that the man is simply a victim of his own charms.

> Today's "womanizers" were yesterday's "roués," "gallants," "ladies men," "Don Juans," and "Casanovas." With the old labels these men could be perceived as romantic figures, as men who were helpless to prevent the adoration that they received from women and the secret envy that they inspired in less-appealing men. (Carpineto 1989, 11)

In some contexts, though, the expression might take a subtle swipe at a man's manliness—why doesn't he spend more time with the guys? Or it may suggest a moral flaw, as does *playboy*, or conceit, as in *God's gift to women.* Many will suspect that the ladies' man is out to break some hearts, and others will regard as trivializing the reference to *la-*

dies, a term that connotes lack of seriousness or worth (see LADY). Although there are many terms for women who tempt, seduce, and destroy men, no female term is parallel in connotations to *ladies' man,* probably because women are still not always allowed to "play the field" to the same degree as are men.

See also CAKE, CASANOVA, DON JUAN, HOOCHIE (hootchie-cootchie man), LADY-KILLER, LOTHARIO, LOUNGE LIZARD, LOVE MACHINE, LOVER, MACK, PLAYBOY, ROMEO, ROUÉ, SCUTZ, WOMANIZER.

lady. Beginning in the ninth century, a word for a mistress in the older, polite sense of that term—a female head of a household. Within about a century, it came to mean the woman whose social position corresponded to that of a lord. This was a title signifying high status, though the lady might often have been expected to "obey her lord" (Gouëffic 1996, 147). It also came to denote a woman to whom a chivalrous man devoted himself. In the same sense of feminine purity, the term came to be used in the phrase *Our Lady* or *Virgin Lady.*

Lady acquired a different tone by the nineteenth century, when it came to designate any properly behaved (by the standards of the day) or admired woman, usually one well placed socially and married to a man who provided some measure of comfort. "You haven't the faintest idea what it means to be a Great Lady" (said to the timid fiancée [Joan Fontaine] of the lord [Laurence Olivier] of the English estate of Manderley in the Hitchcock-directed movie *Rebecca* [1940]).

Here it also had some classist implications. In a now well-known discussion of the usage, Robin Lakoff (1975) argued that the term primarily connoted a lack of seriousness—a "lady" was not likely to be someone who accomplished anything worthwhile. During the burgeoning nineteenth-century so-called Cult of Domesticity, feminine culture was characterized by wearing corsets and other stiff, close-fitting garments and by refined gentility and breeding.

In this context, the term projected an image of ornamentation, uselessness (except to demonstrate one's ability to define the leisure class; see also CORSET CROWD), and being in the service of men. Such a woman, however refined and respected—the exalted "arbiter of morality, judge of manners" as discussed by Lakoff (52)—was not meant to have much influence, especially in public life. Miss Alice Brayton of Newport, Rhode Island, voiced the norm when she said "A lady's name should appear in the papers three times—when she is born, when she marries and when she dies" (in *American Treasury,* 1955).

By the twentieth century, *lady* took a greater downward turn in such expressions as *cleaning lady* and *lady politician,* carrying an ironic sense of condescension (Flexner and Soukhanov 1997). Schulz (1975, 65) refers to this process of change over the years as a "democratic leveling," characteristic of terms for women as opposed to those for men. "The more demeaning the job, the more the person holding it (if female, of course) is likely to be described as a lady. Thus, *cleaning lady* is at least as common as *cleaning woman"* (Robin Lakoff, in McPhee and FitzGerald 1979, 117). Perhaps the worker is supposed to think the title is more meaningful than the wages. *Lady* is also found in slang meaning simply a girlfriend.

When *lady* serves to feminize the name of a role or occupation—such as *lady cop*—the meaning shifts to something slightly out of the usual or even comical; in any case it is not to be taken as seriously as *cop* alone, which may be used for a male cop or applied generically. Also, in spite of its respectable history and traditional use to signal politeness, *lady* has come to acquire sexual connotations in such slang expressions as *foxy lady* (see FOX).

A number of euphemisms employing *lady* have been used at one time or another to signify a female prostitute. These include *lady of the night, landlady* (a "madam"), *lady of a certain description, lady of easy virtue, lady of no virtue, lady of pleasure,* and *lady of the stage* (see also ACTRESS).

Lady also occurs in slang for a man's effeminate homosexual companion or a gay queen (see also DUCHESS), and LADY LOVER has been used to designate a lesbian. In some instances, *lady* might be quite pejorative, as when applied to a male Marine recruit in basic training. (If he's a lady, he's not a man!)

Some *lady* expressions are losing ground, while others seem to be holding on and may serve a purpose or express bias. *Lady of the house,* a cliché from the nineteenth century, is passing away almost everywhere except among salespeople, often phone solicitors, who may still ask for "the lady of the house" (see also HOMEMAKER, MAN [man of the house]). At the same time, however, a female member of the House of Lords is still called a lady. *Our Lady* and perhaps also *ladies' night* also appear to be holding up, though only the perfunctory *ladies and gentlemen* address (one of the few instances where the female term precedes the male) to an audience seems embedded in the language.

It's not over till the fat lady sings, alluding to the stereotypical size of female opera singers, was a 1990s vogue cliché among, for example, sports commentators when asking people to wait until the end of a game or match before predicting who will win (Kirkpatrick 1996). At the same time, patronizing expressions such as *lady doctor* are being replaced by *woman doctor* (see WOMAN for potential bias).

Some women would like to see *first lady* (title since the 1850s for the wife of the president of the United States or other important official, but gradually dropping out of our political language) replaced with *first woman*. They also suggest that the woman's given and surname be used, according to her preference. LITTLE LADY, whether meant for a girl or a woman, is rapidly becoming anachronistic and is often regarded as inappropriate and sexist. Also, *boss lady* is not usually accorded the same respect as *boss man*, and *lady lover* is often ascribed a negative meaning.

Iron lady, used typically for a female authority figure (sometimes today for a female athlete), refers, often derisively, to her hard, masculine qualities (note that *iron chancellor* and *iron duke* were applied to royalty in admiration; and *iron man* refers more exclusively to one's athletic stamina, not personality).

> The so-called Iron Ladies—Indira Gandhi, Golda Meir, and Margaret Thatcher [see also BUTTERFLY]— have all sent men to their deaths at rates not dissimilar to those of the average male leader. (Farrell 1993, 63)

Terms such as *ladybird* (a woman's nickname and also a type of beetle), *ladyfinger,* and *lady's slipper* connote small size or daintiness.

See also BAG (bag lady), DAMSEL, FAIRY (fairy lady), GAL, GIRL, LADIES' MAN, LADY-KILLER, MADAM (landlady), MISTRESS, OLD LADY.

lady-killer. A reference to a man who thinks he is fascinating and irresistible to women, from the early nineteenth century. He devotes himself to their "conquest." "She had a love affair with the Honourable Henry Cust, a tremendous lady-killer whose conquests were, by all accounts, numerous and easy" (Kate Caffrey, *The 1900s Lady,* 1976, 108).

The words closest in meaning, when applied by men to women—such as *bombshell, femme fatale*, and *knockout*—imply that a woman's sexuality can be wielded against men, though one term refers to an object, one to an action, and the third is borrowed from French and assumes an exotic quality. *Lethal Lady* has been adopted by female computer gamers as a persona name suggesting the kind of aggressiveness it takes to confront and beat men in such games. In this context, however, it is a more democratic term than *Lady-Killer. Killer* as used in *lady-killer* actually derives from the sense of a person who is impressive or formidable at what he does, but of course the connotations of aggression and dominance are unmistakable. Yet *The Oxford English Dictionary* (1989) labels the word as "humorous."

See also BLUEBEARD, LADIES' MAN.

lady lover. Slang usage since the early twentieth century for a lesbian. Used outside the lesbian community, as it usually is, it may carry negative connotations or be overtly derogatory. A synonym is *girl kisser* (see also GIRL).

See also LESBIAN.

lady monger. See LADIES' MAN.

lamb; lambchop. *Lamb,* an animal metaphor suggesting a meek or peaceful person, one easily deceived, or a dear person or PET. Such a person may be thought of as passive or soft, thus stereotypically feminine. Whereas CRONE was once a word for an old ewe or female sheep, the younger *lamb* has more positive connotations.

In line with its feminine connotations, *lamb* has also occurred in prison slang for a subordinate homosexual male partner, often one easily abused (see also PASSIVE).

Lambchop is a meat metaphor for a woman considered pretty, dear, or likable.

See also MEAT, WOMEN AS ANIMALS.

latent. Applying to a quality that has not yet developed but is capable of doing so. This term occurred as psychiatric jargon, especially during the mid-twentieth century, to mean homosexual desires that have not emerged to consciousness but show signs of doing so. These desires may be thought of as either dormant (in abeyance only for now) or potential (theoretically, the case with everyone).

According to Sigmund Freud, who spoke of a "latency period" in psychosexual development during which sexuality slows to a virtual standstill, we are all essentially bisexual, although some of us are harsher on our homosexual impulses than others. It is these others—who may have explicitly homosexual dreams or fantasies and find it easier to succumb to same-sex desires, even though they may also be homophobic—who are the so-called latent ones.

Persons with strong latent tendencies may be described psychologically as subject to "homosexual panic," the extreme anxiety experienced by the individual in circumstances where the latent desires may be acted out. In fact, the very notion of latent homosexuality may actually contribute to the occurrence of so-called homosexual panic, since if the desires are present just below the surface, they could erupt into consciousness at any time, posing a threat to those who identify as heterosexual.

Homosexual individuals have also been spoken of as being "latent heterosexuals," a concept that may please those who see gay people as having been "diverted from their true path" (Ruse 1988, 49).

The term *latent* was perhaps first used by the early-twentieth-century English sex researcher Havelock Ellis. In his 1897 book, *Sexual Inversion*, Ellis, who did not quite accept the idea that homosexuality is acquired or the notion of "suggestion," wrote, "The seed of suggestion can only develop when it falls on a suitable soil" (in Mondimore 1996, 49).

For many psychiatrists, the idea of latent homosexuality is now untenable or meaningless. The word *latent* has

been losing ground in both the professional and the popular lexicon, except sometimes for playful reminders of what may now be considered psychobabble: "Better latent than never" (graffiti wordplay reported by Panati [1998, 109]).

See also CLOSET (closet queen), HOMOSEXUAL.

lavender; lavender menace. *Lavender*, a color associated with femininity (as is the fragrance, once worn by men to suggest their homosexuality) and, by extension, with profanity. Since the nineteenth century, *lavender* has been linked with homosexuality. Especially when used by heterosexuals, it has often been intended as a slur on a male's masculinity.

However, the term (and color) has been reclaimed by gay communities, sometimes seeing it as a blend of pink and blue—female and male—symbolizing the integration of gender. Grahn (1990) writes, in affirmation of the gay and lesbian culture, "We lavender folk sprang up, spontaneously flowering in the color we had learned as an identifying mark of our culture when it was subterranean and secret" (6).

Lavender menace, patterned on the Cold War reference to communism as the "red menace," is an epithet for lesbians, in the sense intended by Betty Friedan in 1969 when she used the term. Friedan, author of *The Feminine Mystique* (1963) and at the time president of NOW (National Organization for Women), viewed lesbians as an impediment to the goals of the women's movement, especially, she thought, by endangering the image of feminism.

Lesbians quickly reclaimed the term, some of them forming a group called the Lavender Menace, later called Radicalesbians. They showed up at the Second Congress to Unite Women in 1970 wearing T-shirts emblazoned with "Lavender Menace" and proceeded to charge the women's movement with heterosexism and discrimination against lesbians.

Lavender boy, meaning a gay male, was heard in the early-twentieth-century underground world (see also BOY). *Black lavender* is the color of African American homosexuality (and the name of a midwestern magazine for lesbians of color). An old reference to a heterosexual man believed to have homosexual tendencies is "to have a dash of lavender (in the garden)."

Color has long played a role in the history of homosexual people. In the Nazi German concentration camps, male homosexual prisoners were forced to wear an inverted pink triangle, associated with effeminacy, so they could be identified and called out for special abuse (pink was later used by U.S. gay activists as a symbol of their identity and to belie the myth that gays and lesbians don't face persecution). It was the Jehovah's Witness inmates in the camps who were marked by lavender. Lesbians, along with prostitutes and other so-called antisocial people, were made to wear a black triangle.

See also HOMOSEXUAL, LESBIAN, LILY (lilac).

lay. A slang word suggesting sexual intercourse, often from a male point of view. It connotes aggressiveness: a male laying or placing a woman on a bed or, in dated slang, "laying the log," meaning inserting the penis into the vagina. Rawson (1989), however, notes a possible derivation from the past tense of *lie*, used since the twelfth century in such forms as *lie with* and *lie by* in reference to sexual intercourse. The slang usage of *lay*, first used in the United States in a short story by James T. Farrell, has been around since the 1930s for a woman regarded as sexually available. It is often heard as "She's a good (or lousy) lay" or "an easy lay." The objectification of women is clear.

See also EASY LAY, HUMP, PUNCHBOARD, SCORE.

LBFM. An Asian woman thought of as a *"Little Brown Fucking Machine."* Usually considered very vulgar, the reference is typically to Southeast Asian women, especially those whom U.S. soldiers met during the Vietnam War. *Brown*, alluding to skin color, adds a racist note to the obvious objectification of women.

See also EXOTIC, LOVE MACHINE.

leather; leather boy; leather dyke. *Leather*, referring to leather jackets and the masculinity they symbolize, has, for much of the twentieth century and into the twenty-first, applied to a virile male or to any supposedly sadistic male, gay or straight. A second meaning of *leather* comes from the idea of leather "fetishism," practiced by some gay male sadomasochists, or—without the often unwanted psychological baggage—"leatherfolk." *Boy* is a polite SM term for the subservient partner of a "Master" (or "leather daddy").

Leather boy may be used more generally for a man who is attracted to leather as a fetish or (as *leatherboy*) for male motorcyclists and rockers, regardless of sexual orientation (see also BOY). In use since about the 1950s, *leather boy* for a gay man may be self-descriptive. "Leather queens" are gay men who parody the ultramasculine role in their outfits of tight-fitting leather (see also QUEEN). Both of these words are most acceptable only within the gay communities.

Leather dyke refers to a lesbian who sports leather outfits and accessories and may be into the SM scene or bondage. The term, which finds its most acceptable use in the lesbian community (see also QUEEN and DYKE for potential bias), is not parallel with *leather boy* in some very important ways. Unlike the gay male term, *leather dyke* suggests dominance. This is not to say, however, that she should be considered masculine, a lesbian version of a male. The leather dyke world was described in Kate Allen's 1993 novel, *Tell Me What You Like*. *Leather woman* is a synonym, though lacking some of the connotations of masculinity of *leather dyke* (there may also be straight or bisexual leather women).

See also HOMOSEXUAL.

lecher; letch. *Lecher,* a man known for his lewdness and indulgence in sexual—usually heterosexual—activity; from the twelfth century. *Lecher* is of Germanic origin, related to Old High German *leckōn* (to lick), suggesting sensuality. It connotes not only an inordinate interest in sex but also often an inappropriate one—as that of an older man, as though because of age he is not supposed to have sexual desires. In fact, the relatively recent slang variant *letch* (or *lech*) is often constructed as the disapproving "old letch." As opposed to such words as *Casanova* and *playboy*, which carry positive connotations and deflect blame from men for their promiscuous behavior, *lecher* is highly disparaging, though sometimes ironic. *Letch* is also sometimes heard in reference to a woman.

See also BADGER, BILLY GOAT, CASANOVA, COCK (cock hound), CUNT (cunt hound), DIRTY OLD MAN, DOG, EXHIBITIONIST, GENDER-SPECIFIC ADJECTIVES (randy), GOAT, HEAD (headhunter), HOT (hot nuts), PLAYBOY, RAKE, ROUÉ, SCUTZ.

left-handed. A term used by heterosexuals to mean homosexuality. Because of cultural associations with something crooked or inferior, left-handedness is used here to suggest deviance. In German, *links* (left), is used for gay people.

See also DEVIANT.

leg; leggy; leg man. *Leg,* a term also used (in addition to its primary meaning) in a reductive way to mean sexual intercourse with a woman (from a male point of view) or a woman viewed as sexually available (sometimes any woman, regardless of sexual interest). Through-out much of the twentieth century, this use was often associated with black slang, but today it is also heard among college students of different backgrounds. The word may be heard in use mostly by men in such phrases as "piece of leg" (see also PIECE); it is also constructed as "some leg!"

Leggy, meaning having long and shapely legs, is typically, if not always, used of women and is not derogatory, though it may be considered looksist. A variant expression is "She has legs all the way up to her neck." *Leg man* is male talk for a man who particularly likes women with attractive legs (see also ASS MAN, TIT MAN). *Leggy* may also be used by women for other women, just as *leg man* may sometimes be used by women for men.

See also DIRTYLEG, MEAT, PROMISCUOUS.

les. See LES(S)

lesbian. A term for a female homosexual, from the 1880s. Today *lesbian* would be defined as a woman whose emotional, social, and often political as well as sexual interests lie in someone of her own sex. The noun *lesbian* made its debut in the more-or-less modern sense in an article in 1883 in a U.S. medical journal (*The Alienist and Neurologist*), describing a woman who crossed-dressed. However, only the use of *lesbianism* in the current sense of same-sex orientation between women was new, not the term itself. In earlier centuries, the term carried the meaning of "oral intercourse," without reference to the sex of those engaging in it.

The sexual as well as emotional and social lives of women and ideas about them change over history and vary across cultures, making it difficult to define lesbianism. However, in reference to modern American life, feminist theorist Ann Ferguson has offered three definitions or aspects of lesbianism: a clinical term that is often pejorative; a sociopolitical self-definition of lesbian culture; and a tradition connecting lesbian women transhistorically (Humm 1995).

Lillian Faderman (1981) used *lesbianism* to refer to women thinkers and writers in Western history who had strong feelings of attachment or commitment to other women, though not specifically a sexual interest. This view creates a continuum between exclusive heterosexuality and exclusive homosexuality. To these concepts might be added Eisenbach's (1996) antipathetic take on the word's connotations:

> Some women...revel in the word *lesbian,* either for its pure historical merit or because of the whiff of sleek Catherine Deneuvelike condescension it offers the outsider or novice. Such women...shudder at the word *dyke.* (51)

The word *lesbian* derives from Latin *Lesbius*, in turn from Greek *Lesbios*, from *Lesbos*, for the Greek island in the Aegean Sea. In the seventh century B.C., Lesbos was known for its lyric poets, including Sappho, an aristocratic Greek woman married to a wealthy man by whom she had at least one child. Family life, however, did not keep her from attracting an entourage of female admirers who spent their days with her in the writing and recitation of poetry. Among the themes of her poetry were the loves and jealousies among these women. Yet in spite of the poetry and traditions associating Sappho with lesbianism, we are told that extant works contain no evidence that she or her friends actually practiced it (*The New Encyclopaedia Britannica,* vol. 10, 1993). Others, however, point to the poetic themes, despite lack of identification of specific sexual practices, as strong indications of what can be called lesbianism.

From Sappho and her life we also take the word *Sappho* as used for a lesbian (the name may be mildly disparag-

ing coming from a heterosexual, but often is not) and *sapphism*, which, like *lesbianism*, refers to homosexual relations between women. *Sapphist* was used in the 1920s for a woman believed to be a follower of Sappho.

From the seventeenth century until *lesbian* became generally accepted in the late nineteenth century, the terms sometimes used for a female homosexual were *tribade* (from the Greek *tribein,* "to rub, implying friction between two bodies) and *fricatrice* (the Latin counterpart to *tribein* was *fricare*).

In the nineteenth century, *smashes* and *spoons,* meaning "infatuations," were applied to relations between women. In the nineteenth-century "Boston marriage," two women found emotional intimacy and vowed fidelity together but usually appeared not to have been in a sexual relationship; in any case, they had not yet the homophobic labels to fear. Little was made of such relationships until the advent of Freudian psychology, which spelled out the sexual motives believed to underlie such behavior (Flexner and Soukhanov 1997, 380).

Russ (1998), points out also that when marriage is disconnected from women's personal preferences, as it was when marriage was a social and economic necessity for women, women having crushes on other women was irrelevant to marriage and thus nonthreatening to men and male prerogative (126). Since the changes in the status of women, however, the derogatory language has flowed, including such words as *lesbos.* The term *lesbian* itself is frequently used as a put-down by heterosexuals: "I called the girl at work a lesbian because she hadn't been out on a date in a long time" (cited by Laura Markowitz, *In the Family,* 4:2, October 1998, 19).

The term *lesbian*, in spite of considerable social reform in views of homosexuality since the mid-twentieth century—it is the preferred term of self-identity among many lesbians today—has often been applied as a strong form of censure in the heterosexual world.

Until very recently, and still among many heterosexual people, views of lesbianism have ranged from the notion of being a stage of adolescence to stereotypes of a dark world—twisted, debauched, unnatural, and ridden with neurotic women. Today it is not unusual, for example, for conventional young people to disparage a teenage girl who dresses like a boy as a "lesbian." Nor is it unusual to find certain men applying the term against women who resist their sexual overtures. In the words written by Radicalesbians in 1970: "Lesbian is a label invented by the Man to throw at any woman who dares to be his equal, who dares to challenge his prerogatives...who dares to assert the primacy of her own needs" (in Tuttle 1986). *Lesbian* may also be seen as a weapon wielded to divide women and censure those who associate closely with each other, thereby either neglecting their womanly duties to men or threatening to challenge a male-dominated system. In *Surpassing the Love of Men,* Faderman drew a connection between women becoming economically independent, including being less dependent on men, and the treatment of lesbianism as a threat to the social order.

Daly and Caputi (1987) argue that the terms *gay,* which has almost exclusively come to designate men in everyday language, and *female homosexual* are more appropriately applied to women who, in spite of relating genitally to women, remain loyal to male authority, practices, and ideology. *Pseudo-lesbian* is what Daly would ask us to use to refer to the degraded caricatures of lesbianism disseminated in the popular media and pornography.

Lesbian sometimes appears as the diminutive *lezzie* or is abbreviated to the trivializing *les* (see LES[S]). Other slang variants, also usually carrying derogatory connotations, include *les girls, lesbe-friends, less-than-a-man's,* and *Leslie.* It has also been alluded to as "the L-word," suggesting that it may once have been in bad taste in heterosexual circles to say *lesbian.* Diana Rigg, playing a role in the movie *On Her Majesty's Secret Service* (1969), was said to be "noble yet nubile. [She] intrigues 007 enough to make him say the L-word" (*Maxim,* January/February 1998, 58).

Among other related word forms, *lesbian baiting* refers to equating feminism with lesbianism in order to create an aversion to the former. It may also involve tagging women as *lesbians* as a way of scolding them for wanting the same rights as men or asserting their independence from men. To "Lesbianize" has come to mean licentious sexual practice, and *Lesbia* may suggest a harlot without shame. The acronym LUG (*lesbian until graduation*) came into use in the 1990s, meaning a young woman who tries out a homosexual relationship in college. It is not usually meant to be disparaging.

See also AMAZON, BIRD, BLUFF, BROAD (double-barreled broad), BULL, BULLDAGGER, BULLDYKE, BUTCH, CRUNCHIE, CUNT (cunt-lapper), DADDY, DAISY, DUTCH GIRL, DYKE, FAG HAG, FAGGOT, FAIRY, FEMALE (female-oriented), FEMINIST, FEMME, FINGER ARTIST, FISH, FLAUNT, FRAIL, FRIGID, GAL (gal officer), GAY, GIRL (girl kisser), GODDESS (African goddess), HARPY, HEN (crested hen), HE-SHE, HETEROSEXUAL, HOMOSEXUAL, HORSE (horsewoman), INVERSION, JASPER, JOHN, LADY LOVER, LAVENDER, LEATHER (leather dyke), LESBIGAY, LESBO, LES(S), LIPSTICK LESBIAN, LIZZIE, MAMA, MAN (manny), MAN-HATER, MANNISH, MARIMACHO, MISS ANNE (Amy), MOLL (molly dyke), NELLY, NO-NUTS, ODD, PANSY (pansy without a stem), PANTS (slacks), PASSIVE, PERVERT, PRUDE, QUEEN, QUEER, RUG-MUNCHER, SERGEANT, SHE-MALE, STUD, TOMBOY, TOOTSIE, VEGETABLE, VELCRO, WITCH, WOMAN, WOMANIZER.

lesbie. See LES(S).

lesbigay. A blending of *les*bian, *bi*sexual, and *gay* that attempts to group homosexual women and men together with bisexuals as one community. As long as differences in agendas and identities are acknowledged, this grouping can help create a sense of solidarity among these communities. Also in evidence are *LesBiGay* (which gives more prominence to *Bi*, since the *bi-* in *lesbigay* might more readily be interpreted as the middle syllable in the word *lesbian*) and the abbreviation GLB (gay, lesbian, bisexual). However, these terms are not all-inclusive, since transgendered people are excluded. What are inclusive are such abbreviations as LGBT (lesbian, gay, bisexual, transgendered) and BGLT.

lesbo, lezbo. An often derisive contracted form of *lesbian,* from the Greek *Lesbos,* for the Greek island in the Aegean Sea. *Lesbo* is also used as a term of address (also as *lezbo*). Such words, however, take on different, sometimes positive connotations when used within the lesbian community.

See also LESBIAN, LES(S).

lesbophobia. See HOMOPHOBIA.

les(s), lez, liz, lessie, lezzie, lesbie. Slang variants of *lesbian,* usually taken offensively, especially when used by heterosexuals. *Les(s), lez,* and *liz* (a pun on the abbreviated form of the woman's name, *Elizabeth*) trivialize, and *lessie, lezzie,* and *lesbie* are diminutive forms that often deride. "What I did know was that I was a freak, a pervert, a 'lezzie'" (in Duberman 1997, 266). *Lesbine,* in use in the mid-twentieth century, is listed as a mispronunciation by Wentworth and Flexner (1975); Spears says the mispronuciation is "deliberate and contrived." Relatively jocular is *lesbyterian.* Some of these terms were used throughout much of the twentieth century and may still be current.

See also LESBIAN, LESBO, LIZZIE.

less-than-nothing. A disparaging expression for a gay male regarded as weak and unable to defend himself, a black usage given by Major (1994). It is listed as a late-twentieth-century straight male term.

See also CANDY-ASS, FLOWER, GUSSIE, MILKSOP, MILQUETOAST, PANSY, WIMP.

letch. See LECHER.

lez, lezzie. See LES(S).

libber; lib. Shortened and trivialized forms of *liberationist* or, more specifically, *women's liberationist.* Around 1971 *libber* was first heard and became widespread among antifeminists. Maude Findlay, the assertive feminist played by Bea Arthur in the 1970s TV sitcom *Maude,* was sometimes referred to as a "women's libber" (*Time* once described her as a "libber" with "the voice of a diesel truck in second gear" [in Rowbotham 1997, 460]). Related terms that caricatured the women's movement in addition to *libber* and *lib* (for conservatives, *lib's* negativity is probably reinforced by its alternative meaning, "a liberal") included the diminutive *libbie* (or *libby*) and *libbist* (or *libbest*). *Fem libber* or *fem lib,* meaning the movement itself, is another reduction in meaning; it seems to be restricted to journalism (Lighter 1994). Derision and disrespect led to *women's liberation* yielding ground to *feminism.* That term, though holding up, has also taken a drubbing (see FEMINISM).

See also BRA BURNER, FEMINAZI, FEMINIST, LIBERATED WOMAN, WOMEN'S LIBERATION.

liberated woman. A woman who has been freed of the oppressiveness of society and its male domination. Some feminists, however, may be skeptical of the term, believing that no woman, whatever her personal, economic, or political assets, can liberate herself and be completely free of the constraints of a patriarchal society.

Karen Lehrman (*The Lipstick Proviso,* 1997) notes how *liberated woman* had become a disparaging label by the 1970s, representing the crudest stereotypes of the women's movement:

a saggy-breasted, hairy-legged, man-hating militant who spends her days denouncing capitalism and Western culture and her nights doing God knows what with other women. (7)

To many men, however, *liberated* and, especially, *free* may be construed as "accommodating," sexually, that is. It can suggest a successful woman who nevertheless remains loyal to men and makes herself sexually available to them.

See also FEMINIST, LIBBER.

lifestyle choice. See ALTERNATIVE LIFESTYLE.

lily; lilac. Both terms for a gay or effeminate male, used disparagingly in the straight world. The flower metaphors, implying femininity, suggest a man who is soft and weak, thus sissified. *Lily* comes from *lily of the valley*, the name of an ornamental flower, and also from the woman's first name; it was in use throughout much of the twentieth century and may still be current. It has also seen some use in gay communities in reference to a timid man who is still closeted or hesitant about his homosexuality (see also CLOSET). *Lilac*, a flower that often has a lavender color, is associated with homosexuality but has probably known less use than *lily*.

See also BUTTERCUP, DAFFODIL, DAISY, EFFEMINATE, FLOWER, GLADIOLA, HOMOSEXUAL, LAVENDER, PANSY, SISSY, VIOLET.

limp-dick. See *dick*.

limp-wrist. A gay male, especially one seen as effeminate, or any ineffectual man from the point of view of men who see themselves as more masculine than those they may deride with this term. The reference is to the stereotypical effeminate use of the hand and wrist associated with

male homosexuals. It also suggests softness, that is, the absence of an erection. In use since at least the mid-twentieth century, *limp-wrist* is not as direct in its sexual imagery as is *limp-dick. Wrist* is sometimes also combined into *broken-wrist* and often occurs as an adjective, *limp-wristed.*

See also BUTTERCUP, CANDY-ASS, DAFFODIL, DAISY, EFFEMINATE, FAIRY, FLOWER, FRUIT, GAL, GIRL, GUSSIE, LESS-THAN-NOTHING, LILY, LISPER, MARIPOSA, PANSY, SISSY, SWISH, TWINK (twinkie), TWIT.

lipstick lesbian. A lesbian known for being "feminine," in particular, stylishly dressed and attractive in a traditionally feminine way; chic. The term is not necessarily derogatory, yet it may be used derisively by those who do not condone the associated politics or lifestyle.

The "lipstick lesbians" of the early 1990s, who first emerged on the West Coast, broke the stereotype of the dour, preachy, overall-clad, granola-eating lesbian feminist. (Camille Paglia, *Chronicle of Higher Education,* 25 July 1997, B5, is referring here to the so-called "crunchies.")

See also CRUNCHIE, LESBIAN.

lisper. American slang, used throughout the twentieth century, for a gay male or any male regarded as effeminate. It comes from the heterosexual stereotype of such a man pronouncing sibilants (*s* and *z*) by turning them into a *th-* sound (thus, also known mockingly as a *lithper*).

See also EFFEMINATE, LIMP-WRIST, SWISH.

little lady. Used for either a female adult or a child, usually patronizingly. Women are not necessarily little; nor do many today appreciate the dismissive connotations often surrounding *lady* (see LADY). A girl called a "little lady" is probably expected to behave more daintily than boys, which burdens her with a stereotype. In the earlier twentieth century, *little lady* was also directed disparagingly at a gay male youth.

See also LITTLE WOMAN.

Little Lord Fauntleroy. One of a number of names denigrating a boy for supposed feminine characteristics, this one coming from the title of a children's book written in the late nineteenth century by Frances Hodgson Burnett. The young lord in the story starts out as a child of poverty in New York, his mother an American and his father an English nobleman disinherited for marrying her. The boy doesn't actually inherit the title of lord until he goes to England and charms his grandfather with his winning ways. He is usually depicted as a sissified boy (see also SISSY) with a pretty face and long golden curls and is dressed in black velvet and lace.

The name was better known earlier in the twentieth century, when many young boys still suffered being dressed in this Victorian style. The youth labeled with this name was usually believed to have been mollycoddled by an overprotective mother (see also MOLLYCODDLE, MOTHER). The term is still heard today, sometimes dismissively for any man considered prissy or for an Englishman.

See also EFFEMINATE, FLOWER, MILKSOP, MILQETOAST, NAMBY-PAMBY, WIMP.

little man. See LITTLE WOMAN.

little miss. See MISS.

little shit. An expression, usually considered vulgar, typically used by men to make another man, likely to be smaller in physical stature, feel small and insignificant. It may be applied to a boy, too, but age is not the issue.

See also PUNK.

little woman, the. From the late nineteenth century, a somewhat dated, hackneyed phrase still used by some men to refer to a sexual mistress or, in what Holder (1996) calls "ponderous male humour," literally, a wife. Although it may still be regarded by some as a compliment to a woman's sex, the expression acknowledges neither her individuality nor her status in a world in which the women's movement has enlarged women's roles. There is no exact equivalent for a man. In contrast, when we hear *little man*, it is not for a husband or usually for any adult male (unless he is of small stature); rather, it is used for a boy.

See also LITTLE LADY, MOUSE (mouse queen), MRS. (missus), WOMAN.

liz. See LES(S).

lizard. See LIZZIE, LOUNGE LIZARD.

lizzie; lizzie boy. *Lizzie,* a somewhat dated slur on a male regarded as a sissy (often as *lizzie boy;* see also BOY):

> There's a swell bunch of Lizzie boys…that love to fire off their filthy mouths and yip that Mike Monday is vulgar and full of mush. Those pups are saying now that I hog the gospel-show, that I'm in it for the coin. (Sinclair Lewis, *Babbit,* 1922)

It was also once in use for a homosexual male and a young woman. *Lizzie* is a diminutive form of the nickname Liz from the woman's first name, Elizabeth, and has been used (usually disrespectfully) for a lesbian (*lizzie* is a mid-nineteenth-century alteration of *lesbian*).

Although *lizzie* comes from the personal name for a woman, it also suggests *lizard*, which may be heard in rap songs for a woman (see also LOUNGE LIZZARD).

See also EFFEMINATE, LESBIAN, LES(S), SISSY.

lobby louse. See LOUNGE LIZARD.

lobo. From the Spanish word for a wolf, a term for a young woman seen as unattractive.

See also COOLER, COYOTE, DOG, GANGSTER GIRL, HOGGER, PIG, SCUD, SKAG, YETI.

Lolita. An adolescent girl regarded as seductive, formed from the diminutive of Lola, which in turn is the diminutive of

Dolores. The name comes from Vladimir Nabokov's novel, *Lolita*, first published in 1955 in France. The story tells about the sexual obsession of a middle-aged man, Humbert Humbert, with his twelve-year-old stepdaughter, Lolita. She is portrayed as an archetypal nymphet: flirtatious, manipulative, and sexually precocious. Humbert ends up in jail for killing the man for whom Lolita eventually leaves him.

A young woman, Amy Fisher, convicted in 1992 of shooting the wife of her much older boyfriend, was dubbed in the press the "Long Island Lolita" or the more sensational "Lethal Lolita." (At the same time, the press largely ignored the sad situation of the disturbed Fisher.)

Adolescent boys' sexual desire is not similarly labeled; they are just "boys being boys."

See also BABE (baby pro), BAIT, FORBIDDEN FRUIT, JAILBAIT, NYMPH (nymphet), SEDUCTRESS, TEMPTRESS, VIXEN.

lollipop. A term for a piece of hard candy on the end of a stick that had some use during the nineteenth and early to midtwentieth century as an epithet for a woman viewed as good-looking and for any sweetheart, male or female. It has also been heard in the sense of a gay male or any male regarded as effeminate. The idea of candy and sweetness often suggests femininity and can thus be used to call a man's masculinity into question.

See also CANDY-ASS, HONEY, SWEET.

lone wolf. See WOLF.

looksism. Bias and discrimination based on physical appearance; pressures on people to adhere to particular body norms and cultural "ideals" of beauty. The term runs parallel with HETEROSEXISM as well as SEXISM. Looksism can affect people from all walks of life and all backgrounds or gender, often curtailing access to jobs, respect, and prestigeful forms of social interaction. However, it is still probably true that women are more likely to be judged on appearance (culturally a major factor in the determination of their fundamental worth) than are men. Men are more often sized up by their achievements. While there have been conscious legal, academic, and journalistic efforts to reduce these biases and their impact, researchers report that the large majority of cosmetic surgery patients have been women (although men today, like women, are spending more on plastic surgery than before). Also, women mentioned in the media are considerably more likely to be described in terms of their physical appearance—and criticized for it—than are men.

Fattism, bias and discrimination against people who are considered overweight, is a form of looksism, but many other factors affecting appearance are also relevant in our appearance-conscious culture. Thus, ageism, ablism, heterosexism, racism, and sexism describe biases that are often closely connected with those of looksism.

loose; loose woman. *Loose,* a term suggesting such things as freedom from constraint, moral laxity, and frivolity from nearly the time that it entered English. Since the fifteenth century, *loose* has also meant lewd, unchaste, and dissolute, said of men as well as women, although women have long borne the brunt of the negativity. As Mills (1989) points out, while a man "on the loose" is enjoying a spree, a woman "on the loose" is violating basic rules of decency. Men are known by kinder words or phrases, such as "sowing their wild oats." Men have, however, been known as loose for being involved in crime (see CRIMINALS).

Loose woman, equivalent to the once common "woman of loose morals," has been applied to any woman regarded as unchaste, lacking in moral constraint, or sexually indiscreet. Not surprisingly, it has also referred to a woman working as a prostitute ("on the loose" on the streets). A loose woman (twentieth-century usage) is the antithesis of the "nice girl," who is seen as not getting into trouble because she knows what is right to do. To those who deny the responsibility of men in rape and its seriousness, for example, the female victims are victims of their own immorality. Thus, we sometimes hear in discussions of rape, "'Nice girls' aren't assaulted; 'loose' and 'careless' women are" (Rhode 1997, 120). A judgmental phrase that has seen some use for a loose woman is "no better than she ought to be."

See also ACTRESS, CHIPPIE, COOZIE, DIRTY GERTIE, EASY LAY, FLOOZY, FLY, HARLOT, HAT, HIDE, HOOZIE, HUMP, JOB, KEPT WOMAN, LAY, MATTRESSBACK, MINK, MISTRESS, NYMPH, PROMISCUOUS, PROSTITUTE, PUNCHBOARD, SADIE THOMPSON, SKEEZER, SLAG, SLATTERN, SLUT, TART, TRAMP, TROLLOP, WENCH, WHORE.

lord. See MISTRESS.

lose one's virginity. See VIRGIN.

loser. See BUM.

Lothario. A debonair man and womanizer, especially one said to "love them and leave them." The cliché's allusion is to English playwright Nicholas Rowe's *The Fair Penitent* (1703), in which he says of a character, "Is this that haughty, gallant, gay Lothario?" Rowe's Lothario was a revengeful young cad who seduced a woman whose father had denied him her hand in marriage. After giving up her virginity to Lothario, the devoted young woman found that Lothario had no intention of marrying her.

Although Lothario was killed and illicit love was disapproved of in the story, the euphemistic *Lothario,* whatever its denotation, sometimes rings more with the connotations of *noble cavalier* than with *debauchee*. Carpineto (1989) writes of this word and its siblings:

Today's "womanizers" were yesterdays "roués," "gallants," "ladies

men," "Don Juans," and "Casanovas." With the old labels these men could be perceived as romantic figures, as men who were helpless to prevent the adoration that they received from women and the secret envy that they inspired in less-appealing men. (11)

The use of *gay* to describe a dashing figure of a man began in the seventeenth century. Besides *Lothario,* such related expressions as *gay blade* and *gay deceiver* also gained currency. While the gay Lothario gained a romantic reputation for his wayward ways, however, the woman who succumbed to his charms came to be labeled as *gay,* denoting loose morals. It was largely the negative feminine overtones that carried over to the twentieth-century use of GAY for homosexual men. In this current context of usage, the pairing of *gay* with *Lothario* is likely to taint it. With *gay* carrying almost exclusively the meaning of homosexual, the full expression *gay Lothario* sees little use today.

To more fully understand the significance of the expression, contrast it with equivalent words used for women; for example, see LOLITA and NYMPHOMANIAC.

See also CASANOVA, DON JUAN, LADIES' MAN, LOVE MACHINE, LOVER, PLAYBOY, ROMEO, ROUÉ, SCUTZ, WOMANIZER.

lounge lizard. One of the few animal metaphors for men that conveys worthless or despicable qualities. A lizard is a reptilian creature that enjoys lounging in the sun but is popularly associated with swamps and dark holes. *Lounge lizard* was in use throughout the twentieth century but was probably most popular during the Roaring Twenties. During that decade the term, meaning something like a playboy, had not yet become exactly derogatory but soon became so. This slinky word denotes a vain man who can be seen hanging around hotel or nightclub lounges, where he flirts or dances with women and often tries to pick them up. He may or may not be a gigolo but in any case will often be regarded as one; at best, he is a kind of "ladies' man."

Lizard, suggesting a contemptible person—usually a man (it is also a slang word for the penis)—is also used in this sense. A related species is the "lobby louse," a man who habitually hangs around hotel lobbies. *Barfly*, meaning someone who hangs out at bars, is a more gender-neutral term.

See also GIGOLO, LADIES' MAN, LOUSE, WORM.

louse. A word for a type of small parasitic insect and also long used for a person considered vile. Although the dictionaries suggest it may be applied to anyone, it is, in common practice, restricted to men. A man who is unfair in his dealings with others, untrustworthy, irresponsible, and parasitic is held in low regard as a louse. He may also be known as a "heel" or, in more vulgar vernacular, an "asswipe."

See also ASS (asswipe), LOUNGE LIZARD (lobby louse), PIMP, WORM.

love goddess. See GODDESS.

love machine. A passionate lover, one not easily sexually satisfied, especially a man. The expression was popularized by Jacqueline Susann's 1969 novel, *The Love Machine* (Lighter 1997), although *machine* has, since the early twentieth century, also seen some use for a young woman seen as sexually appealing (see also LBFM). The Susann novel jacket blurb says the book is about a

> man whose dazzling professional triumphs and spectacular sexual conquests can never answer his own questions about himself, the man who is: The Love Machine.

While the suggested mechanical quality of lovemaking and unfeeling nature of the man—he is compared with a "wrecking machine" in the novel—is dehumanizing, compare the connotations of this term with such negative epithets for women: *nymph, slut,* and *whore*. A man is not likely to take offense at being called a "love machine," unless he knows the word is being used ironically.

A synonym used for women as well as men is *sex machine*, which, when it fits, is probably a more honest term than *love machine*, with its oxymoronic tinge.

See also LOVER (loverboy), SCUTZ, STUD.

lover; loverboy. Lover, anyone in love, including often a sexual partner of any sexual orientation or a person in an adulterous relationship. But as *Merriam-Webster's Collegiate Dictionary* (1997) claims, *lover* often means a man in love with a woman. Cameron (1985, 81) says that as a young actress performing in school, she learned that the word *lover* should be restricted to men because it denoted activity; the passionate women in Racine's plays were known as mistresses (see also MISTRESS).

Loverboy, reserved for males, may be used to poke fun at a man for his youthful prettiness (though a loverboy may be a mature man) or attractiveness to women. It also has ironic uses. *Boy* is a way of calling a man's masculinity into question; at the same time it is the subject of interest (see also BOY). Yet a man who shows a sexual interest in women—the loverboy or woman-chaser—is seldom condemned for his behavior, linguistically or otherwise (see exception at SCUTZ). A woman who expresses sexual interest in men is sometimes labeled a slut or a whore, while the female counterpart to the mildly disapproving *philanderer* (from the Greek *philandros*, loving man) is the scornful *adulteress*.

See also CASANOVA, DON JUAN, HOOCHIE (hoochie-coochie man), LADIES' MAN, LOTHARIO, LOVER (loverboy), MISTER (Mr. Groin), PLAYBOY, ROMEO, ROUÉ, WOMANIZER.

love them and leave them. See CASANOVA, HOOCHIE (hoochie-coochie man), LOTHARIO, LOVER (loverboy), PLAYBOY, ROMEO, ROUÉ, WOMANIZER.

L.P. See PUSS.

lug; **lummox**. Terms typically used for men. Both, but *lug* especially, refer to loutishness. *Lug,* which is primarily American slang, is a contemptuous term for a person seen as brutish or a sponger. However, it may be used more affection-ately than a word such as *bum* (e.g., "I love ya, ya big lug"). It has been in use since the 1920s. Older by at least a century, *lummox* refers more to size and awkwardness, suggesting a large, ungainly, or clumsy man, usually also a stupid one.

See also BRUISER, CAVEMAN, GORILLA.

LUG. See LESBIAN.

L-word. See LESBIAN.

M

macho; machismo. Mexican Spanish words having to do with qualities and images of masculinity. *Macho* describes a man who is strong and virile, assertive and self-confident, even to the point of being brutish, and who possesses an attitude of superiority to women. A common Spanish expression is *Es muy macho,* "He's very tough."

Macho, deriving from the Latin *masculus* (male), entered Spanish in a biological context, largely as a reference to male animals. In Mexican Spanish, however, it was reserved mostly for human males, although never losing all of its animal connotations (*Webster's Word Histories* [1989] notes that it denoted a he-male).

The first uses of *macho* in English were limited mostly to descriptions of the behavior of Latino or Hispanic men. As both an adjective and a noun, the word made its way from the western United States early in the twentieth century to the East in a short time, becoming less ethnically specific in its application to men. Later in the century, the women's movement challenged the term, calling into question the stereotypical assigned social roles of men and exposing the problems in the assumption that to be a real man, a man must be strong and assertive. Watergate figure G. Gordon Liddy once griped about how women's liberation had appropriated the term as a code word "twisted into a pejorative Archie Bunkerish caricature of the loutish, leering male" (in Panati 1998, 20). But the term had been used to define extreme, even unnatural masculinity before the mid-twentieth-century women's movement, and it hasn't just been feminists on the attack: according to Hollywood actress Zsa Zsa Gabor, "Macho does not prove mucho" (in James 1984, 88).

The meaning of *macho* became generalized to other situations that might be characterized in masculine terms. A few writers even coined a debatably equivalent term, *macha,* for women, making a feminine noun with the use of the Spanish *-a* ending.

> There was a scene in a movie…in which one girl turns to another girl who's been screwed over and tells her to "be a macha" and take care of herself. Instead of macha being the feminine twin to macho, the bullheaded brute, here it is more like the Yiddish mensch: Be a stand-up guy. (Vanessa Veselka, *Bitch,* Wint-O-Green 1998, 37)

Macho, however, has come to be applied also to women: "Another career-minded Hollywood powerhouse who might well be described as the modern macho woman" (*Elle,* August 1986, in Panati 1998, 21). In gay communities it refers to the presentation of an ostentatious virility, with a touch of "tough guy." The gay "clone" look of the 1960s and 1970s—identified, for example, by workingmen's flannel shirts, button-up Levi's, and a rugged, Nautilus-conditioned body—was often called "macho."

Machismo derives from *macho* and was recorded in English in the 1940s. It is a noun referring to a proud and exaggerated masculinity, an exhilarating sense of power, or an ethos of virility. We seldom hear it used of women. Recently, however, *machismo* has lost some of its connotations of male dominance and has come instead to designate family pride and honor. (This shift in meaning is discussed in Alfredo Mirande's *Hombres y Machos: Masculinity and Latin Culture,* 1998.)

See also BUTCH, CAVEMAN, COWBOY, HE-MAN, HUNTER, MAN, MASCULINE, TARZAN.

mack, mac. A pimp, especially a flashily dressed one or one seen as able to sweet-talk a woman into hustling for him; or, as in rap music, any smooth-talking or persuasive man, especially one who knows how to attract women; often also as *mackman*. *Mac* is also used informally to mean any fellow, as in addressing a man whose name is not known. In the sense of a pimp, especially in black English, *mack* dates to the nineteenth century.

Explanations of the origin of the black usage range from its relation to Middle English *mackerel*, meaning a bawd; to the characteristics of the mackerel fish, which is carnivorous; to an improbable derivation from *mackintosh raincoat* (Major 1994), which is a British rather than an American garment. It may derive from Old French *maquerel*, pimp.

Whatever the exact connotations of the term, which may vary depending on the race or sex of the speaker, they are often more positive than those carried by comparable words for women known for being able to deceive or manipulate men (VAMP), for being interested in men's bank accounts (GOLD DIGGER), or for seeking sexual relations (SLUT, WHORE). The masculinity of the term is also reflected in the lesbian use of the word as a verb, often constructed as "to mack it," meaning to have an aggressive way about oneself.

See also CRACK (crack salesman), EASY RIDER, GIGOLO, HUSTLER, LADIES' MAN, LOUNGE LIZARD, PIMP.

madam; ma'am. *Madam,* a Middle English (fourteenth century) word deriving from the Middle French *ma dame* (literally, my lady). Originally the term was used by children in addressing their mother, especially in the upper classes, and later as a title or a form of address for a French married woman or married woman of any nationality. In some American contexts, still carrying something of an elegant French ring, *madam* has been used as a form of respectful address to a woman whose name is unknown; as a title with a given name or a surname; or

as a designation of rank or office (e.g., Madam President). It has also been applied to the female head of a household, or to businesswomen, and in the South as a way of distinguishing a woman from her daughter-in-law, addressed as "Mrs." In addressing a woman of another (usually European) nation, including when the proper local term is not known, the respectful term is *Madame* (with a final *-e*; *pl. Mesdames;* abbreviation *Mme* or *pl. Mmes*).

While titles of respect or honor for men, such as *sir* and MASTER, have tended to retain their honor, many of those for women have been tainted over the years. *Madam,* though in some contexts still semantically noble, has been among those names that have suffered some degraded meanings. It has acquired the sense of a woman considered overly bold or affected, a mistress, a prostitute (senses largely from the seventeenth and early eighteenth centuries), or, especially common, a woman who keeps a brothel (since the eighteenth century). "Nadia [Frey]…was reportedly linked to Heidi Fleiss, the leading Hollywood madam whose own downfall revealed a black book overflowing with the names of famous men" (John Lata, *National Examiner,* 9 September 1997, 5). In the sense of a brothel keeper, she may also be known as a "housekeeper," MOTHER, or "housemother," *house* in this context meaning a brothel (Spears 1990), or a "landlady" (see also LADY). In gay communities, but restricted largely to the 1960s, *madam* took on the meaning of an older gay man, but it may currently be used for the man who operates an all-male house of prostitution (of which there are apparently very few).

The contraction *ma'am* is considered useful as the equivalent of *sir* ("Excuse me ma'am") and appropriate as the address for English royalty (even the queen).

See also BAWD, MISTRESS, MRS.

Madge. See MARY.

madonna. In its capitalized form, from the Old Italian *ma donna* (my lady), a reference to the Virgin Mary, mother of Jesus; or to a statue or picture representing her. At one time, it was also a polite form of address in Italian for a woman. In the nineteenth century it referred to a hairstyle in which the hair was parted in the center, as in some representations of the Virgin Mary. In lowercase, it is used to represent a nurturing, pure, virtuous woman, a good mother or wife.

The madonna is contrasted with the impure whore. The early Christian church, adopting the Neoplatonic doctrine of the opposition between spirit and flesh, made woman anathema as the embodiment of the flesh. The virgin, represented in highest form by the Christian Madonna, was the only kind of woman worthy of God's grace and man's love. Attitudes toward the two types of women found in so much Western imagery—the madonna and the whore—are also reflected in our language (see, e.g., ANGEL, PROSTITUTE, VIRGIN, WHORE). The word may also be used ironically or sarcastically to suggest that a woman who pretends to be saintly is anything but.

Popular rock star Madonna's erotic performances also give the name an ironic twist. However, some Madonna-ologists would argue, Madonna is not simply a singer who dresses like a whore and conveys a "boy-toy" attitude. Rather she is a postmodern performer who makes videos that blur differences.

In fact, though, the performer Madonna—more completely, Madonna Louise Veronica Ciccone—was given her name at birth, after her mother.

See also NUN, PRUDE.

maid. An unmarried woman (usually a young woman, with no stigma attached, versus an OLD MAID); a VIRGIN (the only appropriate state, traditionally, for an unmarried young woman); and a female servant. From the Middle English *maide*, short for *maiden*, *maid* is now largely restricted to references to houseworkers and cleaners, though to many even this use seems quaint or playful and often sexist.

For more on *maid* and its companion forms, see MAIDEN.

maiden. A Middle English word from which derives the shortened form *maid*, once applied to any woman or girl. *Maiden* is related to Old Irish *mug* (serf). The noun form came to mean a woman or girl who is not married (as female domestic servants were once required to be); the adjective form means unmarried, virginal, or never having borne young. *Maiden* conveys the idea of someone unspoiled or innocent, the qualities that were traditionally those of the ideal young woman, if a man had not yet "violated" her; it may be euphemistic for *virgin*. Even things can be described as "maiden," such as a maiden voyage.

Maiden is a quaint-sounding word today, fading as society takes less notice of "maidenhead"—the quality or state of being a maiden but also referring to the hymen. Also losing ground, as marital status becomes of less interest, is *maiden aunt*, which sometimes connotes a prim and prudish middle-aged or elderly woman (see also PRUDE). Language bias guidebooks today are also recommending the replacement of terms such as *maid of honor* with *best woman*, among other possibilities, and *meter maid* with substitutes such as *meter reader* (see Maggio 1997).

Maiden is now largely reserved for literary contexts. However, in horse racing, *maiden* survives in reference to a horse that has not yet won a race.

See also ANGEL, DAMSEL, GENDER-SPECIFIC ADJECTIVES (chaste), IRON MAIDEN, MAIDEN NAME, MISS, VIRGIN.

maiden name. The surname of a woman

before she is married, from the seventeenth century. The term suggests the status of a virgin, still sometimes expected of the woman before her marriage (see also MAIDEN). The first well-known woman in the United States to keep her own surname after marriage, in protest against the unequal laws applied to married women, was Lucy Stone, who married in 1855. Although she retained her family name, she preferred to be known as *Mrs.* Stone to indicate her marital status. Almost seven decades later, a group of professional women called the "Lucy Stoners" followed her in retaining their own surnames. Their credo was "My name is the symbol of my identity and must not be lost." Around the 1980s *birth name*—or *own name,* as well as *family name*—came to be preferred by many women inclined to eliminate the use of the word *maiden.*

Many women have continued the customary practice of taking their husband's surname. In 1982, when Hillary Rodham Clinton began campaigning for Bill Clinton's reelection as governor of Arkansas, she acquiesced in being called "Mrs. Clinton" for the first time. It has been suggested that she did this on her own; the alternative explanation is that "her husband's aides in the war room told her, 'The gals out there— to say nothing about their husbands— aren't going to buy this maiden name crap! Bake cookies! Stand by your man!'" (Kaplan and Bernays 1997, 157). Other women—African American women in particular—respect the use of a man's name, a practice that had once been legally denied them.

Some women have hyphenated their names (the woman's surname followed by the husband's), although hyphenated names can pose their own problems, length being one of the most obvious. Creating still other solutions to the perceived problem of inegalitarianism, some couples have tried making an ana-

gram out of both the wife's and husband's surnames. It's also possible to abandon both the first and last names, which is what nineteenth-century reformer Sojourner Truth did.

Miller and Swift (1991, 11) note that blue bloods are very interested in a woman's maiden name and her grandmother's maiden name. Their concern in upholding elite culture leads to marriage practices intended to preserve "well-bred" lineage.

See also MRS., NÉE.

mail-order bride. See BRIDE.

make an honest woman of her. See HONEST WOMAN.

male. Ultimately from Latin *masculus,* diminutive of *mas,* a man or boy; as an adjective, relating to men, masculinity, or of the sex that has organs that produce spermatozoa. Like *female, male* categorizes by sex and is not reserved only for human beings but is also applied to animals and used in technical or statistical contexts. As an adjective, it is often supplied without warrant to identify men working in occupations traditionally more or less reserved for women, as in *male nurse* and *male secretary,* when the equivalent *female* is not used to describe the same category.

Today, feminist writers have depicted *male* as a representation of dominance having institutional sanction, as indicated, for example, by its use in the U.S. Constitution (*male citizens* and *male inhabitants*). In her acclaimed book *The Second Sex,* philosopher Simone de Beauvoir addressed the matter of defining *woman* in biological terms. She noted, "In the mouth of a man the epithet *female* has the sound of an insult, yet he is not ashamed of his animal nature; on the contrary, he is proud if someone says of him: 'He is a male!'" ([1952] 1974, 3).

There are some cracks in the term, however, appearing especially in the past few decades, which reflect recent changes in the perceived social value of men versus women. Terms such as *male privilege, male ego,* and *male chauvinist pig,* for example, have all been used for generalizations and stereotypes that are not always fair or accurate or representative of the whole truth about men and male power. Still, these terms have been useful in giving a name to a class of men who have not had to think about the privilege they are accorded compared with other groups and can often unthinkingly and unintentionally wield power over others.

See also FEMALE, MACHO, MALE CHAUVINIST, MALESTREAM, MAN, MASCULINE.

male chauvinist; male chauvinist pig. *Male chauvinist,* meaning a sexist man, from at least the 1960s. *Chauvinist* originally meant a patriot or ultranationalist and, by extension, someone zealously attached to a particular group, often race or sex, or to a place or cause. *Chauvinist* derives from the surname of Nicolas Chauvin, a French soldier whose excessive, simple-minded devotion to Napoleon eventually made him the butt of ridicule among the early nineteenth-century French (he is depicted in the French vaudeville *La Cocarde tricolore,* 1831).

In the United States, when the country was showing its chauvinism during the Vietnam War (1960s), *male chauvinist pig* became a popular expression first in leftist circles and then in the media and populace in general. The usage was patterned after the *pig* in common use by radical students and black power activists in the 1960s to deride the police. Nilsen (1977) suggests that "perhaps one of the reasons that in the late sixties it was so shocking to hear policemen called *pigs* was that the connotations of *pig* are very different from the other [more positive] animal metaphors we usually apply to males" (28). *Male* further suggested an animal because of its common use in biological references.

Male chauvinist pig was commonly applied in the 1970s to men regarded as sexist. However, the epithet quickly came to be applied to some men as a kind of joke. The abbreviation *MCP,* from the late 1960s, also took on a jocular tone; if it is used today at all, it is more likely to be used by men self-descriptively, even with pride. It has also become a way of caricaturing feminists and the women's movement.

Male chauvinist pig is deliberately insulting language and in some contexts, virtually a swear word. It has been used to condemn anyone who criticizes women or who disagrees with feminist beliefs, uses that can quickly put an end to dialogue. It denies the individuality of a man in much the same way that, for example, *bra burner,* directed at feminist women, distorts their intentions. However, there is a difference between epithets for men and those for women: men, probably out of their generally stronger political status, are more likely than women to adopt such epithets for themselves and use them self-descriptively or in humor, as described above. In addition, in spite of the term's appropriation by men, some feminists might argue that while it is a more demeaning term than *sexist,* like that term, *male chauvinist pig* has served to name a class of men engaged in oppressive behavior, helping to bring that behavior to social awareness.

See also MALE, PIG, SEXIST.

male feminist. See FEMINIST.

malestream. A feminist version of *mainstream* meaning that men are viewed as having created the dominant attitudes, standards, and practices of a cultural system that usually benefits men. The term may refer to those cultural patterns themselves, which marginalize and render as deviant, invisible, or inferior the world of feminine behavior that lies outside the patterns.

Women's Studies…proposes a revolutionary remaking of knowledge. Its main areas of activity include critiquing the biases and omissions of "malestream" theories and practices…. (Sue Wise in *The Social Science Encyclopedia,* 2d ed., ed. Adam Kuper and Jessica Kuper, 1996, 293–94)

Some may protest the pegging and tagging of men in this way, but the word, like HERSTORY and other such constructions, has found its place in feminist theory.

mama; momma. A word meaning mother, said to derive from baby talk, though it is closely akin to *mammary,* from the Latin *mamma* (breast). It is often used in the South instead of *mom.* Generally, *mama* is a more intimate and informal word than *mother* in expressing emotional attachment. But like *mother,* it illustrates how a normally wholesome word for a woman can slide into slang usage and even disrepute.

In slang, *mama* has been a name used originally (early twentieth century) by black men for a black woman (sometimes also by the woman for herself) who is not their mother. It is also often meant for a young woman, girlfriend, or wife ("Crazy Little Mama" was the title of a song sung by the Eldorados in the 1950s). As Sharp (1993) indicates, *mama* is frequently preceded by such words as *little, pretty,* or SWEET, often viewed as undignified, connoting the insignificance of feminine qualities (40).

The word also often suggests sexiness, sauciness, or sexual availability, as in "red-hot momma" (see also HOT). "Pistol Packin' Mama" was songwriter Al Dexter's hit song of 1943. *Mama* has also been used for a female member of a motorcycle gang, often suggesting her promiscuity, and has had limited application to an EFFEMINATE gay male (mostly in prison subculture) and, in some contexts, the FEMME lesbian in a butch/femme relationship.

Mama-san (*san* is an honorific in Japanese), in military lingo, has referred to a middle-aged or older Asian woman, especially one who runs a brothel; or a U.S. soldier's female prostitute or girlfriend. *Mamacita,* a familiar Latin American Spanish word meaning mummy, occurs in U.S. slang for a sexy young woman. It is used mostly by men (see also EXOTIC).

In the African American community, especially in the South, *big mamma* has meant "one's grandmother," where *big* refers more to age than to size.

See also MOM, MOTHER.

mama's boy. Since 1850 a boy or young man viewed as dependent on his mother—timid, clinging, and spoiled. Use of the term MAMA, which is baby talk, connotes his alleged immaturity. Boys, who are not motivated to be as emotionally demonstrative and dependent as girls are and who are belittled for being "tied to their mother's apron strings," are harshly—often painfully—reproved for being "mamma's boys." Generally, the term is synonymous with SISSY: "You gotta find me first, you pansy-ass mamma's boy" (film *Scream,* 1997).

See also APRON, BABY (crybaby), BOY, CANDY-ASS (candy kid), CREAMPUFF, EFFEMINATE, FLOWER, GIRL, LITTLE LORD FAUNTLEROY, MILKSOP, MILQUETOAST, MOM (momism), WIMP, WUSS.

man. An adult male person, or humanity in general (controversial). The term comes from the Old English *man,* which originally designated a human being or person or, collectively, humanity, unmarked for gender. Its roots run deep not only in Germanic languages but also in the Slavic languages and other language groups within the Indo-European family. Some etymologists (Gouëffic 1996) believe *man* may ultimately be related to the Latin *mens,* meaning a thinking being, although only the biases of the word over the centuries would support that relationship.

Until around 1000 the Old English *wer* and *wœpman* designated a male person. By the late Middle Ages, as the relative status of men and women changed, with men gaining the upper hand in legal and personal privileges, *man* began to replace the earlier terms for a male (*wer* apparently survives in *werewolf*), while still being used as a generic. From the late Middle Ages to the present, writers and speakers who used *man* ostensibly in the sense of humanity were for the most part referring to males as the norm; thus, women came to be largely erased from history.

About the 1970s there was a growing awareness that *man* as a generic was often a slippery, ambiguous term, sometimes meaning both men and women and sometimes only men. It was capable of causing confusion in writing and speaking as well as giving distorted impressions of gender roles and relations. For instance, a male employer who tells a woman that he is looking for the "best man for the job" might be using the term generically, or he could also be telling her not to bother to apply.

Judged to be a sign of patriarchal dominance, the generic *man* began to give way to the nongendered *person*. In time, however, *person* in turn came to look more like a euphemism for *woman*. This happened as words such as *salesperson* were used for women, while a male salesperson was still called a salesman. Men still came out looking like the standard.

The word *man* has a power and prominence that distinguish it sharply from *woman*. These characteristics reflect, reinforce, and are reinforced by the social advantages and prerogatives of men. As discussed above, *man* became the standard and chief category—and has even been identified with the human species itself (anthropology was long

defined as "the study of man"). The distinctions between *man* and *woman* have been argued to be a product of a patriarchal society (see PATRIARCHY), where men construct their world with women subordinate to it. (Also, compare the connotations of *manly* with those of WOMANLY.)

Among the assymetries: *Man of the world* is used for a sophisticated man, one who gets around (it originally meant a married man). *A woman of the world* is also in use, but in some instances may call into question just what she has been up to to make her so worldly. A "grand old man" refers to a man who long held an eminent position in his field; we seldom hear of a "grand old woman." *Man to man* (honest, treating another man as an equal) dates to the time when it was difficult for men to discuss certain delicate matters with women. *Woman to woman,* on the other hand, suggests the close personal ties found between women.

In the context of marriage, the more common expression is the traditional *man and wife*, which is gradually losing out to the more egalitarian *husband and wife* (see also WIFE). (But try *wife and husband;* the word order doesn't greet the ear quite right.) Of the pair of words *women* and *men, men* usually goes first in the common phrase *men and women*.

The stronger or more positive connotations of *man* relative to woman are consistent with the generally higher stature of men in our culture. But these connotations may often reflect social and psychological pressures placed on men. Thus, the clichéd command "Take it like a man" is advice given to a boy or a man about how to experience something hurtful. Similarly, "Be a man" tells boys and men that their lives may not be easy, but they should take pride in that fact. Anthropologist Lionel Tiger once argued for a biological link between hard military virtues and maleness: "The advertisements instruct us 'Be a Man—Join the Army' not 'Be a Man—Become a Fabric Designer'" (from *Men in Groups*, 1969, 211).

The virtues of "being a man"— strength, character, bravery, steadiness, and maturity—may also be taken as urging a boy or man to "be stupid, be unfeeling, obedient and soldierly, and stop thinking" (Paul Theroux, quoted in August 1998, 428). The "man of action" may be energetic to the point of courting death to accomplish his goals (see also HERO), while "A man's gotta do what a man's gotta do," often heard in western movies, and sometimes used humorously today, refers to a "real" man's ability to do things regardless of his feelings about them or the consequences. Men are also expected to have what it takes to be responsible for themselves— "to be your own man."

Man sometimes also has its less positive connotations, as in such terms as *con man* and *manslaughter,* reflecting the association of men with criminality and, when it is still used, *man's inhumanity to man*. Applied emphatically in direct address, *man* may convey, among other things, impatience or disdain. In black English, *the man* serves as a label for an oppressive white boss or other authority figure or ruling system. *Man* or *manny* may also be used to describe a masculine lesbian (or perhaps any lesbian). For stereotypes of men, see CRIMINALS, MALE CHAUVINIST PIG.

Changes are being made in the use of *man*. For example, physical anthropologists once referred to prehistoric fossil finds by such appellations as *Java Man, Neanderthal Man,* and *Cro-Magnon Man*. Logic dictates that there were women among these prehistoric populations, yet use of the term *man* suggests that men, not women, were being offered as examples of key "types." Thus, it was assumed, men were playing more important roles in the emer-

gence of homo sapiens than were women, including the invention of tools and the discovery of fire. This linguistic practice has changed in scientific writing today, with such finds now being referred to, for example, as *Neanderthals* or *Cro-Magnon people. Java Man* seems to hang on, at least in nonscientific language.

Many terms ending with *-man* are now assumed to refer to an adult male; thus, a nobleman is a male aristocrat; an anchorman, a male newscaster. When it is a woman who is of high birth or is broadcasting the news, she is a noblewoman (a member of the nobility or more specifically, a countess or princess) or an anchorwoman (or an anchorperson). The use of *-person* as a sex-neutral element, however, sometimes sounds euphemistic or forced.

Homo sapiens (the Latin *homo* [man, in a generic sense] with Latin *sapiens*, wise), though inclusive, is not a candidate to replace the ambiguous *man,* since it is associated with scientific jargon and is too "foreign" in form. Also, *homo* may be mistakenly construed as denoting a gay male person (see also HOMOSEXUAL).

In spite of attempts to dislodge the generically applied *man*, however, use of the term still holds up, not only in reference to adult males but also for people or humankind as a whole. This is likely because of centuries of its use in English (and long-standing traditional male influence on it).

Man is still found in a number of expressions. These include *every man for himself* (though "everyone for themselves" can sometimes be substituted if the lack of agreement in number can be tolerated, as might "look out for number one"), *man's best friend* (the faithful canine), *man overboard, man bites dog* (newsworthy story), and *manslaughter* (which carries a definite legal meaning). *Man* also still finds a place in such anthropological or cosmological phrases as *man, myth, and magic* and *man and the cosmos*. *Persons, people,* or *humans* as well as pronouns, such as *we* or *you,* can be substituted. But according to some, such substitutions result in a loss of pithiness or punch, and using *women* as a generic does not yet sound "natural" to most ears; it may even be misleading. Finally, in most published literature, unless it is to be rewritten—an act of sacrilege to many readers—the generic *man* is here to stay.

See also CAVEMAN, GUY, HE-MAN, HERSTORY, MALE, MAN FRIDAY, MANKIND, MANNISH, MAN'S WORLD, MARY, MASCULINE, VIRILE, WOMAN.

mandyke. See DYKE.

maneater; mankiller; mantrap. *Maneater,* when applied to women, a reference to their imagined (by men) power to devour and destroy men. (A related sense of the term is a woman who performs oral sex on a man.) "I'm a man-eater, a ball-buster, a castrator" (Ann-Margret's character in the 1971 movie *Carnal Knowledge*). Similarly, the "mankiller" uses her sexuality to bring men to their ruin, while *mantrap* refers to a woman regarded as someone who snares and then devours men (see also WIDOW). In any variety these women are portrayed as cold and calculating in their selfish pursuit of men and their destruction, largely deviant in their "femininity." "[Julianne] Moore [appears in] the hallowed blond territory of such icy mantraps as Leigh, Kim Novak, Eva Marie Saint, Grace Kelly, and Tipi Hedren" (reference to 1999 remake of Alfred Hitchcock's *Psycho,* in Degen Pener, *Out,* December 1998, 74].

See also BALLBREAKER, BOX (PANDORA'S BOX), CASTRATING, FEMME FATALE, MAN-HATER, SEDUCTRESS, SHE-DEVIL, SIREN, TEMPTRESS, VAMP, VIXEN, WITCH, WOMEN AS STORMS.

man Friday. A willing male assistant or helper, usually in an office. This expression comes from *Robinson Crusoe,* Daniel Defoe's 1719 novel in which the faithful servant and boon companion of the hero, stranded on a desert island, is named Friday because they met on a Friday, Crusoe having saved the man's life that day. The fact that Crusoe was English and Friday, American Indian (Crusoe instructed Friday to call him "master") adds racism to the patronizing tone of the term (see also BOY). The female counterpart does not use the equivalent *woman,* but the less dignified GAL or GIRL.

man-hater. Label sometimes applied to a woman who is believed to question the role and status of men. The underlying criticism is that she has dared to assert her prerogatives and equality with men or to stand up to a man for what she thinks and feels. Feminists and lesbians are those who usually feel the sting of this slur. At the same time, men who oppose feminism or disdain lesbians are seldom known as "woman-haters," though they may be called misogynists. In writing of the reception of her novel *The Golden Notebook,* which was belittled for being about women's liberation, author Doris Lessing wrote that "a lot of very ancient weapons were unleashed, the main ones…being on the theme of 'She is unfeminine,' 'She is a man-hater'" (*The Golden Notebook,* 1981, ix).

See also ANTIMALE, FEMINIST, LESBIAN, MANEATER.

mankind. In its generic sense, a word meaning humanity. However, although *mankind* has traditionally been used synonymously with *humanity, womankind* is not interchangeable in that way.

The variant *humankind* is modeled on *mankind.* Used since the seventeenth century along with *the human race* and *mankind, humankind* and *humanity* came into special favor in the mid- to late-twentieth century among those opposed to the use of *mankind* on the grounds that it excluded women. Thus, it was considered more accurate and inclusive to say, for instance, "Anthropology, the scientific study of humanity, seeks to explain how and why people are both similar and different" (Michael Howard, *Contemporary Cultural Anthropology*, 1996, 3).

In scientific, journalistic, and politically correct discourse, *mankind* in most instances is on its way out, though some would argue it still has a place in the language. Other acceptable terms include *humans, people, the human species*, or *human society*. Although some antisexists have complained that *humanity* contains the word *man*, in this context etymologically the reference is not just to male but male *and* female, since *human* derives from the Latin *humanus*, akin to the Latin generic *homo* (for another point of view, see Gouëffic [1996]).

See also MAN.

manly. See WOMANLY.

mannish. A term commonly used to chide a woman seen as being "overly" assertive, aggressive, or in other ways inappropriately masculine for her sex, especially in her physical appearance or dress. For example, *mannish* may be applied to a woman sporting a man's tie or, in the case of American writer Gertrude Stein, who happened to be a lesbian, to the notoriously "sensible" shoes that she wore. It may also be coded to refer to a lesbian who is not necessarily simply imitating male behavior but indicating her sexual interest in women. In black slang, it may describe the actions of a boy trying hard to be an adult.

See also DYKE, MARIMACHO. For other terms describing women, see GENDER-SPECIFIC ADJECTIVES.

man's man. Generally a reference to a man admired among other men in heterosexual society, where he has many male friends. The term lost some of its meaning in the 1970s and 1980s, however, when it came to suggest homosexuality

as a result of its use among gay men for another gay man.

man's world. The world as a sphere of activities traditionally dominated by men. "It's a man's world. Woman's place is in the home."

If women are confined to only a "place" in the world, it is, as the old saw suggests, because the world itself "belongs" to men. The folk justification of men's pervasive power rests on the idea that such power is "proper," even "natural"—so say men, although many women may feel constrained to disagree. Although *man's world* may be used in a broad sense, it also refers to specific areas—such as politics, big business, and the professions—where men have exercised substantial control (and women have traditionally been excluded). "Don't let the 'man's world' label scare you either. We have to call it by its rightful name because there are mostly men in it" (Letty Cottin Pogrebin, in McPhee and FitzGerald 1979, 116).

See also WOMAN'S PLACE IS IN THE HOME.

mantrap. See MANEATER, WIDOW.

mare. A horse metaphor applied to a woman, usually by men. Especially in British slang, it suggests a NAG, thus, a drab, wearisome woman (Thorne 1990). But it also often implies sexuality—a woman to "mount." This usage has been in English for at least seven centuries.

See also HORSE, WOMEN AS ANIMALS.

Marge. See FEMME.

marimacho. A woman regarded as mannish, a tomboy, or a lesbian, from the Spanish name *Maria* (Mary) plus the word *macho,* meaning masculine. Another Mexican Spanish heterosexual slang term for a lesbian is *loca,* which also has the meaning "madwoman." These terms tend to be disparaging. The standard Spanish word for a lesbian is *lesbiana*.

See also LESBIAN, MANNISH, MARIPOSA, TOMBOY.

mariposa; maricón. *Mariposa* [ˌmar-ə-ˈpō-zə], a term sometimes used to demean a gay man, from the Spanish word for a butterfly. In everyday discourse it suggests effeminacy, passivity, and flightiness, qualities regarded as "feminine" and therefore supposedly inappropriate for a male. It could also, however, be construed positively as meaning emerging from a cocoon into colorful flight (see also BUTTERFLY). Grahn (1990) notes that in many cultures, the butterfly symbolizes the spirit of a person (106).

Maricón is a familiar Spanish word meaning about the same as the English derogatory term QUEER or FAGGOT, though it may be self-descriptive. Among some Latinos *maricón* may be used in some contexts by heterosexuals with a hint of affection. However, as a generally very negative term, it is used less with affection and more as a subtle way men vie for power by casting aspersions, bringing into question the targeted male's masculinity and power. Both *mariposa* and *maricón* may also be heard outside the Latino/a population in the United States.

See also EFFEMINATE, FAIRY, FLOWER, MARIMACHO.

marshmallow. A food metaphor with different meanings; for example, a soft, weak, or very fat person. If said of a man, he would supposedly be deficient in the "manly" qualities of physical strength and courage (see also EFFEMINATE). Other meanings are a man regarded as worthless and, in black slang, a white man.

Mary; Mary Ann; Mary Jane. Mary, a Christian name for a woman. *Mary* (rhyming with the derogatory FAIRY) may also be applied to a man to suggest effeminacy or the playing of a female role. Names such as Mary and Mary Anne were adopted by homosexual men dur-ing the reign of Charles II in England.

Today, *Mary* may be intended and taken offensively when used by nongays for an effeminate or gay man, but gay men have also adopted the epithet as an affectionate nickname or form of self-mocking. "Oh, Mary, it takes a fairy to make something pretty" (*The Boys in the Band,* 1970 movie). It was heard in such vocative forms, especially in the mid-twentieth century, to address other homosexual men. As an adjective, it once served in such expressions as "Is *she* ever mary!" emphasizing one gay man's feeling that another is acting very feminine.

The name has also been applied to lesbians or to any women, and Major (1994) says that in its use among African Americans in Chicago, *Mary* was once a derogatory word for a woman. *Mary Ann* has also been used, often derisively, to mean an effeminate or gay man or a man who helps with household chores (see also BETTY). *Mary, Mary Ann,* and *Mary Jane* (also a slang reference to female genitals) have been heard in slang at least throughout the twentieth century, but all have earlier origins.

Parallel to Mary, another female given name referring to a gay man, especially a dowdy one, is Madge (from Magdalene), which was also once used to mean female genitals and, in nineteenth-century Californian dialectal usage, a female prostitute (Richter 1993).

See also EFFEMINATE, NANCY, NELLY.

masculine; masculinity. *Masculine,* as an adjective, a reference to certain qualities and behaviors believed to be appropriate to or associated with a man. *Masculine* is also used in language study to refer to words and grammatical forms relating to the masculine gender. *Masculine* carries heavy cultural freight, depending on what the culture makes of masculinity, and it is not symmetrical with FEMININE. Not used to refer to biological categories, as is *male,* the word *masculine* carries the more implicit and subjective meanings of that which a man or often boy is expected to be in society. The qualities designated as masculine will vary from group to group, culture to culture, and even among individuals.

In many cultures, the formation and projection of masculinity may be a problem for men. In his study of how the roles and attitudes of masculinity are created in British schools (generally applicable to the U.S. as well), Mairtin Mac an Ghaill (in Abbott and Wallace 1997, 108–09) found that male peer groups were formed out of expressions of hostility toward women and gay men. The young males in these groups showed insensitivity toward women and, although expressing desire for heterosexual sex, did not necessarily want to spend time with women. They also often ridiculed and bullied those males who did not meet the peer group's standards of masculinity. Mac an Ghaill also found a number of different codes of masculinity, varying by class and race, in the school setting. Masculinity, he explains, is a fragile construct; males need to buttress their masculinity by demonstrations of dominance.

See also GENDER AND SEX, MACHO, MAN.

masher. Since 1875, a man considered a flirt, one who makes passes at women, usually in public. *Masher* has carried some positive connotations (usually among men) but may also be used to express annoyance or fear at a man's attentions or insolence. Today the word is also applied to a frotteur (from the French *frotter*, rub), a man who rubs up against a women (or man) in a crowded public place to reach orgasm, or anyone who sexually harasses a woman.

See also SEXUAL HARASSMENT.

masochist. Someone who willingly suffers abuse and cruelty. The term comes from the surname of Leopold von Sacher-Masoch, the nineteenth-century Austrian novelist, some of whose novels depicted characters who derived sexual arousal and satisfaction from their own physical pain and humiliation. *Masochist* has acquired two primary related meanings. One is that of someone who intentionally seeks out pain and humiliation for sexual pleasure, as in a self-identified sadomasochistic (S&M) relationship.

The other, more metaphysical usage signifies someone who, for less conscious reasons, seeks or stays in relationships that are psychologically painful. In the latter sense, the term has been applied especially to women as part of a cultural myth that women are—or are supposed to be—self-denying, self-punishing, and self-blaming. Such women devote themselves, for example, completely to family or remaining in unhappy relationships and blaming themselves for their misery.

Sigmund Freud's notion of masochistic impulses in women—impulses derived, he argued, from suppression of their aggressiveness (Freud called this "feminine masochism")—entered our culture and in the 1940s and 1950s was established as a belief "almost undisputed" (Ehrenreich and English 1978, 271). Young-Bruehl (1990) refutes the common belief that Freud saw women or their activities as naturally or intrinsically masochistic (35).

In *The Myth of Women's Masochism* (1985), Caplan explains that women may get and stay in painful situations, such as unhappy relationships, because they have traditionally had fewer choices than have men. Enduring suffering is "worlds away from wanting to suffer" (21). Many people, men as well as women, even in (or because of) our consumer- and leisure-conscious society, do put themselves into situations of pain and danger. Men may even be rewarded for it; they are glorified as "real men" and applauded as good providers. But women more than men face such treatment as severe physical abuse from a spouse or the degradation reflected in many of the words discussed in this dictionary. To call women masochists for suffering this treatment may only serve to justify or obscure the treatment and adds insult to injury.

master. A strong, masculine word that usually conveys respect. Ultimately from the Latin *magister,* related to *magnus* (large), the word has had many meanings, largely positive. These have included someone with authority or superiority over others, a person whose art or work serves as an ideal, an artist of consummate skill, a venerated religious figure, a worker qualified to teach apprentices, and a male teacher. It has also been applied to the man who headed a household or owned a slave and was used as a title for a boy not considered old enough to be called "Mister."

In prison and in African American talk, *master* has meant that which is the absolute best, including people and drugs. To see the full implications of the connotations, try substituting *mistress,* which is not, as it may seem, an equivalent, in such expressions as *grand master, master of my fate,* or *master mariner.* Although in some instances, *master* may be applied to women, as in the trades, and although related words, such as *masterly,* may be applied to anyone's work, *master* still more often suggests a man. There is no comparable term reserved especially for a woman.

See also HUSBAND, MISTRESS.

maternal. Relating to the mother and mother's side of the family. *Maternal* has very different connotations from those of *paternal,* associated not only with what is often believed to be women's instinctual nature ("the maternal instinct") but also with cultural expectations of motherhood, such as solicitousness, kindheartedness, and nurturance. In the context of the term *maternal dep-*

rivation, it also suggests the special responsibilities our culture attaches to motherhood and with them, blame.

See also MOM, MOTHER, PATERNAL.

matriarchy; matriarch. *Matriarchy,* a family, community, or state ruled by women or by the mother (a system once known as "mother right"). The term, taken from the Latin *mater* (mother) and the Greek *árchein* (to rule), was first recorded about 1885. The closest synonym is *matriarchate,* although also emphasizing government by women are, for example, *gynarchy* and *gynocracy. Matriarchy* also has different, sometimes confusing, misleading and, to some, problematic meanings.

While the term occurs in feminist literature, some of which has idealized the matriarchy as a society more in harmony with nature than is the patriarchy, some feminists take exception to the use of the term. They object to the implication of political hierarchy and control, not true alternatives, they believe, to a patriarchy. For this reason, some feminists prefer the terms *matristic* (woman-centered and -supportive) or *matrifocal* (discussed below). Others define a matriarchy as a form of social organization centered on women who partake in power equally with men.

Matriarchy is also often applied to a social system in which inheritance and descent are traced through the female line, a descent system known as matrilineal. However, in a matrilineal society, brothers and husbands often control women's labor and reproductive powers, so that the matrilineal system, unlike a matriarchy, does not necessarily empower women. Women do not necessarily have a higher status or greater autonomy in matrilineal societies than they do in patrilineal societies.

Other terms often confused with *matriarchy* are *matrilocal,* which describes a pattern of residence in which a married couple lives with the wife's kin; and *matrifocal*, referring to a domestic group in which the mother is present and the father absent.

In the United States, the matrifocal family has been given a bad reputation, especially by those on the political right of the culture wars, as causes of various "social pathologies," including young men's involvement in crime and drug use. Although the matrifocal family may sometimes be a result of poverty, slavery, marriage bars, and labor discrimination, it occurs in all social classes, and there is no evidence that such a domestic group is inherently any more or less socially unnatural or unstable than the nuclear family (Harris 1993, 264).

Some nineteenth-century historians and anthropological theorists believed that a female-governed society appeared as a stage in the evolution of all societies. Influenced in particular by the work of the Swiss anthropologist Johann J. Bachofen, these theorists argued that the matriarchal stage of society, based on women's reproductive powers, was preceded by one of general promiscuity and was followed by patriarchy, or political rule by men. In *The Origin of the Family, Private Property and the State* ([1972] 1884), Friedrich Engels contended that matriarchal societies gave way to societies in which land and goods became private property and in which men found it necessary to ensure the legitimacy of their offspring as a way of transferring their wealth through descent. Patriarchy, according to Engels, thus emerged, allowing men to govern female reproduction.

The twentieth-century feminist perspective picked up on the idea of matriarchy in part as a way to argue that male rule of societies has not been universal. Di Leonardo (1991) notes that feminist writers throughout the 1970s and 1980s wrote a number of histories of gender relations, many suggesting the existence of early matriarchal societies. The no-

tion of a better, female-governed society evoked from the distant past had millenarian appeal, according to di Leonardo, and matriarchies often appear in feminist writing as utopias (8).

However, most anthropologists today, while acknowledging that a matriarchal family might occur idiosyncratically, doubt that institutionalized matriarchies existed at any time or in any stage of social evolution. Yet the absence of matriarchies in world cultures, Harris notes, while a significant historical fact about gender, does not mean that males have always dominated females. There have been a number of societies in which gender roles seem to have been egalitarian. Also, a number of societies have offered women a variety of religious, magical, creative, productive, and political roles, including sharing power with men (349).

The term *matriarch*, originally for a woman who enjoyed considerable authority in a family, has suffered some changes and degradation of meaning, especially in the context of the black family. Collins (1991) says that we now tend to see the black "matriarch," as opposed to the obedient "mammy," as the stereotypical black mother in the African American home—excessively aggressive, unfeminine, and symbolizing the "bad" black mother (74).

The white male, says Collins, sees her as a "failed mammy," an African American woman who flouts the racial rules of submissiveness and hard work. Writer Angela Davis has objected to calling a black woman who heads her household a "matriarch" when she lacks power in the larger society (Rich 1976, 40).

Matriarch is also sometimes used for a black (or any) woman who manages a business without the aid of a man; in this sense, the term is an aspersion on a woman's supposed domineering character.

See also AMAZON, MATRON, MOTHER, PATRIARCHY.

matrifocal. See MATRIARCHY.

matron. A married woman of mature and dignified character, such as a "fine Savannah matron." She may also be a woman who supervises the domestic affairs of an institution such as a hospital or a prison. The word comes ultimately from the Latin *mater* (mother), entering English from Middle French to mean a woman who was married and usually of some social status or character.

Matron is a weaker word than *patron,* reflecting the weaker position of women in society relative to men. A patron may be a man who supports the arts (*patron* is often used for women in this sense, too); a matron is often a woman who looks after a public rest room or women's jail. *Matron* also more obviously connotes middle age, while the adjective *matronly* connotes a conservative and chaste manner or appearance. *Patroness* transfers some prestige from the masculine term, but it is still troubled by the *-ess* ending (see -ESS).

See also MATRIARCHY (matriarch), MOTHER.

mattressback. A woman said to spend a lot of her time on her back on a mattress— that is, a sexually promiscuous woman or prostitute. From the middle of the twentieth century, the word has been usually used by men and meant to be degrading. A synonym is *flatbacker,* though the idea here is a prostitute who limits her services to standard sexual intercourse.

See also CHIPPY, COOZIE, DIRTY GERTIE, EASY LAY, GOOD LAY, HARLOT, HAT, HIDE, HOOZIE, HUMP, JOB, LOOSE, MINK, NYMPH, PROMISCUOUS, PROSTITUTE, PUNCHBOARD, SADIE THOMPSON, SKEEZER, SLAG, SLUT, TART, TRAMP, TROLLOP, WENCH, WHORE.

meat. Usually considered vulgar slang, long a colloquial term for the body. Meat is often also used for someone regarded as a sex object, victim, or conquest. Commonly used to mean a woman as a source of sexual gratification, often with such modifiers as *sweet* (see also SWEET MEAT), *fresh*, or *raw*, it has occurred in English in this sense since at least the sixteenth century. It may also be applied to a man, especially a large or muscular one (a HUNK) or a strong and stupid one. In gay men's slang, it refers to a man or men as sex objects.

A "meat market" is a place, usually a bar, where heterosexual or homosexual men and women go to find sexual partners. *Meat rack* is heard more particularly in the gay male community for a "cruisy" bar, where gay men go to meet other men for sexual purposes. Rodgers (1972) defined it as an outdoor setting where gay men parade their "wares." In these senses, *meat* is a double entendre, playing on the word *meet*.

Meat can also be heard in vulgar slang discourse in the sense of the female genitals or, especially among gay men, the penis. In underworld slang, it refers to a corpse, especially that of a person who suffered a violent death.

Meat has often been seen as a man's food; it connotes and may even celebrate virility. Animals are commonly hunted and butchered by men (see also HUNTER). Although meat is eaten by women (and typically cooked by them), our meat/ food language is filled with allusions to masculinity: "man-sized portions," "hero" sandwiches, "Manhandlers" (a brand name), and so on. Furthermore, the husband is thought of as the person who puts the "meat" (a symbol of the substance of the meal) on the table. Such words as *hunk*, though objectifying and fragmenting of men, may be regarded as flattering, whereas *meat* applied to a woman is almost always considered insulting and evokes male aggression and the idea of women as something to consume.

> To hear a [men's] bull session is traumatic to a woman: So all this

time she has been considered only "ass," "meat," "twat," or "stuff," to be gotten a "piece of." (Shulamith Firestone, *The Dialectic of Sex,* 1974, 170)

In her work on the sexual politics of meat, Carol Adams (1995) has made such connections between meat and masculinity—and male dominance—explicit. She discusses the Greek myth in which Zeus, the divine ruler, chases, coaxes, and then subdues and rapes Metis. Upon finishing his violence on her, he swallows her: the male power consuming the female. As Adams points out, however, we are not told how Zeus manages to fit Metis' body into his mouth. The process of butchering her is muted or hidden in the myth. Just as we mute the process of butchering animals in the slaughterhouse for meat in order to preserve the illusion that what we eat is food—cuisine—and not an animal in name and body, the myth renders the woman invisible or absent. The same applies to the meat language directed at women: the woman is absent in the idea named by the word *meat.* We are left with merely a food metaphor, one so dehumanized it is often used to express women's oppression.

Following is a sampling of the many expressions that operate from this principle of women reduced to meat. In at least one instance, however, gay men are targeted.

Terms such as *breast man, leg man,* and *thigh man* are heard typically among men describing their or others' preferences for specific parts of women's anatomy. See also ASS MAN, LEG (leg man), TIT MAN.

Chunk of meat refers to a woman as a sex object (it may also sometimes be applied to a man, probably because *chunk,* which rhymes with *hunk,* connotes size).

Dark meat, used at least throughout the twentieth century, alludes usually to a black woman (or black women gener-

ally) as a sex object, to her genitals, or to sexual intercourse with a black person. In white supremacist talk, it may suggest the cannibalistic urge to "fry" or "grill" a black person. Variations, all alluding to meat as food, include *piece of dark meat, hot piece of dark meat,* and *rare piece of dark meat* (see also *white meat,* below).

Dead meat and *stale meat,* referring to an older prostitute or older woman regarded as "loose," are ageist as well as misogynistic.

Furburger refers to the vulva (identified in terms of that sexual part, including pubic hair) or to an attractive woman. Conventional images of women's long hair probably reinforce the image.

Government Inspected Meat is a derisive reference to a gay man in the military.

Street meat means a prostitute.

White meat, used at least throughout the twentieth century, alludes usually to a white woman (or white women generally) as a sex object or to sexual intercourse with a white person. Largely in theater use, it can also mean a white female performer for hire (Wentworth and Flexner 1975).

See also BEAST, BEEF, CHICKEN, COW, DISH, EATING PUSSY, FALLEN WOMAN (piece of Eve's flesh), FISH, HAIR (hairburger), LAMB (lambchop), MUTTON, PIECE, PIG, TAIL, TAMALE, TUNA.

megabitch. See BITCH.

menopause. The period of time when menstruation naturally ceases (French *pause* means stop), sometimes used to symbolize a woman's middle age. At this time reproductive capacity in women comes to an end, and qualities that men commonly admire—youth, physical attractiveness, sexuality—may be thought of by men as on the wane. The image is misogynistic, looksist, and ageist. "You dried up menopausal nightmare" (1997 TV drama *Hope*).

Despite the negative images of menopausal women and stereotypes of their physical decline, many women note few or no physical problems or troublesome psychological conditions related to menopause. Many women even claim to enjoy increased sexual satisfaction and are happy about the end of their fertility, which frees them from childbearing and the imposition of using birth control.

The middle-aged male's corresponding period of physiological and psychological change is described medically as "climacteric," or more commonly as "male menopause." By comparison with female menopause, there seems to be a paucity of cultural lore and stereotypes surrounding climacteric, almost suggesting an imposed silence about changes in male sexual functioning.

See also FEMALE PROBLEMS

midnight queen. See DINGE.

MILF. Acronym meaning a "mother I'd like to fuck," that is, an attractive older woman from a young male's point of view; usually considered vulgar. "It singles out older women and expresses the condescension of men toward them" (Sutton 1995, 287). Also as MIF (mother I'd fuck).

milker. See COW.

milk mouth. See COCK (cocksucker).

milksop. Since the fourteenth century, a man regarded as unmanly; a weak or effeminate man or boy. Originally, in Middle English, *milksop* meant a piece of bread soaked in milk, eaten perhaps both by very young children and toothless old people.

See also EFFEMINATE, LITTLE LORD FAUNTLEROY, FLOWER, MILQUETOAST, MOLLYCODDLE, SISSY, WIMP, WUSS.

milquetoast. A label for a meek, timid, or unassertive person, probably more often intended to describe and insult men, who are expected to stand up for themselves, than women. It made its way into slang usage from the spineless comic-strip character, Caspar Milquetoast, created by American cartoonist H. T. Webster. The comic strip, called *The Timid Soul*, first appeared in 1924; the word is still used against anyone regarded as a WIMP. "[Jim] Carrey makes co-star Matthew Broderick, playing mild-mannered architect Steven Kovacs, come across as a saintly milquetoast" (Peter Stark, in *Merriam-Webster's Dictionary of Allusions,* 1999).

See also EFFEMINATE, LITTLE LORD FAUNTLEROY, FLOWER, MILKSOP, MOLLYCODDLE, SISSY, WUSS.

mimbo. See BIMBO.

mince. To walk in a "feminine" manner, probably used in England more than in the United States. It is one of those many female references applied to stereotype a gay man as effeminate, but it may also be used in a camp fashion, for example, "Look at that queen mincing along the street."

See also CAMP, EFFEMINATE, FAIRY, FLAMER, FLOWER, TWINK (twinkle-toes).

miniskirt. See SKIRT.

mink. An animal metaphor applied to a woman since at least the early 1940s, usually implying a lively, provocative, or sexually available woman, including a nymphomaniac; also, a woman's genitalia (see also BEAVER). In the sense of "girlfriend" or "attractive young woman," the term is found primarily in black English (Lighter 1997). The word has also had some use in the sense of a *lecher*.

See also FOX, NYMPH, SLAG, SLUT, WHISKER, WHORE, WOMEN AS ANIMALS.

minx, minxs. A woman viewed as being pert or flirtatious, even wanton or a WHORE, from the sixteenth century and first used for a pet dog or as a proper name. The early meaning of a pet dog may come from or help explain the use for women (see DOG). The term may derive from the Dutch *minneken,* little love, used in the fifteenth century as a term of endearment for a woman.

misfit. See INVERT, PERVERT.

miss. Derived from *mistress,* in the seventeenth century. It was reserved largely for young women or girls or applied to a paramour or prostitute. By the eighteenth century, *miss* was used as a term of address for an unmarried girl or woman who was not addressed as "lady," thus signaling marital status. In the South it retained use as a courtesy title attached to a woman's first name regardless of marital status, as in Margaret Mitchell's Miss Scarlett, of *Gone with the Wind* fame. But in general, whereas *Mr.* designated a man but not his marital status, *Miss,* by the nineteenth century, had come to identify an unmarried woman or girl (thus connoting youth, but when applied to an older unmarried woman, bearing some of the taint of OLD MAID) and *Mrs.,* a married woman. A woman's identity was thus made dependent on whether she was married. The sexism in the term is revealed in this lack of parallelism between the male and the female titles. In the late 1960s feminists began using *Ms.,* also a shortening of *mistress,* as a term that did not identity a woman's marital status or define her in relation to men.

Certain abstractions—such as liberty and justice—have been depicted as female with the use of *Miss* ("Miss Liberty" and "Miss Justice"). But the connotation of virtue in these "Miss" abstractions derives from the idea of virginity and purity implicit in *Miss.* A similar connotation is found in *little miss,* once in common use by older black servants to refer to the daughter, of any age or stature, of their white employer.

Miss has also had numerable uses in referring to gay men. Adopting *miss* as a title—as in Miss Taylor or Miss Gar-

land—or used before the names of other movie stars, is a convention among some drag queens who emulate such performers. *Miss Molly* identifies a man as effeminate or homosexual (see also MOLL).

See also MISS AMERICA, MISS ANNE, MISS SCARLET, MISTER (MR.), MISTRESS, MRS., MS., NANCY.

Miss America. The title for the woman crowned in the beauty contest held live in Atlantic City almost every year since 1921 (shortly after women won the right to vote). The winner was not actually called Miss America until 1922. Depending on the listener, the term may evoke America, embody the worst of the country's evils, or be little more than pretty "girls" strutting around and performing. The term (often in the form *a regular Miss America*) or the theme tune of the pageant, "There She Is, Miss America," may also be used as a way of referring to any very pretty young woman, though this use is often ironical. *Miss* can convey both purity (see MISS, VIRGIN) and availability (she's not married) at the same time.

Throughout the years, Miss America has remained a symbol of American femininity, an exhibition of the U.S. version of the dream of female beauty, crossing two American traditions—the "girly" show (see CHEESECAKE) and apple pie. The pageant today prefers to be known as a scholarship competition rather than a beauty contest. But while still upheld by many Americans, who continue to tune in every year to the pageant, the symbol has been maligned, in particular by religious fundamentalists and other moralists concerned with issues of decency and modesty, but also by those who found it racist and sexist. Many in the women's movement in the late 1960s and 1970s began to complain of the commercialism involved in selling sponsors' products, the expectation that the winner at that time would entertain U.S. troops in Vietnam, and age discrimination. Not the least of their attacks was that against the exploitation of women's bodies.

See also BEAUTY, BELLE, LOOKSISM, QUEEN (beauty queen).

Miss Anne; Miss Amy; Miss Lillian. *Miss Anne* (or *Miss Annie*), an ironical black English usage for a white woman, originally a Southern plantation term of respect for white people. Since the 1920s it has sometimes been used sneeringly, especially to mock any underlying patronizing attitude of a white woman.

Miss Amy, in black use for a young white woman, and *Miss Lillian,* for an older white woman, were coined in the 1970s during Jimmy Carter's presidency. His daughter's name is Amy, and Lillian was the name of his late mother. *Amy* may also be a slang term for a lesbian.

See also MISS.

Miss Nancy. See NANCY.

Miss Saigon. See EXOTIC.

Miss Scarlet. Gay black slang referring to a white racist homosexual.

See also MISS.

mister, Mr. A formal term of address for a man, prefixed to his first and last name or the last name alone; a term of address for a man used instead of a name, usually for a stranger ("Mister, can you do me a favor?"). In certain circumstances, it implies a man who lacks a title of rank or an honorific or professional title. In capitalized form, as a title of respect prefixed to a man's name, *Mister* is usually abbreviated to *Mr. Mister,* an alteration of MASTER, was abbreviated to *Mr.* around the sixteenth century. Unlike the titles MISS and MRS., but like MS., *Mr.* does not identify marital status.

Black people in the traditional South were compelled to address a white male, from about the age of ten, as *Mister,* a sign of respect. In contrast, white people called black men by their first names until late middle age, at which time the patronizing *uncle* was applied. African American actor Sidney Poitier, following up on his *In the Heat of the Night* film role, conveyed the post-civil rights reevaluation of black men in the 1970 movie *They Call Me MISTER Tibbs!*

In more general use *Mr.* can suggest male dominance. "A Louisiana educator told us about a science teacher who called the boys 'Mr.' or 'Professor' but called the girls by their first names, if they were lucky, or 'Blondie'" (Sadker and Sadker 1994, 95). *Mr. Right* refers to a woman's idea of the ideal mate; it may also refer to a gay man's ideal mate. We less often hear of *Miss* or *Ms. Right,* though they are in use. *Mr. Man* is street slang referring to the leader of a gang (there appears to be no female equivalent).

Mr. Groin is used somewhat facetiously for a man with a reputation for sleeping with women. Like other terms indicating a man's interest in sex, it does not carry the negative connotations of such terms as *slut* and *whore.* See also LOVER (loverboy).

mistress. A title of courtesy for women that, unlike *sir* and *master,* has suffered some degradation in meaning over time. From the Middle English *maistresse,* ultimately from Old French, the word *mistress,* in the fifteenth century, was predominantly the female equivalent of *master,* a title that carried respect. It meant someone with authority, usually over the household, its children, and its servants, but it also designated such esteemed positions as a female governor (see also GOVERNESS) or a patroness of the arts.

By the seventeenth century *mistress* also came to mean a woman who is "kept" by a man who is not her husband and with whom she has a sexual relationship; also a man's sweetheart or lover. The word has retained those sexualized meanings, adding others along the way, such as "dominatrix" (this preserves some sense of authority, but in a sexual context). "She is every man's fantasy mistress" (Alistair Cooke, of Greta Garbo, in Stibbs 1992). Unlike *master,* the word *mistress* has acquired such "illicit sexual meaning that it has become an unusable, tongue-in-cheek dirty joke" (Lederer 1991, 55). No one would think of consulting a "grand mistress," applying for a "Mistress card," or owning a painting by an "old mistress."

Mistress has also been used for a nation enjoying supremacy over other peoples (Rome was "mistress of the world") and for something personified as female that directs or reigns, as in the metaphorical title of the Robert Heinlein science fiction work *The Moon Is a Harsh Mistress* (1966). In these instances, however, it is objects that are thought of as women.

See also ARMPIECE, KEPT WOMAN, LOOSE, MADAM, MASTER, MISS, OLD LADY, PET, SCARLET WOMAN.

mo. See HOMO.

model. See ACTRESS, PROSTITUTE.

moll; molly. *Moll,* a seventeenth-century word meaning, primarily, a female prostitute or similarly disreputable woman. A century earlier, however, the word's primary use was as a pet version of the female given name Mary, and at different times it meant simply any young woman (it may derive ultimately from the Latin *mollis,* soft). Connotations of criminality have also been prominent throughout much of the history of the name.

In 1722 Daniel Defoe, in *The Fortunes of Moll Flanders,* described Moll (on the original title page) as "Twelve Year a *Whore,* five times a *Wife* (whereof once to her own Brother), Twelve Year a *Thief,* and Eight Year a Transported *Felon* in Virginia." *Moll* was also, in Defoe's day, the nickname of a notorious woman thief (Moll Cut-Purse),

while *Flanders* reinforced the connotations of ill repute because Flanders had a reputation in England as being the home of skilled prostitutes.

By the nineteenth century, the meaning of *moll* shifted even further to criminality. Female criminals have commonly been thought to be of coarse character and low social status and often to work under the direction of men (see also CRIMINALS), sometimes serving also as their mistresses. In the first half of the twentieth century, a "gun moll" was a female thief or pickpocket, but one often believed to operate under a man's direction; she was sometimes also known as a tramp or a prostitute and might carry a gun.

Moll or *Molly* (see also MISS [Miss Molly]), like other words for women, was once used to designate any man seen as effeminate or a gay man. Molly and other female names were also adopted by homosexual men, especially effeminate ones, during the reign of Charles II in England. Stewart (1995) says this British term may have been one of the first words for gay men popularized from within gay communities. *Molly dyke,* though dated, may still be heard for a femme lesbian.

See also DOLL, EFFEMINATE, FAG HAG (fag moll), FEMME, MOLLYCODDLE.

mollycoddle. To be overprotective or unduly solicitous, especially on the part of a motherly woman. We may speak of a child—especially a boy—or a husband being mollycoddled, or, in noun form, being ridiculed as a mollycoddle. The boy or man so indulged may be believed to be in danger of becoming not just spoiled but "sissified."

See also APRON, LITTLE LORD FAUNTLEROY, MILKSOP, MILQUETOAST, MOLL (molly), SISSY, WIMP.

mom; momism. *Mom,* short for *momma,* meaning mother, from the late nineteenth century. It is almost always an affectionate kin term, although it has also been used nonpejoratively in the lesbian community for a feminine lesbian, or one in a relationship with a butch lesbian (see BUTCH, FEMME). The informal version *mommie* takes on negative connotations, strongly contrasted with those of *mom*, in the expression *Mommie dearest*, meaning an abusive mother. This comes from the title of Christina Crawford's 1978 book about growing up under the alleged tyranny of her mother, actress Joan Crawford.

Supermom usually refers to a woman who holds down a full-time job while also looking after the house and the children. In general, the word refers to any mother who seems to work miracles by meeting what many women know to be the impossible expectations of being a mother and a career woman. She may be open to blame when she can't meet these expectations (see also SUPERMOM).

Momism refers to the domination by a mother of her children and their worship of her. It is the unflattering name, planted in our language by author Philip Wylie, referring to the so-called syndrome in which a man's purported inability to "measure up as a man" is blamed on his mother. Specifically, the problem is believed to be feminine behavior such as "maternal overprotection" (David Levy's term in his 1943 book by that name), or what one commentator discussed as the overpowering mother's "cunning styles" and "gruesome strategies" that result in the "Momistically impaired male."

See also CASTRATING, FREAK (freak mommy), MAMA, MAMA'S BOY, MOTHER, SINGLE MOTHER (Murphy Brown mom), UNCLE MOM.

Mommie dearest. See MOM.

mopsy. A term of endearment, meaning something like sweetheart, for much of the sixteenth through the early eighteenth century. This term has come to mean a woman seen as slatternly, untidy, or homely.

See also SLATTERN.

morphadite, morphrodite, mophrodite. Slang word in use since the nineteenth century meaning a HERMAPHRODITE, or intersexual person. It is also applied to a gay man (sometimes also a lesbian) and may be used to suggest anyone regarded as a sexual PERVERT. Chapman (1998) says it is probably a naive and not a humorous mispronunciation of *hermaphrodite*. A variation is *morphadike*, suggesting what is often the derisiveness of the syllable *dyke* (see DYKE).

morsel. See DISH.

mother; motherhood. *Mother* (from Sanskrit *mātr*), commonly meaning a female parent. The concept of motherhood, the state of being a mother, however, varies with time and culture. In the West motherhood, in the traditional sense of a woman's primary vocation, the source of her identity, and a significant family role, was a middle-class invention associated with the rise of the ideology of homemaking and womanhood during the industrial revolution. In our society women have become so closely linked to the childbearing and socialization roles expected of them that the word *mother* is often identified as "parent." However, in many societies, including our own, while a biological mother is the one who gives birth to a child, other people—older siblings, fathers, the elderly, extended relatives of either sex, foster or adoptive parents, or even au pairs—may do the "mothering."

Theorists such as Dale Spender have argued that, as the controllers of language, men influence the meanings of words such as *motherhood*. According to Spender (1980), men have attached strongly positive meanings to the word, making it out to represent an ordained, even beatific feminine role, one that purports to provide ultimate fulfillment for the woman (54–58).

Mother takes on an almost magical if not religious significance: "Mother is the name of God in the lips and hearts of little children" (William Thackeray, in Dunkling 1990). As such, it is defended against the "barbarian" incursions of liberalism: "Reverence for patriarchal institutions led Phyllis Schlafly to defend motherhood and apple pie from the Equal Rights Amendment" (Hill 1986, 100). Spender argues also that such reverence for motherhood serves to keep women from recognizing or talking about any negative sides of being a mother, such as the practical difficulties of meeting the expectations that come with the role. The word thus may come in conflict with women's experiences.

Whether, how, or how much men control language are controversial issues; nevertheless, the meanings that the words *mother* and *motherhood* have taken on suggest a strong bias. Most of it is positive, as in the African American Protestant church tradition, in which "Mothers of the Church" refers to women venerated for their spiritual character and influence. But in other contexts, reflecting the relative weakness of women's position in our society, blame and disparagement may sneak in. Words such as *mother hen* (see also HEN), *mother-in-law, stepmother*—known to us popularly as the wicked stepmother of fairy-tale fame—demonstrate how the supposedly glowing word *mother* can quickly take on a negative cast.

Mother can also be used for the woman who runs a brothel (see also MADAM) or a despicable person (see MOTHERFUCKER). *Your mother!* is often thought of as a vulgar expression suggesting "go fuck your mother," and *the mother* was once used to designate HYSTERIA in a woman. Some women are also bothered by being described exclusively in terms of motherhood, when they also play other important roles. For example, during her 1992 Illinois senatorial cam-

paign, Carol Mosley Braun was called a "den-mother with a cheerleader's smile"; her experience as a lawyer, prosecutor, and state senator—roles that are highlighted in the case of a male candidate—was sometimes neglected in media accounts (Rhode 1997, 73).

While *to father* a child means to sire one, *to mother* a child carries the weight of caretaking and nurturing responsibilities that a woman must meet if she is not to be censured. In U.S. society women more than men are taken to account for whatever may go wrong in the care and surveillance of their children. *Maternal deprivation* is often used as though only mothers deprive their children (fathers, however, may be called DEADBEAT or "absent").

Men come into the picture of responsibility in different ways than do women. In male-oriented writing or speech, young children still in need of their mother's care are thought of as belonging to their mother, whereas young men viewed as heirs or young women of marriageable age are often thought of as their fathers'.

Terms employing the concept of motherhood are often ambivalent. *Mother Earth,* for example, evokes earth as a divine body, a unity both taking and giving life; all living things are her children. Yet we are not beyond exploiting her to our advantage. The same is true of *Mother Nature,* largely positive.

Earth mother has been in use to mean the earth as the origin of all life, a female spirit symbolizing fertility. In feminism, she is a woman committed to nature and ecology or natural processes, such as natural childbirth; or she is a woman who is warm, instinctive, and always there for her family. Native American women especially have been stereotyped as "earth mothers." Although there is no parallel for a man, whether the concept is linked with any negatives depends largely on who is interpreting it.

The term *Jewish mother* may stand for a kind of "supermother." She supposedly devotes her life to her children, whom she is said, along with her husband, to dominate. She expects her children to meet her expectations, for example, by marrying well and establishing good careers, and to satisfy her everyday needs, such as by phoning her when they're away from home. Dan Greenburg's 1964 novel, *How to Be a Jewish Mother,* regards guilt as the "Jewish mother's" chief means of controlling her children. There is stereotyping both of women and of Jews in the term. Ethnic uses of *mother* extend to other groups, too: an older black woman whose presence in the community is valued may be known as a "queen mother."

Some feminist theorists since at least the 1970s have tried to challenge the assumption that "mothering"—the desire to have children and nurture them—is somehow instinctive. They have also questioned the division of labor between mothers and fathers, although most parenting, in our culture anyway, is probably still carried out by women. Rather than only focusing on mothers as childbearers and -raisers, some studies have also given attention to the mother herself. They have looked at her position in the family and within society at large and her identity as it is related to motherhood. They have also considered the social pressures on her to have children. Whatever the results of feminists' and others' examination of the role of mother, on one thing there is agreement: mothers will continue to play a vital role in raising and nurturing their children.

See also AUNT (auntie), BAREFOOT AND PREGNANT (KEEP THEM), BREEDER, GOSSIP (mothers' meeting), HOMEMAKER, MAMA, MAMA'S BOY, MOM, OLD LADY, PREGO, SINGLE MOTHER, STEPMOTHER, SUPERMOM, WIFE, WOMAN.

motherfucker. A reference to someone or something regarded as mean or despicable—often, or at least typically, and in the literal sense of the word, a man (Oedipus, who in Greek mythology married his mother, was a motherfucker in the literal sense). From the early to mid-twentieth century, said to derive from African American slang, the word is usually considered very vulgar and provocative—a "fighting word" among men—drawing its force from the taboo placed on sexual relations between a son and mother. Although it is a man who is often verbally attacked in this way and whose ambivalence toward his mother is exposed, the image conveyed is also degrading for a woman.

More recently, the word has taken on a new and in fact positive meaning. A "bad-ass motherfucker" may be a man admired by other men. Black Americans have also invented such dialectal variants as *mofo* and *moa-fugg*.

See also FUCKER, MOTHER.

mother hen. See HEN, MOTHER.

mother-in-law. The mother of one's spouse (in use since the fourteenth century). The kinds of jokes and insults surrounding the role of a mother-in-law are seldom if ever heard for fathers-in-law. "Two mothers-in-law" was British statesman Lord John Russell's answer when asked what he would regard as a proper punishment for bigamy (in Stibbs 1992).

From the French term meaning beautiful mother comes the euphemistic *belle mère*, meaning mother-in-law. The idea seems to be to call her the opposite of what one thinks she is to appease her (or one's own guilt about harboring hostility toward her).

See BAT, BATTLE-AX, HAG, HARRIDAN, MOTHER.

mother's meeting. See GOSSIP.

mount. See HORSE.

mouse; **mousy**. *Mouse*, suggesting small stature and timidity, used affectionately in the sixteenth century in addressing a young woman but in the eighteenth, for a woman considered coarse and brawling. By the twentieth century, the term was applied to a wife or girlfriend. Earlier in that century, *mouse* was also used for an EFFEMINATE gay man, as was the often derisive *mouser* for any gay male.

Mouse was also applied affectionately to a child. *Mousy*, meaning resembling a mouse, is usually an unflattering reference to a shy or bland woman or an effeminate, retiring man. "Jake is a blowhard, infatuated with himself and eager to put down his mousy wife" (Joe Collins, *Booklist*, 15 March 1998, 1202, speaking of Frank Manley's novel *The Cockfighter*). A term in the same demeaning category as LITTLE WOMAN, used for a wife, is *mouse queen* (see also QUEEN [woman]). *Mouseburger* was Helen Gurley Brown's (1982) expression for a woman regarded as not pretty or especially educated, well off, or socially privileged.

Mr. See MISTER.

Mr. Brown. See FUDGEPACKER.

Mrs. The title that precedes a married woman's name, which is her husband's surname. It is a contraction of *mistress* (Mis'ess). Before 1800 *Mrs.* had been used as a title prefixed to the name of an unmarried lady or girl (comparable to today's *Miss*) as well as one prefixed to the surname of a married woman. It was often used synonymously with the spelled-out form *mistress* and was most likely pronounced the same (Miller and Swift 1991, 16).

After 1800 *Mrs.* served almost exclusively to mark a woman's status as married, providing information to men about a woman's position at a time when women were beginning to leave home to labor in factories, thereby threatening their husband's control over them. The title *Mrs.* was thus a way of reminding a woman and informing those with whom she worked that her identity was as a wife.

Until recently married women were identified almost exclusively in terms of their husbands' names, and single women were known by the names of their fathers. Thus, for instance, accomplished actress Helen Hayes was once known in print as Mrs. Charles MacArthur. The husband's name was virtually mandated after *Mrs.*, since, as books of etiquette once instructed, *Mrs.* was a shortening of *Mistress*, and a woman was only a mistress of a man (although, of course, *Miss* is also a shortening of *Mistress* [Nilsen 1998, 403]). That traditionally a woman was allowed to keep only her given name may often seem to give it the same function as the man's surname. Thus, Miller and Swift (8) point out that when former Secretary of State Henry Kissinger and Nancy Maginnis were married, newspapers sometimes referred to them as "Kissinger and Nancy."

Today the title is still very significant in representing women. In 1992 educators Myra and David Sadker asked students in different classrooms to write down the names of famous women and men who were not entertainers or athletes. The names of men the students selected came right from their history textbooks, but they had trouble thinking of the names of women, "Mrs. Fields" (of cookie store fame) and "Mrs. Bush" (former first lady) being among the few (1994, 71).

Of the pair of terms of address *Mrs.* and *Mr.*, the masculine form may be viewed as the more powerful on the grounds that it is placed first in the common phrase *Mr. and Mrs.* Some men refer to their wives as *the Mrs.*, suggesting that she is more an assistant than a partner. *The missus* may evoke an image of a subservient woman, though some wives may regard it as simply affectionate (see also LITTLE WOMAN). *Missus* (or *missis*) is mostly Southern in usage, though less so than *missy*, a dated, largely black pronunciation of *Mrs.*

See also BRIDE, FRAU, HOMEMAKER, LADY (lady of the house), MADAM, MAIDEN NAME, MISS, MISTRESS, MS., NÉE.

Ms. *pl.* Mss. or Mses. Most likely a blend of *Miss* and *Mrs.*, both of which are shortenings of *mistress*; usually said to have been first recorded in 1949 (Pei [1978, 143], however, traces it back to 1825). Since either *Mrs.* or *Miss* could give offense if inaccurately applied, and personal information was not always accessible to business-letter writers, the term *Ms.* was recommended to members of the National Office Management Association in a booklet it published in 1952: "Use the abbreviation *Ms.* for *all women* addressees. This modern style solves an age-old problem" (in Barnhart and Metcalf 1997). (This business guideline was revised later to recommend usage only if one was unsure of whether to use *Mrs.* or *Miss.*)

In the late 1960s feminists began using *Ms.* as a term that did not, as opposed to *Miss* and *Mrs.*, identify a woman's marital status, which in many contexts, especially public life, was increasingly considered irrelevant. However, *Ms.*, at first derided as a feminist construct, is no longer linked strictly with the feminist movement and enjoys widespread use among many women, especially single women in business or professional contexts. As a matter of politics as well as taste, however, it remains unpleasant to some ears. Many women still prefer the traditional *Miss* and *Mrs.*, the choice varying with the person or the social or regional setting.

Ms. may be seen without the period (*Ms*).

See also MISS, MISTER (MR.), MISTRESS, MRS.

mudkicker. Since the early twentieth century, meaning a prostitute. It suggests walking the streets (what a "streetwalker" does) but also connotes the lowliness of the occupation. The term is associated with black slang.

See also DIRTY GERTIE, DIRTYLEG, PROSTITUTE.

muffin. Since the mid-nineteenth century, a food metaphor applied to a woman, usually young, regarded as a dear friend or sweetheart. *Muffins,* referring to a woman's breasts, especially if small, dates to the eighteenth century. *Muffin* was also once applied to the female genitals and to a handsome young boy seen as being of sexual interest to a gay man.

See also CAKE, CHEESECAKE, COOKIE, CREAMPUFF, CUPCAKE, DISH, JELLY ROLL, PIE, STUD (stud muffin), SWEET, TART.

mutt. See DOG, MUTTON.

mutton; mutt. *Mutton,* a meat metaphor suggesting a promiscuous woman, prostitute, or women generally as sex objects, until about the twentieth century. The term also referred to female genitals or intercourse with a woman. Although more prominent in British than in American English, in use since at least the early sixteenth century, the term has had similar application in the United States. *Mutt* has been used for a woman regarded as unattractive. In spite of commonly being linked with a DOG (an ugly cur), *mutt* probably derives from *muttonhead,* "a stupid person," from the notion of sheep as unintelligent.

See also BEEF, CHICKEN, MEAT.

N

nag. Since the nineteenth century, a word meaning someone, often a woman, who is always scolding and finding fault (in card gambling it means the queen). Used for a woman, the implication is that she complains endlessly, often about or at her husband for not behaving as she wishes he would. *Nag*, in the sense of a scold, derives from Old Norse *gnaga*, to bite or irritate. One of the closest words in meaning for a man would be CURMUDGEON, only mildly negative if not sometimes affectionate, though a man can do his own share of nagging, grumbling, and scolding. Also usually reserved for a woman is *nag* in the sense of an old horse ("old nag"). *Nag* was also once used abusively for a lewd woman, suggesting the colloquial notion of having been "ridden" around the track a few times.

The scolding nag and the horse nag stem from different words.

See also BITCH, GAB, GOSSIP, HEN (henpecked), PUSSY-WHIPPED, SCOLD, SHREW, TERMAGANT, VIRAGO, WIFE, WITCH.

namby-pamby. Usually reserved for a man who makes an impression as being weak, indecisive, sentimental, or insipid and often perceived as a sissy; also anything feeble, childish, or silly. *Namby Pamby* was the nickname given to Ambrose Philips, an English poet (1674–1749), by one of his critics, Henry Carey. It comes from shortening Philips' first name, *Ambrose,* to the babylike *Amby;* an *n* is placed at the beginning; *p*, the first letter of his last name, is then used to begin the next morpheme. The overall effect is a rhyming nickname (Philips wrote in rhyme, and here the repetition of sound pokes fun at his technique) connoting the diminutive and feminine. Carey coined the word in verse published in 1726:

Namby Pamby's doubly mild,

Once a man, and twice a child…
Now he pumps his little wits
All by little tiny bits.

See also EFFEMINATE, SISSY.

nameless sin. See SODOMY.

Nancy. A woman's name used for a gay man or any man regarded as effeminate or PASSIVE, from the nineteenth century. It is usually a derisive allusion to perceived soft, girlish qualities (*Nancy* rhymes with *fancy*). It has had some currency in both England and the United States but is more likely to be heard in England today than in the United States. *Miss Nancy* is similarly used for a man believed to be effeminate or something of a dandy. While *Miss Nancy* often suggests a gay man, *nancy boy* (see also BOY) makes the referent quite clear. Nineteenth-century U.S. senator William Rufus de Vane King was called a "Nancy boy" for supposedly having a relationship with James Buchanan, and Theodore Roosevelt scolded Woodrow Wilson for refusing to enter World War I by calling him a "white-handy Miss Nancy." The shortened *Nance* carries echoes of MINCE.

See also EFFEMINATE, MARY, NELLY.

Nanette. See PASSIVE.

natural. See NORMAL.

Neanderthal. See CAVEMAN.

née. The feminine French form *née* (born), used to identify a married woman by her birth name (e.g., Mrs. Jim Thompson, née Jones). Those who see this as freighted with sexist implications or who feel the construction is old-fashioned or irrelevant commonly use both names, as in Jessica Jones Thompson. The masculine *né* (or *ne*) is now appearing in obituaries to indicate the original name of a man who later changed his name, which is the only time it applies. The differences in use between the two forms reflect differences in the positions of men and women in our society.

See also MAIDEN NAME, MRS.

needle-dick. See BUGFUCKER.

Negress. See -ESS.

Nelly, Nellie. The familiar form of Helen or Eleanor and also viewed as an old-fashioned name for a woman; in use for much of the twentieth century for someone regarded as effeminate, weak, prissy, or silly. This is often applied to a gay man seen as making a public display of his homosexual identity (sometimes as *nelly fag*) but also sometimes used to refer to a lesbian. Names such as Mary and Nelly were adopted by homosexual men during the reign of Charles II in England. Until the 1950s the name had both humorous and abusive uses.

Although it is still derogatory when applied by heterosexuals, *Nelly* now generally conveys a lighter note than certain words applied exclusively to lesbians, such as *lezbo* or *dyke*. In gay use today, the adjective *nelly* describes effeminacy, especially when regarded as overdone: "You expect them to be mincing, screaming, nelly fairies" (Jonathan Kellerman, *When the Bough Breaks*, 1985, 29). Gay communities have largely reclaimed the word to signal their difference from straight society.

Used for a woman, there may be an implicit comparison with a horse, since *Nelly* has been identified with horses: "Whoa, there, Nelly" (see also HORSE). A "nervous Nelly" is someone who is timid or edgy, and a "nice Nelly" is fastidious or prudish (see PRUDE); either may be used for men or women, but the negativity comes from the implication of femininity or effeminacy, the latter being an accusation made against men that also implicates women.

See also EFFEMINATE, FAG, MARY, NANCY, PANSY.

nerd. See BARNEY.

nervous disorder. Historically, any sort of mental illness or abnormality in a woman; one considered to be caused by her reproductive system. In the nineteenth century, a prevalent belief about women was that their reproductive systems, rather than their brains, governed their thought. Female biology was believed to be more powerful than women's intellect. As a result, medical doctors linked mental illness with the reproductive system, reducing to biological terms a condition that in fact was a result of social constraints placed on women of that day. An epidemic of "nervous disorders," as they were called, was reported during those years, especially for women of the middle and upper classes. Freud's conception of female psychology contributed to beliefs in women's inferiority as witnessed in the frequency of these disorders.

See also FEMALE PROBLEMS, HYSTERIA.

neuter; neuter gender. See GENDER AND SEX.

new woman. See FLAPPER, PRUDE, WOMAN.

nice Nelly. See NELLY.

no-nuts. A slang term meaning "a lesbian." Since *nuts* acts here as slang for the testicles, the idea is a woman who can do without them (or who "acts as though she has them," i.e., claiming privileges granted normally only to men). The term may be jocular, but it is often used by men with intent to slight the lesbian sexual orientation. Twentieth-century usage.

See also LESBIAN.

nooky, nookie. The vagina, sexual intercourse (usually from a man's point of view), or women regarded as sex objects. *Nooky* has been in use in the United States since the early twentieth century, first appearing in the Ben Hecht and Charles MacArthur play *The Front Page*. Its origin is uncertain, perhaps stemming from the obsolete *nugging* (the sex act) or, more likely, from *nook*, meaning a secluded corner (compare with such slang terms as CRACK and CUNT, the Middle English meaning of which was a hollow space). A man may speak of "getting nooky" just as he speaks of "getting a piece of ass."

See also HIDE, PUSSY.

normal; natural. *Normal,* conforming to a standard or occurring naturally or usually. When used for people, their personalities, practices, lifestyles, looks, or physical or mental functioning, *normal* is loaded with problematic implications. Psychologists, for example, have long struggled with the term and have come up with no single criterion to describe what is normal in the human personality.

> Normality highly values its normal man. It educates children to lose themselves and to become absurd and thus to be normal. Normal men have killed perhaps 100,000,000 of their fellow normal men in the last fifty years. (R. D. Laing, *The Politics of Experience,* 1967, 28)

Usage tends to set up a sharp dichotomy between *normal* and *abnormal* that oversimplifies reality. Outside of references to statistical frequencies, these words often suggest that if I'm normal, and you're different from me, then you must be abnormal. For example, if one person's heterosexual orientation is normal, another person's homosexuality is abnormal. Those who are accused of being abnormal may be victimized and even blamed for their own victimization. "After the murder of a gay man in Miami, local newspapers demanded that homosexuals be punished for tempting 'normals' to commit such deeds" (C. Taylor, in Richard Ropers and Dan Pence, *American Prejudice,* 1995, 299).

Ideas of what is abnormal are easily upheld when their assumptions go unquestioned. The assumption that homosexuality, for example, is abnormal is supported by the assumptions that it is sinful or immoral, that it tears the fabric of society, that it hampers human evolution, and that it is nonprocreative. It has been argued by some that the genitals were made in part for procreation and that having descendants fulfills a supposedly innate and normal desire. Others, however, would disagree, stating that such arguments are questionable, at least in the conclusions drawn, and that they are mere judgments that in fact might be turned around. For example, it could also be argued that HO-MOPHOBIA—which often becomes violent—and not homosexuality is destructive to society; and some anthropologists have shown that the nonreproductivity of homosexuality may be acceptable in societies depending on how they regard population growth or having large numbers of children (Werner 1979). What is clear is that a great variation in sexual behavior and attitudes toward homosexuality has been documented across cultures and times, calling into question our ideas of what is normal (and abnormal) about sexuality.

Chauncey (1994) has described how definitions of *normal* and the application of the term change with time. Only a few decades ago, for instance, "normal" men were permitted certain eroticisms that would be taboo to those men considered heterosexual today. Chauncey notes that *normal* was in use in gay communities early in the twentieth century for those men who were not exactly "queer," that is, men who identified themselves largely, though *not* completely, by their heterosexual interest. Writes Chauncey, "'Normal' men only became 'heterosexual' men…when they began to make their 'normalcy' contingent on their renunciation of such intimacies with men" (120).

Close kin to *normal,* and sometimes used in that sense, *natural* usually means innate, of or from nature. When *natural* is applied to people, it packs a wallop— we are supposed to believe that certain behavior or inclinations are in accordance with nature or ordained by God, that they are essential and inborn, simply to be expected (and thus respected). If nature has given them to us in fixed, unchangeable form, the implication goes, who are we to question them? The term is most often used to justify and buttress mainstream or status quo beliefs, practices, and privileges. For example, since only love between two "complementary sexes" (as sex is constructed in Western culture) is considered "natural," homosexuality is deemed "unnatural," thus censured and condemned. Traditional Western society has regarded gender roles defined by certain authorities, often men, as "masculine" and "feminine" and resolute adherence to them as "natural."

See also CRIME AGAINST NATURE, DEVIANT, HOMOSEXUALITY AS DISEASE, OTHER WAY, PERVERT, SICK, SINFUL, TWISTED, UNNATURAL.

nun. A woman said to abstain from sex. Regarded as prudish, she may be derided as much by men who seek sexual pleasure with her (and control of that "right") as by those women whose views of sexuality are less conservative than those of the woman named.

See also MADONNA, PRUDE, VIRGIN.

nymph; **nymphomaniac**. *Nymph* (from a Greek word meaning bride) entered English in the fourteenth century as a word for a lesser divinity of nature. Represented in classical mythology as a beautiful maiden inhabiting the forests, mountains, and waters, the nymph was often depicted as romping with satyrs (whose name acquired associations with revelry and lechery but which we seldom use to label men). *Nymph* later came to mean not only a girl but also a prostitute; then, by the twentieth century, it was used as an abbreviated form of *nymphomaniac*.

Nymphomaniac is used to describe the condition of a woman reputed to have insatiable sexual desire, a sort of female sex fiend. The nymphomaniac manifests a form of aggressiveness (see GENDER-SPECIFIC ADJECTIVES [aggressive]) that causes her to exceed the limit of female sexual expressiveness allowed by her culture, and she is often thought to be afflicted with and degraded by her desires. *Nympho,* meaning nymphomaniac, slang since the 1930s, is often derisive. The definition of *nymphet* —a term used by Vladimir Nabokov (*Lolita,* 1955) in reference to "bewitching" maidens between the ages of nine and fourteen—is a pubescent girl looked upon as sexually desirable.

The nymphomaniac is demeaned for the same behavior that elevates a man in other men's eyes. Compare the connotations of this term with the positive ones in, for instance, STUD or VIRILE. We do have some negative terms for men, though, that are somewhat similar in meaning or at least negative, such as *sex fiend,* but which may also be facetious.

See also EASY LAY, FREAK, HARLOT, HOSE (hose monster), HUMP, JOB, LOLITA, LOOSE, MATTRESSBACK, MINK, MINX, PROMISCUOUS, PUNCHBOARD, SKEEZER, SLAG, SLATTERN, SLUT, STRUMPET, TART, TRAMP, TROLLOP, TUNA, WENCH, WHORE.

O

objectification. See SEX OBJECT.

odd; oddball. Euphemistic expressions for a gay or lesbian person. Though in less use today than formerly, offense is still usually taken.

See also FUNNY, QUEER.

oinker; oink-oink. See PIG.

old bat. See BAT.

old biddy. See BIDDY.

old boy; old girl. Expressions that carry largely different meanings. They have had more currency in England—*old boy* derives from the term for British school alumni. *Old boy* has been characteristic of men's talk as a friendly form of address to another man (it can also mean the devil or the penis). While *old girl* is also used by men, it applies affectionately to women—often of any age—but also to female animals, such as horses.

See also BOY, GIRL, GOOD OL' BOY.

Old girl (or *old hen*) is also a gay term meaning an older gay man. It may be viewed as both ageist and sexist, since it draws on derogatory images of women to communicate the insult.

See also GIRL, HEN, HOMOSEXUAL.

old coot. See BILLY GOAT, COOT.

old fart. An expression for a man (sometimes also a woman) seen as unpleasant, worthless, silly, and thus easily dismissed, used since the sixteenth century. The term may also have affectionate use.

A man regarded as worthless or contemptible does not actually need to be old to suffer the epithet, though our negative attitudes toward old age make it easier to dismiss him. *Fart* resembles other excretory metaphors, such as *snot* or *shit*. Often constructed as *stupid fart, silly fart, boring old fart,* but especially *old fart,* such expressions have been common since at least the early twentieth century. "I have become an old fart with his memories and his Pall Malls..."

(Kurt Vonnegut, *Slaughterhouse-Five,* 1966).

Rawson (1989) notes that *fart* (originally and still meaning a release of gas through the anus) was long accepted as standard English, not being avoided by lexicographers and middle-class writers until Victorian standards pronounced it vulgar.

See also BADGER, BILLY, BUZZARD, COOT, CUSS, DUFFER, FOGY, GAFFER, GEEZER, GOAT.

old fogy, fogey. See FOGY.

old gee. See GEEZER.

old goat. See GOAT.

old hat. See HAT.

old hen. See OLD BOY (old girl).

old lady; old man. Regardless of her age a mother, girlfriend, mistress, or wife may be referred to as an "old lady," usually by her son, boyfriend, or husband. Lighter (1997) traces the use for a mother to the early eighteenth century, in a quotation from Daniel Defoe's novel *Moll Flanders*: "His elder brother was married and we, being then removed to London, were written to by the old lady to come and be at the wedding." *Old lady* has also seen some use for the "feminine" member of a homosexual relationship, for a male cook in Western ranch-hand talk, or for any man regarded as having womanish characteristics. In all these usually sexist senses, *old lady* tends to communicate disrespect, and the word *lady* (see LADY) in the expression is not parallel to *man* in *old man*. The latter, which may apply to a father or a woman's boyfriend, is sometimes used also for a boss, or any man in charge, including God. *Old man,* however, may also be used in the street slang of prostitutes for their pimp (see also PIMP).

See also JOANIE, OLD WOMAN.

old maid. A woman who is not married, especially an older one (see also SPINSTER), usually meant and taken as offensive. It can also mean any person seen as timid, fussy, fastidious, and probably asexual, implying a comparison with the stereotype of an old, unmarried woman. "You find [women] copy editing or reading proof. Old maids mostly, with a pencil behind their ear and dyspepsia" (Mary McCarthy, *The Group,* 1963, 211).

The assumption is that there is something wrong with a woman who has "missed her chance" for marriage. The idea of something left over after the best is gone is reflected in the use of *old maid* to mean the last card in a game played by children or kernels of unpopped popcorn left after the rest has been eaten.

In the sense of an unmarried woman, this term has been used since the sixteenth century. The English once believed that after death, old maids changed into lapwings, a kind of plover noted for its shrill wailing cry and its boldness, so they called the bird as well by the name *old maid.*

Being averse to the term, some women once tried to identify themselves as *bachelorettes* (see -ETTE). But since marital status in many circumstances is no longer regarded in our society as pertinent information, there is usually no need to express it linguistically, and, hence, terms like *bachelorette* never caught on.

Old maid can also be applied to a man for his alleged prudishness, fussiness, or unmanly behavior. Being branded an old maid has been a tactic of male soldiers to get their fellow soldiers to conform to the soldierly idea: "'Whatsa matter, bud—got lace on your drawers?' 'Christ, he's acting like an old maid'" (Samuel Stouffer, in Gerzon 1982, 39).

See also BACHELOR, MAID, MAIDEN, MISS, PRUDE, SCHOOLMARM.

old man. See OLD LADY.

old nag. See NAG.

old stick-in-the-mud. See FOGY.

old wives' tales. Superstitions, folklore, or tales from ancestors. "Old wives' tales" are said to be told by women who, according to sexist-ageist bias, do little more than prattle.

Not everyone adheres to the negative stereotype of old wives' tales: yes, many are nonsense, but some contain time-tested wisdom and are the foundation of successful folk remedies. In many cultures women, often older women, have been the healers, and talking was the way to pass down herbal remedies and traditions through the generations. Though these remedies were proven by observation and experience rather than controlled experiments, some have scientific merit. For example, an old Italian superstition commands that a pregnant woman be allowed to eat all she craves, otherwise her baby will be deformed. This is not as preposterous as it first appears. Current research suggests that a pregnant woman craves certain foods because her body requires the nutrients in those foods.

Bubbe meisers is a related Yiddish term meaning, literally, Grandmother's stories. "It's just a bubbe meiser" is a way to dismiss an assertion as silly. Some stories are indeed far-fetched, while others are meant to teach a lesson, and still others may have a claim to age-old good sense.

See also GOSSIP.

old woman. Used in many of the same ways as *old lady*—for a mother, wife, or girlfriend. *Old woman* has also been used to suggest a fussbudget—who might also be said to be "old womanish"—and to demean men. In a sexist culture that diminishes women, for a man to be thought of not only as a woman, but as an old one at that, is a great insult. He is thus allegedly pitifully weak.

No insult is implied if you refer to a female as an *old man:* it is inaccurate, but the assumption is that there has been a mistake in identity. This is not the case if you call a man an old woman. (Spender 1980, 17)

See also OLD BOY (old girl), OLD LADY, WOMAN.

one-bagger. See BAG.

one of those (them). A euphemism sometimes used among heterosexuals, usually for a male homosexual. The expression puts gay men distinctly outside the speaker's own group, presumed to be the normal one.

The claim made by some heterosexual people that they "can always spot one of them"—that is, a homosexual person—is a result largely of selective perception plus misperception. It may be possible to point to what is called effeminacy in a man or butch qualities in a woman, but such qualities often do not indicate sexual orientation. Even if one's guess turns out to be correct, there are many more homosexuals around who cannot be identified, since they manifest no visible signs whatsoever of their orientation. As Anne Killpack points out, "You claim you can 'always spot one of us'—why, then, were nearly a third of the anti-queer crimes reported last year committed against heterosexuals, by persons so eager to hate that they didn't bother to find out who they were attacking?" (*Anything That Moves*, Fall 1998, 89).

One of us is used in gay and lesbian communities in the sense of being "in the family." Thus, one lesbian might ask another, in reference to a third woman, "Is she one of us?"

See also NORMAL, OPPOSITE SEX (other sex), OTHER WAY.

opposite sex; other sex; third sex. *Opposite sex*, an expression that stresses the differences between men and women, placing them in different—actually, antithetical—categories. The socially constructed opposition alluded to is represented primarily by the genitals, or reproductive organs, which give us our

way of assigning sex. The fact that there are babies born intersexual—with variable, sometimes ambiguous genitalia—does not stop us from imposing a rigid dual-sex system. Medical practice even encourages surgical alteration on such babies to enforce the cultural mandate that there must be only two sexes (see also HERMAPHRODITE). In turn the Western world, at least, aligns the two sexes with two genders. This usage thus reinforces the dual-gender system in U.S. society.

Geneticist Anne Fausto-Sterling says that the dual-sex system, rather than being a fact of nature, is in fact a defiance of it. She recognizes a spectrum running from female to male along which there are at least five sexes (in Feinberg 1996, 103). Given such societies as those of Native Americans, where the "two-spirit," or BERDACHE, adopted the dress and ways of the other sex as actually another gender, the notion of the "opposite sex," based on anatomical differences, is seen as an arbitrary social construct. "The first thing that strikes the careless observer is that women are unlike men. They are the 'other sex'—(though why 'opposite' I do not know; what is the 'neighbouring sex'?)" (Dorothy Sayers, quoted in *On the Contrary,* ed. Martha Rainbolt and Janet Fleetwood, 1984, 10).

To avoid the sense of oppositeness, *other sex* is sometimes preferred. *Other sex* (or *a member of the other sex*), however, may also be heard as a coy reference to someone viewed as attractive or treated as a sex object. *Other sex* has also been used for a wide range of marginalized gender identities and sexualities. *Other* here connotes "one of those people" (see ONE OF THOSE).

Third sex, coined in the nineteenth century in reference to a supposedly innate "intermediate stage" between female and male, has also been widely used, largely synonymous with *other sex*, but in addition covers many other sex or gender categories. *Third sex,* or the more slangy *third sexer,* may be used in particular to designate gay males or lesbians, but it is also used for a diversity of sexualities or gender identities that do not conform to the conventional American bipolar model of the "opposite" sexes. This would include CROSS-DRESSERS, EUNUCHS, androgynes (see ANDROGYNY), and hermaphrodites (see HERMAPHRODITE), although the categorization of these groups may vary at different times and among cultures.

In the 1860s a Prussian lawyer and defender of homosexuality, Karl Heinrich Ulrichs, categorized the homosexual as a "third sex" (*das dritte Geschlecht*), neither sick nor sinful, but a soul that belonged to one sex in a body belonging to another. A few decades later, sexologist Magnus Hirschfeld used *third sex* for homosexuals in an attempt to diminish social prejudices by the construction of a special class of people. The unintended effect, however, may be only to overcategorize the diversity of other expressions of gender and sexuality and even to dismiss them as inferior.

See also GENDER AND SEX; HETEROSEXISM.

oppression; **oppressed**. Terms weighted with the meaning of the root word, *press*: weighing heavily on, applying pressure to, and hence flattening and immobilizing. Groups or individuals that are oppressed are subjugated, persecuted, and left without freedom to move because of the application of the unjust social, political, or economic forces of the oppressors. Although *oppressor* and *oppression* are strong, often inflammatory, and sometimes overused or misused terms, they serve a useful, even essential, place in discussions of marginalized, politically weak, and minority peoples.

Many theorists have argued that the oppression of women is a universal in the present as well as in at least the recent past, although current scholars emphasize the diversity of political relations and argue that women have not been subjugated everywhere. However, whatever the clamor surrounding the idea of oppression and the sometimes misleading implications of the use of the term, for many people, certain forms of constraints and discrimination are realities that they live every day. For women, for example, it may be the general exclusion from powerful political or business positions, physical abuse in the home, rigid expectations regarding sex roles and physical looks, and harassment in the workplace.

Men may suffer the oppression of their own rules that they must be strong, aggressive, and without the "weaker" emotions, while many men, depending on their race or class, are also subjected to exclusion and abuse of different kinds. Some writers, however, have objected to the use of *oppressed* to characterize men. Thus, although granting that sexism and power harm men, too, especially poor men and men of color, men and women are generally seen as occupying very different positions. It would seem easier for many men to divest themselves of chauvinistic attitudes than it is for many women to avoid the impact of male power.

See HETEROSEXISM, HOMOPHOBIA, SEXISM, VICTIM, WOMEN AS A MINORITY GROUP.

other sex. See OPPOSITE SEX.

other way, the. Euphemistic reference to homosexuality, seen by heterosexuals as a deviation from "normal" sexuality.

See also NORMAL, ONE OF THOSE.

owl. A bird metaphor for women, particularly for prostitutes who walk the streets at night, suggesting the nocturnal habits of the owl (mostly nineteenth-century usage). The "wise old owl," on the other hand, is usually seen as male.

See also BAT, BIRD, CHICKEN, GROUSE, QUAIL, WOMEN AS ANIMALS.

P

package. A twentieth-century name for an attractive woman viewed as a sex object, alluding to outside, or superficial, beauty. Also applied to men's genitals, in gay and heterosexual use.

See also BEAUTY, LOOKSISM, SEX OBJECT.

pansy. A type of flower, from Old French *pensée*, the feminine past participle of *penser*, to think (botanists found a human face in the head of the pansy, apparently a pensive one). But the intellectual image behind the term is long lost to history. Directed at a man, *pansy* has been considered disparaging, suggesting weakness and effeminacy, thus homosexuality, since the early twentieth century, especially the 1920s and 1930s. Like food metaphors such as *fruit*, plants—especially flowers, connoting femininity—can be used to call a man's masculinity into question. "Male commentators like Rush Limbaugh and Howard Stern command some 25 million listeners for their tirades against 'feminazis,' 'pansies,' and 'foreigners'" (Rhode 1997, 67). Like other epithets meant to disparage men's masculinity, *pansy* is also a name for a woman.

Pansy raid, meaning an attack on gay groups or a raid on places where they gather, is a pun on *panty raid*. While sometimes meant as jocular, the term is likely to be taken as offensive by gays when used by heterosexuals in reference to discriminatory or punitive actions directed against gay people. *Pansy without a stem,* gay male slang, refers to a lesbian's lack of what men have that "makes them men." *Pansified* means "effeminate." *Ansy-pay,* Pig Latin, is synonymous.

Pansy has also had nonpejorative uses for gay men. For example, in the early 1930s, at the height of what Chauncey (1994, 314–21) describes as the "pansy craze" in New York City, the Pansy Club opened up in Times Square, featuring a gay chorus line and a female impersonator host. The term has also enjoyed more recent positive associations: A Queer Punk band called Pansy Division sings songs about being gay.

See also BOY (pretty boy, Percy boy), BUTTERCUP, CANDY-ASS, DAFFODIL, DAISY, EFFEMINATE, FAIRY, FLOWER, FRUIT, GLADIOLA, LAVENDER, LILY, LIMP-WRIST, LISPER, PEEPING TOM (peeping pansy), POWDER PUFF, TWIT, VIOLET.

pants. Trousers, traditional male clothing. *Pants* carries masculine connotations and may be used metaphorically, or synecdochically, to suggest masculinity. "Who wears the pants in the family?" is asked when there is some question about a man's authority. A cliché dating to the eighteenth century referring to the culturally unacceptable dominance of a woman in a relationship, "wears the pants" may be used to censure her for being overly aggressive, but the expression is also sometimes said ironically or partly in jest. Although dominance has traditionally been regarded as an "unfeminine" quality, women today are learning to assert themselves at home and in the workplace and for some time have literally worn pants.

The usage reflects on men as bearers of power and is not symmetrical with the sexualized slang term, SKIRT, used for a woman. *Pants* may also be sexualized but usually only in the context of an expression such as *hot pants*, also used for women (see also HOT). However, slacks, as applied to an article of clothing worn by women as well as men, lacks the definite masculine cast of *pants*.

Slacks has been used for lesbians, associating them stereotypically with masculine clothing and features.

party girl. A young woman depicted as sexually promiscuous; often, a euphemism for *slut*. In the mid-1990s, when black celebrity O. J. Simpson was on trial for the murders of his wife, Nicole Brown Simpson, and her friend Ron Goldman, the press gave some attention to Nicole's lifestyle. Although sometimes portrayed as a caring mother and family woman, there were also tabloid innuendoes that she sometimes ignored her children, preferring instead the role of a swinging "party girl."

See also GIRL, PROMISCUOUS, SLUT.

passion flower. See FLOWER.

passive. Inactive; being acted upon, often regarded as an attribute of femininity and of certain kinds of gay or lesbian roles. In either sense it is a stereotype and a misleading notion. The idea derives largely from considering women as being sexually penetrated by men (female receptor vs. male inserter) and confusing this role with the passive role that women are expected to play in society. Not only is this notion of female passivity regarded as sexist, but it becomes objectionable to homosexual persons as well. In general, people, regardless of sex, gender, or sexual orientation, engage in varying degrees of active and passive behaviors.

Gay communities abandoned the active-passive distinction some time ago.

> After the almost complete victory of gay liberation in San Francisco…[gay bar] customers were no longer concerned with the distinction between "active" and "passive"; instead, "everybody did everything." (Haeberle and Gindorf 1998, 36)

However, gay slang for the "passive" partner has included such vulgar words as *anus queen* and such disparagements as *Nanette*.

All these labels overcategorize people, ignoring the change and variety that people experience in their sexual and social lives.

See also COOKIE, DAISY, DOLL, DUCH-ESS, EFFEMINATE, FAIRY, FEMME, FOX, FRUIT, FUCKER, GENDER-SPECIFIC ADJECTIVES (aggressive), HALF A MAN, HE-SHE, HOLE, HUMP, MOM, NANCY (Nancy boy), OLD LADY, PUSS, QUEEN (gay man), VEGETABLE, WALLFLOWER, WIFE.

pastry. See CAKE, CHEESECAKE, CHERRY (cherry pie), COOKIE, CREAMPUFF, CUPCAKE, DISH, JELLY ROLL, MUFFIN, PIE, SUGAR, SWEET, TART.

paternal. Like *father*, a derivative from Latin *pater*, meaning like or relating to a father, received or inherited from a father, or related through the male side of the family. Compared with *patriarchal*, which rings with strength and often harshness and occasionally, in some feminist contexts, blame, *paternal* is a soft term ("His was a paternal goodness"). However, it may suggest more severity than does *fatherly*, which implies kindness. Thus, to take a "paternal hand" in a matter is to be firm.

See also MATERNAL, PATRIARCHY.

patient Griselda. See GRISELDA.

pato. A gay man, with connotations of stereotypical effeminacy, apparently from Puerto Rican Spanish. In Spanish, *pato* means duck, perhaps suggesting a type of walk as perceived by those who stereotype gay men.

See also BIRD, EFFEMINATE, HOMO-SEXUAL.

patriarchy. Literally, rule of the father in the family or group, from Latin and Greek (*pater,* father, plus *árchein,* to rule). Once known also as "father right," *patriarchy* refers to the dominance of men over women as a class. The different elements or senses of patriarchy include (1) the legal and economic dependence of wives and children on the male head of the household, (2) reckoning of descent and inheritance through the male line, (3) a society based on male governance and descent through men, (4) the ideas and values on which male authority is based and by which it is legitimized, and (5) the symbolic devaluation of women.

Some theorists have defined *patriarchy* as a universal political and oppressive system, though many others have come to see it as taking on unique historical forms. Some writers have written about it as though it were a natural form of dominance (e.g., Steven Goldberg, *The Inevitability of Patriarchy*, 1974) or a myth (Farrell 1993). But despite differences of opinion about this much used, often confusing, and allegedly inflated term, a patriarchy is generally viewed as a system that subordinates women and privileges men. Patriarchy takes its power from the resources and benefits—political, social, and economic—that men have more access to and control over than do women, generally. The common synonym in this context is *male-dominated society*.

In *Ancient Law* (1861), nineteenth-century evolutionary anthropologist Henry Maine sought the origins of human law in the authority exercised by fathers over the ancient family. While he saw the modern European family as the result of the evolution of this ancient patriarchal family, he nevertheless hedged on the question of whether patriarchy was a universal "stage" in human history (Harris 1968, 143). The primordial family group in Maine's time was often depicted as those Homer envisioned for the mythical race of Cyclops, with a father wielding absolute power over his children and wives. On the other hand, those evolutionary theorists of the family who challenged Maine, such as Johann J. Bachofen (*Mother Right*, 1861), argued that matriarchy was the earliest and universal stage of social development; the chief implication of coming earlier, in Victorian thought, was that matriarchy was more primitive.

The theory of the patriarchal development of society was taken up by other important thinkers. Among these was Sigmund Freud, who equated civilization with patriarchy, whose values a boy internalizes through resolution of the Oedipal complex. Karl Marx and Friedrich Engels also theorized on patriarchy, assuming the existence of early matriarchal societies. Engels' "decisive victory" of monogamy in cultural evolution, which he took as a sign of the rise of civilization, was seen as based on male supremacy (Engels [1884] 1972). He saw the male heads of households as controlling women, as the reproducers of children. "The overthrow of mother right was the *world historical defeat of the female sex*" (87).

In the twentieth century radical feminists saw patriarchal values as structuring relations between the sexes, creating gender inequalities viewed as the paradigm of all other social inequalities (Cannell and Green 1996, 592). Some feminists and academics have taken patriarchy, or specific features of it, as an explanation of women's oppression everywhere. In the linguistic theory of Jacques Lacan, entering into our culture means having to submit to patriarchy, although this theory does not explain why the symbolic order is patriarchal in the first place (Cameron 1985, 124).

On a different track of social thought, anthropologist Margaret Mead, who did not typically take a feminist point of view, criticized the notion of a male conspiracy to keep women in their place. She argued that "this is a world made not by men alone, in which women are unwilling and helpless dupes and fools or else powerful schemers hiding their power under their ruffled petticoats, but a world made by mankind for human beings of both sexes" (*Male and Female*, [1949] 1975, 299–300).

Contemporary anthropology has attempted to rework or refine the idea of universal patriarchy by noting that it is based on a taken-for-granted "natural" distinction between men and women. Non-Western societies do not view the sexes as Westerners do; they often do not share our concept of a biological dichotomy between "male" and "female." As a result, the notion of patriarchal dominance may distort the complex nature of gender relations and identity in the West as well as in the non-Western world (Cannell and Green, 592). Anthropologists today have also stressed how different social affiliations may cut across a patriarchal society. In the United States, for example, where patriarchy is acknowledged as governing relations between men and women, many black men nevertheless enjoy far less prestige or power than white, upper-class women.

Critics of the idea of patriarchy have tried to demonstrate the weak political position in which many men may find themselves. For instance, men may assume obligations or make sacrifices under "patriarchy" that appear to put them in positions of servitude and put their lives in jeopardy. Men have traditionally taken jobs to support their families, including those in the military (not always voluntary), that are hazardous and take their lives (Farrell). Such positions are questionable as signs of universal "patriarchal privilege."

At the same time, however, men, whatever the constraints or hardships of their roles, do not typically find themselves in positions of servitude to women *as a class*. Also, women of one class or race will likely be granted fewer privileges than men of that same group.

Patriarchy and *patriarchal* have also commonly been employed to assign blame to males and disparage men or anything masculine or oppressive. A swift reference to *patriarchy* or *patriarchal structures* allows a detractor to put the blame for society's ills squarely on men while absolving women of all responsibility (August 1998, 432). Simi-larly, Farrell sees *patriarchy*, like *male dominance*, as a code word for male disposability.

Some feminists, with different perspectives, prefer such varied and noninterchangeable language as *sex-gender system* (Gayle Rubin), *the planetary Men's Association* (Mary Daly), and *phallocracy* (dates from the mid-twentieth century).

See also MATRIARCHY, OPPRESSION, PATERNAL.

patron. See MATRON.

pavement princess. See PRINCESS.

peach. Originally, a young woman seen as luscious and good-looking; or sometimes any admirable or attractive person; also in twentieth-century slang, a promiscuous woman (Spears 1991). *Peaches* is also a nickname given to a female or a gay male.

This fruit metaphor is from at least the eighteenth century. The idea is that a peach is soft, sweet, beautiful—in our society, feminine qualities, as is a "peaches and cream" complexion (usually limited to white people). A closely related fruit metaphor applied to women is *plum*.

See also CHERRY, DISH, FRUIT, LOOKSISM, TOMATO.

peacock. A term for a male bird (the peafowl) with a strutting gait and brightly colored plumage; also used metaphorically to suggest a person—usually a man—seen as extremely vain, puffed up in self-image and often ostentatiously dressed. It is a put-down meant to deflate the ego, which our culture has traditionally allowed the male greater range to display, though not typically through dress.

See also BIRD, COCK.

pearl. A gem valued for its luster, an object of beauty, typically traded by men and used in female adornment, and long serving as a lunar symbol. It is not surprising to see this term applied to women. Among the many female associations the term has picked up are the sexual ones deriving from a pearl being inside an oyster, suggesting the female genitals. It is found as a given name, in word compounds, or in such references as "fair as a pearl."

Black pearl has occurred in literary descriptions of beautiful black women, and *pearl of the Orient* stereotypes an attractive Asian woman as exotic. *Ivory pearl* was a largely British usage for a white woman. Such names, however complimentary the user may intend them, tend to allude to women as sex objects.

See also EXOTIC, FLOWER.

pederast. From the Greek *paiderastēs*, meaning lover of boys, a positive term in the ancient Greek context, where such activity was considered healthy for a young (usually adolescent) man's upbringing. Today, however, *pederast* has come to be a term of opprobrium, since it often connotes pedophilia or child molesting. In particular, it would be insulting and inaccurate to refer to a gay man as a pederast when he has as sexual partners consenting young men.

What's more, all scientific evidence today indicates that most pedophiles—adults, usually males, who obtain sexual gratification through sexual contact with young children—are heterosexual.

See also CHICKEN (chickenhawk), HOMOSEXUAL, JOCK, WOLF.

P.E.E.P. See PUSSY.

Peeping Tom. Someone who takes pleasure—usually sexual pleasure—in secretly watching women who are not fully clothed or in prying into their lives with prurient interest. It is usually applied euphemistically to a man who in more blunt terms would be called a "pervert" or a "dirty old man." Unlike *Peeping Tom*, usages such as *peeper* and *voyeur* are supposed to be sex-neutral, but most such terms usually implicate men. The female version, *peeping Thomasina*, is seldom heard. Also rare is the female *peeping pansy*. In gay communities, *peer queer* may be heard as a reference to a gay man who likes to watch others engaging in sex (see also QUEER).

The word apparently derives from the name of the citizen of Coventry, England, who is said to have watched Lady Godiva riding naked. According to the legend, the lady made her ride as a way of persuading her husband to lower taxes. In one version of the story, a local tailor or butcher named Tom enjoyed a peek as she rode by; the other townspeople had shuttered their windows. Some accounts say that Tom was killed by angry townspeople; others say he was struck blind.

W. H. Auden wrote, "Peeping Toms are never praised, like novelists or bird watchers,/For their keenness of observation" (quoted in *The American Heritage Dictionary* [1992]).

See also DIRTY OLD MAN, EXHIBITIONIST, FREAK (peek freak), PERVERT, TOM.

Percy boy. See BOY.

person. See MAN.

pervert; perversion. *Pervert*, usually someone believed to exhibit what the speaker regards as deviant sexual behavior. The Latin *vertere* (to turn), is also the source of the related word *invert,* which unconsciously picks up the late medieval idea of "the world upside down" (Dynes 1990).

Perversion, the word for a so-called aberrant sexual practice, dates to the fourteenth century; *pervert,* for the person practicing it, entered the language about three centuries later. However, the use of *pervert* as a sexual colloquialism dates only to the nineteenth century, associated originally with the 1897 work of sexologist Havelock Ellis, *Studies on the Psychology of Sex.* A contemporary of Ellis, Sigmund Freud distinguished between the neurosis and the perversion:

the former involved the overrepression of childhood impulses; the latter, the lack of proper control of impulses. Thus, homosexuality, according to Freud, was a perversion because it was believed to represent a kind of state of arrested development, homosexuality being a normal phase of childhood growth.

The word *pervert* usually implies a condemnation of what is often believed to be abnormal or unnatural forms of sexual intercourse among humans. Gay men and lesbians especially have been targeted with this loaded word, though anyone, regardless of sexual orientation, may experiment with what a particular society would view as nonstandard sex. In his study of how different historical periods have viewed sexual orientation, Jonathan Katz (1995) reports that in the earliest known use of *heterosexual,* in a Chicago medical journal in 1892, the term was equated not with normal sex but with perversion (see also HETEROSEXUAL).

According to social philosopher/linguist Roland Barthes, the dominant group of a society will promote the belief that the particular norms and institutions of that society—which usually benefit the dominant group—are "nature's way" or "God's way." By this logic, those who challenge these systems with variant beliefs or practices can only be "deviants" or "perverts." According to the "natural" design of the universe, as it is viewed, the sexual pervert is often one who undermines the essential complementarity between male and female. But even a dominant group's views of perversions can be "reconstructed," especially for commercial purposes: "S&M—or B&D, for bondage and discipline—has been mainstreamed from deviant perversion to just another wacky lifestyle choice" (Rich Marin, *Newsweek,* 29 December/5 January, 1998, 85).

Pervert has lost ground since the 1960s, no doubt because of the efforts of gay liberation activists to replace such biased terms with terms of their preference. However, it and the abbreviated *perve* (also *per*) may still be heard in scorn or dismissal of gay men or, sometimes, any men regarded as lascivious. A variant spelling and deliberate mispronunciation is *prevert.* "I think you're some kind of deviated prevert. I think General Ripper found out about your preversions and that you were organizing some kind of mutiny of preverts" (suspicious Keenan Wynn to Peter Sellers in the 1964 Cold War black comedy *Dr. Strangelove or: How I Learned to Stop Worrying and Love the Bomb*).

Since there is no shortage of ways to look down on others' sexual practices or orientations, we have a number of terms like *perversion* in our language, some of which are shown here. Included are euphemisms, meant to blunt certain "disagreeable" truths about sexuality.

Aberration, introduced by French medical writers in reference to kinds of sexual behavior, including same-sex relations, is a euphemism for any nonheterosexual (or nonprocreative) sex act.

Abnormality is a euphemism for homosexuality.

Abomination, something worthy of hatred or disgust, appeared in Jerome's Vulgate translation of the Bible to designate conduct, such as idolatry, believed to be in violation of God's covenant with Israel. Since medieval times, writers have applied it in religious and legal texts synonymously with *homosexuality* after the wording used in the Old Testament. SODOMY and *buggery* (see BUGGER) were also introduced to describe "unnatural," religious "abominations."

Degenerate signals someone whose morals have deteriorated from what is regarded as the standard system of morality; he (the person is often male) is usually known as a sexual deviate. Chauncey (1994) argues against the "myth of internalization," which holds that gay men tend to accept society's view of them as perverts. According to Chauncey, many doctors of the early twentieth century reported that "their subjects rejected the efforts of science, religion, popular opinion, and the law to condemn them as moral degenerates" (6).

Depraved means corrupt or perverted, especially sexually. Sexual "abnormalities" referred to as such are usually acts contrary to procreative heterosexual sex.

Kinky, from the earlier sense of a kink as a twist, has been in use since the early twentieth century, often to describe a gay man or lesbian. *Kink* identifies someone as a sexual deviant, especially someone whose sexual interests or tastes run to what is commonly regarded as bizarre or adventuresome. Although often expressing disapprobation—criminals have been known as "kinks," especially in the early twentieth century—*kink* as applied to someone of unusual sexual practices is not necessarily a term of contempt, and, to some, it may even be flattering.

Misfit was used during the early twentieth century for a homosexual, suggesting sexual deviation. "In Hitler-era Germany...lesbians (grouped with prostitutes, antisocials and 'misfits') wore a black triangle" (Amanda Staab, *Curve,* November 1998, 48).

See also DEVIANT, DIRTY OLD MAN, HOMOSEXUALITY AS DISEASE, INVERT, MORPHADITE, NORMAL, QUEER (queervert), SICKO, STRAIGHT, TWISTED.

pet. A pampered child, someone regarded as a darling person (e.g., *my pet*, as an address often to a female friend or wife), a sexual mistress, or a domesticated animal kept for friendship or companionship. All the senses share the idea of someone (or an animal) meant to please, often someone smaller or subordinate, and all carry a load of condescension.

As in Germany it is said that every gentile has his pet Jew, so it is said in the South that every white has his "pet nigger."...We sometimes marry the pet woman, carrying out the paternalistic scheme. (Myrdal [1944] 1962, 1078)

As a verb, it means to caress.

See also BIRD, BUNNY, DOG, FAWN, KITTEN, LAMB, WOMEN AS ANIMALS.

petticoat; **petticoat chaser**. See SKIRT.

philanderer. See LOVER.

pie; **cutie pie**. *Pie*, a woman regarded as a sex object or a euphemism for female genitalia. This twentieth-century food metaphor suggests women as "passive" items of consumption and is reinforced by the expressions "as easy as pie" (Spears [1991] says it derives from this phrase; see also EASY) and "nice piece of pie" (see PIECE). "As easy as pie" has also served as an expression to note that something is easy to do.

Gay men may also use "pie" language to refer to other men. For example, *blueberry pie* refers to a sailor, alluding to the color of the uniform as well as consumability.

Cutie pie, from at least the early twentieth century, originally meant an attractive, pert young woman, eventually becoming simply *cutie*. *Cutie* implies small and cuddly or charmingly attractive (see also GENDER-SPECIFIC ADJECTIVES [cute]).

See also BISCUIT, CAKE, CHEESECAKE, CHERRY (cherry pie), COOKIE, CREAMPUFF, CUPCAKE, DISH, JELLY ROLL, SWEET, TART.

piece; **piece of ass**. Degrading expressions for a woman (seldom today a man but sometimes used by women), usually a young one, considered as a sex object. *Piece* was used to mean a person as early as the thirteenth century and was also once used for a man ("King James... selecting him as his choicest piece, to vindicate his regality" [1651, cited in *The Oxford English Dictionary* 1989]). It still refers to men in such phrases as the ironic *piece of work*, as might be used by a teacher for a mischievous male student. By the fourteenth century, the term was applied more specifically, though not yet exclusively, to women.

The degraded, sexual sense, often suggesting food, arose by the nineteenth century. Other senses of the expression *piece of ass* (or *tail*) are the vagina and the sex act. A "coarse piece" is a woman considered vulgar (Spears 1991). A "piece of trade" (see also TRADE) may still occasionally be heard for a prostitute. There have also been other variations on the *piece* theme, such as *piece of snatch*, a usually vulgar, demeaning expression for a woman.

A mostly British synonym is *bit*, used for the female genitals, sexual intercourse, or a woman considered sexually. Richter (1993) gives *bitty* as an African American word for a woman.

See also ARMPIECE, ASS, CUNT, FILET, HIDE (piece of hide), LEG (piece of leg), MEAT, PIE (nice piece of pie), POONTANG, PROSTITUTE, PUSS, TWAT.

pig. A popular slur on people with characteristics supposedly resembling those of the animal. The pig itself is known for its value as meat, a quality that contributes to its force as a slur. Today, in the United States, we usually consider pigs as serviceable farm animals. The pig is seldom regarded as a pet, though a few animal lovers have in recent years been seen walking their pet pigs down the urban sidewalks. According to anthropologist Edmund Leach, the pig figures into abusive language because "we rear pigs for the sole purpose of killing and eating them, and this is rather a shameful thing, a shame which quickly attaches to the pig itself" (in Dunayer 1995, 18).

The pig was a religious figure to the ancient Cretans, and among some ancients it was depicted as the sacred companion of the goddess of regeneration (Eisler 1988, 51). To Jews, Muslims, and others, however, the animal has been considered ritually unclean, debased for its voracity and habit of miring in the mud.

Negative links between people, especially women, and the pig and the word itself also go back in time. For example, the Greek word *choiros* means both pig and female genitals, and the two meanings were not always distinguished by the punning ancient Greek man. The use of the word *pig* for people today—we know it as a slur on those regarded as fat and ugly, vulgar, slovenly, or greedy, and especially on females or police—is often vicious. When we hear "She is a pig," the woman referred to is often being disparaged as obese or undesirable. "What a pig she was…pretty vicious face under caked powder and rouge…" (Eugene O'Neill, *Strange Interlude: A Play*, 1928).

Perhaps only 1950s beatniks and other counterculture groups have applied the word to women nonpejoratively (Thorne 1990). On the other hand, "He is a pig," which may mean something similar to the usage as applied to women, would more likely mean the man is messy, coarse, and unclean.

Entertainer Andrew Dice Clay was known for using such slurs as *pigs* and *sluts* to refer to women, marking a rise in linguistic political incorrectness associated with a feminist backlash. Some college fraternities have also made use of the imagery in what are sometimes called "pig contests." The purpose of this competition is to see which man can have sex with a woman considered the least attractive. Among straight men, a pig may also refer to a woman who makes herself sexually available, while in gay communities, *pig* refers to a woman considered to be competing for the attention of a gay man.

Oinker, which supposedly imitates the sound made by pigs, is also used in the sense of fat people or ugly women, while *oink-oink* alludes to the notorious MALE

CHAUVINIST pig. *Porker, hog,* and the adjective *porky* have also been used to disparage people regarded as obese or repulsive. *Porker* is also applied contemptuously to Jewish people, especially men, or to someone, usually a man, known to copulate. *Pig-meat,* especially in black slang, means a woman regarded as sexually loose. *Pork* may be heard in current U.S. slang for copulation with a woman.

See also ANIMAL, BEAST, BEEF TRUST, BIG BERTHA, COW, DOG, HELLPIG, HOGGER, LOOKSISM, MEAT, SOW, WOMEN AS ANIMALS, YETI.

pigeon. A member of a certain family of birds; a person seen as easily duped, often a male victim of a gambler (slang); or a woman, usually a young or sometimes a gentle one (also slang). "And now, my little pigeons, it's time to coo" (Oscar Madison to his dates, the "Pigeon sisters," on TV sitcom *The Odd Couple,* 1997 rerun). The word first indicated a young bird, then in the sixteenth century it was generalized to denote women as well, though often used affectionately. The birds of the Columbidae family, to which pigeons belong, probably serve as analogues for women in sexist thought because of their deep-chested bodies and small heads; also, they are, like quail, hunted and commonly believed to be easy to catch (see also HUNTER).

See also BIRD, CANARY, CHICKEN, GROUSE, OWL, QUAIL, WOMEN AS ANIMALS.

pimp. A man who finds clients for female prostitutes and lives off their earnings. The origin of the term is unknown, but it is believed to date to at least the early seventeenth century, perhaps from the Middle French *pimper,* meaning to dress smartly, as to allure. In the United States, the pimp is often stereotyped in the media as a black man, especially one who wears flashy clothes and drives a big, gaudy automobile that may be known as a "pimpmobile" (see also WELFARE MOTHER [welfare pimp]). The term may

be used as a slur on any man reputed to be without qualms in his sexual dealings with women, or simply any despicable man. "He had all the charm of a lowlife pimp" (TV drama *Silk Stalkings,* 1998).

While few people would regard the application of *pimp* to men who exploit women's sexual services for profit as inappropriate, the word was long taboo, avoided in print. Although commonly seen in newspapers and heard on TV today, it still carries an aversive charge. In May 1998 six fifth-grade boys in a Carpentersville, Illinois, school were suspended for a day for composing a rap song, as part of a school assignment, with such lyrics as "Pimps for life/Bow down to the pimps" and "Capital P-i-m-p, that's the way we got to be." The boys apparently thought that *pimp* meant no more than "cool dude," suggesting a link with the African American stereotype. *Pimp* has also had some use for a man who works as a prostitute serving gay men, and it has had use in gay communities with a hint of disparagement for any married heterosexual man.

See also CRACK (crack salesman), EASY RIDER, GIGOLO, GORILLA (gorilla pimp), LOUSE, MACK, OLD LADY (old man).

pink taco. See TACO.

pink tea. See CLOSET (closet case).

pinup girl. See GIRL.

pixie. See FAIRY.

playboy. A term for a male considered a swinger; a philanderer who considers women as playthings (slang meaning loose women) or fair game. The women serve to give him pleasure. *Playboy* also connotes "playing the field." While moralists will quibble and some may note a hint of moral flaw in it, the image is generally relatively positive. Alleen Pace Nilsen et al. note that although the qualities of a playboy may not typically be those women usually hope to find in a husband, the reason a playboy is considered a *good catch* is that he supposedly has money and sophistication. It is as if we envy unmarried men because of the fullness of the life they lead with their extra freedom and extra money, while we pity unmarried women because we think they live only half a life. (1977, 35)

There are "playgirls," too, devoted to self-indulgent living, but they usually don't get the same attention that the bon vivant playboy attracts.

See also CASANOVA, DON JUAN, LADIES' MAN, LECHER, LOTHARIO, LOVE MACHINE, LOVER, PLAYMATE, RAKE, ROMEO, ROUÉ, SCUTZ, SOW WILD OATS.

playmate. Used since the seventeenth century for a companion in play and also a lover. Since the 1920s this term has acquired the meaning of a young woman who seeks men with whom to have a good time. Hugh Hefner's *Playboy* magazine popularized the term with its "Playmate of the Month" centerfold, featuring photographs of a sexy woman who the magazine continues to deny is simply a sex object. *Playboy* made its debut in 1953, but the Playmate model was not shown nude until the 1970s.

See also BABE, BUNNY, DOLL, FOX, KITTEN, PET, PLAYBOY.

plaything. See PLAYBOY.

plum. See PEACH.

poke. As a verb, to have sexual intercourse with a woman; as a noun, the act of sexual intercourse with a woman or the woman herself considered as an object of the sex act. Vulgar, reductive slang.

See also FUCKER, PUNCHBOARD.

pony. See HORSE.

poontang, poon tang. Sexual intercourse with a woman (from a man's point of view), the female genitals, or a woman regarded as a sex object. In its earlier incarnation, this Southern expression was usually applied to black women and white men's sexual relations with them

(Wentworth and Flexner [1975] give "Negro piece" as a synonym; see also PIECE). Usually considered vulgar "man" talk, now used by white men as well as black and for women in general, *poontang* probably derives ultimately from the French *putain*, meaning whore; it comes to us by way of Louisiana French. John Ciardi (1980) writes, "Spoken with a leering drawl by southerners in the army, *Ahm goin' inta town and ahm gonna git me some poooooon-tang,* it was probably the most lascivious sound I have ever heard out of the mouth of man." Also sometimes abbreviated as *poon*.

See also CUNT.

pop tart. See TART.

pork; porker; porky. See PIG.

potato. Based on the food, a slang term meaning a woman. A "sweet potato" is one regarded as sweet and attractive (see also SWEET). Probably derived from *potato* is the somewhat dated *patootie*, meaning a man's girlfriend or an attractive young woman (sometimes also a boyfriend).

See also DISH, FRUIT, TOMATO, VEGETABLE.

prattle. See GAB.

prego; preggy. *Prego*, possibly a variation of *preggo,* Australian slang meaning pregnant. *Prego* is mid- to late-twentieth-century, often offensive, U.S. slang for a pregnant woman, especially a teenage one. *Preggy* is an earlier version. "There is no attractive adjective in modern English for a woman who is about to give birth" (Miller and Swift 1991, 186). Female reproduction takes an ambivalent place in patriarchal culture, both glorified and disparaged.

See also MOTHER.

pretty boy. See BOY.

prevert. See PERVERT.

prick. From the sixteenth century, a word that still often means penis, usually considered vulgar slang. The word comes from the verb *to prick,* meaning to pierce, with the implication that it is the penis that punctures or pierces a woman's genitals. The word has also come to mean a man (rarely a woman) viewed as obnoxious, foolish, or detestable, often one willing to hurt others' feelings. An old joke recorded in Panati (1998) goes like this: "What's the difference between a penis and a prick? A penis is what a man uses to make babies. A prick is the rest of him" (7). See also BUGFUCKER, COCK, DICK, FUCKER, JACK, SON OF A BITCH.

A "prick-tease(r)" (or P.T.) is a woman who excites a man sexually but will not have intercourse with him. The expression is probably still used largely by young men (see also TEASE), but young women are using such terms today, too.

prima donna. An Italian word meaning first lady, used for the principal female singer in an opera. By the mid-nineteenth century, the meaning was extended to a woman (also frequently a man) considered conceited, temperamental, and used to having her (or his) own way. The word was also once used for an expensive prostitute, who may have put on airs considered inappropriate for her profession.

See also PRINCESS, QUEEN.

prince; Prince Charming. *Prince,* a title which, unlike words of royalty for women—such as PRINCESS, has largely retained favorable connotations. Although it may be used ironically, it can mean a fine and admirable man, appearing in such positive phrases as "He's a prince of a guy" or "a real prince." *Prince* is also heard in gay communities for a man of royal-like qualities.

Prince Charming refers to a man who represents a traditional woman's romantic ideal, white horse and all. "Like most young girls, I had always been vaguely

longing for my 'Prince Charming' to come and awaken me with his magic kiss" (in Phyllis and Eberhard Kronhausen, *Sexual Response in Women,* 1965, 61). From the mid-nineteenth century, this term is patterned on *King Charming,* the earlier answer to how a woman in patriarchal society could avoid a sense of incompleteness through bonding with men.

See also DUKE, KING.

princess. A title for female royalty, which has taken a slide in the vernacular over the years. At best, it may be used simply, and affectionately or paternalistically, as a nickname. For example, the older daughter (played by Elinor Donahue) in the 1950s TV sitcom *Father Knows Best,* known as Betty to everyone else, was Princess to her father. There is a sense of an adornment, as when a man speaks of "his little princess." But the word is also employed to describe a young woman viewed as selfish, demanding, and pampered. *Ice princess* is used for a young woman viewed as cold and often bitchy as well (see also ICEBOX), and the common epithet *JAP,* which stands for "Jewish American princess," stereotypes a young Jewish woman as wealthy, grasping, and self-centered. Brumberg (1997) reports that those adolescent girls who indulge in expressive body piercing in their struggle for autonomy do so to separate themselves from mainstream or affluent youth, especially those they snub as "princesses."

Princess also once had currency for a classy female prostitute, while a "pavement princess" was a prostitute who walked the streets. A "porn princess" is a sexy young woman featured in pornographic displays. *Princess* is also a nickname used self-descriptively by some drag queens (see DUCHESS for a quotation) or a reference to a very young, usually effeminate, gay male.

Indian princess represents an attempt at euphemism in referring to a black woman, blunting more overtly racist images.

See also DUCHESS, -ESS, GOVERNESS, PRIMA DONNA, QUEEN.

prissy. An Americanism from the late nineteenth century, a blend of *prim* and SISSY. Describing someone as prim, finicky, and excessively correct or proper, *prissy* often suggests an overfastidious man regarded as having effeminate characteristics or a "girlie-girl," one who, for example, wears girly stuff—the opposite of a TOMBOY.

See also EFFEMINATE, LA-DI-DA.

pro. See PROFESSIONAL.

profeminist male. See FEMINIST.

professional; **pro.** *Professional,* a man who has a successful career position; a woman who has a successful career, or one who walks the streets. In abbreviated form, *pro* is one of many terms in English for a female prostitute (in this sense, however, *pro* may also derive from *prostitute* and perhaps also be reinforced by *promiscuous*).

See also AMATEUR, HUSTLER, PROSTITUTE.

profligate. See GENDER-SPECIFIC ADJECTIVES.

promiscuous. A description, often maligning, for someone believed to have many sexual partners. It comes from the Latin *pro-* (forth) plus *miscēre* (to mix). Another meaning, which has been somewhat lost as a result of the prominence of the sexual sense of the term, is indiscriminate.

The *promiscuous* label is often applied by men to censure and control the behavior of young women. Lees (1986) has shown how in England, where usage often matches that in the United States, *promiscuous* becomes a slur, along with SLUT and EASY LAY, to be used when behavior deemed "unfeminine" triggers censure. It may not be the ac-

tual sexual behavior of a woman that makes her a target of abusive language so much as swearing or loud behavior—things that "nice girls" are not supposed to do. Poor women and women of color, especially, are blamed for promiscuity. "Black slave women were raped, sexually abused and blamed for their 'promiscuity'" (Jordan and Weedon 1995).

See also ACTRESS, ALLEY CAT, BEDDY, CHIPPY, CUNT, DIRTY GERTIE, FALLEN WOMAN, FAST WOMAN, FLOOZY, GOOD LAY, HARLOT, HOOZIE, HUMP, JOB, LOOSE, MATTRESSBACK, MINK, NYMPH, PARTY GIRL, PROSTITUTE, PUNCHBOARD, SADIE THOMPSON, SKEEZER, SLAG, SLATTERN, TART, TRAMP, TROLLOP, WENCH, WHORE, YES-GIRL.

pross; **prossy**; **prosser.** See PROSTITUTE.

prostitute. From the Latin word *prōstituere*, composed of *pro-* (before) plus *statuere* (to station), suggesting a person stationed somewhere on the streets to offer her (or his) body for sale.

A prostitute is most frequently thought to be a woman. In fact Julia Penelope (1990) has described the prostitute as a "paradigmatic woman." The kinds of slang and disparaging names given to female prostitutes reflect the underlying understandings men have of women and through which women often come to see themselves. The term is so closely linked with women that when we refer to a man in the role of a prostitute, we need a qualifier, and so we speak of a *male* prostitute. Only recently have some courts begun to interpret the word *prostitute* in a gender-neutral way.

As with many other female roles or occupations, men usually exercise some kind of control over prostitutes. For example, many prostitutes—it is estimated up to 90 percent—are dominated by male pimps, who live off the earnings of the women and children they press into service. However, although men are often indeed the exploiters in prostitution, some writers acknowledge the role of the woman's free choice. Others suggest also that the experience of visiting a prostitute can be alienating for a man. He may seek a prostitute because she provides relatively ready and easy access to sexual satisfaction compared with conventional relationships with women, or she serves as a sexual outlet, as when he and his spouse lack access to birth control.

As a paradigm of women's place in the gender system under patriarchy, prostitution has, through the ages, been one of a woman's few traditional alternatives to marriage for securing her economic survival. This is changing as women make their way into the economy. The standard social attitude toward prostitution, however, is not that of an economic activity but as a representation of an immoral activity. Phyllis Chesler (1989) compares prostitution to a "sale of self," but with more than the body for sale: "Prostitutes are degraded and punished by society; it is their *humiliation* through their *bodies*—as much as their *bodies*—which is being purchased" (100).

Ambiguous in definition, prostitution comes in different guises and is defined differently from culture to culture, place to place, or dictionary to dictionary (Bullough and Bullough 1987, x-xiii). In some U.S. state penal codes, for example, *prostitution* is defined as the hiring out of one's body for purposes of sexual intercourse; other states, however, do not stipulate the exchange of money in defining prostitution but rather define it simply as the use of the body for indiscriminate sexual intercourse. When the defining element is simply the "offering of the body to indicate lewdness for hire," as it was in an earlier edition of *The Oxford English Dictionary,* the definition becomes

> so broad that the girl who sells kisses at a church fund-raiser could be labeled a prostitute, since what

constitutes lewdness is just as unclear as what constitutes prostitution. (Bullough and Bullough, x)

Still other considerations point out the difficulty of arriving at a clear, universal definition of the term. For example, the use of a sexual surrogate in sex therapy may be close in practice to prostitution. Does this kind of sex for hire make the surrogate a paraprofessional or a prostitute? What about a married woman, traditionally treated by law as the property of her husband, or a woman or man who marries for money, or a mistress who expects to have her way paid in exchange for sexual services? How indiscriminate does a person have to be in selling her or his body to be considered a prostitute?

Goldman (1981, 153–56) defines prostitution as direct, face-to-face sexual barter that has the following characteristics: promiscuity (the prostitute has sexual relations with more than one partner over time, customers not enjoying exclusive contact); impersonality (prostitute and customer—often called by the generic name JOHN—present superficial facades to one another, rationalizing it as just another service in which each party has an immediate, limited claim); and lack of emotional intimacy.

Society abounds with notions and stereotypes of who prostitutes are and what they are like. For example, white men on city streets often assume young black women to be prostitutes (see also JEZEBEL). In some settings, such as bars or restaurants at night, a woman of any race unescorted by a man may be seen as selling herself. Female independence is read as "prostitute."

The sinfulness or public nature of the prostitute has been suggested in such terms as *girl of the night, woman of easy virtue, public woman,* and *woman of ill repute.* Today she may elevate herself out of the fallen woman or working-class category to the more elegant *model, call girl,* or *escort.* The variety of terms for prostitutes has probably reflected journalists' desire to write with colorful words, but a more significant reason may be the centrality of prostitution to social life in America (Goldman, 57).

Prostitution has long been claimed to be the "oldest profession." Anthropologists once gave weight to this notion. However, some argue that these views are little more than androcentric versions of the origin of prostitution. The idea of the universality and inevitability of prostitution obscures the fact that it is a product of the exclusion of women from public life and of economic discrimination against them.

Pross, prossy (also *prossie*), and *prosser* are abbreviated forms of *prostitute,* and *prosty* is a related variant form. *Sex-care provider* has been regarded a neutral label among some in recent years, a joke by others. *Sex worker* is also in use as a more neutral term.

See also ACTRESS, ALLEY CAT, ASS PEDDLER, BABE (baby pro), BAG, BIDDY, BLOWSER, BOOM-BOOM GIRL, BUSINESS GIRL, CHICKEN, CHIPPY, DIRTY GERTIE, EASY LAY, FAGGOT (bed faggot), FALLEN WOMAN, FLOOZY, GOLD DIGGER, GOOD LAY, HARLOT, HAT, HIDE, HOOKER, HOOZIE, HUMP, HUSSY, HUSTLER, JAG, JANE, JOB, KEPT WOMAN, LOLITA, LOOSE WOMAN, MADAM, MATTRESSBACK, MINK, PROFESSIONAL, PROMISCUOUS, PUNCHBOARD, PUTA, SADIE THOMPSON, SKANK, SKEEZER, SLAG, SLATTERN, SLUT, SPRING CHICKEN, STRUMPET, TART, TOM, TOMATO, TRAMP, TROLLOP, TUNA, WENCH, WHORE.

prude; straitlaced; uptight; repressed. *Prude,* short for the French *prudefemme,* meaning good woman. *Prude* entered English about 1704 to mean a woman said to show or affect excessive attention to modesty or propriety. It may be used for a man, too, but women who appear overly decorous or demure— traits once especially admired in a woman (particularly before the advent

of the "new woman" of the 1920s)— may not be sexually attractive to a man, who, at the same time, may scorn other women for being morally loose. This two-faced attitude can put women in a no-win situation. Women who show any kind of behavior regarded by men as aloofness, independence, or resistance to their advances may be dismissed as prudes.

An adjective conveying a similar idea, and usually reserved for women, is *straitlaced* (also *straightlaced*). This term now describes someone overly concerned with morals and manners but once meant the use of a bodice or tightly laced stays to help women display or prove their leanness and control (at the expense of physical discomfort and even deformity).

Uptight, in the sense of "stiffly conventional," is applied to both men and women, but women seem to bear the brunt of it when it is meant as a reproof for not giving in to a man's demands for sex.

Still another term used to refer to— and often denigrate—people said not to acknowledge their sexual impulses is the Freudian *repressed,* referring to the unconscious suppression of feelings. We hear of the "sexually repressed bigot," making a link, for example, between rigidly conservative views of sexuality, including homosexuality, and a person's inability to come to terms with his or her own sexual feelings.

"In the nineteenth century, most Americans, not just women, became more repressed—or 'uptight'—about bodily functions, including sex" (Brumberg 1997, 12).

Men may dismiss women who seem aloof or sexually unavailable as "lesbians."

See also FRIGID, GOODY TWO-SHOES, LESBIAN, MADONNA, MAIDEN (maiden aunt), OLD MAID, VIRGIN.

pullover. See EASY LAY.

pumpkin. See VEGETABLE.

punchable. See FUCKER (fuckable).

punchboard. A word for a woman regarded as sexually LOOSE. The word derives from the name for a type of board used in gambling; the idea was to try to win a prize by punching a round scroll of paper out of a hole in the board. It is also said to be related to *punch*, a slang expression meaning to deflower.

See also EASY LAY, HARLOT, LAY, MATTRESSBACK, MINK, MINX, NYMPH, POKE, PROMISCUOUS, PROSTITUTE, SCORE, SLAG, SLATTERN, SLUT, TART, TRAMP, TROLLOP, WENCH, WHORE.

punk. A term of unknown origin that has a variety of meanings, often centered on men. The archaic British sense of the word was a female prostitute, but since the mid-twentieth century, *punk,* with some of its feminine connotations intact, has been applied to gay men ("Queer Punk" is self-descriptive in gay communities for someone who listens to and follows the fashions of punk rock), an inexperienced young man, or one regarded as weak or worthless. It was also once used for a young male companion of a tramp, whose relationship to the youth sometimes implied homosexuality, and is still heard in prison for a young man who receives protection in exchange for his sexual services (see also HUSTLER). On the streets, *punk* often means a petty gangster or hooligan, while in the music world it designates a punk rock musician or a fan of punk rock. *Punk kid* may be used to slight any male adolescent.

See also LITTLE SHIT.

pushover. See EASY LAY.

puss; pussy. *Puss,* a name for a cat since the sixteenth century. It seems to derive from an imitation of a catlike sound (it has also been said to come from the Irish Gaelic *pus*, meaning mouth but also once a term for the vagina). The term also has applications to women (during the Middle Ages, it was used platonically, even affectionately) and to men considered EFFEMINATE.

The meanings of both *puss* and *pussy* have largely paralleled those of CAT: female genitals, women defined by men as sex objects, and sexual intercourse with a woman. These meanings derive mostly from the similarities between pubic hair and animal fur, although other associations of women with the cat—including the notion of having a gentle "pet"—reinforce the gender and sexual meanings.

Puss and *Pussy* were actually once nicknames for girls, used until the sexual connotations kicked in. The British actress Honor Blackman went by the blatantly sexual name Pussy Galore in the 1964 movie *Goldfinger,* though she probably took her name as much for her strong manner and sly ways as her sexuality (producers thought about changing it to what they considered the more innocent "Kitty"). Lighter (1997) gives *L.P.* as a term that probably derives from *lousy puss* and means an unattractive or unpleasant woman (limited mostly to the first half of the twentieth century).

Variations on *pussy* in reference to women include the following terms, usually considered vulgar and reflecting sexist attitudes toward women. A "P.E.E.P" is a desirable woman seen as a sex object—a "Perfectly Elegant Eatin' Pussy." *To eat pussy* means to have sexual intercourse with a woman or to perform cunnilingus. A man whose thoughts always stray to women has been called "pussy-struck" (see also CUNT [cunt-struck]). *Pussy posse* means a vice squad that controls and arrests prostitutes.

Pussy power was usually an expression antifeminists in the 1960s and 1970s used to dismiss the women's movement (see also WOMEN'S LIBERATION). Against this tide of antifeminism, Germaine

Greer, who encouraged the expression of women's erotic desires as a way to subvert patriarchy, spoke of "Pussy Power" as "the retrieval of women's capacity for imaginative invention" (Rowbotham 1997, 427).

The feminine connotations of *pussy* or *pussycat* have been transferred, with added scorn, to a supposedly weak or effeminate male or a gay man, especially the one said to take a "passive" role. "Frank's a weak little kid. His daddy taught him how to be a pussy" (1996 film *Sling Blade*). John Higham noted the increasing popularity of the related *pussyfoot* in the late nineteenth century, when masculinity became a guarded focus of male culture (Chauncey 1994, 114). In reference to a man's weakness, however, *pussy* may come from the boxing world, where weak boxers pat rather than punch with their gloves.

A "pussyboy" is a boy "kept" by a PEDERAST. It may also be any man re-garded as easily bossed around or subject to his superiors' whims. See also SCREWBOY. *Pussy-bumping* refers to lesbian behavior.

See also BEARD, BEAVER, BUSH, HAIR, HAT, HIDE, TIGER, TWAT, WHISKER, WOOL.

pussy-whipped. A description for a man said to be henpecked, one who, like a horse, suffers under a whip; a colloquialism from the mid-twentieth century. The term insults the man but also reflects on conventional definitions of women as enjoined to hold their tongues and control their inclinations to dominate.

See also BALL AND CHAIN, HEN (henpecked), NAG, PUSSY.

puta. A usually offensive slang word from the mid-twentieth century meaning a prostitute or loose woman. It comes from the Spanish word *puta,* meaning whore.

See also PROSTITUTE, WHORE.

Q

quail. Since the seventeenth century, now largely obsolete, a bird metaphor for young and attractive women regarded as prostitutes or whores; more recently, in U.S. slang, girls or women in general, but often those considered to be sexually free. According to *The Oxford English Dictionary* (1989), the figurative definition was a courtesan, from the French *caille coifeé,* an allusion to the supposed amorous disposition of the bird. This bird metaphor calls up images of game birds hunted down by predatory males, or "quail hunters" (see also HUNTER). The variation *San Quentin quail* (from the mid-nineteenth century) suggests an attractive girl (or girls) not yet of the age of consent to engage legally in sexual intercourse, fantasies of which she inspires in men. She is regarded as so dangerous that just flirting with her could cause a man to end up in prison—San Quentin, that is—for statutory rape. The man, seeing himself as "seduced," may come across as the victim (see also BAIT, JAILBAIT).

English has created similar meanings out of the names of other game birds. *Game hen, partridge*, and *pheasant*, for example, have all at one time or another lent their names to use for prostitutes. *Covey*, meaning a group of game birds, often quail, is used for a group of prostitutes.

Quail has also had some use for a young boy as seen from the perspective of an older gay man. See also CHICKEN (chickenhawk).

See also BIRD, GROUSE, OWL, PROSTITUTE, WOMEN AS ANIMALS.

quean. See QUEEN.

queen. Historically, primarily a royal title for a woman. The word derives from the Middle English *quene*, which in turn comes from Old English *cwēn*—woman, wife, queen.

While the title *king* has retained its honorableness, *queen,* like many titles for women, has been tainted with bias over the years. *Queen*—which in some contexts, especially crowned heads (e.g., Queen Elizabeth), still remains semantically noble—has undergone some twists and suffered some degradation of meaning in other contexts.

The male title still carries more weight than the female. *King* is thus regarded as stronger than *queen*. The wife of a British king carries the title *queen*. However, a man who marries a woman who holds a royal title is not necessarily given the masculine equivalent of the title. He is considered to come from outside the royal family and thus is not a true heir to the crown. Also, the compound *kingdom* is formed from the masculine *king*, but there is no *queendom*; and note that the male term is placed first when we talk of "kings and queens."

Among the less royal senses, a "sex queen" is a woman known for her special sexual charms. Marilyn Monroe still touches our fancy as a sex queen (she might also be called a "movie queen").

There are also hundreds of beauty queen contests; none of the contest winners are royalty, but the contests may reinforce the narrow view that beauty is an essential, "royal" attribute of the female (see also BEAUTY, LOOKSISM, MISS AMERICA). A "prom queen" is a high-school or college-age woman who is pretty and popular. *Queen* is also applied to an upper-class woman or to any woman seen as narcissistic, insistent on being treated "like a queen," that is, waited upon, especially by men (see also PRIMA DONNA). "What a lady, boy. A *queen,* for Chrissake" (J. D. Salinger, *The Catcher in the Rye,* 1945).

Things that might be personified as a woman have also taken the name "queen." Thus, for example: "Tahiti, queen of the South Seas." *Queen* may also convey an image of wickedness (e.g., see JEZEBEL) or an exotic image (*queen of the jungle*; see EXOTIC), while the term *queen bee*, an insect metaphor meaning a woman who "lords" it over other women, is anything but flattering. A "drama queen" is a woman taken as hysterical (see HYSTERIA) or histrionic or, sometimes also meant disparagingly, a gay man.

In other examples of its linguistic degradation, *queen* also comes in various word combinations as forms of political attack on liberal civil rights policies. A "welfare queen," for example, is a woman stereotyped as running away with welfare money (see also WELFARE MOTHER). She has been depicted as lazy, sexually promiscuous, and fertile, someone who cheats on the system and may even drive a "welfare Cadillac." She is usually assumed to be a black woman and often a single parent. In 1993, around the time that Lani Guinier, a black female professor of law, was nominated and then rejected for the position of assistant attorney general for civil rights, she came to be known by what she called a caricature of her ideas. Even though she did not actually advocate quotas, she

> became a cartoon character, Clinton's "quota queen".... Like the welfare queen, [the] quota queen was a racial stereotype and an easy headline looking for a person. (Guinier 1998, 420)

In spite of such trivializations and diminishments in the meaning of the term, the continuing association of *queen* with royalty has also allowed it to be used to elevate an identity, as in "girls'" gangs (e.g., the Latin Queens of Chicago). Sometimes *queen* means simply a very attractive young woman.

Queen size refers to a large woman, or to other things of large size, for example, a "queen-size bed." But it's still smaller than the "king-size" version.

Queen is also a biased term used by nongay people for a man regarded as gay and effeminate, especially one who is ostentatious with his "femininity."

Queen in this sense was in use in U.S. slang by the 1920s. It probably derives from *quean* (a spelling from the Indo-European word *gwena*), originally meaning woman but whose denotation wandered to cover wanton or disreputable women, including female then male prostitutes, and later to refer to male prostitutes and effeminate gay men (sometimes also lesbians). The *quean* spelling served to preserve the royal sense of *queen* by keeping the two terms distinct in writing.

Queen has been used in particular for the sexual partner categorized as "passive" or for a transvestite, but outside gay communities, it may be heard, often derisively, for any gay man. When effeminacy is really pronounced, the man may be disparaged as a "screaming queen" or a "raging queen," terms sometimes also used for lesbians.

Among gay men, *queen* has come to be self-descriptive. In gay communities, the term is not at all derogatory and does not suggest a feminine gay man—all gay men are queens. *Queenie* is the diminutive form.

There are scores of gay names with *queen*, of which the following are but a small sampling. A "closet queen" (also "closet queer") is a gay man who keeps his sexual orientation secret (usage restricted largely to gay communities since the mid-twentieth century; see also CLOSET). *Queen of the flits in Hoboken* is a disparaging name for a gay man. A gay man who seeks sex in public rest rooms may be put down as a "bog queen." A "Queen of Sheba" is a black homosexual (aka "queen of spades"), while *Queen Mary*, dubbed after the name of the ship, is a gay man considered overweight. A gay man obsessed with the size of penises may be known as a "size queen." "Queen" terms range from contemptible to neutral and self-descriptive, depending on who is using them and on the intent.

See also AUNT (auntie queen), CAMP, DIRTY OLD MAN (dirty old queen), DRAG, DUCHESS, EFFEMINATE, FREAK (watch queen), GAY, GOVERNESS, HOSE (hose queen), ICEBOX (ice queen), KING, LEATHER (leather queen), MOUSE (mouse queen), PASSIVE (anus queen), PRINCESS, WIFE.

queer. A word, now applied largely to homosexuals, that has been used since the early sixteenth century mostly to denote people considered to be odd or eccentric. It has also designated being of unsound mind, the state of drunkenness, and counterfeit money, among other irregular things—things contrasted with the norm. For example, Charles Dickens and Mark Twain have plenty of queer characters, not to mention Robert Frost's horse, "who thinks it queer" to be stopping in the snowy woods. The term may come ultimately from the German *quer* (crooked, awry, or perverse).

In the early twentieth century, *queer* was applied as a kind of euphemism for a homosexual (*odd* has also been used this way). In gay communities, *queer* was not usually derogatory but was an identification among men who saw themselves as different from other men only because of their sexual interest in men. These more conventional queer men clearly distinguished themselves from effeminate men, typically identified in the gay vernacular of that time as "fairies," and from the masculine heterosexual, known as TRADE (Chauncey 1994).

Later *queer* was generally used by heterosexuals as a label of contempt, denoting a "homosexual"—at first male, but now (since about the mid-twentieth century) female as well. Conveying strong prejudice, the word first appeared in print in the United States. In 1922, the Children's Bureau of the U.S. Department of Labor published the results of a survey of personality traits thought to be linked with criminals. It reported that a man with refined physical features and sensibilities, who could color coordinate his room and showed an appreciation of the opera, was headed for a career of crime and was "probably 'queer' in sex tendency" (in Panati 1998, 179). Today it is difficult to use the term, which still carries some sense of "odd," without inadvertently calling up the gay world, from which some heterosexuals would just as soon distance themselves.

In gay communities of the late 1940s, younger gay men were coming to avoid *queer* as disparaging, censuring older gays for using it. A few decades later, in the gay and lesbian communities, the much preferred *gay* acquired more conservative and euphemistic meanings. At the same time, *queer* came to represent subcultural difference, protest, and dissent, a symbol that cut across the traditionally sanctioned lines of sexuality in celebration of the diversity of sexualities. This new sense of the word *queer* is first associated with the aptly named Queer Nation ("We here, we're queer, get used to it") and the AIDS Coalition to Unleash Power, which began its practice of activist politics in the 1980s. From *queer* comes *queering,* which designates the appropriation for gays and lesbians of everyday things and common identities and the representation to others of those things as "queered appropriations" (Leap 1996, 23).

Some lesbians have questioned the use of the word in representing both men and women, since the experiences of women are not necessarily those of men. Other critics dispute the ability of "queer" consciousness and activism to deal with wider issues of racial and class discrimination and gender exploitation. Still, the concept of "queer" remains an important one in the advancement of gay people, including bisexuals and the transgendered, and has been useful in studies of gender and sexuality. As Stewart (1995) says, activists choose to use the word to reclaim the language of antigay bigots—"to disarm their vocabulary and throw it back in their faces." Heterosexuals, too, may be regarded (and self-identified) as having "queer-friendly" politics or social relations.

In the straight world, however, *queer* and its variations continue to project homophobia and negative images. In the 1985 film *The Boys Next Door,* for example, a man called a "queer" becomes a psychopathic killer. *Three-dollar bill* has seen some pejorative use in the sense of a person regarded as "queer," as in the phrase "queer as a three-dollar bill." *Queer-beer* and *queervert* (see PERVERT) target gay men.

Queer fish is slang for any weird person. The sense of *queer* here is usually understood by context. See also FISH (fishy).

See also BIRD (queer bird), FAIRY, FUNNY, GAY, HOMOSEXUAL, INVERT, ODD, PEEPING TOM (peer queer), PERVERT, SISSY.

quesadilla. See TAMALE.

R

rake. From the sixteenth century, a usually derogatory term for a man viewed as dissolute or sexually promiscuous; short for *rakehell,* meaning a libertine or man of immoral character. Unlike words such as CASANOVA or PLAYBOY, which have positive connotations and deflect blame from the man for his promiscuous behavior, *rake* is disparaging.

See also LECHER, GENDER-SPECIFIC ADJECTIVES (randy), ROUÉ, ZIPPER.

randy. See GENDER-SPECIFIC ADJECTIVES.

rape. Unlawful sexual intercourse or unlawful sexual intrusion that occurs without the victim's consent and involves force, the threat of force, intimidation, or deception. *Rape* derives ultimately from the Latin *rapere* (to seize, carry away by force, or plunder).

As a result of feminist redefinitions, the emphasis today has been on rape as an act of violence and power rather than one of sex, though it may be acknowledged as an expressly sexual act of violence. This emphasis is in part a reaction against the idea that men rape simply because they feel lusty, or that they just can't help it. But what constitutes force in the standard definition of *rape* is in dispute, as is lack of consent. These issues are handled in varying ways by different groups and different states.

Although literally a "four-letter word," *rape* is not always seen as a taboo word (Muriel Schulz, in Spender 1980, 178–79). For Schulz, it is a fairly innocuous term used in polite conversation, even applied in everyday conversation as a metaphor for other forms of violence (e.g., "rape" of the planet), and it has not been treated euphemistically as have other words for sexual acts or body parts (the "dirty" words). The explanation for this treatment of the word, according to Spender, is that *rape* is encoded for meaning by men, who rationalize it as neutral. It names the experience as men see it, not as women are traumatized by it. Matters of consent and coercion, as Susan Estrich argued in her 1987 work, *Real Rape,* have largely been defined in the law from a male perspective.

What's more, when speaking about rape, we often seem reluctant to acknowledge men's responsibility; we may use words other than *man* for the rapist.

> Words such as "beast," "monster" and "sex fiend" are commonly used to describe the rapist, yet we rarely see the simple word "man," which the rapist invariably is. (Cambridge Rape Crisis Centre, in Stibbs 1992)

Other commonly worded phrasings, such as the passively worded "The woman was raped" (which, unlike "The man raped her," might make us wonder what she did to bring it on), obscure the role of the male in the crime.

Yet we can acknowledge that the word *rape* strongly signals sexual abuse, a topic so sordid in itself that for a long time the word was not allowed in print. *Forcible assault, molestation,* and *outrage* were the less coarse terms once used by newspapers. Adds Panati (1998), we remain sensitive to the word: "It has become so pejorative that companies that manufacture rape oil or rapeseed oil—from the rape plant…have changed its name to 'canola' oil" (105).

Of course, there have been reasons other than the violation of a woman's human rights why men and society in general have regarded rape as a sordid business. When women were viewed as the property of their fathers and husbands, rape was regarded as a crime against a man's property, and a victimized woman lost not only her reputation but also her value on the marriage market. Yet the dearth of euphemisms today may in part be a result of the fact that the act of rape itself *is* increasingly being confronted as a serious societal problem.

Some critics of feminist positions have questioned the use of the term *rape*, claiming it has been used among some feminists synonymously with political "terrorism." In some instances, these critics argue, it becomes not just an expression of the degradation of women's condition but also an attempt to vilify men. As a "smear tactic," as August (1998) calls it, the word is seen as having loose and metaphorical use to blame men for almost anything reprehensible. Thus, as August illustrates, Andreé Collard's book title *Rape of the Wild: Man's Violence against Animals and the Earth* (if we assume the ambiguous *Man's* means male) suggests that men alone are responsible for the deterioration of the environment. "Such usage trivializes the word *rape* and the suffering of genuine rape victims" (427). Others would argue, however, that the word *rape* is in fact seldom used as a strategy for vilifying men; rather it is typically applied when a vocabulary is required to express the frequency and aggressiveness of men's violation of women.

To some theorists, rape is a manifestation of natural acts of aggression by males throughout history. For example, Susan Brownmiller's *Against Our Will: Men, Women and Rape* (1975) depicted rape as the chief mechanism of men's oppression of women. From prehistoric times to ancient Greek warriors, from the Boston Strangler to U.S. soldiers in Vietnam and the statistics on recent police blotters, rape, claims Brownmiller in her comprehensive indictment of the abuse of male power, has been a crime of violence and power. "It is nothing more or less than a conscious process of intimidation by which *all men* keep *all women* in a state of fear" (5).

Brownmiller's work has contributed to an awareness of the rights and dignity of rape victims, of the relation of socializing women into passive roles to their vulnerability to rape, and of views of women's bodies as men's property. Nevertheless, Brownmiller's conception of rape as a result of male sexuality directed universally against women ignores evidence of boys and men being molested or raped. In prisons, for instance, men may be brutally raped as an act of male dominance, but over other men. Struckman-Johnson (1988) also discusses forced sex on dates as something that "happens to men, too." Elizabeth Wilson (1983) objects to the implications of viewing rape as instinctual and universal, preferring to see it instead as a cultural problem contingent on particular social conditions and capable of being changed.

Attitudes and responses to rape and its frequency do vary across cultures. The Busii of Kenya, for example, use it as a form of social control, while among the Arapesh of New Guinea, rape is almost unknown. Finally, among many antifeminists, the idea of "all men" being rapists has been fashioned into a dismissive caricature of the feminist position on rape, thus contributing to the denial of rape as a serious problem.

In furthering an understanding of rape, many theorists today stress that rape is not, as already mentioned, a question of sex, nor a private issue, but a public issue and a political act of violence. To feminists who find patriarchal values pervasive in our society, rape is an act of power that keeps women subordinate and deprives them of their freedom to do as they will with their own bodies.

Attempts to justify or excuse rape derive from the ideology that sees women in no rightful roles other than as mothers or sex objects available for men's pleasure. Merrill (1995) has reported that rapists often have conservative views of women and their "place" and feel threatened by women who occupy positions of authority or exercise economic control.

As objects in a patriarchal system, women are often accused of enticing men, "leading them on." Men may even claim that women "want it," or "have fantasies of it" and may speak of a woman's appearance as a "wanna-be-raped look." A woman may also be said to "cry rape," that is, to lie about being raped. What a woman may regard as rape may be interpreted by a man as "working around the *no*," talking the woman into having sex, or, after the fact, making the excuse, "She asked for it," supposedly because of her clothes or behavior. Men have also argued that rape is not possible, since women should be able to fight back or run away, regardless of their fear for themselves or others, relative physical weakness, or having a knife pushed into their side (or an economic weapon pointed at their job). To further the unfairness, when a woman has suffered the crime and indignity of being raped, men may even avoid her as DAMAGED GOODS.

Overtly opposed to the idea of patriarchal causes of rape, Warren Farrell (1993) claims that those men who are more powerless in our society, specifically black men, are more likely to be reported as rapists than are white men. To Farrell, this weakens the argument that rape always derives from power. However, it could be argued that these greater numbers of accusations against black men are a part of a wider system of racial oppression that overlaps with or even reinforces patriarchy. In addition, rape victims of white men know the difficulties of winning their case against their rapists in court. Women are probably more likely to report rapes by men outside their own racial group.

In the context of war, rape has historically been regarded as a "natural" consequence of hostilities between peoples and of men out for conquest. Rape has been used consciously and strategically as a war tactic, as by U.S. sol-diers against women in Vietnam. The conquering warriors may regard it as a right or even a duty, since the women of the enemy nation are likely to be viewed merely as the enemy's property. The conquered see it as trespass and humiliation; for the women who are raped, in particular, it is devastating.

Rape is increasingly being regarded as a twisted form of behavior that is all too easily justified by soldiers. Reports of the thousands of rapes committed by Serbian soldiers against Bosnian women in the former Yugoslavia heightened awareness of the deviance of rape and its intentional use as an act of violence and its use to force interbreeding meant to "dilute" an ethnic group.

The language of rape is full of many, often confusing terms. For example, *forcible rape* is defined by the FBI as vaginal penetration by the penis, while state statutes may include a broader scope of nonconsensual sexual contact. The use of the term *forcible* is sometimes considered a redundancy, though some rapes falling under this rubric may not involve clear physical force but threats of force or other forms of coercion. *Statutory rape* means sexual intercourse with or without the victim's consent but involving someone under the statutory age of consent, as defined by state law, or those deemed physically or mentally incapacitated. *Gang rape* is yet another usage, reflecting the fact that there may be multiple assailants.

Sexual assault is a broad term that widens the category of prosecutable offenses to include not only vaginal penetration but other forms of sexual intrusion as well. Finally, although *rape* usually suggests the victimization of a woman (Black 1990 defines rape as "unlawful sexual intercourse with a female"), this does not encompass all instances of rape. All states have come to define *rape* without reference to the sex of either the victim or the perpetrator

(*West's Encyclopedia of American Law* 1998).

The fact that women may have more to fear from men they know than from strangers gives us the distinction between *stranger rape* and *acquaintance rape*. In acquaintance rape, a person known to the victim applies force or intimidation to coerce the victim into having sex. A subgroup of acquaintance rape, *date rape* (an Americanism from at least the late 1970s, inspired by the repetition of the long *a* vowel), means rape by a man of a woman with whom he is acquainted, and usually during a social engagement. It does not necessarily mean only a man and a woman, since it can occur among homosexuals as well.

Often in the case of date rape, a woman may be perceived as really wanting sex; the man may argue that she made it somehow apparent that she wanted sex even though she said *no*, which the perpetrator may have interpreted as a form of encouragement. But there can be more to date rape than miscommunication: it may involve brutal batterings.

Finally, in the context of rape in which rapists are familiar with the victim, mention should be made of *marital rape*. Historically, rape has not been defined as something that a husband could do to his wife; in fact, he was viewed as having a right to "sex on demand." More recently, however, most states have criminalized coercing a spouse into having sex.

See also SEX OBJECT, SEXUAL HARASSMENT, WANNA-BE-RAPED LOOK.

ravishing. See GENDER-SPECIFIC ADJECTIVES.

raw meat. See MEAT.

real man. See MAN.

repressed. See PRUDE.

rib. See FALLEN WOMAN.

rice queen. See DINGE.

rich bitch. See BITCH.

roach. From *cockroach*, an insect metaphor for a prostitute (regarded as a low creature) or for a woman viewed as ugly.

See also LOOKSISM, PROSTITUTE, QUEEN (queen bee), WOMEN AS ANIMALS.

Romeo. From the name of the hero in Shakespeare's play *Romeo and Juliet*, an epithet for a male lover or a "ladies' man." Although *Romeo and Juliet* has also entered the language to represent a pair of devoted lovers, *Juliet* has different connotations. To say a woman is a Juliet, suggesting a young and affectionate beauty, would not get the same reaction as does calling a man a Romeo. *Romeo* has suffered some pejoration since Shakespeare's time.

> Once Shakespeare's Romeo caught sight of Juliet, he never looked at another woman; today's Romeos are less interested in the quality of their relationships than in the quantity. (Corey 1997, 286)

See also CASANOVA, DON JUAN, LADIES' MAN, LECHER, LOTHARIO, LOVE MACHINE, LOVER, PLAYBOY, RAKE, ROUÉ, SCUTZ.

rooster. See CHICKEN, COCK.

rose. See FLOWER.

roué. A rake, scamp, or lecher; a man viewed as unprincipled, especially one devoted to a life of sensual pleasure. "The character he [Frank Sinatra] plays—the champion roué—is disgustingly brazen and blasé (*New York Times Film Reviews*, 1970, 3392, referring to the 1963 movie *Come Blow Your Horn*). The word comes ultimately from Medieval Latin *rotare* (to turn a wheel), through the French *rouer* (to turn a wheel), but also with the idea of turning *on* a wheel, specifically, to break on the wheel. The reference is to the practice of being broken on the wheel in eighteenth-century France, a form of capital punishment reserved for the roué, a man who had committed an abominable crime. Today, although the term is mildly derogatory, a man's seeking sensual pleasure is considered more "natural" than abominable.

See also CASANOVA (quotation), CRIMINALS, DON JUAN, LADIES' MAN, LECHER, LOTHARIO, RAKE, SCUTZ.

rug-muncher. A name for someone who engages in cunnilingus. Although it might be a man, the word is typically used for a lesbian and is usually (especially among heterosexuals) derogatory. See also LESBIAN.

S

sack artist. See CASANOVA.

Sadie Thompson. From a character in a play based on a 1927 short story by Somerset Maugham, in which a fiery woman with a dissolute past refuses to repent to a hellfire-and-damnation preacher on a South Seas island, a term now synonymous with *tramp* or *hussy*. Although in the story Sadie Thompson is a woman of definite strength and untamed qualities and the preacher is a sanctimonious hypocrite, we remember her name only for its negative associations.

See also HARLOT, HUSSY, LOOSE, SKEEZER, SLAG, SLATTERN, SLUT, STRUMPET, TART, TRAMP, TROLLOP, WENCH, WHORE.

San Quentin quail. See QUAIL.

Sappho. See LESBIAN.

satyr. See NYMPH.

saucy. See GENDER-SPECIFIC ADJECTIVES.

scag. See SKAG.

scank. See SKANK.

scarlet woman; scarlet letter. *Scarlet woman,* a euphemism for a prostitute, first recorded in the sixteenth century. The color scarlet has been associated with immorality and flagrant unchasteness for centuries, as recorded in the Bible. According to Isaiah 1:18, "Though your sins are like scarlet, they shall be as white as snow"; Revelations 17:3 speaks of "a woman sitting on a scarlet beast which was full of blasphemous names" (probably a reference to Rome). We still encounter the term, especially in writing. "He was especially opposed to dancing, which, he claimed, 'scarlet women use to tempt men'" (James A. Michener, *Texas*, 1985, 850). Also, *scarlet lady* and *scarlet sister.*

Scarlet letter refers to a red letter, once sewn or branded on a woman's dress as a sign that she had been convicted of adultery. In Nathaniel Hawthorne's novel, *The Scarlet Letter* (1850), the heroine Hester Prynne is forced to wear an embroidered red *A* on her breast while she stands in the pillory with her illegitimate child: "She turned her eyes downwards at the scarlet letter, and even touched it with her finger, to assure herself that the infant and the shame were real." Hester refuses to name her partner in sin—a minister who suffers mental torment but not the application of an epithet as stigmatizing as "scarlet woman." However, throughout the punishment and condemnation, she retains her soundness of mind by an act of appropriation of the symbol: she embroiders the letter into a thing of beauty.

The idea of a scarlet letter dramatized by Hawthorne was imported to America from England's penal code. Adulterers might wear badges of sin for six months, since public shaming was believed to purge the soul. A statute of Plymouth Colony of 1658, for example, made adultery a violation of God's law; the adulterer was severely whipped and forced to wear the letters *AD*.

See also ACTRESS, FALLEN WOMAN, MISTRESS, PROSTITUTE, SEDUCTRESS, TEMPTRESS, TRAMP, WENCH, WHORE.

schmuck, schmock; schmo(e); schtoonk. From the Yiddish *shmok*, meaning penis (the German *Schmuck* means jewel), a slang usage since the late nineteenth century for a man viewed as detestable, oafish, obnoxious, or a dullard. It is often synonymous with BASTARD and PRICK and also with the related *schmock*, also Yiddish. Non-Jewish speakers may use it with little intention of abuse, but to point out, even sometimes affectionately, something they don't like about a man. The Yiddish-derived *schmo(e)* is an American euphemism for *schmuck*, and *schtoonk*, also from Yiddish, means a man rated as a terrible stinker.

See also DICK, JACK.

schoolmarm. A female schoolteacher, from the nineteenth century (an American variation of *schoolma'am*) and no longer much in use except sometimes as a disparagement. The taint to the word comes from the projected image of a conservative, old-fashioned woman, perhaps one thought to teach children because that was the only way the stereotypical SPINSTER could be close to children (it might also be the only way she could make a living). When it is a *schoolmaster* who presides over the school, the schoolmarm is his subordinate. As Miller and Swift (1991, 38) suggest, the schoolmarm was also thought of as the fussy, misinformed woman who told her students not to use a preposition at the end of a sentence. Editor Theodore Bernstein's imaginary fussbudget, "Miss Thistlebottom," for example, liked to prescribe "good" English: "For years and years Miss Thistlebottom has been teaching her bright-eyed brats that no writer would end a sentence with a preposition if he knew what he was about" (*The Careful Writer,* 1965, 342). Bernstein appropriately gave his schoolmarm a prickly name.

See also OLD MAID.

scold. From the twelfth century, a word used for anyone who habitually finds faults in others or rebukes them in ill temper; however, it is commonly directed at women seen as quarrelsome and abusive. Unruliness and lack of control of the tongue have traditionally been much maligned and even feared characteristics in women. There is no dearth of words for women seen as scolds.

See also BALLBREAKER, BITCH, CASTRATING, FISH (fishwife), HARPY, HARRIDAN, MOTHER-IN-LAW, NAG, SEEN BUT NOT HEARD, SHREW, VIRAGO, WITCH.

score. To count a sexual conquest as a way of gaining esteem. *Scoring,* which comes from the mid-twentieth century, is usually associated with the man, whose role is traditionally cast as the active one. The man, rather than the woman, is believed to act on, to perform, to "make it" in the bedroom as well as on the football field.

Men go out to "score" as part of an assigned cultural role, and they evaluate one another in terms of their success at sexual conquest. "[Athlete] Jamison knew that the following day he would hear boasting about who scored the quickest and most often—not on the basketball court, but with the women" (quoted in Jeff Benedict, *Public Heroes, Private Felons,* 1997, 73). The term is also used by prostitutes, male as well as female, for their clients, or "johns" (see JOHN). When applied to men by female prostitutes, it almost seems a called-for act of retribution.

See also LAY.

scrag. See SKAG.

screaming fairy (queen). See FAIRY, QUEEN.

screwboy. A man seen as being bossed around or subject to his superiors' whims. In another sense, not common to gay communities but probably restricted mostly to subcultural contexts, he is a young man viewed as being "kept" by a PEDERAST.

See also BOY, FUCKBOY, FUCKER, PUSS (pussyboy).

scud; scuzz. A woman seen as unattractive. Both terms sound like *scum. Scuzz* also appears to be related to *scuzzy,* meaning dirty and foul. *Scuzzball* means any despicable person.

See also COOLER, COYOTE, DOG, GANGSTER GIRL, HOGGER, LOBO, LOOKSISM, PIG, SKAG, YETI.

scumbag. See BAG.

scutz. A man who seeks out women only for sexual intercourse; from the mid-twentieth century, origin unknown. This is a slangier and, because of its relation to *scuzzy* ("dirty, foul," origin also unknown but from about the same time) and possibly also to *scum,* a much more derisive term than, for example, CASANOVA or PLAYBOY.

Compare with *scuzz* (see SCUD), used for a woman, where the emphasis is on bad looks.

See also LECHER, ZIPPER.

seafood. See FISH.

second sex, the. Originally, the title of Simone de Beauvoir's book (first published in French in 1949, appearing in English translation in 1952), which examines the problems, myths, and possibilities in women's lives. De Beauvoir's "second sex" is women, the "Other," whom men define relative to themselves and to whom they have been reluctant to grant the full rights of humanity. Men, she says, think of women as sexual beings, unlike men; they are inessential rather than essential. "He is the Subject, he is the Absolute—she is the Other" (de Beauvoir [1952] 1974, xix).

While de Beauvoir was writing *The Second Sex*, people frequently asked her about her subject matter. She would answer, "Just something about the other sex." One night, Jacques-Laurent Bost, her and Jean Paul Sartre's friend, commented on homosexuals as "the third sex, and that must mean women come in second." She then had the title of her book (Bair 1989, xvii, footnote 8).

The book has been criticized for its middle-class and autobiographical influences and its association of the "male principle" with progress. However, it is still read and continues to provoke thought.

See also WOMAN.

seductress. From Latin *seducere* (to seduce), a woman said to be capable of leading a man astray, especially, to entice into sexual intercourse. Associated with evil—we sometimes hear of a woman being "fiendishly seductive"—she is the one to be blamed for any shame or ruin brought to a man; he escapes responsibility.

See also FACE THAT LAUNCHED A THOUSAND SHIPS, FEMME FATALE, LOLITA, MANEATER, SCARLET WOMAN, SHE-DEVIL, SIREN, TEMPTRESS, VAMP, VIXEN, WITCH.

seen but not heard. An expression referring to silencing children, who have traditionally been subjected to rules restricting their speech around adults. In other words, children can be in adult company, but they are supposed to be quiet and well-behaved. The idea also captures some of women's relation to language. Drawing on the work of Cora Kaplan, Cameron (1985) notes that boys gain public speaking rights around puberty, at the onset of manhood, while girls continue to be restricted (154). Adult women have also traditionally been enjoined to silence (and still are) in some conservative quarters, especially in relation to political, literary, formal, ritual, and public discourse. Public, formal conversation has traditionally been the prerogative of men and a way of enhancing their status over women. Such practices of womanly deference, however, have been changing as women increasingly take their place in public life. For insults referring to women who do not know how to "hold their tongues," see also BITCH, GOSSIP, HARPY, HARRIDAN, NAG, SCOLD, SHREW, TERMAGANT, VIRAGO, YENTA.

senior. A reference to the father, when the son is named after him. There is no parallel in our patrilineal society for a woman named after her mother. As Margaret Mead ([1949] 1975) once pointed out, we are more likely to name a son for the father than to name a daughter for the mother, a practice reflecting our patrilineal customs and "reinforced by the complications of having to refer to the mother as 'big' or 'old' Susan, neither adjective being attractive to women" (266).

sergeant; **top sergeant**. Expressions used for a lesbian, alluding to stereotypical dominance or masculinity; usually derogatory when used by heterosexuals.

See also GAL (gal officer), LESBIAN.

sex. See GENDER AND SEX.

sex bomb. See BOMBSHELL, SEXPOT.

sex-care provider. See PROSTITUTE.

sex-change operation. See TRANSSEXUAL.

sex fiend. See RAPE.

sex goddess. See GODDESS.

sexist; sexism. *Sexist*, a standard English word meaning a man who is prejudiced against women and who, because of his greater authority as a male, is able to discriminate against or disparage and objectify them in such a way that accrues to his advantage. In general, the sexist's understanding of gender leads him to support the widespread cultural assumption that the generally differing social, political, and economic stations of men and women in the United States and around the world are "natural" and justifiable.

The word *sexist* has been used in feminist rhetoric as a deliberate political choice and strategy since the mid-1960s. It is patterned after *racist* and invites comparison between sexist and racist behaviors. The original emphasis in the use of *sexist* was on demonstrating a parallel between negative attitudes toward women and those toward black people (see also WOMEN AS A MINORITY GROUP). Although not strictly parallel, both kinds of attitudes evolve out of doctrines of the biological inferiority of others and uses of such doctrines in justifying the exploitation or the degradation of others.

Sexism, coined in 1968, means prejudicial attitudes and discrimination against women on the basis of their sex. Sexism ranges from the individual to the institutional level and includes beliefs, behavior, policies, and language reflecting and conveying a pervasive view that women are inferior. All forms of sexism are seen as contributing to inequality between the sexes. The prejudice and discrimination identified as sexism can also be blatant or covert and indirect. In any case it may be traced to early socialization into the gender system and is often unreasoned or below the level of consciousness and impervious to fact.

Studies of sexist language—for example, the sexualized words, animal metaphors, trivializations, belittlements, and euphemisms reported in this dictionary—indicate how words, however taken for granted, can degrade, diminish, and control women. Many sexist men objectify women (i.e., identify them in terms of their body parts) or assume that maleness is the standard or that it subsumes women.

In their chronology of our society's consciousness of linguistic sexism, Nilsen et al. (1977) begin with Benjamin Bradlee, then executive editor of the *Washington Post,* who, in 1970, issued a memo to his staff informing them of his views of sexual equality and women's dignity. He advised against the use in print of such words as *divorcée* and *blonde* for a woman and trivializing or dismissive adjectives such as *pert, dimpled,* and *cute* (2).

The term *sexist* today is often perceived as being overworked and stereotypically applied. For one thing, it does not acknowledge differences in levels of privilege between men based on class and race. For another, it is easy to ignore, because men who hold beliefs of male superiority accept male privilege as normal or natural and will not acknowledge their sexism.

There are also many men today whose "sexism," as they see it, consists only of such habits as opening doors for women or chauffeuring them on dates. Such behavior may or may not be associated with firm convictions of female inferiority, so calling someone a sexist merely on the basis of such a habit may be regarded as unfair.

A woman, too, may be called sexist, either because she is prejudiced against men or treats them unfairly or because she favors them and has beliefs or feelings disparaging her own sex or acknowledging women's subordinate position as natural and right. For example, a claim of the New Right is that what is called men's sexism against women does not disadvantage women but rather privileges them, as when views that assume a lack of physical strength and courage among women help to keep them out of military combat. Feminists would charge those who take this point of view as having accepted the sexist assumptions of male dominance.

Use of *sexist* for a woman, however, is infrequent and nonstandard, reflecting the minority status of women in U.S. society and the influence of the feminist movement as well as media interpretations of it. Yet some critics of feminist positions argue that defining sexism solely as male prejudice against women may be regarded as sexist itself. August (1998) for example, is troubled by the fact that sexism is generally held to be a "male-only fault" (431). A long tradition of women's subservience to men, however, in family and, especially still today, in public life and of male objectification of women in art, the media, and language makes this a difficult position to defend.

Terms that have been used more specifically for prejudice and discrimination against men are *inverse sexism* or *reverse sexism*. These expressions may be used as code words among those who criticize advances in civil rights and employment that offer the same advantages to women that men have long enjoyed.

Sexist, however condemning it may sound to some today, is not as disapproving an epithet as *racist,* nor does it carry the harshness of *male chauvinist pig,* as that expression was once applied. Like *male chauvinist pig*, *sexist* has lost its impact from use over the years and has taken on ironical meanings and may even be jocularly self-descriptive, espe-

cially among men who wish to dismiss their own sexism. Finally, those who are accused of being sexists may defend themselves against the charge by attacking the accuser as holding "radical feminist" views, thereby avoiding consciousness of their sexist assumptions and even preserving the culture's presumption of male superiority.

Whatever the difficulties in use of the term *sexist*, it can be argued that it has played a productive role in raising women's consciousness. By naming oppressive behavior, it has served to bring that behavior to awareness and thus subject to political, legal, and social remedy.

See also FEMINISM, GENDER AND SEX, HETEROSEXISM, HOMOPHOBIA, MALE CHAUVINIST, OPPRESSION, SEX OBJECT, SEX SYMBOL.

sex machine. See LOVE MACHINE.

sex object. First recorded in 1911, a term referring to someone regarded only as an object of sexual interest, not as an individual human being. We hear it mostly in reference to women, commonly treated in our culture as though they are things to be looked at and judged for their beauty (usually read "sexuality"), which tends to become synonymous with their value. Actor Roger Moore seemed to think it was a passive role that women played with relish: "My real attitude toward women is this… basically, women like to be treated as sex objects" (in Fikes 1992).

Moore notwithstanding, women suffer from objectification. A woman sought out only for sexual gratification is not a subject belonging to herself but rather the means to an end from the point of view of male onlookers.

MacKinnon (1982) finds no difference between objectification and alienation. As represented especially in the media, women can become so accustomed to seeing themselves as sexual objects that they stop feeling that they are anything else. They seem to be designed to please men: body parts on exhibit, a conquest or score, a pet, a doll, or a pretty young thing—something less than human. In addition, the sexual or beauty standards promoted by the culture are unattainable by most women. When women strive to meet these standards, they may be dismissed as "vain"; if they don't, they may be scorned with the use of even more negative words (see, e.g., PIG, SLATTERN).

Feminists have placed special emphasis on the objectification of women in rape and pornography. Much of traditional Western painting also depicts women as objects of male spectators, while prostitution is an example of how women's bodies have become commodified. The word *commodity* is even used to mean a woman as a sex object. In pornography women are stereotypically presented as desirable, alluring, subservient, childlike, trusting, dominant, or resistant, images that are used by the man to arouse his particular sexual fantasies. Thus, the male viewer of pornography invents the woman he views as he pleases.

See also BEAUTY, FEMININE (Eternal Feminine), SEXIST, SEX SYMBOL, WOMEN AS ANIMALS.

sexpot. From 1948, a woman (seldom a man) conspicuous by her sexuality. Speaking of Marilyn Monroe and other sexually provocative film actresses, Weitz (1977) wrote, "The sexpot had no self; her definition was in the eyes of the male beholder" (198). Men may use the term in a teasing or partly joking manner toward a woman they regard as flaunting her physical attractiveness and whom they seek to dismiss as disreputable.

See also BOMBSHELL (sex bomb), SEX OBJECT, SEX SYMBOL.

sex symbol. In use especially since the mid-1950s, though recorded as early as 1911, a term for a person well known for sex appeal. The word has occurred in the language especially to capture the sexual glamour of such female stars as Marilyn Monroe, Brigitte Bardot, and Madonna. "A sex symbol becomes a thing. I hate being a thing" (Marilyn Monroe, in James 1984, 119).

See also SEXIST, SEX OBJECT, SEXPOT.

sexual harassment. As coined by the Working Women United Institute in 1974, unwanted, unsolicited, unreciprocated, and offensive sexual attention that tends to reduce the person (usually a woman) to a sex object. Some definitions of the term place sexual harassment in situations where there is unequal authority or power or define the attention as "deliberate and repeated"; but the limits of the term are still very much debated and contested. In any case, such attention is seen as inhibiting a person's freedom by making the environment—whether school, work, or public place—inhospitable, hostile, or intimidating.

Lawyers dealing with cases of sexual harassment are especially interested in abusive or discriminating behavior that influences promotions, pay raises, or other conditions in the work or school environment. Feminists look at sexual harassment as not simply a matter of someone seeking sexual gratification but as a way men have of guarding their favorite lines of work "as preserves of male competence and authority" (Schultz 1998, 11) and of generally asserting male dominance.

Sexual harassment takes a variety of forms, including leering, flattery, teasing, verbal abuse (denigration resulting from the use of such terms as those in this dictionary), demands and threats, displays of sexually explicit or suggestive material, bodily contact (see also MASHER), and assault. However uncomfortable or even harmful some of this behavior may be, it is still sometimes dismissed by men as innocent fun ("boys being boys") or responses to invitations ("She wanted me to"; "She asked for it").

Women are often blamed for the advances made against them and may even think or be persuaded to think that they brought them on. One myth about successful women in the workplace is that they "sleep their way to the top," a belief that stereotypes women as "available" and that can then be used against them when they complain of harassment.

Business and government did not take sexual harassment seriously until Congress passed the Civil Rights Act of 1964, prohibiting discrimination based on gender, race, or religion. Title VII, following in 1977, forced the issue of sexual harassment as a form of discrimination to the attention of the courts.

The term has been criticized, especially by the political right, for lacking clear definition. The Equal Employment Opportunity Commission has defined conduct as sexual harassment if it

> has the purpose or effect of unreasonably interfering with an individual's work or academic performance or creating an intimidating, hostile, or offensive working or academic environment.

However, what constitutes hostility or offensiveness, it is sometimes argued, is left to subjective measures, and responses will vary. Speaking of conditions in the military, for example, Elaine Donnelly, president of the Center for Military Readiness, said, "One woman may take a male recruit's gaze and words to be encouragement and support, while another may take them as harassment" (in Dennis Byrne, *Chicago Sun-Times*, 24 December 1997, 23).

What's more, definitions that include such forms of behavior as leering, ogling, or whistling are seen as increasing the roster of victimhood without teaching the attendant social skills—such as being able to take aggressive action—that may be required to empower women in any such situation. On the other hand, the use of the term to describe these forms of behavior, and of legislation to protect women, could be seen as a way of taking "aggressive action" and as empowering. Moreover, women have won a number of sexual harassment cases that have helped to change workplace rules and improve often intolerable working conditions.

The term *sexual harassment* names behavior that is a public issue, not simply a woman's personal problem—behavior that as a result of this naming can no longer be dismissed simply as expected male behavior.

sexual preference; sexual orientation. *Sexual preference,* a commonly used term with a grounding in legal usage: "The Alabama Court of Appeals reversed the trial court decision and held that 'custody should be determined on individual character and parenting skills, and not on the basis of sexual preference'" (*National Center for Lesbian Rights Newsletter*, Fall 1998, 56). However, it is also an ambiguous and controversial term referring generally to what many gays or lesbians would prefer to call *sexual orientation.*

In some contexts, *sexual preference* reinforces a heterosexual stereotype of gay, bisexual, or transgendered people by conveying the impression that their sexual orientation is selected rather than being intimately connected with their personhood. Also, because many people do not act on their preferences, this is a vague term; Young-Bruehl (1996) speaks of "psychological homosexuals...in whom homoerotic desires and fantasies preponderate—who are heterosexual in object choice and may not even be conscious of their homosexuality" (142). As is true with homosexuality, there was no concept of sexual orientation, at least not as we know it today, until the late nineteenth century.

The term also has its detractors. Pei (1978) once remarked that this psychologist's term has "weasely connotations," since it has been "used to cover up homosexuality" (126). In general, however, *sexual orientation* is today the "preferred term to use to refer to an individual's romantic and physical attraction to the same and/or other sex" (*GLAAD Media Guide,* n.d., 37).

See also ALTERNATIVE LIFESTYLE, BISEXUAL, HETEROSEXUAL, HOMOSEXUAL, GENDER AND SEX.

seymour. Used for much of the twentieth century and mostly restricted to heterosexual use, a name for a gay male seen as effeminate. The usually offensive idea is that the given name Seymour sounds sissified.

See also EFFEMINATE, SISSY.

she asked for it. See RAPE, SEXUAL HARASSMENT.

Sheba. See EXOTIC.

she-devil; **she-demon**. From the early nineteenth century, expressions used for a woman regarded as very difficult to deal with. She may be considered ill-tempered or even wicked (the former "unfeminine" attribute may suggest the latter).

Western culture has produced its share of personifications of shrewish women and feminine evil. The she-devil has enjoyed some popularity, especially in Hollywood filmmaking. Silent film star Theda Bara, for example, played a menacing role in *The She-Devil*, which allowed her to gain sexual power over her male "prey" long enough to present the image of forbidden sensuality.

Although wickedness is often attributed to women, the constructions *she-devil* and *she-demon* suggest that a female prefix is needed to make a feminine noun out of a masculine term. August (1998) argues that in our culture,

evil is commonly masculinized (431–32). (Perhaps, but usually only when it is associated with power or dominance.)

"The evil white woman," often depicted as a whore in black Muslim thought, is a compensatory parallel to white male sexist conjuring of black women as evil whores (see JEZEBEL).

See also BITCH, CASTRATING, FEMME FATALE, HARPY, HARRIDAN, SHREW, VAMP, VIRAGO, VIXEN, WITCH, WOLF (she-wolf).

she-he; **shim**; **s/he**. *She-he,* an expression used for an effeminate or gay male, also known as *shim* (a blend of *she* and *him*). The derogatory implication is that his masculinity is compromised by his femininity.

In some written contexts, however—when constructed as *s/he*—the bigendered notion is acceptable and even preferred. "S/he [Leslie Feinberg]…has been fighting for the rights of transgendered persons for decades" (*Girlfriends,* December 1998, 9).

See also ANDROGYNY, BUTCH, EFFEMINATE, GENDER BENDER, HE-SHE, HIM-HER, SHE-MALE.

she-male; **she-man**. Twentieth-century references to a man seen as EFFEMINATE, a male cross-dresser or other type of male-to-female individual, a lesbian, or almost anyone who appears to have bridged gender lines. The hyphen joining the two words is a sign of an apparent contradiction, "since sex and gender expression are 'supposed' to match" (Feinberg 1996, 97). Restricted to heterosexual use, the terms are not flattering.

She-male, in particular, occurs in the context of pornography; there is a whole subcategory of visual porn known as "she-male porn." It features people with both penises and breasts who appear feminine in dress and demeanor. Some of these people are preoperative male-to-female transsexuals trying to earn their surgery money. Some are people who construct their identity specifically as "she-males" and who do not plan on having any genital surgery, though they may have augmentation mammoplasties as well as other feminizing cosmetic surgery. The term may also refer positively to androgyny, often spelled without the hyphen (*shemale*), as in this statement in respect to mythology: "The Divine Itself was a shemale" (Ganapati Sivananda Durgadas, *Anything That Moves,* Fall 1998, 40).

See also AMAZON, ANDROGYNY, CROSS-DRESSER, GENDER BENDER, HE-SHE, HIM-HER, LESBIAN, SHE-HE.

shero(e). See HERO.

she-wolf. See WOLF.

shim. See SHE-HE.

shit. See OLD FART.

shit-ass. See ASS.

shrew. A small mouselike animal that is regarded as vicious and good at fighting. It eats relentlessly, even other shrews. In a society in which women are expected to be mild-mannered servants, this animal metaphor came to be applied to a woman regarded as having a scolding, nagging temperament. Such a woman was even once believed to be a mistress to the devil. In the fourteenth and fifteenth centuries, the term stood for a difficult man as well as a woman; it acquired the meaning of a virago in the sixteenth century.

Shrew is often the label thrown at a woman who lacks power but "scolds" or "nags" to get her way. Women considered as having *too much* power may also be known as shrews. When women are no longer subordinated to men and are charged with responsibilities that compel them to act assertively, they are often disparaged with this small-animal metaphor.

Speaking of home and garden author Martha Stewart, Will Manley writes that she has sometimes been characterized as a demanding boss, manipulative dealmaker, cutthroat competitor, ruthless negotiator, and selfish profiteer—that is, as a shrew. But "you would never call [Donald] Trump a shrew, you'd call him a tough capitalist" (*Booklist,* 1 November 1997). There is no close male parallel to the term, a fact noted in 1924 by writer Elizabeth Robbins: "If there is no word for *shrew*...in male form, is it because there were no bad-tempered, no slovenly men? Or is it because only the male tongue might safely point out defects?" (in McPhee and FitzGerald 1979, 115). Both *shrew* and *shrewd* derive from the same Middle English term, *shrewe,* meaning an evil or scolding person. *Shrewd,* however, meaning discerning or sharp in practical affairs, has more commonly been associated with men.

See also BALLBREAKER, BARRACUDA, BITCH, CASTRATING, HARPY, HARRIDAN, NAG, SCOLD, SHE-DEVIL, VIRAGO, WITCH, WOMEN AS ANIMALS, YENTA.

shrinking violet. A floral metaphor for a woman, specifically a shy one. "I'm no shrinking violet. I refuse to let my hair color fade into the background" (woman in TV advertisement for Preference, November 1997). In a *Life* magazine article on sexist language in 1970, Ann Bayer wrote of a fictionalized woman concerned with "rampant sexism" in our society. Hyperia, as she was called, complained of how close men's insulting language is to their compliments: "When we're not *fauna,* we're *flora: clinging vines, shrinking violets, wallflowers"* (in Nilsen et al. 1977, 2).

The term may also be applied to men, making them into withdrawn, timid creatures—the inverse of what men are supposed to be in our society.

See also FLOWER, VIOLET, WALLFLOWER.

sick; **sicko**; **sickie**. Names applied indiscriminately to almost anyone who is not conventional or agreeable or to someone regarded as "mentally ill." *Sick* has even been used to refer to a woman having her menses, who might be accused of and stigmatized for being all these things (see also CURSE). Sexual "perversion" as well as mental disturbance and other forms of social or political marginality has often been cause for labeling someone "sick."

When used for homosexuals or the transgendered, *sick* draws on the medical model, often tinged with moralism. "They [homophobic straight people] get more worked up talking about the immorality, the depravity, *the sick and twisted nature* of gays, than they ever do about murderers, rapists or child molesters" (Richard Roeper, *Chicago Sun-Times,* 20 October 1998, 11).

Since about the 1960s, the idea that behavior that is unconventional, "deviant," or "inappropriate to the situation" harbors pathology has been increasingly replaced by an emphasis on seeing the world from the subject's own point of view. In regard to the so-called mentally disturbed, the sociologist Erving Goffman (1961), who studied mental asylums, wrote that "the student of mental hospitals can discover that the craziness or 'sick behavior' claimed for the mental patient is by and large a product of the claimant's social distance from the situation that the patient is in, and is not primarily a product of mental illness" (130).

From the idea of being mentally "sick" come the slang terms *sicko* and *sickie.* Both originated in the United States in the mid-twentieth century and can disparage and dismiss a person or behavior that others regard as falling outside the pale of normality. For example, a conference sponsored by the women's studies program at the State University of New York at New Paltz included two workshops, one on sex toys and one on sadomasochism, that were condemned in *The Wall Street Journal* as "A Syllabus for Sickos."

See also DEVIANT, HOMOSEXUALITY AS DISEASE, INVERSION, NORMAL, PERVERT, SINFUL, TWISTED.

sinful. When used for homosexuals or others whose sexual orientation or gender behavior is not "straight" or conventional, a judgmental term that draws upon religious thinking. However, while many U.S. religious denominations regard homosexuality as a sin, the mainline denominations tend to enjoin their members to treat gay people with humane respect. "The Bible contains six admonishments to homosexuals and 362 to heterosexuals. This doesn't mean God doesn't love heterosexuals. It's just that they need more supervision" (Lynn Lavner, in Witt 1995, 31).

See also DEVIANT, HOMOSEXUALITY AS DISEASE, NORMAL, SICK, SODOMY (nameless sin), TWISTED.

single. Unmarried man or woman. As a result of efforts in recent decades to deemphasize the differences between men and women, *singles* has taken on a larger workload. It is often heard today instead of the gendered and often biased words BACHELOR, DIVORCÉE, OLD MAID, SPINSTER, WIDOW, and *widower.*

See also SINGLE MOTHER.

single mother; Murphy Brown mom. *Single,* commonly used in the United States descriptively. When linked with *mother* (and often also with *parent,* which may suggest a woman), however, the term has sometimes taken on biased connotations. *Single mother* is still sometimes a stigmatizing term for a woman who, because she raises children without the aid of a father, is depicted as a threat to traditional family life. Yet at the same time, in certain circumstances, it is possible for a woman to use the label in pride for her self-reliance and independence from men.

In 1998 in an Illinois political race for Cook County board president, a female candidate produced an ad in which she proclaimed, "I'm a single mom, too, with three great kids" and noted in reference to her office's efforts in child-support collection that "raising a family is hard enough," that is, even with a man's help. (Her opponent claimed that she was trying to give the impression that she had been struggling without help to support her family.)

Single mothers comprise a diverse group, including widows, divorced women, women who are separated, those who keep a baby after an accidental conception, and those who opt to bear or adopt children to raise alone. Some of these various women are well educated and may hold better jobs than many of the men they know. But many others, though often employed, fall short of financial stability and face problems of providing child care on meager incomes.

Single women, especially those who experience financial difficulties, are commonly scorned for what is believed to be their moral shortcomings. Many mainstream Americans still view single motherhood as a certain source of social and moral problems, while lesbian mothers have been charged with being inadequate custodians even though they may provide the same kind of parenting as other mothers (*Women's Studies Encyclopedia* 1989).

Although this term does not necessarily allude to race, as a social issue it has gained virulence in part because of its frequent association in some contexts with racial notions. Regarding *single parent*, Zellah Eisenstein has argued that the term is encoded "racially" in political talk: it often refers to a black teenage girl or black women on welfare. "Because the imagery of black single and often teenage mothers was already in place for [Vice President Dan] Quayle, he did not have to speak of race" (Eisenstein, *The Color of Gender*, 1993, 78).

Murphy Brown mom refers to a single, professional woman who has given up on becoming a wife but still seeks to be a mother. The expression, like others of this ilk, comes from the 1980s–90s TV sitcom *Murphy Brown*, in which the unmarried professional woman, played by Candace Bergen, has a baby and draws criticism (in real life) from the religious right (see Melissa Ludtke, *On Our Own: Unmarried Motherhood in America*, 1999).

Some scholars and writers have viewed single motherhood as, potentially, a route to greater freedom for women from patriarchal constraints and even as helping to create an alternative to the conventional nuclear family (Hanscombe and Forster 1982).

See also MOTHER, SINGLE, WELFARE MOTHER.

siren. Feminine creature in Greek fables said to lure mariners to their death by melodious singing (in this classical sense, the word is often capitalized). These creatures frequently took form as bird-women or mermaids. Embodying both animal and human features, the Sirens synthesized water and earth, beauty and terror, the tangible and the metaphysical. Seamen who heard the "siren song" were sometimes said to forget everything and die of hunger. In Homer's *Odyssey,* the hero Odysseus managed to escape the Sirens' enticement by lashing himself to the ship's mast and filling his shipmates' ears with wax. Homeric myth told of two Sirens; later stories increased the number.

Since the fourteenth century, the name in English, which comes ultimately from Greek *seirēn* (entangler), has been used in literature, but has also been applied to any woman regarded as seductive and dangerous. The image is of a woman capable of overpowering men with her sexuality and leading them astray (rendered helpless, men are thus "victims"). A headline in the October 27, 1998, issue of the *National Enquirer,* referring to glamorous 1950s Hollywood star Mamie Van Doren, said, "Legendary screen siren talks candidly about her life—and lovers!"

Recently, however, some women have redefined *siren,* for example, as the name of a women's magazine: "*Siren,* the hip magazine for 'women who get it,' landed on *Spin* magazine's blacklist this year, so we love them even more" (Diane Anderson-Minshall, *Girlfriends,* December 1998, 15).

See also BEAUTY, BOX (Pandora's box), FALLEN WOMAN, FEMME FATALE, LOLITA, MANEATER, SEDUCTRESS, TEMPTRESS, VAMP, VIXEN, WILES (FEMININE), WITCH.

sis. See SISSY, SISTER.

sissy. Usually, a boy or man considered weak, effeminate, or cowardly. From the late nineteenth century, *sissy* (the diminutive of *sis*) is the informal form of *sister.* At one time, it was a term of address for girls and a self-reference among gay men who compared themselves with gossipy sisters. But among heterosexuals, especially men, it became a contemptuous term associated with feminine roles. The person called a sissy is accused of having supposedly undesirable childish or feminine characteristics, such as passivity, softness, artistic sensitivity, and dependence. More broadly, but still disparaging characteristics that are assigned to females, the put-down may be used for anyone lacking in strength or courage. "Growing old isn't for sissies" (attributed to Bette Davis).

When applied to a man, a sissy is a male who doesn't measure up to manhood (see also MAN). Being called a sissy or a girl is part of the sanction against males looking or acting in feminine ways. The word was especially popular during the late nineteenth and early twentieth century, when, as Rotundo (1993) has argued, men were trying to rebuild the crumbling walls between manly and womanly characteristics and

were increasingly in conflict over their own feminine qualities.

In contemporary U.S. society, ideas of gender are linked symbolically with sexual orientation (Thorne 1993). A man who engages in cross-dressing, for example, even though he is likely to be heterosexual, or in other so-called gender-disturbed behavior may be put down as a "fag," "queer," or "sissy." Like *tomboy* for females, *sissy* appears to be less frequently heard today, in part because gender stereotypes have been increasingly challenged in recent decades.

Imitating the stereotypical lisping sound of a gay man, *thithy* is a variant pronunciation, likely to give offense. *Cissy* is a British spelling, also meaning an effeminate or gay man (see also CLOSET [cedarchest sissy]). Also *sissy-britches.*

See also APRON, BABY (crybaby), CANDY-ASS, CREAMPUFF, EFFEMINATE, GAL, GIRL, LIZZIE, MAMA'S BOY, MILKSOP, MISS NANCY, MOLLYCODDLE, PANSY, PRISSY, QUEEN, SEYMOUR, TOMBOY, WIMP, WUSS.

sister; sisterhood. *Sister,* related to the Latin *soror* (sister), usually used in the sense of a female sibling who has the same mother and father (a "half-sister" shares only one parent). More generally, it has been used to denote a female who shares with other females a common ancestry, cause, character, or allegiance. A sister may also be a member of a religious order of women, a fellow member of a sorority, or something identified as female and closely related to another (e.g., a "sister ship," now considered sexist).

Sister needs to be contrasted with its sibling word, *brother,* to understand its full meaning and bias. Often connoting solidarity, loyalty, and mutual respect, *brother* has traditionally been placed before *sister* when both are referred to ("brothers and sisters"). When the connotations of *brother* are more suitable for a subject, the speaker may refrain from using *sister*, even though it may be more accurate. Gersoni-Stavn (1976) for instance, reported a preponderantly female Red Cross Unit referred to in a children's reader as "brothers" (199).

In the gay male community *sister*, usually meaning a man not regarded as a sexual partner—a comrade or confidante (see also AUNT)—is normally preferred to *brother*. In this case, the feminine term is probably used as a form of resistance to male heterosexual images. *Sis* is used similarly among gay men, with respect and affection, although heterosexual men may use it pejoratively for those men they believe to be effeminate or gay (see also SISSY).

Among other instances of the uses of these sibling terms, *blood brother*, meaning a biological brother or one of two men who pledge their mutual loyalty through a ritual mixing of blood, enjoys more powerful connotations than the less often heard *blood sister*. Philadelphia, whose name comes from the Greek *phil* (love) plus *adelphos* (brother), is known as the City of Brotherly Love. Although we do have the expression "sister cities," this expression is part of a long tradition that equates the idea of "woman" with cooperation and stereotypes her as relationship-oriented.

There are no male parallels to such usually negative expressions as *sob sister* and *weak sister* or the everyday *sissy*, and *brother* is not likely to form sexualized expressions such as *street sister* and *sister of the night*, once referring to female prostitutes, or *sister act*, a gay term for sexual relations between a straight woman and a gay man. Similarly, the expression "We're all brothers under the skin" may serve as generic, but "We're all sisters under the skin" does not work when there are men in the audience.

Sister is used by feminists for a woman who supports the women's movement (see also FEMINIST). The choice of the term in the feminist com-

munity, dating from its inception in the nineteenth century, has been self-conscious, strategic, and political, forging solidarity against what was often a tide of resistance to women's solidarity. "'Sister' really means something like: 'You who are one with me in our oppression,' rather than merely being an expression of pure unity" (Robin Lakoff in McPhee and FitzGerald 1979, 189). It has also been used by the feminist movement to critique a status quo in which women have been taught to mistrust and compete against one another. "The time has come…to see other women not as competitors, but as sisters whose problems are our problems" (Berkeley Women's Liberation New Monday Night Group 1969).

Sister is used similarly among black women and among Native Americans and other minority groups as a way women have of identifying with a common political cause. In these contexts, however, she may be someone who is subordinate to a "brother" (Marcia Ann Gillespie wrote of women in the black civil rights movement, "We were 'Good Sisters' if we dutifully followed orders, or mouthed the party line laid down by the brothers" [in *Getting There*, compiled by Diana Wells, 1994, 129–30]). *Sister* is also heard on the political right, though arguably a co-option of the feminist use of the term for a very different agenda. At the Women of Faith conference in Pittsburgh, September 1997, a consciousness-raising event for Christian women, an antifeminist group used the language of sisterhood and solidarity: "'We're sisters…and we're on this journey together!' cried Sheila Walsh, onetime cohost of Pat Robertson's *700 Club*" (Tanya Erzen, *Nation*, September 8/15, 1997, 7).

Sisterhood has come to imply positive female bonding and the self-affirmation that comes with a "woman-centered vision and definition of womanhood" (Humm 1995). "Sisterhood is

Powerful" is a phrase coined by feminist Kathie Sarachild and which first appeared in a leaflet distributed at the Burial of Traditional Womanhood demonstration, Washington, D.C., in January 1968. Black feminists such as bell hooks (1981), however, have replaced *sisterhood*, which they see as obscuring such differences as those between white and black women, with *solidarity*, seen as denoting a political agenda.

skag, scag. In slang use mostly among young African Americans since at least the 1920s, a disparaging name for a girl or woman regarded as promiscuous and, in more recent usage, ugly. "The dumb pimps are losing all their flatbackers to bad skag" (Nelson De Mille, *The Smack Man*, 1975, 121) (see MATTRESSBACK [flatbacker]). Also used in this sense is young people's slang *scrag*. "If we don't score by Thursday, those two scrags are going to start looking good" (one man to another in regard to young women, in the 1986 movie *Club Paradise*).
See also SKANK.

skank, scank. An unattractive woman or one regarded (especially by men) as cheap-looking, promiscuous (she may be a prostitute), malodorous, or scraggly; in use mostly among African Americans, among whom the term may have arisen, from the mid-twentieth century. *Skank* may refer generally to anything unpleasant. Major (1994) says it is a variant of *stank* or *skunk*, referring to foul body odor (see also FISH, ZOO). Also as *skank ho* (see HO).
See also PROMISCUOUS, PROSTITUTE, SKAG, SKEEZER.

skeezer. Late-twentieth-century slang term, associated with student use, for a woman viewed as sexually promiscuous.
See also EASY LAY, HARLOT, LOOSE, MATTRESSBACK, MINK, NYMPH, PROMISCUOUS, PUNCHBOARD, SLAG, SLATTERN, SLUT, TART, TRAMP, TROLLOP, WENCH, WHORE.

skippy. Now mostly African American euphemistic slang meaning a gay male, especially one seen as EFFEMINATE. The term was also once used by U.S. soldiers in the Pacific to refer to Japanese women or female prostitutes. It originally meant a sexually dissolute woman.

skirt. *Skirt*, a piece of clothing worn by a woman, representing the woman. The term, meaning a woman, including one regarded sexually, occurred in standard English from the sixteenth to the nineteenth century, at which time it began to acquire negative and more overt sexual connotations.

In the twentieth century, *skirt* took on its current meaning, not intended as negative (in fact, usually connoting attractiveness) but nevertheless still objectifying women. The word is most commonly used by men, especially among themselves. "I've seen her around. [She's] some society skirt" (man on the TV show *Diagnosis Murder,* 1997). The skirt is a sign of femininity in Western culture. The usage also sometimes alludes to the parts of the female anatomy under the skirt, thus signifying a woman as sexual prey.

Skirt-chaser (*woman-chaser* or simply *chaser*) means a man habitually in amatory pursuit of women (see also CHIPPY [chippy chaser]). If the woman he is pursuing has special sexual appeal, she may be reduced to a "superskirt," while a "miniskirt" (after the short skirt popular in the 1960s for accenting the idealized lean, leggy look) also means an attractive woman but almost always a young one.

First skirt refers to the ranking female noncommissioned officer of a unit in the Army, and during World Wars I and II, women recruited mostly for clerical work were known as "skirt marines." *Grass skirt* is a nickname, often offensive, for Hawaiian or other Polynesian females that alludes both to a stereotypical feature of Polynesian dress and to gender. A man said to "hide behind skirts" is regarded as too unmanly to dare it on his own.

The quaint-sounding *petticoat* (from the name of the skirtlike garment worn by women) has been used since the seventeenth century for a woman viewed as a sex object, and *petticoat-chaser* refers to a man who seeks her out. *Petticoat* can also refer dismissingly to domination by a woman, as in *petticoat government,* a household controlled by a female.

See also APRON, FLUFF, HOT (hot pants), HUNK (hunk of skirt). For a comparison with language for a man, see PANTS.

skirt-chaser. See SKIRT.

slacks. See PANTS.

slag. A slang term for a woman believed to be of low morals and to be sexually available. It suggests both slackness, meaning an unwillingness to work, and the obsolete *slagger*, once applied to a woman who ran a brothel. Sutton (1995) defines this slang term in current use as "an overweight female who is sexually promiscuous" (288), thus giving emphasis to personal appearance along with sexuality, which is also what the word *slattern* does (see also LOOKSISM). She reports also that her data from California undergraduate students indicate that *slag* is used almost exclusively by women. Holder (1996) wonders if the word is not back slang for *gals.*

Probably because of some of the negative associations, *slag* was also used in the science-fiction TV series *Alien Nation* for any one of the extraterrestrials who came to reside on earth, seen by xenophobic Californians as bald, foul-smelling, and simultaneously repugnant and sexy.

See also EASY LAY, FLOOZY, HARLOT, LOOSE, MATTRESSBACK, MINK, MINX, NYMPH, PROMISCUOUS, PROSTITUTE, PUNCHBOARD, SKEEZER, SLATTERN, SLUT, STRUMPET, TART, TRAMP, TROLLOP, WENCH, WHORE.

slattern. A woman seen as untidy, or a slovenly housekeeper; also, a slut or prostitute. According to *Merriam-Webster's Collegiate Dictionary* (1997), the word probably comes from the German *schlottern* (to hang loosely, to slouch), probably entering English with the poor and working classes

> when most lower-class girls were making a living as domestics, struggling to keep clear of the sexual exploitation of the males in the household.... The concept of sluttishness or slatternliness with its compound implication of dirt and dishonor gave rise to a great family of nasty words, like *drab, slut, slommack, slammerkin, traipse, malkin, trollop, draggletail.* (Greer 1970, 260–61)

Men thus managed to keep both their homes and their names clean by having a domestic in the household whose powerlessness made her an easy scapegoat. The term was formerly used for men, too, but today there seem to be few terms beyond *slob* that designate slovenly men.

See also BAG, BIDDY, EASY LAY, FLOOZY, GENDER-SPECIFIC ADJECTIVES (blowsy), HARLOT, LOOSE, MATTRESSBACK, MINK, MOPSY, NYMPH, PROMISCUOUS, PROSTITUTE, PUNCHBOARD, SKEEZER, SLAG, SLOVEN, SLUT, STRUMPET, TART, TRAMP, TROLLOP, WENCH, WHORE.

slave. See BOY.

slit. See GASH.

slob. See SLATTERN.

sloven. A person viewed as disreputable or a woman unconcerned with cleanliness, neatness, and personal appearance. From the Middle English *sloveyn* (rascal), which may come from the Flemish *sloovin* (a woman of low repute).

See also SLATTERN.

slut. A usually derogatory slang word for a woman regarded as sexually promiscuous and immoral. Although this may include a prostitute, who is paid for her services, the term often implies a woman of "easy" virtue, one who "gives it away." This usually constitutes a vicious slander on a woman, since "a woman who thinks so little of herself as to not get something in exchange for sex is perceived as pitiful, the lowest of the low" (Penelope 1990, 121). The common British sense of the term, that is, of a slovenly woman, or slattern, relates neatness and cleanliness with morality (see also SLATTERN).

Slut derives from the Middle English *slutte*; comparisons may be made with the dialectal *slut* (mud) and the Norwegian dialectal *slutr* (sleet, impure liquid). It did not acquire its sexualized application to women until the sixteenth century. The initial consonants may suggest those of the etymologically unrelated but semantically allied *sleaze*, a person of low character. "Marc became obsessed with the men I worked with. He called me a slut, a sleaze, and threatened to ruin me" (Kelly Flinn, the female Air Force pilot charged in 1997 with adultery and disobeying an order, speaking of her boyfriend in *Newsweek,* 24 November 1997, 55). Use of the word serves only to induce anxieties in women over their sexuality and to promote bias and misinformation in rape cases.

A current version of the word is *turboslut*, a woman seen as performing like a sex engine.

Like so many slurs against women, *slut* has enjoyed some reclamation in recent years. For example, in the 1991 movie *Chopper Chicks in Zombietown,* a group of female motorcyclists refer to themselves proudly as "Cycle Sluts." Recent changes in our language have also made *slut* available for tongue-lashing men. Risch (1987) found it in use among female college students as a "dirty word" referring to men.

Slut may also be applied to a gay man regarded as sexually promiscuous (used mostly in gay communities since the mid-twentieth century). More specifically, among gays *butt slut* is a name for a man who enjoys anal intercourse with other men. Used outside the gay community, this expression would usually constitute a strong insult.

See also ACTRESS, EASY LAY, FLOOZY, HARLOT, HOOZIE, LOOSE, MATTRESSBACK, MINK, MINX, NYMPHO, PROMISCUOUS, PROSITUTE, PUNCHBOARD, SADIE THOMPSON, SKEEZER, SLAG, SLATTERN, STRUMPET, TART, TRAMP, TROLLOP, WENCH, WHORE.

snake. See WORM.

snot. See OLD FART.

snow queen. See DINGE.

snow white. From the name of the heroine of the famed folk tale, a young woman of supposed virginal purity. There are racial tones, too: black women, given white America's racial stereotypes, are not as likely as middle-class white women to be thought of as "snow whites" (compare, e.g., JEZEBEL). The term may also be used jocularly or ironically. "I used to be Snow White…but I drifted" (Mae West, *The Wit and Widsom of Mae West,* 1967, in Stibbs 1992).

See also ANGEL, VIRGIN.

social butterfly. Metaphor used of women stereotyped as flitting about their little social circles. The triviality of a butterfly—an image of fickleness and frivolity—is emphasized. As Dunayer (1995) notes, "The phrase would confer very different traits if the butterfly's flight from flower to flower were perceived as life-sustaining rather than trivial" (12).

See also BIRD, FLAPPER, MARIPOSA, WOMEN AS ANIMALS.

sodomy. A term with a long history of changing meanings and connotations, deriving from Middle English, in turn from Old French *sodomie*, from Late Latin *Sodoma* (Sodom), referring to the biblical city. In chapter 19 of Genesis, the fate of the city of Sodom is sealed when men of the city demand that two angels, whom they have trapped in the house of Lot, show themselves. While some scholars claim that the men of the city were simply being inhospitable to strangers, others hold that they wished to subject the angels to homosexual acts.

Working from the latter point of view, Miles (1996) argues that homosexuality is not really the relevant issue in the story, however, nor is sodomy as an intrinsic evil. The point, says Miles, is that the two angels are God. The men of the city have demanded access to God's genitals just as, in an earlier Bible episode, God had demanded that Abraham be circumcised. By demanding illicit sexual relations, the men of the city were infringing on a divine prerogative (57). The issue, then, is not morality, but power. Although probably the majority of Jews and Christians today would not agree with this interpretation, it is important to enter it into the dialogue, since the story of the destruction of Sodom and Gomorrah has played a substantial role in shaping oppressive American attitudes toward homosexuality.

John Boswell (in Gomes 1996) says that sodomy has varied in meaning from

> ordinary heterosexual intercourse in an atypical position to oral sexual contact with animals. At some points in history it has referred almost exclusively to male homosexuality and at other times almost exclusively to heterosexual excess. (150)

We can identity various common, related senses of the term *sodomy*. First, it can mean copulation with someone of the same sex. Some dictionaries define it explicitly as anal or oral copulation between *men*, though female-female activities are also often included in definitions.

The word should not, however, be identified exclusively, or even primarily, with homosexuality, since in its broader sense it means anal or oral copulation (under common law, sodomy was iden-

tified with anal intercourse) between a man and a woman, copulation with an animal, or any sex act legally defined as "unnatural." Much discourse on sodomy today takes place within legal institutions, where the act of sodomy is debated as that which is punishable as a criminal offense.

The expressive force of the word *sodomy* comes from the strong taboo placed on any of the forms of behavior so labeled. The common traditional rationale condemning sodomy is that it is against the "natural order" and that only sexual activity that leads to conception is natural, thus permissible. But if this strict interpretation carries any moral weight, then the majority of lovers who engage in such activities as passionate kissing, which does not result in pregnancy, are sinners against nature. "Undoubtedly, Nature has wider and more varied erotic purposes than those prescribed by any neat catechism" (Arango 1989, 65).

Homosexual activity has long carried the stigma of "sodomy," including state statutes that have historically outlawed consensual homosexual sex. The criminalization of sodomy in the United States dates to colonial times, when being found guilty of "a crime against nature" (as sodomy was typically regarded in the courts and statutes) could result in a death sentence, although it is doubtful anyone was ever actually executed for it.

In the nineteenth century, some reports, far from empirical, suggested that sodomy was primarily a "perversion" of the English and the French. Many Americans believed themselves blessedly free of this "foreign corruption." Katz says, "Anti-sodomite discourse supported the nationalistic rhetoric of young America" (1997a, 223).

As of the turn of the twenty-first century, twenty-one states still had some form of criminal provision against same-sex sodomy on the books, although these laws are difficult to enforce because the sexual act takes place in privacy. Gay and lesbian activists have argued that although many of these laws apply to heterosexuals as well as to gay people, "they are primarily used to deny lesbians and gay men a range of other rights" (*Advocate,* 27 October 1998, 45). Activists have made the repeal of these statutes a major objective of their rights campaigns. They enjoyed a victory in 1998 when the high court of the state of Georgia struck down its law against sodomy (which had been upheld by the U.S. Supreme Court twelve years earlier) on the grounds that the law violated the state constitution's provision of the right of privacy.

In the course of revising their criminal codes and recognizing that heterosexuals as well as homosexuals may engage in anal and oral sex, twenty-seven states have either repealed sodomy laws through legislative action or had them struck down by state courts. Still, the Supreme Court has found that state laws that proscribe sodomy are not unconstitutional. The Court has rejected certain critical arguments that would support homosexual rights. Although the argument that a right of privacy does not extend to homosexual activity has been weakened by the demise of the Georgia state sodomy law, some people still argue that the right to engage in such activity is not protected by the due process clauses of the Fifth and Fourteenth Amendments (*West's Encyclopedia of American Law* 1998).

Other references to sodomy with obvious negative or euphemistic overtones have been *that crime, unmentionable vice, nameless sin,* and *unnatural sexual intercourse.* There was once a taboo on mentioning the word in proper Christian society.

Sodomite, dating from the fourteenth century, means either an inhabitant of the ancient city of Sodom, which God destroyed for its sinfulness (Gen. 18–19),

or, when lowercased, someone who engages in sodomy (though *sodomite* referred to the sexual activity before coming to mean one who engages in it). For many in the United States, *sodomite,* linked with the "sin of Sodom," is a code for immorality and perversion and is used as justification to limit or deny the rights of individuals and groups defined as "immoral" and "perverse," especially homosexuals. "We are standing with the G.O.P. against the Sodomites" (the Reverend O. N. Otwell, cited in *Time,* 26 October 1998, 34).

Outside of far right rhetoric, however, the term has lost ground and may be considered dated and moralistic in tone. A later version of the word is *sodomist,* while a slang truncation is *sod. Sodomitess,* meaning a female sodomite, is obsolete.

See also BUGGER, DAISY (daisy chain), HOMOSEXUAL, NORMAL (natural), PERVERT.

softer sex. See WEAKER VESSEL.

software. A computer-age demeaning reference to a woman, alluding to her sexual organs. There are also overtones here of "the softer sex" (see WEAKER VESSEL).

son. From the Old English *sunu,* a male child in a family or a male descendant. The term is also used for a man regarded as though he were a child in relationship to a parent (e.g., a son of the city), a person personified as a male descendant, or a form of address for a young man. As an inclusive designation for both male and female descendants, it is ambiguous and likely to be regarded as sexist.

In Judeo-Christian theology, a son has a preeminent role. In Christianity, the Son is the second member of the Trinity. *Son of God* is used in the Old Testament to refer to Israel, kings, and even the messengers of God. It means Jesus in the New Testament. *Son of Man* as used in the Bible may designate a human being, an exalted apocalyptic figure, or Jesus. The concepts have been rendered in inclusive language, though there will be disagreements about how or whether that can be done. Thus, Maggio (1997), in treating the language used for Jesus, suggests such expressions as *Beloved of God* or *Only Begotten* for *Son of God*, and *the Incarnate One* or *the One made flesh* as two of several possibilities for *Son of Man*.

See also SON OF A BITCH.

son of a bitch. A man regarded as contemptible; sometimes also a pitiful man or simply any fellow. The term is also used to express strong emotion, especially anger or disgust but also sometimes pity, as in "the poor son of a bitch." In the sense of a despicable man, the term dates to the early eighteenth century.

Although usually used for men, the term, in all its opprobrium, reflects back on women: the "bitch" is the man's mother.

Also sometimes spelled *son-of-a-bitch, sonuvabitch, sonofabitch*. Euphemisms are *son-of-a-bee* and *son of a gun,* which is also used to express surprise or disappointment.

See also BASTARD, BITCH, COCK (cocksucker), FUCKER, PRICK.

sow. From Latin *sus*, meaning swine. *Sow* means an adult female pig and also, in what is usually considered sexist slang, a woman (it was once applied to men, too). The image conjured is of a fat, dirty, lazy, dull animal. *Sow* adds to the well-known and often vicious use of *pig* (also applied to men; see PIG) the idea of a female, an idea that often equates with piggishness in linguistic abuse.

The only thing lowlier than a sow may be a "swamp sow," also used for a woman seen as fat and ugly. But also on the low linguistic rung is *swine*, referring to any kind of pig, hog, or boar but also to someone regarded as brutish or contemptible. The insult *swine* is usually reserved for men.

See also BEEF TRUST, BIG BERTHA, COW, HOGGER, WOMEN AS ANIMALS, YETI.

sow wild oats. Originally a British phrase dating to the sixteenth century, referring either to youthful, often irresponsible, play or (more recent) to having sexual intercourse in a cavalier way, especially before marriage. *Sow* here alludes to planting and plowing, and *oats*, to seeds (i.e., semen). *Wild* conveys the idea of being carefree or not playing by the usual rules. "'OK, so I've sown a few wild oats.' 'A few? You can qualify for a farm loan!'" (1962 movie *Lover Come Back*).

The reference is etymologically, and almost always in practice, to young men. Traditionally, *boys* and young men were allowed—even expected—to enjoy some sexual freedom, while girls were held to a narrow line leading to respectable, steady relationships and marriage. Today, in dealing with sexual harassment at work, phrases such as "boys will be boys" or "sowing wild oats" may be used to dismiss gender issues.

See also PLAYBOY.

space girl. A young woman (sometimes a woman of any age) seen as acting silly or mindlessly; from the mid-twentieth century. She may be perceived as giddy and "spaced-out," out of touch with reality. "Get out of my way, you nutty old broad—I mean it, space girl" (TV crime drama *Walker, Texas Ranger*, 1997).

Pejorative or dismissive synonyms also associated with women are, for example, *airhead, bubblehead,* and *ditz,* all emphasizing the stereotypical view of women as lacking in intelligence. *Space cadet,* meaning someone crazy or eccentric, may be applied to a man or woman.

See also BLONDE (dumb blonde), BUNNY (dumb bunny), DAME (dizzy dame), DITZ, DUMB DORA, GIRL, TWINK (twinkie).

spare rib. See FALLEN WOMAN.

special rights. See GAY AGENDA.

speciesism and women. See WOMEN AS ANI-MALS.

spice. From the idea of the zest, flavor, or perfume of the plant-derived spices, a term used for sexual appeal, often that of women. As the poet Robert Southey said, "Sugar and spice/And all that's nice,/That's what little girls are made of."

See also DISH, HOT, SUGAR, TAMALE.

spinster. Originally, a woman or man whose occupation was spinning. The term eventually came to be applied exclusively to women spinners, since although men spun, spinning was traditionally looked upon as women's work. The word derives from the Middle English *spinnestere* (a woman who spins). In his will, Alfred the Great, ninth-century king of Wessex, referred to the women in his family as the "spindle side," that is, the female line of descent.

During Saxon times in England, spinning was the occupation of the women of the household, done especially during the winter. Young women were believed not to be ready for marriage until they had spun and woven for themselves fabric for a set of body, bed, and table linen. As a result, the maiden was called a spinner, or spinster. By the seventeenth century, the term had acquired formal legal status in reference to an unmarried woman.

Views of spinsters have often been ambivalent. Grahn (1990) mentions a European folk belief that a pregnant woman's baby could be cursed by the evil (apparently envious) glance of a spinster. But Grahn also tells of a belief among Welsh mothers who regarded their child as blessed by the presence of a spinster in the room during childbirth (111). The connotations and even denotations of the word have also varied. At one time, the word (mostly in British usage) was a euphemism for a mistress or prostitute, women who were of marriage-able age or beyond but not married, thus being viewed as deviant. These women were perceived as having no husband in their lives to make them "virtuous." Since the eighteenth century *spinster* has denoted a woman who has remained unmarried longer than convention dictates in the culture. Today, however, the word carries Victorian overtones that make it sound somewhat quaint.

The negative valence of *spinster* reflects on the traditional—and sometimes still forced—dependence of a woman on marriage. Without marriage and the clearly defined social position it gives her, she might be regarded as lacking in integrity (contrast with VIRGIN, also used for an unmarried woman, but one traditionally held in high esteem). The term often connotes prissiness, sexlessness (being "dried up"), sublimation, and someone who has "had her chance." "His office [had]...two desks, one for himself and one for Miss Giles, his secretary, a middle-aged, efficient spinster" (Irwin Shaw, *Rich Man, Poor Man,* 1969). An even more degrading synonym is OLD MAID. See also FRUMP and SCHOOLMARM for similar, staid, old-fashioned connotations.

Spinsters have been condemned as women who may have tried but failed at love, maladjusted females with no chance at all (or who lost their chance after being jilted and hurt too much to resume a love life), women who have been either unattractive to or inept with men, or those kept from love by the dictatorial demands of a parent. There has also been the notion of a woman who specializes in love affairs with married men, thus sabotaging her own efforts to find a husband.

Psychological literature once commonly stereotyped the spinster as childlike, with complexes that were impediments to marriage. She was considered fearful of men (as perhaps she was of her father), easily hurt by disappointments with men, and held back by a cringing inferiority complex.

Spinsters were once identified—and often admired—as teachers, but it was believed that spinsters were attracted to teaching because it satisfied their need, being denied motherhood, to be near children (in fact, they had few other outlets for making a living). They kept pets supposedly for the same reason. The younger spinster may have been attractive and kind, but the older one was often stereotyped as nagging and hypochondriacal.

In the 1960s these stereotypes began to lose force, for which Helen Gurley Brown, who elevated the "spinster" into "the newest glamour girl of our time" in her 1962 book *Sex and the Single Girl,* is given much of the credit.

Spinster is not parallel with BACHELOR, which is not derogatory; the bachelor may be seen as enviably independent, perhaps even a sexual libertine. The man has traditionally had a choice whether to marry, and the bachelor may be thought of only as a man who has eluded his pursuers. However, once women were able to divest themselves of some of the negative image of being single, *spinster* no longer served to designate, and thereby limit, them. *Single,* a nongendered word, is common today and usually preferred (see also SINGLE).

Against the tide of disparagement, the unmarried woman might be thought of as establishing a role for women beyond that of the family and of dependence on men. Along these lines there has been some attempt to reclaim the word *spinster.* For example, Spinsters Ink is the name of a book publisher owned and operated by women. For a view of spinsters as women who help "spin" women's culture, weaving its connections, see Daly (1978).

spitfire. A term for a person seen as fiery-tempered, emotional, and easily provoked to anger. *Spitfire* is typically used for women, who are often stereotyped as being controlled by their emotions. "The Hungarian spitfire [Zsa Zsa Gabor] claimed she belted Beverly Hills Police Officer Paul Kramer after 'he dragged me out of the car and called me a whore'" (*National Enquirer,* 29 September 1998, 26). Attractive Mexican women or other Latinas have in particular been dubbed "spitfires" for their stereotypical Latin emotionalism.

See also HOT.

spring chicken. See CHICKEN.

squaw. From various Algonquian words meaning woman, an epithet for an Indian or Inuit woman or wife, often connoting old age and sexlessness—from a male perspective, good for little else but cooking for "her man." In many ways, *squaw* is the opposite of the male "brave" and the reverse of the "Indian princess," seen as an attractive young Native American women. This term, used in English since at least the early nineteenth century, has perpetuated a stereotype of the Native American woman as docile and subservient, and this sense of the word has, since about the mid-twentieth century, been transferred to a more general meaning of any woman or wife or even a prostitute. *Squaw* and *squaw-man* have both been applied abusively to a man seen as effeminate or an effeminate gay man.

See also WIFE.

squid bait. See BAIT.

squirrel. A slang term usually relating to women—the female genitals or pubic hair (compared here with fur) and a woman regarded as a sex object. However, *squirrel* has also had some currency for a psychiatrist, said to thrive on "nuts."

See also BEAVER, BUNNY, CAT, HAIR, HAT, MINK, PUSS, WOMEN AS ANIMALS, WOOL.

stag. From Middle English *stagge*, meaning first a drake (male duck), then an adult male red deer. By the mid-nineteenth century, this term for a male animal known for its striking behavior when in heat came to be applied to the human male (who, since the eighteenth century, has been said colloquially to "be in rut" when sexually excited). Since 1935 it has meant "for men only." *Stag party* refers to a party restricted to men, as a party held for a bachelor before his wedding (bachelor party) or a more risqué gathering where "stag films" are shown. (When women gather, for whatever reason, the get-together may be trivialized in language as a "hen party" [see HEN].) *Stag line* refers to a line of men at the side of a dance floor waiting to claim a dance partner from among the women. With its heavy freight of masculinity and absence of negative connotations, the name was also appropriated as the title of a men's magazine featuring nude women:

> We can well understand why an army of publications has sprouted with healthy Anglo-Saxon titles such as *Stag*. They are desperately needed to bolster Hemingwayman-ship. (Eve Merriam, in Adams and Briscoe 1971, 146)

See also ANIMAL, BULL, CORK, HAG (hag and stag party), STALLION, STUD, TIGER, WOLF.

stallion. Since the seventeenth century, an animal metaphor—a stallion is a male horse kept for breeding—applied to men viewed as very sexually active. It usually carries positive connotations of sexual power: "a real stallion" is a man who performs sexually the way most men are said to aspire to. *Italian stallion* is how the media has dubbed Hollywood actor Sylvester Stallone. There are no comparable positive animal images for women, although in African American use since the mid-twentieth century, *stallion* has meant an attractive and sexually appealing black woman. In some contexts, *stallion* may suggest a horse ridden by a woman, and in British usage, it once denoted the client of a female prostitute or a man kept by a woman for her sexual pleasure.

See also ANIMAL, BULL, COCK, HORSE, KING (king of the jungle), STAG, STUD, TIGER, WOLF.

star fucker. See GROUPIE.

stepmother; **stepfather**. *Stepmother*, the spouse of one's father by a later marriage, long stereotyped as a wicked person in children's stories, such as *Cinderella* and *Snow White*. "As a stepmother, you are initially perceived, falsely or not, as a rival to the most traditionally revered and respected biological forces in the family—the mother" (Cherie Burns, *Stepmotherhood*, 1985, 3). The *step-* prefix may imply "second best"; it can also suggest meanness. The male counterpart, *stepfather,* is sometimes stereotyped as an uncaring disciplinarian. Among his critics, George Washington was known as the "Stepfather of His Country."

The term *blended family* was coined in the 1970s as a less biased substitute for *stepfamily*.

See also MOTHER, MOTHER-IN-LAW, WITCH.

stimey hole. See HOLE.

stone fox. See FOX.

straight. An informal term often used for a heterosexual person, suggesting properness and a correct standard. Those who are not straight, as this directional metaphor implies, are TWISTED, DEVIANT, or bent out of shape (see also directional antonyms INVERSION, PERVERT [aberration, kinky]). "We were all so young that we arrogantly assumed that all of us were straight and they were bent" (sailor speaking of gay people, from Pete Hamill, in Katz 1995, 168).

Applied to women, *straight* has often meant "chaste," thus suggesting that women (and, by extension, gay people) who are not straight are lascivious and morally "loose" (*straight* in the culture of female prostitution has also signaled a woman who does not give oral sex).

Straight dates to at least the early twentieth century. It emerged in the gay male community, where it was originally applied to a gay person who wanted to go "straight up," as it were, or to be "set straight," that is, to give up homosexuality for the "straight and narrow path" of heterosexuality. Later it acquired the current meaning of a heterosexual, in common use implying someone who never engages in homosexual activity.

The concept of a straight person may take on negative meanings in gay communities: "With a bit of therapy or prayer, they [homosexuals] could change and become as wretched as those sad straights, half of whom are doomed to undergo divorce, battles over child custody, and charges of overpopulating the planet" (Gore Vidal, *The Advocate,* 24 November 1998, 9). The heterosexual may be dismissed as "straighty," and the metaphor often carries the connotations of someone whose orientation lacks interest or imagination.

Vanilla, referring to what is thought to be an unimaginative choice of flavors, is used for a heterosexual person with the same hint of blandness. An abbreviated form of *heterosexual, het,* heard in informal contexts, may also, when used by a gay person, carry mild disrespect (see also BREEDER).

In the hippie subculture of the 1960s, those who comprised the mainstream society were also known, usually with some derision, as "straight people." Similarly, among drug users, a person who does not take drugs may be described as "straight," as are honest people from the point of view of a criminal. The expression *straight as a virgin* draws from the notion of the dullness of the virginal status to reinforce the idea

of the unimaginativeness of moral rectitude. "Since when did you drink, man? I thought you were as straight as a virgin" (1991 movie *Across the Tracks*).

See also HETEROSEXUAL.

straitlaced. See PRUDE.

street meat. See MEAT.

strident. See FEMINISM.

strumpet. A woman taken to be a prostitute or morally debauched. The etymology is unknown, but the word apparently entered English in the fourteenth century. "Such a bold, shameless way to dress!... You strumpet!" (Theodore Dreiser's father to his daughter, in *Dreiser,* W. A. Swanberg, 1965). *Strumpet* has also been used figuratively, as when Shakespeare wrote of "That strumpet Fortune" (*King John* III. i. 61). Today, when heard at all, it is often in a jocular or ironic vein. Abbreviated to *strum.*

See also PROSTITUTE, SLATTERN, SLUT, WHORE.

stud. Ladies' man; since the late nineteenth century, a man viewed as handsome, virile, and usually sexually promiscuous. Once applied in England to places where horses were bred, in the United States the word came to identify a stallion or male horse used for breeding. Later it also took on the meaning of a kind of poker in which every card after the first is dealt face up, revealed to the other players.

In black usage *stud* may denote any young man, not necessarily a promiscuous one. It is also applied in gay communities to gay men and male prostitutes. A handsome man admired for his body but not his brain may also be called—or dismissed as—a stud. In the African American lesbian community, it has had use in the sense of BUTCH.

The word would seem to objectify men, and indeed it does. In fact, it suggests how patriarchy, so often distorting of women's relations to their bodies, has done something similar to men. Yet when words for men are sexualized, they tend to highlight men's status and masculinity rather than demean the person named, as so many sexualized epithets do for women. Many people respond only to the positive connotations in the term—a man who is accomplished at being a man and excels in sexual performance. A number of men have even used the term as a first name, for example, Studs Terkel.

A "studhammer" is a man regarded as being very successful with the women (or men), especially sexually (see also HAMMER), and a "studmuffin" is known for his sexual appeal.

See also ANIMAL, BULL, COCK (cocksman), HOSE (hoseman), LOVE MACHINE, STAG, STALLION, TIGER, TOM, VIRILE.

stuff. See HOT (hot stuff).

stunner. See KNOCKOUT.

suffragist; suffragette. *Suffragist,* a woman or man who advocates suffrage, especially women's right to vote. It was first used in the early 1820s but gained currency around the 1880s (often as *woman-suffragist*).

Suffragette was coined in London in 1906 as part of the English opposition to female British suffragists, who, however, came to adopt *suffragette* for themselves. In the United States, *suffragette* was seen in writings that disparaged women's rights, and it did not really catch on among American women in the suffrage movement, who preferred *suffragist. Suffragette*, still often seen in print, came to be regarded as a trivialized form of *suffragist* (see also -ETTE).

See also FEMINIST.

sugar. A slang term meaning a dear one or sweetheart, frequently occurring as a term of address for a woman. Although the word may be used affectionately by a woman for a man, it often has a paternalistic ring. In a *Life* magazine article

on sexist language in 1970, Ann Bayer wrote of a fictionalized woman concerned with "rampant sexism" in our society: "[She] didn't like 'devious paternalistic devices' which men use in calling women *cookies, gumdrops, sugar, honey,* or *cheesecake"* (Nilsen et al. 1997, 2). W. C. Fields knew the value of the term in ingratiating himself to a woman when he referred to Mae West, after their marriage in the 1940 comedy film *My Little Chickadee,* as "My little sugar-coated wedding cake."

See also CAKE, CHEESECAKE, CHERRY, COOKIE, CUPCAKE, DEAR, DISH, HONEY, JELLY ROLL, MUFFIN, PIE, SPICE, SWEET.

sugar daddy. See DADDY.

supermom; superwoman. A mother or woman who is efficient, competent, and on the go. These terms came out of the eighties, when women were making gains in the workplace. The supermom starts up where Betty Friedan's dissatisfied homemaker (*The Feminine Mystique* [1963]) left off—little has improved in the homemaking domain, but now she is employed at the office as well as in the home. "Supermoming was a common working mother's strategy for coping with the work at home *without imposing* on their husbands" (Hochschild 1989, 195).

The supermom, or superwoman, is played up as the woman who "has it all" but in fact ends up struggling to juggle her career and her duties at home with a husband and children. She may be open to blame when she fails to meet the conflicting expectations. According to Hochschild, the idea of the supermom disguises the strains and minimizes the personal needs of women. As long as the myth puts her in a position of envy, society is not likely to acknowledge those strains. Whereas *superwoman* may also denote a woman who has superhuman powers (sometimes it simply suggests obsessiveness), *superman* almost never carries the family-career meanings of *superwoman* but means either a man of superhuman powers or philosopher Friedrich Nietzsche's superior creative being.

See also MOM, MOTHER.

survivor. See VICTIM.

sweater girl. See GIRL.

sweet; **sweetie**. *Sweet,* a common metaphor for women. Although often used affectionately, it may also be used in such degrading pornographic lines as "soft, sweet, and ready to eat!"

Sweetie is often thought of as an endearment, but it can often be annoying and paternalistic. *Sweetie* and *sweetie-pie* are also used endearingly by a woman for a man, suggesting kindness or gentleness, traditionally feminine qualities, but nonsexual in connotation (contrast with the degrading sexual connotations of PIE, applied to women). Carrying feminine connotations, *sweetie* is also used for a gay male.

See also CAKE, CHEESECAKE, COOKIE, CUPCAKE, DEAR, DISH, HONEY, JELLY ROLL, MAMA (sweet mama), MUFFIN, PIE, SUGAR, SWEET MEAT, TART.

sweet meat. A term once used for the penis and also for a young mistress, both in British slang. In the United States this term came to refer to any girl or woman. Although it may be relatively affectionate, unburdened from the blatant degradation of terms such as *dark meat* or *horseflesh* (see MEAT), it has definite sexist implications. It may also be applied to gay men with implications of effeminacy.

See also SWEET.

swine. See PIG, SOW.

swish. From around the turn of the twentieth century (some dictionaries say mid-twentieth century, which is when it became popular), a slang word applied to obviously effeminate gay men, often those thought to be overly delicate, refined, or narcissistic. It may derive from an imitation of the sound that a dress makes when a woman walks. The connotations are often taken as pejorative. The usage occurs in both the gay and the straight communities.

Adj. swishy.

See also EFFEMINATE, FAIRY, FLAMER (second quotation), GIRL, HOMOSEXUAL, LIMP-WRIST, LISPER, MARIPOSA, PANSY.

T

table grade. A usually vulgar reference to a woman seen as sexually available. The reference is to food, a substance to be consumed; in particular, though, table grade is the more ordinary variety of "food," less pricey than the better brands. See also DISH, PROMISCUOUS.

taco. A food-based epithet of Mexican Spanish origin applied especially to Mexicans or Mexican Americans, often women. Mexican Americans popularized the term, as they did the synonymous *taco belle*. *Pink taco* is a vulgar epithet used for a Mexican or Mexican American woman or any Latina, alluding to the vagina. See also DISH, SPICE, TAMALE.

tail. See ASS, BEAVER, BUNNY, SQUIRREL.

tamale. A food-based epithet for a Mexican woman—or any young woman. *Hot tamale,* a play on the spiciness of the food, refers to a young woman seen as provocatively sexy. The word objectifies women and reduces them to something to be consumed.

After the same fashion, *enchilada* and *quesadilla* (as in the alliterative *cute quesadilla*) have seen some use for a woman. See also DISH, HOT, SPICE, TACO.

tart. Originally a Middle French word meaning a small pie or sweet pastry. *Tart* came to be used in the Victorian era as a male term of endearment for a woman, especially a female partner. (Because of its early meanings and sound, it is also sometimes said to be a contraction of *sweetheart*.) As it became attached to women, it acquired, by the late nineteenth century, the meaning of a young woman regarded as a sex object, a woman of loose morals, and then a prostitute. The term comes loaded with sexual suggestiveness: the English dessert tart is a pastry shell filled with jelly or cream. As a kind of pie, it suggests the female genitalia, long known euphemistically as "pie." *Tart* reduces a woman to a soft, sweet morsel to be consumed. This feminine meaning carries over to gay usage, where it means the young gay companion of an older man or a male prostitute.

Based on the feminine sense of *tart* and the brand name of a breakfast pastry, *pop tart* may be used for a young woman seen as cute or sexy. "The spicy pop tart [Madonna] authored an entire book about 'Sex' that exposed her erotic fantasies, depicting her in pornographic and sadomasochistic poses" (*National Enquirer,* 29 September 1998, 21). See also CAKE, CHEESECAKE, COOKIE, CUPCAKE, DISH, HONEY, JELLY ROLL, MUFFIN, PIE, SUGAR, SWEET.

Tarzan. Now a word for any strong man, a man regarded to be of physical or sexual prowess, or a man of nature. "My wife said it was like I was Tarzan" (man who had been impotent before trying an oral drug to restore sexual function, quoted in the *Chicago Sun-Times*, 28 October 1997, 4).

Tarzan was the vine-swinging jungle hero of a series of stories written by Edgar Rice Burroughs in the early twentieth century. His adventures began when, as a noble English family's son, Lord Greystoke, he was lost in Africa and raised by apes who helped him to understand the ways of nature. He grew up with the brawn and talents necessary to foil the plans of the many evil people he encountered in his adventures. A kind of Anglo-Saxon "noble savage," Tarzan's class nobility by birth was transformed into a natural nobility untainted by civilization. His relationship with women may be summed up in the apocryphal line: "Me Tarzan, you Jane" (Jane being Professor Archimedes Q. Porter's daughter, who was charmed by Tarzan and married him). Besides being accused of treating Jane as a helpless woman he must continually rescue from danger, the Tarzan character has also drawn criticism as a racist depiction of a "superior" white man in a jungle full of black people

See also CAVEMAN, HE-MAN, HUNTER, JANE, KING (king of the jungle), MACHO.

tease. A word used for a woman who is said to make amatory advances. To be called a tease is usually an insult, in part because a woman's traditionally assigned role does not allow her to make sexual advances (sometimes considered tacky). Also, a woman who "tempts" men without allowing sex to culminate in intercourse is said to frustrate men and may open herself to charges of being a "temptress" (see TEMPTRESS). "*YM* [teen magazine] shows girls 100 asinine ways to be supersexy.... If *YM* ever changes its name again, I suggest *Dicktease*" (Anastasia Higginbotham, *Ms.,* March/ April 1996, 86). *Cybertease* refers to a "netgirl," a woman who goes on-line for long-distance sexual fantasy and arousal.

Teaser, from the mid-twentieth century, is used for a woman who is perceived as being sexually available but is in fact not.

See also COCK (cockteaser), CUNT (cunt-teaser), PRICK (prick-tease[r]).

temptress. Since the sixteenth century, a term for a woman seen as tempting or enticing a man and capable of bringing him to ruin. "Was she [Cleopatra] really the evil temptress that we've all heard about? Or was she simply a brilliant, ambitious ruler trying to do the best for her kingdom?" (TV series *Biography,* 1997). The -ESS ending, often regarded today as sexist, signals the word's use for women; *tempter* is a sex-neutral term. *Temptress* is part of a long tradition of viewing women, their sexuality in particular, as threatening to men, who may wield the term to try to escape any responsibility for their own sexual con-

duct. In recent years the media have called attention to this double standard of sexuality for women and men.

See also BAIT, BITCH (bitch goddess success), BOX (Pandora's box), COQUETTE, FEMME FATALE, HOMEWRECKER, JEZEBEL, MANEATER, SCARLET WOMAN, SEDUCTRESS, SHE-DEVIL, SIREN, VAMP, VIXEN.

termagant. From Middle English, a woman perceived as overbearing; a nag or shrew. *Termagant* (capitalized) originally referred to a male deity or idol believed by the Crusaders and other medieval European Christians to be Islamic. He was introduced into early Christian drama as having a violent and turbulent character and depicted in long, flowing "Eastern" robes that gave him the look of a woman. Since the seventeenth century, this term has come to mean a shrewish female, a creature despised because she does not allow herself to be controlled by men.

See also BITCH, HARPY, HARRIDAN, MOTHER-IN-LAW, NAG, SHREW, VIRAGO, WITCH.

that crime. See SODOMY.

thigh man. See MEAT.

third sex. See OPPOSITE SEX.

thithy. See SISSY.

three-dollar bill. See QUEER.

three-letter man. See FAGGOT (fag).

thumper. See FAWN.

Tinker Bell. A man believed to be effeminate or gay. Often derisive, the allusion is to the name of the unseen female fairy in James Barrie's play *Peter Pan.* Although this name has more currency in British slang, it is also heard and understood in the United States.

See also BELLE, EFFEMINATE, FLOWER, LA-DI-DA, LIMP-WRIST, LISPER, LITTLE LORD FAUNTLEROY, NELLY, SWISH.

tit man. A reference applied to a man who describes his sexual fantasy as a woman with attractive and, usually, big breasts. The term is not usually derogatory and may even be flattering to a man proud of his particular fetish. Given American men's obsession with female breasts, it is not surprising to find *tit* occurring in vulgar use for a woman viewed as a sex object.

See also ASS MAN, BRA-BUSTER, HOOT-ERS GIRLS, LEG (leg man), MEAT (breast man).

tom; tomcat. *Tom*, from the nickname for Thomas, meaning the male of some animal species (e.g., tomcat), the penis, or any man (not usually derogatory). *Tom* may also mean a female prostitute (see ALLEY CAT) or any woman, linking her with conventional male behavior—in particular, aggressiveness (see GENDER-SPECIFIC ADJECTIVES [aggressive]). *Tomcat* is a name for a man who prowls around for a (female) "tom." Women may use the term to express their disapproval of a man who "roams." Aggressive animals are likely to be used as metaphors for men or masculinity.

See also ANIMAL, CAT, STUD, TOMBOY, WOLF.

tomato. A reference to a woman regarded as good-looking; sometimes also a prostitute, from the early twentieth century. As a food metaphor, it suggests a luscious (thus, *luscious tomato*) fruit ready to be eaten. The tomato's cherished properties of redness, tautness, and juiciness add to the sexual and sexist connotations.

See also DISH, FRUIT, HOT (hot tomato), POTATO, VEGETABLE.

tomboy. A girl or young woman who behaves in a manner that suggests boyishness. The word was originally (during the sixteenth century, when it meant boisterous or rude) applied to boys (Tom is short for Thomas). Then it was attached to girls as well as boys and eventually narrowed in meaning to girls only (also formerly in British slang meaning STRUMPET). Unlike *sissy*, by which a man is derided as having feminine characteristics, the word *tomboy* may carry favor-

able connotations; however, the meaning is not always straightforward. "The word," note Rivers, Barnett, and Baruch (1979), "can be an insult or a badge worn proudly" (109). Today, with rapid social change, especially in gender stereotyping, *tomboy* seems to be losing ground, especially in certain regions or urban centers.

Struggling against the confinements of femininity, the tomboy may be something of a gender rebel. Some researchers (e.g., Lees 1986) have noted that becoming a tomboy is one of a number of strategies a young woman can choose to resist conventional images of femininity. Any pride borne by the word, however, derives largely from comparison with a boy, not from extolling the girl herself for being spirited and adventuresome.

According to a *WomenSports* correspondent, active women for some years now have been describing themselves as athletes. Many young women interviewed did not use or even understand the term *tomboy*, which was apparently being replaced in some contexts by *jock* (noted in Rivers, Barnett, and Baruch, 111). Applied to a female, *jock*, derived from the slang name for a male athlete and evoking sweat and muscularity, signals the widening of the domain of female activities beginning in the second half of the twentieth century.

Fictional tomboy figures have been more or less enduring characters in American children's literature. There was, for instance, Caddie Woodlawn, who lived on the nineteenth-century frontier; Charlie Boy (Charlotte) Carter, a 1920s "Texas tomboy"; and Grace Jones, who climbed trees in a post-Depression story. As Thorne (1993) has outlined, the fictional tomboy is spirited and adventuresome, rejects dresses and good manners, and likes to move freely, especially out of doors in the company of boys (112–13). Other girls, especially the more "ladylike" ones, become objects of scorn to the tomboy, though she may eventually succumb to the "softer" values of her defined gender.

Tomgirl is a variant form of the word.

See also BOY, GIRL, HOYDEN, JOCK, MARIMACHO, SISSY, TOM.

tootsie. Since the late nineteenth century, a slang endearment and term of address or nickname for a girl or young woman, synonymous with *sweetheart* or DOLL. The word has also been seen as *tootsy* or *tootsie-wootsie*. By connoting babyishness (see also BABY), *tootsie* is likely to be offensive to many women, as the drag character played by Dustin Hoffman in the 1982 movie *Tootsie* learned. *Tootsie* also serves as a reference to a masculine lesbian, usually meant as an affront outside lesbian circles.

The origin of the term is not known. However, Chapman (1987) notes that it might have developed from the playful fun a parent may have with a baby's toes (also called "tootsies"), thus leading to associations with a baby or doll, then a woman. He also sees a relation to the Yiddish *zees tushele* (sweet bottom), said endearingly of babies. The trade name Tootsie Roll, for a candy, comes into play also, as in the sexaul slang pun "to have a roll with a tootsie" (see also SWEET).

Toots is the shortened form, from the early to mid-twentieth century. "Sure— I can give you a part in *Hearts and Spades,* Toots. But I don't do favors for kids that don't play ball" (Jack Hanley, *Let's Make Mary,* 1937, 81).

top sergeant. See SERGEANT.

tornado. See WOMEN AS STORMS.

toyboy, toy boy. An often demeaning term for a good-looking young man seen as existing solely for the pleasure of those older women, often celebrities, whom he dates. The term dismisses him as having no serious adult male role other than

the sexual one; he is viewed as just a plaything, a role American society has typically assigned to women (see PLAYMATE). The woman is likely to keep him around by lavishing gifts on him. *Toyboy* is the masculine equivalent of *kept woman* or *bimbo*. *Toyboy* may also be used for a handsome male youth kept by an older man.

See also BOY, GIGOLO.

trade. In general, a reductive commerce metaphor that was applied throughout much of the twentieth century for a man or woman viewed as a sex partner, especially the customer of a prostitute. In particular, however, this has been a term of the male homosexual community for a heterosexual man willing to have sex with another man for some remuneration.

Around the first decade of the twentieth century, *trade* came to mean a man regarded by a gay man as sexually desirable but was used specifically for men who demanded payment for a sexual service offered another man as well as for "heterosexual" men willing to accept a gay man as a sexual partner for pleasure rather than profit. (*Heterosexual* is in quotation marks because today such a man, given his interest in a homosexual relationship, whatever his own sexual identity or economic motives, would most likely be regarded as homosexual, by gay communities as well as straight. Bisexuals, however, might see him as one of their community.)

The term enjoyed currency early in the twentieth century, before the ascendancy of *gay* and when it was regarded as more important in gay communities to distinguish the masculine heterosexual man willing to accept a homosexual man's advances from the more effeminate (FAIRY) homosexual and from the more conventional one (QUEER, having a homosexual interest but no effeminate characteristics). Chauncey (1994) has made this point, arguing that the boundaries separating these gay groups have now shifted, the categories reconfigured under the umbrella term *gay*. Speaking of the pre-World War II homosexual culture, he writes, "Many fairies and queers...considered the ideal sexual partner to be 'trade,' a 'real man,' that is, ideally a sailor, a soldier, or some other embodiment of the aggressive masculine ideal...neither homosexually interested nor effeminately gendered" (21–22).

The trade can refer to prostitution or the customers of a prostitute (see JOHN, TRICK).

See also PIECE (piece of trade).

tramp. A term from the sixteenth century originally meaning someone whose poverty restricted him (or her) to getting around on foot, now usually with different meanings depending on whether it is applied to men or women. The male tramp is a poor, aimless wanderer or vagabond; a female tramp is any woman considered promiscuous or a prostitute. "Once a tramp, always a tramp" (Ingrid Bergman, protesting the stigma in her role in Alfred Hitchcock's film *Notorious*, 1946). The application to a woman regarded as promiscuous, regardless of social class, is relatively recent, though when this U.S. slang sense came into use is uncertain.

See also EASY LAY, FLOOZY, HARLOT, HOOZIE, LOOSE, MATTRESSBACK, MINK, MINX, NYMPH, PROMISCUOUS, PROSTITUTE, PUNCHBOARD, SADIE THOMPSON, SCARLET WOMAN, SKEEZER, SLAG, SLATTERN, SLUT, TART, TRASH, TROLLOP, WENCH, WHORE.

transgenderist; transgender. Terms that can be used in both a narrow and a broad sense having to do with gender identity and embodiment. When *transgenderist* was coined in the mid-1980s by Virginia Prince, herself a transgenderist and a gender researcher who established support groups in the mid-twentieth century for transvestites, it had a narrower mean-

ing than it does today. It designated those individuals who permanently changed their gender—that is, characteristics conventionally associated with biological sex (e.g., born male = masculine gender)—through their use of clothing, hair styles, makeup, and mannerisms that are socially normative for the "other" or "opposite" sex. This distinguished the transgenderist from the transvestite, who changed clothes only at certain times or places, and the transsexual, some of whom changed genitals or altered their bodies in other ways.

In the 1990s, however, *transgenderist* came to be an umbrella term encompassing all the many possibilities of gendered embodiment, in the sense of a pan-gender spectrum. In this broad sense it would include transsexuals, cross-dressers, drag queens, drag kings, butch lesbians, androgynes, intersexuals, and transvestites, among others who in so many different ways cross the socially normative gender lines.

Because *transgenderist* or *transgender* in the original sense implied the repudiation of genital surgery, some transsexuals now refuse to be lumped into the category. Nevertheless, *transgender,* in particular, is a fairly widely adopted term within the transgender community, which is a concept largely of the 1990s.

MacKenzie (1994) notes that the term is self-generated and not medically applied and is not a term of disempowerment. Rather, *transgender* is a way of acknowledging the sense of community and common interest among those individuals in society who adopt different kinds of gender-transposed identities. "I've been called a he-she, butch, bulldagger, cross-dresser, passing woman, female-to-male transvestite, and drag king. The word I prefer to use to describe myself is *transgender"* (Feinberg 1996, x). Coming into currency in the transgender community is the construction *TS/TG*, meaning transsexual and transgender.

Taken together, as Anne Bolin (in Herdt 1994) has written, the diverse transgender identities "challenge the dominant American gender paradigm with its emphasis on reproduction and the biological sexual body as the sine qua non of gender identity and role" (447). Yet in societies that insist on conformity to dual gender roles and are not in most contexts tolerant of crossing or tinkering with established gender lines, the transgendered represent a threat to dominant practices and ideologies. The negative stereotypes of and associations with the transgendered are quite pervasive. For example, in movies such as *Psycho* and *The Silence of the Lambs*, maniacal killers have been depicted as transgendered.

See also ANDROGYNY, BERDACHE, BUTCH, CROSS-DRESSER, DRAG, GENDER AND SEX, HERMAPHRODITE, INVERSION, OPPOSITE SEX, TRANSSEXUAL, TRANSVESTITE.

transphobia. See HOMOPHOBIA.

transsexual. A term describing persons who feel they properly belong to a sex other than the one to which they were born and who often alter their bodies with surgery and hormones so that other people can see them as they see themselves. Transsexuals express themselves according to the same gendered styles of dress, hair, mannerism, and speech—and embodiment—that a majority of people in their culture use to communicate a masculine or feminine sense of self. But this style is *theirs* and should not be thought of as a style that does not properly belong to them, which is how the transsexual is so often defined.

The word *transsexualism* (now usually spelled *transsexualism),* originally as *psychopathia transexualis* (*psychopathia* today is dated, inaccurate, and offensive), was first used in 1949, appearing in an article by David O. Cauldwell in a sex education magazine

called *Sexology.* Harry Benjamin, who made the term current through his published medical work, claims to have coined the term independently.

The related expression "sex-change operation" is now considered an anachronistic and misleading term, especially problematic because most transsexuals do not consider it to be a change but a process of manifesting a preexisting identity. "It is not the surgeon's knife that makes the transsexual, but rather the transsexual's identity that brings the knife to bear" (Dr. Susan Stryker, personal communication, January 1999). What's more, transsexuality cannot be reduced to a "sex change" operation, because about half the transsexual population—the so-called FTMs (female-to-males)—do not typically have genital surgeries. In any case, the operation or, as is especially true for female-to-males, series of operations is currently known as "sex reassignment surgery."

Transsexualism itself is now regarded as an outdated term in some quarters. As still used among many psychotherapists, the term does not refer to what is considered a separate clinical entity but rather to the most extreme form of "gender dysphoria," a problematic term first proposed by psychiatrist Norman Fisk in 1974. *Gender dysphoria* entered the *Diagnostic and Statistical Manual of Psychiatric Disorders (DSM)* to name an official psychopathology in 1980.

This term refers to a sense of unhappiness about incongruities between how one perceives one's own gender and how one's gender is perceived by others. However, many transsexuals who simply feel that they somehow have the "wrong body" resent this psychiatric labeling and feel that transsexuality is no more psychopathological than homosexuality, which was dropped from the *DSM* after decades of lobbying by gays, lesbians, and their allies. There is some transsexual support for inclusion in the

DSM, however, because some transsexuals have health insurance policies that will pay for their surgery if it is considered a "cure" for a "disease."

The concept of transsexualism, which embraces a diversity of individuals, lifestyles, and sexualities, is commonly misunderstood to the extreme. To begin, transsexuals, in spite of their crossing of gender boundaries, are not usually homosexual and may resent that identification. They are frequently heterosexual but may also be bisexual. A transsexual woman (a woman born biologically male), for instance, would regard her attraction toward men as heterosexual, since she regards herself as a woman. She would think of herself as lesbian only if attracted to women. Transsexuals may also object to being labeled "impersonators" of the other gender. In her research on male-to-female transsexuals and male transvestites, Anne Bolin (in Herdt 1994) found that male-to-female transsexuals did not see themselves as engaging in parody or play, illusion or impersonation, "but rather in a true expression of a feminine gender identity" (451).

Along with these misunderstandings of transsexuality comes a sometimes virulent stigmatization. To make a point about how transsexuals are often perceived as a threat, Randi Ettner wrote, "The transsexual is [regarded as] a leper in modern society, and the parents are considered to be the breeders of the contagion" (*Confessions of a Gender Defender,* 1996, 28–29).

In referring to transsexuals, it is appropriate to speak of "she" in the case of the male-to-female transsexual, and "he" in the case of the female-to-male. However, the commonly accepted terms *male-to-female* and *female-to-male* have been called into question as medically derived and suggestive of the role of genitals in indicating gender and the value of biological transformation. They

serve to strengthen the conventional, rigid notion that there are only two sexes. *Transgenderist* is commonly accepted within the transsexual community (but see TRANSGENDERIST for the confusion over these terms). Like *transsexual, transvestite* has been criticized for being a medically applied label; both terms may be problematic because they are still often used interchangeably.

See also CROSS-DRESSER, GENDER AND SEX, OPPOSITE SEX, TRANSVESTITE.

transvestite. A person who engages in cross-dressing, wearing clothes suitable to the gender role of the other sex. The goal, especially for male transvestites, may be to achieve some sort of erotic arousal from the clothes (the sometimes objectionable psychological concept applied is that of a "fetish" or "obsession" with the garments). Other transvestites, however, are motivated to cross-dress because passing in public as the opposite gender helps to free them from the pressures of acting out the roles of the gender they seek to escape through cross-dressing. Many claim simply that it brings out another side of themselves, allowing them to express another gender. However, *cross-dresser* is often the term preferred in the transgender communities, *transvestite* apparently carrying too heavy a load of psychological and medical pathologizing.

The term *transvestite* comes ultimately from the Latin *trans* (across), plus *vestire* (to clothe) and dates to 1910, coined by the German sexologist Magnus Hirschfeld and used in his book *Die Transvestiten.* However, the verb *transvest* appeared in the seventeenth century, applied in the theatrical sense of dressing oneself in other garments, including those of the other sex. Sexologist Havelock Ellis expressed dissatisfaction with the term because it focused on clothing to the neglect of the "feminine" identity aspect of male cross-dressing.

Transvestite is most often applied to men, specifically those who sometimes dress and behave as women, thus "passing" as feminine. In our culture men have traditionally had fewer options for dressing like the other gender than have women, especially in recent decades, and parents have shown more concern for boys acting feminine than girls carrying on as "tomboys." However, there are female transvestites, a category that is seldom heard about and apparently excluded from much of the discourse about transvestitism. Another reason, then, that the term *transvestite* is sometimes regarded as objectionable is because it is so often used only to describe males.

The transvestite is not to be confused with a homosexual; the term does not imply sexual orientation, although most transvestites are heterosexual. Neither is the transvestite a transsexual, that is, someone who has had or desires surgical or hormonal treatment, or both, in order to be as physiologically consistent with his or her gender role identity as possible.

See also BERDACHE, CROSS-DRESSER, DRAG, GENDER AND SEX, INVERSION, KNOBBER, OPPOSITE SEX, QUEEN, SHE-MALE, TRANSGENDERIST, TRANSSEXUAL.

trash. A woman regarded as promiscuous and sexually available. Spears (1991) says she is considered "worse than a tramp." From this female sense, dating to the seventeenth century, comes the mid-twentieth-century gay use for a gay man regarded as sexually free.

The word carries strong connotations of low social class, which (especially as *poor white trash*) stigmatizes people for being poor and short on moral standards. A related classist expression also linked with women is *trailer (park) trash.* "Spurlock's defenders won't get to portray these women as trailer trash, emotionally disturbed or sluts to undermine

their credibility" (regarding a judge facing sexual charges, *Chicago Sun-Times,* 31 December 1998, 33).

See also CHIPPY, COOZIE, DIRTY GERTIE, EASY LAY, FLOOZY, HARLOT, HAT, HIDE, HOOZIE, HUMP, JOB, LOOSE, MATTRESSBACK, MINK, MINX, PROMISCUOUS, PROSTITUTE, PUNCHBOARD, SLATTERN, SLUT, STRUMPET, TART, TROLLOP, WHORE.

trick. Slang applied by prostitutes to their customers or to the sexual transaction. In prison talk, it is a woman's slur on a man who is willing to send her money or gifts. Among gay men, it is any casual sex partner. Heterosexual men, too, use the term for women regarded as easy to pick up and "bed" (see also EASY LAY). Holder (1996) says the word does not derive from the use of deception (trickery) so much as "from the limited turn of duty" (originally, *trick* referred to the time allotted a sailor on duty at the helm).

See also JOHN, TRADE.

troll. From Old Norse *troll*, meaning giant or demon—usually depicted as a monster who lurks in caves—a slang term for a man regarded as hideously ugly. It is one of the few words reserved for men that stresses unattractive appearance, but it is seldom used (among heterosexuals), and when it is, it may be intended as facetious (see LOOKSISM). In the gay male community, however, it is an ageist expression for the kind of gay man no young gay male wants to turn out to be: the so-called predatory, older homosexual who is usually alone but cruises the bars for partners.

trollop. A woman seen as vulgar, immoral, or sexually promiscuous; a prostitute. This word appears to be related to *troll,* meaning "to lure or hook (see also HOOKER) a fish" (the Old French *troller* meant to hunt for game without purpose) and akin to German *trulle* (prostitute). *Trollop* has been in use since the seventeenth century, when it meant a slovenly woman, or slattern, thus adding to the words that deride women as immoral because of their association with dirt or untidiness. "Harlot. Hooker. Trollop.... These words evoke either nervous laughter or serious social condemnation—but always images of the 'bad' woman" (Phaye Poliakoff, in Alexander 1984, 143).

See also CHIPPY, COOZIE, DIRTY GERTIE, EASY LAY, FLOOZY, HARLOT, HAT, HIDE, HOOZIE, HUMP, JOB, LOOSE, MATTRESSBACK, MINK, MINX, NYMPH, PROMISCUOUS, PROSTITUTE, PUNCHBOARD, SADIE TOMPSON, SLAG, SLATTERN, SLUT, TART, WENCH, WHORE.

tuna. A woman believed to be promiscuous, a prostitute, or a woman generally considered as a sex object. The reference is to a woman as meat and as smelly (influenced by the idea of the odor of a woman's genitals). Sutton (1995) reports this sense in use among California Asian male students; while in Hawaii, female Euroamericans apply it to a girl considered ugly (292). The notion of there being a fishy odor to women's genitals is reflected in particular in African American slang.

See also FISH, LOOSE, MEAT, PROMISCUOUS, PROSTITUTE.

turbobitch. See BITCH.

turd burglar. See FUDGEPACKER.

tutti-frutti, tootie-fruitie. From the name of the ice cream or confection that contains pieces of chopped or candied fruits (*tutti frutti* is Italian, meaning all fruits), an expression meaning an effeminate or gay man. It is a play on the derogatory use of the word *fruit* to mean a gay man.

See also EFFEMINATE, FRUIT.

twat. Used since the seventeenth century for the vulva. This slang word also came to be applied to a woman regarded as a sex object.

See also ASS, BEAVER, CUNT, HIDE, PIECE, PUSS.

twink; twinkie. *Twink,* a word used for someone regarded as socially odd or DEVIANT, such as, among some heterosexuals, a gay person. *Twinkie* is probably more often intended for a young woman seen as flaky (see also SPACE GIRL). In gay communities *twinkie* refers, with mild disparagement, to a young gay man, usually one who is superficial and nonpolitical, whose main concern is pop culture.

The suggested origins are interesting if uncertain. Chapman (1987) links the term to Twinkies, trade name for a kind of a pastry with a sweet cream filling; to the nubile *Tinker Bell,* name of the unseen female fairy in James Barrie's play *Peter Pan;* to the idea of twinkling stars; and to *twinkle-toes,* applied to a dainty, mincing person (see MINCE). *Twinkie* has also had some use in gay communities for an attractive straight man.

See also FAIRY, TINKER BELL

twinkle-toes. See FAIRY, TWINK.

twisted; twisty. Slang terms, from at least the mid-twentieth century, referring to someone regarded as sexually perverted.

See also DEVIANT, HOMOSEXUALITY AS DISEASE, INVERSION, PERVERT, SICK, SINFUL, STRAIGHT.

two-bagger. See BAG.

U

udder. See COW.

Uncle Mom. A term for a woman, patterned after *Uncle Tom* (a slur for a subservient black man), connoting servility and docility. In particular, she may be seen as overly accommodating to patriarchal expectations. "Cropped-down Afros are to Uncle Tom what skirts are to Uncle Mom" (Robert Baker, in Vetterling-Braggin 1981, 170).

See also AUNT TOM, MOM, UNCLE TOM.

Uncle Tom. From the 1852 novel *Uncle Tom's Cabin*, by Harriet Beecher Stowe, an African American ingroup slur for a black man viewed as subservient to white people. Used in this sense since the 1940s, and especially popular among African Americans in the 1960s for those black people who continued to call themselves Negroes, the label also came to be applied to any obsequious member of a subordinate group. Thus, in gay communities it is heard as a slur on a gay man believed to have sold out to heterosexual society.

See also CLOSET.

undamaged goods. See DAMAGED GOODS, VIRGIN.

undercover fag. See CLOSET (closet case).

unmentionable vice. See SODOMY.

unnatural. A euphemism meaning homosexuality or sodomy, often regarded as inaccurate, prejudiced, and offensive. The term is heard particularly in such legal expressions as *unnatural crime* or *unnatural practice*. The implication is that the heterosexual orientation is natural, that is, a fixed part of nature, while other sexual orientations are seen as existing outside that acceptable domain.

Philosophers and churches have often condemned homosexuality for being "unnatural" because it is a nonprocreative activity, though probably the majority of marriages involve sexual activity, such as kissing or intercourse with contraception, that is also not procreative. If *natural* refers to something all-embracing, then it would be difficult to exclude homosexuality, especially when it is as widespread across cultures as it is. Dynes (1990) argues that "only things that do not exist at all, such as centaurs and phlogiston, would be unnatural."

"Why should any of us [gay men] hide? What we do is natural, if not 'normal,' whatever that is" (Gore Vidal, *The City and the Pillar,* [1948] 1965, 90).

See also DEVIANT, NORMAL, PERVERT, SODOMY.

unt-cay. See CUNT.

uppity. See GENDER-SPECIFIC ADJECTIVES.

uptight. See PRUDE.

V

vamp; **vampire**. *Vamp,* from the eighteenth-century word *vampire*, and once applied to persons of either sex seen as having predatory or vile ways. It appeared in English by 1910 in reference to a woman believed to use her charms to seduce and then exploit or ruin a man. Invested with exoticism and danger, the gender-specific *vamp* and the type of woman it designates were popularized and symbolized by silent movie star Theda Bara in the 1914 movie *A Fool There Was,* based on Rudyard Kipling's poem "The Vampire," and then by Pola Negri in *Passion,* a 1919 German film.

Vampire, usually meaning the revived dead who suck the blood of the living, has also been used in the sense of "a seductive female." Referring to men's dread of women (of female genitals specifically), psychologist Karen Horney wrote of a man's striving to objectify his dread: "'It is not,' he says, 'that I dread her; it is that she herself is malignant, capable of any crime, a beast of prey, a vampire'" (quoted in Hays 1964, 53).

Some psychologists have referred to the behavior of little girls, such as smiling back at their fathers when being held, cuddling with them, or sitting in their laps—believed to be more common among girls than boys—as "vamping." It may also be called "flirtatiousness, although the father's own behavior when cuddling with his daughter is never labeled as seductive or eliciting the flirtatiousness" (Miriam Ehrenberg, in *Women's Issues,* vol. 1, 1997, 314). Such logic assumes that inappropriately aggressive sexual behavior (even if indicated merely by little girls' displays of affection) is innate in women and implies that all men are at risk of being deviously seduced by all women, even fathers by their daughters. Such logic has been used to excuse and justify incest and rape.

Rodgers (1972) lists *vampire* as a gay male usage meaning an older gay man who preys on younger ones. See CHICKEN (chickenhawk).

See also BAT, BOX (Pandora's box), FALLEN WOMAN, FEMME FATALE, LOLITA, MANEATER, SEDUCTRESS, SHE-DEVIL, SIREN, TEMPTRESS, WITCH.

van dyke. See DYKE.

vanilla. See STRAIGHT.

vegetable. Regarded as soft, passive, and dull, a word used as a metaphor comparing plants with women, employed to convey disdain. Women have condescendingly been referred to as "tomatoes," "potatoes," and "pumpkins" (the last, because of size and shape, is also used for women's breasts). In gay camp language, *vegetable* is also applied to a lesbian in the same way that *fruit* is used for a gay man (see also DISH, FRUIT, POTATO, TOMATO).

Vegetable is also used for a person lacking in acceptable levels of intelligence or responses. In this sense, it is synonymous with the almost always offensive *retard.*

velcro. A fastener comprising a piece of fabric that adheres to another, similar piece of fabric. Dating from the 1980s, the term also came to be used for lesbians: two female pubic areas pressed together are thought to resemble the Velcro fastener. The term reduces women to a sexual practice. *Velcro* also sometimes refers to the hair texture of African Americans and may be used with intent to offend.

See also LESBIAN.

venereal; **Venus**. See GODDESS.

victim. Someone who suffers as a result of social or political forces beyond his or her control or from events or actions of other people, though one can also be a victim of one's own actions. In common usage today, the word refers to someone who suffers prejudice and discrimination or oppression.

Victim is useful in pointing out the

effects of socioeconomic and political systems and as a way to express anger over oppressive practices. Thus, African Americans who wish to borrow money and are denied loans by dint of racism are victimized by bank and mortgage company practices known as redlining; Jews have been victims of assaults by neo-Nazis; and women are victimized by glass ceilings and sexual harassment.

Some social critics, however, especially on the political right, are exasperated over the word's implications, especially the promotion of minority claims against the dominant group for its alleged victimizing actions. Definitions of who are victims, and of what, vary with the social theory or political perspective of the observer. What's more, claiming that actions or conditions have created victims can affect the perception that victimhood has occurred and promote identification with it. For example, whether people with lung cancer from smoking are victims of their self-imposed addiction or of corporate campaigns to promote smoking has been debated.

Some have argued that the concept of victimization can become a double-edged sword that carves out a self-defeating system of claims and counterclaims. Victims are those who define themselves as such—and they can be anybody who feels injured or excluded. Not just women, homosexuals, and ethnic minorities but also white supremacists and other bigots can claim to be victims (see ANGRY WHITE MALE). Other social observers, however, suspect that attempts to contest the word and its definitions only detract from focusing on the problems of minorities who are *in fact* victimized and hurt by historical and current pervasive prejudice and discrimination.

Although it has been identified as a useful term that directs our attention to inegalitarianism, exclusion, and oppression, *victim* is often not prescribed be-

cause it implies weakness and passivity and may suggest that the group one belongs to is characterized by some kind of problem or pathology. The view of women as victims of rape and sexual harassment, for instance, may imply a sexist Victorian notion that women need protection because of some "natural" weakness (many women may occupy politically and economically vulnerable positions in society, but women as a whole are not morally, intellectually, or even necessarily physically weaker than men).

Survivor is frequently used by feminists for women who have had to deal with male abuse or rape; it is also used to designate individuals who have been tortured by totalitarian regimes for their political beliefs. *Survivor* is often preferred because it connotes toughness and courage, though it does obscure what may have been a brutal, victimizing experience.

Victimhood also fails to stress the personal worth of an individual, and the usage is commonly avoided today; rather than *AIDS victim, person living with AIDS* is preferred (see AIDS).

Although *victim* may itself be a victim of today's climate of linguistic sensitivities, it is still found in such expressions as *child-abuse victims, crash victims,* and *victims' rights group.*

See also OPPRESSION.

violet. A term that, when directed at a man, is considered disparaging, suggesting weakness and effeminacy or homosexuality as undesirable characteristics. "Oh swift, what are you two guys, a couple of violets?" (sailor addressing Frank McHugh and James Cagney when McHugh blows a kiss to naval officer Cagney, from 1934 movie *Here Comes the Navy).*

See also BUTTERCUP, DAFFODIL, DAISY, EFFEMINATE, FLOWER, GLADIOLA, LAVENDER, LILY, PANSY, SHRINKING VIOLET.

virago. A reference to a woman regarded

as scolding or domineering. In the fourteenth century, *virago* meant a woman as a heroic figure or woman warrior. Its derivation from the Latin *vir* (man) suggests a woman who is "manlike"; however, since women, traditionally, were not supposed to be heroic or warlike, manliness may be disturbing when seen in a woman (see also AMAZON).

As a term connoting male strength and courage, *virago* was sometimes used also for men, but the link with women grew too strong and too negative to be popularly applied to men. As the word became female-specific, it also became more derogatory.

> When [scholars]…are bound by the necessity for accuracy or logic to include a woman's *name* in the unfolding of a national event, her name is invariably coupled with a belittling adjective.… Thus all outstanding women become in the history books "viragos" (Boadicea), "hussies" (Matilda of Flanders), "hysterics" (Joan of Arc), "monstrosities" (Tomyris), or merely myths (Martia and Pope Joan). (Elizabeth Gould Davis 1971, 270–71)

Some feminists have made a serious but not generally successful attempt to reclaim the word.

See also BALLBREAKER, CASTRATING, HARPY, HARRIDAN, NAG, SCOLD, SHE-DEVIL, SHREW.

virgin. A person who has not experienced sexual intercourse. Although a man today may be called a virgin, the word originally and still usually implies a woman. *Virgin* comes from the Latin *virgo* (young woman), entering English in the twelfth century, often to refer to the Virgin Mary.

In ancient Greece, however, an unmarried woman who had the freedom to mate with whomever she pleased was a virgin. Modesty and chastity—virtues imposed on women by many religious codes and institutions (the words are reserved mostly for women)—were not characteristic of the ancient Greek goddesses. Artemis, the divine huntress, cherished her virginity as a sign of her self-sufficiency and freedom from being possessed by a man.

Because of Christian influence, from at least the fifth century Common Era (about the same time that monasticism became popular), we have come to take *virgin* to mean a chaste woman, one not yet "deflowered." The early Christian church, with its adoption of the Neoplatonic doctrine of the opposition between spirit and flesh, had made woman, the embodiment of the flesh, anathema. Symbol of innocence and undeveloped possibilities, the virgin, with the asexual angel, was believed to be the only kind of woman worthy of God's grace—and man's love. But this Western sense of virginity is by no means universal today. Some cultures see virginity as a matter of a married woman not having children, while others take virginity as signifying an unmarried woman. Still others, such as some traditional Polynesian societies, where sexual play is allowed virtually from infancy, might not find any reason to prescribe it at all.

Virgin typically defines a woman in relation to men. Speaking of men's interest in virginity, de Beauvoir ([1952] 1974) wrote, "What he [a man] alone is to take and to penetrate seems to be in truth created by him" (174). For much of Western history, the virgin—or at least her condition—was highly valued. A virgin slave, for instance, commanded a higher price at the slave market, and the dower was known as "the price of virginity." As a marketable commodity, the virgin became known as "unspoiled goods." The protection of girls' virginity, undertaken vigilantly, was elaborated into an institution.

Today, as women have become more independent, virginity is downplayed, especially compared with its role in Victorian America, but it remains an idea that carries significance for many men and women. Brumberg (1997, 141) tells of an adolescent girl who in 1993, experiencing social pressures to indulge in early sexual activity, wrote to a national columnist asking, "Why isn't there a virgin support group?"

Anatomically, the virgin is a woman viewed as having preserved the thin fold of skin at the opening of the vagina, called the hymen, or (at one time) metaphorically, the "maidenhead" or "virgin knot." (In classical mythology, Hymen was the god of marriage.) Although in some cultures its presence is viewed as a sign that a young woman is a virgin, the hymen in fact can easily be broken by means other than sexual intercourse.

The term *defloration,* still used today but having a Victorian ring to it, means the act of "deflowering" a woman, or rupturing the hymen. A woman, thought of as playing the passive role, is deflowered by a man. She *loses* her virginity, while the man, expected to play the active role vis-à-vis the woman, *takes away* her virginity. We still talk of a woman losing her virginity, or "virtue," as though she has been deprived. Many writers and feminists prefer "had sexual intercourse for the first time."

The term *virginity* is also not as straightforward as it may seem. Maggio (1991) says it is heterosexist, euphemistic, and impractical. Technically, by definition, a person who has experienced oral or anal sexual activity, but not genital penetration, is a virgin. Also, there are such problems as not being able to use the same definitions for male virginity (there is no physical indication of virginity in men) or that of lesbians. Maggio asks, "How virginal is a practicing lesbian with an intact hymen?"

Women may be condemned for their sexual status, whatever it is. A woman who has premarital sex may be derided as loose or even a whore, while a virgin may be accused of being uptight (see PRUDE) and puritanical about her sexuality. Expressions for women believed to be cherishing their virginity, such as *saving it, sitting on it,* or *planning to take it to Heaven with her,* reflect men's disparagement of a woman considered "stingy with her charms" (Aman 1987, 17). A related term, *undamaged goods*—meaning property that has not yet been touched—is extremely objectifying (see DAMAGED GOODS).

From a feminist point of view, virginity might be regarded positively as the original integrity of a woman, free of patriarchal restrictions. She belongs to herself, not to a man. Chesler (1989) gives a matriarchal turn to the story of the Catholic Virgin birth: it represents the special, "miraculous" ability of women to conceive and bear children, an ability independent of men. Others, however, would point out that the Virgin Mother is defined in her relation to her divine Son.

See also CHERRY, FRUIT (unripe), GENDER-SPECIFIC ADJECTIVES (chaste), MADONNA, MAIDEN, MISS, NUN, PRUDE, SPINSTER, SNOW WHITE, STRAIGHT (straight as a virgin).

virile. A word describing the qualities believed to make a man masculine: energy, sexual vigor, masterfulness, and forcefulness. The Latin *vir* (man), is the source of the words *virtuous* and *virile.*

Our language has no exact female equivalent, although obviously a woman, too, may be energetic, vigorous, forceful, and strong.

See also MAN, STUD.

vivacious. See GENDER-SPECIFIC ADJECTIVES.

vixen. A female animal metaphor for a woman, from the Old English *fyxe,* feminine of *fox.* Since the sixteenth century the term has meant a shrewish woman (Shakespeare, in *A Midsummer Night's Dream,* wrote, "O when she's angry, she is keene and shrewd, she was a vixen when she went to schoole").

The fox is an animal that preys on farm animals and fowl. The vixen is thus a female animal that trespasses on human property to take what belongs to humans. A vixen may also be a formidable animal when protecting her cubs. Like the dread-inspiring or threatening intruder that the vixen is, a woman may also be perceived as threatening a man's security, furtively intruding into his domain and "outfoxing" him (Dunayer 1995, 15).

But however aggressive or off-putting she may be considered to be, she can also be regarded as sexy. For example, actress Heather Locklear, of television's *Melrose Place,* has been known in TV publicity as "Melrose vixen, Amanda," and Monica Lewinsky, the young woman alleged in 1998 to have had an affair with President Clinton, was described by an informant in the *Globe* (17 February 1998) as being a "sultry temptress," a "vixen." Men's fear and resentment are expressed in these descriptions, while women, too, may be afraid or resentful of women they perceive as vixens.

See also BOX (Pandora's box), FEMME FATALE, FOX, LOLITA, MANEATER, SEDUCTRESS, SHE-DEVIL, SIREN, TEMPTRESS, VAMP, WOMEN AS STORMS. Compare also with the male-specific WOLF.

voyeur. See EXHIBITIONIST, PEEPING TOM.

W

walk-up fuck. See EASY LAY.

wallflower. A person too shy, homely, or unliked by others to be chosen in social activities, such as at a dance. The term usually suggests a woman being ignored by men; the image is of passivity and inertness.

> Wallflower, wallflower
> Won't you dance with me?
> I'm sad and lonely too.
> Wallflower, wallflower
> Won't you dance with me?
> I'm fallin' in love with you.
> —Bob Dylan, "Wallflower,"
> 1971, 1976, Ram's Horn Music
> (www.aiconnect.com, February
> 2000)

See also FLOWER, SHRINKING VIOLET.

wanna-be-raped look. A reference to the kinds of clothing—for example, revealing or skintight—that a woman may wear that is used as an excuse by men who rape or harass her. The blame for rape is thus deflected from the man to the woman. *Wanna-be* is based on "want to be." This is a student usage, late twentieth century (Spears 1991).

See also RAPE.

warden. A man's wife, seen as imprisoning him. Twentieth-century demeaning slang.

See also BALL AND CHAIN.

warhorse. See BATTLE-AX, HORSE.

warlock. See WITCH.

weaker vessel; softer sex; weaker sex. Expressions dating to a few centuries ago that represent the view that women's supposedly inferior character is biologically determined. Their purpose is to deny and disguise as well as prohibit the development of women's physical and mental skills and accomplishments. They define man as the norm (strong) and woman as the "other" (weak).

Fraser (1985) notes that *the weaker vessel*, meaning women, originated with William Tyndale's translation of the New Testament into English in 1526. St. Peter, founding his comments on those of St. Paul, encouraged husbands to give "honour unto the wife, as unto the weaker vessel" (1). Shakespeare later told us, "Frailty, thy name is woman." During the seventeenth century, "phrases like 'the softer sex'—used by John Locke, for example—and 'the fair sex' hung delicately like perfume in the air" (4).

Women have been considered soft physically, emotionally, and intellectually; the female brain was once characterized as soft relative to men's. When women are portrayed as physically and mentally soft or weak, they are also believed to be in need of protection.

> On the excuse of protecting the weaker sex, they (men) placed woman under male tutelage; henceforward she must serve her father's or husband's domestic needs as though not only spiritually but mentally inferior to him. (Robert Graves, *Mammon and the Black Goddess,* 1965, 104)

The linguistic and cultural stress on women's supposed weakness not only denies women's abilities and feats but also denies and disguises women's capacity for aggression (Pearson 1997). Violence is considered to be the province of men, buttressing their power over others. The myth of the gentler sex causes us to ignore such phenomena as women's abuse of children, their assaults on husbands (see WIFE [wife abuse]), and the rising rates in crime by women, when most crime statistics are dropping (see CRIMINALS). However, while many women are capable of overt acts of aggression, cultural roles often constrain them, leaving them to express aggression in less direct ways than are allowed for men, including turning it against themselves.

See also FAIR SEX, FLUFF, FRAIL, GENDER AND SEX.

weak sister. See SISTER.

wear the pants. See PANTS.

weekend ho. See HO.

welfare mother. An epithet that stereotypes a woman receiving welfare money (living off the "dole") as lazy, dependent, sexually promiscuous, and fertile; one who cheats on the system, perhaps even in possession of a "welfare Cadillac"; often a black woman or other woman of color and a single parent. She may also be known as a "welfare queen" (see also QUEEN). The male version may be called a "welfare pimp" (see also PIMP).

The welfare mother may be perceived as lacking in initiative, character, and other so-called core American virtues. Some writers substitute *welfare client* or *welfare recipient* (which is more often used for men than for women), seeing it as less loaded with prejudice than *welfare mother*. Major (1994) says that in black usage, the meaning of *welfare mother* shifts to a black woman who dresses in cheap, tacky clothes.

See also MOTHER, SINGLE MOTHER.

wench. From the Old English *wencel* (by the thirteenth century), a child of either sex; later as *wenche*, a young woman or girl, but especially one of low birth or rustic background. By the late fourteenth century, a female servant or a lewd woman or prostitute (see also SLATTERN for a link between female domestics and sexuality).

Today *wench* is usually considered offensive and may be used by men to suggest the subordinate status of women and to deny their abilities. "When monkeys and serving wenches begin to write, can the Eumenides [Furies] be far behind?" These are the words of F. Scott Fitzgerald about his wife Zelda, whose writing he resented (in Chesler 1989, 9).

In the United States the term was commonly applied historically to female slaves and mulattas. "In overt contempt for slaves, the masters used *buck* and

wench till they became trade terms, like *filly* and *shoat*" (J. C. Furnas, *Goodbye to Uncle Tom,* 1956, 120). In black usage today, the word may be ironical, and it is also used in jest or mockery in some contexts, such as in *Wayne's World* humor.

Buxom wench is still sometimes heard for a shapely woman, in particular, one with large breasts and perhaps who is also full-figured. A man who is said "to wench" is one who womanizes or sleeps around.

See also CHIPPY, COOZIE, DIRTY GERTIE, EASY LAY, FLOOZY, HARLOT, LOOSE, MATTRESSBACK, MINK, MINX, NYMPH, PROMISCUOUS, PROSTITUTE, SADIE THOMPSON, SCARLET WOMAN, SKEEZER, SLATTERN, SLUT, STRUMPET, TART, TRAMP, TROLLOP, WHORE.

wet smack. See FRIGID.

whisker. Referring to female pubic hair, an epithet for a woman viewed by men as a sex object, a prostitute, or any woman of allegedly loose morals (Wentworth and Flexner 1975).

See also BEARD, BEAVER, BUSH, CAT, HAIR, MINK, PUSS, WOOL.

whiteboy. See BOY.

whore. A harlot or promiscuous person, almost always a woman, from Old English *hōre* (prostitute), and related to certain Germanic words meaning one who desires or adulteress or adulterer. Outside its many Germanic cognates, *whore* can be traced to the Latin *cārus* (beloved), and is also the source of our modern *cherish* and *charity.*

Whore has been in use since the twelfth century to mean a prostitute or promiscuous woman. Besides carrying sexist implications, the word today also resonates with classist images of cheap or tacky settings and educationally backward women: "You're a low-life trailer park whore" (white female prostitute to another white prostitute on TV talk show *Jerry Springer,* 31 October 1997). "You can lead a horticulture, but you can't make her think" (Dorothy Parker, in John Keats, *You Might as Well Live*, 1970, 46). Racial images may also come into play (see, e.g., JEZEBEL).

There are other negative uses of the word, but they tend to derive from the original sense of a promiscuous woman or at least are reinforced by it. For example, *whore* may be used for a male prostitute or any person regarded as venal or corrupt (Risch [1987] found it in use among female college students as a "dirty word" referring to men). The verb *to whore* means to have sexual relations with prostitutes or to associate with them, to seek numerous sexual encounters in general, to accept payment for sexual relations, or to compromise one's principles for profit.

Whoremaster (also *whoremonger*), seldom used anymore, refers to a man who associates with prostitutes, pays to have sexual relations with them, or pimps for them. *Forty-four*, which rhymes with *whore*, means a prostitute, while *whore-chaser* refers to a man seen as habitually seeking prostitutes or other women for sexual encounters.

Gay men, referring to other gay men, may use the term *whores* loosely in barroom talk; it may be offensive or intimate, depending on the context. *Whoreson*, meaning the bastard son of a woman regarded as a whore (or any contemptible man), impugns the mother as much as the son (see also BASTARD).

Even the most pejorative monikers can be worn as badges by some people.

> They're whores, and that's not a term of abuse. It's a good honest biblical word for an honourable profession of ancient lineage. They make love with men for a living.... Any woman worthy of the name would do the same if her children were hungry. (Allegra Taylor, *Prostitution*, 1991, in Stibbs 1992)

Writing of women's involvement in computer games, Cassell and Jenkins (1998) note that organizations of female gamers have embraced an ethos of empowerment through competing with men in an area that is typically male turf. One such group of gamers call themselves "Crack Whores" (32). In politics, *whore* may be used endearingly by one politician for another politician who has wealthy supporters.

See also CHIPPY, COOZIE, DIRTY GERTIE, EASY LAY, FLOOZY, HARLOT, HE-WHORE, HO, HOOZIE, HUSTLER, LOOSE, MATTRESSBACK, MINK, MINX, NYMPH, PROMISCUOUS, PROSTITUTE, PUNCHBOARD, SADIE THOMPSON, SCARLET WOMAN, SKEEZER, SLAG, SLATTERN, SLUT, STRUMPET, TART, TRAMP, TROLLOP, WENCH.

whoreson. See BASTARD, WHORE.

wicked witch of the west. A woman regarded as a "bitch," that is, she is considered temperamental, uncontrollable, and evil—characteristics that make her unattractive and usually untouchable to men, who may resent her autonomy.

See also BITCH, WITCH.

widow; widower. *Widow*, a woman whose husband has died and who has not remarried. *Widow* comes ultimately from the Latin *-videre* (to separate), which is related to the Sanskrit *vidhavā*, void. The etymology suggests the loneliness and meaninglessness the widow was once expected to feel without a husband. To some women the word may still have these connotations, which are resented. "*Widow*...means 'empty.' I resent what the term has come to mean. I am alive. I am part of the world" (Lynn Caine, in Kramarae and Treichler 1985).

Widower, a man who has lost his wife, is a term formed by adding the *-er* suffix to *widow*. It is one of the few words for a man that derived from the corresponding term for a woman. This suggests the greater social and economic significance of marriage to a woman relative to a man. Also reflecting our concern for women without husbands are other differences between the two terms in form and use. For example, unlike *widower*, *widow* appears in a number of compound words or phrases. These include *widowhood, widow's walk*, and *widow's peak* (an old superstition had it that a woman with such a hairline was doomed to an early widowhood, thus, she was to be avoided as a wife). Although *widowerhood* (or *widowership*) may occasionally be heard, that is about the extent of the compounding. Also, *widow* may be used as a verb, whereas *widower* is always a noun.

The term *widow* has other meanings, too, but all suggest undesirable isolation. In print production, for instance, a "widow" is a line that is left over because it doesn't fit on the page; it has to be carried over to the top of the next column or page. In cards, similarly, a "widow" is an extra hand or part thereof dealt face down—thus separated from the other cards—and used by the highest bidder.

Although a woman might be widowed at an early age, the term often connotes an older woman, someone in a socially weak position and nonintimidating to men. Although the rules have changed now, in some traditions she was blamed (especially by men) for remarrying, supposedly neglecting loyalty to her husband's memory in favor of her own happiness. Widowers felt no such social pressures.

> The networks only seemed willing to support single-women shows when the heroines were confined to the home in nonthreatening roles in a strictly all-female world—like the elderly widows in (the TV sitcom) *The Golden Girls*. (Faludi 1991, 159)

When she does express an interest in remarrying, a widow has sometimes been disparaged as a "mantrap" (see also MANEATER).

Grass widow and *grass widower* overlap in meaning, both referring to a divorced or separated person or someone whose spouse is away for a while. However, *grass widow* sees more use and has some negative senses not shared by the male form: a woman who has had an illegitimate child or is a discarded mistress. The *grass* in *grass widow* alludes to hay; as the story goes, the farmer's daughter "marries" (has sex with) her boyfriend in the hay, so to speak, but is just as quickly "widowed" when he finds out that she is pregnant.

Evoking the image of woman-as-evil, *black widow* refers to a women who pairs up with or marries a man so she can get his money when he dies—which she hopes will be soon. The expression comes from the common usage for a type of venomous spider, the female of which is known to devour its mate (see also MANEATER, VAMP).

Widow is often used colloquially today for a woman whose husband spends a great deal of time away from home to engage in his work or other activities.

See also HUSBAND, SINGLE, WIFE.

wife. A female spouse, from Old English *wīf* (adult female). The term has had various meanings over the centuries. These include the often derogatory ones of a woman of low social standing, a mistress (in the sense of a kept woman), a middle-aged or elderly woman, the senior prostitute of a pimp, a leg shackle (prison slang; see also BALL AND CHAIN), and a "passive" gay man (gay slang; see also PASSIVE).

Wife and *husband* are not parallel words, nor are the roles they designate ones of equivalency or equity. Linguistically, so to speak, the man often walks ahead of the woman; for example, we say *husband and wife*, just as we honor men first in *brother and sister* and *son and daughter* (see also MAN [man and wife]). It was also once standard practice, and is still found today, to refer to a man by his name and the woman as "his wife" (a man may also refer to *"the* wife," but the woman seldom reciprocates with *"the* husband").

Expressions such as *faculty wives* and *Thou shalt not covet thy neighbor's wife* also imply the man as the norm. Supposedly the man is the more important member of the "partnership," while what is important for the woman is her marital status. The woman is not recognized as an individual, nor is her role valued as highly as that of the traditional husband. There are also strong hints of subordination in *wife* when it refers to a female prostitute who works for a pimp or a "passive" partner in a homosexual relationship. With the expression *wife-swapping*, the suggestion is men's ownership of their wives; there is no comparable expression *husband-swapping.*

Legal authorities, viewing marriage as natural and ordained, once referred to women as "wives" and as such might be complementary to husbands but not equal. Wives were not, for example, allowed to own property. Expressions such as "men and their wives" and "the farmer's wife" connote men's ownership of their wives. Also, in the latter case, the woman herself is not acknowledged as a farmer, though in fact she may participate directly in farm life.

Things are improving, however. As a result of *Frontiero v. Richardson,* in which a female physical therapist in the Air Force filed a lawsuit alleging sex discrimination, the Department of Defense altered its policies regarding entitlements to dependents of persons in the service. The Supreme Court ruled that the dependents of women in the armed forces were to receive the same entitlements as those given to dependents of servicemen, causing the Department of Defense to change the words *wife* and *husband* to read *spouse* in pertinent documents (Sherrow 1996).

The commonly heard terms *battered*

wife and *wife abuse* refer to domestic violence, specifically male violence against women. It may be acknowledged that there is some bias in these usages. Since we seldom hear the words *battered husband* or *husband abuse*, the fact that women, too, are sometimes abusive and men victimized in the family (though with less frequency than the reverse) is obscured. The term *domestic violence* itself may imply female victimization, ignoring the male as anything but the abuser, though it also points out the sphere in which violence so often takes place—the home.

There is clearly a strong need for terms that recognize both male and female domestic violence. However, it is frequently argued that unlike husband abuse, wife abuse has historical significance as a way men have of controlling their wives and ensuring their subordination. Indeed, until recently, wife abuse was both legal and socially sanctioned (e.g., "rule of thumb" meant a husband could beat his wife, but not with a stick larger than the thickness of his thumb). Husband abuse was never sanctioned.

In addition, because of women's traditional economic dependence on men and former lack of right to own property or to instigate legal divorce proceedings, they had few or no alternatives but to tolerate abuse. Reports also indicate that women may suffer more serious types of physical abuse than do men and that when women are abusive, it may be out of self-defense (Jean Reight Schroedel and Sharon Spray, *Women's Issues,* vol. 1, 1997, 234). Finally, there are also statistics suggesting a fairly high rate of domestic abuse among gay and lesbian couples.

Among the many traditional colloquialisms that have been applied disparagingly or ironically by husbands for their wives are OLD LADY (see also LADY), HAG, NAG, BALL AND CHAIN, and boss.

See also BAREFOOT AND PREGNANT

(KEEP THEM), FISH (fishwife), FRAU, HOME-
MAKER, HUSBAND, SQUAW, WIDOW.

wiles (feminine). Special artifices women
are often viewed as having for beguil-
ing, deceiving, and trapping men.

See also BOX (Pandora's box), FEMI-
NINE, FEMME FATALE, MANEATER, SEDUC-
TRESS, SIREN, TEMPTRESS.

wimmin, wimyn. A coinage meaning
women. A stab at a phonetic spelling, it
was in jocular use in the early twentieth
century before it was adopted by feminists in the 1970s. Many feminists preferred the term because it lacked the suggestion that *women* stemmed from the
affix *-men* but also because it served to
provoke the reader to think about gender relations and the power of patriarchal society to define women's roles.

However, the *-men* element in the
word *women* does not derive from or
mean men in the sense of the male, nor
is it pronounced the same as *men*. This
objection is minor, however, and hardly
the reason that the word *wimmin* has not
caught on in the general writing community. Its lack of popularity is probably the result of the spelling's link to
what some fear or stereotype as "radicalism" in the women's movement.

See also HERSTORY, WOMANIST,
WOMEN'S LIBERATION, WOMYN.

wimp. A person, traditionally and still usually a male (though increasingly used for
females as well), regarded as weak or
ineffectual. Though he is considered
unmanly, overt homosexuality is not
necessarily implied.

Although possibly from *whimper,* the
term is sometimes also said to derive from
the name of the meek character, Wimpy,
in the "Popeye" comic strip or from *wimp*,
meaning young woman in Cambridge
University slang earlier in the twentieth
century. It is probably also related to, or
reinforced by, such words as *limp, simp*,
and *gimp* (all suggesting some kind of
weakness, and often insulting). *Wimp* first

occurred in its derisive slang sense for a
weak person in 1970s student use.

The usage is often heard among
males, especially in male-dominated institutions, groups, or occupations, such
as soldiering and many sports. In national defense discourse, Cohn (1998)
has pointed out, *wimp* is used as a
gendered pejorative and polarizes human characteristics in terms of male and
female, the former being valued and the
latter, scorned. Wimpishness in this discourse is a female characteristic and derided as such; when applied to individuals, it impugns their masculinity and
weakens their point of view so it does
not have to be taken seriously. "'Those
Krauts are a bunch of limp-dicked
wimps' was the way one U.S. defense
intellectual dismissed the West German
politicians who were concerned about
popular opposition to Euromissile de-
ployments" (227). Cohn illustrates the
consequences of this labeling with the
example of how then President George
Bush's military intervention in Panama
and the Persian Gulf War enabled him
to overcome the "wimp factor."

In an illustration that has frequently
appeared in white supremacist WAR
(White Aryan Resistance) publications,
a white woman is shown bare from the
waist up, toting an automatic rifle. The
captions reads, "My man is a white racist. If yours is a whimp [sic], dump him
and get a real White man and screw the
system" (in Daniels 1997, 60).

Daniels points out the linkage in this
imagery between gender, sexuality, and
race: white women, valued for their
sexual attractiveness, are able to resist
"the system" only by means of having
access to "real" white men. At the same
time, this sexuality is implicitly heterosexual and meant for the pleasure of
white men, while those who are not
white male racists are implicitly rendered not only as nonwhite but also as
weak, perhaps even homosexual.

See also APRON, BABY (crybaby),
CANDY-ASS, CREAMPUFF, EFFEMINATE,
FLOWER, GIRL, LIMP-WRIST, LITTLE LORD
FAUNTLEROY, MAMA'S BOY, MILKSOP,
NANCY, MOLLYCODDLE, NAMBY-PAMBY,
PRISSY, PUSSY-WHIPPED, SISSY, SKIRT, WUSS.

witch. Generally and stereotypically applied to a woman thought to have supernatural powers and to be in service to
the devil or aided by spirits or a familiar. The word's earliest roots, *wicca* (wizard) and *wicce* (witch), have a kinship
with Old English *wigle* (divination), and
perhaps Old High German *wīh* (holy).

The history of this word suggests that
witch once referred to someone who was
a diviner or sage, a beneficent practitioner of the occult arts. The word is also
used for a believer in Wicca, a nature
religion with origins in pre-Christian
Europe that has nothing to do with devil
worship. But the sense of wickedness
remains strong in the term, especially to
many conservative Christian people,
who accept the biblical injunction "Thou
shalt not suffer a witch to live" (Exodus
22:18).

Connotations of evil are reinforced
when we consider that *wicked* has been
traced to the same Indo-European root
(*weik-*) as *wicce,* the Old English word.
The negative implication of women as
supernatural danger is picked up in other
senses of the term: a HAG, a HARPY, or a
woman considered to have bewitching
charms.

In some societies, accusing people of
practicing witchcraft allows for the ver-
balization of suspicions and conflicts,
sometimes leading to their resolution. In
Europe, however, in the sixteenth and
seventeenth centuries, and in colonial
Salem, witchcraft fantasies came to suggest pacts whereby witches enjoyed
sexual intercourse with demons; such
fantasies were given legal standing and
snowballed into mass hysteria (*Dictionary of Anthropology* 1997). Thousands
of people were denounced, tortured, and
executed.

Although many—perhaps the vast
majority—of those accused were
women, suggesting their politically
weak position relative to men, the patterns of accusation and execution were
not always a matter of men against
women. Many men, including Quakers,
homosexuals, the mentally disturbed,
and so-called heretics, were burned at
the stake with women.

In Salem, Massachusetts, in 1692, it
was the accusations of a group of teenage girls that led to convictions of at least
thirty women, some of whom were tortured. Still, it is frequently argued that
when men are accused, it is usually because of certain specific social or economic rivalries or conflicts rather than
men's general position in society (Weitz
1977, 167–68). By contrast, the social
position of women alone often invites
accusations of dangerous magical powers. When women occupy powerless
positions, especially when they lack a
definite social niche related to men, they
and their conduct are open to suspicion.

Society imputes wicked powers to
and victimizes particularly those women
regarded as a threat to the social order.
For example, such women are believed
to be smarter than women are supposed
to be, to reject (or seduce) men and subvert male authority, or to bear grudges
against men or their families. Or they
are old; mentally disturbed; poor; lesbian; single or living alone and nonre-
productive; or practicing forms of pagan worship, healing, or midwifery that
invoke hostility from the religious and
medical establishments.

Such women have been linked with
mystical darkness throughout history:
woman was the Chimera, the Sphinx, the
Isis whose veil mortals feared to lift; we
find her depicted in the story of Pandora,
the Fates, Hecate, the Harpies, Medusa,
the Valkyrie, among other Western

myths. While she may serve a master, Lucifer—in Judeo-Christian tradition, the "Evil One" is masculine—she is able to do so through rebellious free choice. In twentieth-century England and the United States, wicca groups (or covens) of all-female membership appeared, often seeking to affirm feminine spirituality by finding the female divinity within. They practice rites similar to those that grew out of pre-Christian nature religions. These worshipers have tried to reclaim the term *witch*.

In 1997, for example, Rosemary Keefe Curb, a lesbian ex-nun, self-described as a witch, created a controversy as a candidate for a position as a dean at the State University of New York–New Paltz. She wrote in a book she edited, *Lesbian Nuns: Breaking Silence* (1985):

> I've never been initiated into a coven, but I like to call myself a witch because the word carries such patriarchal taboo, and I feel a solidarity with the women who were burned as witches. (in Courtney Leatherman, *The Chronicle of Higher Education*, 30 May 1997, A21)

The term *wicca* is considered a euphemism by many conservative religious people who view witchcraft as immoral. *Witch* is not parallel with either *warlock* or *wizard*. Even though both male and female terms commonly refer to a person who practices the black arts, *witch* is a more common symbol of moral darkness in the popular imagination and, besides connoting deviltry, as does *warlock*, is also used to describe a woman considered mean and cruel (synonymous with BITCH).

In addition, while *witch* may mean an ugly old woman or a seductive woman, *warlock* does not designate a man with these characteristics but in fact may suggest someone of strength, even character. *Wizard* may have altogether different connotations. In L. Frank Baum's novel *The Wizard of Oz*, for in-

stance, the wizard was "mysterious," the witch, "wicked." *Wizard* can also mean a man with control over both magic and wisdom. We speak, for instance, of a man who is a "computer wizard" or "corporate wizard."

See also BAT, BOX (Pandora's box), SHE-DEVIL, STEPMOTHER, VAMP, WICKED WITCH OF THE WEST.

wizard. See WITCH.

wolf; she-wolf. *Wolf,* a carnivorous animal that preys on other animals and an animal metaphor. We are ambivalent about this animal. The wolf is admired for its handsomeness, wildness, strength, and (when not caged) freedom. It has been represented as a helper and protector (it was a female wolf that suckled Romulus and Remus of Roman legend). At the same time, the wolf has been reviled as evil, ravenous, and devouring. Our notions about both women and men have also taken shape in terms of the ambivalent imagery of wolves.

Men are linguistically linked with evil in several wolf expressions. For example, such phrases as *wolf man* (the Hollywood werewolf, as played by Lon Chaney Jr.), *wolf in sheep's clothing*, *lone wolf* (not necessarily evil, but his aloneness may be threatening or seductive), and *big bad wolf*, derived from the story of the evil wolf who devoured Little Red Riding Hood of folklore, convey danger or the morally suspect.

A popular masculine sense of the term, from the early twentieth century, is a sexually aggressive or flirtatious man, one known to "prey" on women (see HUNTER). Part of the womanizer's repertory of seducing behavior is the "wolf whistle," a whistle made to express his sexual admiration for a girl or woman nearby. Also, especially in prison talk, a wolf is a man regarded as an aggressive or promiscuous male or rapist. *Wolf* has also been used to mean a gay man who takes the more "active" role in a relationship (his subordinate sex partners may be referred to as *kids* or *lambs*; see also DADDY, JOCK) and a masculine lesbian.

In folklore and literature, the she-wolf, the supernatural connection between witches and wolves (women during the Inquisition were accused of being lupine shape-shifters) and the werewolf (which may be male as well as female) testify to the use of the wolf image to demonize women. Like SHE-DEVIL and she-demon, *she-wolf* personifies woman as evil. The Italian poet Dante used the idea of the *she-wolf* to symbolize avarice in the *Inferno*.

In more everyday use, *she-wolf* refers to a woman regarded as difficult to get along with, a HARPY. William Herndon, law partner of Abraham Lincoln and severe critic of Lincoln's wife, Mary Todd Lincoln, once wrote of her that she was "a she-wolf" who "woman-whipped and woman-carved" her suffering husband (in *The Life and Writing of Abraham Lincoln*, 1940, 30). Also, the Latin word *lupa*, which means whore, sounds very much like the Latin *lupus*, meaning wolf.

The reclaiming of wolves as metaphors for women's freedom and intuition is seen in such works as Clarissa Pinkola Estés' *Women Who Run with the Wolves*, 1992.

In fairness to wolves, who are maligned in our language and folklore and have been exterminated in so many places, they are not unpredictably vicious or philandering. Unlike the human wolf, the animal generally establishes steadfast monogamous relations (Dunayer 1995, 17).

See also ANIMAL, BITCH (bitch-wolf), CAT, DOG, FOX, TIGER, TOM, WOMEN AS ANIMALS.

woman. From Old English, *wīfman, wif* (woman, wife) plus *man* (human being). *Wifman* became gendered, while *man* represented the standard. With the rise of Middle English, *wifman* became *wimman; wif* lives on in English as *wife*. The vowel sound in *wifman* has been preserved in the pronunciation of *women*. Folk etymologies that derive *woman* from such male-biased explanations as "woe to man" confirm how stereotypes have been attached to the word.

The different, but related, meanings of *woman* over the centuries include an adult female person, a female servant, a mistress (also a kind of servant), a wife (usually informal), a female partner in sexual intercourse, a girlfriend, womankind or womenfolk (women in general), and womanliness. In the nineteenth century, the term even came into slang use for the female pudenda. *Women* also sometimes serves as a reference to lesbians, as in "women's bar," which lesbians would call a "lesbian bar" unless the code word was necessary.

The questions of what a woman is, who is said to possess womanhood, and when a person becomes a woman are answered differently in different cultures. Even within the same culture, the meaning of womanhood can vary by age, class, race, or geographic region. For example, at one time, black women were not perceived as "women" in the same sense as white women were (hooks 1981). In antebellum America, biologists tried to confirm notions that sex differences existed not just between men and women but between, for example, Jewish women and white upper-class Protestant women.

In American culture the term *woman* has been sexualized. At least until fairly recently, *woman* has carried sexual connotations, as in "That's his woman" or "He's a womanizer." It may also imply negative qualities, as in "Vanity, thy name is woman!" As a result, a number of more delicate or sexist expressions—such as *ladies' room, lady of the house*, and *girls' school*—have sometimes been substituted (Nilsen 1998, 401). Feminists, however, who helped give us the more independent, assertive "new woman" of the late nineteenth and early twentieth centuries, have had some success in reclaiming *woman* as a positive, nonsexual term.

There are other problems associated with the use of *woman*. For example, it is commonly used as an adjective to indicate the sex of an occupational or related noun (e.g., "woman dentist"). In using such terms, the speaker seems to tacitly acknowledge the male as the standard. *Fowler's* (1996) noted a decline during the late twentieth century in the use of compounds formed with *-woman*, giving way to genderless equivalent terms. Yet *Fowler's* also points out that many such compounds remain in use, for example, *chairwoman, policewoman, saleswoman*, and *spokeswoman*.

Feminists have noted that women have traditionally been defined in terms of men (Abbott 1996). The definition, it is pointed out, stems from men's control of the production of knowledge and historical dominance in most professions. Women thus become the "other" to men, lacking in male characteristics or virtues and thus, by way of contrast, supply men with a means of defining themselves (i.e., as better, dominant).

In some of the more extreme views in Western intellectual history, women have been depicted as deformed men (Aristotle), "misbegotten males" (Thomas Aquinas), defective men (Sigmund Freud), or even as a frightening caricature of the male. According to many theorists, men have also produced an image of women as subordinate to men, often in order to benefit from women's domestic labor, emotional support, and sexual favors.

The construction of manhood through the idea of female inferiority and subordination is enabled in a number of ways. For example, men may speak of handling a tool "like a woman" or the Army drill sergeant may disparage his

male recruits as "women" to suggest that they lack manhood—the goal and norm of life—until they become soldiers. *Woman* may also refer disparagingly to a gay man. English writer Rudyard Kipling was even more dismissive: "And a woman is only a woman, but a good cigar is a smoke" (from *The Betrothed*, in Stibbs 1992).

Women are also commonly defined as a biologically determined category. Women are assumed to be the childbearers, mothers, and homemakers, often thought of as biologically governed by emotion and lacking in reason, supposedly the true or "natural" domain of men. The rhetoric of "moral motherhood" has appealed not only to men but also to some twentieth-century feminists, not to mention conservative antifeminists, attracted, for different reasons, to the image of an innately nurturing woman.

Many feminists and social scientists today reject the kind of universalism that says that women are as a whole devalued and oppressed in preference to looking at how women are situated in particular times and places.

Definitions that treat women as a single category tend to ignore the diversity of women's experience. Women, it is increasingly being realized, are shaped by such factors as race, class, ethnicity, age, sexual orientation, disability, and the life cycle. Also, differences of power exist among women as well as between men and women: differences between white and black, working and middle class, first and third world (Abbott).

Women-identified-women was apparently coined by a group called the Radicalesbians in the 1970s to refer to women who prefer to relate to other women, emotionally, sexually, or both, than to men. The term may apply to feminist heterosexual women as well as to lesbians.

See also HONEST WOMAN, LADY, LITTLE WOMAN, MAN, MOTHER, OLD WOMAN, SECOND SEX, WIFE, WIMMIN, WOMANIST, WOM-

ANLY, WOMAN'S PLACE IS IN THE HOME, WOMEN AS ANIMALS, WOMEN AS A MINORITY GROUP.

woman-chaser. See SKIRT (skirt-chaser).

woman-hater. See MAN-HATER.

womanish. Resembling a woman (fourteenth century). Unlike *womanly, womanish* is usually somewhat disparaging, referring to characteristics in a woman not generally valued in our society, such as weakness. When applied to a man, which may more often be the case, *womanish* implies effeminate, traits—for example, a manner of walking—that may seem appropriate for women but are socially frowned upon in men (the sexist notion here is that there is something inferior about the trait, belonging as it does to women).

See also EFFEMINATE, WOMAN, WOMANIST, WOMANLY.

womanist. "Like a woman," often used as an adjective but also appearing in noun form. More specifically, the term relates to writer Alice Walker's understanding of a woman who takes her identity from what both her sex and her ethnicity offer. Walker (1984) coined *womanist* to describe a black feminist, defining the term in the preface to her collection of essays, *In Search of Our Mothers' Gardens: Womanist Prose*. It is also applied self-descriptively by other feminists of color, with the intent of avoiding any racism implied in *feminist*, which, when applied to black women, often requires a qualifier, e.g., *black feminist*. Derived from WOMANISH—meaning characteristic of a woman and considered unsuitable for a man (e.g., "womanish tears")—it nevertheless has a very different meaning.

Illustrating women-centered critical thinking, and her departure from white feminist thought, Walker defines the term as "acting grown-up. Being grown-up. Interchangeable with another black folk expression: 'you trying to be grown.' Responsible. In charge. *Serious*" (xi). Walker notes that it is the opposite of *girlish*. Her womanist appreciates and cares for other women regardless of class or race, while she is committed to all people, female *and* male. Walker argues that being womanist is also the means for recovering black women's history and culture, essential to the wholeness of both women and men.

See also FEMINIST, WIMMIN, WOMYN.

womanizer. A man seen as habitually pursuing women to seduce them; in more blunt terms, a lecher.

> Glen Charles, coproducer of *Cheers* (the 1980s TV sitcom)…turned his show's bartender Sam into a chauvinistic womanizer because "he's a spokesman for a large group of people who thought that [the women's movement] was a bunch of bull and look with disdain upon people who don't think it was." (Faludi 1991, 144)

Although typically used to describe men, it may also be a label for a lesbian.

Many men, especially those who tend to objectify or mistreat women, do not view the term as necessarily derogatory; it may even signal their "charm." Others see the womanizer as shallow and offensive, if not dangerous. Carpineto (1989) says that the word suggests that men's use of their inescapable charm is not simply harmless; men are doing something to women, for which these men are responsible (12).

See also CASANOVA, DON JUAN, LADIES' MAN, LECHER, LOTHARIO, LOVER, PLAYBOY, ROMEO, ROUÉ.

womanly. An adjective (thirteenth century) describing those qualities that have traditionally been associated with women as opposed to men (e.g., "woman's intuition"); it also means feminine as opposed to girlish. Regarded by many as an approving term, it may suggest such admirable characteristics as self-possession, modesty, maintenance of personal relations, and motherliness (*Merriam-Webster's Collegiate Dictionary* 1997).

These are, however, largely attributes of women that accord with their historically assigned social roles. As Miller and Swift (1991) have argued, the difference between such words as *manly* (see MAN) and *womanly* is that the former often signifies those traits regarded as valuable for humans in general, whereas "womanly" qualities are those more closely associated with women as females. *Womanlike* may be synonymous but sometimes connotes traits, such as tending to cry, that are not always held in high esteem.

See also FEMININE, WOMAN, WOMANISH.

woman of easy virtue. See EASY LAY.

woman's place is in the home. An old saying conveying a set of attitudes, ways of doing things, restrictions, and responsibilities that traditionalists, antifeminists, and proponents of traditional values believe are proper and even innate to women. Some women may hold the same belief vis-à-vis where women "belong," as long as society can find a place there for men, too. Nonetheless, the expression justifies as "natural" women's role as childbearer, nurturer, and homemaker, while the word *place* suggests exclusion or subservience (as when white racists talk about black men keeping their "place").

Gender theorists claim that by making these roles out to be "natural," Western ideology disguises the realities of subordination and domination that characterize male-female relations. For example, as Rose (1976) argues, women often put a lot of hours into domestic labor, but women are said to do it because it's fitting and natural, they are better at it than men are, and they love doing it.

This view, of course, is consistent with the fact that women's housework is unpaid labor that, many sociologists

argue, benefits capitalists as well as husbands. Yet while benefiting from it economically, society also tends to look down on women's domestic roles, often viewed, for example, as less engaging, challenging, or romantic than many traditional male roles. Male anthropologist Elman Service once explained that he titled his book about small-scale band societies *The Hunters* because it sounded more interesting than "Woman's Work" (Nelson 1997, 32)

The paternalism of the view was articulated by sociologist Gunnar Myrdal ([1944] 1962), when he compared the historical position of African Americans with that of women:

> As the Negro was awarded his "place" in society, so there was a "woman's place." In both cases the rationalization was strongly believed that men, in confining them to this place, did not act against the true interest of the subordinate groups. (1077)

Myrdal called this belief the "myth of the 'contented women.'"

The view of women's place being in the home is actually an invention of middle-class, industrial society. Societies in which women spend all or most of their time in the home are few, and there are many cultures in which women spend much of their time outside the home (Nelson, 86). For example, many poor or immigrant women and women of color have worked as "domestics" in the homes of middle- or upper-class women.

In many societies women make substantial contributions to the food supply and maintenance of the economy. In addition, "motherhood" is far from universally restricting, requiring women to be at home. Women do not all become mothers, and child care, which in many cultures may be taken up by siblings or other children, elderly relatives, adult males, and au pairs, among others, is not always only a female or mother's task. Even when women do become biological mothers, their tasks with children are limited to only certain years of the life cycle.

Today, as people increasingly acknowledge the creative and intellectual potential of women and as women enter the workplace in greater numbers, the concept of "women's place" as homebound seems anachronistic to many. Awareness of this change comes in such forms as the bumper sticker that reads "A woman's place is in the house—and in the Senate."

See also BAREFOOT AND PREGNANT (KEEP THEM), HOMEMAKER, MOTHER, WIFE.

women and children first. A Victorian tradition, originally associated with maritime practice, that allows women and children to go to safety before men. The practice began with the English in 1852. When a ship named *Birkenhead* ran aground off the southernmost tip of Africa and began to sink, the soldiers aboard stayed behind, letting the women and children get on the few seaworthy lifeboats available. Only the women and children were saved.

Victorian values see the tradition as noble and honorable of men. However, the fact that "women and children" are uttered in the same breath suggests not only the protectiveness of males but also the lumping together of those that men regard as weaker. At the same time, the practice does not suggest that all societies, or even ours at all times, have regarded women or children as inferior; that belief is historically specific. For that matter, women and children regarded as inferior or less than human for such reasons as class or race—such as black women and children in a context of slavery or racism—may be treated as though they were undeserving of safety or care, unless they are being protected as mere property.

See also FAIR SEX, WEAKER VESSEL.

women as a minority group; women as niggers. Phrases suggesting that women are members of a category of people that are subject to prejudice and discrimination, excluded from the economic or political mainstream, and in possession of less power over their lives than the dominant male category.

One of the few sociologists of her day to look at women as a minority group, Helen Mayer Hacker ([1951] 1969) found women to occupy a marginal status in a male-dominated society that compared in some basic ways with that of black people's status, though when talking about women she unfortunately meant only white women, to the exclusion of all women of color.

She argued, for example, that both white women and African Americans are visible, though in somewhat different ways; have been regarded by society as being of inferior intelligence; have adapted to their status through behavioral accommodation to white male society; and have suffered similar kinds of educational, employment, and political discrimination. Hacker also noted a historical relation: in the seventeenth century, the legal status of black servants was derived from that of white women and children. (See also Gunnar Myrdal's comments under WOMAN'S PLACE IS IN THE HOME.)

Yet Hacker also took account of some significant differences: marriage can act as a social elevator for white women but not for blacks, and the dominant group ascribes greater importance to (white) women than to blacks in general. She also acknowledges that greater discrimination is suffered by black people than by women.

What she did not recognize is that certain affiliations, such as class and race, cut across gender, creating significant differences among women. As mentioned, Hacker talked about women as though they were only white women;

similarly she made no distinctions among categories of men.

At the same time that John Lennon sang "Woman Is the Nigger of the World," psychologist Naomi Weisstein discussed the same concept in an article in *Psychology Today:*

> The list [of female attributes] adds up to a typical minority-group stereotype—woman as nigger. If she knows her place (the home), she is really quite a lovable, loving creature, happy and childlike. ("Woman as Nigger," *Psychology Today,* October 1969)

Black feminist bell hooks (1981) writes that when white women compare themselves with black people, they evoke "the sufferings and oppressions of non-white people to say 'look at how bad our lot as white women is, why we are like niggers, like the Third World'" (141–42). hooks goes on to argue that these "metaphors" would not be necessary if middle- and upper-class white women truly resembled the oppressed people of the world.

If white women's oppression were the same as blacks' oppression, it would be sufficient merely to describe white women's oppression without appropriating the black experience. hooks' point is that white feminist women have tended to compare themselves with black people as a result of aspiring to equality with middle- and upper-class white men.

The implication of the "woman as nigger" metaphor, as hooks sees it, is that unless white women enjoy full rights along with white men, they will be at the same level with black men. The alleged subtle plea is for racist white men to protect the innocent, virtuous white woman from that degradation (143–44). What's more, the comparison between race and sex discrimination implicitly assumes that all women are white and all blacks are men, effacing the realities of black women.

One white feminist response to this criticism is an appeal to "sisterhood," stressing the "common oppression" of women. Other white feminists, however, have advocated greater sensitivity to issues of how race and class intersect. It is arguable that a white woman advantaged with a good education and middle- or upper-class background will find it easier to combat sexism than will a poor black or a poor white woman.

See also OPPRESSION, WOMAN.

women as animals; women and speciesism. Traditional matching of women with animals by way of expressing or justifying beliefs in women's inferiority. The practice of identifying women with animals and animal qualities ranges from the sexist philosophy of Aristotle (who regarded women as being the softer of the sexes in disposition, more impulsive, and comparatively deficient in rational faculties) to today's man on the street who insists on applying animal metaphors (e.g., BAT, COW, and FOX) to describe or demean women.

Along with animals, women have long been excluded from the community of "man" on the grounds that they are more corporeal than rational, rationality being the working criterion of choice for determining human worth. Women of color in particular have been portrayed in the popular media as animal-like.

Men, too, may be described in animal terms—*wolf* and *buck* or *worm* and *rat*—but in many cases, especially when the men being described are white, words such as *stud* express what are often considered to be positive attributes. In any case, the male epithets are seldom as sexualized or as ageist as are those for women. Negative terms such as *rat* or *worm* are probably just as commonly in use among men as among women in referring to men.

According to Donovan and Adams (1995) the different feminist responses to this historical matching of women with animals range as follows: (1) Women are not animal-like, but distinctly human. Women need to affirm their intellectual powers, thus severing their identification with animals. (2) The argument that the distinction between body and soul, between women/children/animals on the one hand and men in their allegedly superior rational or divine faculty on the other, should be rejected, since it is at the source of the exploitation of both women and nature. (3) The feminist perspective must consider nonhuman life-forms, since all human groups (viz. women) will not be free—of exploitation, abuse, or commercialization—until all life-forms are free. (4) Other feminists believe that there is no need to consider animals in feminist perspectives and that focusing on animals only diverts attention from the political needs of women (1–8).

Regarding this last response, Donovan and Adams say that the rendering of other animals as unimportant "is a haunting repetition of the traditional trivializing of women's issues" (3).

Speciesism, from the 1970s, means human bias against other species of life, specifically the belief that humans are superior to other species and that human exploitation of animals is justifiable. Many social critics have seen a connection between this kind of bias and the bias against women and have started developing perspectives exploring that connection and what it means to women and society at large.

See also ANIMAL, BARRACUDA, BEAST, BEAVER, BIRD, BUTTERFLY, CAT, CHICKEN, DOG, FILLY, FISH, HEIFER, LAMB, MARE, MINK, MINX, NELLY, OLD GIRL, PET, PIG, PUSS, SEXISM, SHREW, SOCIAL BUTTERFLY, SOW, SQUIRREL, TUNA, VIXEN, WOLF, WOMEN AS STORMS, ZOO.

women as storms/ships/cars. A common linguistic practice in English has been to refer to certain classes of things as feminine or to name them after women. For example, storms, especially hurricanes and tornadoes, have often been regarded as feminine and named after women. This practice is consistent with the patriarchal view of women as sinister, threatening, stormy in their rage (see also SPITFIRE), and potentially ruinous—a powerful, negative physical force. However, the act of naming something very powerful as feminine may also serve as a subtle way to calm it, control its force.

The National Weather Service bestowed women's names on storms beginning in 1953, although this practice actually began with military meteorologists using female names for storms in the Pacific during World War II. In 1979 feminists convinced the World Meteorological Organization to begin using men's names for storms as well as women's, alternating the two. Actually, gender balance was provided earlier, in 1978, when men's names were assigned to Pacific storms.

Another common practice is for men to regard their boats, ships, cars, engines, and like objects as feminine. These are largely objects that traditionally have served men's uses or entertained them or which men may produce, cherish, control, or command. In the case of a battleship, in particular, the idea is of a military tool to be controlled by powerful men, but the comparison is also with something regarded as destructive.

The practice of referring to objects as women has been criticized as part of a long tradition of using "woman" as a symbolic category. This practice has worked to further objectify women and efface their roles as historical actors.

See also WOMAN, WOMEN AS ANIMALS.

women's liberation (movement); women's lib. The former, a 1968 term, part of the revival of feminism in the 1960s, referring to the movement (also known as *the women's movement, the women's* *rights movement,* and *second wave feminism*) to fight sexist male attitudes and institutions and to win full political, social, legal, and economic rights and opportunities for women on a par with those of men. Those women (and men) involved in the movement dealt with broad public issues of discrimination and sexuality, encouraged activism in such areas as abortion rights and violence against women, and promoted the raising of women's consciousness.

The term *women's liberation* was apparently not coined by any one person. The idea of liberation, including that of third world countries from colonial occupation—witness the National Liberation Front in Vietnam—was in the air during this decade in leftist politics, influencing the adoption of the word for domestic groups seeking to free themselves from traditional roles and restraints (Mankiller et al. 1998). Ridicule of the women's movement, including fear and dismissal of its accomplishments, and of the term led in a few years to the fading of the expression from the national vocabulary.

The shortened form *women's lib* came to carry even more derision, though it has probably also been used simply as an abbreviation. James (1984) cites this anonymous, dismissive graffiti from 1971: "Women's Lib? Put them behind bras."

The women's liberation movement coined such words and expressions as SEXIST, *sexual politics* (from the title of Kate Millett's book [1970]), WIMMIN, and WOMYN, while women in the movement were often derided as "women's libbers" and BRA BURNERS. Negative stereotypes of feminist "radicalism," including alleged disrespect for men and traditional gender roles, also emerged in the popular media, and women in general have not always accepted what they perceive or stereotype as the conduct of some of the women in the movement or its prem-

ises: "On the question of 'women's liberation' Golda Meir [said:] 'Do you mean those crazy women who burn their bras and go around all disheveled and hate men?'" (Oriana Fallaci, in Carolyn G. Heilbrun, *Reinventing Womanhood,* 1979, 111).

Although *women's liberation* is still heard, it has lost ground to *feminism* and the long-standing *women's rights* as references to women's efforts to combat barriers to equality with men and to gain support for those matters in which women differ from men, such as women's health. *Women's liberation* differs from these other terms in connoting a more aggressive form of feminism, espousing more radical issues than those of feminism or the women's movement.

See also FEMINISM, LIBBER, PUSS (pussy power).

women's movement. See FEMINISM, WOMEN'S LIBERATION (MOVEMENT).

women's work. See WOMAN'S PLACE IS IN THE HOME.

womyn. A 1970s (and still in use) variant of *women,* designed to avoid the suggestion of masculinity that some find in the affix *-men* in *women.* The purpose behind the coinage is to help divorce the user from any hint of patriarchy and also to better reflect women's experience. Of the standard English-language dictionaries used in research for this dictionary, only *Webster's College Dictionary* (1991) had an entry for this word, which is rarely seen outside women's studies programs, feminist writing, and lesbian publications (e.g., "Womyn Finder" is a personal ad section in *The Lesbian News*).

Womon and *woperson* are singular forms; the plural variants are *wimmin* and *wimyn.* Such neologisms, sometimes short-lived, have been derided and made the butt of jokes by those opposed to the women's movement and by those not able to forgive the reform and politicization of the language, although the latter critics have not convincingly argued that they are free of their own political and linguistic agendas.

See also HERO (shero[e]) HERSTORY, WIMMIN, WOMANIST, WOMEN'S LIBERATION (MOVEMENT).

wool. Reference to a woman as a sex object, probably based on the comparison of a woman's pubic hair with wool.

See also BEARD, BEAVER, BUSH, CAT, HAIR, HAT, SQUIRREL, WHISKER.

woperson. See WOMYN.

working girl. See GIRL, PROSTITUTE.

worm. An old animal metaphor referring to a despicable person, often a man. He may be thought of as a jerk or someone who acts ungentlemanly toward women, or contemptibly toward anyone, like a "snake"; but in general he is considered spineless, groveling, creeping lowlife.

See also LOUNGE LIZARD, LOUSE.

wuss. A weak person or coward, traditionally a man; a combination of the *w* in *wimp* with the last three letters in *puss* (*wussy* is even more like *pussy,* since they rhyme). Like *wimp* and *pussy,* this is a hurtful term for a male, used with the implication that he lacks strength and other virtues of masculinity (it compares a man with a woman, thus demeaning women in general as well as the particular male targeted). *Wuss,* from the 1960s, is most common in young people's talk, where it is coming into use for females as well. Some current dictionaries even describe it as a virtually gender-neutral term. It may also mean a dupe.

See also APRON, BABY (crybaby), CANDY-ASS, CREAMPUFF, EFFEMINATE, GIRL, MAMA'S BOY, MILKSOP, NANCY, MOLLY-CODDLE, PANSY, PRISSY, PUSSY-WHIPPED, SISSY, SKIRT, WIMP.

Y

yenta. A Yiddish word meaning a woman regarded as a gossip or a shrew.

See also GOSSIP, NAG, SHREW.

yes-girl; **yes man**. The former, a woman believed to be sexually PROMISCUOUS; the latter, "a toady." The lack of symmetry is characteristic of the culture's different expectations of men and women.

yeti. An epithet for a woman seen as fat and homely. Sutton (1995, 294) reports male high school student use in Pennsylvania, but usage is probably more widespread.

See also BEEF TRUST, BIG BERTHA, BUFFALO, COOLER, COYOTE, DOG, GANGSTER GIRL, HOGGER, LOBO, LOOKSISM, PIG, SOW.

Z

zipper. Referring to the zipper on pants, a term used for a man viewed as PROMISCUOUS. It is one of the few terms used for men in this sense that doesn't connote a positive quality (compare, e.g., with STALLION, STUD). Nor does it suggest a ROMEO or a CASANOVA.

See also LECHER.

zoo. A brothel. There are different possibilities for explaining this sometimes jocular, sometimes derisive term. It may result from the animal smell stereotypically associated (typically among men) with women and female genitals, female prostitutes in particular, or just the association of women and sex with things of animal nature (see also SKANK, SLAG, WOMEN AS ANIMALS). More often it is said to derive from a racist and sexist image of the varied kinds of "colorful" and "multicultural" women and sexual experience available—"on display"—in a brothel.

Core Works Consulted

Abbott, Pamela. 1996. "Women." In *The Social Science Encyclopedia,* 2d ed., edited by Adam Kuper and Jessica Kuper. London: Routledge.

Abbott, Pamela, and Claire Wallace. 1997. *An Introduction to Sociology: Feminist Perspectives.* London: Routledge.

Adams, Carol J. 1995. *The Sexual Politics of Meat: A Feminist-Vegetarian Critical Theory.* New York: Continuum.

Adams, Elsie, and Mary Louise Briscoe. 1971. *Up Against the Wall, Mother: On Women's Liberation.* Beverly Hills, CA: Glencoe.

Alexander, Maxine, ed. 1984. *Speaking for Ourselves: Women of the South.* New York: Pantheon.

Allen, Irving Lewis. 1990. *Unkind Words: Ethnic Labeling from Redskin to WASP.* New York: Bergin & Garvey.

Aman, Reinhold. 1987. *The Best of Maledicta: The International Journal of Verbal Aggression.* Philadelphia: Running Press.

American Heritage Dictionary of the English Language, The, 3d ed. 1992. Boston: Houghton Mifflin.

American Treasury, 1455–1955, The, selected by Clifton Fadiman with assistance from Charles Van Doren. 1955. New York: Harper.

Andersen, Margaret L., and Patricia Hill Collins, eds. 1992. *Race, Class, and Gender: An Anthology.* Belmont, CA: Wadsworth.

Arango, Ariel. 1989. *Dirty Words: The Expressive Power of Taboo.* Northvale, NJ: Aronson.

Ashcraft, Donna M., ed. 1998. *Women's Work: A Survey of Scholarship by and about Women.* New York: Harrington Park.

August, Eugene R. 1998. "Real Men Don't: Anti-Male Bias in English." In *Exploring Language,* edited by Gary Goshgarian, 424–34. New York: Longman.

Ayto, John, and John Simpson. 1992. *The Oxford Dictionary of Modern Slang.* Oxford: Oxford University Press.

Bair, Deirdre. 1989. "Introduction to the Vintage Edition." In *The Second Sex,* by Simone de Beauvoir, translated and edited by H. M. Parshley, vii–xviii. New York: Vintage.

Baring, Anne, and Jules Cashford. 1991. *The Myth of the Goddess: Evolution of an Image.* London: Penguin.

Barnhart, David K., and Allan A. Metcalf. 1997. *America in So Many Words: Words that Have Shaped America.* Boston: Houghton Mifflin.

Barnhart, Robert K., ed. 1988. *The Barnhart Dictionary of Etymology.* Bronx, NY: H. Wilson.

Beauvoir, Simone de. 1973. *The Coming of Age.* Translated by Patrick O'Brian. New York: Warner.

———. [1952] 1974. *The Second Sex.* Translated and edited by H. M. Parshley. New York: Vintage.

Bell, Robert E. 1991. *Women of Classical Mythology: A Biographical Dictionary*. Santa Barbara, CA: ABC-CLIO.

Beneke, Timothy. 1997. *Proving Manhood: Reflections on Men and Sexism*. Berkeley: University of California Press.

Bentley, William K., and James M. Corbett. 1992. *Prison Slang: Words and Expressions Depicting Life behind Bars*. Jefferson, NC: McFarland.

Black, Henry Campbell. 1990. *Black's Law Dictionary: Definitions of the Terms and Phrases of American and English Jurisprudence, Ancient and Modern*. St. Paul, MN: West Publishing.

Blockbuster Entertainment Guide to Movies and Videos 1998. 1997. New York: Island.

Bly, Robert. 1990. *Iron John: A Book about Men*. Reading, MA: Addison-Wesley.

Boles, Janet K., and Diane Long Hoeveler. 1996. *From the Goddess to the Glass Ceiling: A Dictionary of Feminism*. Lanham, MD: Madison.

Brah, Artur. 1986. "Unemployment and Racism: Asian Youth on the Dole." In *The Experience of Unemployment*, edited by S. Allen et al. London: Macmillan.

———. 1991. "Questions of Difference and International Feminism." In *Out of the Margins: Women's Studies in the Nineties*, edited by Jane Aaron and Sylvia Walby. London: Taylor and Francis.

Brewer's Dictionary of Phrase and Fable, Centenary Edition. Revised by Ivor H. Evans. 1970. New York: Harper & Row.

Brown, Helen Gurley. 1982. *Having It All: Love, Success, Sex, Money*. London: Sidgwick & Jackson.

Brownmiller, Susan. 1975. *Against Our Will: Men, Women and Rape*. New York: Bantam.

Brumberg, Joan Jacobs. 1997. *The Body Project: An Intimate History of American Girls*. New York: Vintage.

Buchwald, Emilie, Pamela R. Fletcher, and Martha Roth, eds. 1993. *Transforming a Rape Culture*. Minneapolis, MN: Milkweed Editions.

Bullough, Vern, and Bonnie Bullough. 1987. *Women and Prostitution: A Social History*. Buffalo, NY: Prometheus.

———. 1992. *Cross Dressing, Sex, and Gender*. Philadelphia: University of Pennsylvania Press.

Cahill, Spencer E. 1986. "Language Practices and Self-Definition: The Case of Gender Identity Acquisition." *Sociological Quarterly* 27, no. 3 (Fall): 295–311.

Cameron, Deborah. 1985. *Feminism and Linguistic Theory*. London: Macmillan.

Campbell, Robert Jean. 1989. *Psychiatric Dictionary*, 6th ed. New York: Oxford University Press.

Cannell, Fenella, and Sarah Green. 1996. "Patriarchy." In *The Social Science Encyclopedia*, 2d ed., edited by Adam Kuper and Jessica Kuper. London: Routledge.

Caplan, Paula J. 1985. *The Myth of Women's Masochism*. New York: Signet.

Carpineto, Jane. 1989. *The Don Juan Dilemma: Should Women Stay with Men Who Stray?* New York: Morrow.

Caskey, Noelle. 1986. "Interpreting Anorexia Nervosa." In *The Female Body in Western Culture: Contemporary Perspectives,* edited by Susana Rubin Suleiman. Cambridge, MA: Harvard University Press.

Cassell, Justine, and Henry Jenkins, eds. 1998. *From Barbie to Mortal Kombat: Gender and Computer Games.* Cambridge, MA: MIT Press.

Chafe, William H. 1972. *The American Woman: Her Changing Social, Economic, and Political Role, 1920-1970.* London: Oxford University Press.

Chapman, Robert L., ed. 1987. *American Slang.* New York: Harper & Row.

———. 1998. *American Slang,* 2d ed. New York: HarperPerennial.

Chauncey, George. 1994. *Gay New York: Gender, Urban Culture, and the Making of the Gay Male World, 1890–1940.* New York: Basic.

Chesler, Phyllis. 1989. *Women and Madness.* San Diego: Harvest.

Churchill, Wainwright. 1967. *Homosexual Behavior among Males.* New Jersey: Prentice-Hall.

Ciardi, John. 1980. *A Browser's Dictionary and Native's Guide to the Unknown American Language.* New York: Harper & Row.

Cohn, Carol. 1998. "Wars, Wimps and Women: Talking Gender and Thinking War." In *Exploring Language,* edited by Gary Goshgarian, 222–32. New York: Longman.

Coleman, Jennifer A. 1998. "Discrimination at Large." In *Exploring Language,* edited by Gary Goshgarian, 364–66. New York: Longman.

Collins, Patricia Hill. 1991. *Black Feminist Thought: Knowledge, Consciousness, and the Politics of Empowerment.* New York: Routledge.

Concise Oxford Dictionary of Sociology, The. 1994. Edited by Gordon Marshall. Oxford: Oxford University Press.

Corey, Dale. 1997. *Inventing English: The Imaginative Origins of Everyday Expressions.* New York: Berkley Books.

Daly, Mary. 1973. *Beyond God the Father: Toward a Philosophy of Women's Liberation.* Boston: Beacon.

———. 1978. *Gyn/Ecology: The Metaethics of Radical Feminism.* Boston: Beacon.

Daly, Mary, and Jane Caputi. 1987. *Webster's First New Intergalactic Wickedary of the English Language.* Boston: Beacon.

Daniels, Jessie. 1997. *White Lies: Race, Class, Gender, and Sexuality in White Supremacist Discourse.* New York: Routledge.

Davis, Elizabeth Gould. 1971. *The First Sex.* New York: Putnam's.

Davis, Philip G. 1998. *Goddess Unmasked: The Rise of Neopagan Feminist Spirituality.* Dallas: Spence.

Deford, Frank. 1971. *There She Is: The Life and Times of Miss America.* New York: Viking.

Delaney, Janice, Mary Jane Lupton, and Emily Toth. 1988. *The Curse: A Cultural History of Menstruation,* rev. ed. Urbana, IL: University of Illinois Press.

Dictionary of American Regional English. 1985 (vol. 1), 1991 (vol. 2). Edited by Frederic G. Cassidy (vols. 1 and 2) and Joan Houston Hall (vol. 2). Cambridge: Belknap Press.

Dictionary of Anthropology. 1997. Edited by Thomas Barfield. Oxford, UK: Blackwell.

Dillard, J. L. 1976. *American Talk: Where Our Words Came From.* New York: Random House.

Donovan, Josephine, and Carol J. Adams, eds. 1995. *Animals and Women: Feminist Theoretical Explorations.* Durham, NC: Duke University Press.

Douglas, Susan J. 1994. *Where the Girls Are: Growing Up Female with the Mass Media.* New York: Times Books.

Duberman, Martin, ed. 1997. *A Queer World: The Center for Lesbian and Gay Studies Reader.* New York: New York University Press.

Dunayer, Joan. 1995. "Sexist Words, Speciesist Roots." In *Animals and Women: Feminist Theoretical Explorations,* edited by Carol J. Adams and Josephine Donovan. Durham, NC: Duke University Press.

Dunkling, Leslie. 1990. *A Dictionary of Epithets and Terms of Address.* London: Routledge.

Dynes, Wayne R. 1990. *Encyclopedia of Homosexuality.* New York: Garland.

Eckert, Penelope. 1989. *Jocks and Burnouts: Social Categories and Identity in the High School.* New York: Teachers College Press.

Ehrenreich, Barbara, and Deirdre English. 1978. *For Her Own Good: 150 Years of the Experts' Advice to Women.* New York: Anchor.

Eisenbach, Helen. 1996. *Lesbianism Made Easy.* New York: Three Rivers.

Eisler, Ríane. 1988. *The Chalice and the Blade: Our History, Our Future.* San Francisco: HarperCollins.

Encarta World English Dictionary. 1999. New York: St. Martin's.

Engels, Friedrich. [1884] 1972. *The Origins of the Family, Private Property and the State.* London: Penguin.

Evans, Arthur. 1977. *Witchcraft and the Gay Counterculture.* Boston: Fag.

Faderman, Lillian. 1981. *Surpassing the Love of Men: Romantic Friendship and Love between Women from the Renaissance to the Present.* New York: William Morrow.

Faludi, Susan. 1991. *Backlash: The Undeclared War against American Women.* New York: Crown.

Farrell, Warren. 1993. *The Myth of Male Power.* New York: Berkley Books.

Feinberg, Leslie. 1996. *Trans Gender Warriors: Making History from Joan of Arc to Dennis Rodman.* Boston: Beacon.

———. 1998. *Trans Liberation: Beyond Pink or Blue.* Boston: Beacon.

Fikes, Robert Jr., ed. 1992. *Racist & Sexist Quotations: Some of the Most Outrageous Things Ever Said.* Saratoga, CA: R & E Publishers.

Flem, Lydia. 1997. *Casanova: The Man Who Really Loved Women.* Translated by Catherine Temerson. New York: Farrar, Straus and Giroux.

Flexner, Stuart Berg, and Anne H. Soukhanov. 1997. *Speaking Freely: A Guided Tour of American English.* New York: Oxford.

Foucault, Michel. 1978. *The History of Sexuality, Vol. 1, An Introduction.* Translated by Robert Hurley. New York: Pantheon.

———. 1985. *The History of Sexuality, Vol. 2, The Use of Pleasure.* Translated by Robert Hurley. New York: Pantheon.

Fowler's Modern English Usage. 1996. First edition by H. W. Fowler; 3d edition edited by R. W. Burchfield. Oxford: Clarendon Press.

Fraser, Antonia. 1985. *The Weaker Vessel.* New York: Vintage.

French, Marilyn. 1992. *The War against Women.* New York: Ballantine.

Freud, Sigmund. 1953. "The Taboo on Virginity." In *The Standard Edition of the Complete Psychological Works of Sigmund Freud,* edited by James Strachey, vol. 11, 192–208. London: Hogarth.

———. 1966. *The Complete Introductory Lectures on Psychoanalysis.* Translated and edited by James Strachey. New York: Norton.

Friedan, Betty. 1963. *The Feminine Mystique.* New York: Norton.

———. 1998. *The Second Stage.* Cambridge, MA: Harvard University Press.

Gay, Peter. 1980. *Thy Neighbor's Wife.* Garden City, NJ: Doubleday.

Gefou-Madianou, Dimitra, and A. M. Iossifides. 1996. "Gender and Sex." In *The Social Science Encyclopedia,* 2d ed., edited by Adam Kuper and Jessica Kuper. London: Routledge.

Gentz, William H., ed. 1986. *The Dictionary of Bible and Religion.* Nashville, TN: Abingdon.

Gersoni-Stavn, Diane. 1976. *Sexism and Youth.* New York: R. R. Bowker.

Gerzon, Mark. 1982. *A Choice of Heroes: The Changing Faces of American Manhood.* Boston: Houghton Mifflin.

Gittelson, Natalie. 1972. *The Erotic Life of the American Wife.* New York: Delacorte Press.

GLAAD Media Guide to the Lesbian and Gay Community. n.d. New York: Gay & Lesbian Alliance against Defamation.

Goffman, Erving. 1961. *Asylums.* New York: Doubleday & Company.

Goldberg, Herb. 1976. *The Hazards of Being Male: Surviving the Myth of Masculine Privilege.* New York: Signet.

Goldman, Marion S. 1981. *Gold Diggers and Silver Miners: Prostitution and Social Life on the Comstock Lode.* Ann Arbor: University of Michigan Press.

Gomes, Peter J. 1996. *The Good Book: Reading the Bible with Mind and Heart.* New York: Avon.

Goshgarian, Gary, ed. 1998. *Exploring Language,* 8th ed. New York: Longman.

Gouëffic, Louise. 1996. *Breaking the Patriarchal Code.* Manchester, CT: Knowledge, Ideas & Trends.

Graham, Alma. 1975. "The Making of a Nonsexist Dictionary." In *Language and Sex: Difference and Dominance,* edited by Barrie Thorne and Nancy Henley. Rowley, MA: Newberry House.

Grahn, Judy. 1990. *Another Mother Tongue: Gay Words, Gay Worlds.* Boston: Beacon.

Green, Richard. 1987. *The "Sissy Boy Syndrome" and the Development of Homosexuality.* New Haven, CT: Yale University Press.

Greer, Germaine. 1970. *The Female Eunuch.* New York: McGraw-Hill.

Griffin, Susan. 1981. *Pornography and Silence: Culture's Revenge against Nature.* New York: Harper & Row.

Guild Dictionary of Homosexual Terms, The. 1965. Washington, DC: Guild.

Guinier, Lani. 1998. *Lift Every Voice: Turning a Civil Rights Setback into a New Vision of Social Justice.* New York: Simon & Schuster.

Hacker, Helen Mayer. [1951] 1969. "Women as a Minority Group." In *Masculine/Feminine: Readings in Sexual Mythology and the Liberation of Women,* edited by Betty Roszak and Theodore Roszak, 130–48. New York: Harper & Row.

Haeberle, Erwin J., and Rolf Gindorf, eds. 1998. *Bisexualities: The Ideology and Practice of Sexual Contact with Both Men and Women.* New York: Continuum.

Hanscombe, G. E., and J. Forster. 1982. *Rocking the Cradle—Lesbian Mothers: A Challenge to Family Living.* London: Sheba.

Harding, M. Esther. 1976. *Woman's Mysteries.* New York: Colophon.

Harris, Marvin. 1968. *The Rise of Anthropological Theory: A History of Theories of Culture.* New York: Thomas Y. Crowell.

———. 1993. *Culture, People, Nature: An Introduction to General Anthropology,* 5th ed. New York: HarperCollins.

Hays, H. R. 1964. *The Dangerous Sex: The Myth of Feminine Evil.* New York: G. P. Putnam's.

Hendrickson, Robert. 1993. *Whistlin' Dixie: A Dictionary of Southern Expressions.* New York: Facts On File.

Herder Dictionary of Symbols, The. 1993. Wilmette, IL: Chiron.

Herdt, Gilbert. 1989. *Gay and Lesbian Youth.* New York: Haworth.

———, ed. 1994. *Third Sex, Third Gender: Beyond Sexual Dimorphism in Culture and History.* New York: Zone.

Higgins, Patrick, ed. 1993. *A Queer Reader.* New York: The New Press.

Hill, Alette Olin. 1986. *Mother Tongue, Father Time: A Decade of Linguistic Revolt.* Bloomington, IN: Indiana University Press.

Hochschild, Arlie, with Anne Machung. 1989. *The Second Shift: Working Parents and the Revolution at Home.* New York: Viking.

Holder, R. W. 1996. *A Dictionary of Euphemisms.* Oxford: Oxford University Press.

hooks, bell. 1981. *Ain't I a Woman: Black Women and Feminism.* Boston: South End Press.

Horney, Karen. 1939. *New Ways in Psychoanalysis.* New York: Norton.

Humm, Maggie. 1995. *The Dictionary of Feminist Theory,* 2d ed. Columbus, OH: Ohio State University Press.

James, Simon, ed. 1984. *A Dictionary of Sexist Quotations.* Sussex, Great Britain: Harvester.

Jordan, Glenn, and Chris Weedon. 1995. *Cultural Politics: Class, Gender, Race and the Postmodern World.* Oxford: Blackwell.

Kaiser, Charles. 1997. *The Gay Metropolis: The Landmark History of Gay Life in America since World War II.* Harvest: San Diego.

Kantor, Martin. 1998. *Homophobia: Description, Development, and Dynamics of Gay Bashing.* Westport, CT: Praeger.

Kaplan, Justin, and Anne Bernays. 1997. *The Language of Names.* New York: Simon & Schuster.

Katz, Jonathan Ned. 1995. *The Invention of Heterosexuality.* New York: Plume.

———. 1997a. "Coming to Terms." In *A Queer World: The Center for Lesbian and Gay Studies Reader,* edited by Martin Duberman, 216–35. New York: New York University Press.

———. 1997b. "'Homosexual' and 'Heterosexual': Questioning the Terms." In *A Queer World: The Center for Lesbian and Gay Studies Reader,* edited by Martin Duberman, 177–80. New York: New York University Press.

Kheel, Marti. 1995. "License to Kill: An Ecofeminist Critique of Hunters' Discourse." In *Animals and Women: Feminist Theoretical Explorations,* edited by Carol J. Adams and Josephine Donovan. Durham, NC: Duke University Press.

Kirkpatrick, Betty. 1996. *Dictionary of Cliches.* London: Bloomsbury.

Kramarae, Cheris, and Paula A. Treichler. 1985. *A Feminist Dictionary.* London: Pandora.

———. 1992. *Amazons, Bluestockings and Crones: A Feminist Dictionary.* London: Pandora.

Lakoff, Robin. 1975. *Language and Woman's Place.* New York: Colophon.

Lakoff, Robin Tolmach. 2000. *The Language War.* Berkeley: University of California Press.

Lakoff, Robin Tolmach, and Raquel L. Scherr. 1984. *Face Value: The Politics of Beauty.* Boston: Routledge & Kegan Paul.

Laqueur, Thomas. 1990. *Making Sex: Body and Gender from the Greeks to Freud.* Cambridge, MA: Harvard University Press.

Lawrence, Barbara. 1975. "Four-Letter Words Can Hurt You." In *Philosophy & Sex,* edited by Robert Baker and Frederick Elliston, 31–33. Buffalo, NY: Prometheus Books.

Leacock, Eleanor Burke. 1978. "Women's Status in Egalitarian Society: Implications for Social Evolution." *Current Anthropology* 19: 247–75.

Leap, William L. 1996. *Word's Out: Gay Men's English.* Minneapolis, MN: University of Minnesota Press.

Lederer, Richard. 1991. *The Miracle of Language.* New York: Pocket Books.

Lees, Sue. 1986. *Losing Out: Sexuality and Adolescent Girls.* London: Hutchinson.

Leonardo, Micaela di, ed. 1991. *Gender at the Crossroads of Knowledge: Feminist Anthropology in the Postmodern Era.* Berkeley: University of California Press.

Lewin, Esther. 1994. *The Thesaurus of Slang.* New York: Facts On File.

Lighter, J. E., ed. 1994 (Vol. 1, A–G), 1997 (Vol. 2, H–O). *Historical Dictionary of American Slang.* New York: Random House.

MacKenzie, Gordene Olga. 1994. *Transgender Nation.* Bowling Green, OH: Bowling Green State University Popular Press.

MacKinnon, Catharine. 1982. "Feminism, Marxism, Method and the State: An Agenda for Theory. In *Feminist Theory,* edited by N. O. Keohane et al. Brighton, England: Harvester.

Maggio, Rosalie. 1988. *The Nonsexist Word Finder: A Dictionary of Gender-Free Usage.* Boston: Beacon.

———. 1991. *The Dictionary of Bias-Free Usage: A Guide to Nondiscriminatory Language.* Phoenix, AZ: Oryx.

———. 1997. *Talking about People: A Guide to Fair and Accurate Language.* Phoenix, AZ: Oryx.

Mainard, P. 1970. "The Politics of Housework." In *Sisterhood Is Powerful,* edited by Robin Morgan. New York: Vintage.

Mairs, Nancy. 1998. "On Being a Cripple." In *Exploring Language,* edited by Gary Goshgarian, 355–58. New York: Longman.

Major, Clarence, ed. 1994. *Juba to Jive: A Dictionary of African-American Slang.* New York: Penguin.

Mankiller, Wilma, et al., eds. 1998. *The Reader's Companion to U.S. Women's History.* Boston: Houghton Mifflin.

Martin, Nancie S. 1998. "An Interview with Nancie S. Martin." In *From Barbie to Mortal Kombat: Gender and Computer Games,* edited by Justine Cassell and Henry Jenkins. Cambridge, MA: MIT Press.

Max, H. 1988. *gay(s)language: a dic(k)tionary of gay slang.* Austin, TX: Banned Books.

McPhee, Carol, and Ann FitzGerald, comps. 1979. *Feminist Quotations: Voices of Rebels, Reformers, and Visionaries.* New York: Thomas Y. Crowell.

Mead, Margaret. [1935] 1963. *Sex and Temperament in Three Primitive Societies.* New York: Marrow Quill.

———. [1949] 1975. *Male and Female: A Study of the Sexes in a Changing World.* New York: William Morrow.

Members of the Gay and Lesbian Historical Society of Northern California. 1998. "MTF Transgender Activism in the Tenderloin and Beyond, 1966–1975." *GLQ: A Journal of Lesbian and Gay Studies* 4, no. 2: 349–72.

Mencken, H. L. 1962. *The American Language: An Inquiry into the Development of English in the United States,* supplements 1 (1945) and 2 (1948). New York: Knopf.

Merriam-Webster's Collegiate Dictionary, 10th ed. 1997. Springfield, MA: Merriam-Webster.

Merrill, William F. 1995. "The Art of Interrogating Rapists." *FBI Law Enforcement Bulletin* 64, no. 1 (January): 8–12.

Michener, Anna J. 1998. *Becoming Anna: The Autobiography of a Sixteen-Year-Old.* Chicago: University of Chicago Press.

Miles, Jack. 1996. *God: A Biography.* New York: Vintage.

Miller, Casey, and Kate Swift. 1991. *Words and Women.* New York: HarperCollins.

Millett, Kate. 1970. *Sexual Politics.* Garden City, NJ: Doubleday.

Mills, Jane. 1989. *Womanwords: A Dictionary of Words about Women.* New York: Henry Holt.

Mondimore, Francis Mark. 1996. *A Natural History of Homosexuality.* Baltimore: Johns Hopkins University Press.

Moore, Robert, and Douglas Gillette. 1990. *King Warrior Magician Lover: Rediscovering the Archetypes of the Mature Masculine.* New York: HarperCollins.

Morgan, Robin. 1989. *The Demon Lover: On the Sexuality of Terrorism.* New York: Norton.

Myrdal, Gunnar. [1944] 1962. "A Parallel to the Negro Problem." Appendix 5 in *An American Dilemma: The Negro Problem and Modern Democracy,* 1073–78. New York: Harper & Row.

Nanda, Serena. 1990. *Neither Man nor Woman: The Hijras of India.* Belmont, CA: Wadsworth.

Nelson, Sarah Milledge. 1997. *Gender in Archaeology: Analyzing Power and Prestige.* Walnut Creek, CA: AltaMira.

Nilsen, Alleen Pace. 1998. "Sexism in English: A 1990s Update." In *Exploring Language,* edited by Gary Goshgarian, 398–407. New York: Longman.

Nilsen, Alleen Pace, Haig Bosmajian, H. Lee Gershuny, and Julia P. Stanley, eds. 1977. *Sexism and Language.* Urbana, IL: National Council of Teachers of English.

Nowlan, Robert A., and Gwendolyn W. Nowlan. 1994. *Film Quotations: 11,000 Lines Spoken on Screen, Arranged by Subject, and Indexed.* Jefferson, NC: McFarland.

Oakley, Ann. 1972. *Sex, Gender and Society.* London: Temple-Smith.

Orr, Catherine M. 1997. "Charting the Currents of the Third Wave." *Hypatia* (Summer) 12, no. 3, in *Periodical Abstracts* 2945.

Oxford Dictionary of Modern Slang, The. 1992. Compiled by John Ayto and John Simpson. Oxford, UK: Oxford University Press.

Oxford Dictionary of New Words: A Popular Guide to Words in the News. 1991. Compiled by Sara Tulloch. Oxford: Oxford University Press.

Oxford English Dictionary, The. 2d ed. 1989. Oxford: Clarendon Press.

Ozick, Cynthia. 1971. "Women and Creativity: The Demise of the Dancing Dog." In *Women in Sexist Society: Studies in Power and Powerlessness,* edited by Vivian Gornick and Barbara K. Moran, 431–51. New York: Mentor.

Panati, Charles. 1998. *Sexy Origins and Intimate Things: The Rites and Rituals of Straights, Gays, Bi's, Drags, Trans, Virgins, and Others.* New York: Penguin.

Partridge, Eric. 1984. *A Dictionary of Slang and Unconventional English.* 8th ed. New York: Macmillan.

Pattee, Fred Lewis. 1940. *The Feminine Fifties.* New York: D. Appleton-Century.

Pearson, Patricia. 1997. *When She Was Bad: Violent Woman and the Myth of Innocence.* New York: Penguin.

Pei, Mario. 1978. *Weasel Words: The Art of Saying What You Don't Mean.* New York: Harper & Row.

Pellegrini, Ann. 1992. "S(h)ifting the Terms of Hetero/Sexism: Gender, Power, Homophobias." In *Homophobia: How We All Pay the Price,* edited by Warren J. Blumenfeld. Boston: Beacon.

Penelope, Julia. 1990. *Speaking Freely: Unlearning the Lies of the Fathers' Tongues.* New York: Pergamon.

Pharr, Suzanne. 1988. *Homophobia: A Weapon of Sexism.* Oakland, CA: Chardon.

Plotnik, Arthur. 1996. *The Elements of Expression: Putting Thoughts into Words.* New York: Henry Holt.

"'Political Economy' of Sex." In *Toward an Anthropology of Women,* edited by Rayna R. Reiter, 157–210. New York: Monthly Review.

Queen, Carol, and Lawrence Schimel. 1997. *PoMoSexuals: Challenging Assumptions about Gender and Sexuality.* San Francisco: Cleis.

Rand, Erica. 1995. *Barbie's Queer Accessories.* Durham: Duke.

Rawson, Hugh. 1989. *Wicked Words: A Treasury of Curses, Insults, Put-Downs, and Other Formerly Unprintable Terms from Anglo-Saxon Times to the Present.* New York: Crown.

Raymond, Janice G. 1993. *Women as Wombs: Reproductive Technologies and the Battle over Women's Freedom.* San Francisco: HarperSanFrancisco.

———. 1994. *The Transsexual: The Making of the She-Male.* New York: Teachers College Press.

Rhode, Deborah L. 1997. *Speaking of Sex.* Cambridge, MA: Harvard University Press.

Rich, Adrienne. 1976. *Of Woman Born: Motherhood as Experience and Institution.* New York: Bantam.

———. 1980. "Compulsory Heterosexuality and Lesbian Existence." *Signs* 5, no. 4: 631–60.

Richter, Alan. 1993. *Sexual Slang: A Compendium of Offbeat Words and Colorful Phrases from Shakespeare to Today.* New York: HarperPerennial.

Risch, B. 1987. "Women's Derogatory Terms for Men: That's Right, 'Dirty Words.'" *Language in Society* 16, no. 3: 353–58.

Rivers, Caryl, Rosalind Barnett, and Grace Baruch. 1979. *Beyond Sugar and Spice: How Women Grow, Learn, and Thrive.* New York: G. P. Putnam's Sons.

Rodgers, Bruce. 1972. *Gay Talk: A (Sometimes Outrageous) Dictionary of Gay Slang.* New York: Putnam's.

Rogers, James. 1994. *The Dictionary of Clichés.* New York: Wings Books.

Roiphe, Katie. 1993. *The Morning After: Sex, Fear, and Feminism on Campus.* Boston: Little, Brown.

Rose, Hilary. 1976. "Women's Work: Women's Knowledge." In *The Rights and Wrongs of Women,* edited by Juliet Mitchell and Ann Oakley. Harmondsworth, England: Penguin.

Roszak, Betty, and Theodore Roszak, eds. 1969. *Masculine/Feminine: Readings in Sexual Mythology and the Liberation of Women.* New York: Harper & Row.

Rothblatt, Martine. 1995. *Apartheid of Sex: A Manifesto on the Freedom of Gender.* New York: Crown.

Rotundo, E. Anthony. 1993. *American Manhood: Transformations in Masculinity from the Revolution to the Modern Era.* New York: Basic.

Rowbotham, Sheila. 1977. *A Century of Women: The History of Women in Britain and the United States.* London: Viking.

Ruse, Michael. 1988. *Homosexuality: A Philosophical Inquiry.* Oxford, UK: Basil Blackwell.

Russ, Joanna. 1998. *What Are We Fighting For? Sex, Race, Class, and the Future of Feminism.* New York: St. Martin's.

Sadker, Myra, and David Sadker. 1994. *Failing at Fairness: How America's Schools Cheat Girls.* New York: Charles Scribner's.

Schultz, Vicki. 1998. "Sex Is the Least of It: Let's Focus Harassment Law on Work, Not Sex." *Nation* (25 May), 11–15.

Schulz, Muriel R. 1975. "The Semantic Derogation of Women." In *Language and Sex: Difference and Dominance,* edited by Barrie Thorne and Nancy Henley. Rowley, MA: Newberry.

Sharp, Saundra. 1993. *Black Women: For Beginners.* New York: Writers and Readers Publishing.

Sherrow, Victoria. 1996. *Women and the Military: An Encyclopedia.* Denver, CO: ABC-CLIO.

Shilts, Randy. 1987. *And the Band Played On.* New York: Harper & Row.

Singer, June. 1976. *Androgyny: Toward a New Theory of Sexuality.* Garden City, NJ: Anchor.

Smith-Rosenberg, C. 1972. "The Hysterical Woman: Sex Roles and Conflict in Nineteenth-Century America." *Social Research* 39: 652–78.

Smitherman, Geneva. 1994. *Black Talk: Words and Phrases from the Hood to the Amen Corner.* Boston: Houghton Mifflin.

Sorrels, Bobbye D. 1983. *The Nonsexist Communicator: Solving the Problems of Gender and Awkwardness in Modern English.* Englewood Cliffs, NJ: Prentice-Hall.

Spears, Richard A. 1981. *Slang and Euphemism: A Dictionary of Oaths, Curses, Insults, Racial Slurs, Sexual Slang and Metaphor.* Middle Village, NY: Jonathan David.

———. 1990. *Forbidden American English.* Lincolnwood, IL: Passport.

———. 1991. *Slang and Euphemism.* 2d rev. ed. New York: Penguin.

Spender, Dale. 1980. *Man Made Language.* London: Routledge.

Stange, Mary Zeiss. 1997. *Woman the Hunter.* Boston: Beacon.

Stanley, Lawrence A., ed. 1992. *Rap: The Lyrics.* New York: Penguin.

Stewart, William. 1995. *Cassell's Queer Companion.* London: Cassell.

Stibbs, Anne, ed. 1992. *A Woman's Place: Quotations about Women.* New York: Avon.

Strainchamps, Ethel. 1971. "Our Sexist Language." In *Women in Sexist Society: Studies in Power and Powerlessness,* edited by Vivian Gornick and Barbara K. Moran, 347–61. New York: Mentor.

Struckman-Johnson, Cindy. 1988. "Forced Sex on Dates: It Happens to Men, Too." *Journal of Sex Research* 24: 234–41.

Suárez, Juan A. 1996. *Bike Boys, Drag Queens, and Superstars: Avant-garde, Mass Culture, and Gay Identities in the 1960s Underground Cinema.* Bloomington, IN: Indiana University.

Sullivan, Andrew. 1995. *Virtually Normal: An Argument about Homosexuality.* New York: Knopf.

Sutton, Laurel A. 1995. "Bitches and Skankly Hobags." In *Gender Associated Language and the Socially Constructed Self,* edited by Kira Hall and Mary Bucholtz. London: Routledge.

Talese, Gay. 1980. *Thy Neighbor's Wife.* Garden City, NJ: Doubleday.

Tannen, Deborah. 1990. *You Just Don't Understand: Women and Men in Conversation.* New York: Ballantine.

Tenenbaum, Joseph. 1936. *The Riddle of Woman: A Study in the Social Psychology of Sex.* New York: Lee Furman.

Thorne, Barrie. 1993. *Gender Play: Girls and Boys in School.* New Brunswick, NJ: Rutgers University Press.

Thorne, Tony. 1990. *The Dictionary of Contemporary Slang.* New York: Pantheon.

Toner, Barbara. 1977. *The Facts of Rape.* London: Hutchinson.

Tuttle, Lisa. 1986. *Encyclopedia of Feminism.* New York: Facts On File.

Tyler, Carol-Anne. 1991. "Boys Will Be Girls: The Politics of Drag." In *Inside Out: Lesbian Theories, Gay Theories,* edited by Diana Fuss, 32–70. New York: Routledge.

Veblen, Thorstein. [1899] 1953. *The Theory of the Leisure Class: An Economic Study of Institutions.* New York: Mentor.

Vetterling-Braggin, Mary, ed. 1981. *Sexist Language: A Modern Philosophical Analysis.* Totowa, NJ: Littlefield, Adams.

Waldman, Carl. 1994. *Word Dance: The Language of Native American Culture.* New York: Facts On File.

Walker, Alice. 1984. *In Search of Our Mothers' Gardens.* London: The Women's Press.

Webster's College Dictionary. 1991. New York: Random House.

Webster's Word Histories. 1989. Springfield, MA: Merriam-Webster.

Weeks, David, and Jamie James. 1996. *Eccentrics: A Study of Sanity and Strangeness.* New York: Kodansha.

Weideger, Paula. 1975. *Menstruation and Menopause: The Physiology and Psychology, the Myth and the Reality.* New York: Alfred A. Knopf.

Weitz, Shirley. 1977. *Sex Roles: Biological, Psychological, and Social Fondations.* New York: Oxford University.

Wentworth, Harold, and Stuart Berg Flexner. 1975. *Dictionary of American Slang,* 2d supplement [i.e., 3d] edition. New York: Thomas Y. Crowell.

Werner, Dennis. 1979. "A Cross-Cultural Perspective on Theory and Research on Male Homosexuality." *Journal of Homosexuality* 4: 345–62.

West's Encyclopedia of American Law. 1998. St. Paul, MN: West Group.

White, Edmund. 1994. In *The Burning Library: Essays,* edited by David Bergman. New York: Alfred A. Knopf.

Williams, Walter L. 1986. *The Spirit and the Flesh: Sexual Diversity in American Indian Culture.* Boston: Beacon.

Wilson, Elizabeth. 1983. *What Is to Be Done about Violence against Women?* Harmondsworth, England: Penguin.

Witt, Lynn, Sherry Thomas, and Eric Marcus. 1995. *Out in All Directions: A Treasury of Gay and Lesbian America.* New York: Warner Books.

Wolf, Naomi. 1991. *The Beauty Myth: How Images of Beauty Are Used against Women.* New York: William Morrow.

Women's Issues. 1997. Margaret McFadden, consulting ed., vols. 1–3. Pasadena, CA: Salem Press.

Women's Studies Encyclopedia. vol. 1, edited by Helen Tierney. 1989. New York: Greenwood.

Young-Bruehl, Elisabeth, ed. 1990. *Freud on Women: A Reader.* New York: Norton.

Zucker, G. S., and B. Weiner. 1993. "Conservatism and Perceptions of Poverty: An Attributional Analysis." *Journal of Applied Social Psychology,* 23: 925–43.

Zweig, Paul. 1974. *The Adventurer.* New York: Basic Books.